£29.50

THE COLLECTED LETTERS OF
THOMAS HARDY

VOLUME SEVEN

1926–1927

WITH

ADDENDA, CORRIGENDA,
AND GENERAL INDEX

Already published

The Collected Letters of Thomas Hardy

Volume One: 1840–1892

Volume Two: 1893–1901

Volume Three: 1902–1908

Volume Four: 1909–1913

Volume Five: 1914–1919

Volume Six: 1920–1925

The first page of Hardy's last letter, written in pencil to Sir Edmund
Gosse, 25 December 1927

THE COLLECTED
LETTERS OF
THOMAS HARDY

EDITED BY

RICHARD LITTLE PURDY

AND

MICHAEL MILLGATE

VOLUME SEVEN

1926–1927

WITH

ADDENDA, CORRIGENDA,
AND GENERAL INDEX

CLARENDON PRESS · OXFORD
1988

Oxford University Press, Walton Street, Oxford OX2 6DP

Oxford   New York   Toronto
Delhi   Bombay   Calcutta   Madras   Karachi
Petaling Jaya   Singapore   Hong Kong   Tokyo
Nairobi   Dar es Salaam   Cape Town
Melbourne   Auckland

and associated companies in
Berlin   Ibadan

Oxford is a trade mark of Oxford University Press

Published in the United States
by Oxford University Press, New York

British Library Cataloguing in Publication Data
Hardy, Thomas, 1840–1928
The collected letters of Thomas Hardy.
Vol. 7: 1926–1927: with addenda,
corrigenda and general index
1. Hardy, Thomas, 1840–1928—Biography
2. Novelists, English—19th century—Biography
I. Title   II. Purdy, Richard Little
III. Millgate, Michael
823'.8   PR4753
ISBN 0–19–812624–7

Library of Congress Cataloging in Publication Data
(Revised for vol. 7)
Hardy, Thomas, 1840–1928.
The collected letters of Thomas Hardy.
Includes indexes.
Contents: v. 1. 1840–1892.—[etc.]—v. 5. 1914–1919.—
v. 7. 1926–1927, with addenda, corrigenda, and general index.
1. Hardy, Thomas, 1840–1928—Correspondence.
2. Novelists, English—19th century—Correspondence.
I. Purdy, Richard Little, 1904–   II. Millgate,
Michael.   III. Title.
PR4753.A42   1978   823'.8 [B]   77–30355
ISBN 0–19–812624–7

Set by Rowland Phototypesetting Ltd.
Printed in Great Britain
at the University Press, Oxford
by David Stanford
Printer to the University

CONTENTS

Preface   vii

Chronology: Thomas Hardy 1840–1928   ix

Acknowledgements for Volume Seven   xi

List of Abbreviations   xiv

Letters 1926–1927   1

Additional Letters   90

Undated Letters and Fragments   165

Corrections and Amplifications   171

Index of Recipients   179

General Index   182

PREFACE

THE distinctive contents and organization of this seventh and final volume of *The Collected Letters of Thomas Hardy* perhaps warrant a few words of description and explanation. Of the first section little need be said, for it simply continues for the last two years of Hardy's life the chronological procession of letters that has been maintained throughout the edition as a whole; a number of drafts in his hand have also been included in accordance with the principles set out in 'A Note on Hardy's Drafts' at the beginning of Volume 5. The second section of the present volume, 'Additional Letters', consists primarily of items which became available only after the volume in which they should ideally have appeared had already gone to press, and the editors wish particularly to record their gratitude to those interested users of the edition who took the trouble to report the existence of unnoticed letters or were generous enough to supply copies of unpublished letters they had themselves recently obtained. Also in this section are a few items that were initially omitted from the edition but have upon reconsideration been judged appropriate for inclusion, together with a few others that it has proved possible to date with a degree of confidence that once seemed unattainable.

Given the wide dispersal of Hardy's letters, the relatively short period of time that has elapsed since his death (as work on the edition draws to a close a few letters still remain in the hands of their original recipients), and the certainty that additional letters will continue to 'surface' during the years ahead, the editors have persisted in their original policy of not reproducing quotations from Hardy letters in booksellers' and auctioneers' catalogues or incomplete transcriptions appearing in published books. Exceptions have, however, been made for documents believed to survive only in the form of excerpts printed in *Early Life* and *Later Years* and for the available transcriptions of significant letters to the firm of Harper & Brothers that seem to be no longer in existence. Letters which do exist in manuscript but only in fragmentary form have been included, together with complete letters which have proved impossible to date with any precision, in a third section that is headed 'Undated Letters and Fragments' and organized in a necessarily speculative chronological sequence.

The fourth section, 'Corrections and Amplifications', has provided the editors with an opportunity to make good the errors and oversights detected —by themselves and by others—in the first six volumes. The section also supplies additional information about some of the documents edited earlier —noting, for example, the existence of previously unrecorded envelopes, some of which have become separated from the letters they once enclosed —and replaces or expands upon annotations that information subsequently acquired has revealed to be inadequate or even misleading. Changes in the ownership of individual letters have not been systematically recorded, and in only a very few instances has it seemed necessary to replace a text derived from a transcription by one derived from the newly available manuscript of the same letter.

The volume continues with an index to the recipients of the letters contained within it and—finally, and much more substantially—with the General Index to the entire seven-volume edition.

CHRONOLOGY

THOMAS HARDY 1840–1928

1840	2 June	Born, eldest child of Thomas and Jemima (Hand) Hardy, at Higher Bockhampton, Dorset.
1856	11 July	Articled to John Hicks, Dorchester architect.
1862	17 Apr	Goes to London; soon employed in architectural office of Arthur Blomfield.
1867	20 July	Returns to Dorset because of ill health; again employed by Hicks.
1868	9 June	Completes final draft of 'The Poor Man and the Lady' (later destroyed).
1869	May	Employed by Weymouth architect, G. R. Crickmay.
1870	7 Mar	Goes to St. Juliot, Cornwall, to inspect church; meets Emma Lavinia Gifford for the first time.
1871	25 Mar	*Desperate Remedies* pub. (3 vols.) by Tinsley Brothers.
1872	March	In London lodgings, working for the architect T. Roger Smith.
	June	*Under the Greenwood Tree* pub. (2 vols.) by Tinsley Brothers.
	15 Aug	First instalment of *A Pair of Blue Eyes* in September number of *Tinsleys' Magazine*.
1873	late May	*A Pair of Blue Eyes* pub. (3 vols.) by Tinsley Brothers.
	21 Sept	Suicide of Horace Moule at Cambridge.
	December	First instalment of *Far from the Madding Crowd* in the *Cornhill Magazine*.
1874	17 Sept	Marries Emma Lavinia Gifford at St. Peter's Church, Paddington; honeymoon in France.
	6 Oct	Takes rooms at St. David's Villa, Hook Road, Surbiton.
	23 Nov	*Far from the Madding Crowd* pub. (2 vols.) by Smith, Elder.
1875	22 Mar	Moves to 18 Newton Road, Westbourne Grove, London.
	15 Aug	Moves to West End Cottage, Swanage, Dorset.
1876	early March	Moves to 7 Peter (or St. Peter) Street, Yeovil, Somerset.
	3 Apr	*The Hand of Ethelberta* pub. (2 vols.) by Smith, Elder.
	3 July	Moves to Riverside (or Rivercliff) Villa, Sturminster Newton, Dorset.
1878	22 Mar	Moves to 1 Arundel Terrace, Trinity Road, Upper Tooting.
	4 Nov	*The Return of the Native* pub. (3 vols.) by Smith, Elder.
1880	23 Oct	Beginning of serious illness.
	26 Oct	*The Trumpet-Major* pub. (3 vols.) by Smith, Elder.
1881	25 June	Moves to Lanherne, The Avenue, Wimborne, Dorset.
	early December	*A Laodicean* pub. (3 vols.) by Sampson Low.
1882	late October	*Two on a Tower* pub. (3 vols.) by Sampson Low.
1883	June	Moves to Shire-Hall Lane, Dorchester.

1885	29 June	Moves to Max Gate (designed by himself), just outside Dorchester.
1886	10 May	*The Mayor of Casterbridge* pub. (2 vols.) by Smith, Elder.
1887	15 Mar	*The Woodlanders* pub. (3 vols.) by Macmillan.
	March–April	Visits Italy.
1888	4 May	*Wessex Tales* pub. (2 vols.) by Macmillan.
1891	30 May	*A Group of Noble Dames* pub. by Osgood, McIlvaine.
	late November	*Tess of the d'Urbervilles* pub. (3 vols.) by Osgood, McIlvaine.
1892	20 July	Death of Thomas Hardy, sen.
1893	19 May	In Dublin; first meeting with Florence Henniker.
1894	22 Feb	*Life's Little Ironies* pub. by Osgood, McIlvaine.
1895	4 Apr	First vol. of Wessex Novels edn. pub. by Osgood, McIlvaine.
	1 Nov	*Jude the Obscure* pub. by Osgood, McIlvaine.
1897	16 Mar	*The Well-Beloved* pub. by Osgood, McIlvaine.
1898	December	*Wessex Poems* pub. by Harper & Brothers.
1901	mid-November	*Poems of the Past and the Present* pub. by Harper & Brothers.
1904	13 Jan	*The Dynasts*, Part First, pub. by Macmillan.
	3 Apr	Death of Jemima Hardy.
1906	9 Feb	*The Dynasts*, Part Second, pub. by Macmillan.
1908	11 Feb	*The Dynasts*, Part Third, pub. by Macmillan.
1909	3 Dec	*Time's Laughingstocks* pub. by Macmillan.
1910	June	Receives the Order of Merit.
1912	30 Apr	First two vols. of Wessex Edition pub. by Macmillan.
	27 Nov	Death of Emma Lavinia Hardy.
1913	24 Oct	*A Changed Man and Other Tales* pub. by Macmillan.
1914	10 Feb	Marries Florence Emily Dugdale at St. Andrew's Church, Enfield.
	17 Nov	*Satires of Circumstance* (including 'Poems of 1912–13') pub. by Macmillan.
1915	24 Nov	Death of Mary Hardy, the elder of his sisters.
1917	30 Nov	*Moments of Vision* pub. by Macmillan.
1922	23 May	*Late Lyrics and Earlier* pub. by Macmillan.
1923	15 Nov	*The Famous Tragedy of the Queen of Cornwall* pub. by Macmillan.
1925	20 Nov	*Human Shows, Far Phantasies, Songs, and Trifles* pub. by Macmillan.
1927	21 July	Address at Dorchester Grammar School stone-laying: last public appearance.
1928	11 Jan	Dies at Max Gate.
	2 Oct	*Winter Words* pub. by Macmillan.
	2 Nov	*The Early Life of Thomas Hardy* pub. under the name of Florence Emily Hardy.
1930	29 Apr	*The Later Years of Thomas Hardy* pub. under the name of Florence Emily Hardy.

ACKNOWLEDGEMENTS FOR VOLUME SEVEN

IN the course of collecting and editing the letters in this seventh and final volume the editors have incurred many obligations. Our thanks are due first of all to the authorities of the following institutions for the assistance they have given and for permission to publish manuscripts in their possession:

Aberdeen Art Gallery; Aberdeen University Library, and Mr. Colin A. McLaren; Albert A. and Henry W. Berg Collection, New York Public Library, and Mrs. Lola L. Szladits; B.B.C. Written Archives Centre; University of Birmingham; Bodleian Library; University of Bristol; British Library; British Theatre Association; Cambridge University Library, and Mr. A. E. B. Owen; Case Western Reserve University, and Ms. Sue Hanson; Cecil Sharp House; University of Chicago Library, Department of Special Collections; Clifton College, Bristol; Colby College, Waterville, Maine, and Dr. J. Fraser Cocks III; Columbia University, and Mr. Kenneth A. Lohf; Cornell University; Duchy of Cornwall, by kind permission of His Royal Highness the Prince of Wales;

Dorset County Museum, Dorchester, and Mr. R. N. R. Peers; Dorset County Library; Edinburgh City Library; Essex Institute, Salem, Massachusetts; Eton College, School Library, and Mr. Michael Meredith; Folger Shakespeare Library; Georgetown University; Harvard University, Houghton Library; University of Illinois, Urbana; Indiana University; Iowa State Historical Department; Keats–Shelley Memorial Association; University of Keele; University of Kentucky, W. Hugh Peale Collection, and Ms. Claire McCann; King's College, London, by permission of the College Secretary;

University of Leeds, Brotherton Library, and Mr. Christopher Sheppard; University of London Library; Manchester Central Library; Miami University of Ohio; National Library of Scotland; Newberry Library; New York University, Fales Library, Bobst Library, and Dr. Theodore Grieder; Historical Society of Pennsylvania; Princeton University Library; Queen's College, Oxford; Society for the Protection of Ancient Buildings; Somerville College, Oxford; Syracuse University;

University of Texas at Austin, Harry Ransom Humanities Research Center, and Ms. Cathy Henderson; the Master and Fellows of Trinity College, Cambridge; University of Vermont; State Library of Victoria; Washington and Lee University; Wiltshire Record Office; Yale University, Beinecke Library, and Miss Marjorie G. Wynne; Yale University, Sterling Library.

We owe a special debt of gratitude to the following collectors and private owners who have made manuscripts in their possession available to us:

Mr. Frederick B. Adams, Professor Masao Akagi, Mr. R. Barrie, Lord Bridges, the Hon. David Lytton Cobbold, Mr. Morton N. Cohen, Canon C. P. Cowley, Mr. J. Stevens Cox, Mrs. A. M. Dilke, Mr. Kildare Dobbs,

Mrs. Norton Downes, Mr. Patrick Gardiner, Mr. R. Greenland, Mrs. Lilian Hamlyn, Mr. David Holmes, Miss Imogen Holst, Mr. H. G. Wood Homer, Mr. and Mrs. William Jesty, Mr. W. King, Mr. Rodney Legg, Miss Norma Millay, Mr. Ronald Moore, the Revd. G. R. K. Moule, Mr. Denis O'Malley, Mr. A. D. C. Peterson, Mr. W. M. Purvis, Mr. Gordon N. Ray, Mr. P. C. Roscoe, Mrs. M. Stewart-Mackenzie, Lord Stockton, Miss Barbara Sturgis, Mr. Robert H. Taylor, Mr. T. Trafton.

To the following we offer our grateful thanks for help of many kinds, especially in tracing manuscripts and resolving problems of annotation:

Mr. and Mrs. Frederick B. Adams, Professor Peter Allen, Mr. John Antell, Miss J. V. Ayton, Mr. Simon Bailey, Mrs. Celia Barclay, Dr. and Mrs. C. J. P. Beatty, Mr. Alan Bell, Mr. Michael Bott, Professor Kristin Brady, Dr. Iain G. Brown, Mrs. Gertrude Bugler, Mrs. Fiona Clark, Mr. Alan Clodd, Professor Michael Collie, Professor Philip Collins, Mrs. Jane Cooper, Professor Pierre Coustillas (and the staff of the Service de la Scolarité de l'Université de Lille III), Mr. Nigel Cross, Ms. Pamela Dalziel, Mr. H. Lovat Dickson, Mrs. Jo Draper, Mr. Fraser B. Drew, Mr. Paul Ensom, Mr. John Fowles, Dr. Ian H. C. Fraser, Mrs. Christine Fyfe, Dr. Howard Garber, Mr. Patrick Gardiner, Miss Helen Garton, Dr. James Gibson, Mrs. Carole Gillin, Dr. Robert Gittings, Mr. George T. Goodspeed, Mr. Brian Green, Mr. Ronald Green, Professor Phyllis Grosskurth, Mr. James Gwinn, Dr. M. A. Halls, Mr. G. V. Hardyman, Dr. Graham Haslam, Dr. Desmond Hawkins, Mr. David Holmes, Professor Samuel Hynes, Professor Heather Jackson, Professor J. R. de J. Jackson, Professor Mary Jacobus, Mr. D. Johnson, Mr. Richard Colles Johnson, Professor Christopher Jones, Mr. Denys Kay-Robinson, Professor W. J. Keith, Professor Martin Kreiswirth, Mr. Richard Landon, Mrs. Patience-Anne W. Lenk, Mr. Peter Lennon, Professor Charles Lock, Mrs. Jennifer Macgregor, Canon Roy McKay, Ms. Glenise A. Matheson, Mr. Michael Meredith, Professor Nancy Milford, Professor Jane Millgate, Dr. Rosemarie Morgan, Professor W. W. Morgan, Professor Desmond Neill, Mr. Richard Nemesvari, Professor Norman Page, Mr. Stephen R. Parks, Mr. John Pentney, Mr. A. D. C. Peterson, Mr. Charles P. C. Pettit, Dr. F. B. Pinion, Miss Helen Powell, Mr. Michael Rabiger, Dr. Martin Ray, Mrs. Isabelle Robinson, Professor J. M. Robson, Dr. R. Robson, Mr. P. C. Roscoe, Professor S. P. Rosenbaum, Professor Eric Salmon, Professor Robert C. Schweik, Mrs. Carola Shephard, Mrs. Sofija Skoric, Professor Paul Stevens, Lord Stockton, Mrs. Virginia Surtees, Mrs. Lillian Swindall, Mrs. Ann Thwaite, Professor P. H. Waddington, Miss H. M. Webb, Mr. Brian Weight, Mr. Tom Wightman, Professor Keith Wilson, Professor Donald Winslow, Professor Judith Wittenberg, Mr. C. M. Woolgar, Miss Marjorie G. Wynne, the Revd. J. M. C. Yates.

It seems appropriate, in this final volume, to express our gratitude to Mr. Nicholas Barker, whose design for the volumes has proved both elegant and serviceable in every respect, to Dr. David C. Sutton and the Location Register of Twentieth-century English Literary Manuscripts and Letters, for guiding us to documents otherwise undiscovered, and especially to Miss Catharine Carver, whose superlative editorial skills were of the greatest assistance to the edition in its earlier stages.

Professor Millgate has again been aided in his work by the generous and sustained support of the Social Sciences and Humanities Research Council of Canada. That support helped to make available the expert typing services of Mrs. Freda Gough and the efficient research assistance of Ms. Christy Robson and especially of Ms. Lesley Mann and Dr. Lawrence Miller, both of whom have made substantial contributions to the present volume. Professor Millgate also particularly acknowledges the invaluable editorial participation of Ms. Pamela Dalziel and the researches so willingly and ably undertaken on his behalf by Mr. and Mrs. William Jesty and the late Mr. Malcolm Tomkins.

Our best thanks, finally, must go to the Trustees of the Hardy Estate for their grant of an 'exclusive licence' to collect, edit, and publish Hardy's letters, and to Mr. R. N. R. Peers, Curator of the Dorset County Museum and its Hardy Memorial Collection, for assistance of every sort, most generously given.

December 1987   R.L.P.
                                                          M.M.

LIST OF ABBREVIATIONS

TH	Thomas Hardy
ELH	Emma Lavinia Hardy
FEH	Florence Emily Hardy

Adams	Frederick B. Adams, private collection
Berg	Berg Collection, New York Public Library
Berkeley	University of California, Berkeley
BL	British Library
Buffalo	State University of New York, Buffalo
Colby	Colby College, Waterville, Maine
DCM	Dorset County Museum
LC	Library of Congress
Leeds	University of Leeds, Brotherton Collection
NLS	National Library of Scotland
NYU	New York University, Fales Library
Taylor	Robert H. Taylor, private collection
Texas	University of Texas at Austin, Humanities Research Center
UCLA	University of California, Los Angeles

D.N.B.	*Dictionary of National Biography*
EL	Florence Emily Hardy, *The Early Life of Thomas Hardy* (London, 1928)
LY	Florence Emily Hardy, *The Later Years of Thomas Hardy* (London, 1930)
Millgate	Michael Millgate, *Thomas Hardy: A Biography* (New York, 1982; Oxford, 1982)
Purdy	Richard Little Purdy, *Thomas Hardy: A Bibliographical Study* (London, 1954, 1968, 1978); where no page is indicated, the reference is to the editor's private collection.
Wessex edn.	Wessex Edition, 24 vols. (London, 1912–31)

For the full names of other private and institutional owners of Hardy letters see Acknowledgements, pp. xi–xiii.

1926

To H. W. LEE

Dear Sir:

I am obliged to you for information about the Hyndman Club & Institute, as I was a personal friend of the late Mrs Rosalind Hyndman, & to a less extent of Mr Hyndman himself.

As to the inquiry you make, I am sorry to say that I am unable for several reasons to enter into associations of a political nature, actively or merely nominally. I became a member of the Hyndman Memorial Committee solely on account of the personal friendship I mention, but I never discussed with Mr Hyndman how much, or how little, we agreed in social or political views. I may add that, apart from this, age prevents my joining any new societies.

H. W. Lee Esq. | Hon. Sec. Hyndman Club. | 54, Colebrooke Row, Islington. N. 1.

Text   MS. (pencil draft) DCM.
Lee: Henry William Lee (1865–1932), formerly secretary of the Social Democratic Federation and editor of its journal, *Justice*; in his letter to TH (1 Jan 26, DCM) he identified himself as an associate of Hyndman's since 1884.   *the late . . . Hyndman himself*: for TH's acquaintance with Henry Mayers Hyndman, the socialist leader, and his second wife Rosalind (*née* Travers), see V.270. Mrs. Hyndman committed suicide in April 1923, shortly after completing *The Last Years of H. M. Hyndman* (London, 1923).   *Memorial Committee*: TH (together with Lady St. Helier, George Bernard Shaw, Sir James Frazer, and others) had accepted membership of this Committee when it was established in March 1922, following Hyndman's death; like the S.D.F. itself, the specifically political Hyndman Club and Institute, located in north London, did not long survive the outbreak of the Second World War.

To SIR FREDERICK MACMILLAN

MAX GATE, | DORCHESTER. | Dorset. | 4 January: 1926

Dear Sir Frederick Macmillan:

Mrs Doyle Jones's sketches for the illustrations to "Tess" seemed very promising when I saw them some time ago. A finished one she has sent lately (Tess leaning against a tree) I like very much.

With regard to the suggested édition de luxe besides the ordinary edition, I think I can manage to sign the 325 sheets if the edition is practicable in other respects. Indeed, I feel sure I can, so agree to undertake it, and to accept the sum of £300, which seems to me quite liberal. Whenever therefore you send on the pages I will begin. It is, I believe, advisable in such cases, and easier for the writer, that each sheet should not be absolutely blank, but should have some words printed upon it referring to the edition, so that the name be written immediately under them. But you are probably aware of all this.

I am glad to hear that "Human Shows" is going on well, and am obliged for the American copy. I have not detected any misprint as yet.

My wife and I reciprocate your good wishes for the New Year. I don't mind the wet, mild weather, preferring anything to bitter cold.

Yours very sincerely,
Thomas Hardy.

P.S. I want to put a foot-note to the "Apology" in "Late Lyrics" whenever you include the volume in the Wessex edition. Perhaps you will let me know. T.H.

Text   MS. (typewritten) BL.
Macmillan: Sir Frederick Orridge Macmillan (see I.132), publisher.   *illustrations to "Tess"*: Macmillan wrote 1 Jan 26 (Macmillan letterbooks, BL) to report that Mrs. Doyle Jones (Vivien Gribble; see VI.292) was making good progress with the woodblocks for the forthcoming illustrated issue of *Tess of the d'Urbervilles*.   *against a tree*: see opp. p. 108 of the illustrated *Tess*, pub. by Macmillan later in 1926.   *édition de luxe*: of the illustrated *Tess*; Macmillan had suggested that TH could take as long as a month to sign the 325 statement of limitation sheets for the fee of £300.   *"Human Shows"*: TH's *Human Shows, Far Phantasies, Songs and Trifles*, pub. by Macmillan in November 1925, had already gone into a third printing; a reset American edn. was pub. by Macmillan in New York in December 1925 (see Purdy, 248).   *My wife*: Florence Emily Hardy (FEH), *née* Dugdale, whom TH married, as his second wife, in 1914; see III.179 and V.8.   *Wessex edition*: Macmillan replied (6 Jan 26, Macmillan letterbooks, BL) that the Wessex Edition vol. (London, 1926) containing *Late Lyrics and Earlier* was already being printed and that TH should send copy for the footnote at once; it appears on p. xiv and regrets the continuing conservatism of the Church of England.

To SIR FREDERICK MACMILLAN

MAX GATE, | DORCHESTER, | DORSET. | 9th. January 1926.

Dear Sir Frederick:

I have looked up "The Thomas Hardy Dictionary" by F. O. Saxelby that you mention, which was sent to me when it appeared in 1911. It is, I think, rather a useless book, being a compilation of commonplace ingenuity, for which I should imagine there would be little demand, after it was found to be what it ought to have been called, a Dictionary of the fictitious characters in the novels (which I cannot conceive the use of,) and a synopsis of each story (which rather gives the novels away by making people content with it, without reading the originals.) In addition to this it tells the supposed real places concealed by the fictitious names, which is merely an overlapping of Mr Lea's book. And it omits "The Dynasts" entirely, with its hundreds of characters and places which, as they are all real, would be more useful than any. And of course it omits all references to books published since 1911. So that it would have to be entirely recast and enlarged before it could be offered to readers. On the whole I should prefer that it be not taken up, and I imagine few people would buy it.

The question arises whether the compiler could get another publisher to do it. But in that case there would be no appearance of its being authorized, and I should have a free hand in asserting it to be incomplete, ill-proportioned, erroneous, or what not.

I am sending up the footnote I spoke of, and a correction of a word or two elsewhere. The words you are going to print on the autograph-sheets will help the signing,

Yours very sincerely,
Thomas Hardy.

Text MS. (typewritten) BL.

you mention: Macmillan (6 Jan 26, Macmillan letterbooks, BL) asked if TH approved of F. Outwin Saxelby's proposal for a new and revised edn. of his *A Thomas Hardy Dictionary*; see IV.133–4.   *Mr Lea's book*: *Thomas Hardy's Wessex* by TH's friend Hermann Lea (see II.232), pub. by Macmillan in 1913 (see IV.164, etc.).   *the footnote*: see letter of 4 Jan 26; Macmillan sent a proof showing the correction on 15 Jan 26 (Macmillan letterbooks, BL).   *the signing*: Macmillan said in his letter that the statement of limitation sheets for the illustrated *Tess* would carry the printed words, 'This is one of three hundred and twenty-five copies on large paper printed in 1926'.

To J. H. MORGAN

MAX GATE, | DORCHESTER, | DORSET. | 12 Jan. 1926

Dear General Morgan:

I was by chance looking into your article in the English Review to-day, & it suddenly occurred to me that I had never thanked you for sending it. But I am doing such things continually now, owing to increasing age, except when using the typist's services, and I get, I daresay, a sad character for neglect.

The question of the Polish "corridor" has always been interesting to me—I fear rather from its ingenious appearance on the map, as a means of making an inland country a sea-bord one, than from any real understanding of the means & practicability of the scheme. We might save Shakespeare's reputation, for making Bohemia a country with a coast, in the same manner.

That must have been a pleasant dinner at F. Pollock's. Ld Balfour is more brilliant at such gatherings than he is in his philosophic writings. I was reading his article in "Science & Religion" a week or two back, & found it hopelessly old fashioned, leaving you after studying it "as you was," (as the drill-serjeants used to say when I was a boy).

Sincerely yours
Thomas Hardy.

Text MS. Berg.

Morgan: John Hartman Morgan, lawyer and author; see V.187.   *your article*: 'First Thoughts on the Security Pact', *English Review*, November 1925.   *Polish "corridor"*: allowing Poland access to the Baltic Sea; this issue was, in fact, only briefly touched upon in Morgan's discussion of the Pact of Locarno, initialled 16 Oct 1925.   *Bohemia . . . coast*: TH first wrote 'Bohemia an isla', then struck through everything after 'Bohemia'; the allusion is to *The Winter's Tale*, III. iii. 1–2.   *F. Pollock's*: Sir Frederick Pollock, jurist; see VI.170. Since Morgan's letter has not survived the exact occasion cannot be identified.   *Ld Balfour*: Arthur James Balfour (see II.185), former prime minister, created Earl of Balfour in 1922.   *his article*: Balfour wrote the Introduction to *Science, Religion and Reality*, a collection of essays edited by Joseph Needham (London, 1925).   *when I was a boy*: Dorchester was a garrison town during TH's childhood, and after.

To G. HERBERT THRING

MAX GATE, DORCHESTER. | 16th. January 1926.

Dear Mr Thring:

The Return of the Native (Czech trans.)

I agree with you in seeing no reason why I should sign certain copies of the Czech translation. The actual readers of the book are not likely to value an autograph, so that it would profit only the publishers. Please therefore reply to this effect. You may also, if you think it desirable, say that signing books is troublesome to me on account of increasing age.

Yours sincerely,
T. Hardy.

Text MS. (typewritten) BL.
Thring: George Herbert Thring (see III.8), secretary to the Incorporated Society of Authors, Playwrights, and Composers, of which TH was president.   *the Czech translation*: published in Prague in two volumes, 1924–5; see VI.251.

To JOHN HUTCHINSON

[Ans]   [Mid-January 1926]

Dear Sir:

Mr Hardy says in reply to your inquiry that in the Greek Anthology the epitaph is a mournful one on an unhappy man. (A neater translation than that you cite is given in Mackail's Select Epigrams, & a rhymed one in Stebbing's Greek Epigrams.) In the French rendering (author forgotten) it is changed to humorous, as also in Mr Hardy's, and the French version was alluded to on that account.

Yours truly
. . . .
Secretary

John H. Hutchinson Esq. | Dublin

Text MS. (pencil draft) DCM.   *Date* Replies to letter of 18 Jan 26.
Hutchinson: John H. Hutchinson, of 55 Hollybank Road, Dublin; he wrote 18 Jan 26 (DCM).   *[Ans]*: TH's square brackets.   *the epitaph*: TH's 'Epitaph on a Pessimist', first collected in *Human Shows* with the annotation, 'From the French'. Hutchinson asked TH if he could identify his source and pointed out that any French version must have derived from a very similar epigram in the Greek Anthology (VII, 309). TH subsequently changed the annotation to read, 'From the French and Greek'.   *that you cite*: Hutchinson referred to the Loeb Classics edition of the Greek Anthology, with a translation by W. R. Paton (5 vols., London, 1917), II.169.   *Mackail's . . . Stebbing's*: see Purdy, 244; for Mackail and Stebbing see V.174 and IV.273 respectively.   *Secretary*: May O'Rourke (see V.271), who did a good deal of secretarial work at Max Gate during these years, says in her *Thomas Hardy: His Secretary Remembers* (Beaminster, 1965), 43, that she was in Italy until late February 1926; if so, this letter would have been typed and initialled by FEH and sent out as if from a secretary (see 'A Note on Hardy's Drafts', V.[vii]).

To LADY PINNEY

MAX GATE, | DORCHESTER. | 20 Jan. 1926

My dear Lady Pinney:

My sincere thanks for the details you have been so indefatigable as to obtain about that unhappy woman Martha Brown, whom I am ashamed to say I saw hanged, my only excuse being that I was but a youth, & had to be in the town at the time for other reasons. I gather from your description that the house of the murder has quite disappeared. I daresay it was pulled down as much on account of its tragic associations as from its dilapidated state. I wonder if there are any remains of it. I remember what a fine figure she showed against the sky as she hung in the misty rain, & how the tight black silk gown set off her shape as she wheeled half-round & back.

I hope you have not felt the cold much: we have somewhat. Young people love frost, but I for one don't. We shall be glad to see you later on.

Affectionately yours
Thomas Hardy.

Text   MS. (with envelope) Univ. of Bristol.
Pinney: Lady Hester Pinney, wife of Maj.-Gen. Sir Reginald John Pinney, of Racedown, Dorset (see VI.375), and sister of TH's friend Dr. Henry Head (see VI.129).   *Martha Brown*: correctly, Browne; TH was present when she was publicly hanged in Dorchester, 9 Aug 1856, for the murder of her husband. She came from Birdsmoorgate, near Racedown, and Lady Pinney, at TH's request, had been gathering information about her from local inhabitants; see Millgate, 63, and Lady Hester Pinney, *Thomas Hardy and the Birdsmoorgate Murder 1856* (Beaminster, 1966).

To G. HERBERT THRING

Encl.   22 January 1926

Dear Mr Thring:

I enclose herewith a circular letter from the Duke of Portland as President of the Alexandra Memorial Committee, asking if the Society of Authors can participate in the Memorial. I am telling him that I have sent his letter on to the Council of the Society, & that they will give it their consideration, but that I cannot say what its Members may be disposed, or able to do in the matter.

Yours very truly

. . . .

Text   MS. (pencil draft) DCM.
Portland: Sir William John Arthur Charles James Cavendish-Bentinck, 6th Duke of Portland (1857–1943), whose wife was a former Mistress of the Robes to Queen Alexandra. He had addressed TH as the President of the Society of Authors and TH's draft reply to him is also in DCM.   *the Memorial*: to Queen Alexandra (1844–1925; *D.N.B.*); it took the form of a fund to support the work of Queen Victoria's Jubilee Institute for Nurses, of which Queen Alexandra was patron.   *the Council*: Thring reported on 2 Feb 26 (DCM) that the Council, meeting the previous day, had expressed its sympathy but decided that it would be 'outside the legitimate work of the Society' to accede to the Duke's request.

To SIR FREDERICK MACMILLAN

MAX GATE, DORCHESTER. | 25 January 1926.

Dear Sir Frederick:

I duly received the sheets, and have signed 180 of them. I will go on till I have signed all of them, and send them back in the same box to Clarks, unless you write to say otherwise.

Very sincerely yours,
Th: Hardy.

Text   MS. (typewritten) BL.
the sheets: see letters of 4 and 9 Jan 26.   *Clarks*: the Edinburgh printing firm of R. & R. Clark.   *say otherwise*: Macmillan did in fact write (26 Jan 26, Macmillan letterbooks, BL) to ask that the signed sheets be sent to the Macmillan & Co. offices in London.

To CHRISTINE SILVER

MAX GATE, | DORCHESTER. | 26: 1: 1926.

Photograph returned. Good luck to you & the play.

T.H.

Text   MS. (correspondence card) Barbara Sturgis.
Silver: Christine Silver (1884–1960), the actress who played Tess in the Barnes Theatre touring production of *Tess of the d'Urbervilles*; later in 1926 she played Susan Henchard in the Barnes Theatre production of *The Mayor of Casterbridge*. In *Who's Who in the Theatre* for 1957 she listed Tess as her favourite part.

To SIR FREDERICK MACMILLAN

MAX GATE, | DORCHESTER. | 27th. January 1926.

Dear Sir Frederick:

Here I am writing again. The British Broadcasting Company ask permission to broadcast three scenes from The Dynasts. I have told them I will consult you; but I do not see there can be any objection, as the scenes are mere extracts from a long drama. I am not aware if a charge is usually made in these cases, and do not wish to make any, the publicity given being I suppose of some value, but I will hear what you say about it.

I am creeping on with the signatures, and will send the sheets to you when finished.

Sincerely yours,
T.H.

Text   MS. (typewritten) BL.
what you say about it: Macmillan replied (28 Jan 26, Macmillan letterbooks, BL) that, under the terms of an agreement between the B.B.C. and the Society of Authors, TH should receive a minimum fee of six guineas for the broadcast. The projected performance appears not to have taken place, although TH did accept a fee of two guineas for a reading from *The Dynasts* broadcast in October 1927 (B.B.C. Written Archives Centre).

To SYDNEY NICHOLSON

February 16. 1926

Dear Sir:

I have received your interesting circular letter, enclosing the Review of the Abbey "Special Choir's" recent doings, which I found attractive reading, for though I have never had anything to do with the Abbey music I have known the building with a certain intimacy for a good many years (ever since in fact, I was present at Lord Palmerston's funeral in 1865) & was at one time connected with old church music & musicians.

However I am compelled on account of age & other reasons to decline the honour of becoming a Patron of the Special Choir, being forced nowadays to cut off many desirable associations. With my thanks & many regrets I am

Yours very truly

Sydney H. Nicholson Esq. M.A. Mus.Bac.

Text   MS. (pencil draft) DCM.
Nicholson: Sydney Hugo Nicholson (1875–1947), organist and master of the choristers, Westminster Abbey, 1918–28, and founder of the Royal School of Church Music; *D.N.B.*   *circular
letter*: of 13 Feb 26 (DCM).   *"Special Choir's"*: the Westminster Abbey Special Choir,
trained not only for the Abbey services and for recitals but also for performances on national
occasions.   *Palmerston's funeral*: see I.5–6.   *old church music & musicians*: through the
participation of his father, grandfather, and uncle in the old Stinsford 'Quire'; see *Under the
Greenwood Tree, passim*, and *EL*, 12–17.

To THE REVD. H. G. B. COWLEY

23 February 1926

Dear Mr Cowley:

In respect of the report by the bellfounders on the Stinsford bells I am thinking you might reply with some queries on these points:—

1. As the parish is not a rich one, could the difficulty & expense of re-casting the treble be got over by cutting out the crack, as was done, I believe, with "Big Ben"? Even if the tone thus recovered should not be inferior to that of a new bell, there would be the great advantage of retaining the actual old bell, which is of pre-Reformation date.

2. Could not some of the oak from the old beams & bell-carriages be re-used, as it can scarcely be entirely decayed?

3. It is understood that, in re-hanging, the canons need not be cut off from the heads of the bells, which would be fastened to the head-stocks in the old manner. As they would not be re-hung for ringing peals, there would be no object in mutilating them in the modern fashion to make them swing more easily.

I did not know that the old bells had such historic interest till I read the report, & if anything should be done I will subscribe something. I wish I could afford to pay for the whole job. The report is returned herewith.

Sincerely yours

Text   MS. (pencil draft) DCM.
Cowley: the Revd. Henry Guise Beatson Cowley (see IV.237), vicar of Stinsford since 1911.   *with "Big Ben"*: the great bell of the clock in St. Stephen's tower of the Palace of Westminster cracked within a few months of first becoming operational in 1859 but was repaired without recasting.   *not be inferior to*: TH first wrote, 'not be so good as'.   *retaining . . .* *pre-Reformation date*: although the Parochial Church Council, meeting on 12 Mar 1926, decided against either recasting or even rehanging the treble bell (which probably dated from the 15th century), it was in fact recast and then rehung with the other two bells (dating from the 17th century) in 1927.   *canons*: a canon (or cannon) is the 'metal loop or "ear" at the top of a bell, by which it is hung' (*O.E.D.*).   *head-stocks*: the blocks of wood from which bells are hung; TH made the same point with reference to the Stinsford bells in 1909 (see IV.20).   *subscribe something*: see letter to Cowley of 27 Feb 26.

To SIR FREDERICK MACMILLAN

MAX GATE, | DORCHESTER. | February 24th. 1926.

Dear Sir Frederick:

To have "green malt in floor" means to have a daughter in childbed before she is married—green malt meaning immature malt, and a floor of malt meaning the outspread malt for steeping. I am not surprised at the Japanese gentleman being puzzled as there is hardly anyone left in Dorset who would know the meaning of the saying, it having quite passed out of use. I will have a line of explanation sent him, since he is so persevering.

The new volume of the Wessex edition has just come. The Late Lyrics and the Queen of Cornwall fit in very well. One other copy will be quite enough at present, for a set my wife is making up.

Thanks, my cold went off when the wind changed from east as it mostly does.

Very sincerely yours,
Thomas Hardy.

Text   MS. (typewritten) BL.
"green . . . floor": see *Tess of the d'Urbervilles* (Wessex edn.), 29.   *Japanese gentleman*: Macmillan (23 Feb 26, Macmillan letterbooks, BL) forwarded his letter but did not cite his name.

To R. GOLDING BRIGHT

MAX GATE, | DORCHESTER, | DORSET. | February 27th. 1926.

Dear Mr Golding Bright:

I have received the application I enclose herewith, and have no objection to the performance of "Tess" by Mr Stirling's company, though I am not anxious for them to do it, as the novel is already well-known in France. I do not know what terms a Repertory Theatre expects, but I am willing to be quite reasonable. Perhaps you could enquire particulars for me, if you think it worth while.

With regard to the copies of the play that were sent, if you remember, to the Belgian manager at his earnest request, and also to Mr Ames of New York, who was in the same haste, everything has lapsed into silence. Don't you think we had better get back the copies?

> Yours very truly,
> T. Hardy.

Text   MS. (typewritten) Adams.
Bright: Reginald Golding Bright (see III.272), the dramatic agent to whom TH had entrusted the play-version of *Tess* the previous year (see VI.303, etc.).   *Mr Stirling's company*: Edward Stirling (1891–1948), actor and producer, director of the English Players, a professional company performing outside England itself; there is, however, no mention of a *Tess* play in Stirling's autobiographical *Something to Declare* (London, 1942).   *Belgian manager*: Jules Delacre of Le Théâtre du Marais; see VI.357–8.   *Mr Ames*: Winthrop Ames, American theatrical producer; see VI.302.

To THE REVD. H. G. B. COWLEY

27 February 1926

Dear Mr Cowley

I have been thinking over your suggestion that something could be done to raise subscriptions for the bells by a paragraph or so in the English & American papers to the effect that Stinsford is the Church I have described under the name of Mellstock (it is not *exactly* so in trifling details, but never mind that). As I cannot very well draw attention to my own writings personally, all I can do is to furnish you with the facts enclosed, that you may make use of them in any way you choose with the above object. I hope it will be with some effect.

> Sincerely yours

"Mellstock Church", in T.Hs novel "Under the Greenwood Tree" is well known locally to be Stinsford Church under a very thin disguise. The sub-title of the story is "The Mellstock Quire", the description of which as it used to be before the substitution of an organ for stringed instruments fills a large part of the book. The old west gallery, which also appears in the story, was removed when the old quire was abolished in the latter part of the last century.

Several of Mr Hardy's poems also refer to the same church & churchyard. "The Dead Quire" for example, treats of the ghostly reappearance of the same Quire. "Afternoon service at Mellstock" describes the congregation of those old days, & "Voices in a Churchyard" brings in several names that are to be still read on the tombstones there.

It is for the bells of this interesting Church that the appeal is made. They are in wretched condition, & the old oak bell-carriages & mechanism quite decayed. The tenor is of very fine tone, & the treble, which is cracked, is of pre-Reformation date. [Any details from the Report that may be necessary can be added.]

Text   MS. (pencil draft) DCM.
your suggestion: Cowley (24 Feb 26, DCM) had asked TH to write a few lines supporting an appeal for the £123 needed to repair the Stinsford church bells (see letter of 23 Feb 26).   *facts enclosed*: included here in the form of a postscript.   *any way you choose*: see, however, letter to Cowley of 13 Apr 26.   *latter . . . century*: the quire seems in fact to have been disbanded in the early 1840s; see Millgate, 14.   *[Any . . . added.]*: TH's square brackets.

To CHARLES BATES

1 March 1926

Dear Sir:

I have received your account of the movement for a Memorial to Blake, which much interests me & has my approval. I am quite willing to be associated with any plan for carrying it out, so that you may place my name in the list of supporters when you apply to the Dean & Chapter. The exact form of the memorial to be left for future consideration.

Yours very truly
(Signed) T.H.

Text MS. (pencil draft) DCM.
Bates: Charles H. Bates, of Bedford Park, London, was Hon. Secretary of the Blake Centenary Memorial Fund; he wrote 26 Feb 26 (DCM) to seek TH's support for a formal application to the Dean and Chapter of St. Paul's Cathedral for a memorial to be placed there 100 years after William Blake's death in 1827. Once the application had been granted TH joined in signing a letter to *The Times*, 20 Mar 1926, which invited contributions to the scheme.   *The exact . . . consideration*: TH took over this sentence almost verbatim from Bates's letter. The memorial, executed by Henry Poole, was unveiled in the crypt of St. Paul's 6 July 1927.

To J. C. SQUIRE

MAX GATE, | DORCHESTER. | 1 March 1926

Dear Mr Squire:

I have been dipping into your poems during the last few days, & ought to have thanked you for them before this time, though you should have made me buy a copy & not have presented it. However *I* don't object to your plan, because I get an inscription by it.

I cannot tell you which of the number I like absolutely the best; likings vary with "the season & the mood" as Tennyson says—at least they do with me. But some of those I put in a row on a mental shelf as it were are "Winter Nightfall" "To a Bull-dog" "The Three Hills", "Song," "To a Musician", "Rivers"; & (I think) "A Far Place", & "The Lover Comforts himself." One I dare not read again, "The Stockyard".

I hope you did not include any good ones in your rejections: but that is rather a risky process I find.

With renewed thanks believe me

Always sincerely yours
Thomas Hardy.

P.S. My wife says I must congratulate you on a domestic increase, of which she has seen a notice. T.H.

Text MS. NYU.
Squire: John Collings Squire, man of letters; see V.322.   *your poems*: Squire's *Poems in One Volume* (London, 1926).   *as Tennyson says*: line 71 of 'Aylmer's Field' reads 'But subject to the season or the mood'.   *"To a Bull-dog"*: see VI.86.   *"The Stockyard"*: see VI.137, 199.   *a notice*: the birth of a daughter to Squire's wife Eileen was announced in *The Times*, 26 Feb 1926. ·

To G. HERBERT THRING

MAX GATE, | DORCHESTER. | 2 March 1926.

Dear Mr Thring:

"Tess of the d'Urbervilles" (Czech rights.)

So far as I know, no translation of this novel has been published in Czech. It is of course possible that one may have appeared without my knowledge, as it was done into Russian, German, Italian, and I cannot say what other languages. I should think the publisher himself could find out if it has been translated more easily than anybody, as there would be copies in the Prague shops; and in any event no *exclusive* right of translation has ever been granted. I am willing to accept the offer, if Dr Marven decides to go on with the book.

In respect of "Far from the Madding Crowd" it must have been translated without my knowledge.

Should Dr Marven hesitate over "Tess", there are plenty of others. "A Pair of Blue Eyes", for instance, is a great favourite with French readers in their translation.

Yours very truly,
Th: Hardy.

G. Herbert Thring. Esq. | Society of Authors.

Text   MS. (typewritten) BL.
Dr Marven: evidently TH's misreading of the name of Dr. Štorch-Marien (1897–1974), Czech writer and publisher, whose Prague publishing house brought out *Tess z D'Urbervillů*, trans. Jos. J. David, in 1927.

To PERCY SMALLMAN

5 March 1926

Dear Sir:

In reply to your letter of the 4th to Mr Hardy I write for him to say that he is glad to hear that representatives of the Weymouth Town Council have accepted an invitation to visit the citizens of their namesake town of Weymouth, Massachusetts, & hopes that the visit will be entirely successful.

In respect of your suggestion that Mr Hardy should afford you an interview on the subject, he considers such an interview would be unnecessary in view of the very small claim he has to be associated with the proposed visit. He could, however, give a small written message to the representatives before they start, that may be delivered to the citizens of the Massachusetts Weymouth.

Yours very truly
E.F.
Secretary

Percy Smallman Esq. | Town Clerk's Office | Weymouth.

Text   MS. (pencil draft) DCM.
Smallman: Percy Smallman (d. 1982, aged 93), town clerk of Weymouth 1926–56; he wrote 4 Mar 26 (DCM) to ask if he might call to discuss the possibility of TH's sending a message to Weymouth, Mass.   *small written message*: TH in fact sent Smallman two versions of the message; a copy of the one selected for transmission is in DCM. See Purdy, 323, and *The Personal Notebooks of Thomas Hardy*, ed. Richard H. Taylor (London, 1978), 282.   *E.F.*: apparently

an inversion (for the sake of disguise) of the initials 'F.E.' often used by FEH when acting in a secretarial capacity.

To MARGARET BRADISH

[Ans]   11 March 1926

Dear Madam:

In reply to your circulars Mr Hardy wishes me to say that he has already notified in public prints, &c, his opposition to the practice of keeping animals & birds in captivity. A message from him was therefore not necessary, & undesirable, since it is a mistake to be over-emphatic even in a good cause.

Yours truly
M. O'R.   Secy

Text   MS. (pencil draft) DCM.

Bradish: Margaret Julia Bradish (d. 1944), of Chiswick, an active member of the Royal Society for the Prevention of Cruelty to Animals; see E. S. Turner, *All Heaven in a Rage* (London, 1964), 303. Her duplicated letter (dated February 1926) asked for messages of sympathy to be sent to a public meeting of protest 'against keeping animals and birds in life-long close captivity'; in a hand-written addition she appealed specifically to TH as 'a lover of freedom, & hater of cruelty'.   *[Ans]*: TH's square brackets.

To THOMAS J. WISE

MAX GATE, | DORCHESTER, | DORSET. | 21 March 1926.

Dear Mr Wise:

My great thanks for the seventh volume of the Catalogue. You really ought not to bestow these valuable books upon me.

I am thinking of your troubles ahead even yet, since a little further on in the Ws you will have to encounter Wordsworth.

I have glanced at p. 29, where Bartolini's Hotel is mentioned as the meeting place of the "Cannibal Club", & you may be surprised to hear that I used to lunch there in my younger days (as Tennyson did earlier, I think), before Swinburne knew the place. In my time the floors were of stone, sanded, & the front of squared ashlar, just as in Dr Burney's day, &, no doubt, Sir Isaac Newton's. I wonder who was fool enough to pull down such an interesting building.

Sincerely yours
Thomas Hardy.

Text   MS. (with envelope) BL.

Wise: Thomas James Wise, bibliographer and forger; see V.192.   *the Catalogue*: Wise's *The Ashley Library: A Catalogue of Printed Books, Manuscripts and Autograph Letters*, Vol. 7 (London, 1925); Wise had already sent TH the earlier vols.   *further on in the Ws*: vol. 7 concludes with the entries for Wollstonecraft.   *Bartolini's Hotel*: see *EL*, 55, and letter of 23 Mar 26.   *"Cannibal Club"*: the reference appears in the Catalogue entry (28) for Wise's own 1913 private printing of Swinburne's poem 'The Cannibal Catechism', written to be recited or sung at Club meetings.   *Dr Burney's*: Charles Burney (1726–1814), musician and author, father of Fanny Burney; *D.N.B.*   *Newton's*: Isaac Newton (1642–1727), scientist, mathematician, and philosopher; *D.N.B.*

To THOMAS J. WISE

MAX GATE, | DORCHESTER. | 23 March 1926

Dear Mr Wise:

Yes: I should like a copy of the C.C. if you have one to spare.

That old house—it was, by the way B*e*rtolini's, not B*a*rtolini's—must have seen an extraordinary number of interesting people in it from Newton onward. I must ask the Macmillans how it came to be pulled down. It was exactly opposite their offices.

Sincerely yours
Th: Hardy.

Text MS. (with envelope) BL.
copy of the C.C.: Wise's pamphlet of Swinburne's 'The Cannibal Catechism' (see letter of 21 Mar 26) had been limited to 20 copies; his offer to TH was made in a letter of 22 Mar 26 (DCM).   *opposite their offices*: in St. Martin's Street, just S. of Leicester Square.

To HENRY ARTHUR JONES

MAX GATE, | DORCHESTER. | 26: 3: 1926

We (Baldwin, Macdonald, Asquith, & Self) have not appealed for a "National Theatre",—only for the *rebuilding* of the Shakespeare Theatre burnt down at Stratford-on-Avon.

Am glad to hear you are recovering.

T.H.

Text MS. (postcard) Taylor.
Jones: Henry Arthur Jones, dramatist; see II.31.   *We . . . Self)*: TH had joined with Stanley Baldwin (1867–1947; *D.N.B.*), the current prime minister, James Ramsay MacDonald (1866–1937; *D.N.B.*), the Labour leader, and Lord Oxford and Asquith (see III.353), the former Liberal prime minister, in signing an appeal for funds to build a new theatre in Stratford-upon-Avon to replace the original Shakespeare Memorial Theatre, destroyed by fire earlier in the month; the appeal was pub. in *The Times*, 25 Mar 1925. Jones's letter (25 Mar 26, DCM), apparently based on a misunderstanding, argued that no National Theatre should be built until there were actors who could speak blank verse.   *recovering*: Jones said that he had been in bed for six months but was now improving; he underwent a major kidney operation, however, in July 1926.

To THE BISHOP OF SALISBURY

MAX GATE, | DORCHESTER. | 27 March 1926

Dear Bishop of Salisbury:

I will look into the Dilapidations question, as a matter of interest (I had to report upon & schedule them in my younger days!) but I fear there are too many starving authors knocking at the door to allow me to do anything for the burdened clergy.

I hope your throat is improving. I have all my life suffered from a weak throat, hindering all speech-making (a good thing). I find that *honey* for breakfast, & at odd times is rather beneficial.

Sincerely yours
Thomas Hardy.

Text   MS. Wiltshire Record Office.
Bishop of Salisbury: the Right Revd. St. Clair George Alfred Donaldson (1863–1935), Bishop of Salisbury; *D.N.B.* He and TH were both Honorary Fellows of Magdalene College, Cambridge; see VI.194.   *Dilapidations question*: Donaldson had evidently sent TH an appeal for funds to meet the costs of church repairs, especially insofar as these fell upon the shoulders of incumbents.   *in my younger days*: i.e., during his career as an architect.

To SIR FREDERICK MACMILLAN

MAX GATE, | DORCHESTER. | 3rd. April 1926.

Dear Sir Frederick:

I am glad to hear that the limited edition of "Tess" promises to be so successful. I did not think that it would be bought up so soon.

As to what you tell me of the prospects of a limited edition of "The Dynasts", I am really more interested in that than in the other. And with regard to the autographing, I did not find the "Tess" autographs to be any particular burden, so that I feel sure I can get through this 500 without much effort—by doing, say, about 30 a day. Whenever you send them I will begin.

I am quite in your hands about the terms, a fee of £1 per copy, since you know all the details on which the amount should be based, and I do not. So I accept your judgment without hesitation on what will be proper in the circumstances.

I wonder whether you are proposing to illustrate "The Dynasts" as you are doing with "Tess". I have never considered what might be done in this way with a limited edition. But I have often thought that if you ever should wish to bring out a popular, people's, college, or school edition of the drama (as was done with some of Victor Hugo's books, I think) all that would be necessary would be to get photographs of the various capitals, public buildings, battle-fields, and other historic sites of Europe that come into the drama (a large number), and get an artist to reproduce them, which would result in an attractive picture-book, apart from the text. This, however, is outside the present question. I am,

Very sincerely yours,
Thomas Hardy.

Text   MS. (typewritten) BL.
bought up so soon: Macmillan (29 Mar 26, Macmillan letterbooks, BL) reported that orders had been received ahead of publication for all 325 copies of the limited, signed, large-paper issue of *Tess of the d'Urbervilles* illustrated with wood engravings by Vivien Gribble; see letter of 4 Jan 26.   *limited . . . Dynasts*": Macmillan asked whether TH would be prepared to sign 500 copies of a projected three-vol. limited edn. of *The Dynasts*.   *Victor Hugo's books*: although numerous school edns. of Hugo's works had been pub. in Britain by this date, none of those examined has proved to be illustrated in the way TH suggests.   *outside the present question*: Macmillan (6 Apr 26, Macmillan letterbooks, BL) did not greet this suggestion with particular enthusiasm, and it was not followed up.

To JOHN PINNEY

MAX GATE, | DORCHESTER. [6 April 1926]

Thank you for the beautiful Easter egg, John.

T.H.

Text MS. (postcard) Univ. of Bristol. *Date* From postmark.
Pinney: John Pinney (see VI.375), the young son of Lady Hester Pinney and her husband, of Racedown, Dorset; see letter of 20 Jan 26. *Thank . . . T.H.*: the hand, though large, rounded, and strongly slanted, does indeed appear to be TH's.

To SIR FREDERICK MACMILLAN

MAX GATE, | DORCHESTER. | 7 April 1926.

Dear Sir Frederick:

In respect of the illustrated small-paper "Tess", you are probably right in supposing buyers will be more active in securing a copy if they think the edition may soon be exhausted. I should myself; so that I have nothing to say against your doing as you propose, i.e., limiting the edition to 1500. On this edition you will pay me £250.

As to date of payment, many thanks for your suggestion to send cheque at any time. I really don't much mind, so suppose we say about Midsummer for the autographed and unautographed editions of "Tess" illustrated, and for the autographed "Dynasts" some time later on—or at the same time as may be convenient, if I have finished them by then.

Very sincerely yours,
Thomas Hardy.

Text MS. (typewritten) BL.
limiting . . . to 1500: a statement to this effect appears on the verso of the half-title of the standard-sized vols. of *Tess* containing the Vivien Gribble illustrations; see letter of 3 Apr 26. *pay me £250*: Macmillan (6 Apr 26, Macmillan letterbooks, BL) explained that this would be a down-payment; the original plan had envisaged payment of the standard Wessex edn. royalty of 1s.6d. on each of up to 3,000 copies. *finished them*: i.e., finished signing the sheets for the limited edn. of *The Dynasts*.

To G. HERBERT THRING

FROM TH. HARDY, | MAX GATE, | DORCHESTER. | 8 April 1926

1 Copy of the Czech agreement for translating Tess of the d'Urbervilles signed & returned herewith. Many thanks.

Text MS. (correspondence card) BL.
Czech agreement: see letter of 2 Mar 26.

To THE REVD. H. G. B. COWLEY

MAX GATE, | DORCHESTER. | 13 April 1926

Dear Mr Cowley:

I think the appeal for help with the bells will do very well, & return it herewith: also attached to it what I understand you thought I might say. If however no remark from myself is necessary, please pull off the strip of paper, which can easily be done.

I hope something will result, & am

Sincerely yours
T. Hardy.

Text MS. Canon Cowley.
appeal . . . bells: Cowley had apparently declined TH's suggestions (see letter to Cowley of 27 Feb 26) as to the form the appeal for the Stinsford bells might take and secured his approval of the quite differently worded appeal pub. in the Paris edn. of the New York *Herald*, 25 April 1926. *I might say*: the reference is evidently to TH's brief letter of endorsement, requested by Cowley in his letter of 9 Apr 26 (DCM) and also pub. in the *Herald* on 25 April. *something will result*: in October 1926, however, a printed statement issued by the Stinsford Parochial Church Council reported that no contributions whatsoever had resulted from the *Herald* appeal.

To F. W. SLATER

13 April 1926

Dear Mr Slater:

I return Mr Canfield's letter, & am sorry to say that the suggestion of Mr Hardy being interviewed by the lady correspondent of the New York World is impracticable. He has often been asked by interviewers to let them come, but for many years past increasing age & other reasons have rendered him unable to receive them.

Mr Bowker of New York, whom you mention, is remembered by Mr Hardy very well as the agent who started Harper's Magazine in England. As he, unlike the press lady, is presumably not coming to take notes we shall be pleased to see him when he happens to be in this part of England during his stay.

Thank you for inquiries. We have kept fairly well through the winter, & hope you have also.

Yours sincerely

Text MS. (pencil draft) DCM.
Slater: Frederick William Slater, London representative of Harper & Brothers for many years. *Mr Canfield's letter*: Cass Canfield (1897–1986), American publisher, currently manager of Harper's London office; his letter had accompanied Slater's own letter to FEH of 10 Apr 26 (DCM). *lady correspondent*: referred to by Slater as 'Miss Merrill' and perhaps to be identified with Sarah Lawrence Penny Merrell (d. 1966), a free-lance reporter at this date. *Mr Bowker*: Richard Rogers Bowker, publisher and bibliographer; see I.77. He was the editor with whom TH dealt when writing *A Laodicean*.

To MARIE STOPES

MAX GATE, | DORCHESTER. | 16 April 1926

Dear Dr Marie Stopes:

I have read, or rather had read to me, your play, with much interest, and sympathize with you in your troubles over it, especially as it is obviously written with great skill and care.

My knowledge of the theatre nowadays is very slight—I have only been once these seven years—and I don't at all know what is in the tradition of modern plays. So I can only judge yours as a work of literary art, and even in that may be entirely wrong.

It seems to me that the situation and events are improbable: not too improbable to have happened, but too improbable for art, which must keep far within actual truth. I cannot conceive a young woman not an imbecile who has been married three years being in such crass ignorance of physiology, especially with a young man just through the party-wall ready to teach her. If she had been married only three days, or even three months, it would not have thrown such a strain upon one's credulity. However, taking the case quite seriously, the position of the pair is painful without reaching to the tragic. I may say in passing that if you had ended it as I thought you were going to, and made her, out of kindness to her husband, and her own and her father the bishop's horror at an unchristian scandal, resign herself to a living death with her husband you would have made it a tragedy.

A play acts so differently from how it reads that I can express no opinion on the censor's refusal to license. I believe some words had to be softened when "Tess" was staged which were quite unexceptionable in the reading.

The question arises, is an abnormality ever a fit subject for a work of art, even though not immoral.

You won't want to see me in the Lighthouse after this cold douche, but will wish me at the dark house rather. But with renewed sympathy I am

Sincerely yours,

T. Hardy.

P.S. Play returned in separate parcel.

Text   MS. (typewritten) BL.
Stopes: Marie Charlotte Carmichael Stopes (1880–1958), scientist and reformer; *D.N.B.* TH had known her at least since 1923, when he and FEH visited the lighthouse on Portland Bill in which she spent much of her time.   *your play*: *Vectia*; in her letter of 14 Apr 26 (DCM) Marie Stopes reported that the play had been denied a performance licence and expressed the hope that TH would write, for publication, a statement to the effect that a licence should in fact be granted.   *within actual truth*: Vectia's ignorance of sexual realities even after marriage was in fact closely autobiographical; see Ruth Hall, *Marie Stopes: A Biography* (London, 1977), 95–9.   *in the Lighthouse*: Stopes had issued such an invitation in her letter.

To A. R. POWYS

18 April 1926

Dear Mr Powys;

I will write a line to Mr Watkins the Secretary of the Dorset Men in London asking him to give attention to your suggestion that the Society should subscribe to purchase the building known as Judge Jeffries's Lodgings, which whether his lodgings or no is a most interesting old building, & very suitable for an annexe to the Dorset County Museum.

I should have thought that the Corporation of Dorchester could have bought it, & rented it to the Museum.

Yours very truly

Text   MS. (pencil draft) DCM.
Powys: Albert Reginald Powys (see V.296), secretary of the Society for the Protection of Ancient Buildings; he wrote 16 Apr 26 (DCM).   *Mr Watkins*: William Watkins (see below, letter of 14 May 08), founder of the Society of Dorset Men in London.   *Jeffries's Lodgings*: the early seventeenth-century half-timbered building (now a restaurant) in High West Street, Dorchester, at which Lord Jeffreys (1648–89; *D.N.B.*) is said to have lodged while holding a 'bloody assize' following the suppression of the Monmouth rebellion of 1685.

To THE REVD. E. M. WALKER

MAX GATE, | DORCHESTER, | DORSET. | 19 April 1926

Dear Dr Walker:

I have just sent to you a sketch of myself by the late William Strang, on the chance of its finding a nail on some wall in the College. I suddenly felt ashamed at what seemed a great piece of vanity till I thought you would understand that as I had nothing at all valuable to present to a rich & ancient institution like Queen's, it was sent to show in a feeble way my sense of the hospitality mental & corporeal I have experienced there.

I hope you & Mrs Walker continue well. We often think of you, & my wife sends kind regards to both.

Believe me

Yours sincerely
Thomas Hardy.

Text   MS. Queen's College, Oxford.
Walker: the Revd. Edward Mewburn Walker (see VI.168), Pro-Provost of Queen's College, Oxford, of which TH had been an honorary fellow since 1922.   *Strang*: William Strang, painter and etcher; see I.284.   *in the College*: Walker replied (1 May 26, DCM) that the portrait-etching would be hung in the Common Room Gallery; for a reproduction of the portrait and TH's inscription, see the frontispiece to William R. Rutland, *Thomas Hardy* (London, 1938).

To THEODORE MAYNARD

[22] April 1926

Dear Sir:

I beg to acknowledge the receipt of the April number of "The Catholic World" containing your article on the Poetry of Thomas Hardy, & he asks me to thank you for the same, & for your appreciation of his writings. He does not find, as you expected he might, anything to disagree with in your criticisms. He thinks you may discover as you get older that the harshness you say you notice in some of his poems is deliberate, as a reaction from the smooth alliterations of the Victorian poets.

Yours truly

. . . .

Secretary

Mr Theodore Maynard | The Gibson Apts | Northern Boulevard at 149th Street. | Flushing, Long Island. U.S.A.

Text   MS. (pencil draft) DCM.   *Date*   From typewritten letter sent over initials of May O'Rourke (Georgetown Univ.).
Maynard: Theodore Maynard (1890–1956), currently professor of English at St. John's College, Brooklyn, later professor at Georgetown Univ. and president of the Catholic Poetry Society of America; he wrote 3 Apr 26 (DCM) but sent the magazine under separate cover.   *your article*: Maynard's 'The Poetry of Thomas Hardy', *Catholic World* (April 1926), 46–54.   *harshness . . . you notice*: Maynard speaks of 'the uncouth and grotesque style of so many of the poems' and of the 'awkwardness' of their diction.

To PHILIP RIDGEWAY

23 April 1926

Dear Mr Ridgeway:

In reply to your letter & telegram I can only remind you that you already have copies of all the plays written by Mr Hardy. He gave you a small printed copy of "The Queen of Cornwall", telling you you might produce it if you chose. And we sent you "The Three Wayfarers"—a typewritten copy I believe.

Such of the novels as have been dramatized by amateurs he could not consent to have put on the regular stage.

The two short plays above-mentioned—"The Famous Tragedy of the Queen of Cornwall," & "The Three Wayfarers"—both by himself—would almost make out a full-length performance.

Yours very truly
F.H

Philip Ridgeway Esq. | 19 Buckingham Street | Strand: London. W.C. 2

Since writing the above have received your second telegram. The so-called "Hardy" plays as produced down here were, with two exceptions, *not* written by Mr Hardy, & absolutely unfitted for the London stage. But if Mr Drinkwater or Mr St John Ervine cared to dramatize "The Mayor" or "Jude" Mr Hardy would have no objection. Two London theatre managers have expressed a desire to produce "The Queen of Cornwall" & indeed one made a definite offer which was refused—F.H.

Text MS. (pencil draft, with postscript in FEH's hand but probably dictated by TH) DCM.
Ridgeway: Philip Ridgeway, theatrical producer; see VI.334. He had been responsible for the 1925 production of *Tess*.   *letter & telegram*: both dated 22 Apr 26 (DCM) and addressed to FEH, both requesting the immediate dispatch of all scripts of plays based on TH's works, whether dramatized by TH himself or by others.   *by amateurs*: Ridgeway's telegram had referred specifically to the versions performed by the 'Hardy Players'.   *second telegram*: dated 23 Apr 26 (DCM), it repeated Ridgeway's previous requests and enquired specifically about *Jude the Obscure* and 'Drinkwater dramatisations'.   *Mr Drinkwater*: John Drinkwater; see letter of 11 Sept 26.   *Ervine*: for Ervine and his attempted dramatization of *Jude the Obscure* see letter of 9 Sept 26.   *no objection*: an extensive correspondence with Ridgeway, conducted by FEH, led to Drinkwater's dramatization of *The Mayor of Casterbridge* being produced by Ridgeway at the Barnes Theatre; see letter of 27 July 26 to Ervine.   *Two . . . managers*: unidentified.

To J. H. MORGAN

MAX GATE, | DORCHESTER. | 24 April 1926

Dear General Morgan:

I have read your interesting letter about Napoleon I., but am sorry to say I am compelled to answer it by the typewriter, on account of increasing weakness of sight, which limits my handwriting to short notes only. However I must not complain, as my eyes have served me well in their time.

As to the points about Waterloo, to which you draw my attention, I fear my memory does not enable me to say what foundation I had for that legend I called "The Peasant's Confession", beyond the passage in Thiers prefixed to the verses. Of course Thiers says a great deal more about the mystery of

Grouchy's movements than I quoted from him—in fact he argues it out at length if I remember, so as to prove if possible that it was not Napoleon's fault the battle was lost.

I think Napoleon himself said that, after all, the issue of a battle was a matter of chance, and that it set all foresight and calculation at defiance. Anyhow, he himself trusted far more to chance than is generally supposed. Ney's enthusiasm must have been risky, once he got out of control. It has always been a mystery to me that he did not get killed; it bears out the saying they have hereabouts: "Nought (care-not?) is never in danger."

I believe it was never exactly known how Napoleon got off, or precisely what he did, on the night after Waterloo. Probably he himself was not quite aware. I recall that the accounts were very puzzling.

Modern wars do not lend themselves to scenic drama. Old Waterloo men have told me how close they were to the French, and of course one can see for one's self that they were by looking at the field. What you say about the sunken road is quite true.

Many thanks for inquiries. My wife sends kind regards.

Sincerely yours
Th: Hardy.

Text   MS. (typewritten) Berg.
interesting letter: of 20 Apr 26 (DCM).   *Confession"*: first pub. in *Wessex Poems* (1898); Morgan had asked whether it was purely imaginative or based on some oral tradition.   *passage in Thiers*: i.e., from the *Histoire du Consulat et de l'Empire de Napoléon* (21 vols., Paris, 1845–69), by Louis Adolphe Thiers (1797–1877), of which TH had in his library a set in French (DCM), for reference purposes, and a set in translation (Purdy), for actual use.   *Grouchy's*: Emmanuel Marquis de Grouchy (1766–1847), one of Napoleon's generals at the battle of Waterloo.   *Napoleon himself*: it is not clear that Napoleon ever spoke in just these terms; see, however, le Comte de Las Cases, *Memorial de Sainte-Hélène*, ed. Joël Schmidt (Paris, 1968), 110, 573 (first English translation 1823).   *Ney's*: Michel Ney (1769–1815), marshal of France; he personally led several charges at Waterloo.   *the sunken road*: Morgan remarked that a modern battle would not have been fought in so restricted a terrain as Waterloo and that aerial reconnaissance would have rendered impossible Napoleon's crucial ignorance of the sunken road behind La Haye Sainte.

To ARTHUR SYMONS

MAX GATE, DORCHESTER. | 26 April 1926

Dear Symons:

The letter enclosed herewith will explain my difficulty about seeing anybody at present, and why I find personal interviews so trying, particularly with strangers. So that I don't like your coming so far, in case I should be in bed and your journey wasted. I have read your thoughtful introduction to Miss Mason-Manheim's poems.

I am glad to hear that you had such a successful circular trip in France last year, and with best wishes for your health in this

I am

Sincerely yours
Th: Hardy.

Text MS. (typewritten, with envelope in FEH's hand) Adams.
Symons: Arthur William Symons, poet and critic; see II.90. *letter enclosed*: perhaps a reply to Mason-Manheim's letter to TH of 20 Apr 26 (DCM). *Mason-Manheim's poems*: Madeline Mason-Manheim (b. 1908), American writer; her *Hill Fragments* (London, 1925) contained a preface by Symons and five drawings by Kahlil Gibran. See Karl Beckson, *Arthur Symons: A Life* (Oxford, 1987), 311–12.

To ROY McKAY

27 April 1926

Dear Mr McKay:

I have read your letter with interest: also the enclosure that you & your friends sent to The Manchester Guardian, particularly because, when I was young, I had a wish to enter the Church.

I am now too old to take up the questions you lay open, but I may say that it has seemed to me that a simpler plan than that of mental reservation in passages no longer literally accepted (which is puzzling to ordinary congregations) would be just to abridge the creeds & other primitive parts of the Liturgy, leaving only the essentials. Unfortunately there appears to be a narrowing instead of a broadening tendency among the clergy of late, which if persisted in will exclude still more people from church. But if a strong body of young Reformers were to make a bold stand, in a sort of New Oxford Movement, they would have a tremendous backing from the thoughtful laity, & might overcome the retrogressive section of the Clergy.

Please don't attach much importance to these casual thoughts, & believe me

Very truly yours

R. McKay Esq. | Ripon Hall (or Magdalen Coll:) | Oxford

Text MS. (pencil draft) DCM.
McKay: Roy McKay (b. 1900), candidate for ordination at Ripon Hall, Oxford, subsequently Canon of Chichester Cathedral and head of religious broadcasting for the British Broadcasting Corporation. *your letter*: of 26 Apr 26 (DCM). *Manchester Guardian*: McKay sent a cutting of the letter, signed by himself and three colleagues, pub. in the *Manchester Guardian*, 26 Apr 1926, under the heading 'Anglicans and the Creeds'; it urged the Church of England to face the fact that many sincere members of both the clergy and the laity could not give literal assent to all elements of the regularly recited Creeds. *(or Magdalen Coll:)*: McKay had written to TH from Ripon Hall but signed the *Guardian* letter as from Magdalen College.

To G. HERBERT THRING

MAX GATE, DORCHESTER. | 27 April 1926

Dear Mr Thring:

I have read your lawyer's letter from Prague, and I do not see that anything better can be done than to let him deal as best he may with any of the short stories that are required or suggested for Czech serial publication. I have not parted with the copyright of any except "Under the Greenwood Tree".

Yours very truly
Th: Hardy.

G. Herbert Thring Esq. | Society of Authors, | 11 Gower Street | London. W.C. 1

Text   MS. (typewritten) BL.
Czech serial publication: it is not clear that anything came of these negotiations.

To DOROTHY ALLHUSEN

MAX GATE, | DORCHESTER. | 7 May 1926

My very dear Dorothy:

I have hunted up these I enclose, as being more or less suitable for that sweet child, but I don't know if you will care for either of them: if you don't I can find plenty more, & shall be delighted to do it: it is all I can do for her. If you choose one from the English poets his name need not be attached to the epitaph. I have only put the poet's name that you may know where I took the sentence from.

Of course I would write one myself, but mine would not be so good as one of these.

You must never mind asking me these things, as you may be sure I like to do them.

I don't know when this will get to you on account of the strike.

Ever affectionately
T.H.

Florence has been talking about Elizabeth, & how much she liked her. You know how much I did. T.H.

Text   MS. Mrs. M. Stewart-Mackenzie.
Allhusen: Osma Mary Dorothy Allhusen (see I.257), daughter of Lady St. Helier (see I.144 and III.167) by her first marriage; TH had known her since her childhood.   *these I enclose*: accompanying the letter is a separate typewritten sheet of quotations potentially usable as epitaphs, four from the Old Testament, one from the Book of Wisdom, one from Matthew Arnold, three from Wordsworth, and two from Charles Lamb; markings suggest that Mrs. Allhusen chose Wordsworth's 'She seem'd a thing that could not feel | The touch of earthly years'. TH's draft of this sheet is accompanied by a separate list of possible epitaphs from TH's own poems; both are annotated 'as submitted to D.'   *that sweet child*: Mrs. Allhusen's daughter, Dorothea Elizabeth (see V.241), who had recently died after a long illness.   *the strike*: i.e., the British General Strike of 3–12 May 1926.

To R. GOLDING BRIGHT

MAX GATE, DORCHESTER. | 10th. May 1926.

Dear Mr Golding Bright:

I am much obliged by your reminder, and find the account for Hammersmith had been passed through as you say. I fear your opinion of my book-keeping will have sunk very low, or of my memory.

This strike will, I suppose, have a disastrous effect on theatres.

Yours sincerely,
T. Hardy.

Text   MS. (typewritten) Adams.
passed through as you say: TH had evidently enquired as to his share of the receipts of the Hammersmith performances of the touring production of *Tess of the d'Urbervilles* (see letter of 26 Jan 26) and been told that payment had already been made.   *This strike*: see letter of 7 May 26.

To EDWARD PRICE BELL

MAX GATE, | DORCHESTER, | DORSET. | 17 May 1926

Dear Sir:

The copy of "World Chancelleries" you have been so kind as to send me through Mr Walter G. Strong has come to hand, though its arrival has been delayed by the recent strike in the trades and industries of England. Many thanks for a volume on a subject into which Mr Victor F. Lawson entered so enthusiastically, and for which you yourself travelled and laboured—the coming to some conclusion as to how the cause of world-peace may be advanced and served.

I am personally unable, as you will well understand, to take up actively at my time of life a question of such moment; but I quite agree with President Coolidge in believing that these carefully wrought statements of opinion and fact are a valuable aid to the great though laborious cause.

Yours very truly
Thomas Hardy.

Edward Price Bell, Esq. | Chicago Daily News | 15 North Wells Street | Chicago. U.S.A.

Text MS. (typewritten) Newberry Library.
Bell: Edward Price Bell (1869–1943), American journalist and author, London correspondent of the Chicago *Daily News* 1900–23; his *World Chancelleries* (Chicago, 1926) was based on personal interviews with political leaders throughout the world. *Strong*: i.e., Walter Ansel Strong (1883–1931), editor and publisher of the Chicago *Daily News*; the *Daily News* pub. *World Chancelleries* and Strong presumably distributed copies to notable figures who might conceivably lend their support to the campaign for world peace his paper was currently promoting. *Lawson*: Victor Fremont Lawson (1850–1925), the former editor and publisher of the Chicago *Daily News*, to whom *World Chancelleries* is somewhat fulsomely dedicated. *with President Coolidge*: TH refers to the introduction to *World Chancelleries* written by Calvin Coolidge (1872–1933), the current President of the United States.

To EUGENE FIELD II

17 May 1926

Dear Sir:

In reply to your letter Mr Hardy desires me to say that he may have received a communication from you in the autumn of last year, but he has no recollection of it, his correspondence being very heavy & troublesome.

He regrets to say that he is unable to make a manuscript copy of his poem "Men who march away" for your mother, being compelled to get his writing done by typewriter at this time of his life.

Mr Hardy sends his thanks for the offer of one of your father's manuscripts, though he thinks that America is the proper home for them.

Yours very truly

. . . .

Secretary

Mr Eugene Field | Congress Hotel | Congress Street | Chicago. U.S.A.

Text MS. (pencil draft) DCM.
Field: Eugene Field II (d. 1946, aged 67); the son of Eugene Field (1850–95), American

journalist and poet, he is said in his New York *Times* obituary (4 Jan 1947) to have 'devoted most of his attention to collecting and sale of manuscripts and acting as author's agent'.   *your letter*: of 29 Apr 26 (DCM).   *father's manuscripts*: Field said that his mother wanted to distribute the MSS. 'amongst those whom we feel will appreciate and love them'; in effect, however, he was offering one in exchange for a TH manuscript.   *Secretary*: the letter as sent (Texas) is typewritten and signed 'M. O'R.' (May O'Rourke; see letter of mid-Jan 26).

To ARTHUR HIND

                    MAX GATE, | DORCHESTER, | DORSET. | 22nd. May 1926.
Dear Sir:

   The drawing of the barn that you have been so kind as to send has arrived uninjured, and I thank you much for the gift. I think it a charming picture, and a characteristic reproduction of that part of Dorset.

   As to the spot being the "Little Hintock" of "The Woodlanders"—that is another question. You will be surprised and shocked at my saying that I myself do not know where "Little Hintock" is! Several tourists—mostly American —have told me that they have found it, in every detail, and have offered to take me to it, but I have never gone.

   However, to be more definite, it has features which were to be found fifty years ago in the hamlets of Hermitage, Middlemarsh, Lyons-Gate, Revels Inn, Holnest, Melbury Bubb, &c.—all lying more or less under the eminence called High-Stoy, just beyond Minterne & Dogberry Gate, where the country descends into the Vale of Blackmore.

   The topographers you mention as identifying the scene are merely guessers, and are wrong. The only authorized book of the kind is "Thomas Hardy's Wessex" by Hermann Lea (Macmillan's Highways & Byways Series). It contains nearly 250 photographs of places which "obviously suggested" the fictitious places, (as he rightly puts it) though, as the author carefully states, the latter are by no means photographs of them. With renewed thanks I am,

                                            Yours very truly,
                                            Thomas Hardy.
Arthur M. Hind. Esq. O.B.E. | 24 Campden Hill Square, | Kensington. London. W. 8.

Text   MS. (typewritten) Dennis O'Malley.
Hind: Arthur Mayger Hind (1880–1957), historian of engraving; *D.N.B.*   *drawing of the barn*: Hind had told TH (undated letter, DCM) that he was sending a drawing he had made of an old barn at Minterne Parva, Dorset, 'as a token of my devotion to your novels & poems'.   *another question*: Hind had speculated on this point in his letter.   *topographers you mention*: Hind cited F. O. Saxelby's *A Thomas Hardy Dictionary* (see letter of 9 Jan 26) and Charles G. Harper's *The Hardy Country* (London, 1904).   *by Hermann Lea*: see letter of 9 Jan 26.

To HAROLD LASKI

                         MAX GATE, | DORCHESTER. | 26th. May 1926.
Dear Mr Laski:

   In reply to your inquiry I can say quite readily that I have a high opinion of Mr H. M. Tomlinson as a writer of English prose, not to speak of his other capabilities; and nothing would gratify me more than that greater recognition of his excellence should be shown than is shown at present—possibly owing to his own diffidence.

Yours very truly,
Thomas Hardy.

(Glad to hear of S.S.)
Harold J. Laski. Esq. M.A.

Text   MS. (typewritten) Syracuse Univ.
Laski: Harold Joseph Laski (1893–1950), political theorist and university teacher; *D.N.B.*   *your inquiry*: Laski wrote from the London School of Economics (undated, DCM) to seek from TH a confidential letter of support for Henry Major Tomlinson (1873–1958; *D.N.B.*), the writer, who was being considered for a literary prize in the United States. For Tomlinson on TH, see his *Out of Soundings* (London, 1931), 246–73.   *S.S.*: Siegfried Sassoon (see V.201), cited by Laski as his source for the information that TH thought well of Tomlinson's work.

To JOHN ACLAND
(Private.)   3 June 1926

Dear Capt. Acland:
Would you be so kind as to caution the attendant Kibby whenever convenient against letting strangers who visit the Museum draw from him any personal particulars about myself? I am sorry to trouble you with this trivial matter, but gossiping journalists in England & America print all sorts of rubbish, mostly false, that they were told by "the porter at the Museum", as they state, though no doubt they largely exaggerate what he really may have said under pressure of their questions in their eagerness for news, which is, of course, money to them.

    Please mention it to him kindly, as I have no objection to him whatever to make. I hope you are well, & with our kind regards I am

Yours sincerely

Text   MS. (pencil draft) DCM.
Acland: John Edward Acland, curator of the Dorset County Museum; see III.262.   *Kibby*: correctly Kibbey; Albert Kibbey (d. 1948, aged 87), doorkeeper at the Museum for many years, had been quoted in a newspaper article (see letter of early June 26 below) as saying that TH, 'a sad man', had never exchanged a word with him.   *mention . . . kindly*: Acland (4 June 26, DCM) replied that Kibbey had himself drawn attention to the offending article and denied the statements attributed to him.

To HARLEY GRANVILLE BARKER

Max Gate, | Dorchester. | 4. June 1926.

My dear H.G.B.
My very warmest thanks for your kind wishes about my birthday, and Helen's. You might just as well have come along to see us, whether you thought to do so on June 1, 2, or any other day of the year. I have been rather shaky, but am getting right by degrees.

    I have just noticed on taking up the new number of the Sphere the remark of a writer in it that some estimate of "The Madras House" by a well-known critic was inadequate. Yes: to paraphrase Stevenson, one says "Golly, what a crew these critics are!"

Always yours,
Th. H.

Text   Typed transcript DCM; Barker's name and address, appearing at the top of the transcript in FEH's hand, were probably not part of the original letter and have not been reproduced (see VI.344).
Barker: Harley Granville Barker, actor, producer, dramatist, and critic; see III.257.   *Helen's*: Barker's second wife; see below, letter of 29 Dec 26.   *any other day*: Barker (1 June 26, DCM) confessed that confusion over dates had led him and his wife to send their birthday telegram a day early and abandon a plan they had had for paying TH a visit.   *Sphere . . . inadequate*: Arnold Palmer, reviewing James Agate's *The Contemporary Theatre, 1925* in the *Sphere* of 5 June 1926, cited the 'very inadequate notice' of Barker's play *The Madras House* as an instance of Agate's tendency not to 'see a play as a whole'.   *to paraphrase Stevenson*: an apparent reference to the exclamation about the *Athenaeum*, '"Golly, what a paper!"' in Robert Louis Stevenson (see I.147) and Lloyd Osbourne's *The Wrong Box* (London, 1889), 273.

To EDWARD, EMMA AND CONSTANCE DUGDALE

MAX GATE, | DORCHESTER. | 4 June 1926

Many & sincere thanks for birthday good wishes. The same to you all.

Affectionately,
T.H.

Text   MS. (correspondence card, with envelope) Purdy.
Dugdale: Edward and Emma Dugdale (see V.33 and IV.246 respectively) were FEH's parents, Constance (see IV.103) one of her sisters.

To WILFRID HODGES

MAX GATE, | DORCHESTER, | DORSET. | 4 June 1926

Dear Sir:
    I send sincere thanks to the inhabitants of Dorchester, including yourself personally, and the Corporation, for your good wishes and congratulations on my birthday.

Yours very truly
Thomas Hardy.

To | His Worship the Mayor of Dorchester.

Text   MS. (typewritten, with envelope in May O'Rourke's hand) R. Greenland.
Hodges: Wilfrid Francis Hodges (see IV.314), Dorchester wine merchant, currently mayor.

To H. O. LOCK

[Early June 1926]

To Major Lock:
    All that is required from Hopkins is,
    1. That he makes absolute withdrawal of his statements in the Westminster

Gazette on Mr Hardy's relationships & on his silence being "a byword in Dorchester". Also what he wrote in an article in an American paper that has been sent here by disgusted friends of Mrs Hardy, that she runs the house at Max Gate by the help of a maid of all work (or words to that effect) there never being less than four servants to do the work of the premises.

2. That he pays the legal expenses to which Mr Hardy has been put. He does not require damages.

3. That he ceases to annoy Mr Hardy in future in this manner.

Text MS. (pencil draft) DCM. *Date* See letter of 11 June 26.
Lock: Henry Osmond Lock (see IV.11), Dorchester solicitor. *Hopkins*: Robert Thurston Hopkins (1883–1958), journalist and miscellaneous writer, author of *Thomas Hardy's Dorset* (London, 1922); TH had been angered by his article, 'Thomas Hardy and His Folk', pub. in the *Westminster Gazette* of 2 June 1926 and extracted in the *Dorset Daily Echo* the same day. *in an American paper*: *Book Notes*, in which Hopkins's 'Thomas Hardy at Home' had recently appeared.

To SIR EDMUND GOSSE

[6 June 1926]

My dear Gosse:
What with weak eyesight & other complications incidental to my age I send only this miserable postscript of thanks for your letter. I have however managed to read your illuminating review of Mr Priestley's book on Meredith.

Ever yrs
T.H.

Text MS. (with envelope in FEH's hand) Leeds. *Date* Written as a postscript to FEH's letter to Gosse of 6 June 26.
Gosse: Edmund William Gosse (see I.110), man of letters, one of TH's oldest friends. *illuminating review*: Gosse's review of J. B. Priestley's *George Meredith* (London, 1926), *Sunday Times*, 6 June 1926; see letter of 8 Aug 26.

To DOROTHY ALLHUSEN

MAX GATE, DORCHESTER. | 8 June 1926

My dear Dorothy:
I am sending with this, what I ought to have sent before, some suggested inscriptions for the room, either of which I hope, gets over the difficulty of expressing clearly what you want to say. I am glad you like one of the epitaphs for dear regretted Elizabeth. I write in a great hurry to get this posted.

Always yours
T.H.

Text MS. Mrs. M. Stewart-Mackenzie.
for the room: the Junior Combination Room of Trinity College, Cambridge, restored by Mrs. Allhusen in memory of her husband, Henry Allhusen (see II.249), and their son Henry Christian Stanley Allhusen (1899–1922); the suggested inscriptions no longer accompany this letter and the Latin inscription on the chimney-piece of the renovated room seems not, in any case, to have been of TH's composition. *epitaphs for . . . Elizabeth*: see letter of 7 May 26.

To SIR FREDERICK MACMILLAN

MAX GATE, | DORCHESTER, | DORSET. | 8 June 1926

Dear Sir Frederick:

I have received the sheets for signature, and am going to plunge into them to-day.

I have also received a letter from Sir Henry Newbolt asking if he may include the story of "The Three Strangers", (in Wessex Tales,) in a "little one-and-ninepenny volume of Short Stories for use in Secondary Schools", (he does not state the publishers). When a request of this kind comes from an old friend it is very difficult to refuse, but I wish friends would not make such requests all the same, which are really asking for money. Will you suggest what answer to send? I don't mind what.

Sincerely yours
Th: Hardy.

Text   MS. (typewritten) BL.
the sheets: see letter of 3 Apr 26.   *letter . . . Newbolt*: Newbolt (see letter of 11 June 26 to him) wrote 7 June 26 (Texas), referring to the story as 'The Three Visitors'.   *answer to send*: Macmillan (9 June 26, Macmillan letterbooks, BL) recommended that Newbolt's request be refused, adding that his own firm might pub. a vol. of TH's stories arranged for school use if TH were interested.

To H. O. LOCK

11 June 1926

Dear Major Lock:

I have received your letter of yesterday & enclosures. I quite approve of your asking Hopkins to repeat his withdrawal also in the Bournemouth & Dorset Echo, & to send you a copy of the Westminster.

I prefer not to ask him to pay the legal costs, for the reason given in my note of yesterday; so please also state this in your letter to him, & that I acquit him of any malicious intention in publishing the article.

I enclose the article by Kathleen Woodward in the New York Times Magazine from which he derived his statements, that you may return it to him as he requests.

Yours very truly

Text   MS. (pencil draft) DCM.
& enclosures: Lock (10 June 26, DCM) sent a copy of a letter he had received from Hopkins (see letter of early June 26) together with the Woodward article (see below), which Hopkins had supplied.   *Bournemouth . . . Echo*: i.e., the *Dorset Daily Echo*, where the Hopkins article had been quoted 2 June 1926; no further retraction seems to have appeared there.   *copy of the Westminster*: i.e., of the 11 June issue in which Hopkins's (second) letter of retraction appeared.   *article by . . . Woodward*: 'Thomas Hardy Cleaves to His Solitude', *New York Times Magazine*, 22 Nov 1925; before returning this article TH copied out substantial portions of it (DCM), including those referring to FEH's lack of domestic assistance (see letter of early June 26) and to TH's having 'a half-brother up Bockhampton way' who wrote poetry some thought better than TH's own—apparently a garbled description of his first cousin John Antell (see I.92). This last point, repeated by Hopkins almost word for word, was particularly stressed in the editorial apology pub. at TH's insistence—conveyed over the telephone by FEH in words drafted by TH himself (DCM)—in the *Dorset Daily Echo* of 3 June.

To SIR HENRY NEWBOLT

MAX GATE, | DORCHESTER, | DORSET. | 11 June: 1926

My dear Newbolt:

I have inquired of the Macmillans about your including "The Three Strangers" in your volume of short stories for Secondary Schools—which I was obliged to do before replying, as the publishers have a joint right with me in such questions—& they unfortunately answer that they themselves are thinking about a volume of my stories arranged for school use, & so they do not see their way to agree to the permission. I am sorry, & should be more so if it really mattered much to you, which it will not, as there are hundreds of short tales that will do equally well for your purpose.

We shall be pleased to see you & the John Buchans in July, if you will let my wife know when you are arriving, so that we may not be out. Many thanks for your kind congratulations on my birthday, which we got through in spite of a disconcerting invasion by strangers. I hope you & Lady Newbolt keep well. I have had an attack of lumbago, but it is a little better, though not gone. Kind regards

Yours very sincerely
Thomas Hardy.

Text   MS. (with envelope) Texas.
Newbolt: Sir Henry Newbolt, poet and man of letters; see III.21.   *of the Macmillans*: see letter of 8 June 26 to Macmillan.   *it will not*: TH, turning the page, wrote 'it will will not'.   *for your purpose*: Newbolt seems to have abandoned the project, however.   *John Buchans*: John Buchan (see V.220), later Lord Tweedsmuir, and his wife.   *invasion by strangers*: FEH reported to Sydney Cockerell (21 June 26, Purdy) that Arthur Symons had arrived with his American friends (see letter of 26 Apr 26) just as she and TH were sitting down to tea on his birthday.

To SIR FREDERICK MACMILLAN

MAX GATE, | DORCHESTER. | 12 June 1926.

Dear Sir Frederick:

I have told Newbolt that there are difficulties about his printing "The Three Strangers", and I think he will consider this as quite probable and natural, and not mind, especially since I have already obliged him by letting him have several poems and prose extracts for his Anthology published some time ago.

I have received the cheque safely, and am much obliged. I have done about 200 of the new signatures, which reminds me to ask if, were I to send up half-a-dozen words in The Dynasts which I have discovered from time to time to be clerical errors, etc., they could be put in. But the matter is not of great importance.

Respecting Mr Wolmark, as it is possible that a sketch by him might come in useful for some edition or other of the books, I don't mind giving him a sitting of an hour or so, though I am afraid it could not be (unless he is leaving England or anything of that sort) till July, so many things chancing to be coming along this month—one of the events, by the way, being what would interest your cousin George as he is a Greek enthusiast—a performance of the Hippolytus of Euripides on our lawn by undergraduates from Balliol.

As Mr Wolmark may want his drawing of Mr Zangwill, I return it herewith.
My wife sends kind regards, and I am

Always sincerely yours,
Thomas Hardy.

Text   MS. (typewritten) BL.
his Anthology: see VI.92.   *the cheque*: Macmillan (9 June 26, Macmillan letterbooks, BL) sent
£550 for the signed and unsigned edns. of the illustrated *Tess*; see letters of 3 and 7 Apr
26.   *new signatures*: for the limited signed edn. of *The Dynasts*; see letter of 3 Apr 26.   *not
of great importance*: Macmillan (14 June 26, Macmillan letterbooks, BL) assured TH that the
corrections would be made in the new edn. and in the plates of existing edns.   *Mr Wolmark*:
Alfred Aaran Wolmark (1877–1961), artist; he came to Dorchester to make his pen-and-ink sketch
of TH on 5 July 1926.   *cousin George*: George Augustin Macmillan; see II.108.   *from
Balliol*: the Balliol Players (see VI.256) paid this second visit to Max Gate on 29 June 26 (see *LY*,
247–8).   *of Mr Zangwill*: Macmillan had sent a drawing of Israel Zangwill, the writer (see
III.84), as a specimen of Wolmark's work; the original is now in the National Portrait Gallery.

To R. GOLDING BRIGHT

MAX GATE, | DORCHESTER. | 17th. June 1926.

Dear Mr Golding Bright:
I have this morning received your cheque for £49. 5. 2., covering fees for
Glasgow, Liverpool, and Harrogate, in the weeks ending May 22, 29, and June
5. Respecting the two weeks May 8 & 15, which are not paid, Mr Ridgeway
writes persistently about his losses in those weeks through the strike, and as no
doubt he did badly during that time I don't mind letting him off half. I think he
said my dues for the fortnight when they played at Sheffield and Manchester
would come to about £30 odd, so that they would be reduced to £15 or £16. He
wants to be excused paying anything for that fortnight, but it seems to me that a
reduction to half is as much as he can reasonably expect. However, if you think
otherwise please let me know.

Yours very truly,
Th: Hardy

Text   MS. (typewritten) Adams.
fees: for the touring production of *Tess*; see letter of 26 Jan 26.   *the strike*: see letter of 7 May
26.

To ERNEST BARKER

19 June 1926

Yes. French eveng classes 1865–66. Jelf, Principal (a man of dignified
humour). Stièvenard, French lecturer (a charming character whom I remember very well). It was when I was working at architecture with Sir Arthur
Blomfield at Adelphi Terrace; & what with that, & my being also engrossed in
English poetry, I did not do much in class, I fear (though I recall the old room
& desks clearly), & Stièvenard must have had a low opinion of my progress.
Am pleased to give this information.

T.H.

Text   MS. (postcard, King's College stationery) King's College, London.
Barker: Ernest Barker (1874–1960), political philosopher, principal of King's College, London, 1920–8; *D.N.B.* He wrote TH 18 June 26 (DCM), enclosing a postcard addressed to himself, to ask if it were true that TH had once attended classes at the college.   *Jelf*: Richard William Jelf (1798–1871), principal of King's College 1844–68; *D.N.B.*   *Stièvenard*: Léonce Stièvenard, lecturer in French at King's College; see *EL*, 65.   *Blomfield*: see I.3.

To DANIEL MACMILLAN

MAX GATE, | DORCHESTER. | 23 June 1926

Dear Mr Macmillan:

I have received your letter & enclosed cheque. Many thanks. I am getting ready the list of corrections to The Dynasts that I told you about, & will send it in a day or two.

Thinking over the question of printing the head-lines in red or black, I am personally in favour of black after all. But please let the consideration of what buyers would prefer have weight in deciding.

Sincerely yours
Thomas Hardy.

Text   MS. BL.
Macmillan: Daniel de Mendi Macmillan, publisher; see IV.201.   *your letter*: of 21 June 26 (Macmillan letterbooks, BL).   *head-lines . . . black*: the question of printing portions of the limited edn. of *The Dynasts* in red had evidently been discussed during the 19 June visit to Max Gate mentioned in Macmillan's letter; his letter of 25 June 26 (Macmillan letterbooks, BL) deferred a final decision, and red was in fact used for the shoulder headlines (showing act and scene numbers), and for some other elements of the vols. as published.

To DANIEL MACMILLAN

MAX GATE, | DORCHESTER. | 24 June 1926.

Dear Mr Macmillan:

Herewith the corrections to The Dynasts, which, as you will perceive, are of a very trifling kind.

One list refers to the small type editions, and I don't think it has been sent up before.

The other list, referring to the Wessex edition, may have been sent up before, but I fancy not all the words.

By setting these right the two editions will be exactly alike, never to be touched again, which is highly desirable. In composing for the large paper forthcoming edition, it does not much matter which of the two is used for copy by the printers, provided the enclosed corrections have been made first. If they think it would be safer for me to look at the corrections when made I will do so, on their sending proof of the particular words affected.

Sincerely yours,
Thomas Hardy.

Text   MS. (typewritten) BL.
particular words affected: Macmillan (25 June 26, Macmillan letterbooks, BL) promised that the proofs of the corrected passages would be read very carefully, making it unnecessary to trouble TH 'unless doubtful points arise'.

To EDWARD CLODD

MAX GATE, | DORCHESTER. | 1 July 1926

My dear Clodd:

I have just got back from Devonshire soon enough to remember before post-time that this is your birthday, so I will supplement what my wife said a week or two ago & wish you as many returns of the day as you can conveniently enjoy.

We had a letter from Clement Shorter a little while back, but do not gather from it the exact nature of his illness. We are sorry to miss him in The Sphere, & don't think the literary part so well done now that he has retired.

I am compelled by weak eyes to write very little, as I may have already told you. I understand that you have no sight difficulties. I have to stop all at once sometimes when I have strained mine.

I fear rational religion does not make much way at present. Indeed the movement of thought seems to have entered a back current in the opposite direction. These however are not uncommon in human history.

Sincerely yours
Thomas Hardy.

Text   MS. Berg.
Clodd: Edward Clodd (see I.237), rationalist author and retired banker; he had known TH for many years.   *from Devonshire*: where he had perhaps been visiting the Granville Barkers at Netherton Hall, near Colyton.   *conveniently enjoy*: Clodd was now, like TH, 86 years old.   *Shorter . . . illness*: Clement King Shorter (see I.245), journalist, died 19 November 1926.   *retired*: Shorter, as editor of the *Sphere*, had contributed a weekly 'Literary Letter'; in the issue of 29 May 1926 his 'temporary retirement' was announced on a 'Books of the Week' page signed by Arnold Palmer.   *opposite direction*: Clodd (6 July 26, DCM) agreed that rationalism was declining and sacerdotalism reasserting itself.

To CLEMENT BONE

3 July 1926

Dear Sir:

As increasing age prevents my giving that personal attention to the County Library Sub-Committee business which its importance entitles it to expect from those who are connected with books, I write to propose that I resign the membership with which I have been honoured, & that Mrs Hardy should take the place I vacate, as being eminently the better qualified at the present time & onwards. You may possibly be aware that she is & has been for many years active in all matters pertaining to literature, has written & published several books, has had a large experience as a reviewer & magazine writer, & was at one time on the staff of a London daily paper. I do not know the exact proceedure necessary for carrying out my idea, but at any rate make the suggestion to the Committee. I should add that she is quite willing to serve.

Yours very truly

Clement G. Bone Esq. M.A. | County Education Office | Dorchester

Text   MS. (pencil draft) DCM.
Bone: Clement George Bone (d. 1936, aged 65), Director of Education for Dorset 1920–36.

Sub-Committee: TH's draft is written on the verso of a formal notice, dated 26 June 26, of a forthcoming meeting of the sub-committee.   *Mrs Hardy ... vacate*: Bone replied, 5 July 26 (DCM), regretting TH's decision but welcoming the prospect of FEH's participation in the future.

To SIR EDMUND GOSSE

MAX GATE, | DORCHESTER. | 6: 7: 1926

Great excitement here listening in last night. Very impressive.

T.H.

Text   MS. (postcard) Leeds.
last night: as Gosse has noted on the MS., the reference is to his reading Wordsworth's 'Immortality' ode as part of a B.B.C. programme devoted to poems from Francis Turner Palgrave's famous anthology *The Golden Treasury*.

To JANE POPHAM

MAX GATE, | DORCHESTER. | 6 July 1926

Dear Mrs Popham:
    Many thanks for sending on the letter. An expert will be here later on, who will know how to mount it & put it in good condition for the Museum.
    We drove past your Stinsford encampment a few days ago, & thought of you there in the rain. I am glad you had better weather afterwards.

Sincerely yours
Thomas Hardy.

Text   MS. DCM.
Popham: Jane (Jeanne) Susanna Popham, of Bournemouth; see V.1.   *the letter*: written from Berlin by her father, George Tilley Gollop, in June 1815; see VI.160, 161.   *the Museum*: i.e., the Dorset County Museum, where it now accompanies this present letter.   *Stinsford encampment*: as Mrs. Popham wrote in the Max Gate visitors' book (BL) on 13 June 1926, she was currently 'gipsying' in a caravan at Stinsford.

To RUTLAND BOUGHTON

MAX GATE, | DORCHESTER. | 9 July 1926

Dear Mr Boughton:
    On looking into our Music Agreement for the Queen of Cornwall (which I had quite forgotten) I am of Mr Thring's opinion that it nowhere empowers you to publish the music and words of any of the songs apart from the whole opera. At the same time I have no objection to your doing so—in fact I wish you would, as I think they are buried if they never are heard unless the opera is performed—and I agree to your doing just as other composers do, that is, publish separately whichever songs you want to—printing each on a separate sheet with the music in the ordinary way, and paying me on publication a small fee for the use of the words in this separate manner. The other composers or their publishers pay two to four guineas each song—never offering less than two. In your case I will say two guineas each, which is low, considering that

you will be able to sell as many copies as you like without paying more. But I shall, of course, be getting a little whenever either song is performed as a part of the whole music drama.

  This addition to the contract will, I imagine, meet your views.

Yours sincerely
Th: Hardy.

Text MS. (typewritten) BL.
Boughton: Rutland Boughton, composer; see VI.225.   *Agreement . . . Cornwall*: for the evolution of Boughton's music-drama based on TH's *The Famous Tragedy of the Queen of Cornwall* see VI.225, etc.   *Mr Thring's*: he had been consulted, as secretary to the Society of Authors, Playwrights, and Composers, when the agreement was first drawn up; see VI.271.

To THE REVD. NORMAN BENNET

12 July 1926

Dear Sir:
  I write for Mr Hardy, whose letters are numerous, to say in reply to your inquiry that he cannot remember to what birds he referred in the passage you quote from Tess or that he referred to any special ones. Strange birds do undoubtedly appear on the uplands of Dorset in winter time, as on other uplands, & they might be identified by watching for them through a glass in cold weather.

Yours very truly
. . . .
Secretary

Revd. Norman Bennet | The Vicarage | Crewkerne

Text MS. (pencil draft) DCM.
Bennet: the Revd. Norman Robert Ottiwell Gifford Bennet; he became vicar of Crewkerne in 1924 after returning from extended service in India.   *passage you quote*: Bennet (5 July 26, DCM) had expressed ornithological scepticism as to the 'strange birds from behind the North Pole' referred to in *Tess of the d'Urbervilles* (Wessex edn., 367).

To RUTLAND BOUGHTON

MAX GATE, DORCHESTER. | 15th. July 1926.

Dear Mr Boughton:
  I find that Clause 3 in my copy of the Agreement runs: "The Licensee reserves all rights in the Musical setting of the version."
  If that means anything it means that I cannot publish your music and means nothing more. But as I don't wish to publish it I cannot see what it has to do with the question of your publishing the songs separately from the opera.
  However, I don't wish to make any profit out of the Opera, so please do what you like.

Yours very truly,
T. Hardy.

Mr Thring's letter returned herewith.

Text   MS. (typewritten) BL.
the Agreement: see letter of 9 July 26; Boughton (11 July 26; copy, BL) had disagreed with TH's interpretation of this part of the agreement.

To SIR FREDERICK MACMILLAN

MAX GATE, | DORCHESTER. | 15th. July 1926.

Dear Sir Frederick:

I have received a letter from Mr Newman Flower, manager of Cassells, whom I know very well, as he is a Dorset man and calls here sometimes. He writes to ask if I would be prepared to allow them to run "The Mayor of Casterbridge" as a serial through T.P.'s Weekly (which I suppose they own); and if so what would be my fee. He thinks it would be a good thing to run it there when the play by Mr Drinkwater based on the novel—to which we decided when you were here that there would be no objection—comes on the stage. I have replied briefly that I will ask you what you think about it, and let him know.

If you consider that no harm will be done by letting the story run as a serial as he wishes, perhaps you will arrange terms, as you did for "Tess" with "John o' London". Should this be the case I will either tell him to write to you about it, or you can inform him at once that I have communicated the above facts to you and ask him what he offers.

He seems anxious to have it, but the story, as you know, was never so popular as "Tess", so that I don't expect we should get nearly as much for the serial right as we did for that.

I have been asked for a copy of Moments of Vision, and cannot find one. Please let me have one of the uniform edition at your convenience.

Very sincerely yours,
Thomas Hardy.

Text   MS. (typewritten) BL.
Flower: Newman Flower; see letter of 24 Feb 27 to him.   *as a serial*: see letter of 28 July 26.
play by Mr Drinkwater: see letter of 23 Apr 26.   *with "John o' London"*: see VI.356; it seems in fact to have been Maurice Macmillan (see III.261) who handled the negotiations with *John o' London's Weekly*.

To RUTLAND BOUGHTON

MAX GATE, | DORCHESTER. | 17: 7: 1926

Yes: certainly.—

T.H.

Text   MS. (postcard) BL.
certainly: see letter of 9 July 26 and letter to Boughton of 15 July 26, although Boughton himself has annotated the card, 'Reply to request for permission re extra cuts'; his operatic version of the *Queen of Cornwall* does not appear to have been revived following its last Glastonbury Festival performances in 1925.

To VERE H. COLLINS

[20] July 1926

Dear Mr Collins:

I am sorry that I cannot answer the questions, though less sorry when I doubt if Shakespeare, Shelley, or any of the greatest poets, could have answered them or ever thought of them.

Poetry being in the main a spontaneous product that comes of itself, I don't even suppose that the least spontaneous of poets, Goethe, could have answered them.

Yours truly
Thomas Hardy
per . . . .

Text MS. (pencil draft) DCM. *Date* From the typewritten letter (Texas) sent out over the initials of May O'Rourke.
Collins: Vere Henry Gratz Collins, on the publishing staff of the Oxford University Press; see IV.145. *answer the questions*: Collins (8 July 26, DCM) forwarded on behalf of Professor Edward Wheeler Scripture, an American psychologist teaching at the Univ. of Vienna, a series of thirteen questions (DCM) about TH's metrical practice (e.g., 'How does the verse-form come to you?'). In October 1927 TH did make a brief response to a direct appeal from Scripture, his remarks being subsequently quoted in the opening chapter of Scripture's *Grundzüge der Englischen Verswissenschaft* (Marburg, 1929).

To R. GOLDING BRIGHT

MAX GATE, | DORCHESTER. | 27 July 1926.

Dear Mr Bright:

I have received the enclosed letter about the Tess play. I don't at all wish to have it produced in America unless there were some very strong reason for such a thing. You may know something of the Copley Theatre, and be able to give me an opinion on the proposal.

Yours very truly,
T. Hardy.

P.S. You may have seen that Mr Drinkwater is going to put his dramatization of The Mayor of Casterbridge on the stage. I have nothing to do with the arrangements beyond giving him permission. T.H.

R. Golding Bright. Esq.

Text MS. (typewritten) Adams.
enclosed letter . . . Copley Theatre: see letter of 5 Aug 26. *on the stage*: it was produced at the Barnes Theatre 8 Sept 1926; see *LY*, 248.

To SIR FREDERICK MACMILLAN

MAX GATE, | DORCHESTER. | 28th. July 1926.

Dear Sir Frederick:

I am pleased to hear that you have agreed with Mr Newman Flower about The Mayor of Casterbridge for Messrs Cassell's paper. I consider the amount to be quite as large as could be expected, and you must settle how much is due to yourselves.

I suppose that in printing an old-established story in that sort of periodical the aim is to get at the young man in the street, or the young woman, who never looks at anything but the moment's publications, and was unborn when the novel first appeared.

Believe me,

Yours sincerely,
Th: Hardy.

Text MS. (typewritten) BL.
pleased to hear: Macmillan's letter was written while he was holidaying in Norfolk and no copy appears in the letterbooks in BL.   *Flower*: see letter to Macmillan of 15 July 26.   *Cassell's paper*: *The Mayor of Casterbridge* appeared as a weekly serial in *T.P.'s Weekly* 11 Sept 1926–2 Apr 1927.

To FREDERIC WHYTE

[Late July 1926]

Dear Sir:

As Mr Hardy is much pressed by correspondence he asks me to say in reply to your inquiry that he does not know how "Desperate Remedies" came into the hands of Mr Heinemann, whom he met only once for a few minutes so far as he knows & never did any business with.

All he remembers about the book is that some years after its first publicn. by Tinsleys, Ward & Downey had a lease of it for five years; when it came back again to Mr Hardy. The only correct text, with a new Preface is now published by Messrs Macmillan. Mr Hardy is glad to hear of your view of "The Dynasts," &c.

Yours truly

. . . .
Sec.

Text MS. (pencil draft) DCM.
Whyte: Frederic Whyte (1867–1941), journalist and author; he wrote 25 July 26 (DCM) seeking information for his *William Heinemann: A Memoir*, pub. 1928.   *Heinemann*: William Heinemann, publisher; see letter of 16 July 05.   *never did any business with*: see, however, letter of 16 July 05 below and I.286, related specifically to Heinemann's pub. of a 'Popular Edition' of *Desperate Remedies* in 1892.   *for five years*: the Ward & Downey 'New Edition' appeared in 1889.   *"The Dynasts," &c.*: Whyte mentioned *The Dynasts* and *Tess* as two of TH's works by which he had been especially 'thrilled and delighted'.

To R. GOLDING BRIGHT

MAX GATE, | DORCHESTER. | 5th. August 1926.

Dear Mr Golding Bright:

My thanks for your letter, and I shall be much obliged if you will send a line to Mr E. E. Clive, telling him that I regret to say there are difficulties in the way of having Tess of the d'Urbervilles performed by the Copley Theatre Company.

With regard to The Mayor of Casterbridge, the only arrangement I have with Mr Drinkwater is that he pays me half his receipts, (which I think fair;) and as there were no details, and nothing to see to further, I did not trouble you about it.

In respect to Mr St John Ervine he was asked, I believe by Mr Ridgeway, to dramatize Jude the Obscure, and I have had no objection; but as only pourparlers have passed, and he is busy with other work, and very vague as to when he can take up Jude, if at all, I hardly expect much will come of the idea.

A notion seems to have spread—to judge from the papers—that more of my novels are to be dramatized; but I have given no such permission, and if you should be approached on the subject kindly state, what is quite true, that I am by no means anxious to have *any* novel of mine staged, and that these one or two dramatic productions have come about rather by the wish of others than by mine.

Yours very truly,
Th: Hardy.

Text   MS. (typewritten) Adams.
Clive: Edward E. Clive (1884–1940), English-born American actor and theatrical producer, actor-manager of the Copley Theatre, Boston, for many years; he was evidently the author of the letter TH forwarded to Bright 27 July 26.   *of Casterbridge*: see letter of 27 July 26.   *Ervine . . . Jude the Obscure*: see letter of 9 Sept 26 to Ervine.

To J. B. PRIESTLEY

MAX GATE, | DORCHESTER. | 8 August 1926

Dear Mr Priestley:

I send my warm thanks for your kind gift of the "George Meredith" book, & should have done so before if I had not fallen into the sere, & weak eyesight did not trouble me. I have read your essay, or rather have had it read to me, & have been much interested in the bright writing of one in whom I had already fancied I discerned a coming force in letters.

I am not at all a good critic, especially *of* a critic, & when the author he reviews is a man who was, off & on, a friend of mine for 40 years; but it seems to me that you hold the scales very fairly. Meredith was, as you recognize, & might have insisted on even more strongly, & I always felt, in the direct succession of Congreve & the artificial comedians of the Restoration, & in getting his brilliancy we must put up with the fact that he would not, or could not—at any rate did not—when aiming to represent the "Comic Spirit", let himself discover the tragedy that always underlies Comedy if you only scratch it deeply enough.

I was going to tell you some passages I particularly liked in your book, but must leave off, & with renewed thanks I am

Sincerely yours,
Thomas Hardy.

Text   MS. Texas.   *Date*   In *LY*, 257, this letter is wrongly dated 1927.
Priestley: John Boynton Priestley, novelist, dramatist, and critic; see VI.281.   *"George Meredith"*: Priestley's inscribed copy of his *George Meredith* (see letter of 6 June 26) was sent to

TH with a covering letter dated 30 July 26 (Mount Saint Vincent Univ.); for Meredith himself, see IV.23.   *fallen into the sere*: *Macbeth*, V. iii. 20.   *much interested*: FEH, however, told Cockerell (21 June 26, Purdy) that TH was not finding the book very interesting.   *especially of*: TH first wrote, 'especially when'.   *Congreve*: William Congreve (1670–1729), dramatist; *D.N.B.*   *tragedy . . . underlies Comedy*: a favourite observation of TH's; see I.190 and *Thomas Hardy's Personal Writings*, ed. Harold Orel (Lawrence, Kansas, 1966), 154.

To PHILIP GUEDALLA

MAX GATE, | DORCHESTER. | 16 Aug. 1926

Dear Mr Guedalla:

The book has come, & I owe you many thanks for it, as it is one I shall much like to read when the evenings get longer, though I will not delay my acknowledgment of your gift till then.

Napoleon III. is a little associated with these parts. He used in his English days to visit at a house a mile from the front of this, whose daughter refused his offer of marriage—not thinking a mere adventurer good enough.

Sincerely yours
Thomas Hardy.

Text   MS. (with envelope) Masao Akagi.
Guedalla: Philip Guedalla (1889–1944), historian and essayist; *D.N.B.*   *The book*: Guedalla's *The Second Empire: Bonapartism, the Prince, the President, the Emperor* (London, 1922), with a presentation inscription from the author dated 14 Aug 1926.   *Napoleon III.*: Louis Napoleon (1808–73), emperor of France 1852–70.   *a house*: Came House; see *EL*, 229–30.

To JOHN GALSWORTHY

MAX GATE, | DORCHESTER. | 29 Aug. 1926

My dear Galsworthy:

We have already read several chapters of the book, but I don't wait till the end before writing since, owing to the weakness of my eyes, I am at the mercy of my wife's reading it aloud, & she can only do so in the evening when the house is quiet & trippers cease from troubling.

So far I find the story moves along very briskly & brightly.

I had nearly forgotten to say how much I thank you for it, & for the inscription. Kindest regards.

Sincerely yours
Thomas Hardy.

We should be pleased to see you & Mrs Galsworthy at any time you may be coming this way. T.H.

Text   MS. Univ. of Birmingham.
Galsworthy: John Galsworthy, novelist and playwright; see III.202.   *the book*: *The Silver Spoon* (London, 1926).   *the inscription*: Galsworthy used the phrase 'affectionate homage'. *Mrs Galsworthy*: see VI.71.

To THE REVD. G. H. MOULE

MAX GATE, | DORCHESTER. | 31 August 1926

Dear Mr Moule:

I am much obliged to you for the Japanese magazine you send, which incidentally shows what a progressive people the Japanese are. M. Romain

Rolland, who was here some time ago, thinks that ultimately Japan will be the leading country of intellectual light. I don't know enough about the quality of their minds, and the lines on which their thinking and feeling are developing, to have an opinion about it.

It seems strange that, bringing news from the other side of the world you should express yourself from such a homely and secluded corner as Abbotsbury, but I am told that you are settled or likely to settle there.

In respect of your allusion to the character in "Tess of the d'Urbervilles" called the Revd. Mr Clare, I remember taking some features of Mr Moule's *public* life in constructing the fictitious personage—features I much admired in the Vicar of Fordington. I do not think I had Mrs Moule in mind when describing Mrs Clare, and if there were any resemblances they would probably have been accidental.

Believe me

Sincerely yours
Th. Hardy.

Reverend G. H. Moule | Manor House | Abbotsbury.

Text   MS. (typewritten) the Revd. G. R. K. Moule.
Moule: the Revd. George Herbert Moule, later vicar of Stinsford; see VI.5.   *Japanese magazine*: Moule had served as a missionary in Japan 1902–11, and currently held a teaching position at the Central Theological College, Tokyo.   *Rolland*: Romain Rolland (1866–1944), French novelist, playwright, and essayist; his sister, Madeleine, was well known to TH as the translator of *Tess* (see II.145).   *Abbotsbury*: the Dorset village, SW of Dorchester, where his brother Walter was vicar; Moule did not remain there but returned to Japan until 1936.   *Mr Moule's*: Moule's grandfather, the Revd. Henry Moule, vicar of the Dorchester suburb of Fordington 1829–80; see I.70.   *Mrs Moule*: Mary Mullett Moule, *née* Evans (1801–77), wife of the Revd. Henry Moule.

To H. G. WELLS

MAX GATE, | DORCHESTER. | 5 Sept. 1926

Dear Mr Wells:

I have a half-ashamed feeling at accepting this beautiful edition of your new book, as I have done nothing to deserve it, & an ordinary copy would have been good enough for me. However, I thank you much for such a handsome gift.

I have begun it, but perceiving it to be a book of much more solid & philosophic quality that I at first expected I find it will not be one to hurry over. No book worth reading is. Although I do not see far into it as yet, I anticipate that you will get some buffets from the thoughtless—which happily you are well able to bear.

It is a most depressing business to endeavour to advance thought ever so little along the road to rationality. Your arguments are read or listened to—sometimes with respect—& twenty years later you find you may just as well not have written a line—except, of course, for a certain satisfaction that comes of having been no hypocrite & in having expressed your views sincerely. It may not always be thus; but I don't know.

Very sincerely yours
Thomas Hardy.

Text   MS. Univ. of Illinois, Urbana.
Wells: Herbert George Wells, author; see V.280.   *beautiful edition . . . new book*: *The World of William Clissold* (3 vols., London, 1926); Wells sent TH a set of the limited signed issue.   *quality that*: TH means 'quality than'.   *not . . . hurry over*: for TH's final response see letter of 19 Nov 26.

To N. O. M. CAMERON

MAX GATE, | DORCHESTER. | 7 Sept. 1926

Dear Mr Cameron:

I return the proof, which is all right, but I have added a paragraph, if you think it worth while to put it in. If not, let the proof stand.

Yours very truly
Thomas Hardy.

You may have already solved the problem I mention. T.H.

Text   MS. Cecil Sharp House.
Cameron: N. O. M. Cameron, editor of the English Folk Dance Society's *E.F.D.S. News* and founder of the Greensleeves Morris Dancers, worked in the Department of Printed Books, British Museum. He wrote 6 Sept 26 (DCM).   *return the proof*: of a letter about English country dances which TH had said might be published in *E.F.D.S. News*, no. 12, September 1926; see Purdy, 323.   *added a paragraph*: the third paragraph of the letter as pub.; TH kept a copy of his insertion (DCM) and the proof itself survives at Cecil Sharp House.   *the problem I mention*: that of the relationship between the so-called Country dances and the dances fashionable in London during the eighteenth century; see letter of late Mar 27.

To ST. JOHN ERVINE

MAX GATE, | DORCHESTER, | DORSET. | 9th. September 1926.

Dear Mr Ervine:

I am happy to send you the authorization you ask for—that is, that you have the sole right to dramatize "Jude" for twelve months from the beginning of November next.

I may say that I am not keen on the new mode (as I suppose it is regarded, though really Elizabethan) of giving a series of episodes in the film manner instead of set scenes. Of the outlines I sent you which suggested themselves to me many years ago, I thought the one I called (I think) "4th Scheme" most feasible. If you wanted to begin further back than the First Act of this, you could split the act up into 2 or 3 scenes.

Would not Arabella be the villain of the piece?—or Jude's personal constitution?—so far as there is any villain more than blind Chance. Christminster is of course the tragic influence of Jude's drama in one sense, but innocently so, and merely as crass obstruction. By the way it is not meant to be exclusively Oxford, but any old-fashioned University about the date of the story 1860–70, before there were such chances for poor men as there are now. I have somewhere printed that I had no feeling against Oxford in particular.

I hope you keep well as we do.

Sincerely yours,
Th: Hardy.

Text   MS. (typewritten) Texas.
Ervine: St. John Greer Ervine, playwright and author; see VI.85.   *authorization you ask for*:
in an earlier version of this letter (DCM), not sent, TH deferred such authorization until
Drinkwater's current dramatization of *The Mayor of Casterbridge* had proved successful; see
Personal Notebooks (see letter of 5 Mar 26), 283n.   *outlines I sent you*: they were in fact sent by
FEH, 17 July 26 (Texas), and are now at Texas (drafts in DCM); the '4th Scheme' reflects quite
closely the action of the novel itself.   *Oxford in particular*: the reference is perhaps to the
implication in the 1912 Preface to *Jude* (Wessex edn., ix) that TH was surprised to discover that
'some readers' considered the Christminster sections of the novel 'an attack on venerable
institutions'.

To AUGUSTA EVERETT

9 Sept. 1926

Dear Mrs Everett:
    I write for Mr Hardy, who is suffering from weak eyesight, to say in reply to
your letter that he quite remembers you when you were living at the Rectory in
Dorchester.
    Respecting your request that he will sign the Caricature of him which
appeared in Vanity Fair thirty years ago, he regrets to tell you that he has been
compelled for many years to decline to give autographs for various reasons.
    He is glad to hear that you are thriving, & returns the print.

Yours vy trly

Text   MS. (pencil draft) DCM.
Everett: Augusta Stewart Everett, widow of the Revd. Henry Everett, rector of Holy Trinity,
Dorchester, 1870–95; TH appears to have been friendly at one time both with her and with her son
Herbert (see TH's letter to Besant tentatively dated Spring 86, below).   *your request* . . .
Vanity Fair: Mrs. Everett wrote from London 8 Sept 26 (DCM) to ask if TH would autograph a
copy of the 'Spy' cartoon of himself pub. in *Vanity Fair*, 4 June 1892.

To JOHN DRINKWATER

[11 September 1926]

Yes. T.H. will come to matinee. Keep the actors from indulging in dialect: it is
not really necessary to do more than just hint it. T.H. says he is afraid they
overdo it. You will find the Weymouth theatre a very convenient one, but I
suppose the scenery will require fitting.

Text   MS. (pencil draft) DCM.   *Date*   From internal evidence.
Drinkwater: John Drinkwater, poet and playwright; see IV.34. He wrote to FEH (10 Sept 26,
DCM) to say that Ridgeway was bringing the play of the *Mayor* to Weymouth on 20 September for
a 'flying' matinée so that TH could see it in comfort; TH's telegram to Ridgeway accepting the
invitation to attend is dated 11 Sept 26 (Adams).

To JOHN GALSWORTHY

MAX GATE. | 13 Sept., '26.

My dear G.,
    Have finished the book. One of the very best you have done!

T.H.

Text   H. V. Marrot, *The Life and Letters of John Galsworthy* (London, 1935), 578.
the book: *The Silver Spoon*; see letter of 29 Aug 26.

To ST. JOHN ERVINE

MAX GATE, | DORCHESTER. | Wed. morning 15: 9: '26

Yes: "The Ring" is the Roman Amphitheatre close to Dorchester—called locally "Maumbury Rings". Maiden Castle, or "Mai Dun" is a huge enclosure a mile further on—said to be the largest fortress in the world.

T.H.

Text   MS. (postcard) Texas.
Yes: Ervine (14 Sept 26, DCM) asked if he had been wrong, in a review of the *Mayor of Casterbridge* play, to identify 'the Ring' with Maiden Castle.

To ROBERT PEARSALL

17 September: 1926

Dear Sir:

I have received your letter of the 12th, informing me that you are an old pupil of the late Sir Arthur Blomfield's. As for the accounts of myself you see in the papers, you must accept them with extreme caution, the penny-a-liners who write them being in the habit of inventing what they do not know for the sake of effect, particularly so in my own case.

I am interested to hear of the assistants & pupils at Blomfield's. I knew Streatfield & W. O. Milne; also John Lee & his brother. What became of the 2 last I cannot tell. I also just remember Green. The other names are strange to me.

Yours truly

Robert Pearsall Esq.

Text   MS. (pencil draft) DCM.
Pearsall: Robert Pearsall, of Uxbridge, Middlesex, formerly an assistant architect with the London County Council; he wrote 12 Sept 26 (DCM).   *Blomfield's*: the architect (see I.3), TH's employer 1862–7; Pearsall entered Blomfield's office in September 1868.   *in the papers*: Pearsall had seen an article in the *Star*, 10 Sept 1926, which gave a partly accurate, partly inaccurate account of TH's early experiences as an architect in London.   *Streatfield*: T. E. C. Streatfield's is one of several names mentioned in Pearsall's letter; he remains otherwise unidentified.   *Milne*: who often visited theatres with TH; see Millgate, 99.   *Lee*: John T. Lee, the senior assistant in Blomfield's office in TH's time and in Pearsall's.   *his brother*: with whom TH attended Lord Palmerston's funeral; see I.5–6.   *Green*: Pearsall calls him Herbert Green.

To ARCHIBALD FLOWER

MAX GATE, | DORCHESTER, | DORSET. | 30th. September '26.

Dear Mr Flower:

I have read with interest your account of the progress made so far towards the rebuilding and endowment of the Shakespeare Memorial Theatre, and I ought to have replied before this. But I have unhappily reached an age at which I begin to find it impossible to do more than an infinitesimal part of what I used to do, and though I am glad to hear that there is to be a Drury Lane performance in aid of your objects, I fear I cannot be of any assistance in the effort. I have not, in fact, written an original line for months.

In 1916 I wrote some verses to Shakespeare, and I should not at all mind making a copy or replica of the MS. of a dozen lines of those, and sign them, if they would be of any use. But of course they would not be much, and my feeling is that you can get some original lines from some other writer or writers which would quite suit your purpose,

Yours sincerely,
Th: Hardy.

Archibald Flower. Esq. | Stratford-upon-Avon.

Text   MS. (typewritten) Folger Shakespeare Library.
Flower: Archibald Dennis Flower (1865–1950), former mayor of Stratford-upon-Avon, chairman of the council of the Shakespeare Memorial Theatre 1900–50.   *your account*: in his letter of 18 Sept 26 (DCM); for TH's support for an earlier appeal for funds see letter of 26 Mar 26.   *an original line*: Flower had asked TH to write 'a stanza or two' which could be reproduced in the souvenir programme of the forthcoming Drury Lane special matinée in aid of the rebuilding fund.   *verses to Shakespeare*: TH's 'To Shakespeare After Three Hundred Years'; see Purdy, 177–8.   *of any use*: TH's offer was taken up, however; see letter of 12 Oct 26.

To MALCOLM WATSON

MAX GATE, DORCHESTER. | 12 October 1926.

Dear Mr Watson:

I am sending under another cover a copy of a part of the MS. I wrote in 1916, as offered to Mr Flower—18 lines, and have signed them as you request. I cannot suppose that they have much value, as the poem has been printed several years.

Yours very truly,
Th: Hardy.

P.S. I found it beyond me to write out the whole six verses. T.H.
Malcolm Watson. Esq.

Text   MS. (typewritten) Folger Shakespeare Library.
Watson: Malcolm Watson (1853–1929), dramatic critic and playwright; he wrote 4 Oct 26 (DCM) after Archibald Flower had forwarded to him TH's letter of 30 Sept 26.   *18 lines*: increased, at Watson's request, from the 12 lines TH had offered to Flower; the MS., though incomplete, was reproduced in facsimile in the souvenir programme of the Grand Matinée in Aid of the Shakespeare Memorial Fund, held at the Theatre Royal, Drury Lane, 9 Nov 1926.

To MARIE STOPES

FROM TH. HARDY, | MAX GATE, | DORCHESTER. | 16 Oct. '26

Dear Dr Marie Stopes:

I should have told you earlier that I was quite glad to hear how successful the meeting at Portland about the Museum turned out to be. It is very strange that nobody shd have had the bright idea of forming it earlier.

I cd not have been present, the play at Weyth being enough for me.

Yrs v. sincly
T.H.

Text MS. (correspondence card) BL.
about the Museum: Marie Stopes (9 Oct 26, DCM) reported that a public meeting on Portland had given unanimous support to the creation of a local museum in 'Avice's cottage', associated with TH's *The Well-Beloved*, which she had bought and was in the process of restoring. *enough for me*: the meeting was held on 20 September, the same day as the Weymouth performance of *The Mayor of Casterbridge* (see letter of 11 Sept 26).

To WILFRID HODGES

17 October 1926

Dear Mr Hodges:

I ought to have answered your letter before on the question of my continuing to be a Vice-President of the Dorchester Old Grammarians Club. On account of age & incompetence I have retired from several Clubs & other Societies, & therefore think I ought also to retire from this, as for the same reasons I am unable to attend any dinners or meetings, or, in short, do anything for the Club.

Of course, if you & the other officers really care for a merely nominal membership on my part I shall be quite pleased to continue such a very shadowy connection. But I hardly think it is worth while to keep my name on the books on such terms.

Yours very truly
[Signed] T—— H——

Wilfrid Hodges Esq

Text MS. (pencil draft) DCM.
Old Grammarians Club: Hodges, writing as president of the club, reported (9 Oct 26, DCM) that at the recent annual meeting he had been instructed to ask TH to stay on as a vice-president. TH did not attend the school as a boy but had served on its board of governors for several years. *[Signed]*: word and brackets in TH's hand.

To O. H. FORSYTH-MAJOR

. . . . [Mid-]October: 1926

Dear Sir:

In reply to your letter of 14 Oct. concerning the story which you tell me is in circulation, to the effect that when staying at an Hotel at Amsteg, Switzerland in the seventies or eighties, I made the acquaintance of Miss Rosine Indergand, & presented her with some of my books, I can state that it is entirely fictitious. I have never in my life set foot in Amsteg, & the only time I ever passed through the place was when returning from Italy by the St Gotthard route in April 1887, the train not stopping between Geschenen & Lucerne. I have never known any lady of that attractive name, which is quite new to me.

It is a pity to spoil the story, but I cannot help it, even though the dates somewhat correspond.

Yours truly
[Signed] . . . .

Major O. H. Forsyth-Major | Connaught Club.

Text MS. (pencil draft) DCM. *Date* From internal evidence.
Forsyth-Major: Major O. H. Forsyth-Major, son of the late Dr. Charles Immanuel Forsyth Major, F.R.S., told TH (14 Oct 26, DCM) that he was interested in the history of the Major family and specifically in the story, current within the family, that TH had known his father's sister-in-law, Rosine Indergand, in Amsteg in the 1870s or 1880s. *in April 1887*: when returning with ELH from a holiday in Italy; see *EL*, 257–8. *[Signed]*: all in TH's hand.

To W. STEBBING

[Mid-October 1926]

Dear Mr Stebbing:

I return the paper signed (I believe correctly), & thank you for sending me the £30 left me by your kind father, who really ought not to have taken the trouble, as I knew of his goodness without it, though no doubt it was a pleasure to him to do so.

It was somewhat singular that we should have got so attracted to each other, since one has a long acquaintance with so many men without getting any sort of warm feeling towards them.

Well, as to what I told him of my instinct having been originally rather towards verse than novel writing, I was correct in saying so, whatever good results may have come from my being forced to take to prose; & I still feel that I have in many cases concentrated into a page or two of verse what in the novels filled scores of pages.

I did as a boy see a woman hanged at Dorchester, &, it rather shocks me now to remember, without much emotion—I suppose because boys are like it. I might have seen more hangings if I had wished, for I was living in London when 5 pirates were hanged in a row at Newgate, & met the crowds returning from the spectacle.

Yours very sincerely

Text MS. (pencil draft) DCM. *Date* Replies to letter of 17 Oct 26.
Stebbing: W. P. D. Stebbing, of Deal, wrote 17 Oct 26 (DCM), to send the £30 left to TH by his father, William Stebbing (see IV.273), leader-writer for *The Times* for many years, who had died in May at the age of ninety-five. *a woman hanged*: Martha Browne, in 1856; see letter of 20 Jan 26. *5 pirates … spectacle*: on 22 Feb 1864; see Newman Flower, *Just as It Happened* (London, 1950), 91–2, and, for the execution itself, *The Times*, 23 Feb 1864.

To SIR FREDERICK MACMILLAN

MAX GATE, | DORCHESTER. | 23 October 1926.

Dear Sir Frederick:

My wife will have acknowledged the receipt of the copy of "Tess" as illustrated by Mrs Doyle Jones, and said how much we like the look of it, and her cows and milkmaids. I also duly received the statement of sales some months ago.

In looking over the latter I believe I am right in gathering, with regard to the volumes of *poetry*, that the American sales are included in the English sales, no American sales by the Macmillan Company being entered, except in the case of the last published volume, Human Shows, which was printed over there.

I enclose a letter from a lady Dr. of Philosophy in Germany, which I imagine to be of no importance.

> Very sincerely yours,
> Th: Hardy.

Text   MS. (typewritten) BL.
"*Tess*" . . . *Jones*: see letter of 4 Jan 26; Macmillan wrote to FEH, 22 Oct 26 (Macmillan letterbooks, BL), to report that the book had been pub. that day.   *some months ago*: TH perhaps meant 'weeks'; see letter of 29 Jan 27.   *American sales*: Macmillan replied (26 Oct 26, Macmillan letterbooks, BL) that the statement of sales did in fact show that 343 copies of *Collected Poems* had been sent to and sold in the United States; he added that the book was now being printed in America and that future royalties would be based on the American price.   *in Germany*: unidentified; Macmillan thought the letter was probably intended to elicit an autograph and promised to deal with it.

To SIR FREDERICK MACMILLAN

> MAX GATE, | DORCHESTER. | 27th. October 1926.

Dear Sir Frederick:

My thanks for the explanation of the sale of the poems in America. I did not understand that the second numbers under "Collected Poems" referred to that country, owing to your clerk having accidentally drawn his pen through the word "America".

As people seem to be reading the poems in the U.S. more than they did, I think the plan you are adopting of printing them over there quite desirable.

I leave the question entirely to you of Messrs George Newnes including "The Three Strangers" in their library, the reasons for and against being practical ones. I never think that a passage extracted from a novel for an anthology does the novel any harm, but as to borrowing a whole story I cannot say.

> Very sincerely yours,
> Th: Hardy.

Text   MS. (typewritten) BL.
poems in America: see letter of 23 Oct 26.   *practical ones*: in his letter of 26 Oct 26 Macmillan noted that Newnes' desire to print a complete TH story in their 'World's Library of Best Books' was on a different scale from their earlier use of extracts in the same series.

To JOHN DRINKWATER

> MAX GATE, | DORCHESTER. | 5 Nov. 1926

Dear Mr Drinkwater:

Thank you much for the copy of your Book for Bookmen, which has already tempted me to look into it, though I have not really read it yet—my reading nowadays being very intermittent, for physical reasons.

Your letter drew my attention to the paragraph in the Hawker article. What I may have told you was that a relative of mine was the rector of St. Juliot, on the same coast as Morwenstow, & on neighbourly terms with Hawker, & that on my frequent visits the St. Juliot people often said they would drive me across to see him. But we put off & put off going, & then heard that Hawker was dead.

Whether your impressions were derived from this, or from some other account
I cannot say. Believe me

Sincerely yours
Thomas Hardy.

Text   MS. Yale.
for Bookmen: Drinkwater's *A Book for Bookmen: Being Edited Manuscripts and Marginalia with Essays on Several Occasions* (London, 1926).   *Your letter*: it has not been traced.   *Hawker article*: Drinkwater's essay on the Revd. Robert Stephen Hawker (see IV.327), the poet and antiquary, ascribed to TH (175) what was in fact Edmund Gosse's story of travelling to Hawker's Cornish parish of Morwenstow only to hear upon arrival the sound of the passing-bell announcing his death. See Ann Thwaite, *Edmund Gosse: A Literary Landscape 1849–1928* (London, 1984), 160, 532n.   *may have told you*: as he certainly told John Lane in 1913; see IV.328.   *relative of mine*: his first wife's brother-in-law, the Revd. Caddell Holder (see IV.276).

To SIR FREDERICK MACMILLAN

MAX GATE, | DORCHESTER. | 10 November 1926.

Dear Sir Frederick:

I don't at all mind signing the copy for the bookseller if he or you will send it.

As I am writing I may mention another matter that occurred to me one day. You may perhaps be able to recall that when the Wessex edition of the novels was started I wrote brief postscripts to some of the old Prefaces of 1895, to bring the edition up to date. These postscripts were I believe never added to the same old Prefaces in the Uniform and Pocket editions, so that the latter still have only the old Osgood & McIlvaine Prefaces of 1895. The postscripts are not perhaps of great importance—certainly not in more than 4 or 5 of the novels; but as there is mostly a blank space on the page under the old prefaces, it seems to me it would be worth while, requiring no type-shifting, to add the postscripts from time to time whenever you are reprinting any of the volumes. The prefaces of the Uniform and Pocket editions would then be nearer to date than they are now, giving the volumes a more recent appearance.

Perhaps you will give this your consideration and let me know at any time. Believe me,

Very sincerely yours,
Thomas Hardy.

Text   MS. (typewritten) BL.
for the bookseller: Macmillan (9 Nov 26, Macmillan letterbooks, BL) asked if TH would sign a copy of *Jude* for a bookseller in Hereford who was very interested both in reading TH's books and in selling them.   *reprinting any of the volumes*: Macmillan (12 Nov 26, Macmillan letterbooks, BL) promised that no more copies would be printed in the Uniform and Pocket formats without incorporating the revisions and additions made to the Wessex edn. prefaces of 1912–13.

To SIR FREDERICK MACMILLAN

MAX GATE, DORCHESTER. | 16th. November 1926.

Dear Sir Frederick:

I have signed the book with pleasure, and posted it back.

I am glad to hear that you are going to set the prefaces right. I am sending herewith a few Memoranda on trifling points, to which my attention has been drawn from time to time, that it will be as well to see to at the same time as when the Prefaces and Postscripts are made uniform.

Yours very sincerely,
T.H.

Text MS. (typewritten) BL.
the book: see letter of 10 Nov 26. *prefaces right*: see letter of 10 Nov 26. *Memoranda*: Macmillan acknowledged these 18 Nov 26 (Macmillan letterbooks, BL) and undertook to see that they were acted upon immediately.

To J. D. PARSONS

17 November 1926

Dear Sir:

Mr Hardy has received your letter on his poem entitled "To Shakespeare after three hundred years."

The question you raise on the antecedent unlikelihood of Shakespeare of Stratford-on-Avon having written the plays attributed to him has been raised many times, & is too large a one for Mr Hardy to enter into in a letter, although eternally interesting. And whatever may be said against its probability, the testimonies of Heminge, Condell, Jonson (vide Dedicatory Epistle to the First Folio) & many other of his contemporaries as to the authorship of the plays are weighty enough to set at rest all doubts on the point that may be based merely on conjectures formed from the Burbage family petition of 1635.

Yours very truly
for Th. Hardy

. . . .

J. D. Parsons Esq. | Chiswick.

Text MS. (pencil draft) DCM.
Parsons: John Denham Parsons, author of the privately printed *Report on the Poet Shakespeare's Identity Submitted to the Trustees of the British Museum* (Chiswick, 1930) and other such pamphlets. *your letter*: Parsons, writing from Chiswick 16 Nov 26 (DCM), wondered whether TH, in composing the poem, had taken sufficiently into account the possibility that 'Shakespeare the Actor was, so far as poems & plays be concerned, but a stalking horse for some one yet to be determined'. *Heminge, Condell*: John Heming or Hemminge (1556–1630; *D.N.B.*) and Henry Condell (d. 1627; *D.N.B.*), editors of the First Folio edn. of Shakespeare, 1623. *Jonson*: Ben[jamin] Jonson (1573?–1637; *D.N.B.*), poet and dramatist. *Dedicatory Epistle*: 'To the memory of my beloved, The Author Mr. William Shakespeare: And what he hath left us'. *Burbage family petition*: Parsons drew particular attention to this petition's reference to Shakespeare as an actor only.

To H. G. WELLS

MAX GATE, | DORCHESTER, | DORSET. | 19 Nov: 1926

Dear Mr Wells:

I am writing to let you know that we have finished Clissold with great regret, & that we wish there was a Volume IV coming along next month.

Though I own that the ideas bursting out of the pages everywhere interested me more than the story proper, & that I am full of visions of the World Republic, the tale itself was arresting nevertheless. I felt sorry for the two chief characters. As for him, you gave him a dignity by putting an end to him that he would not otherwise have had, so that you were artistically right in doing it some way or other. But Clementine: well, I really wish she had lived on. It is strange that a figure so lightly sketched should be so real.

With best thanks & kindest regards I am,

Sincerely yours
Thomas Hardy.

Text   MS. Univ. of Illinois, Urbana.
Clissold . . . a Volume IV: The World of William Clissold, first pub. in three vols.; see letter of 5 Sept 26.   *ideas . . . story proper*: Clissold's schemes for world government in fact occupy the bulk of the third volume, although always framed within the narrative of his relationship with Clementine Campbell, thirty years his junior.   *gave him a dignity*: TH apparently saw the deaths of Clissold and Clementine in a car accident just after it had become obvious that they would marry as bestowing upon the former a tragic status he could not otherwise have achieved; it is less clear whether he saw the impending marriage as potentially comic (because of the age difference) or as too conventionally 'happy'.

To SIR ALFRED RICE-OXLEY

22 November 1926

Dear Sir Alfred Rice-Oxley:

I have not the slightest objection to telling you the exact situation of houses in which I lived in Kensington—as nearly as I know it.

1894 & 1896. 16 Pelham Crescent S.K. (We had the whole house)

1898–1899. Wynstay Gardens. I cannot remember the number of the flat, but it was in the front row, facing the main street. We lived there mainly because the concerts at the Imperial Institute were within easy access.

Yours very truly

P.S. I should also add that in 1887 I lived in Campden Hill Road—number forgotten.

Text   MS. (pencil draft) DCM.
Rice-Oxley: Sir Alfred James Rice-Oxley (1856–1941), distinguished physician and former mayor of Kensington; in his letter of 20 Nov 26 (DCM) he recalled TH's telling him he had once lived in Kensington and asked if he might now have more precise details for the benefit of the 120 members of the London Society he would shortly be guiding round parts of the borough.   *16 Pelham Crescent*: see II.55.   *Wynstay Gardens*: correctly 'Wynnstay'; the Hardys stayed at no. 20 (see II.193), as Rice-Oxley himself discovered (18 Dec 26, DCM).   *number forgotten*: no. 5; see I.165.

To ERNEST BARKER

MAX GATE, DORCHESTER. | 23 November 1926

Dear Dr Barker:

Many thanks for the invitation to the Annual College dinner, for even though, as you say, a matter of form only, it keeps alive a sense of my old relationship with you. I wish I could come, but I am getting more and more every year like a vegetable that will not bear transplanting.

Yours sincerely
Thomas Hardy.

Text MS. (typewritten) King's College, London.
matter of form only: Barker's handwritten addition to the formal invitation (19 Nov 26, DCM) to the King's College annual dinner recognized that TH would not in fact be able to come but assured him that he would be remembered on the occasion. *relationship with you*: i.e., with the College; see letter of 19 June 26.

To DOROTHY ALLHUSEN

MAX GATE, | DORCHESTER. | 26 Nov. 1926

My dear Dorothy:

The book has come: many thanks for it. I have begun to read it already, as the type is a good size. You ought not to have taken the trouble to send it, all the same. But you were always so good-natured—more than you ought to be, for other people are not.

We shall, of course, be glad to see you at any time. Our poor dog seems to be in a bad way, but we don't like to put an end to him: a neighbour did to hers when he was ill, & she has regretted it ever since.

We think of you these dark days, & I am

Ever your affectionate
T.H.

Text MS. (with envelope) Purdy.
The book: *A Book of Scents & Dishes* (London, 1925), compiled by D. Allhusen; it contains several recipes supplied by FEH. *glad to see you*: a response to her letter of 25 Nov 26 (DCM). *Our poor dog*: see letter of 29 Dec 26; Mrs. Allhusen wrote back, 29 Nov 26 (DCM), to urge that Wessex be put to sleep.

To JOHN GALSWORTHY

MAX GATE, | DORCHESTER.| 1 Dec. 1926

My dear Galsworthy:

I am sending this brief reply at a venture, as you may be vanishing across the Bay of Biscay before it reaches your house. Another friend of ours is crossing the Bay this very week, but he, poor fellow, is in a troop-ship.

We hope the change will benefit you both, & that we shall see you when you get back. My own travels are limited to a radius of about 50 miles from here, & have been for many years.

We wish you luck in weather & everything else. The autumn has been exceptionally cold here.

Always yours sincerely
Thomas Hardy.

Text MS. Univ. of Birmingham.
Bay of Biscay: Galsworthy and his wife sailed from Southampton for Cape Town 3 Dec 1926, returning to England in late March 1927. *Another friend*: T. E. Lawrence ('Lawrence of Arabia'); see VI.291. The *Derbyshire*, the troop-ship taking him to Karachi, sailed 7 Dec 1926.

To G. HERBERT THRING

MAX GATE, | DORCHESTER. | Dorset. | 2. December 1926.
Dear Mr Thring:

"Jude the Obscure."

The right of translating the above novel into the Czech language has not been disposed of, and I have no objection to its being done by the Co-operative Publishing Society of Prague. I think your judgment in the matter is better than mine, and therefore will leave you to make terms. I am more interested in having the book well-translated than in getting money from it, so that what you suggest will quite meet my views.

Sincerely yours,
Th: Hardy.

G. Herbert Thring, Esq. B.A. | Society of Authors.

Text MS. (typewritten) BL.
into the Czech: the translation, *Neblahý Juda*, by Josef Hrůša, was pub. in Prague in 1927.

To BASIL DALTON

7 December, 1926
Dear Sir:

I fear I have not the time or energy to take up the question of submerged books of a noteworthy kind—though it is an interesting one. But if such a book occurs to me I will let you know. Of modern books I can only think of one at the moment—Charles C. Colton's "Lacon" (published about 1820) that might possibly be included in your category, though it can scarcely be called a *great* book.

Yours very truly

Basil Dalton Esq. M.A. | Oxford.

Text MS. (pencil draft) DCM.
Dalton: Basil Imlay Dalton, author of books on card games; he wrote from Oxford (6 Dec 26, DCM) to seek a contribution to a proposed but apparently never-published volume devoted to 'lost' books, works of genuine merit that had somehow slipped into oblivion.   *submerged books*: TH first wrote 'submerged or still-born books'.   *Colton's "Lacon"*: Charles Caleb Colton (1780?–1832; *D.N.B.*); his collection of aphorisms, *Lacon, or Many Things in Few Words: Addressed to Those Who Think*, was pub. in two vols., London, 1820–22.

To PHILIP MACER-WRIGHT

<u>Private</u>   MAX GATE, DORCHESTER, DORSET. | 14th. December 1926.
Dear Sir:

I am sorry to say that a contribution to the Westminster Gazette on Christmas reminiscences is out of my power, but I do not doubt that you will by this time have found more than enough to fill your Saturday page,

Yours truly,
T. Hardy.

P. Macer-Wright. Esq.

Text MS. (typewritten) Univ. of Vermont.
Macer-Wright: Philip Macer-Wright, journalist and author; he wrote 7 Dec 26 (DCM), as editor of the *Westminster Gazette*'s 'Saturday Page', to ask TH for 'a short article of Christmas reminiscence'.

To L. S. AMERY

19 December: 1926.

Dear Sir:

In reply to your letter of the 17th December I am sorry to say that my age & state of health are such that I must forgo the opportunity you offer me of writing a poem for the use of the Empire Marketing Board.

The chill from which I have not yet recovered prevented my seeing Mr Heath when he called last week to propose my undertaking the verses, so that perhaps he gathered that it was more likely I should do so than it really was. But apart from my temporary indisposition I have found of late that increase of years compels me to withdraw from all new engagements. And though small productions of mine are still being issued they are not newly written.

I regret the less my inability to compose the poem in that I know you will be able to avail yourself of plenty of writers equally, & more, efficient for your purpose.

I am charmed with the design you enclose, & as it will probably be useful in other directions I return it herewith.

Believe me, with thanks for your request

Yours truly
[Signed] Th: Hardy

The Rt. Hon. L. S. Amery. P.C.

Text MS. (pencil draft) DCM.
Amery: Leopold Charles Maurice Stennett Amery (1873–1955), statesman and journalist; *D.N.B.* As Colonial Secretary and Secretary of State for Dominion Affairs in the current Conservative government he was responsible for creating the Empire Marketing Board, designed—as he said in his letter of 17 Dec 26 (DCM)—'for the furtherance of the sale in this country of Empire products, among which home agricultural produce is given pride of place'. *writing a poem*: Amery wanted a poem that could be set out on a poster, together with 'a special pictorial map of the United Kingdom illustrating the varied activities of home agriculture and fisheries', and prominently displayed throughout the country. *Mr Heath*: not, apparently, a civil servant but Frederick W. Heath, editor of *The Bermondsey Book*, a magazine to which Amery had already contributed an article and TH a poem ('The Weary Walker', in the issue of December 1925). *[Signed]*: TH's word and square brackets.

To W. H. PARKER

22 Dec. 1926

Dear Sir,

Your inquiry has been received. Mr Hardy is at present too unwell to attend to correspondence, but will probably be able to do so after Christmas.

Your book is doubtless one of those in the heap sent by other strangers with similar requests for autographs, & search shall meanwhile be made for it amongst them.

Yours truly

. . . .

Secretary

W. H. Parker Esq. | Central Library | Hackney, London. E. 8

Text   MS. (pencil draft) DCM.
Parker: Walter H. Parker, chief librarian of the Hackney Public Libraries, wrote 20 Dec 26 (DCM) to ask if TH had received the copy of *Late Lyrics and Earlier* sent some weeks previously in the hope that he would sign and return it; Parker added that Shaw, Galsworthy, Wells, and others had already responded positively to such requests.

To HARLEY AND HELEN GRANVILLE BARKER

Max Gate, | Dorchester. | 29 Dec. 1926.

Dear H.G.B. and Helen.

This is intended to be a New Year's letter, but I don't know if I have made a good shot at it. How kind of you to think of sending me Raymond Guyot's *Napoleon*. I have only glanced at it, at the text that is, as yet, but what an interesting collection of records bearing on the life of the man who finished the Revolution with "a whiff of grapeshot," and so crushed not only its final horrors but all the worthy aspirations of its earlier time, made them as if they had never been, and threw back human altruism scores, perhaps hundreds of years.

We have had a sad aftering to our Christmas. Our devoted (and masterful) dog Wessex died on the 27th, and last night had his bed outside the house under the trees for the first time for 13 years. We miss him greatly, but he was in such misery with swelling and paralysis that it was a relief when a kind breath of chloroform administered in his sleep by 2 good-natured Doctors (not vets) made his sleep an endless one—A dog of such strong character required human doctors!

Best wishes for the coming year that the scheme, or no scheme, of the universe will permit from both and with many thanks believe me

Very sincerely yours

Thomas Hardy.

P.S. Sight bad: accounting for this scrawl of a letter. T.H.

Text   Typed transcript DCM; names and address in FEH's hand at top of letter not reproduced (see letter to Barker of 4 June 26).
Helen: Granville Barker's second wife, *née* Gates; see VI.124.   *Guyot's* Napoleon: pub. in Paris in 1921, it was a folio vol. composed of plates and facsimiles of documents.   *of grapeshot,"*: from Thomas Carlyle, *Frederick the Great*, book V, chap. 3.   *dog Wessex*: for Wessex see V.8 and *LY*, 250–1.   *under the trees*: in the Pets' Cemetery at Max Gate.

1927

To SIR HENRY NEWBOLT

MAX GATE, | DORCHESTER. | 1 Jan: 1927

My dear Newbolt:

This is a great pleasure to me—to have those good wishes from you this morning—for I can welcome them even though I may have misgivings as to deserving your generous estimate of my services to literature. It curiously happened that just before I saw your letter I took up by accident your book of Essays in Green & Gray, & said to my wife, "we will go on reading this to-night." One of them, about Poetry & Time I think I shall like very much.

Yes: do drive over in the coming summer. I go nowhere now, but a mere boy like you have no excuse for staying at home.

My wife sends best remembrances & good wishes with mine.

Always yours
Thomas Hardy.

Text   MS. (with envelope) Texas.
good wishes: in Newbolt's letter of 31 Dec 26 (Texas).   *Green & Gray*: Newbolt's *Studies Green and Gray* (London, 1926); the essay, 'Poetry and Time', is the first item in the book's second part.   *drive over*: Newbolt lived near Salisbury.   *boy like you*: Newbolt was born in 1862.

To G. HERBERT THRING

MAX GATE, DORCHESTER, DORSET. | 4 January 1927

Dear Mr Thring:

"Jude the Obscure" (Czech Rights)

I have signed the Agreement, as it appears to me to be satisfactory, and return it herewith. I will expect in due course from you the duplicate signed by the Prague publishers. I am obliged to you for attending to the matter.

Sincerely yours
Th: Hardy.

P.S. Please find subscription to the Society enclosed.

G. Herbert Thring Esq. B.A. | Society of Authors.

Text   MS. (typewritten) BL.
Prague publishers: see letter of 2 Dec 26.   *the Society*: TH was still president of the Incorporated Society of Authors, Playwrights, and Composers; see IV.27–9.

To FREDERICK MEDWAY

6 January, 1927

Dear Sir:

I write for Mr Hardy in reply to your letter of the 4th, asking him for a foreword to your intended book on the Royal Navy as a career. Mr Hardy is sorry to say that his advanced age, state of health, &c renders it impossible for him to write such a foreword, a sort of thing he has not been able to do for several years. Moreover it would appear that some eminent naval officer or politician with knowledge of the subject would be more suitable for such a foreword or introduction.

With regard to your statement that one of the chapters is entitled "The Prince, yourself" &c. you seem to mean that the chapter refers to Mr Hardy & the Prince of Wales, though he can hardly think you would be so very unwise as to write about either one personally; seeing that it has nothing to do with the Royal Navy. In case you do mean this, however, Mr Hardy must caution you against such a breach of good faith as printing any account of what he may have casually said to you on that or any other matter when you introduced yourself to him here, as he would be compelled to inform the Prince's secretary that he did not authorize the publication of such details, & it might get you into trouble, the Prince strongly objecting to all such reports. Mr Hardy does not, however, remember speaking on the subject when you called.

But he gives you permission to quote anything he may have said about the Royal Navy in his books, notably "The Trumpet Major," & thanks you for your New Year's good wishes.

Yours truly

M O R

Secretary

Commander Medway R.N. (retired)

Text   MS. (pencil draft) DCM.

Medway: Frederick Medway, a former Royal Navy officer, had lived in Dorchester as a child and been friendly with the Kindens (see III.340), who lived in the old Mack's Gate tollhouse. His letter of 4 Jan 27 (DCM), written from 'Max Gate', Lennox Road, Southsea, asked if TH would supply a foreword to a book, to be called 'H.M.S. Opportunity', which would 'place before the parents and youth of the country, the wonderful career that the Royal Navy has to offer'; the project seems not to have materialized.   *"The Prince, yourself" &c.*: Medway had offered to send 'chapters re, The Prince, Yourself, and "The Winston Touch"'; TH was fearful of allusions to the visit the Prince of Wales had made to Max Gate in 1923 (see VI.205), but Medway (9 Jan 27, DCM) explained that these were separate chapters, the one about the Prince referring to a time when he and Medway had served aboard the same ship.   *introduced yourself*: Medway's full-dress signature ('Lt Commander Frederick Medway. Admiralty') appears in the Max Gate visitors' book (BL), 21 Apr 1926.

To THE REVD. J. H. DICKINSON

MAX GATE, | DORCHESTER. | 14 Jan: 1927

Dear Mr Dickinson:

I am greatly obliged to you for sending me the Records of St. Juliot & Lesnewth that you have compiled, with the excellent sketches by your sister. It is very pleasant to read the details unearthed by your labours. I should like to see the place again, but I hardly suppose I shall.

I see that the Elizabethan Wm Rawle who directed that he should be buried in the Chancel, would have lain in the old Chancel that was pulled down in 1870–72, so that the workmen might have come across his grave, though I never heard that any such thing happened.

We both send kindest regards to Miss Dickenson & yourself.

Believe me

Yours sincerely
Th: Hardy.

Text MS. Berg.
Dickinson: the Revd. John Harold Dickinson, rector of St. Juliot, Cornwall; see IV.262.   *Records*: i.e., Dickinson's *Records of St. Juliot and Lesnewth* (Launceston, n.d.).   *sketches by your sister*: they are signed M. F. Blyth.   *see the place again*: TH had restored the church at St. Juliot in the early 1870s and met his first wife there; his last visit was in 1916 (see V.176–9 and *LY*, 172).   *I see . . . Chancel*: Dickinson's pamphlet records this of an ancestor of Bishop Richard Rawle (1812–89; *D.N.B.*), bishop of Trinidad, who was the chief benefactor of the church at the time of the restoration in the early 1870s.   *Dickenson*: i.e., Dickinson; she was another, unmarried, sister of Dickinson's, living at St. Juliot and presumably to be identified with the Miss L. M. Dickinson mentioned in the pamphlet as the author of *Cornish Saints*.

To SIR FREDERICK MACMILLAN

MAX GATE, | DORCHESTER. | 29 Jan. 1927

My dear Macmillan:

Cheque received, for which I am much obliged. I suppose that though I can hardly be called a "best-seller", I may be called a long-seller, seeing that some of the books were published fifty years ago.

I don't at all mind John o' London's Weekly printing a poem a week during 25 weeks for 100 guineas, since the publication thus will probably be a sort of advertisement, so I agree to your making the arrangement. The Editor will probably choose such as are suitable to his paper rather than those intrinsically the best; however I should be glad if he would let me know which of them he selects.

A friend has asked me for a copy of Wessex Poems with the illustrations that were reproduced from my drawings. I think the Uniform Edition still retains them: if so please let me have one. By the way if it should ever be necessary to print them afresh on account of their being worn, or owing to any fancy of collectors, or you should want to get at the originals for any reason, I may mention that they are in the Birmingham Museum.

I hope you have kept clear of influenza.

Very sincerely yours
Thomas Hardy.

Text MS. BL.
Cheque received: Macmillan (27 Jan 27, Macmillan letterbooks, BL) enclosed a cheque for £5,392.2s.6d. in payment of the royalties shown in the account of the previous October.   *The Editor*: not, apparently, Wilfred Whitten ('John o' London'), who founded the magazine in 1919,

but George Blake (1893–1961), novelist, acting editor 1924–28.   *which of them he selects*: the *John o' London*'s announcement (26 Mar 1927) of the forthcoming weekly series of TH poems claimed that its selection had 'received the approval of Mr. Hardy himself'.   *still retains them*: the drawings were also included in the Pocket format, though not in the Wessex or Mellstock edns.

To SIR FREDERICK MACMILLAN

MAX GATE, DORCHESTER. | 10 February 1927.

Dear Sir Frederick:

I am always delighted to hear that anybody wants a poem or poems. So please oblige the Girl Guides Association and let them have the "Oxen".

The book of poems came promptly. Many thanks. I hope Tunbridge Wells carried off the remains of Lady Macmillan's influenza.

Sincerely yours,
T.H.

Text   MS. (typewritten) BL.
have the "Oxen".: corrected from 'have them.' in TH's hand; Macmillan (9 Feb 27, Macmillan letterbooks, BL) reported that the Girl Guide Association wished to reprint the poem 'in card form' for sale to its members.   *book of poems*: as requested in the letter of 29 Jan 27.   *Lady Macmillan's*: Georgiana Elizabeth Macmillan, *née* Warrin, Sir Frederick's American-born wife.

To THOMAS J. WISE

MAX GATE, | DORCHESTER. | 11 Feb. 1927

Dear Mr Wise:

The eighth volume has arrived, & I have been looking into it all the morning with much interest, as you will know. Many thanks, & kind regards.

Sincerely yours
Thomas Hardy.

Text   MS. BL.
eighth volume: of Wise's *Catalogue* of the Ashley Library; see letter of 21 Mar 26.

To R. GOLDING BRIGHT

MAX GATE, DORCHESTER. | 16 February 1927.

Dear Mr Golding Bright:

Many thanks for your letter, enclosures, and cheque. I daresay Mr Ridgeway will pay up the balance when he is inclined to.

If he should do so, but not unless he does, I am thinking of returning to him the £50 he paid for the option of taking the play to South Africa, since he says he is quite unable to do so as he had hoped.

Sincerely yours,
Th. Hardy.

Text   MS. (typewritten) Adams.
your letter: Bright's letter is not in DCM, but Ridgeway had evidently fallen behind in paying TH's share of the box-office receipts for the *Tess* play; see letter of 10 May 26.

To SIR FREDERICK MACMILLAN

MAX GATE, | DORCHESTER, | DORSET. | 18 February 1927.

Dear Sir Frederick:

I am thinking whether a slight addition to the Selection from my poems in the Golden Treasury Series might not be made. The original edition having been published a good many years ago there are several—perhaps a dozen or twenty—I should like included in it to bring it up to date, people telling me quite truly that it does not contain any specimens from recent volumes.

If you assent I will begin looking over these recent volumes and in the course of this year let you know which seem to be the best to put in.

Mr Newman Flower has asked me on behalf of Messrs Cassell, who re-issued The Mayor of Casterbridge as a serial in T.P.'s Weekly, if they can have two of my old short tales for another magazine of theirs, The Argosy, offering a payment of course. As their publication of the other story seems to have done no harm, and as these are only short ones, I did not trouble you about it, and agreed to let him have the stories,

Sincerely yours,
Thomas Hardy.

Text   MS. (typewritten) BL.
Selection from my poems: i.e., TH's *Selected Poems* (London, 1916); the revised version was pub. in 1929, after TH's death, as *Chosen Poems* (see letter of 18 Sept 27 and Purdy, 187–8).   *If you assent*: Macmillan (21 Feb 27, Macmillan letterbooks, BL) welcomed the prospect of a new edn. of *Selected Poems*.   *Newman Flower*: see letter to him of 24 Feb 27.   *have the stories*: Macmillan replied that he would make terms with Flower for the two stories. *Argosy* had already pub. 'A Mere Interlude' in October 1926, and not just two but several TH stories were reprinted there over the next few years; see letter of 22 Feb 27.

To SIR FREDERICK MACMILLAN

MAX GATE, | DORCHESTER, | DORSET. | 22nd. February 1927.

Dear Sir Frederick:

The Messrs Cassell have sent a cheque for the use of the two Wessex Tales (The Withered Arm & The Distracted Preacher) in their Magazine, before I could tell them to negociate through you. But as it appears to be in about the same proportion as that they paid for The Mayor, it is not worth while to send it back, since you can deduct from our next account what is owing to you, or I will forward it now, just as you choose. The amount for the two is £131-5-0.

I will tell Mr Newman Flower to arrange through you if they want any others, and to put in the Magazine that they are published by your permission.

I am glad you like the idea of a new edition of the Selected Poems. I will go through the recent volumes at leisure, and let you know which seem most suitable to add. It is rather a difficult job.

Yours very sincerely,
Thomas Hardy.

P.S. Mr Newman Flower has also I believe, or had, some scheme in his head for a book of illustrations in colour to the Wessex Novels & Poems, with quotations. If he writes about it I will tell him to communicate with you. He is a Dorset man, which I suppose accounts for his interest in the books. T.H.

Text   MS. (typewritten) BL.
Distracted Preacher: on 23 Feb 27 TH sent Macmillan a telegram (BL) reading, 'For the distracted preacher in letter read the three strangers Hardy'.   *negociate through you*: see letter of 18 Feb 27; Macmillan (23 Feb 27, Macmillan letterbooks, BL) made clear his wish that TH would allow his firm to conduct any dealings with other publishers.   *just as you choose*: Macmillan said that his firm's one-third share would be charged against TH's next account.   *book of illustrations*: this proposal appears not to have materialized.

To NEWMAN FLOWER

MAX GATE, | DORCHESTER. | 24th. February 1927.

Dear Mr Newman Flower:

As you possibly know, I am obliged nowadays to get my letters written by machinery whenever possible, (a sort of thing unheard of in my earlier years) and I am sorry to reply to yours by the same means.

I congratulate you on the very interesting information you give of having purchased Cassell's publishing business, though I fear that any supposed influence I may have unconsciously exercised towards promoting such a desirable result is due rather to a lively imagination on your part than to any actual effect on mine, and that the real influence has been simply your own natural energy.

I may have told you that I remember when John Cassell was first talked about. There is an account of him in the Dictionary of National Biography, and he well deserves his place there. For his date he must have been quite an unusual sort of man, and a pioneer of invaluable merit. I daresay you have copies of the earliest books he published: you ought to keep them in a glass case!

Wishing you every success, and with kindest regards,

I am, sincerely yours,
Thomas Hardy.

Text   MS. (typewritten) Texas.
Flower: Newman Flower, Dorset-born publisher; see II.164.   *information you give*: in his letter of 21 Feb 27 (DCM).   *supposed influence*: Flower said that TH's establishment of so high a standard for Wessex writing had strengthened his own ambition to own a publishing business.   *Cassell*: John Cassell (1817–65; *D.N.B.*), publisher specializing in works of self-education; in *EL*, 32, he is referred to as 'that genius in home-education'.

To SIR FREDERICK MACMILLAN

MAX GATE, | DORCHESTER, | DORSET. | 24th. February 1927.

Dear Sir Frederick:

I have looked through the list of poems which it is proposed to select for "John o' London's Weekly," and it appears to be very judiciously chosen; so that I have no emendation to suggest upon it, which please let the editor know at your convenience.

Sincerely yours,
T.H.

Text   MS. (typewritten) BL.
list of poems: see letter of 29 Jan 27; Macmillan sent the list 21 Feb 27 (Macmillan letterbooks, BL).

To A. G. SYMONDS

24 February 1927

Dear Major Symonds:

Dorchester Grammar School

I had already heard that the new Grammar School is soon to be begun, though I did not know exactly when.

As for the foundation or dedication-stone laying it is well that it should take place in better weather than we have at present, so that, as you say, later on would be advisable.

I must thank the Governors for the honour of their considering me a fit person for the ceremony, though it occurred to me at first that the Minister for Education would have been better. However, as far as I remember, these ceremonies are very brief, with only a few formal words to utter, & perhaps I can easily add a few more on my own account, so that I accept their kind invitation with the proviso (which I am obliged to add on account of advancing age) that should the weather be bad I may be allowed to do it by proxy, somebody, such as yourself for instance, reading what I should have said if I had been able to come. This will be just as good for any reporters that may be present, & will prevent the affair from being a fiasco.

Believe me,

Yours very truly

Text   MS. (pencil draft) DCM.
Symonds: Arthur George Symonds (see IV.234), solicitor; he wrote 22 Feb 27 (DCM) as clerk to the Dorchester Grammar School.   *new Grammar School*: i.e., the new buildings on the outskirts of the town, not far from Max Gate.   *later . . . advisable*: the stone-laying ceremony was performed by TH 21 July 1927; see *LY*, 254–6.

To G. HERBERT THRING

FROM TH. HARDY, | MAX GATE, | DORCHESTER. | 25 Feb. 1927

"Jude the Obscure". Copy of Agreement received. Many thanks.

Text   MS. (postcard) BL.
the Obscure": see letter of 4 Jan 27.

To CHARLES LACEY

MAX GATE, | DORCHESTER, | DORSET. | 17th. March 1927.
Dear Mr Lacey:

Many thanks for the copy of the Dorset Chronicle and for your letter drawing my attention to the paragraph.

I was just going to let you know that in clearing out a cupboard I have found a bundle of old Chronicles lent me many years ago, which I thought had been returned at the time. However, they have been perfectly safe, and I will send them back in a day or two.

Yours very truly,
T. Hardy.

C. Lacey. Esq. | Dorset Chronicle Office, | Dorchester.

Text MS. (typewritten) J. Stevens Cox.
Lacey: Charles Lacey, proprietor of the *Dorset County Chronicle*; see II.237.   *the paragraph*: the *Dorset County Chronicle*, 17 Mar 1927, reprinted as a single paragraph the entirety of TH's contribution to the pamphlet, *The Preservation of Ancient Cottages*, just pub. by the Royal Society of Arts (see Purdy, 323).   *bundle of old Chronicles*: TH had returned a similar parcel of back issues just ten years previously; see V.210.

To W. D. CROFT

. . . . [Late] March. 1927.
Dear Sir:

In the pressure of Mr Hardy's correspondence I write for him in reply to your letter. He has no objection to your publishing his letter to Mr Cameron on the subject of English Country Dances, but has nothing further to say about it.

The indisputable fact that the Country dance was the fashionable dance of London society in the middle of the eighteenth century might enable inquirers to determine from chronicles & dance-books of the date how it came to be so—whether its sometimes intricate figures were a town development from some simple form of dancing in a row of couples that prevailed in rural districts, or an importation from Paris.

Mr Hardy adds that he is no authority on the subject, & has only been able to speak of what came under his notice in this part of the country eighty years ago.

Yours truly

. . . .
Secretary

W. D. Croft Esq. | 11 Ellerdale Road | Hampstead. N.W. 3

Text MS. (pencil draft) DCM.   *Date* Replies to letter of 20 Mar 27.
Croft: W. D. Croft, a senior civil servant in the India Office; he wrote an English Folk Dance Society pamphlet, *English Folk Dances* (London, n.d.), and approached TH 20 Mar 27 (DCM) as editor of the Society's newly established *Journal*.   *letter to Mr Cameron*: TH's letter of 26 Oct 26 (Cecil Sharp House), responding to comments N. O. M. Cameron had made when publishing TH's earlier letter on country dances in the *E.F.D.S. News* (see letter of 7 Sept 26). TH had clearly written with publication in mind, and the letter duly appeared, shorn of its opening paragraph, in the *Journal of the English Folk Dance Society* (1927), 53–4.   *nothing further to say*: Croft had suggested that TH might like to amplify his views on one or two points.

To SIR FREDERICK MACMILLAN

MAX GATE, | DORCHESTER, | DORSET. | 24 March 1927.

Dear Sir Frederick:

I am glad to hear that you are getting on with the large edition of *The Dynasts*, and I can sit to Mr Francis Dodd for the frontispiece at any time almost, though I suppose that I am beginning to look rather aged by this time, and it is years since I was photographed. If you will ask him to let me know what date will suit him I will be prepared for his coming.

A German scholar—Dr. phil. Weltzien of Berlin—is writing "a big book" on the "Wessexromanen" (as he calls my novels) of which he sends me the first part. He seems to be such a well-known and thorough critic that I have thought it would be worth while to forward him a copy of *The Dynasts* with my reply to his letter. A good many Germans read English, and his writing about it may be the means of getting the book asked for over there. The most portable edition would be the easiest to send, if you will be kind enough to send him a copy. His address is: Dr. phil. Weltzien,

> Studienrat,
> Charlottenburg 5
> Friedrich-Karl-Platz 10
> Fernspr. Wilhelm 2426.
> Berlin.

I am,

Sincerely yours,
Thomas Hardy.

Text MS. (typewritten) BL.
to hear: from Macmillan's letter of 23 Mar 27 (Macmillan letterbooks, BL).   *Dodd*: Francis H. Dodd (1874–1949), landscape and portrait painter; his etched portrait of TH was used as the frontispiece to the first vol. of the three-vol. limited signed edn. of *The Dynasts* pub. later in 1927.   *Weltzien*: see letter of 18 Apr 27.   *send him a copy*: Macmillan (25 Mar 27, Macmillan letterbooks, BL) promised to do so.   *Fernspr. Wilhelm 2426*: TH misread Weltzien's telephone number as part of his address; Macmillan (or some other member of the firm) has struck these words through and made other adjustments to the address—evidently prior to sending off the copy of the one-vol. *Dynasts*.

To WALTER J. BERKOWITZ

[Ans.]   [Late March 1927?]

It is with much regret that owing to the great inconvenience caused by strangers sending books & other articles in large numbers for signature & return, it has been found necessary to discontinue the giving of autographs.

Mr Hardy has never written a book called "Utopia", which you ascribe to him.

Mr W. J. Berkowitz.

Text MS. (pencil draft) DCM.   *Date* Replies to letter (from United States) of 7 Mar 27.
Berkowitz: Walter J. Berkowitz (1892–1966), of the Berkowitz Envelope Co., Kansas City, Missouri, wrote 7 Mar 27 (DCM), to ask if TH would sign copies of two of his books, '"Utopia", and "Tess of the D'Urbervilles"'.   *[Ans.]*: TH's square brackets.

To EDNA ST. VINCENT MILLAY

MAX GATE, | DORCHESTER, | DORSET. | 4 April: 1927

Dear Miss Millay:

I found myself one morning the possessor of your beautiful gift of "The King's Henchman", & if I had been a young man instead of an old one I should have read it straight off & written to you forthwith. But age makes us laggards, & what I would have done I do somewhat later, but no less heartily.

An opinion, from a reading, on a play meant for acting, is not worth much, & I do not attempt to write one: indeed I have not formed one. I have simply let you carry me back to those old times outshadowed, & enjoyed the experience.

I think I was among the early readers on this side of the Atlantic to be struck by your lyrics: & I am not sure that I do not like you better in that form than in the dramatic. But if you like exercising your hand—I mean fair hand—on drama I suppose you must. Believe me

Sincerely yours
Thomas Hardy.

Text   MS. (with envelope) Norma Millay.
Millay: Edna St. Vincent Millay (1892–1950), American poet and writer.   *Henchman"*: Millay's *The King's Henchman: A Play in Three Acts* (New York, 1927). The copy Millay inscribed to TH ('with the admiration and love of many years') is at Colby; see *Colby Library Quarterly*, series 5 (1961), 284–5.   *old times outshadowed*: the play is set in southern England during the tenth century.   *struck by your lyrics*: TH had praised them when writing to Amy Lowell in 1923; see VI.186.

To ERICH WELTZIEN

18 April 1927

Dear Dr Weltzien:

I am sending a small portrait of myself as you request in your letter. Though not very good it is the best I can find, & I hope it will suit your purpose.

In respect of the question you put—whether the men of the middle & upper classes here are almost free from fear—I am not able to give a definite reply, but I am inclined to think that they feel it whenever occasion arises, much as other men do, but have acquired a habit of not expressing it outwardly. I doubt if Dr Morsbach's opinion that sport has brought about this development is well-founded, since young men of other nations have also a love for sport, though perhaps it is not so intense as the English. For my part I think too much attention is given to sport in this country, distracting the minds of our youth from more important matters.

Believe me

Yours sincerely

Text   MS. (pencil draft) DCM.
Weltzien: Erich Weltzien, of Berlin, currently completing a doctoral thesis, *Die Gebärden der Furcht in Thomas Hardys Wessexromanen* (Berlin, 1927).   *small portrait*: Weltzien (28 Mar

27, DCM) begged a likeness of TH for the place of honour in his study.   *free from fear*: Weltzien suggested in his letter—as in his thesis—that characters from the middle and upper classes in TH's novels (e.g., Clym, Angel) displayed a distinctively English self-control and freedom from fear.   *Dr Morsbach's opinion*: Weltzien asked if TH agreed with Dr. Lorenz Morsbach, former professor of English at the University of Göttingen, in thinking that it was sport that had brought about 'this wonderful development of the English character'.

To LISBETH DENIS

    . . . . [Early] May 1927

Dear Madam:

I have received your letter of the 30th April, & will answer your inquiries as well as I can.

Unfortunately I am not able to state which of my novels & stories are as yet untranslated into French, some having been done without my knowledge. It might be possible to ascertain this by applying to the Paris publishers, who would probably know the names of those that have been already rendered into your language.

In any event, no *exclusive* permission to translate any of my books has been given, so that if you should by chance translate one that has been already done & forgotten, there would be no great harm in it.

I do not think that either "The Woodlanders", or "The Return of the Native" has appeared in French. If not, I should not object to a judicious cutting out of passages here & there, if Madame Duclaux approved. "The Hand of Ethelberta" has not, I think, been translated.

As to "Wessex Tales", I do not remember that the volume has been done in its entirety, though it is probable that some of the tales have been translated separately in periodicals.

In respect of the poems, your proposal to bring out a small volume of them, with illustrations by M. Marcel Poncet, after letting them appear in the Revue Hebdomadaire, is, I think, excellent, & I wish it success.

Yours sincerely

[Signed] Th. H———y

Madame Maurice Denis | La Prieuré | Saint-Germain-en-Laye | France

---

Text   MS. (pencil draft) DCM.   *Date*   From internal evidence.
Denis: TH appears to be addressing Lisbeth, *née* Graterolle, second wife of the French artist Maurice Denis (1870–1943); she was a musician by training.   *your letter*: it appears not to have survived.   *appeared in French*: TH was wrong about *The Return of the Native*, of which a French translation had appeared in 1923, but right about *The Woodlanders*—as about *The Hand of Ethelberta* and *Wessex Tales*.   *Madame Duclaux*: Agnes Mary Frances Duclaux, *née* Robinson, woman of letters; see I.165, 232. Her second husband, Professor Émile Duclaux, director of the Pasteur Institute, died in 1902.   *small volume*: it seems not to have materialized; for a previous translation of TH's poems see VI.75, 77.   *Poncet*: Marcel Poncet, glassmaker and artist, pupil and son-in-law of Maurice Denis.   *Revue Hebdomadaire*: the *Revue* was planning a special issue devoted to TH and his work; when he died in January 1928, however, the material thus far assembled was absorbed into the 'Hommage à Thomas Hardy' pub. in the January–February 1928 double issue of *La Revue Nouvelle*.   *[Signed]*: TH's word and square brackets.

To SIR FREDERICK MACMILLAN

MAX GATE, | DORCHESTER, | DORSET. | 8th May 1927.

Dear Sir Frederick:

I am sending back the pages of "The Dynasts" with the marked words, which are of course errors, as your reader divines. Whether they occurred in the original MS. (which is now in the British Museum) I don't know, but I doubt it, though I find they are in the first edition.

Please send along anything the reader questions, as I am not doing much now.

The printing seems quite correct, except that the printers have left out some of the accents over proper names that appear in the other editions (such as Trafalgár, &c.) I should wish them to be retained.

If they have not yet printed the titlepage I think I should like to insert an additional short quotation to improve its appearance. Perhaps you can send me a proof of the page, that I may write in the quotation. If however they have done with it, the matter is not important.

Sincerely yours,
Thomas Hardy.

Text MS. (typewritten) BL.
errors: Macmillan (6 May 27, Macmillan letterbooks, BL) drew TH's attention to two apparent misprints (i.e., grammatical errors) in *The Dynasts*.   *accents over proper names*: Macmillan (9 May 27, Macmillan letterbooks, BL) assured TH that these would be properly printed in the forthcoming three-vol. edn.   *additional short quotation*: despite Macmillan's reluctance (in his 9 May letter) to disturb the existing design, the title-page as pub. did include the quotation 'Desine fata Deûm flecti sperare precando' ('Cease to hope that God's will can be deflected by prayer') from Book VI of the *Aeneid*.

To SOTHEBY & CO.

20 May. 1927

Dear Sirs:

Mr Hardy has read the copy of his letter to Mrs Smith which you have enclosed to me. He says that as it is a letter of a very intimate kind, written many years ago, & referring to his life as a bachelor, he would rather it should have been destroyed. But if the executors of the late Mr R. Bosworth Smith want to sell it, he does not wish to hinder their doing so, though he is a little surprised at their proposing to do it, considering its personal nature.

In any case Mr Hardy cannot permit the letter or any part of it to be printed in a sale catalogue or elsewhere.

With thanks to you for submitting the copy I am

Yours truly

Messrs Sotheby & Co. | 34 & 35 New Bond Street

Text MS. (pencil draft) DCM.
Sotheby & Co.: the auction house wrote to FEH, 19 May 27 (DCM), enclosing a copy of TH's letter to Geneviève Smith of 6 Jan 74 (see I.26) and asking if TH would object to its being sold at auction.   *Bosworth Smith*: Reginald Bosworth Smith, Harrow master and son of Geneviève Smith, died 1908; see I.26. The letters he himself received from TH appear to have been

destroyed.   *cannot permit . . . elsewhere*: when the letter was auctioned on 27 July 1927 the catalogue description included the warning 'THE COPYRIGHT OF THIS LETTER IS RESERVED'—as did the description of TH's letter to Mrs. Smith of 4 Jan 74 (see I.26), sold at the same time.

To HARLEY GRANVILLE BARKER

Max Gate, | Dorchester. | 23. May: 1927.

Dear H.G.B.

At last I am able to let you know how much I have liked "Waste", which I could have told you nearly a fortnight ago, as I had finished it then.

It is so much like a novel in the reading that I could not help wishing it had been one. It holds you to the end—just as a good novel does———

Eyes weak, so must leave off!

Ever sincerely
Th. Hardy.

Text   Typed transcript DCM; Barker's name and address, appearing at the top of the transcript in FEH's hand, have not been reproduced (see letter to Barker of 4 June 26).
"Waste": Barker had recently pub. a revised edn. of his *Waste: A Tragedy in Four Acts* (London, 1927).   *wishing it had been one*: Barker replied (26 May 27, DCM) that he himself sometimes wished he had not become involved with the theatre, yet he still hoped for the realization of the theatre of his dreams.

To HARRY LAWRENCE

29 May 1927

Dear Sir:

I am much obliged to you for the inquiries you have caused to be made by the Ashburton Police as to the man Alfred John Hardy who was stated by Mr James Mortimer to have represented himself as being Mr Hardy's nephew, & of having been cast off by Mr Hardy for a crime the said A. J. Hardy's father—Mr Hardy's brother—had committed; the whole story being a fabrication, Mr Hardy having no nephew or great-nephew of his name, never having cast off any relation, & no crime having ever occurred in his family—in short that the man was an absolute impostor, if Mr Mortimer speaks the truth.

Should the police have been put to any expense in this inquiry please inform Mr Hardy who is willing to defray it.

Yours very truly
[Signed] F. E. Hardy

Mr Supt Lawrence | Dorset Constabulary | Dorchester

Text   MS. (pencil draft) DCM.
Lawrence: Harry Tom Lawrence, superintendent of the Dorchester station of the Dorset Constabulary 1923–27.   *inquiries . . . Ashburton Police*: TH had received from James Mortimer of Ashburton, Devon, former grammar school headmaster, a letter (21 May 27, DCM) accusing him of being unforgiving towards his brother ('the perpetrator of a terrible crime') and his brother's family (as represented by the informant, 'a nephew of yours') and of having allowed his bitterness to enter his work and thus 'spread like poison into so many other lives'. Lawrence reported (28 May 27, DCM) that Mortimer had apparently exaggerated the significance of a 'casual statement', although it was possible that the informant, identified as Alfred John Hardy, of Ashburton, had indeed referred to a deathbed claim by his father, John Hardy, a Royal Marine

pensioner living in Dartmouth, to be TH's brother.   *of his name*: i.e., of the name Alfred John Hardy.   *[Signed] F. E. Hardy*: TH's words and square brackets.

To SIR HENRY NEWBOLT

MAX GATE, | DORCHESTER. [10 June 1927]

My dear Newbolt:

Many thanks for your letter, even though the personal subject is unimportant, & getting less so every year! My wife sends her kind regards. We shall be glad to see you whenever you come this way again.

Always yours
T.H.

Text   MS. (correspondence card) Univ. of Kentucky.   *Date*   Supplied by Newbolt on MS. *the personal subject*: TH's birthday, 2 June.

To JOHN KENYON

23 June 1927

Dear Sir:

I reply to your letter for Mr Hardy on account of his age & the pressure of his correspondence.

Though he does not know anything of the American sound of R he has long been interested in the sound of that letter in England, & has been sorry in the past to observe its gradual silencing in what are called centres of education, so that in the speech of well-bred people it is tabooed & hardly exists. The disadvantage of this disappearance is that words like "boa" and "bore", "adorning" and "a dawning", "caw" and "core" are indistinguishable.

On the other hand, here in Wessex the distinction is kept up by the peasantry & tradespeople, & the R words are recognized in a moment. How long this will last can not be foretold.

The name of "Smiler" for a horse used to be not infrequent here, & "Wey" for "Whoa" is still used by waggoners.

Yours very truly
. . . .
Secretary

John S. Kenyon Esq. | 118 Finchley Road | London. N.W. 3

Text   MS. (pencil draft) DCM.
Kenyon: John Samuel Kenyon (1874–1959), phonetician, professor of English at Hiram College, Ohio.   *your letter*: he wrote from London, 19 June 27 (DCM), to express his interest in the relations between British and American vernacular speech and specifically in the reference in *Tess* (Wessex edn., 13) to the Wessex pronunciation of 'r'.   *"Smiler"* . . . *"Wey"*: Kenyon compared his Ohio grandfather's naming his mare 'Old Smiler' and calling out 'Ho-wey-hey-there' when she began to run away with, e.g., '"Wey, Smiler!"' in *Under the Greenwood Tree* (Wessex edn., 112).

To SIR ROBERT PEARCE EDGCUMBE

MAX GATE, | DORCHESTER. | 24 June 1927

My dear Edgcumbe:

Yes: I have agreed to lay the foundation-stone of the new Grammar School if all's well. It is really but a formal job of a few minutes, as I understand: at any rate that's all I shall make of it.

I must have been living in London or elsewhere when the existing school was altered; & I was not aware till now that the question of a new site had arisen so long ago as that. Of course, I understand the burghers' sentimental feeling for the old site—which, indeed, I have shared; but the old order changeth.

I reciprocate your good wishes, & hope you keep well: you ought to at such a place as Newquay.

Sincerely yours
Thomas Hardy.

Text   MS. Texas.
Edgcumbe: Robert Pearce Edgcumbe, former Dorchester banker and politician; see I.180. He wrote from his home in Newquay, Cornwall, 21 June 27 (DCM).   *new Grammar School*: see letter of 24 Feb 27 to Symonds.   *new site . . . old site*: Edgcumbe recalled a debate in his father's time between those who wished to move the school to the outskirts of the town and those, successful at the time, who wanted it kept 'on the pavement'.   *I have shared*: see, e.g., VI.174–5.   *old order changeth*: an allusion to Tennyson's 'Morte d'Arthur'.

To SIR FREDERICK MACMILLAN

MAX GATE, DORCHESTER, DORSET. | 25 June 1927.

Dear Sir Frederick:

The enclosed has come to me from the Oxford University Press, and I am telling the manager that I have sent it on to you, who will doubtless reply to them on the point. I suppose that in the case of an extract of that kind it does not make much difference either way.

Yours sincerely,
Th: Hardy.

Text   MS. (typewritten) BL.
extract of that kind: the Press had sought permission to reprint a passage from *Far from the Madding Crowd* in a school reader; Macmillan (27 June 27, Macmillan letterbooks, BL) reported that he was granting permission without fee so long as acknowledgement was made.

To UPTON SINCLAIR

25 June 1927

Dear Sir:

I write for Mr Hardy on account of the pressure of his correspondence to say that your novel entitled "Oil!" has just arrived, & that he hopes to read it soon. He thanks you for the copy, but as he reads slowly nowadays on account of his age, he will not be able to get through it just yet.

He is glad to hear that notwithstanding your difficulties with its publication it has already been so successful as to have been translated into several European languages.

Yours very truly
. . . .
Secretary

Upton Sinclair Esq. | c.o. Messrs A. & C. Boni | 66 Fifth Avenue, New York

Text   MS. (pencil draft) DCM.
Sinclair: Upton Beall Sinclair (1878–1968), crusading American novelist.   *"Oil!"*: pub. in
1927—originally by the author himself in Pasadena, then by A. & C. Boni in New York—it attacks
corruption in the oil industry from a socialist standpoint; Sinclair wrote 1 June 27 (DCM) to say
that he was sending TH a copy of the book and hoped that he would join in protesting against its
having been withdrawn from sale in Boston.

To EDWARD CLODD

MAX GATE, | DORCHESTER. | 26 June: 1927

My dear Clodd:

My best thanks for your letter on my birthday. As you know, & probably feel
with me, birthdays have not that entrancing glamour nowadays that they used
to have in early life, & really there is no reason why they should.

As yours is, too, just about now, I wish you as many returns of it as you care
to have, & hope that this letter finds you again well—"as it leaves me at present,
thank God for it", (to use the phrase which formerly adorned so much rural
correspondence.)

I was sorry to hear about the bronchitis. I had a sort of feeling that you could
not be ill. However, as the doctor lets you go sailing again I trust you have got
rid of it. At the same time I would remind you that one is able to get more chilly
sailing than rowing.

My trouble is weak eyes, which prevents my writing any but short notes
now. What a pretty view of your house. Surely the artist chose it because you
live there?

Most sincerely yours
Thomas Hardy.

Text   MS. BL.
your letter: of 1 June 27 (DCM).   *just about now*: specifically, 1 July.   *could not be ill*: TH
presumably meant, 'I always thought you were invulnerable to illness'.   *pretty view*: Clodd
was using a sketch of the sea-front at Aldeburgh, Suffolk, as a heading for his stationery.

To SIR GEORGE DOUGLAS

Max Gate, | Dorchester. | 9 July 1927.

My dear Douglas:

I don't think I thanked you and your sister for your kind telegram on my
birthday? If I didn't I do so now.

However, why I write at this moment is owing to a casual incident.
Yesterday at a garden party I talked to one of the pipers of the Scots Guards
(who were hired to play there, my friends being Scotch). This set me thinking
of Annie Laurie, and you: and to ask you if you could not write an article for,
say, The Fortnightly Review, entitled "The truth about Annie Laurie". I have
been looking into Grant's "Scottish Cavalier", and I am reminded that
"Douglas of Finland" (whatever Finland means) was her lover, &c. &c., the
whole story being very vague. It is possible that this Douglas was an ancestor of
yours: if so, all the more reason why you should write the article.

Kind regards to your sister, and from my wife to yourself.

Sincerely yours,
Thomas Hardy.

Text Typed transcript DCM.
Douglas: Sir George Brisbane Douglas, Bt., Scottish landowner and author; see I.166.   *your sister*: Mary Helena Henrietta Douglas; see III.82.   *garden party . . . Scotch*): one of the Scottish friends was probably Charlotte Helene Patterson of Parkstone, a J.P. and borough councillor, active in local charities.   *Annie Laurie, and you*: TH and Douglas had presumably discussed the song and its origins on previous occasions.   *"Scottish Cavalier"*: TH had been familiar since childhood with *The Scottish Cavalier: An Historical Romance* (London, 1850) by the Scottish novelist James Grant (1822–87; *D.N.B.*); its somewhat sketchy account of the Annie Laurie story identifies Richard Douglas, laird of Finland, as having composed the famous ballad after losing Annie to his rival Fergusson of Craigdarroch. See first letter of 18 Oct 27 to Maxwell.   *Finland*: the standard spelling appears to have been 'Fingland'; see first letter of 18 Oct 27 to Maxwell.

To SIR FREDERICK MACMILLAN

MAX GATE, DORCHESTER, DORSET. | 9 July 1927.

Dear Sir Frederick:
   I am sending back the pages of The Dynasts, with the queries answered, and am glad to hear that you are getting on with the printing.
   I find I have no copy of the second edition of The Queen of Cornwall, as revised, and shall be obliged if you will let me have one at any time.
   Believe me,

Sincerely yours,
Th: H.

Text   MS. (typewritten) BL.
queries answered: Macmillan (7 July 27, Macmillan letterbooks, BL) forwarded proof pages marked to show six queries relating to the forthcoming three-vol. edn. of *The Dynasts*.

To SIR FREDERICK MACMILLAN

MAX GATE, | DORCHESTER. | 14 July 1927

Second edn of Queen of Cornwall received. Many thanks.

T.H.

Text   MS. (postcard) BL.
Cornwall received: see letter of 9 July 27.

To C. BORLASE CHILDS

[Mid-July 1927]

Dear Mr Childs:
   I am interested to hear of your new start, & hope it will be successful. I know practically nothing about literary agencies, as they were not much employed in my busy years, arrangements between publishers & authors being mostly entered into in a hap-hazard manner by letters or conversations between the principals themselves.
   The only agency business in my own affairs was concerning a small theatrical matter some time ago, & I do not suppose such a thing will happen again; but if I should come across anyone who wants an agent I will not forget to mention you.

I am sorry to learn that your father is getting feeble. I have not heard from him lately. Old people do not correspond much.

Yours sincerely

Text MS. (pencil draft) DCM. *Date* Replies to letter of 14 July 27.
Childs: Christopher Borlase Macrae Childs (see VI.317), a distant relative of TH's; he wrote 14 July 27 (DCM) to say that he had left publishing to become a director of the Grosvenor Literary Agency. *small theatrical matter*: the *Tess* play, for which he had employed the agent R. Golding Bright. *your father*: Christopher Childs (see VI.317); he died in 1928.

To W. M. MEREDITH

MAX GATE, | DORCHESTER. | 16 July 1927

Dear Mr Meredith:
Many thanks for your note. I am glad to hear that you enjoyed your trip through the country of my imaginary personages, & hope you will come again.

As soon as I get through a few more summer engagements I will try to say something about your father, though what I say will, I fear, not be of any great value.

Sincerely yours
Thomas Hardy.

Text MS. (correspondence card) Adams.
Meredith: William Maxse Meredith (1865–1937), publisher, son of George Meredith, the novelist and poet (see IV.23). *your note*: of 14 July 27 (DCM); it referred to his recent visit to Dorset and to Max Gate itself. *about your father*: TH had agreed to write what became 'G.M.: A Reminiscence', pub. in the *Nineteenth Century and After*, February 1928, the centenary of Meredith's birth; see Purdy, 250–1.

To SYDNEY COCKERELL

[23 July 1927]

My dear Cockerell:
It is very nice of you to like the speech: but it was only intended for local consumption, & in fulfilment of a rash promise made months ago. Best wishes.

Always yrs
T.H.

Text MS. (correspondence card) Adams. *Date* Supplied by Cockerell on MS.
Cockerell: Sydney Carlyle Cockerell (see IV.178), director of the Fitzwilliam Museum, Cambridge; he corresponded regularly with FEH during TH's last years and made numerous visits to Max Gate. *the speech*: on the occasion of TH's laying the commemoration stone of the new Dorchester Grammar School, 21 July 1927; it had been pub. in *The Times*, 22 July 1927, and FEH may already have sent Cockerell the telegram of 23 July 27 (Adams) which asked him to undertake a private printing of the speech at the University Press, Cambridge (see Purdy, 248–9). In a letter to Cockerell of 24 July 27 (Adams) she explained that she had acted urgently upon receiving two unsolicited applications for permission to reprint the speech in pamphlet form.

To GUSTAV HOLST

MAX GATE, | DORCHESTER. | 6 Aug. 1927

Dear Mr Holst:

We shall be delighted to see you on Tuesday next, & my wife says will you come to lunch at one o'clock.

I will not go into the news you give me of the musical creation you have contrived on Egdon Heath. I am sure it will be very striking. I accept the dedication with pleasure.

Sincerely yours
Thomas Hardy.

Text   MS. Imogen Holst.
Holst: Gustav Theodore Holst (1874–1934), composer; *D.N.B.* He wrote 4 Aug 27 (DCM) to ask if he might dedicate to TH his new orchestral work, *Egdon Heath*, 'the result of reading the first chapter of "The Return of the Native" over and over again and also of walking over the country you describe so wonderfully'; he added that he would be walking through Dorset during the next few days and hoped to reach Dorchester by Monday night, 8 August. Holst's signature, dated 9 Aug 1927, appears in the Max Gate visitors' book (BL).

To J. C. SQUIRE

MAX GATE, | DORCHESTER. | 6 Aug. 1927

Dear Mr Squire:

I have not been to Stonehenge for nearly 20 years, & so have not seen what has happened there since, but I wrote an appeal of some kind for it before then. Having said so much about it one way & another I will hold my tongue now. The letter in the Times of yesterday is quite enough I think.

We are glad to hear you are coming this way. When you do so let us know.

Sincerely yours
Th: Hardy.

Text   MS. Colby.
Stonehenge: Squire (3 Aug 27, DCM) hoped that TH would write a letter of his own to *The Times* in support of an appeal in the 5 Aug 1927 issue for funds to purchase land close to Stonehenge and so prevent the encroachment of modern buildings.   *appeal of some kind*: the interview —substantially TH's own composition—pub. in the *Daily Chronicle*, 24 Aug 1899, under the heading 'Shall Stonehenge Go?'; see *Thomas Hardy's Personal Writings* (see letter of 8 Aug 26), 196–201.

To SIR FREDERICK MACMILLAN

MAX GATE, DORCHESTER, DORSET. | 15 August 1927.

Dear Sir Frederick:

(or, if absent, Messrs Macmillan.)

I am enclosing to you an application from a Mr Elsworth, which reached me a little time ago. It is of no great importance, but I have no objection to his including the poem "Waiting Both" that he mentions. I send on the letter that you may reply to him in any way you think desirable.

Yours very sincerely,
T.H.

Text   MS. (typewritten) BL.
if absent: Sir Frederick was on holiday and his cousin, George A. Macmillan (see II.108), replied
(17 Aug 27, Macmillan letterbooks, BL).   *Elsworth*: correctly Ellsworth; the American author
William Webster Ellsworth (1855–1936), editor of *Readings from the New Poets* (New York,
1928).   *think desirable*: Macmillan agreed that permission should be granted.

To A. W. FREUND

[Late August 1927]

Dear Sir:

Mr Hardy desires me to say in reply to your letter of the 15th August that he gives you permission to translate into German & publish the two tales "The Waiting Supper" & "A mere Interlude" if you undertake to pay a fee of two pounds (£2) for the right on the day of publication.

. . . .

Secretary to T. Hardy

Herrn A. W. Freund | Widerhofergasse 4/3 | Vienna IX | Austria

Text   MS. (pencil draft) Adams.   *Date*   Replies to letter of 15 Aug 27.
Freund: Adolf Walter Freund, translator, wrote from Vienna 15 Aug 27 (Adams) to seek
permission to translate the two TH stories for the Leipzig publisher Insel-Verlag.   *day of
publication*: in 1928 Insel-Verlag pub. 'The Waiting Supper' by itself in a handsomely produced
vol., *Der angekündigte Gast*, with illustrations by the Austrian artist Alfred Kubin (1877–1959).

To THE REVD. N. C. RAAD

9 Sept. 1927

Dear Sir:

I write for Mr Hardy in answer to your letter, on account of the pressure of his correspondence. He is sorry to say that he has been compelled of late years to decline writing introductory words to books by young authors, both on account of his age, & the great number of requests of the kind that he receives.

He regrets this the less because he is of opinion that such patronage does a poet no good, since it leads the public to think he has not merit enough to be read on his own account.

The sonnets seem promising, particularly No 39. The proofs are returned herewith.

Yours truly

. . . .

Secretary

N. C. Raad Esq. | Grosvenor House | Shaftesbury

Text   MS. (pencil draft) DCM.
Raad: the Revd. Nicholas Charles Raad (1888–1962), minor poet, proprietor of the Girls' High
School, Grosvenor House, Shaftesbury, Dorset.   *your letter*: of 31 Aug 27 (DCM); Raad
explained that he was sending proofs of his forthcoming vol. of poems, all of them 'written and
conceived' in Shaftesbury (the 'Shaston' of *Jude the Obscure*), in the hope that TH would 'write a
few lines that would serve as an introduction'.   *No 39*: the poem numbered 39 in Raad's *Life
and Love: Sonnets* (London, 1927) begins, 'All has been felt before and said and done!'

To SIR FREDERICK MACMILLAN

MAX GATE, | DORCHESTER, | DORSET. | 18th. September 1927.

Dear Sir Frederick:

At last I am sending the enlarged copy of my selected poems for the new edition in the Golden Treasury series, which you will remember to have decided some time ago to bring out. As you have now the copy you will be able to print it whenever you may choose. I am not at all anxious about it, but felt it best to make sure you had the corrections in case anything should happen.

I don't know if I have inserted too many extra ones. In the G. T. Wordsworth you have included about 170, and in the Byron 125 (some of the latter rather long). My own I make 159 altogether.

As I have used up my only old copy in arranging for the new edition I should be glad if you will send me another for reference.

Sincerely yours,
Th: Hardy.

Text   MS. (typewritten) BL.

Treasury series: i.e., the revision of TH's *Selected Poems* of 1916; see letter to Macmillan of 10 Nov 27.   *whenever you may choose*: Macmillan's letter of 26 Sept 27 (DCM) referred to the copy as being already in the printer's hands.   *send me another*: a note on the MS. records that a copy was sent.

To LOUIS UNTERMEYER

MAX GATE, | DORCHESTER, | DORSET. | 21st. September 1927.

Dear Mr Untermeyer:

I remember your edition of "Modern British Poetry" published a few years ago, and thought the selection a good one.

I have no objection to your including in the new edition "Snow in the Suburbs", and "When Dead", from my last volume entitled "Human Shows etc." If you wish to add "Yuletide in a Younger World" you will have to wait, as I have promised the publishers not to reprint that for some time. It is not a poem I value, and I should prefer, if I were making the selection, "The Carrier", or "Waiting Both", or "Song to an Old Burden"—in the same volume—either of which you have permission to include. As the whole additional selection will only be the three in number it is not necessary to ask the publishers.

Yours very truly,
T. Hardy.

Louis Untermeyer Esq. | 10 Culford Mansions, | Culford Gardens. London. S.W. 3.

Text   MS. (typewritten) Indiana Univ.

Untermeyer: Louis Untermeyer, American author and editor; see VI.158.   *I remember*: TH was responding to Untermeyer's letter of 19 Sept 27 (DCM) requesting additional TH poems for a revised and expanded third edn. of his *Modern British Poetry*, first pub. 1920.   *"Snow . . . Dead"*: specifically requested by Untermeyer, although only the first was in fact included.   *Younger World"*: this poem, also mentioned by Untermeyer, had appeared four weeks earlier in booklet form as the first of the Ariel Poems (see Purdy, 249–50); it was not included.   *permission to include*: of these three poems, none of which he had himself mentioned, Untermeyer selected 'Waiting Both'.   *the three*: only two poems were in fact added.

To SIR FREDERICK MACMILLAN

MAX GATE, | DORCHESTER, | DORSET. | 27 September 1927.
Dear Sir Frederick:

I think I had better read through the proofs of the Selected Poems, new edition, in case of any oversight, and I will therefore be ready for them at any time.

In respect to your suggestion of a volume of my short stories at 7/6, I quite agree to such a volume on the terms you mention, since it seems likely to do well, and I am willing for you to put it in hand whenever convenient. The order in which you have written them down is as good as any I think. The text of the Wessex Edition is the most correct to print from, and I hope the printers will be able to use that. If any expression in either of the Prefaces or Introductory notes should not apply to the intended edition I will put it right on receiving a proof of the page on which it occurs.

Another matter. I enclose herewith a letter that has just been sent me by Mr John Drinkwater, which explains itself. I don't myself see that his proposed inclusion in his book of the six short poems of mine that he names will do any harm though I think that Messrs Houghton & Mifflin ought to pay something, which indeed they appear quite ready to do. I remember your telling me that John O'London is paying £100 for the 25 poems they are printing, and it has occurred to me that the same ratio might not be too high for Messrs Houghton, —so that the amount would be £24 for the six poems, if they want to sell the book in England as well as America. However I don't much mind what it is, and will ask you to settle the matter. I will let Mr Drinkwater have a line telling him that he will hear from you on the point. Our best regards, & believe me,

Yours Sincerely
Th: Hardy.

Text   MS. (typewritten) BL.

new edition: see letter of 18 Sept 27; Macmillan (26 Sept 27, DCM) had suggested that TH might not wish to be troubled with the proofs.   *the terms you mention*: Macmillan had proposed a one-vol. edn. of TH's short stories and anticipated that TH's royalties would amount to £600.   *The order*: the same non-chronological sequence—*Wessex Tales*, *Life's Little Ironies*, *A Group of Noble Dames*, *A Changed Man*—was followed in *The Short Stories of Thomas Hardy* as pub. in March 1928.   *in his book*: Drinkwater was the co-editor, with Henry Seidel Canby and William Rose Benét, of the Houghton Mifflin anthology, *Twentieth-Century Poetry* (Boston, 1929); Macmillan wrote back (28 Sept 27, Macmillan letterbooks, BL) to propose a fee of £5 for each of the six poems.   *the point . . . Sincerely*: because there was insufficient space for another typed line TH wrote these words in his own hand.

To SIR EDMUND GOSSE

MAX GATE, | DORCHESTER. | 29 Sept. 1927 | (Michaelmas Day)

My dear Gosse:

I have been giving anxious attention to you all through your alarming illness, though I have not said a word, having got every day information (almost) through the family. But you will know all this. We are delighted now to find that you are not only round the corner but speeding on as usual. But surely it was not typhoid, was it? Well, let that drop. I find I am beginning at the wrong end of things. I am writing today that you may get some kind of answer, even if F. does not write herself. She is in the middle of a bad cold, which may be real influenza: I don't know. And I am sniffy & sneezy. So I fear there is no chance of either of us being able to get to B. before you leave: it would have been very pleasant if we could have gone.

I wish I had learnt to use a typewriter when it was practicable years ago. Since I did not I am compelled to send the most meagre letters nowadays, or none at all, on account of weak eyes, &c. But I am fairly well at most times, though no younger, as they say here.

I repeat my relief at finding you have recovered, & end my Scrawl.

Always yours sincerely
Thomas Hardy.

We shall look out for you next Sunday in the "S.T."   T.H.

Text   MS. (with envelope) Adams.
alarming illness: Gosse had been suffering from typhoid.   *through the family*: FEH had been corresponding with—and perhaps telephoning—Gosse's wife; her letter to Lady Gosse of 6 Aug 27 (Leeds) responds on her own and TH's behalf to the first news of Gosse's illness.   *to B.*: to Bournemouth, where Gosse was recuperating.   *the "S.T."*: the *Sunday Times*, for which Gosse was the chief reviewer; see VI.197.

To LADY KEEBLE

MAX GATE, | DORCHESTER. | 3 Oct. 1927

My dear Lady Keeble:

We are shocked to hear of your accident, & send our deepest sympathy. Why *did* you go tennising in such a wild way! I am really angry with you—or should be if I did not know what pain you have been suffering—poor thing!

I am interested in your choice of poems, but send this off immediately without going into that matter, on which I will write again. With every hope for your recovery I am

Yours very sincerely
Thomas Hardy.

Text   MS. Adams.
Keeble: Lillah McCarthy (see IV.100), the actress; in 1920, after her divorce from Harley Granville Barker, she married Sir Frederick William Keeble, civil servant and scientist (*D.N.B.*). Her visit to Max Gate with her husband on 19 Sept 1927 was the last event recorded by TH in his "Memoranda II" notebook; see *Personal Notebooks* (see letter of 5 Mar 26), 97.   *your accident*: Lady Keeble wrote 1 Oct 27 (DCM) to say that she had broken her ankle while playing tennis.   *choice of poems*: Lady Keeble listed the page numbers of the approximately forty TH poems she was memorizing for public performance.

To CARROL ROMER

4 October 1927

Dear Sir:

As you say, Mr W. M. Meredith has suggested to me that I should write something about his father, to be printed on the centenary-month of his birth, & that I thought I could do a few words on my early knowledge of him—a page or two at the outside—which you can have almost whenever you want it.

I understood it was to be a contribution to a sort of Symposium that he or you were going to get together. Unfortunately I am not physically able to write anything that can be dignified by the title of an article! But, as I say, I will get it ready when wanted, though it will be a poor thing, I fear, much as I could have wished, for the late Mr Meredith's sake, that I could have done something worthy of his memory.

Yours truly

Carrol Romer Esq. | "19th Century & After"

Text   MS. (pencil draft) DCM.
Romer: Carrol Romer (1883–1951), barrister, editor of *The Nineteenth Century and After* 1925–30, subsequently King's Coroner and Attorney.   *As you say*: Romer wrote 3 Oct 27 (DCM) to welcome the prospect of 'an article' on George Meredith by TH for publication in his February 1928 issue; see letter of 16 July 27.

To WILLIAM MAXWELL

MAX GATE, | DORCHESTER, | DORSET. | 6 Oct. 1927
Dear Mr Maxwell:

How clever of you to spot the author of the Mary Q. of Scots poem so quickly. I had a feeling that the phraseology was later than that of Mickle: & yet I fancied there was a tone of "Cumnor Hall" about it.

I must thank you much for taking the trouble to print the copies. I had borrowed Mickle from the Library of Queen's, Oxford, & had just written to my friend there to say we had drawn a blank, & that I could not divine who wrote the piece, when your letter came. I am going to send him one of the copies, & he will probably be amused at the solution. However, if you should take up Mickle's "Mary Q. of Scots", you will find that Henry Glassford Bell's, though not by a professional poet, can hold its own against it—Mickle's being really a slavish imitation of Gray.

I hope you had a pleasant journey home. We did not realize till too late that Mrs Maxwell was within hail; but perhaps shall have better luck next time.

Sincerely yours
Thomas Hardy.

Text   MS. (with envelope) Purdy.
Maxwell: William Maxwell (1873–1957), master printer, managing director of the Edinburgh firm of R. & R. Clark, printers of virtually all of TH's books from 1902 onwards.   *Mary Q. of Scots poem*: 'Mary Queen of Scots', first pub. in *Summer and Winter Hours* (London, 1831) by the Scottish judge and poet Henry Glassford Bell (1803–74; *D.N.B.*). TH had evidently mentioned the poem, learned in childhood, and his ignorance of its author during a recent visit of Maxwell's to

Max Gate, and Maxwell (3 Oct 27, DCM) sent copies of a specially printed pamphlet containing the poem and a biographical note on Bell; see *The Thomas Hardy Year Book 1971*, 99.   *Mickle ... Hall"*: TH had been interested as a child in the work of the eighteenth-century Scottish poet William Julius Mickle (see VI.266), whose 'Cumnor Hall' was praised by Scott in his introduction to *Kenilworth.*   *my friend there*: Godfrey Elton (1892–1973), the historian; see *LY*, 232–4. Elton's letter of 13 Sept 27 (DCM) speaks of sending from Queen's College (of which TH was an honorary fellow) two books which contained Mickle's poem on Mary Queen of Scots.   *Gray*: Thomas Gray (1716–71), poet; *D.N.B.*

To W. M. MEREDITH

12 October: 1927

Dear Mr Meredith:

I have posted to the Editor of the Nineteenth Century the few pages I have been able to write about your father. But if there is anything in them that you would prefer to have omitted, please strike it out, or let me know & I will delete it in proof. I have put a provisional title, which can be altered as the Editor or you suggest. I am sorry the article is no better, but though I am well I am not very vigorous at writing nowadays.

I need hardly say that the tribute is sent gratuitously to the magazine.

Yours sincerely

Text MS. (pencil draft) DCM.
the Editor: Carrol Romer; see letter of 4 Oct 27.   *delete it in proof*: Meredith replied (14 Oct 27, DCM) that he had read TH's remarks 'with very deep appreciation' and wished nothing to be omitted.   *provisional title*: 'G.M.: A Reminiscence', the title of the MS. (DCM), was also used in *The Nineteenth Century and After*, February 1928.

To NEWMAN FLOWER

[Mid-October 1927]

Dear Mr Newman Flower

. . . .
Last week we had a young Chinaman—Mr Yu Shou Kuo—call upon us, with an introduction from the Secretary of the P.E.N. club. He told us of an extraordinary tragedy that had occurred in his family in China when he was a boy of 13. The tragedy was quite equal to a Greek tragedy in its events. He knows several languages—English in particular—& is I believe a student at the Sorbonne at present—& his idea seemed to be that he should write out the events as a sort of autobiography, in as good English as he could—& that my husband should correct it for the English press. T.H. could not of course do that, but we were so much struck with the young man that we thought we might give him the name of a publisher—yourself—who, if there were anything in his narrative when written could easily get it corrected for publication. If he should call for your advice you will quite understand that this was all we suggested, & will not mind giving him a few minutes of your valuable time. The tragedy is too terrible for me to write down, but he will probably tell it to you—though he is very shy of telling the actual facts.

Text   MS. (pencil draft) Texas.   *Date*   From internal evidence.
Last week: Kuo's visit to Max Gate occurred on 8 Oct 1927 (Max Gate visitors' book, BL); it is, however, clear from Flower's[?] note on the MS. that no letter was typed or sent but that FEH gave the draft itself to Flower after TH's death.   *Kuo*: Kuo Yu Shou, Chinese scholar and writer, currently studying in Paris; he worked for UNESCO in Paris shortly after the Second World War. Two letters written prior to his visit are in DCM.   *Secretary . . . club*: Herman Ould wrote 7 Oct 27 (DCM), identifying himself as the general secretary of the P.E.N. Club and explaining that Kuo wished to translate some of TH's works into Chinese.   *too terrible . . . down*: FEH did, however, record (a little sceptically) in the diary she was then keeping the story Kuo told of murdering his sister's illegitimate baby in the name of family honour and then forcing the sister to commit suicide; see *Personal Notebooks* (see letter of 5 Mar 26), 292–3.

To WILLIAM MAXWELL

MAX GATE, | DORCHESTER, | DORSET. | 18 Oct. 1927

Dear Mr Maxwell:

I don't think I have acknowledged the receipt of your "Annie Laurie" versions & researches—for which I thank you now. The very interesting details that you have been able to muster show that my idea of somebody writing an article called "The truth about Annie Laurie" was not such a bad one after all. It would certainly attract the public. How one would like to know more of the unhappy Douglas of Fingland, & his love-making, & his end: also of Annie's life with her husband Ferguson of Craigdarroch. Possibly it was a prosy commonplace life, which if known would spoil our romantic tradition of her: still, I shd like to know it. Alicia, Lady John Scott, must have been a gifted woman, not only in music, but as a poetess, for the 3rd verse of the song is a beautiful one.

I daresay the impression we have of Annie as being something of a coquette—if not a heartless flirt—has some basis of truth. A faithful woman would not have become famous: that's how things are! My vision of her & her lover Fingland was derived mainly from James Grant's romance, "The Scottish Cavalier" which I read in my boyhood. You are probably familiar with it.

I am greatly obliged to you for letting me have these particulars, which may lead to more. But possibly the present day Lauries (if there are any) would object to having them raked up—people are so queer sometimes, though not always.

Sincerely yours
Thomas Hardy.

Text   MS. (with envelope) Purdy.
"Annie Laurie" versions: Maxwell had also followed up TH's curiosity as to the origins of the song 'Annie Laurie' and sent him (7 Oct 27, DCM) a version of the poem as given in Allan Ramsay's *Scots Songs* (Edinburgh, 1718) and a more modern version modified by Lady John Scott (see below).   *Douglas . . . Craigdarroch*: these details derive from a note copied by Maxwell from Ramsay's *Scots Songs*.   *Lady John Scott*: Alicia, Lady John Scott, *née* Spottiswood (1810–1900), Scottish poet; she changed the words of the two existing verses of the song and added a third verse of her own.   *Scottish Cavalier*": for this and other references in the present letter see the letter of 9 July 27 to Douglas.

To WILLIAM MAXWELL

MAX GATE, | DORCHESTER. | 18 Oct. 1927.

Your letter of the 17th has arrived just after I had posted mine to you. Many thanks for the correction, which I will note.

T.H.

Text   MS. (postcard) Adams.
the correction: Maxwell (17 Oct 27, DCM) said that so far as he could now discover 'Annie Laurie' must be reckoned a traditional song and 'ascribed to that very gifted gentleman, "Anon."'

To ST. JOHN ERVINE

MAX GATE, | DORCHESTER. | 21 Oct. 1927

Dear Mr Ervine:

As I see that "The Wayward Man" (good title) will take some reading I write at once to acknowledge the arrival of your kind gift, which I have only as yet looked into, though far enough to see that there is sound stuff in it. I hope you & Mrs Ervine are well in your snug quarters up there.

Sincerely yours
Thomas Hardy.

Text   MS. Texas.
Wayward Man": Ervine's novel *The Wayward Man* (London, 1927).   *snug quarters up there*: Ervine lived in Whitehall Court, lying between Whitehall and the Victoria Embankment.

To SIR EDMUND GOSSE

MAX GATE, | DORCHESTER. | 10 Nov. 1927

My dear Gosse:

It is really very kind & prompt of you to enter into J.M.M.'s case so readily: though I confess I should have been terrified if I had supposed I should be the means of sending you personally into the perils of the Lord Mayor's Show! We have briefly signified to him that something may be done: I don't think he is in a position to be touchy, poor fellow; & still more, poor little thing his wife! Many many thanks.

Always sincerely
Th: H.

Text   MS. (with envelope) Eton College.
J.M.M.'s . . . Show!: John Middleton Murry, critic and author; see V.298. With Violet (*née* le Maistre, d. 1931), his second wife, who was acutely ill with tuberculosis, he was spending the winter in a cottage at Abbotsbury, SW of Dorchester, experiencing severe financial difficulties, and arousing the active sympathy of FEH. TH had asked if Murry could be assisted by the Royal Literary Fund, of which Gosse was a committee member, and Gosse wrote twice on 9 Nov 27 (both DCM) to report on his visit to the Fund's offices in the City of London that afternoon—despite the crowds attending the annual Lord Mayor's Show. His second letter explained that the application procedure took five weeks and that he had in the meantime invoked TH's name in making a confidential application to the prime minister (Stanley Baldwin) for a grant to Murry from the Privy Purse; see letter to Gosse of 20 Nov 27.   *to be touchy*: Gosse observed in his first letter that the '*pride* of applicants' often complicated the work of the Fund.

To SIR FREDERICK MACMILLAN

MAX GATE, | DORCHESTER, | DORSET. | 10 November 1927.

Dear Sir Frederick:

I am much obliged for the proof of the new edition of Selected Poems, and will read them through. I think the objection that they were not representative enough is now met.

I find that some stupid people confuse "Selected" with "Collected"—the name given to the 1 vol. edition of the whole lot. Could this selection be called "Selections from the Poems of T.H." "Select Poems of T.H." or "Chosen Poems of T.H." to make more difference? I leave you to settle the point if you kindly will. Perhaps "Chosen" is most distinct.

Many thanks for sending on the letter from the Japanese enthusiast.

Very sincerely yours,
Thomas Hardy.

Text   MS. (typewritten) BL.
Selected Poems: see letters of 18 and 27 Sept 27.   *read them through*: Macmillan acknowledged return of the proofs, with a 'few further corrections', 17 Nov 27 (DCM).   *Perhaps . . . distinct.*: added in TH's hand; Macmillan replied (11 Nov 27, DCM) that the title *Chosen Poems of Thomas Hardy* would certainly be adopted for the revised vol.—not pub. until August 1929.   *Japanese enthusiast*: Macmillan (31 Oct 27, DCM) forwarded a letter and accompanying poem, 'To Thomas Hardy' (both DCM), sent by Shigeo Yoshiwara of Kanagawa, Japan.

To LADY KEEBLE

MAX GATE, | DORCHESTER. | Dorset. | 13 Nov. 1927

Dear Lady Keeble:

I feel rather neglected by your not letting me know how you have been getting on about that accident: I hope well.

I cannot go thinking about that recital business till I know you are physically the same as ever.

Always yours
T.H.

Text   MS. Adams.
accident . . . recital business: see letter of 3 Oct 27; Lady Keeble replied (14 Nov 27, DCM) that while she felt well in herself the pain in her leg had prevented her from working—specifically, from memorizing more than four of TH's poems.

To FLORENCE BULLEN

. . . . [Mid-]Nov. 1927

Dear Madam:

In respect of your inquiry if Mr Hardy was influenced by Guy de Maupassant in writing his short stories, you appear to possess a very slight knowledge of literary chronology, or you would be aware that many of Mr Hardy's novels & stories preceded in date those of the French novelist, & that in any event Mr Hardy would not have been likely to imitate a writer ten years younger than himself, whose works were not much known in England till Mr Hardy had nearly finished his prose writings. (I should add that the dates attached to Mr Hardy's short stories do not represent the time they were written, many of them having appeared in magazines from ten to twenty years earlier).

Yours truly

. . . .

Secretary

Miss Bullen | 18 Allerton Road | Wallasey—Cheshire

Text   MS. (pencil draft) DCM.   *Date*   Replies to letter of 14 Nov 27.
Bullen: Florence T. Bullen wrote 14 Nov 27 (DCM) to ask if she would be correct, in the thesis she was writing (but seems not to have completed), to trace an influence from Guy de Maupassant upon TH's short stories.   *de Maupassant*: Henri René Albert Guy de Maupassant (1850–93); his best known short stories were written in the early 1880s.   *dates . . . stories*: TH evidently means the dates when the stories were first collected into volumes.

To YVONNE SALMON

[Mid-November 1927]

Dear Mlle Salmon:

I am returning to you the copy of Time's Laughingstocks which my husband has signed for the University.

The translation of Pitt's speech in "The Dynasts" he thinks very exact, & is much obliged to you for letting him see it. You may be interested in knowing that the speech is the one that Pitt actually made on that occasion.

The preface to the translation, which Mr Hardy said he would write, is nearly finished & will reach you in 2 or 3 days. If there should be any passage in it about Napoleon that you think will not be liked by French readers, please strike it out. The play of "Tess" will also arrive about the same time.

Text   MS. (pencil draft) DCM.   *Date*   Replies to letter of 14 Nov 27.
Salmon: Yvonne M. Salmon, university lecturer in French; see VI.305.   *for the University*: i.e., for the library of University College, Reading, where Mlle Salmon was teaching; she acknowledged the book's arrival 18 Nov 27 (DCM).   *translation . . . Dynasts"*: Mlle Salmon was translating two segments of *The Dynasts* for inclusion in the planned special TH issue of *La Revue Hebdomadaire* that was in fact realized by *La Revue Nouvelle*; see letter of early May 27. In her letter to FEH of 14 Nov 27 (DCM) she explained that she was sending the part of Pitt's speech (Part First, Act I, Scene 3) which TH had thought might be difficult to translate because of its use of technical terms from brewing.   *preface to the translation*: TH's short preface, translated by Mlle Salmon, appeared as the first item in the January–February 1928 special issue of *La Revue Nouvelle*; see Purdy, 324.

To CHARLES LACEY

MAX GATE, | DORCHESTER. | 16 Nov. 1927

Dear Mr Lacey:

Many thanks for forwarding Sir Stephen Collins's letter, which I will read & return, as I think you ought to keep it yourself.

Yours very truly

T. Hardy.

C. Lacey Esq. | Dorset Chronicle, | Dorchester.

Text   MS. (with envelope) J. Stevens Cox.
Collins's letter: Sir Stephen Collins (1847–1925), Dorset-born Liberal M.P. and temperance advocate; the letter (Cox) was one in which Collins, not long before his death, had told Lacey of his pleasure at having recently encountered TH and found him 'so hale and hearty'.

To LADY KEEBLE

MAX GATE, | DORCHESTER. | 18 Nov. 1927
My dear Lillah:
    I had no idea you had suffered so much, & am very sorry! Please suspend all thoughts of the readings till you get back from abroad, quite strong.

Ever sincerely
Th: H.

Text   MS. Adams.
the readings: see letter of 13 Nov 27.   *from abroad*: Lady Keeble (14 Nov 27, DCM) said that she and her husband were going to Beauvallon in the South of France for a month from mid-December; her dating of this episode in her *Myself and My Friends* (London, 1933), 270, is not precise.

To DOROTHY ALLHUSEN

MAX GATE, | DORCHESTER. | Sunday. [20 November 1927]
My dear Dorothy;
    The flowers have come—quite fresh. How thoughtful of you. I hope you are well, & am

Ever yrs
T.H.

Text   MS. (correspondence card, with envelope) Purdy.   *Date*   From postmark.

To SIR EDMUND GOSSE

MAX GATE, | DORCHESTER. | 20 Nov. 1927
My dear Gosse,
    I am so glad to get your good news anent J.M.M., & believe it will do all that can be done for him. I have not heard from him yet, but doubtless shall in a day or two.

Always yrs
T.H.

Text   MS. (with envelope) Leeds.
good news: Gosse wrote 17 Nov 27 (DCM) to report that the Prime Minister had sent Middleton Murry the sum of £250; see letter of 10 Nov 27.   *not heard from him yet*: FEH wrote to Gosse 28 Nov 27 (Leeds) to express her own and TH's astonishment that Gosse had not himself received any acknowledgement from Murry by that date; Gosse replied 30 Nov 27 (Adams) that he had received an embarrassed but 'very nice' note from Murry just that morning.

To J. T. GODWIN

[Late November 1927]
Dear Sir:
    In reply to your inquiry as to the Arms of the Hardys of Dorset they can be

found described in Hutchins's History of Dorset, Vol II. p. 385, & Vol IV, 433. Mr Thomas Hardy the author, though he is one of the Dorset Hardys, has never used the arms of the family.

Yours truly
F.E
for T.H.

Text   MS. (pencil draft) DCM.   *Date*   Replies to letter of 18 Nov 27.
Godwin: John Thomas Godwin (1879–1952); his china shop, part of a building originally designed and used as a theatre (see VI.248), was in High West Street, Dorchester.   *your inquiry*: Godwin (18 Nov 27, DCM) explained that he had received a request 'for a piece of Heraldic Porcelain with your Coat of Arms on it' but was anxious not to stock anything that was incorrect.   *Hutchins's . . . Dorset*: John Hutchins, *The History and Antiquities of the County of Dorset*, third edn. (Westminster, 1861–73); the first of TH's references is to the arms of the Elizabethan Thomas Hardy who endowed Dorchester Grammar School (see *EL*, 6), the second to the more fully described arms ('Sable, on a chevron between three escallops or, three wivern's heads erased of the field') of the Hardy family of Toller Whelme and Wolcomb-Matravers.

To GEORGES LASSELIN

23 November 1927

Dear M Lasselin:

I am glad to learn from your letter that there is soon to be an article in the "Revue Hebdomadaire" on my writings, by the two eminent French critics that you mention, & their contributors. Your help will be invaluable in the translations of the short specimens, not one of which has, I think, appeared in the French language before.

I cannot for the moment remember any photograph that would be of interest to readers of your forthcoming book. If I should recall anything of the kind I will forward it.

My wife sends her kindest regards to Mme. Lasselin, as I do also, & we hope you both keep in good health.

Sincerely yours

Text   MS. (pencil draft) DCM.
Lasselin: Georges Lasselin, French critic; he wrote 13 Nov 27 (DCM) to inform TH that the critics Charles Du Bos and Ramon Fernandez were gathering contributions for a special TH issue of *La Revue Hebdomadaire* early in 1928; for the eventual outcome of this scheme see letter of early May 27.   *forthcoming book*: *Le Couple humain dans l'œuvre de Thomas Hardy*; originally written by Lasselin as a thesis at the University of Lille, it was pub. in Paris in 1928 over the name of Pierre d'Exideuil. An English translation appeared in 1930.   *keep in good health*: Lasselin and his wife visited Max Gate 3 July 1927 (Max Gate visitors' book, BL), an occasion recalled by 'Pierre d'Exideuil' in his 'Foreword to the English Translation'.

To HARLEY GRANVILLE BARKER

Max Gate, | Dorchester. | Dorset. | 30 Nov. 1927.

Dear H.G.B.

We are slow readers here, and I only yesterday got to the end of the "Preface" which interested me most—that to Lear.

As you may have supposed from my antecedents, I have always held that terrible play to be unactable, even though William himself thought the reverse, in which I have been with Lamb and Bradley. But after reading your essay, I am bound to defer to some extent to your great authority in the matter, so that I am left in a tantalizing mid-space between the two views. I have not yet read the other prefaces, but we are going to tackle them soon.

I am sorry to hear that Helen is not well—I hope it is not much. At any rate she will not go killing herself hunting, as it seems to be the fashion for young women to do nowadays. Best love to her.

Always sincerely
Thomas Hardy.

Many thanks for the other books also. T.H.

Text　Typed transcript DCM; Barker's name and address in FEH's hand at head of letter not reproduced (see letter to Barker of 4 June 26).
that to Lear: TH's reference is to the final section of Barker's *Prefaces to Shakespeare* (London, 1927).　*from my antecedents*: TH presumably refers to his long-standing scepticism regarding the performance of Shakespeare's plays; see, e.g., III.313.　*with Lamb and Bradley*: these opinions of Charles Lamb's (from his essay 'On the Tragedies of Shakespeare') and A. C. Bradley's (from his *Shakespearean Tragedy*) are cited in the opening pages of Barker's own 'preface' to *King Lear*.　*the other prefaces*: to *Love's Labour's Lost* and *Julius Caesar*.　*fashion for young women*: the death following a hunting accident of Lady Victoria Bullock, aged 35, was reported in *The Times* of 28 Nov 1927.　*other books also*: they perhaps included *Four Plays by Serafin and Joaquin Álvarez Quintero*, in English versions by Helen and Harley Granville Barker (London, 1927), and Helen Granville Barker's *Wives and Celebrities* (London, 1927), a collection of short stories described in a prefatory note as concerned with 'the lot of women lucky enough—or it may be unlucky enough—to be married to celebrated men'.

To SIR FREDERICK MACMILLAN

MAX GATE, | DORCHESTER, | DORSET. | 30 Nov. 1927

My dear Macmillan:

I am delighted to receive the two copies of The Dynasts. There was great excitement here when they came, & they are all that I expected. Leslie Stephen used to say that all modern books & newspapers would have perished in 100 years, but I fancy these volumes will hold out. I notice that you have embodied all the latest corrections, & I hope the booksellers will do well with their stock.

I hope you are getting through these fogs without discomfort.

With kind regards

Yours sincerely
Thomas Hardy.

Text　MS. BL.
The Dynasts: the three-vol. limited signed edition.　*Stephen*: Leslie Stephen (see I.27), man of letters; TH is apparently recalling remarks made in conversation.　*do well with their stock*: Macmillan (28 Nov 27, Macmillan letterbooks, BL) reported that the whole edn. had been subscribed for by booksellers and was now technically out of print.　*these fogs*: heavy fog had covered southern England, including the London area, for the past several days.

To SIR FREDERICK MACMILLAN

MAX GATE, | DORCHESTER, | DORSET. | 3 December 1927.

Dear Sir Frederick:

The proposal, or rather suggestion, made by the Messrs Harper, which they appear to have let drop, was that they should issue an edition of the short story called "The Romantic Adventures of a Milkmaid" (which in our editions is bound up with "A Changed Man"). It was to be for America only, of course, and to be illustrated by the young lady you mention. They wanted me to sign a certain number of copies, which I should have been rather loth to do, the story, though readable enough, being but of a slight nature. However, if they want to bring out an illustrated edition I cannot prevent them, as the tale was published in 1883, before copyright with the United States, which naturally they know, and that they are quite free to do as they choose, or any other publisher over there. But I have heard nothing of the matter lately.

Believe me,

Sincerely yours,
Th: Hardy.

Text   MS. (typewritten) BL.

proposal . . . Harper: Macmillan (2 Dec 27, Macmillan letterbooks, BL) said that he had recently learned of TH's discussions with Harper & Brothers about an illustrated edn. of one of his short stories, adding that if there were to be such edns. his own firm would like to have the honour of publishing them.   *lady you mention*: Macmillan's informant, the artist Clare Leighton (b. 1899), was to have illustrated the proposed vol.; she later illustrated for Harper & Brothers a limited edn. of *The Return of the Native* (New York, 1929).   *published in 1883*: and frequently pirated in the United States; see Purdy, 47–9.   *free to do as they choose*: Macmillan, in what appears to have been his last letter to TH (5 Dec 27, Macmillan letterbooks, BL), agreed that this was so but hoped that TH would not agree to sign any copies of such edns.

To DORIS THORNE

5 Dec. 1927

Dear Mrs Thorne:

My husband has received your letter & enclosure, & I am obliged to reply for him, as at his age he finds letter-writing very irksome, & trying to his eyes. He says that as you assume, he is quite in sympathy with Mr Henry Arthur Jones's many movements & writings for the advancement of dramatic art, though at present attempts of that kind look rather hopeless. As to suggesting some practical recognition of what Mr Jones has done, Mr Hardy unfortunately must leave that to younger men, who ought to be dramatists & persons more connected with the stage than he is himself; they will be able to speak more authoritatively on the subject of Mr Jones's plays than one who was never much of a theatre-goer, & also on the subjects mentioned in the resumé you send a copy of.

We are sorry to hear that your father has been unwell with that very painful malady angina, & hope it will disappear entirely, which it does sometimes.

Yours very truly

Text   MS. (pencil draft) DCM.
Thorne: Jenny Doris Thorne, *née* Jones, daughter of Henry Arthur Jones, the playwright (see II.31), and author of *The Life and Letters of Henry Arthur Jones* (London, 1930). She wrote 2 Dec 27 (DCM) to enlist TH's support in seeking from the prime minister 'some public recognition' of her father's past achievements.   *resumé*: Mrs. Thorne enclosed a typed summary of her father's contributions to Anglo-American friendship and other public issues as well as to the theatre.   *disappear entirely*: Jones died, however, 7 Jan 1929.

To JOHN HIGNETT

[Ans.]   [Early December 1927]
Dear Sir:
    Your Poems are returned by Mr Hardy with thanks. He regrets that he is not aware of any method of getting a publisher, except that of sending the manuscript to one who publishes the same kind of matter, & asking his terms.

                                                                              Yours truly

                                                                              . . . .
                                                                              Secretary

Text   MS. (pencil draft) DCM.   *Date*   Replies to letter of 4 Dec 27.
Hignett: John Marcus Hignett wrote from London 4 Dec 27 (DCM), sending examples of his verse and seeking advice as to how to find a publisher for 'a volume of my poems, or a novel of 60,000 words, entitled, "The Mystery of Greycrag."' None of Hignett's work seems ever to have been pub. in book form.   *[Ans.]*: TH's square brackets.

To THE REVD. G. B. CRONSHAW

                                                                    10 December 1927
Dear Mr Cronshaw:
    The invitation to the Needle & Thread Dinner is very attractive, & I should much like to accept the honour of joining the Pro-Provost & Fellows on New Year's Day, as well as the very kind offer of accommodation in College. But I have to forgo all these pleasures nowadays for reasons which you will very well understand, & must make spiritual presence do for the real thing. With best thanks

                                                                              Yours very truly

The Bursar | The Queen's College, Oxford

Text   MS. (pencil draft) DCM.
Cronshaw: the Revd. George Bernard Cronshaw (see VI.172), fellow and bursar of Queen's College, Oxford; his duplicated letter of 6 Dec 27 (DCM) invited TH, as an honorary fellow, to attend on New Year's Day the traditional 'Needle and Thread Dinner', at which each guest is presented with a needle and thread—the colour of the latter varying with academic field—and wished a 'thrifty' (i.e., prosperous) future. See J. R. Macgrath, *The Queen's College* (2 vols., Oxford, 1921), II.240.

To SIR EDMUND GOSSE

MAX GATE, | DORCHESTER, | DORSET. | Xmas Day 1927

Dear Edmund Gosse:

I must thank you for your very kind letter as well as I can. I am in bed on my back, living on butter-broth & beef tea, the servants being much concerned at my not being able to eat any Christmas pudding, though I am rather relieved.

As to those verses in the *Times* you inquire about & gratify me by liking, I can only go by the dates attached in fixing their history: the poem having been begun in 1905 (possibly when I was in the Elgin Room, though I don't remember being there) & then abandoned, & not finished till last year.

I am sorry to hear of your cold on the chest—whatever you do, don't go out against an east wind. I think my aches are diminishing. J.M.M. called here last week, but I did not see him. F. says he is much more cheerful, & he & his young wife are both hoping she will get well again, but the doctors say it is next to impossible—

Best wishes to you & your house for the New Year—& believe m

Always your sincere
T.H.

Text MS. (pencil) BL.
very kind letter: of 24 Dec 27 (DCM). *in bed on my back*: TH's final illness began 11 Dec 1928, ending with his death on 10 Jan 1928; see Millgate, 570–2. *verses in the* Times: TH's 'Christmas in the Elgin Room', *The Times*, 24 Dec 1927; see *LY*, 264. *dates attached*: TH placed the dates 1905 and 1926 following the end of the poem. *the Elgin Room*: the room in the British Museum devoted to the display of the 'Elgin Marbles'. *J.M.M.*: John Middleton Murry; see letters to Gosse of 10 and 20 Nov 27. *next to impossible*: Violet Murry died in 1931. *believe m*: TH did not complete the intended 'me'.

Additional Letters

To CHATTO & WINDUS

1 Arundel Terrace, | Trinity Road, | Upper Tooting. S.W. |
March 22. 1878.

Dear Sirs,

I have removed from Sturminster Newton to the above address, which please use in all future correspondence.

Yours very faithfully
Thomas Hardy.

Messrs Chatto & Windus

Text MS. (all except signature in ELH's hand, Sturminster Newton letterhead struck through) State Library of Victoria.
Chatto & Windus: publishers of *Belgravia*, in which TH's *The Return of the Native* was currently being serialized.

To J. WINTER JONES

1, ARUNDEL TERRACE, | TRINITY ROAD, UPPER TOOTING. S.W. |
April 30. 1878

Dear Sir,

I beg leave to apply to you for a Reader's Ticket.

My object in wishing to make use of the library is to obtain such materials, historical & otherwise, as will be of service to me in preparing the books I publish from time to time.

I am

Yours very faithfully
Thomas Hardy.
(novelist)

P.S. A recommendation from my publishers accompanies this note.

The Principal Librarian. | British Museum.

Text MS. BL.
Jones: John Winter Jones (1805–81), principal librarian of the British Museum (in succession to Sir Anthony Panizzi) 1866–78; *D.N.B.* *Reader's Ticket*: an application by ELH, of the same date and in almost the same words, is also in BL; TH was first admitted to the Reading Room 27 May 1878. *books I publish*: TH was currently working on *The Trumpet-Major*; see *Personal Notebooks* (see above, letter of 5 Mar 26), 120, etc. *my publishers*: Smith, Elder, & Co.

To FRANCIS HUEFFER

1, ARUNDEL TERRACE, | TRINITY ROAD, UPPER TOOTING. S.W. | May 9, 1878

My dear Sir,

I will endeavour to make the story cover at least 40 pages—& it may possibly be longer; but I mention that length in case the subject I have thought of may not safely bear extension further. Of course if it should naturally work out to a greater length I will not curtail it.

Believe me

Yours very truly
Thomas Hardy.

Text   MS. Manchester Central Library.
Hueffer: Francis Hueffer, German-born music critic, currently editor of the *New Quarterly Magazine*; see I.57.   *the story*: pub. in the *New Quarterly*, July 1878, as 'An Indiscretion in the Life of an Heiress'; see Purdy, 274–6.

To AN UNIDENTIFIED CORRESPONDENT

1, ARUNDEL TERRACE, | TRINITY ROAD, UPPER TOOTING. S.W. | Feb 19. 1879

My dear Sir,

I am truly sorry that you should have been put to the trouble of asking if the volume that you were so kind as to send reached me safely. You will perhaps forgive me for not acknowledging the receipt of it when I tell you that I was moving house at the time it arrived, &, in the confusion, your poems were packed up with the rest of my books. As there was no letter from you I had nothing to remind me afterwards of the necessity of a reply.

On reading the poems—which I have been doing this afternoon—I am tempted to ask why a writer who can express himself so felicitously does not venture upon a volume of original verse. But perhaps you have already done this. In any case believe me, with best wishes & thanks for the book

Yours very truly
Thomas Hardy.

Text   MS. Eton College.
moving house: TH must be referring to his move from Sturminster Newton to Tooting in March 1878; see I.55.

To ALEXANDER MACMILLAN

1 Arundel Terrace. May 19. [1879]

Dear Mr Macmillan,

I have sent you by hand the MS. of the story I spoke of the other day—as far as it is written. I have not sent a sketch of the ending, but perhaps it will be sufficient to say that everything winds up well & happily, & that the tale in general is to be of a cheerful sort. There are several reasons why I should wish it to appear as a serial before it is published in a complete form; & you may

possibly know of an opportunity. At any rate I shall be glad to hear what you
think of it so far—

Believe me

Very truly yours
Thomas Hardy.

Text MS. Adams.   *Date* See notes below.
Macmillan: TH's intended recipient was his Tooting neighbour (see *EL*, 158, 167) Alexander
Macmillan (see I.7), the current head of the Macmillan publishing house, although the acknowledgement of the receipt of his MS. (20 May 79, DCM) was in fact sent by Alexander's son
George Augustin Macmillan (see II.108), who had entered the firm five years previously.   *the
story*: evidently *The Trumpet-Major*, which had already been declined by Leslie Stephen for the
Cornhill (see *EL*, 167).   *an opportunity*: TH presumably hoped the novel would be accepted
for *Macmillan's Magazine*, currently edited by George Grove (1820–1900; *D.N.B.*), but by
9 June he was offering it to *Blackwood's Magazine* in very similar terms (see I.65) and it was
eventually serialized in *Good Words* (see letter of 5 July 79).

To WILLIAM ISBISTER

1, ARUNDEL TERRACE, | TRINITY ROAD, UPPER TOOTING. S.W. | July 5. 1879
My dear Sir,

I have been considering the circumstances you state in your letter, & can
quite understand, though I much regret, that the depressed state of trade & the
fact that you already have one story for next year somewhat limits your offer for
mine. However, I like the Magazine & January is a convenient month for me to
begin in, so I agree to the £400, if you will allow me this slight modification on
my side, that I supply 10 pages a month instead of 11—to which I think there
can be no objection, as the story will read the brisker by being a little more
condensed.

I hope you will provide me with a skilful artist, & that he or she will not be
above accepting from me rough sketches of any unusual objects that come into
the tale. I have done this with the Cornhill & other artists, with a very good
result.

I trust that there will be a few days at least of summer weather before you
return. Hail & hurricanes are the rule here, & we are thinking of beginning
fires again.

Believe me

Yours very truly
Thomas Hardy.

Text MS. Eton College.
Isbister: William Isbister, proprietor of *Good Words*.   *your offer for mine*: TH's *The Trumpet-
Major*; see I.66.   *skilful artist*: see I.66–7.   *beginning fires again*: the weather had been
poor over the whole of the British Isles for several days, with rain, gales in the Channel, and
unseasonably low temperatures.

To WALTER POLLOCK

1 Arundel Terrace | Up: Tooting | Nov 5. [1879?]

My dear Pollock,

I will come with pleasure.

Yours sincerely

Thomas Hardy.

Text MS. David Holmes.   *Date* See below.
Pollock: Walter Herries Pollock, barrister and author; see I.121.   *come with pleasure*:
perhaps to the inaugural meeting of the Rabelais Club, 13 Dec 1879 (see *EL*, 172), although an
1878 dating cannot be ruled out.

To JOHN COLLIER

1 Arundel Terrace | Up. Tooting. | Nov 22 [1879]

Dear Collier,

I am glad to hear that the sketches are likely to be useful. They are of course
subject entirely to your revision, the figures being inserted merely to show the
position they seemed to occupy as I wrote the chapter. I could not quite decide
where the trumpet-major ought to be standing, so perhaps you will stick him in
where he looks best. The mounted figure is from a very doubtful sketch on the
covers of a book of the period, supplemented by a description; but I think it is
quite near enough.

I will call at the U.S.M. when in Whitehall—& let you know the result.

Yours truly

Thos Hardy.

Text MS. Eton College.   *Date* Year from internal evidence.
Collier: John Collier, artist (see I.67), was illustrating the serial of TH's *The Trumpet-Major*, due
to begin in the January 1880 number of *Good Words*.   *likely to be useful*: TH was replying
to the letter of 20 Nov 79 (DCM, quoted Purdy, 33) in which Collier thanked him for sending a
series of sketches suggestive of scenes in the early instalments of the novel.   *where he looks
best*: evidently in the scene in the mill kitchen which Collier drew for the February
instalment.   *mounted figure*: of the trumpet-major, intended not for an illustration but for a
possible advertisement; see Purdy, 33.   *book of the period*: unidentified.   *description*:
presumably the one from the 1795 *Standing Orders* of the Queen's Dragoon Guards which TH
copied into his notebook; see *Personal Notebooks* (see above, letter of 5 Mar 26), 146–8 and
146n.   *U.S.M.*: United Service Museum, located in Whitehall Yard; it displayed naval and
military accoutrements and memorabilia from the Napoleonic and other periods.

To ALEXANDRA SUTHERLAND ORR

THE AVENUE, | WIMBORNE, DORSET. | December 14, 1881

Dear Mrs Orr,

I wish all my critics were as appreciative as you, & so well able to express
their appreciation—though, as this seems rather a selfish wish, I may add that
I regret not having you for a reviewer quite as much in thereby missing the
opportunity of getting an instructive light upon my work as in losing a kindly
notice. I am much pleased to find that you feel De Stancy *might* have proved
a very satisfactory husband for Paula, & that poetic justice did not demand
Somerset's success too exclusively. That much may be said on both sides is my

continual feeling, on real situations as well as on ideal ones in life, & if the story exhibits this feeling I have thus far succeeded in it.

The architectural portion of the novel embodies, as you will have guessed, much of my own experience, which enabled me to write the story with, I think, less effort than others have cost me. If you should ever have time to look into the library form of the book you will find that some crudities in Paula's character &c. (which invariably occur in writing from month to month) have been smoothed out—I hope to her advantage.

I sincerely hope your little working power, as you modestly term it, is not to be suspended or interrupted in any way. Your critical writing seems to me to possess a quality singularly absent from the mass of such writings in these days—the quality of gracefulness—which when I first observed it quite charmed me. This being the case you must in common kindness write as much as you can, & develope your speciality still further.

Your kind inquiry about my health reminds me to tell you that it is quite re-established. The fact is I have lived too much in the country to bear transplanting to town, while curiously enough I seem to see more of London now than when we lived in the suburbs. I very frequently run up, & enjoy those very commonplaces of town life which used to be a weariness.

With best wishes I am

Yours sincerely
Thomas Hardy.

Text   MS. Eton College.
Orr: Alexandra Sutherland Orr, *née* Leighton (1828–1903), biographer and critic; *D.N.B.* She was the sister of Lord Leighton, president of the Royal Academy, and the widow of Sutherland George Gordon Orr (d. 1858); TH seems first to have met her in 1878 (see *EL*, 159).   *losing a kindly notice*: Mrs. Orr wrote 12 Dec 81 (DCM) in praise of TH's *A Laodicean* and regretted that by waiting until the appearance of the final instalment (in the December 1881 number of *Harper's New Monthly Magazine*) she had 'missed the proper time' for asking to be allowed to review it.   *De Stancy . . . Paula . . . Somerset's*: characters in *A Laodicean*.   *library form*: i.e., the three-volume first edn., pub. earlier that same month.   *quite charmed me*: Mrs. Orr wrote a long and positive article on TH's own work in the *New Quarterly Magazine*, October 1879; see I.67–8.   *my health*: TH was still recovering from the serious illness he had suffered during the composition of *A Laodicean*; see Millgate, 214–9.

To SAMPSON LOW, MARSTON & CO.

Wimborne. March 3. 1882
Dear Sirs,

The renewed discussion about "Far from the Madding Crowd" which appears in the *Times* of today, & other papers for this week, may cause another demand for the novel—so I would ask you to be ready to meet any such demand.

Will you make known to booksellers that you are the present publishers of the book, since, owing to the recent change they may be puzzled as to where to apply. The *Strand* booksellers should be asked to take copies, owing to the vicinity of the theatres. Also the Liverpool & Manchester booksellers—long articles on play & novel having appeared in all the newspapers there.

I should be glad with a few copies of the book, as I have not a single one. Please let me know what you have done about *Ethelberta*.

Yours faithfully
T. Hardy.

Text   MS. David Holmes.
Sampson Low, Marston: as TH's new publishers (see I.109) they were bringing out his existing novels in cheap one-vol. edns.   *Times of today*: *The Times* of 3 Mar 1882 alluded in one of its leading articles to the persistence of the controversy aroused by the similarities between Pinero's play *The Squire* and TH's own earlier dramatization of *Far from the Madding Crowd*; see I.99–101, etc.   *Liverpool & Manchester*: where J. Comyns Carr's adaptation of TH's *Far from the Madding Crowd* play had recently been performed.   *Ethelberta*: Sampson Low had recently purchased more than half of the 1,000 copies of the one-vol. edn. of TH's *The Hand of Ethelberta* originally pub. by Smith, Elder in 1877; see Purdy, 23.

To MISS FRITH

Wimborne: April 16. 1882

Dear Miss Frith,
    I am glad to hear from you, & in expressing the same send what you require, as also one on the back.
    With best regards

Yours sincerely
Thomas Hardy

Text   MS. R. Barrie.
Frith: it has proved impossible to establish which of the several daughters of William Powell Frith, the painter (see I.129), TH is here addressing.   *what you require*: evidently TH's autograph.

To WALTER BESANT

13 Rue des Beaux Arts | Paris | Oct 12. 82

My dear Besant,
    I am sorry that I shall be unable to attend the dinner this time. We are over here for a while, & hope to stay on till the weather gets cold—unless anything unexpected occurs. Believe me

Yours truly
T. Hardy.

Text   MS. Adams.
Besant: Walter Besant (see I.63), novelist, man of letters, and founder of the Incorporated Society of Authors.   *Paris*: it was at this address (that of the now-fashionable L'Hôtel, scene of Oscar Wilde's death in 1900) that TH and ELH spent several weeks in the autumn of 1882; see *EL*, 200–1.

To GEORGE WILMSHURST

The Avenue, Wimborne, Dorset— | & Savile Club, 107 Piccadilly, W. |
30th Novr 1882

Fordington.

Sir,
    I beg to apply for a Building Lease for 99 years from Michaelmas 1883 or earlier—for the purpose of erecting within three years a villa Residence and

Offices, Stabling &c. on plans to be approved of & to cost £1000 at least—of the site indicated on the enclosed tracing plan, in area 1a..2r..0p., or thereabout, but to be correctly measured & plotted on the ground when a Lease may be prepared; at the rate of Ten pounds per acre rent per annum. The Lease to be drawn up in the Duchy office in the usual form at my cost, and to contain a Covenant reserving to me the option of purchasing the fee simple of the property after the Completion of the Buildings, or within Five years of the date of the Lease, at a price to be computed at the rate of £300 per acre. In that case the Minerals below 60 feet from the surface to be reserved to the Duchy, but without right of surface entry.

I would undertake to properly fence the Plot from the adjacent land—the Duchy to be at liberty to remove the present wire fence adjoining the Highway.

I am, Sir,

Your obedient servant,
Thomas Hardy.

To G. Wilmshurst Esqre

Text MS. (all except signature in an unidentified hand) Duchy of Cornwall.
Wilmshurst: George Wilmshurst (d. 1886), since 1873 Secretary and Clerk to the Council of the Duchy of Cornwall and Keeper of the Records. *the site indicated*: i.e., the one-and-a-half-acre (1 acre, 2 rods) piece of open field, on the Wareham Road just SE of Dorchester, on which Max Gate was subsequently built. TH had first made enquiries about Duchy of Cornwall land as early as the spring of 1880 (see I.73) and a note (apparently contemporary) at the foot of this present MS. indicates that he was known to the Duchy officials as the author of *Far from the Madding Crowd*.

To GEORGE WILMSHURST

THE AVENUE, | WIMBORNE, DORSET. | March 14. 1883

Sir,

Manor of Fordington.

I beg to acknowledge the receipt of your letter of the 12th inst. in reference to my application for a plot of land. I gather from it that, though a clause giving option of purchase cannot (for some technical reason) be inserted in the lease, the practical result will be the same to myself by recording the permission in the Minute of Council. On this understanding I forward Cheque for £6. 6. 0 in payment of duty & office fees upon the Lease, as you request.

I should wish there to be a clause in the lease to the effect that the Duchy will not use the land adjoining my piece in such a way as to create anything of the nature of a nuisance to a private dwelling. Also that I may be permitted to erect on the ground, in addition to my residence, stable &c, a man's cottage, if at any time it should be desirable.

I am, sir,

Your obedient servant
Thomas Hardy.

Geo. Wilmshurst Esqre

Text MS. Duchy of Cornwall.
your letter: of 12 Mar 83 (copy, Duchy files); TH's letter of 30 Nov 82 appears to have been sent in the first instance to the local Duchy agent, George Herriot (see below, letter of 23 Sept 86), who

forwarded it to Wilmshurst in London, with a supporting letter of his own (Duchy files), only in February 1883.   *Council*: of the Duchy of Cornwall.

To THORNHILL HEATHCOTE

SAVILE CLUB, | 107, PICCADILLY. W. | May 28. 1883

Sir,

Manor of Fordington.

I beg to acknowledge the receipt of your letter of the 21st inst, together with the draft of the proposed building lease, which I return to you as requested, the same being approved.

I am, sir,

Your obedient servant
Thomas Hardy.

P.S. After Saturday next, my address will be The Avenue, Wimborne.

Text   MS. Duchy of Cornwall.
Heathcote: Thornhill Bradford Heathcote (d. 1928, aged 89); solicitor to the Duchy and deputy steward for Dorset, Somerset, and Wiltshire.   *your letter*: of 21 May 83 (copy, Duchy files).   *building lease*: this had been prepared on the basis of a new survey of the Macks Gate site (as it was still called) submitted by George Herriot (Duchy files).

To THORNHILL HEATHCOTE

THE AVENUE, | WIMBORNE, DORSET. | June 2. 1883

Sir

Manor of Fordington.

Since writing to you my letter of the 28th ult. it has occurred to me that it would be advisable, in preparing the lease, to add to my address as given in the draft, the words "and of the Savile Club, 107 Piccadilly, London"—my name being such a common one in this county as occasionally to lead to mistakes, & my residence here being but temporary.

I trust that this addition can be made without inconvenience, & am, Sir,

Your obedient servant
Thomas Hardy.

Thornhill B. Heathcote Esq.

Text   MS. Duchy of Cornwall.
my name: it is perhaps significant that TH was writing on his birthday; he had also been embarrassed the previous year by the publication of a bad poem over the name of another Thomas Hardy (see I.108–9).   *but temporary*: see letters of 12 and 14 June 83.   *without inconvenience*: Heathcote, however, replying 6 June 83 (copy, Duchy files), did not feel that TH's concern was sufficiently well-founded to justify an interlineation in a document that had already been engrossed.

To EDMUND GOSSE

Wimborne | June 12. 1883

My dear Gosse,

I will join you with great pleasure. Your very kind invitation to stay with you I am sorry to decline; but as I shall be in Town for some days just then (as I believe) at a place already arranged for my accommodation, your further hospitality must be abandoned with regret. We leave this place in the latter part of the month—much to my exhilaration. A man has been here to look at our furniture, which he "carries in his eye" (so he says) till he has made an estimate for removing it. Looking forward to our meeting I am,

Yours very sincerely
Thomas Hardy.

Text   MS. Eton College.
join you: Gosse (11 June 83, DCM) invited TH to dine at the Savile Club on 25 June and meet the American novelist William Dean Howells (see I.156); see *EL*, 208–9, and *Transatlantic Dialogue: Selected American Correspondence of Edmund Gosse*, ed. Paul F. Mattheisen and Michael Millgate (Austin, 1965), 115.   *to decline*: despite, or perhaps because of, Gosse's enthusiastic comment that he would be alone in his house 'and we would talk, Lord! how we would talk'.   *leave this place*: TH and ELH were moving to a rented house in Shire-Hall Lane, Dorchester.

To THORNHILL HEATHCOTE

The Avenue: Wimborne. | June 14. 1883

Sir,

Manor of Fordington.

Herewith I return the Lease, with signatures attached.
I beg to state that after July 1st & till further notice my address will be
Shire Hall Lane
Dorchester.
& remain, Sir,

Your obedient servant
Thomas Hardy.

Thornhill B. Heathcote Esq.

Text   MS. Duchy of Cornwall.
signatures attached: TH's signature was witnessed by his friend Henry Tindal Atkinson (see below, letter of 5 May 84).   *Shire Hall Lane*: the house rented by the Hardys was called Shire-Hall Place; see I.119 and Millgate, 239–40.

To JOHN BOWEN

Shire-Hall Place | Dorchester, Dorset. | Oct 16. 1883

Dear Sir,

I have received your letter of the 14th Sept., together with a copy of the Independent. I will take your offer into consideration, & let you know as soon as possible if I can send you a story, such as you describe, on the terms proposed.
I am, dear Sir,

Yours truly
T. Hardy.

Text MS. Univ. of Kentucky.
Bowen: John Eliot Bowen (see I.132), assistant ('office') editor of the New York *Independent*; it is possible that the addressee was in fact Bowen's father, Henry Chandler Bowen, proprietor of the magazine, although TH seems to have corresponded with him only after his son's death in 1890 (see I.220).   *a story*: TH's story 'Emmeline, or Passion versus Principle' appeared in the *Independent* 7 Feb 1884; see Purdy, 63–4.

To WALTER BESANT

Dorchester. | Oct 30. 1883

My dear Besant,

I received your telegram, & understood in a moment what had happened—I hope you understood my reply—which was sent off about 3 o'c. I have been trying to recollect since more particularly about the Trumpet Major—but I can only recall the fact that I was disappointed in the number Mudie subscribed for—considering the general success of the book—& it is probable that I now know for the first time the true reason—that they were waiting for the magazine—but did not say so. I know this that, as I said in the telegram, Blackmore's sale of Christowell was ruined by the magazine—but this was partly owing to his delay in producing the 3 vol. form—so that the magazine had a good start of him. Now that nearly all the magazines are pubd at 6d it will be very awkward for us—Country subscribers to the libraries are often supplied with a serial story cut from the magazine—& bound up. I have received novels thus treated—even bound without the last number—this not being out till later. The magazines must be largely used in this way, else why is it that a given amount of success in a story which has never appeared in a magazine ensures a larger sale than the same success in a story which has so appeared? e.g. if John Inglesant, Vice Versâ, &c, had been reprinted from magazines, we should have heard nothing of their large sales.

I intended to be at the Rab. dinner—but could not get to town. I hope to be at the next—& to see you well.

Yours sincerely
Thomas Hardy.

Text MS. P. C. Roscoe.
what had happened: Besant followed up his telegram with a letter of 29 Oct 83 (DCM) which explained that although he was bringing out the three-vol. edn. of his new novel, *All in a Garden Fair*, at the usual interval of six weeks before the appearance of the final serial instalment in *Good Words*, he had discovered that the bound vol. containing a year's issues of *Good Words* (hence a complete text of his novel) was appearing even earlier and at a much cheaper price and therefore being purchased by the circulating libraries in preference to the book itself.   *the Trumpet Major*: this novel of TH's appeared in *Good Words* January–December 1880.   *Mudie*: Mudie's lending library, founded by Charles Edward Mudie (1818–90; *D.N.B.*).   *Blackmore's sale of Christowell*: Richard Doddridge Blackmore (see I.38); his novel *Christowell: A Dartmoor Tale*, serialized in *Good Words* January–December 1881, did not appear in its three-vol. form until the very end of 1881. Besant (31 Oct 83, DCM) expressed regret that Blackmore and TH had 'sat down quiet under your wrongs!'   *John Inglesant*: Joseph Henry Shorthouse's *John Inglesant: A Romance* went through many printings following its first commercial publication in 1881.   *Vice Versâ*: *Vice Versâ, or A Lesson to Fathers* by F. Anstey (i.e., Thomas Anstey Guthrie; see II.123), first pub. 1882.   *Rab. dinner*: i.e., Rabelais Club dinner; see above, letter of 5 Nov 79.

To THORNHILL HEATHCOTE

SHIRE-HALL LANE, | DORCHESTER. | November 22. 1883

Dear Sir,

Manor of Fordington.

I beg to acknowledge receipt of the Lease of the plot of building land adjoining the Wareham Road, as sealed by the Duchy.

I am, dear Sir,

Yours faithfully
Thomas Hardy.

Text MS. Duchy of Cornwall.
as sealed by the Duchy: the lease, bearing an indenture date of 16 Oct 1883, is recorded in the Duchy of Cornwall's Inrolment Book (Country Leases), vol. LXXXV.

To HENRY TINDAL ATKINSON

Dorchester May 5. 1884

My dear Serjeant,

I am glad to hear that the little story was attractive enough to interest your listeners & yourself: we'll see what we can do upon a larger scale before many years have passed. I am glad to hear that you will attend the club meeting: the dinner is mostly interesting when it is held at an inn; members feel more independent there. For my part I wish the club made a point of never dining at other people's expense, as it becomes awkward for those members who are not acquainted with the entertainer. They will, I suppose, read some paper or papers at the table, after the dinner—at least, they have done so on former occasions; so I shall try to attend. My wife will not be there—so would Miss Atkinson prefer to lunch with her here? If so she may be sure my wife will be glad to entertain her. But we shall meet earlier in the morning than that, no doubt—why not come straight here in the morning before the meeting.

I believe the club day is also your court day—I hope the cases will be light. Believe me

Yours very sincerely
T. Hardy.

Text MS. David Holmes.
Atkinson: Henry Tindal Atkinson, Serjeant-at-law and judge; see I.111. *little story*: presumably TH's 'Interlopers at the Knap', *English Illustrated Magazine*, May 1884. *upon a larger scale*: TH was already working on *The Mayor of Casterbridge*. *club meeting*: the meeting of the Dorset Natural History and Antiquarian Field Club, held at the King's Arms, Dorchester, 13 May 1884. *some paper or papers*: it was at this meeting, in fact, that TH read his own paper 'Some Romano-British Relics Found at Max Gate, Dorchester'; see Purdy, 61. *Miss Atkinson*: Atkinson's daughter Louisa; see *EL*, 195. *cases will be light*: Atkinson, sitting in Dorchester as a County Court judge on 13 May, had only cases of a financial nature to dispose of.

To T. M. DRON

Shire Hall Lane, Dorchester, | 22nd May, 1884.

Dear Sir,

I have only to-day learnt that you are the author of the pleasant "Lines written after reading," &c., in the D.C.C. The imagination of the reader had, I suspect, no small share in the effect of the story; for the prosperity of a tale, like that of a jest, lies largely in the recipient.

The initials "T. M. D." recall to my mind that other lines which have impressed me, have appeared thus signed in the same paper.

Accept my congratulations upon them, and the ease with which, apparently, they are produced; and believe me,

Yours truly,
Thomas Hardy.

Text   Dorset Year Book, 1929, 144.
Dron: Thomas Middleton Dron (d. 1931, aged 82), schoolmaster, local government official, and author.   *in the D.C.C.*: Dron's 'Lines Written after Reading "Interlopers at the Knap"' —including the line, 'These characters are folks we've seen and known'—appeared over the initials 'T.M.D.' in the *Dorset County Chronicle*, 8 May 1884.   *other lines*: Dron pub. a poem entitled 'In Memoriam' in the issue of 10 Apr 1884.

To R. H. HUTTON

Dorchester | January 28, 1885

Dear Sir,

I have derived so much pleasure from the perusal of an article entitled "Silence is Gold" in your last number that I am unwilling to let the moment of reading pass by without expressing as much to you. To find that paths of thought which one's own mind has travelled in imagined solitude are the familiar haunts of another, who can, moreover, extend & enlarge those paths, is most impressive. The article must, I am sure, be a means of education to thousands.

With thanks I am, dear Sir

Yours truly
Thomas Hardy.

Text   MS. Univ. of Keele.
Hutton: Richard Holt Hutton (see I.178), joint editor of the *Spectator*.   *in your last number*: 'Silence Is Gold', pub. anonymously in the *Spectator*, 24 Jan 1885, 112–4; the apparent association of this MS. at Keele with the papers of Frances Julia Wedgwood (1833–1913, a niece of Charles Darwin's and a frequent contributor to the *Spectator*) provides some grounds for thinking that the essay may have been her work.

To LADY WINIFRED HERBERT

MAX GATE, | NEAR DORCHESTER. | Jan 3. 1886

Dear Lady Winifred Herbert,

You will recollect my promise to introduce "Winifred" as heroine of one of my novels. I am just beginning to write the story, but alas—according to my plot her destiny is a tragic one. Now it seems a cruel return for your friendship to associate your name with tragedy—& I confess that I have not the heart to do it unless you assure me that you would really like it to be done. So will you be so good as to let me know your commands: is my heroine with a sombre destiny to be Winifred, or shall I reserve that excellent name for some future heroine whose career may be of a brighter kind?

I have pleasure in sending Lady Carnarvon a copy of *The Graphic* containing the opening Chapters of "The Mayor of Casterbridge"—a portion of which I read to you from the MS. at Eggesford.

Yours sincerely
Thomas Hardy.

Text MS. Eton College.
Herbert: Lady Winifred Anne Henrietta Christine Herbert (1864–1933), eldest daughter of the 4th Earl of Carnarvon (see below, letter of 5 July 88); she is mentioned several times in *EL*.   *the story*: evidently *The Woodlanders*. Lady Winifred (9 Jan 86, DCM) appreciated TH's remembering his promise to 'immortalise my name' but was less enthusiastic about the 'tragic destiny'; she seems to have repeated her request at the end of the year, however (see *EL*, 242).   *Lady Carnarvon*: Lady Winifred's mother; see I.133 and *EL*, 242.   *of Casterbridge"*: the first instalment of the novel, containing chap. 1 and 2, appeared in the *Graphic*, 2 Jan 1886.   *at Eggesford*: Eggesford House, Devon, the seat of the Earl of Portsmouth; Lady Winifred, a niece of Lady Portsmouth's, was staying there at the time of TH's visit in March 1885 (see I.131 and *EL*, 221–2).

To LAURENCE ALMA TADEMA

Max Gate, | near Dorchester. | April 5. 1886.

Dear Miss Alma-Tadema,

You have given me a very great pleasure in so considerately sending a copy of your handsome book, which I am going to read with interest as soon as possible. I have as yet only just looked into it, but from what I see there I imagine it to contain some tempting reading for evenings to come. There is I fancy, some sadness in it; but we will not anticipate: The notices have, I believe, been very favourable so far; and altogether your start seems an excellent one.

With best wishes for its success, and many thanks, believe me,

Yours sincerely,
Thomas Hardy.

Text Typed transcript Bodleian Library.
Tadema: Laurence Alma Tadema (d. 1940), novelist and poet, elder daughter of Lawrence Alma-Tadema, the painter (see I.192), by his first wife; his second wife was Edmund Gosse's sister-in-law, and Ann Thwaite's *Edmund Gosse* (see above, letter of 5 Nov 26) contains several references to Laurence and a photograph of her as a child.   *your handsome book*: *Love's Martyr* (London, 1886), a novel pub. in one volume; the author's name appears on the title-page without a hyphen.

To EDMUND GOSSE

Max Gate, Dorchester. | 21.8.86

My dear Gosse,

Monday the 30th will suit us excellently—& you may be sure that the longer you can stay the better we shall be pleased—I am always afraid friends from Town may feel they are wasting themselves down here, so I don't venture to name more than a day or so on that account.

If it should unfortunately happen that you are detained on that day I trust you will be able to name another.

Yours sincerely
Thomas Hardy.

Text MS. (with envelope) David Holmes.
suit us excellently: Gosse had responded positively to TH's invitation of 18 Aug 86; see I.150–1.

To GEORGE HERRIOT

MAX GATE, | NEAR DORCHESTER. | Sept 23. 1886

Dear Sir,

This week the men finish the permanent fencing of my plot of land here (delayed till now on account of the crops outside)—according to the requirements you expressed on your last visit—viz—a flat iron 5 bar fence at the back, & a brick wall at the west side. As Michaelmas is at hand I write to ask if I shall send up the money agreed on for the purchase.

Possibly my mere assertion that the work is complete may not be sufficient to enable you to certify the same. Therefore, as I do not wish to trouble you to get it inspected at an inconvenient time, I could send the purchase money on account, till you have been here—if by so doing I can be relieved of further rental.

Awaiting your instructions I am, dear Sir,

Yours truly
Thomas Hardy.

The necessary plans, as you may recollect, were sent some time ago.

Text MS. Duchy of Cornwall.
Herriot: George Herriot (d. 1910), Scottish-born land steward for the Duchy of Cornwall's western district 1865–99; his office was in Shepton Mallet, Somerset. A year earlier TH had told Wilmshurst (1 Sept 85, Duchy files; draft at I.135) that he was ready to buy the land on which Max Gate now stood; Herriot, as the local agent, then wrote 4 Sept 85 (DCM) to ask that TH send plans of the house itself, so that purchase arrangements might go forward. The one-year interval presumably resulted from TH's decision, once he had paid his annual rent at Michaelmas (29 September) 1885, to delay the purchase until Michaelmas 1886.   *money agreed on*: see letter of 7 Oct 86.

To MAURICE HOLZMANN

MAX GATE, | NEAR DORCHESTER. | October 7. 1886

Sir,

Fordington Leasehold Tenancy No 11.

I enclose herewith the Bank of England Cashier's receipt for 450£, as requested in your letter of Sept 29, the sum being the purchase money of the above mentioned Tenancy.

I also enclose Cheque for £7..7..0 in payment for the Conveyance fees &c. as signified in the same letter.

I am, Sir,

Your obedt Servt
Thomas Hardy.

Text   MS. Duchy of Cornwall.
Holzmann: Maurice Holzmann (1835–1909), formerly Prince Albert's German secretary and librarian, had been appointed Secretary to the Duchy and Keeper of the Records, positions left vacant by the death of George Wilmshurst.   *your letter*: Herriot had written to Holzmann 25 Sept 86 (Duchy files), forwarding and supporting TH's letter of 23 Sept 86, and Holzmann sent TH 29 Sept 86 (DCM) a memorandum allowing him to purchase 'the villa and gardens now completed according to the terms of your lease'.

To MAURICE HOLZMANN

MAX GATE, | NEAR DORCHESTER. | Oct 12. 1886

Sir,

Fordington: Leasehold Tenancy No 11.

I have received from the Bank of England a Bank Cashiers receipt, as required in your letter of the 29th ult. & now enclose it to you that the deed of conveyance may be prepared.

Your obedt servant
Thomas Hardy.

Text   MS. Duchy of Cornwall.
Bank Cashiers receipt: Holzmann (8 Oct 86; copy, Duchy files) explained that the Duchy required a form of receipt different from the one TH had sent with his letter of 7 Oct 86. The rejected receipt, dated 2 Oct 1886, is in DCM.

To MAURICE HOLZMANN

MAX GATE, | NEAR DORCHESTER. | October 30. 1886

Sir,

Manor of Fordington.

I return herewith the Draft Conveyance approved. A trifling inaccuracy in the description of the boundaries has been marked for correction, in coloured pencil. I have also added a few words to my personal description, for insertion if there is no objection to the same.

I am, Sir,

Your obedient servant
Thomas Hardy.

Text   MS. Duchy of Cornwall.
trifling inaccuracy . . . personal description: see letter of 4 Nov 86.

To MAURICE HOLZMANN

MAX GATE, | NEAR DORCHESTER. | Novr 4th 1886

Sir,

I am obliged for the draft lease & conveyance enclosed with your letter of yesterday. The lane from Loud's Mill is almost due east of the plot of land, as shown on the map, but I leave you to decide whether the word south-east should stand, the point being, I suppose, immaterial, since the map will appear in the margin.

I adopt your suggestion of "Author" in the personal description—though I have added the words "of books"—this being, I believe, the full designation as I have seen it in other documents.

I enclose the drafts herewith & am, Sir,

Your obedt servant
Thomas Hardy.

Text MS. Duchy of Cornwall.
from Loud's Mill: the former cloth mill, now the property of the Dorchester Borough Council, still stands on the banks of the River Frome; the lane is now known as Syward Road.   *in the margin*: like all such Duchy records, the conveyance of Max Gate as entered in the Duchy's Inrolment Book (Sales and Purchases), vol. LXXXVI, is accompanied by a small but elegant sketch map of the site and its immediate surroundings. The toll house on the S. side of the Wareham Road is shown as 'Macks Gate' (see Millgate, 256 and n.) but Max Gate itself is annotated '(formerly Louds Gate)'.   *your suggestion*: in letter of 3 Nov 86 (Duchy files).   *"of books"*: TH is named in the conveyance as 'Thomas Hardy of Max Gate near Dorchester in the County of Dorset Author of Books'.

To MAURICE HOLZMANN

MAX GATE, | NEAR DORCHESTER. | December 18. 1886

Sir,

Manor of Fordington.

I beg to acknowledge receipt of the deed of Conveyance to myself of the dwelling house & premises & 1a. 2r. 0p. of land in the Wareham Road, as purchased.

I am, Sir,

Your obedient servant
Thomas Hardy.

M. Holzmann Esqre

Text MS. Duchy of Cornwall.
deed of Conveyance: see letter of 4 Nov 86; the deed is dated 7 Dec 1886 and was sent by Holzmann 16 Dec 86 (DCM).

To JOHN SCARLET

May 6. [1887]

Mr Hardy is not aware if any of his works have been dramatized without his authority.

Text MS. (postcard, with address apparently in ELH's hand) Gordon N. Ray.   *Date* From postmark.
Scarlet: the name (spelled 'Scarlett') and address have been partly erased, but the addressee would appear to be the John Scarlet listed in an 1887 street directory as living at 24 Cramer Terrace, Gateshead-on-Tyne.

To [C. J. LONGMAN?]

MAX GATE, | NEAR DORCHESTER. | May 6. 1887

My dear Sir,

I have been spending the last two months in Italy—which will partly account for my neglect. The notes for your story are still preserved, & it will be a great pleasure to me to write them out as soon as I can during the present year.

Yours very truly
T. Hardy.

Text   MS. Essex Institute.
Longman: Charles James Longman (see I.107), editor of *Longman's Magazine*; the reference is apparently to TH's story 'The Withered Arm', rejected by Longman 27 Sept 87 (DCM) as being too grim and unrelieved—'especially as I believe that the majority of magazine readers are girls'.

To KATHERINE BRONSON

5, Campden Hill Road, | London. W. | May 31. '87

Dear Mrs Bronson,

I have received a nice little roll of music which corresponds so closely with what you proposed to send when we were in Venice that I conclude it comes from your kind hands. As soon as I get back to the country the strains will be heard issuing from the windows of my house—though not in my voice I fear. Perhaps a parcel in my handwriting will come to you some day. But we will not anticipate.

London has been wretchedly cold till to-day—when there is a slight improvement. If we could only get rid of the smoke the sun would have a chance. Our recollections of Venice seem of the essence of romance in these surroundings. Past scenes have a way of mellowing thus. We quite forget that we had some cold days too there.

My wife sends kindest regards, & I am

Yours sincerely
Thomas Hardy.

Text   MS. Eton College.
Bronson: Katherine Colman Bronson, *née* De Kay (1834–1901), widow of Arthur Bronson (d. 1885). An American living in Venice (Casa Alvisi) and Asolo, she was a close friend of Henry James and especially of Robert Browning: see the introduction to *More Than Friend: The Letters of Robert Browning to Katherine De Kay Bronson*, ed. Michael Meredith (Waco, 1985). For her hospitality to TH and ELH during their recent visit to Venice, see *EL*, 254–5, and *Emma Hardy Diaries*, ed. Richard H. Taylor (Ashington, 1985), 181–2, 184.   *music*: presumably of some Italian song TH had heard and remarked upon while in Venice.   *in my handwriting*: TH evidently proposed to send Mrs. Bronson a copy of one of his books.

To JUSTIN McCARTHY

5 Campden Hill Road. W. | June 28 [1887]

Dear Mr McCarthy,

I am quite disengaged on Friday next—& shall have much pleasure in joining you if you will let me know the hour.

Yours very truly

Thomas Hardy.

Text MS. Washington and Lee Univ.   *Date* TH stayed at this address only in 1887 (see I.165).
McCarthy: Justin McCarthy (see II.162), Irish politician and historian, currently M.P. for Derry City.

To LORD LYTTON

5 Campden Hill Road | July 12. 1887

My dear Lord Lytton,

I can hardly tell you how highly I value your letter containing your impressions of The Woodlanders. Indeed, I have been so much struck with the picture that your imagination has raised of the scene of the story that it seems a new revelation, quite transcending my own imperfect view of sylvan life. It is not often one gets a reader who helps out a conception in this way by his own creative power.

The misfortune of novelists nowadays is that they seldom can learn the opinion of competent judges—still less imaginative ones—printed criticism of light literature being for the most part from the pens of beginners, any of whom are considered good enough to review a novel. I fear too that the same fate usually attends writers of verse: I hope your new volume may not suffer from any such cause.

It is somewhat singular—and if one believed in prevision more might be said—but nearly twenty years ago, or quite, before I knew that Owen Meredith was not a real name, I was much attracted by it, & by the peculiar vein of feeling in the verse, so different from anything I had ever read before. One might remark now that it was a grateful sense of favours to come in the shape of highly suggestive & stimulating criticism of my own work from the pen of that author.

I need not say how much pleasure I shall have in receiving your book, & the fact of its publication seems to imply, as I hope, that you mean to be faithful after all to the old "idle trade."

I should much like to see Knebworth & its surroundings, & I must express my warmest thanks for the opportunity of doing so that you offer me. But I fear I shall have to hold aloof from such temptations this autumn. I have done absolutely nothing since February, & for the remainder of the year I shall be compelled to retire to a cottage in the south of England where I do most of my writing.

I hope your journey will be a pleasant one. I leave town myself in about a week, when my address will be Max Gate, Dorchester, till after Christmas. From what I have seen of Herts I am inclined to think that the woods there are of a grander type—at any rate the trees themselves—that those in the part of England in which my story is supposed to take place. But I find that in such matters—indeed in any matter—it is not absolute size but the attitude of the observer which makes things great or small. Believe me,

most sincerely yours
Thomas Hardy.

P.S. The poems have arrived since I began writing. Accept my renewed thanks.

Text MS. the Hon. David Lytton Cobbold.
Lytton: Edward Robert Bulwer-Lytton, 1st Earl of Lytton (see I.240), former Viceroy of India.   *impressions of The Woodlanders*: in his letter of 10 July 87 (Berkeley) Lytton said that in the imagination of any sensitive reader of the novel 'the English Woodland must live permanently—and familiarly—as an animated entity—a mysterious but perfectly sentient and busily occupied Being, with a distinctly personal character of its own'.   *your new volume*: *After Paradise; or, Legends of Exile, with Other Poems* (London, 1887), pub. under the pseudonym of 'Owen Meredith'.   *"idle trade."*: from Alexander Pope's 'Epistle to Dr. Arbuthnot', line 129.   *to see Knebworth*: Lytton's country seat in Hertfordshire; he had invited TH to stay there later in the year.   *a cottage*: i.e., Max Gate.   *seen of Herts*: TH spent approximately two months in Hatfield, Hertfordshire, as a boy of nine; see Millgate, 44–5.   *that those*: TH means 'than those'.   *supposed to take place*: i.e., in NW Dorset.

To LUCY BAXTER

Max Gate: Dorchester. | 26. 1. 88

Dear Mrs Baxter,

I must deny the soft impeachment contained in your note received this morning: I did not write the review in The Athenaeum; nor am I aware who the writer was. I read the article at the time it appeared; & in my mind its commendatory tone was not at all more than the book deserved. As to the few inaccuracies you allude to they are quite unimportant, & can easily be corrected in a new edition. My wife had a note from the editor a few days ago on another matter, but he did not mention the review: if she had thought of it she might have asked him the writer's name.

Though I have not reviewed the Life I have had the pleasure of recommending my correspondents to read it. It is a kind of book likely to have a good many readers, particularly as you have not introduced a mass of heavy detail which requires skipping—but have touched each section lightly, yet sufficiently for clearness.

To-morrow—no, the day after—there is to be a meeting of the Memorial Committee, at which the Site of the Statue is to be finally discussed & settled. Both places suggested are good ones—& it will make little difference to the appearance of the statue which is chosen. You have, I dare say, heard that the full size model is considered an admirable likeness.

Believe me, with kind regards to Mr Baxter,

Yours sincerely
Thomas Hardy.

Text MS. Purdy.
Baxter: Lucy Baxter (see I.158), writer on art, had just pub. a biography of her father, William

Barnes (see I.120), the Dorset poet.   *soft impeachment*: a phrase from Sheridan's *The Rivals*, V. iii.   *review in The Athenaeum*: Mrs. Baxter's *The Life of William Barnes, Poet and Philologist* was reviewed anonymously—but by someone who knew Dorchester well—in the *Athenaeum* of 31 Dec 1887; TH's signed obituary of Barnes appeared in the *Athenaeum* 16 Oct 1886.   *the editor*: Norman MacColl; see I.153, where TH agrees to write the obituary of Barnes for the *Athenaeum*.   *the Statue*: of Barnes, by Roscoe Mullins; it was eventually erected outside St. Peter's Church, Dorchester.   *Mr Baxter*: Samuel Thomas Baxter, whom she married in 1867; TH and ELH had been entertained by the Baxters in Florence in the spring of 1887.

To AN UNIDENTIFIED CORRESPONDENT

SAVILE CLUB, | 107, PICCADILLY. W. | 7. 4. 88

Dear Sir,

I should very much like to contribute something: but I fear it is not in my power to do so, owing to a serial novel looming in the near future which rather terrifies me. If ever I have a short paper I will send it. Believe me

Yours very truly
Thomas Hardy.

Text   MS. T. Trafton.
a serial novel: evidently *Tess of the d'Urbervilles*.

To WILSON BARRETT

SAVILE CLUB, | 107, PICCADILLY. W. | May 11. 1888

Dear Sir,

Owing to an accident I have only received your telegram within the last few hours.

I presume it is now too late to reply; but if not I very readily accept your kind offer of a seat.

Yours very truly
Thomas Hardy.

Text   MS. Texas.
Barrett: Wilson Barrett (1846–1904), actor, dramatist, and theatrical manager.   *a seat*: for *The Ben-my-Chree*, by Hall Caine and Wilson Barrett, with Barrett himself in the principal part; TH attended the opening night at the Princess's Theatre, 17 May 1888.

To WILSON BARRETT

SAVILE CLUB, | 107, PICCADILLY. W. | May 17. 1888

Dear Sir,

Best thanks for the stalls. I hope to have a pleasant evening.

Yours very truly
Thomas Hardy.

Text   MS. Texas.
a pleasant evening: see letter of 11 May 88.

To LORD CARNARVON

SAVILE CLUB, | 107, PICCADILLY. W. |
Max Gate | Dorchester} country address. | July 5. 1888—

Dear Lord Carnarvon,

I had hoped to be able to speak to you this summer on a small personal matter: but as I fear I may not have the opportunity I write a line. For some time I have felt that I should like my name to be put up at the Athenaeum Club. I imagine my chance of election to be infinitesimal, but if anything could help in the case it would be that one occupying your lordships threefold position of prominence as a man of letters rank & politics should be my proposer. With such a beginning I think I could get some supporters.

There may however be reasons which would prevent your acceding to this; but in any event I should highly value a word on the question from you—Believe me

Yours very faithfully
Thomas Hardy.

Text MS. BL.
Carnarvon: Henry Howard Molyneux Herbert, fourth Earl of Carnarvon (1831–90), statesman; *D.N.B.* See I.132–3.   *man of letters*: Lord Carnarvon had pub., among several other works, a verse translation of the *Odyssey*.

To LORD CARNARVON

SAVILE CLUB, | 107, PICCADILLY. W. | July 9. 1888

Dear Lord Carnarvon,

My sincerest thanks for your note. I will leave the matter quite to your judgment.

I did not go out of town as I expected to do when giving my country address, but am staying on till the latter part of this month. With renewed thanks believe me,

Very faithfully yours
Thomas Hardy.

Text MS. David Holmes.
quite to your judgment: TH was proposed by Carnarvon, and elected in 1891, Carnarvon himself having died the previous year; see *EL*, 298, 307.

To ELIZA LYNN LINTON

MAX GATE, | NEAR DORCHESTER. | Dec. 24. 1888

Dear Mrs Lynn Linton,

It was a very great pleasure to me this morning to receive your kindly letter, & I hope that now the ice has been broken we shall be able to exchange an occasional word, if only on a post-card. The little story I sent was not at all worthy of your critical powers, but it was the only new thing I had written this Christmas, & I particularly wanted to keep you in mind of my existence, along with the rest of your friends, at this time. My wife and I live in comparative solitude in our little house here for six months of the year & more, & we sometimes think that though we meet a good many people when we are away, we secure very few real & permanent friends, people in London having a habit of looking upon you as dead if you are outside the 4 mile circle. I now know that there is one, at least, who will not be of that way of thinking. If ever you come down into these parts, & I hope you will do so some summer, I shall be able to show you the exact spot—a green slope in a pasture—on which I used to sit down & read your renowned articles in the S.R. In my innocence I never suspected the sex of the writer. I always thought that the essay which became most celebrated was not quite so fine & incisive as some of the others that you wrote in the series: but that's how things go in this world. I am just in the worrying stage of coming to a decision upon my leading idea of a long story planned sometime ago; & between my own conviction of what is truest to life, & what editors & critics will tolerate as being true to their conventional principles, bless them! I get an unpleasant time, till the thing is settled. I wish I could sometimes consult you!

Believe me, dear Mrs Lynn Linton,

> Yours always sincerely
> Thomas Hardy.

Text Typed transcript (from the typescript catalogue of the library of George Barr McCutcheon) Adams.

Linton: Eliza Lynn Linton (see II.73), novelist.   *kindly letter*: of 21 Dec 88 (DCM).   *little story*: TH's 'A Tragedy of Two Ambitions', *Universal Review*, December 1888; Mrs. Linton praised it highly.   *articles in the S.R.*: during the period 1866–68 Mrs. Linton wrote anonymously for the *Saturday Review* a series of controversial essays on the 'woman question'.   *most celebrated*: 'The Girl of the Period', pub. 14 Mar 1868.   *consult you!*: they seem not to have met until January 1891; see Herbert van Thal, *Eliza Lynn Linton: The Girl of the Period* (London, 1979), 183.

To THOMAS HUTCHINSON

> New Years Eve, | 1888.

I thank you for your genial verses, which I have read with much interest.

> Yours truly
> T. Hardy.

Text MS. (postcard) T. Trafton.

Hutchinson: Thomas Hutchinson, of Morpeth, Northumberland, minor poet.   *your genial verses*: presumably Hutchinson's *Ballades and Other Rhymes of a Country Bookworm* (London, 1888), a vol. dedicated to Andrew Lang.

To WALTER BESANT

> MAX GATE, | NEAR DORCHESTER. | 22. 11. 89

My dear Besant,

I have read the scheme of publication matured by your busy brain; & I will consider it carefully. It is a trades-union, indeed, or something like it. Anything more delightful than to form a ring to keep up prices cannot be presented to the mind of yr avaricious author.

If I have anything to throw into the lottery at some future time I will communicate with Watt. At present I am quite in a muddle, & hardly know how I stand committed by promises &c. And I have cut the tip of my thumb with my new pocket-knife & write with difficulty.

Yours always sincerely
Thomas Hardy.

Text   MS. Eton College.
scheme of publication: Besant had apparently outlined to TH what became shortly afterwards the Authors' Syndicate, essentially a literary agency working in co-operation with the Incorporated Society of Authors.   *Watt*: evidently Alexander Pollock Watt, the literary agent (see I.113), although it was in fact another agent, William Morris Colles (see I.241), who conducted the Authors' Syndicate.

To CHARLES ALDRICH

MAX GATE, | NEAR DORCHESTER. | Dec 31. 1889
Dear Sir,

In response to your request of last summer I send herewith 3 pages of MS. & a photograph. The story is a short one which will appear during the coming spring.

Yours faithfully
Thomas Hardy.

Charles Aldrich, Esq.

Text   MS. (with envelope) Iowa State Historical Department.
Aldrich: Charles Aldrich (1828–1908), founder and curator of the Iowa State Historical Department.   *3 pages of MS.*: these, the first three pages of a draft MS. of 'The Melancholy Hussar', still accompany this letter.   *during the coming spring*: its syndication by Tillotson in fact began in early January 1890; see Purdy, 82.

To T. M. DRON

January 24, 1890.
My Dear Sir,

I have just seen in the *Dorset County Chronicle* a brief report of your lecture, which I read with interest. I have been out of doors so little this winter, except when away from home, that I have not known anything of what has been going on around me, and the newspaper report is my only intelligence of your performance—certainly unique for this county; for, though the novels have been read from, and lectured on in other parts of England, and in the United States, they have not received that honour hereabout till now.

I was absolutely puzzled as to Higgins, the Carpenter, having quite forgotten him. Your knowledge of the novels is, therefore, closer than mine.

With best wishes, believe me,

Yours sincerely,
T. Hardy.

Text   *Dorset Year Book, 1929*, 143.
your lecture: 'The Wit and Wisdom of the Dorset Novelist', Dron's one-hour lecture to the Congregational Mutual Improvement Society, was reported in the *Dorset County Chronicle*, 23

Jan 1890; a cutting of it is pasted into TH's 'Personal' scrapbook (DCM). *Higgins, the Carpenter*: Dron was reported as saying that the description of Higgins's house in *Desperate Remedies* (Wessex edn., 350) was reminiscent of 'the power of Dickens'.

To HARPER & BROTHERS

[7 March 1890]

In answer to your request for a description of the plot of its story, I may say that it is to be a Tale of Tales—a series of linked stories—of a somewhat different kind from the mass of my work of late, excepting The First Countess of Wessex, which comes near it in character. The scenes, which are numerous, will be laid in the old mansions and castles hereabouts: the characters are to be proportionately numerous, & to be exclusively persons of title of the last century (names disguised, but incidents approximating to fact). Like the Wessex-Folk stories, these may be divided easily into parts. The whole Tale of Tales will consist of 30,000 words. There is, of course, much more incident in a scheme of tales of this kind than in a single story of the same length; but I believe the result will be commensurate with the added labour.

Text Partial transcript (by R. L. Purdy) Purdy; present whereabouts of letter unknown. *Date* As recorded on transcript.
Harper & Brothers: the New York publishing house; see I.54. *its story*: that of *A Group of Noble Dames*, subsequently pub. in *Harper's Weekly*, 29 Nov–20 Dec 1890; in the earlier part of the letter TH had accepted terms for the serial pub. of *Tess* in *Harper's Bazar* and spoken of the forthcoming serialization of *A Group of Noble Dames* in the Christmas number of the *Graphic* and simultaneously in Paris. *near it in character*: 'The First Countess of Wessex', pub. in *Harper's New Monthly Magazine*, December 1889, was included in the expanded *A Group of Noble Dames* pub. in volume form in 1891. *approximating to fact*: see Purdy, 66–7. *Wessex-Folk stories*: TH's 'Wessex Folk', already accepted for pub. in *Harper's New Monthly Magazine*, March–June 1891, was later collected, as 'A Few Crusted Characters', in *Life's Little Ironies*.

To HAVELOCK ELLIS

SAVILE CLUB, | 107, PICCADILLY. W. | July 10. 1890

My dear Sir,

I recognise your name, not only as that of the author of the review in the Westminster, but as the writer of "The New Spirit", a book which I have lately read with much interest.

Shall I write the particulars you require: or will you be in Town shortly? I am often lunching here: & if you would lunch with me, say the day after to-morrow, (Saturday), at 1.30, I should be glad to see you. Or if you prefer, can you call about 4, Monday afternoon, at where I am temporarily staying? (5 Chapel Place, Cavendish Square). I could then tell you what may be necessary for your article—though I fear I cannot tell much.

Yours very truly
Thomas Hardy.

Text   MS. Yale.
Ellis: Henry Havelock Ellis, psychologist and critic; see I.118.   *in the Westminster*: 'Thomas
Hardy's Novels', *Westminster Review*, April 1883; see I.117–18.   *lately read*: for TH's notes
(dated May 1890) on Ellis's *The New Spirit* (London, 1890), see *The Literary Notebooks of
Thomas Hardy*, ed. Lennart A. Björk (London, 1985), II.14–17.   *particulars you require*:
Ellis (9 July 90, DCM) sought details of TH's parentage and physical characteristics for an
investigation he was conducting into 'the ancestry of our chief recent poets & imaginative
writers'.   *5 Chapel Place*: the P.O. directory for 1890 shows a Miss Norman as living at this
address.   *your article*: the substance of TH's response, whether given orally or in writing,
appeared in Ellis's 'The Ancestry of Genius', *Atlantic Monthly*, March 1893, 386–7; Carl J. and
Clara Carter Weber, in *Thomas Hardy's Correspondence at Max Gate: A Descriptive Check List*
(Waterville, Maine, 1968), 46, wrongly identify as addressed to Havelock Ellis in early July 1890
the 9 June 17 draft to S. M. Ellis that appears, below, in this present sequence.

To C. W. JARVIS

Max Gate, Dorchester. | 31. 7. 90.

Dear Sir,

   I left town some days ago—& shall probably not return till Nov. or Dec. If
any idea as to placing the play should reach me I will let you know.

Yours truly
T. Hardy.

Text   MS. (correspondence card) T. Trafton.
Jarvis: Jarvis (see I.195) had collaborated with J. T. Grein in a dramatization of TH's *The
Woodlanders*; see I.195, 210–11, 212.   *placing the play*: it was never performed.

To J. J. FOSTER

MAX GATE, | DORCHESTER. | Sept 1. 1890

My dear Sir,

   You will probably have guessed that I was away from home when your letter
& Review arrived. I am much obliged for the list, which must have cost you a
good deal of labour. Of course, though so many remains have been discovered
& tabulated, they represent but a small proportion of those still underground. I
feel certain that there are barrows-full on my place here, if I only had time to
search for them.

Yours very truly
T. Hardy.

P.S. I hope you will call when you next come to Dorchester.

Text   MS. David Holmes.
Foster: Joshua James Foster, Dorchester-born antiquary and art historian; see I.160.   *Review
. . . list*: Foster had sent the August 1889 issue of the *Archaeological Review* containing his article,
'Roman Remains. No. 7.—Dorsetshire', an alphabetical listing of Roman 'finds' in the
county.   *on my place here*: TH's discoveries at Max Gate (see above, letter of 5 May 84) were
mentioned by Foster in his entry for Fordington.

To THE HON. JANE ASHLEY

[2 December 1890]

<u>Stratton Ch:</u>

Madam,

As the most influential member of the committee, and probably the most appreciative of the past history of the abovenamed church we venture to address you on certain points in the proposed restoration. These are so greatly at variance with the best archaeological opinion that we cannot but suppose they must have been adopted from a misapprehension of the true procedure in such cases. We are the more emboldened to do this in that we have reason to suppose that one of the worst features in the suggested re-erection—the insertion of an entirely new chancel arch—is not strictly in accordance with your wishes.

The present chancel arch is as you are aware, blocked up; but as far as can be judged it is an interesting specimen of 13th century work, with one, if not two, hagioscopes attached, the whole, both in details and in narrowness, being a characteristic example of the locality & of the date. The proposed arch, on the other hand, has no local quality in it: nothing which expressly appertains to Stratton, or even to Dorset: it will be a feature with no history: while the old arch & hagioscopes are consecrated by the village life of the last six hundred years. Moreover the devotional value to worshippers in the church of this venerable relic, under which so many generations of the parish have passed to the altar, is too obvious to need pointing out to one so deeply interested in & connected with the history of Stratton as yourself.

The next point of importance is the retention of the present floor level. To raise that level means to stunt the tower. The construction of an open area, with a damp course to the walls, would effectually intercept dampness.

The third point is the retention of the windows in their present positions. Irregularity is the genius of Gothic architecture, & it is an act of sacrilege to obliterate an arrangement of the old builders, until at least we know what their reasons were for adopting it.

Fourth, the new roof should be of a kind similar to the present—a form frequent in the district, or a simply constructed modern roof—either obviating the introduction of the corbels which in the plans cause a displacement of the windows.

We may add that an excellent model of the principles which should be observed in the rebuilding of Stratton Church is afforded by the church of Bere Regis near Dorchester; the restoration of which was carried out by one of the best church architects of our time—the late Edmund Street, F.S.A. In this building occurs, as at Stratton, the simple Early English chancel arch; which many persons wished to replace by a more ornate one; but the good taste of the architect prevented such a grave mistake.

The question also of raising the floor occurred at Bere: it had indeed already been raised by churchwardens of a past period. But the architect directed the earth to be cleared out, & the old level restored, though the churchyard without is five or six feet above it.

From what we have learnt of Mr Crickmays architectural practice we feel assured that, if invited by the rebuilding committee to arrange his plans with a single eye to the archaeological interest of the church, he will willingly respond. And we are convinced that he can do this without in the least degree impairing its utility as a place of worship—or sacrificing any artistic beauty.

Text MS. (pencil draft) SPAB. *Date* See I.221.
Ashley: the Hon. Mrs. Jane Frances Ashley (see I.221), lady of the manor of Stratton, just NW of Dorchester. TH wrote 29 Nov 90 (I.220–1) to Thackeray Turner, secretary of the Society for the Protection of Ancient Buildings, about the proposed 'restoration' of Stratton church, and was asked to draft a letter that could be sent to Mrs. Ashley; he sent the draft to Turner 2 Dec 90 (see I.221). An extensively revised version in a copperplate hand is also at SPAB, but whether the letter in any form was actually sent to Mrs. Ashley is not entirely clear (see I.225). The church was in fact demolished (apart from the tower), although the original chancel arch (apparently of the late twelfth century) was re-erected as part of the new chancel's N. wall; see I.233. *Street*: George Edmund Street (1824–81), architect; *D.N.B.* He directed the work at Bere Regis in 1875. *Mr Crickmays*: George Rackstrow Crickmay (1830–1907), F.R.I.B.A., the architect for the restoration; he had been TH's employer in the late 1860s (see *EL*, 83–4, etc.).

To [HENRY WILSON?]

MAX GATE, | DORCHESTER. | March 14. 1891

Dear Mr Wilson:

I am sorry to say that the Manor-house I spoke of has been sold—for, I think £1,200—As there were grounds, lodge, stabling &c., it was cheap.

I do not know of any other in the market. They do not often change hands, unless with a good deal of land attached. If I should, however, hear of another I will let you know.

I am glad you like the short stories. The one you mention is in the main true.

Yours vy faithfuly
T. Hardy.

Text MS. Clifton College.
Wilson: TH's correspondent was probably Henry Francis Wilson (1859–1937), barrister, Colonial Secretary for the Orange River Colony 1901–7, knighted 1908; he read Classics at Cambridge, won the Chancellor's Medal for English verse, and was, like TH, a member of the Savile Club. Although the location of this MS. suggests that its addressee could have been the Revd. James Maurice Wilson (1836–1931; *D.N.B.*), headmaster of Clifton College 1879–90, subsequently vicar of Rochdale and archdeacon of Manchester, no link between Wilson and TH has been discovered, nor is it clear why he should have been interested in a Dorset manor-house. *the Manor-house*: presumably Rew Manor, Winterborne St. Martin, which TH had inspected on Edmund Gosse's behalf the previous September; see I.217. *the short stories*: TH's 'For Conscience' Sake' appeared in the *Fortnightly Review*, March 1891, and a total of five 'Wessex Folk' ('A Few Crusted Characters') stories in the March and April 1891 issues of *Harper's New Monthly Magazine*.

To JAMES OSGOOD

MAX GATE, | DORCHESTER. | 27. 3. 91.

Dear Mr Osgood:

We congratulate you on your safe arrival. I expect to be in Town in a week or ten days, & will call upon you.

Yours very truly
Thomas Hardy.

Text   MS. David Holmes.
Osgood: James Ripley Osgood, London-based American publisher; see I.182.   *safe arrival*: after his transatlantic voyage.

To J. J. FOSTER

12 Mandeville Place. W. | 27. 6. 91.

Dear Mr Foster:

Your kind invitation has reached me; but I fear that owing to my having been unwell, & so got behindhand with many things, I cannot have the pleasure of accepting it till I am in town again. You will I am sure allow this to be considered as only a postponement.

I hope London has not been so trying to you as it has to us this spring & summer. If you come to Dorchester later on please do not forget to call.

Yours faithfully
T. Hardy.

Text   MS. (Athenaeum Club stationery) David Holmes.
Mandeville Place: rented by the Hardys for the 'season'; see I.234–5.   *unwell*: TH had a heavy cold at the beginning of June; see I.236–7.

To W. E. HENLEY

MAX GATE, | DORCHESTER. | 21 Oct. 1891 | 8½ p. m.

My dear Henley:

The only thing I can possibly send is a character-sketch entitled "Saturday Night in Arcady". It is nearly written, & is to form an additional chapter to a story which (exclusive of this chapter) is appearing as a serial, & will be issued complete at the end of November. So that unless you would mean to publish it before that date—at any rate before the volumes get into circulation—it will be useless to you.

I should explain that it is rather a brutal scene (not indecent)—dancing, getting drunk, & a woman's fight by moonlight. If however you telegraph that you accept the conditions I will finish it up & send it.

As to price I dont know what to say. They pay me about £6 per 1000 words for Great Britain only—£10 if they print in America also. Probably you want to print it in England only.

Now—would you not rather wait till some time (late) next year? I am pregnant of several Noble Dames (this is an unnatural reversal I know, but my constitution is getting mixed)—I mean I have thought of several more sketches of that sort, but can't touch one yet on account of an incubus of a syndicate story which weighs me down.

Believe me

Sincerely yours
Thomas Hardy.

Text   MS. Eton College.
Henley: William Ernest Henley (see I.214), poet, critic, dramatist, and editor of the *National Observer* (formerly the *Scots Observer*).   *in Arcady"*: this segment omitted from the current *Graphic* serial of *Tess of the d'Urbervilles* was accepted by Henley (as he noted on this MS.) and pub. in the *National Observer* 14 Nov 1891; see Purdy, 69.   *Noble Dames*: Henley (22 Oct 91, DCM) invited TH to send him 'the most *risquée* of the bunch', but nothing else by TH seems to have appeared in the *National Observer*.   *syndicate story*: *The Pursuit of the Well-Beloved*, which he was currently writing for Tillotson's Newspaper Fiction Bureau; see I.204, 249, etc.

To HARPER & BROTHERS

[10 December 1891]

The suggestion of Mr. Henry Harper (with whom I had the pleasure of a conversation when he was in England) that fifteen per cent. on published price of the book form of this story would be preferable to a definite sum, in our ignorance of the probable sale, I quite agreed with in accepting the proposal.

Text   Partial transcript (in Harper & Brothers Contract Book 7) Columbia Univ.   *Date*   As clerically recorded.
Henry Harper: Joseph Henry Harper, American publisher; see I.76.   *fifteen per cent.*: underlined in red ink in the transcription but not, presumably, in the original.   *this story*: *Tess of the d'Urbervilles*.

To WILLIAM WATSON

MAX GATE, | DORCHESTER. | 9 Feb. 1892

My dear Sir:

I have read your review with deep interest, which, though some of it is naturally owing to the subject, is largely caused by the knowledge of the reviewer's independent works, & therefore of how much lies behind that review. I may say without affectation that I have misgivings whether the story of Tess justifies a poet's examination of its texture with such powerful vision.

Your generous remarks make me think of the story as it originally rose in my imagination when I said to myself, I have it; which imagination the pen lamentably failed to get upon paper.

It is curious that I share your objection to what are called scientific words—more truly recent words only.—The difficulty is how to express complicated ideas, for the first time reduced to speech by these words, without them—unless by occupying three times as much space.

I am looking out for a volume of poems from you which shall be a help in these & many other matters.

Yours vy truly
Thomas Hardy.

Text MS. David Holmes.
Watson: William Watson (see I.241), poet.   *your review*: under the heading 'Literature',
Academy, 6 Feb 1892; reprinted in R. G. Cox, ed., *Thomas Hardy: The Critical Heritage*
(London, 1970), 197–202.   *scientific words*: Watson had criticised TH's occasional use of
'over-academic phraseology' and questioned whether the technical names for old ideas were
'necessarily more accurate instruments of thought'.   *complicated ideas*: TH first wrote
'complicated modern views'.   *looking out . . . from you*: Watson had apparently promised to
send a copy of his *Poems*, pub. just eight days after the date of this letter.

To OSGOOD, McILVAINE & CO.

Max Gate, Dorchester, Feb. 14/ 92.

Dear Sirs,
   With regard to your inquiry of the 10th instant concerning the "Pursuit of
the Well-Beloved" I am quite willing to arrange with Messrs Harper for their
publication of the American Edition in book form on the terms they offer, a
royalty of fifteen per cent. upon the published retail price of all copies sold;
subject to the following contingency: That the story being short & slight &
written entirely with a view to serial publication, it may be found on consideration to be inadvisable in the interest of future novels to issue this as a book at
all; hence I reserve the right to withhold it in that form either altogether, or
until the story can be re-written. . . .
   I am under the impression that I have until now omitted to acknowledge
Messrs Harper's confirmation (in their letter of the 8th Jan:) of Mr. Henry
Harper's verbal arrangement with me for the 15 per cent. royalty on "Tess" in
book form. . . .

Yours faithfully
Thomas Hardy.

Messrs. Osgood McIlvaine & Co.

Text Partial transcript (in Harper & Brothers Contract Book 6) Columbia Univ. The two
paragraphs appear on different leaves of the contract book and ellipses have been editorially
supplied to register the possibility that still other segments of the original letter were left
untranscribed.
Osgood, McIlvaine & Co.: the London publishing house (see I.219) with which TH pub. shortly
afterwards *A Group of Noble Dames*, *Tess of the d'Urbervilles*, etc.   *re-written*: the novel was
indeed extensively revised before being pub. in 1897, as *The Well-Beloved*, by Osgood, McIlvaine
in London and its American parent-company, Harper & Brothers, in New York.   *royalty on
"Tess"*: see above, letter of 10 Dec 91.

To MARY HARRISON

MAX GATE, | DORCHESTER. | Feb 26. 1892

My dear Madam:
   It gives me much pleasure to receive a letter from you, and to find I have won
such golden opinions from a writer whom I regard as a thoroughly skilled
artist.
   I have read two of your novels—"Colonel Enderby's Wife", & "Mrs
Lorimer," with the deepest interest. The former I consider one of the finest
works of fiction of late years. There is not a threadbare place anywhere in it.

You are one of the few authors of the other sex who are not afraid of logical consequences.

I hope we may some day meet. I think we narrowly missed meeting once at Eggesford.

Yours very truly
Thomas Hardy.

Text   MS. Eton College.
Harrison: Mary St. Leger Harrison (see I.264), daughter of Charles Kingsley, wife of the Revd. William Harrison, writing as a novelist under the pseudonym of 'Lucas Malet'.   *letter from you*: she wrote in praise of *Tess* 22 Feb 92 (DCM).   *Enderby's Wife"*: *Colonel Enderby's Wife: A Novel* (three vols., London, 1885).   *Lorimer,"*: *Mrs Lorimer: A Sketch in Black and White* (two vols., London, 1882); TH owned a set purchased from W. H. Smith's Subscription Library.   *some day meet*: TH called on her in early April, following her invitation of 2 Apr 92 (DCM), and found 'A striking woman: full, slightly voluptuous mouth, red lips, black hair and eyes: and most likeable'; see *The Life and Work of Thomas Hardy*, ed. Michael Millgate (London, 1984), 258.   *Eggesford*: see above, letter of 3 Jan 86.

To MARY HARRISON

MAX GATE, | DORCHESTER. | March 18. 1892

Dear Mrs Harrison:

I find myself the possessor of a novel which I am now glad I did not buy, though I have had its name on a list for a long time. You are very generous to send it, & when "Tess" comes out in one volume, which will be in the late summer, or autumn, I must ask you to let me send you a copy of her. I have read the first chapter of your book already & shall go straight on—without peeping—a trick I particularly detest. I know, of course, that the story is a tragedy.

I know what it is to write in illness. I once had to dictate a novel, or rather half of one, in a reclining position, with my feet higher than my head. But that was when I lived in London.

I have long seen what you say about a woman's disadvantages. And the worst of it is that even when, by accident, she does gain knowledge of matters usually sealed to her sex people will not believe that she knows at first hand. However, you have a counterpoise in other matters: there being many scenes in life —though not so many as in the other case—wherein the knowledge is to the woman only.

I sincerely hope you will feel vigorous again soon. Pain—that is our enemy. Believe me

Yours very truly
Thomas Hardy.

= Whenever you want to drive a bargain for a new novel I can recommend you to a man who will get you the best price possible. T.H.

Text   MS. Newberry Library.
a novel: *The Wages of Sin*, by 'Lucas Malet' (London, 1891).   *to write in illness*: Mrs. Harrison said in her letter of 16 Mar 92 (DCM) that she had been 'suffering from an old enemy—malarial fever—which has left me little peace or pleasure in life, for a long time now'.   *a novel*: *A Laodicean*; see above, letter of 14 Dec 81.   *recommend you to a man*: the literary agent A. P.

Watt (see above, letter of 22 Nov 89), who had recently arranged the publication, on both sides of the Atlantic, of TH's story 'On the Western Circuit'; see I.251. Harrison mentions Watt in her letter of 19 Sept 92 (DCM).

To WILLIAM SHARP

MAX GATE, | DORCHESTER. | 25 March 1892

Dear Mr Sharp:

I am glad to find you have reached home safely.

It happens that I am just getting ready to go to Town next week—Thursday I think—& this may perhaps modify your plans. But if you want to see this place (it is bare enough of green at present) we shall be happy to receive you Monday as you propose, to stay the night. The quickest train leaves Waterloo at 2.20 in the afternoon, reaching Dorchester 6.13. My house is half a mile into the country.

If Town however is more convenient I will let you know where I shall be—Savile Club, Piccadilly will always find me.

As your choice will a little affect my movements to-morrow will you kindly send telegram saying which suits you best?

Yours sincerely
Thomas Hardy.

I know *The Forum*: very good critical papers in it.

Text MS. NLS.
Sharp: William Sharp (see I.277) wrote under his own name and under the pseudonym of 'Fiona Macleod'. *reached home safely*: Sharp had just spent several weeks in New York. *your plans*: Sharp wished to interview TH for his article, 'Thomas Hardy and His Novels', pub. in the *Forum* (New York), July 1892. *critical papers in it*: TH himself pub. 'The Profitable Reading of Fiction' there in March 1888.

To SIR GEORGE DOUGLAS

MAX GATE, | DORCHESTER. | 13. 4. 92

My dear Douglas:

Yes—your letter *did* reach me duly; there lies the guilt of your unhappy friend. As I was just starting for London I resolved to delay my answer till I got there, not quite thinking that I should be able to say Yes to your proposal, but having a glimmer of expectation that something might occur to modify the simple "can't," which I should have sent from here. I was intending to go on as far as Oxford, & I was not absolutely sure what I might do next. However last evening I was obliged to return here rather suddenly, giving up Oxford: so that really I kept back my answer for nothing, & much regret that I have to forego the pleasure of stepping northward.

The few days that I spent in town were pleasant enough. I met among many other people "Lucas Malet" Frederic Harrison, Ellen Terry, Lord Randolph, Miss Norris (ballet dancer), Arthur Balfour, &c. &c. For the due improvement of the mind I went with Mr Justice Jeune to hear Lottie Collins in "Ta-ra-ra-boom de-ay" at the Gaiety. It is really a very unusual performance, & not altogether so silly as people say. My companion was spotted by Fred Leslie (who sings a sort of patter song), & he put in (I think *extempore*) a verse about going to the Divorce Court, & the judge saying to him "You have beha-ved nob-ly!" The verse may possibly, however, have been in the original.

I hope your Burns does not drag. It struck me that you would coquet with the pen till you were caught. I should not be surprised if you were to become as perfect a hack as I am before you have done.

Our plans are uncertain just now, owing to my wife's continued weakness, but if she quite recovers her strength we shall go to Town, & hope to meet you there. With best regards to all,

Yours ever
Thomas Hardy.

Text MS. Eton College.
Oxford: TH did go there, as part of his preparation for the writing of *Jude the Obscure*, in October 1892; see Millgate, 328–9.   *return . . . suddenly*: perhaps because of ELH's illness; see final paragraph of this letter and I.263–4.   *"Lucas Malet"*: i.e., Mary Harrison.   *Frederic Harrison*: the positivist (see I.134), whom TH had known for some time.   *Ellen Terry*: the actress (see II.147); TH had met her in January 1891 (see I.227 and *EL*, 305).   *Lord Randolph*: Lord Randolph Churchill, statesman; see II.53.   *Miss Norris*: unidentified, although TH could perhaps have been confusingly introduced to Rose Norreys, currently taking the leading (but not balletic) role in Henry Arthur Jones's long-running play *The Dancing Girl*.   *Arthur Balfour*: the statesman and philosopher; see II.185.   *Justic*: TH means 'Justice'.   *Jeune*: Sir Francis Henry Jeune (see I.144), divorce court judge, husband of TH's friend Mary Jeune; it was probably at their house that TH met most of the people mentioned in this letter.   *Lottie . . . Gaiety*: Lottie Collins (1866–1910), the music-hall performer, currently making guest appearances at performances of *Cinder-ellen Up Too Late*, a three-act burlesque playing at the Gaiety Theatre, London; see *LY*, 7. TH went to see her again at the London Pavilion, in company with Edward Clodd and others, on 29 April 1892 (Clodd diary, Alan Clodd).   *Leslie*: Frederick Leslie, *né* Hobson (1855–92; *D.N.B.*), actor, specialising in light opera and burlesque; he was the co-author of *Cinder-ellen Up Too Late*.   *your Burns*: Douglas's selected edn. of *Love-Songs of Robert Burns* (London, 1892); it was not, however, the earliest of his numerous publications.

To MONTAGUE GUEST

MAX GATE, | NEAR DORCHESTER. | 15. 5. 92

My dear Sir:

It was no trouble to sign the photograph, nor will it be to do so with the books.

As to the real place-names, "Marlott" bears some resemblance to Marnhull or East Stower; and Trantridge Cross may be supposed to be where the road from Shaftesbury to Cranborne crosses the road from Blandford to Salisbury; Cranborne having suggested "Chaseborough." "Kingsbere" is, as you may know, Bere Regis.

Yours very truly
Thomas Hardy.

P.S. I am to be heard of at the Athenaeum when in Town, where I expect to be again soon. T.H.

Text MS. (with envelope) BL.
Guest: Montague John Guest (1839–1909), M.P. for Wareham 1880–5; he was a younger brother

of the first Lord Wimborne.   *real place-names*: of fictional places in *Tess of the d'Urbervilles*,
pub. November 1891.

To EDWARD CLODD

ATHENAEUM CLUB | PALL MALL S.W. | Thursday. [2 June 1892]
My dear Clodd:
I am so sorry to have delayed answering your letter till now, & am appalled at
what you think of me. I thought I might see you Saturday & talk over your kind
proposal; but I find I have to leave Town rather suddenly, & I fear I may not be
back again just yet: so that it is doubtful if I shall see quaint old Aldeburgh this
year. If I do get back again for any length of time this summer I will let you
know.

I shall think of you down there all the same, & smell in imagination the sharp
salt breeze of that coast—so different from ours southward.

Yours sincerely
Thomas Hardy.

Text MS. Cambridge Univ. Library.   *Date* From internal evidence.
see you Saturday: probably at the Savile Club, of which they were both members.   *kind*
proposal: evidently an invitation to stay with Clodd at his sea-front house at Aldeburgh, Suffolk;
see I.237.   *rather suddenly*: on account of his father's (fatal) illness; see I.271.

To AN UNIDENTIFIED CORRESPONDENT

MAX GATE, | DORCHESTER. | June 24. [1892]
Dear Sir:
I have just received your letter. I shall be here to-morrow (Saturday) aftern
about 5, as you propose.

Yours truly
Thomas Hardy.

Text MS. Morton N. Cohen.   *Date* The address on this letter is blind-stamped, indicating
a relatively early date, and 1892 was the only year prior to 1921 when 24 June fell on a Friday and
found TH at Max Gate.

To LOUISE CHANDLER MOULTON

MAX GATE, | DORCHESTER. [6 July 1892]
My dear Mrs Moulton:
We have been called away from London into the country, & I am not sure
when we shall be back again.

If I return for more than a day or two I shall aim to give myself the pleasure
of calling on you: & if my wife should go she will, I am sure, do likewise. (At
the present moment she is away.)

You will probably find that the elections have broken up the season's
routine. My absence, though it has nothing to do with them, happens to
coincide, & so I find myself in the midst of local politics.

Believe me

Yours sincerely
Thomas Hardy

Text MS. (with envelope) Essex Institute. *Date* From postmark.
Moulton: Ellen Louise Chandler Moulton (see I.194), American author. *called away*: see
above, letter of 2 June 92. *the elections*: a general election, on the issue of Gladstone's policy of
Home Rule for Ireland, was currently in progress. *local politics*: although TH had declined to
sign the nomination papers (see I.272) for his friend Robert Pearce Edgcumbe, the local
Gladstonian candidate, he was deeply interested in the closely fought battle—which had
occasioned what the *Dorset County Chronicle* called a '*melée*' in the Dorchester Corn-Exchange on
2 July and ended with Edgcumbe's defeat by 168 votes on 7 July.

To LADY DOROTHY NEVILL

Max Gate, Dorchester. [14 November 1892]

Dear Lady Dorothy Nevill:

I am sorry to say that I have not been able to get to London since I received
your kind note, & therefore have had no opportunity of bringing about the
meeting you suggested.

When I do arrive I shall not forget 45 Charles Street, & will write your name
in the book with pleasure.

Sincerely yours
T. Hardy.

Text MS. (correspondence card, with envelope, mourning stationery) W. King.
Date From postmark.
Nevill: Lady Dorothy Nevill, Dorset-born daughter of the third Earl of Orford; see
II.53. *your kind note*: Lady Dorothy's habit of not dating her letters has made it impossible to
determine whether any of the several to TH in DCM is the one in question. *Charles Street*:
Lady Dorothy's address in London. *the book*: one of her undated letters acknowledges TH's
gift of a copy of *Tess*.

To FREDERICK WHITEHEAD

70, HAMILTON TERRACE, | N.W. | 29 April, 1893

Dear Sir:

I am much obliged for the photograph. It does not, and of course could not,
do justice to the original picture, which we saw yesterday at the Private View.
It is well hung, and attracted the attention of a great many people. Both in
drawing and colour it is in my opinion a telling piece of work.

We are at home here on Monday afternoons till July (except Whitsun week),
and shall be glad to see Mr. and Mrs. Whitehead whenever they may be in
town.

Yours faithfully
T. Hardy.

Text Typed transcript (by Harold Hoffman) Miami Univ. of Ohio.
Whitehead: Frederick William Newton Whitehead, painter; see II.74. *Private View*: of the
Royal Academy Summer Exhibition. 'Tess of the D'Urbervilles' Ancestral Home' was one of three
landscapes by Whitehead in the Exhibition; for further references to Whitehead's paintings of
Dorset see below, letter of 6 Feb 94, and II.74. *Mrs. Whitehead*: Beatrice Whitehead, *née*
Case, the daughter of a Dorchester bookseller; see II.272.

To EDMUND GOSSE

70 Hamilton Terrace | N.W. | Wedny [31 May 1893]

My dear Gosse:

I have just returned from Ireland, where my wife & I have been staying for nearly a fortnight: and find your letter awaiting me.

Owing to this absence I have unfortunately an engagement at lunch-time to-morrow in the City, & cannot get to you. I should have had much pleasure in meeting Norris.

Yours sincerely
Thomas Hardy.

Text MS. (mourning stationery) Georgetown Univ. *Date* From internal evidence. *from Ireland*: see *LY*, 18–20. *Norris*: William Edward Norris, barrister and novelist; see I.271.

To LORD HOUGHTON

70 Hamilton Terrace N.W. | May 31. 1893

Dear Lord Houghton:

I have been in rapid motion almost ever since we parted, or I would have sent a line sooner to thank you for the very charming volume you have presented to me. I have read several of your renderings, and knowing the immense difficulty, if not impossibility, of conveying the aroma of verse into another tongue, am struck with your many felicitous turns of phrase—suggesting long experience in the art of translating, which I did not suspect you to possess. However you do not want criticism, I am sure; and my regret is that I have no volume of my own just ready that I can send you in return.

My wife and I have not yet lost the sense of the romantic atmosphere which surrounded us during our stay with you at the Lodge—thanks to your hospitality. Believe me

Sincerely yours
Thomas Hardy.

Text MS. (mourning stationery) Cambridge Univ. Library.
Houghton: Robert Offley Ashburton Crewe-Milnes, second Lord Houghton (see II.3), currently Lord-Lieutenant of Ireland. *since we parted*: TH and ELH had been staying in Dublin, at the Viceregal Lodge, as Lord Houghton's guests; see *LY*, 18–20. *charming volume*: evidently *Gleanings from Béranger* (privately printed, 1889), Lord Houghton's translations of the French poet Pierre Jean de Béranger (1780–1857). *romantic atmosphere*: it perhaps contributed to TH's instant attraction to Lord Houghton's sister, Mrs. Florence Henniker (see II.11), whom he met for the first time during the Dublin visit.

To FREDERICK WHITEHEAD

MAX GATE, | DORCHESTER. | Feb 6, 1894

Dear Mr. Whitehead:

I enclose herewith the quotation, which Mrs. Hardy found would exactly apply to the picture. I agree with you in thinking a quotation helps a painting.

If you should be disposed to make a small copy of this Bulbarrow scene

—size of the Woolbridge Manor House picture, or a trifle larger—I would pay for it the price you mentioned for the latter: and would use it as an illustration, with your name attached as painter, when an illustrated edition of the book is published.

Yours faithfully
T. Hardy.

Text   Typed transcript (by Harold Hoffman) Miami Univ. of Ohio.
the quotation: also transcribed by Hoffman was an accompanying passage in ELH's hand, headed 'Blackmoor Vale from Bulbarrow' and consisting of a quotation from the opening paragraph of chap. 50 of *Tess of the d'Urbervilles*.   *Manor House picture*: evidently the one TH had seen at the Royal Academy; see above, letter of 29 Apr 93.   *illustrated edition*: this idea materialized only in 1926, and in a form quite other than here envisaged; see above, letter of 4 Jan 26.

To FREDERICK WHITEHEAD

16, Pelham Crescent, | South Kensington | May 22, 1894

Dear Mr. Whitehead:

The picture has arrived, and we are much pleased with it. It will remain on view in our drawing room here till we leave London, and I hope some day to use it as an illustration to one of my novels. I enclose herewith the amount agreed on, and only wish I could make it twice as much. Believe me,

Yours truly
T. Hardy

We are usually at home at ½ past 5: if Mrs. Whitehead and yourself should find it convenient to call we shall be glad to see you.

Text   Typed transcript (by Harold Hoffman) Miami Univ. of Ohio.
The picture: see above, letter of 6 Feb 94.

To DOUGLAS SLADEN

SAVILE CLUB, | 107, PICCADILLY. W. | June 20. 1894

Dear Mr Sladen:

I had seen the kind review you wrote of my book, but I am very glad to have a copy of it. Many thanks.

Yours sincerely
T. Hardy.

Text   MS. David Holmes.
Sladen: Douglas Brooke Wheelton Sladen (see II.194), miscellaneous writer.   *my book*: presumably *Life's Little Ironies*, pub. 22 Feb 1894; no review signed by Sladen has been discovered but he had perhaps written to TH precisely in order to draw an unsigned review to his attention.

To LUCY CLIFFORD

16, PELHAM CRESCENT, | SOUTH KENSINGTON. | Thursday. [5 July 1894]

Dear Mrs Clifford:

On discovering your card in my pocket I find the date on it to be the same as I have for a previous engagement. I will come if I can, as I shd like to do, but if I cannot you will forgive me I am sure.

Yours sincerely
Thomas Hardy.

Text   MS. Mrs. A. M. Dilke.   *Date*   See below, letter of 6 July 94.
Clifford: Lucy Clifford, usually known as Mrs. W. K. Clifford, novelist; see II.109.   *come if I can*: evidently to a social occasion at 26 Colville Road, Bayswater, where Mrs. Clifford was then living.

To LUCY CLIFFORD

16, PELHAM CRESCENT, | SOUTH KENSINGTON. | Friday eveng. [6 July 1894]

Dear Mrs Clifford;

The only way out of my difficulty is to bring with me the friend with whom I have the engagement. I will endeavour to do so. Do not answer unless you object.

Ever sincerely
Thomas Hardy.

Text   MS. (with envelope) Mrs. A. M. Dilke.   *Date*   Envelope bears postmark for 7 July 94, a Saturday.
the friend: unidentified.

To CLEMENT SHORTER

MAX GATE, | DORCHESTER. | March 1. 1895

My dear Shorter:

I send you what I consider to be an artistic & tender little tale, which would suit the English Illustrated. But please read it for yourself, & let me know if you can accept it for either of your publications.

Sincerely yours
T. Hardy.

Text   MS. Case Western Reserve Univ.
Shorter: Clement King Shorter (see I.245), currently editor of the *Illustrated London News* as well as of the *English Illustrated Magazine*.   *little tale*: 'A Page from a Vicar's History', by TH's friend Florence Henniker (see above, letter of 31 May 93); it appeared in the *English Illustrated*, August 1895 (see II.71–2).

To J. J. FOSTER

MAX GATE, | DORCHESTER. | March 18. 1895

My dear Mr. Foster;

I shall have much pleasure in appearing in your projected series, if you think it worth while to put me there. Unfortunately, I have no photograph I can send: but one can easily be got from Elliott & Fry:—the best, I think, of the two or three they have taken of me is the three-quarter length showing both hands. However, you can judge best. W. & D. Downey (Ebury St.) have also some of me. But please don't use those taken by the Stereoscopic Co. as they are unlike.

We shall be soon leaving for London, but have not found a house yet.

Yours faithfully
T. Hardy

P.S. It will be necessary to ask permission of the photrs—but they never make any objection. T.H.

Text   Typed transcript (carbon) R. Greenland.
projected series: Foster had evidently asked if he might include TH in his series of essays on 'Wessex Worthies', a project which resulted in the book, *Wessex Worthies*, of 1921; see Purdy, 320–1.   *a house*: for the duration of the London 'season'; the Hardys eventually rented a flat near Victoria Station (see II.76).

To LAURENCE ALMA TADEMA

Max Gate, | Dorchester. | Jan 21. 1896.

Dear Miss Tadema:

I have read your generous estimate of *Jude* with much interest and feeling. When one gets an imaginative reader like you, his work is lighted up with an irradiation not its own: and the faults are covered.

The book has, as you may know, been misapprehended in some quarters. The difficulty attending the appearance of a story aiming at sincerity among the "novels of the season" is that the prior expectation of readers who want something comfortable, resigned and conforming, is disappointed; while it is some time before the book settles down into the hands of those for whom it was intended.

Ever sincerely yours,
Thomas Hardy.

Text   Typed transcript Bodleian Library.
estimate of Jude: apparently in a letter (no longer extant) rather than in a published review.   *misapprehended in some quarters*: for the initial reception of *Jude the Obscure*, see Millgate, 368–75.

To LAURENCE ALMA TADEMA

Max Gate, | Dorchester. | Jan 29. 1896.

Dear Miss Tadema:

Yes, I have dramatized *Tess*—less by my own wish than at the request of friends—and if you should meet a theatrical manager who wants it, please send him along. Several asked me for it; but it was not then ready.

I should, of course, be delighted to see it in Italian: indeed it would be a pleasant novelty to produce it *first* in Italian. I intend to be in London on and after Saturday next—and will try to call upon you.

Ever sincerely
Thomas Hardy.

Text   Typed transcript Bodleian Library.
dramatized Tess: although TH completed the dramatization in the spring of 1895 he had not been
able to arrange for its production on acceptable terms; see Millgate, 363–4, 375–6.   *in Italian*:
see below, letter of 30 Mar 96.

To LAURENCE ALMA TADEMA

16, Pelham Crescent, | S. Kensington. | 30. iii. 96.

Dear Miss Alma Tadema,

My best thanks for your letter. We are now living in the house in
S. Kensington that we used to have, and shall be glad to see you at any time.

Meanwhile I will think over what you say about doing "Tess" into Italian for
Madame Duse. Rather singularly, the play as I have arranged it is pre-
eminently a "starring" drama—a certain difficulty I have about it with London
actor-managers lying in the very fact that Tess herself predominates the
piece—she practically doing the whole tragedy.

Ever sincerely,
Thomas Hardy.

Text   Typed transcript Bodleian Library.
your letter: written from Brussels, 25 Mar 96 (DCM).   *used to have*: the Hardys had rented
the same house in the spring and summer of 1894; see II.55.   *for Madame Duse*: Eleonora
Duse, the Italian actress (see II.21); Miss Tadema reported that Duse had expressed great interest
in TH's play but would only be able to read it if translated into French or Italian.   *a "starring"*
drama: Miss Tadema warned that Duse was interested only in plays in which the heroine was
on the stage almost all the time, adding that if Duse produced *Tess* TH would have to submit
to 'the inevitable mangling of *every part of it* save that in which she herself is directly
concerned!'   *London actor-managers*: specifically Johnston Forbes-Robertson, with whom he
had been negotiating in July 1895; see II.82–3 and III.107.

To DÉSIRÉE LEAKE

Savile Club | Piccadilly. | 9. 5. 96

Many thanks. But I fear I shall be out of town.

T. Hardy.

Text   MS. (postcard) Ronald Moore.
Leake: Désirée Mary Leake, *née* Image (d. 1949), author of *The Ethics of Browning's Poems*, with
an introduction by the Bishop of Winchester (London, 1897).

To J. H. NAPIER

MAX GATE, | DORCHESTER. | Dec 3. 1896

Dear Sir:

I regret that distance will prevent my being present at the meeting which is
to be held on the 10th, to take steps towards the erection of a memorial to the
late R. L. Stevenson. But I need hardly say that in am in cordial agreement
with the proposal of the Committee, & feel that no more fitting place could be
found for the inception of their design that the city he knew & loved so well.

Yours faithfully
Thomas Hardy.

Text MS. (with envelope) Yale.
Napier: J. Harold Napier, Edinburgh solicitor, acting secretary and treasurer of the Stevenson Memorial Fund.   *distance*: a public meeting to launch the appeal was to be held in Edinburgh, 10 Dec 1896; in subsequent reports of the progress of the Fund TH's name was listed among those on 'the first subscription list'.   *Stevenson*: see I.146.   *that in am*: TH means 'that I am'.   *design that*: TH means 'design than'.   *the city*: it had been agreed that a monument to Stevenson (in the event, the Augustus Saint-Gaudens relief in St. Giles' Cathedral) should be erected in Edinburgh.

To A. G. GARDINER

MAX GATE, | DORCHESTER. | 12. 6. 97

Dear Sir:

I have been away from home all this month, or I should have replied to your letter sooner. My sincere thanks for your kind congratulations & good wishes: & believe me

Very truly yours
T. Hardy.

Text MS. Patrick Gardiner.
Gardiner: Alfred George Gardiner (see III.307), journalist, currently on the staff of the *Northern Daily Telegraph*.   *congratulations*: on TH's fifty-seventh birthday, 2 June 1897.

To THOMAS WENTWORTH HIGGINSON

MAX GATE, | DORCHESTER. | 29. 3. 98

Dear Mr Higginson:

I have never thanked you for the copy of your Procession of the Flowers, which my wife & I have read with much pleasure. I was not previously aware that you were such an observer of nature. Latterly, as I know from your articles in Harper's Weekly, you have turned your attention more particularly to studies in social life. As that periodical reaches us regularly, my eye has been attracted by your signature therein, since we met in such a chance way at Salisbury. In reading your paper contrasting the mental equipments of Europeans with that of Americans (I am not sure that this was precisely the subject) I ventured to think that while old countries have much to learn from the Americans, what the latter have yet to learn from old civilizations is the art of being ignorant: i.e., of boldly rejecting certain sections of knowledge, even at the risk of narrowness. However it was only a passing thought by way of corollary to your interesting article.

With kind regards I am

Yours very truly,
Thomas Hardy.

Text Typed transcript (from the typescript catalogue of the library of George Barr Mc-Cutcheon) Adams.
Higginson: Thomas Wentworth Higginson (1823–1911), American reformer, soldier, and author; for TH's encounter with him in August 1897, see note below.   *of the Flowers*: Higginson's *The Procession of the Flowers and Kindred Papers* (New York, 1897).   *Harper's Weekly . . . signature therein*: no articles signed or initialled by Higginson had appeared in recent issues of

Harper's Weekly; TH apparently means the *Atlantic Monthly* (see note below).   *at Salisbury*: in August 1897; see *LY*, 71–2, and Mary Thacher Higginson, *Thomas Wentworth Higginson: The Story of His Life* (Boston, 1914), 352–3.   *your paper . . . the subject)*: TH seems to have in mind the generalizations about Anglo-American relations at the beginning of Higginson's article, 'Literary London Twenty Years Ago', *Atlantic Monthly*, December 1897.   *equipments*: so the transcript reads.

To E. HALPÉRINE-KAMINSKY

MAX GATE, | DORCHESTER. | October 4. 1898

My dear Sir:
   I am greatly obliged to you for sending me your pamphlet on "Le Rôle de l'Art", which I am just reading with much pleasure.

Yours truly
Thomas Hardy.

Text   MS. (correspondence card, with envelope) T. Trafton.
Halpérine-Kaminsky: Ely [Ilia] Halpérine-Kaminsky (1858–1936), Russian-born French writer and translator, specializing in Russian-French and French-Russian translations.   *de l'Art"*: Halpérine-Kaminsky's *Le Rôle de l'art d'après Tolstoï* (Paris, 1898), apparently a reprinting of a journal article.

To HAMLIN GARLAND

SAVILE CLUB, | 107, PICCADILLY. W. | 26. 5. 99

Dear Mr Hamlin Garland:
   I shall have much pleasure in making your acquaintance, both on your own account & as being a friend of my valued but too seldom seen friend Mr Howells. I am in London for a short time, at 20 Wynnstay Gardens, just off the High Street, Kensington; & I am at home there any day about 5, except Sunday. But to guard against accidents please send a post-card to let me know the afternoon I may expect you.

Yours truly
Thomas Hardy.

Text   MS. Eton College.
Garland: Hamlin Garland, American novelist; see VI.205.   *Mr Howells*: William Dean Howells (see I.136), American novelist, whom TH had first met in 1883 (see above, letter of 12 June 83).

To EDWARD CLODD

[20 Wynnstay Gardens] | 29. 5. 99.

My dear Clodd:
   Certainly we will go. As I rather dreaded the pit (!) I have secured places in the Upper Circle—so that we need not dress—for Wedny the 7th. They are not very good, but I could get nothing better all through June without bothering Hare, which I preferred not to do.
   When are you coming to see us? I shall be at Stoke Poges from Sat. to Mon. next, & out Friday afternoon; but at home any other day.

I have been so ungrateful as not to thank you for the very pleasant time you gave me at Aldburgh; but I do it now, sincerely. My companions disappeared in the rush for seats at Saxmundham.

Always yours truly
Thomas Hardy.

Text MS. (Athenaeum stationery) T. W. and V. Jesty.
[20 . . . Gardens] : TH's square brackets.   *we will go* : Clodd's diary (Alan Clodd) records that on 7 June 1899 he and TH went together to a performance of Pinero's *The Gay Lord Quex* (see II.219) at the Globe Theatre and enjoyed it very much.   *Hare* : John Hare (see I.103), actor, playing the title-role in Pinero's play.   *Stoke Poges* : to visit Dorothy Allhusen and her husband; see II.222 and letter of 8 June 99.   *at Aldburgh* : correctly, Aldeburgh; see above, letter of 2 June 92.   *My companions* : they included Walter Besant and Flinders Petrie, the Egyptologist; see II.222.   *at Saxmundham* : the railway station at which TH would have changed from the Aldeburgh branch line to the main London line.

To LADY BEATRICE LISTER-KAYE

THE ATHENAEUM, | PALL MALL. S.W. | 8. 6. 99

Dear Lady Beatrice:
    If you will have the books ready I will call tomorrow or Saturday afternoon & sign them. No trouble.

Yours truly
Thomas Hardy.

Text Typed transcript (from the typescript catalogue of the library of George Barr McCutcheon) Adams.
Lister-Kaye : Lady Beatrice-Adeline Lister-Kaye (1862–1935), elder daughter of the sixth Duke of Newcastle, wife of Cecil-Edmund Lister-Kaye; her husband's elder brother was married to the sister of Consuelo, Duchess of Manchester. TH had met the Duchess, and presumably Lady Beatrice herself, at the Allhusens' on 4 June; see *LY*, 82, and letter of 29 May 99.

To CLEMENT SHORTER

MAX GATE, | DORCHESTER. | 26. 12. 99

My dear Shorter:
    "Under the G. Tree" was first published in 2 volumes, not having appeared in any periodical.
    On New Years day I am going to begin shaping the story. May you & Mrs Shorter have a happy 1900.

Yours sincerely
T.H.

P.S. I like "The Sphere".

Text MS. (correspondence card) Yale.
the story : TH's 'A Changed Man', pub. in the *Sphere* 21 and 28 Apr 1900; see II.246.   *I like "The Sphere"* : the first issue of the *Sphere*, edited by Shorter, was dated 27 Jan 1900, and it is not clear whether TH had seen an advance copy or was simply responding positively to the title—which he especially praised in an approving comment on the new magazine pub. in the *Sphere*, 3 Feb 1900.

To [MAX BEERBOHM?]

MAX GATE, | DORCHESTER. | March 3. 1900

My dear Sir:

I am much obliged for the information you send in respect of the dramatiz-ation of "Tess", & I have forwarded it to Mr Fiske, who had written to me on that very subject.

I am, my dear Sir,

Yours very truly

Thomas Hardy.

P.S. I have pleasure in reading your remarks on the Wessex Novels.

Text MS. David Holmes.
Beerbohm: Henry Maximilian (Max) Beerbohm (1872–1956), author and cartoonist, currently dramatic critic of the *Saturday Review*; *D.N.B.* *dramatization of "Tess"*: by H. A. Kennedy, recently produced at the Coronet Theatre; a letter of TH's disclaiming any participation in the adaptation appeared in *The Times* 21 Feb 1900. *Mr Fiske*: Harrison Grey Fiske (see II.110), who with his wife Minnie Maddern Fiske had been responsible for producing the Lorimer Stoddard adaptation of *Tess* in the United States. *your remarks*: if the identification of Beerbohm as the addressee of this letter is indeed correct, the reference must be to his '"Tess", the Footlights and the O.U.D.S.', *Saturday Review*, 3 Mar 1900, which comments positively on *Tess* as a novel and negatively on the Kennedy adaptation.

To THE EDITOR OF THE *BUILDER*

MAX GATE, | DORCHESTER. | 13. 1. 1902

Dear Sir:

As an old reader of the Builder I venture to send you by accompanying Parcel post a drawing & description of the Gateway of Cerne Abbey in this county, believing the relic to be but little known, & worthy of illustration in your pages. I am aware that Architecture has moved considerably onwards towards Classicism since I made a study of the art, but I believe·that genuine old English examples of mediaeval work are still interesting to the profession.

I need hardly add that the drawing & description are gratuitously offered, the spot being one in which I have long taken an interest, as you may know.

Yours truly

Thomas Hardy.

P.S. For convenience I send a reproduction instead of the original drawing, but it has been privately made, & is the only one existing. T.H.

The Ed. of *The Builder*.

Text MS. W. M. Purvis.
Editor: Henry Heathcote Statham (1839–1924), architect, editor of the *Builder* for many years. *Gateway of Cerne Abbey*: in Cerne Abbas, Dorset; the drawing was by ELH's nephew Gordon Gifford, whom TH had instructed in architecture (see II.245 and V.27), and appeared in the *Builder*, 8 Feb 1902.

To CLEMENT SHORTER

MAX GATE, | DORCHESTER. | July 4. 1902

My dear Shorter:

The answer to your question is given at length in the Bibliography by John Lane at the end of Lionel Johnson's book.

<u>Private</u>. The lines enclosed with this have been handed to me by a local wit, who thought of putting them in our paper here. But they seem good enough for London. The idea really originated with a lady we know. If you choose to print them in the Sphere or Tatler it is on condition that you don't say how you got them. Of course they are gratis.

Yours sincerely
T.H.

Please return if you don't want them.

Text   MS. Case Western Reserve Univ.
Johnson's book: Lionel Johnson's *The Art of Thomas Hardy* (London, 1894), to which its publisher, John Lane (see below, letter of 6 Aug o8), appended a list of TH's first edns. (see I.239); Shorter's letter has not survived, but TH had responded to an earlier bibliographical enquiry from him 26 Dec 99.   *Private*: the underlining, extending in the MS. down the left-hand margin of the entire paragraph, appears to be TH's.   *lines enclosed*: unidentified and perhaps unused, although they could conceivably have been the satirical verses, 'Mount Chamberlain', by 'G.E.R.', in the *Tatler* (edited by Shorter) of 6 Aug 1902, 216.   *lady we know*: it is not clear whether by 'we' TH means Shorter and himself or ELH and himself; in either case, the lady remains unidentified.

To WALTER T. SPENCER

Max Gate | 2. 10. 1902

Dear Sir:

I am much obliged to you for sending the list of Vulgates. The first one (1839, Half Calf) would I think suit, if the type be fairly clear for eyes not so strong as they were. But if this should not be the case, & you are of opinion that a better one could be got by waiting, I will wait, as the matter is not pressing. A quarto copy would not be objected to.

Yours truly
T. Hardy.

Text   MS. T. Trafton.
Spencer: Walter T. Spencer (see III.33), antiquarian bookseller.   *list of Vulgates*: for TH's 27 Sept o2 request to Spencer for a Vulgate Bible, see III.33.

To [ALBERT KINROSS?]

FROM THOS. HARDY, | MAX GATE, | DORCHESTER. | Feb 8. 1904

Dear Sir:

Please accept my best thanks for your letter, & the one enclosed from newspaper,

Yours truly
T. Hardy.

Text   MS. (correspondence card) R. Greenland.
Kinross: Albert Kinross (1870–1929), journalist and novelist; a tentative identification, based on

the appearance of the signature 'A. Kinross' and the date 'Jan 14. 04' in the copy of the first edn. of *The Dynasts*, Part First, into which this MS. has been inserted.   *from newspaper*: unidentified, but presumably a review of *The Dynasts*, Part First.

To BLANCHE CRACKANTHORPE

MAX GATE, | DORCHESTER. | 10. 4. 04

Dear Mrs Crackanthorpe:

I am so sorry to say that I am both by nature & circumstance unequal to the interesting task you propose—too far outside "the swim" to be able to do it.

Yes: I have lost my dear mother. She was essentially a literary woman —nearly blinded herself by reading—& took a keen interest in the fortunes of "The Dynasts," down to 3 or 4 weeks ago—

Ever sincerely
Thomas Hardy.

Text   MS. (mourning stationery) Univ. of Chicago.
Crackanthorpe: Blanche Alethea Crackanthorpe, literary hostess; see IV.89.   *task you propose*: unidentified, although TH did later write, at Mrs. Crackanthorpe's request, a preface to the poems of 'Laurence Hope'; see below, letter of 16 July 05.   *lost my dear mother*: on 3 Apr 1904, the occasion of TH's use of mourning stationery.

To THE EDINBURGH PHILOSOPHICAL INSTITUTION

THE ATHENAEUM, | PALL MALL. S.W. | May 18, 1904

Dear Sir:

I am honoured by your request that I should lecture at the Philosophical Institution, but have to inform you that lecturing is beyond my powers & province—otherwise the platform of your Institution would have been an attractive one.

Yours truly
T. Hardy.

Text   MS. Edinburgh City Library.
Institution: the Edinburgh Philosophical Institution, founded in 1846, was especially notable for its annual lecture series; Macaulay, Emerson, Ruskin, and Dickens spoke there, and during the 1902–3 session Sir George Douglas lectured on "Thomas Hardy". See W. Addis Miller, *The "Philosophical": A Short History of the Edinburgh Philosophical Institution* (Edinburgh, 1949).   *your request*: TH was presumably responding to an invitation (no longer extant) from either the secretary, W. Addis Miller, or the chairman of the lecture committee, John F. McLennan.

To CLEMENT SHORTER

THE ATHENAEUM, | PALL MALL. S.W. | June 12. 1904

My dear Shorter:

I am much obliged to you for sending on the titles of those books, as I have long thought that something of the sort would be useful for reference.

I am sorry that you could not call yesterday: but fortunately there will be more opportunities.

Truly yrs
T. Hardy.

Text   MS. (mourning stationery) Univ. of Kentucky.
those books: unidentified.

To WILLIAM ARCHER

MAX GATE, | DORCHESTER. | Nov. 1. 1904

My dear Archer:

I have read the Blue Book so far as is necessary for understanding the general principles of the Scheme; & I can say, as you wish, that it seems to me to be a desirable one in its main points.

On details I will express no opinion, except to remark cursorily that the bodies proposed for nominating the Board of Trustees, &c., do not seem divergent enough in character, & may produce a net result of Philistinism. Indeed, it is in this direction that the *crux* will be found to lie: Where are you to get in England people with ideas detached enough to form, or nominate, the working committee. "Quis custodiet ipsos custodes?"

But this *may* be got over; & I must say that it is most praiseworthy devotion in you to theatrical art to labour so sincerely in its cause.

To my mind a humorous feature in the movement has been the earnestness in supporting it of those living English dramatists who, by writing bad plays, are piling up vast fortunes through the absence of such a theatre. They are like smugglers who should earnestly entreat the Government to establish a more efficient system of Coastguarding. Believe me

Yours sincerely
Thomas Hardy.

P.S. I will return the book.

Text   MS. (mourning stationery) British Theatre Association.
Archer: William Archer, critic and journalist; see I.287.   *Blue Book . . . Scheme*: i.e., the detailed proposal for the establishment of a national theatre, written by Archer and Harley Granville Barker (see above, letter of 4 June 26), privately printed and circulated in 1904, and pub., as *A National Theatre: Scheme & Estimates*, in 1907; in his 1907 preface Barker referred to the vol. as 'this unofficial blue-book' (vii).   *bodies . . . Trustees, &c.*: it was proposed that two of the fifteen members of the theatre's governing Board of Trustees should be nominated by the London County Council and one each by the Royal Academy and the universities of Oxford, Cambridge, and London.   *the working committee*: the Board of Trustees, however, was to have no direct involvement in the management of the theatre.   *"Quis . . . custodes?"*: 'Who is to guard the guards themselves?'; from Juvenal, *Satires*, vi.347.   *living English dramatists*: those endorsing the scheme included J. M. Barrie (see I.200), Henry Arthur Jones (see above, letter of 26 Mar 26), and Arthur Wing Pinero (see I.101).

To CLEMENT SHORTER

FROM THOS. HARDY, | MAX GATE, | DORCHESTER. [Mid-November 1904]

My dear Shorter:

My best thanks for the magazine containing the article, which I should not have seen if you had not kindly sent it.

What you say & show about Milton & Cripplegate in the *Sphere* prompts me to send the enclosed.

Yrs
T.H.

Text MS. (correspondence card) Berg. *Date* From internal evidence.
the article: unidentified. *in the* Sphere: evidently the photograph and brief account in the *Sphere*, 12 Nov 1904, of the recent unveiling of a statue of Milton at St. Giles Cripplegate, where he is buried. *the enclosed*: unidentified.

To THE REVD. S. E. V. FILLEUL

MAX GATE, | DORCHESTER. | 25: 11: '04

Dear Mr Filleul:

I have been searching everywhere for a print of myself, but cannot lay my hands on one as yet: I know I have some lying about, & as soon as I light upon either I will send it on.

As to a *good* etching: one has been done, & published as a frontispiece to Lionel Johnsons "Art of Thomas Hardy" (John Lane). I am sorry that I do not possess it detached; but the book is not dear: & you might find it at a second hand booksellers at a nominal price. Why I recommend this is that, whatever the demerits of its subject, it has a value by reason of the repute of the etcher, (Strang), a well-known artist. Lane, the publisher, might be able to let you have one loose—his address is The Bodley Head, Vigo St. Regent St. I will autograph it with pleasure if you meet with it.

It is interesting to hear about the Upwey "dungeon". I am thinking of a press-gang scene for "The Dynasts"—(I had one in the "Trumpet Major" as you may know).

Yours very truly
T. Hardy.

P.S. I do not know if a print of my mother's house, where I was born, would be of service. There is one in "The Gentlewoman" for April 16. 1904., though the letterpress accompanying it is inaccurate. A good (the best) engraving of my late mother's portrait appears in "The Sphere", April 23. 1904. T.H.

Text MS. (mourning stationery) H. G. Wood Homer.
Filleul: the Revd. Samuel Edward Valpy Filleul (see III.35), rector of All Saints' Church, Dorchester. *Lionel . . . Lane)*: see above, letter of 4 July 02. *(Strang)*: William Strang; see I.284. *Lane, the publisher*: see below, letter of 6 Aug 08. *Upwey "dungeon"*: evidently a hiding-place once used by men threatened with forced enlistment in the Royal Navy; Upwey village is near Weymouth. *for "The Dynasts"*: TH did not in fact do so, although there is a (humorous) reference to a press-gang in *The Dynasts*, Part First, Act V, Scene 1. *in the "Trumpet Major"*: in chap. 31. *inaccurate*: it stated that the Bockhampton cottage had passed out of the hands of the Hardy family 'some years back', but TH's brother and two sisters were in fact still living there. *mother's portrait*: by her daughter Mary; see III.118–19.

To J. M. BULLOCH

Max Gate | 19: 3: 05

Dear Mr Bulloch:

I have accepted Mr Murray's invitation to travel by the sleeping-train. But surely I ought to pay the fare, as I have nothing to do with the Sculpture Gallery?

If you are going by it also, we could meet, either at Euston, or anywhere earlier if advisable.

I have been wanting to go north for some time, & feel that I may as well do so on this occasion.

Yours very truly
T. Hardy.

Text MS. (mourning stationery) Aberdeen Art Gallery.
Bulloch: John Malcolm Bulloch (see III.160), journalist, author of a history of the University of Aberdeen.   *Mr Murray's . . . Gallery*: the special honorary degree ceremony at the Univ. of Aberdeen was being held in conjunction with the opening of a new sculpture section at the Aberdeen Art Gallery, and James Murray (see III.163), chairman of the Gallery Committee, had arranged for a special sleeping-car train to transport the degree recipients and other distinguished visitors from London to Aberdeen and back again.

To FREDERICK GREENWOOD

THE ATHENAEUM, | PALL MALL. S.W. | May 1st. 1905.

Dear Mr. Greenwood,

I am so glad to get your letter, as it shows, at any rate, that you do not lay upon my head any blame for the comments of the newspapers or my letter to the Spectator of last Saturday—most unwillingly written, but as I thought, almost compulsorily. I wrote solely to contradict the odious suggestion in Mr. Downey's book—that after knowing the price Mr. George Smith was willing to pay for "Far from the Maddening Crowd" I had told it to Tinsley with a view to getting him to offer more—a thing I have never done in my life, the mention of one publisher's figures to another seeming unfair. In contradicting this I was, of course, obliged to adhere to the strict letter of events, and therefore could only say that Mr. Stephen wrote to me as editor, and made all the arrangements with me, except the mere price. I now know by hearsay, and have no doubt of the truth of it (though I did not know it for many years) that Mr. Stephen's attention was drawn to Under the Greenwood Tree by yourself, either directly or through Mr. George Smith, that he thereupon read the story, and on the strength of it wrote to me for one for the Cornhill. This however, as you see, was irrelevant to my subject, but the papers have dragged it in.

It would be a satisfaction if you were to write to some paper and show the silly commentators that there is nothing in my letter which contradicts the general belief, that you were the instigator of the communications made to me by Stephen, and the publishers.

I was so sorry not to be at that dinner—but I was in Aberdeen at the time. Believe me,

Sincerely yours,
Thomas Hardy.

Text   Typed transcript Leeds.
Greenwood: Frederick Greenwood (see III.165), journalist and editor.   *or my letter*: so the transcript reads, although TH presumably wrote, 'on my letter'.   *Spectator . . . Saturday*: *Spectator*, 29 Apr 1905; as TH goes on to explain, in challenging statements about *Far from the Madding Crowd* in Edmund Downey's *Twenty Years Ago* (London, 1905) it had not occurred to him to mention the part Greenwood had played in drawing his work to the attention of Leslie Stephen (see I.27), who then, as editor, solicited the novel for the *Cornhill Magazine*. See letter of 1 May 05 to Shorter.   *Smith*: George Smith (see I.35), head of the publishing firm of Smith, Elder.   *Maddening*: evidently a transcription error for 'Madding', repeated in letter of this date to Shorter.   *Tinsley*: William Tinsley (see I.9), TH's first publisher.   *that dinner*: held on 8 Apr 1905 to mark Greenwood's seventy-fifth birthday.

To CLEMENT SHORTER

PRIVATE.   1, Hyde Park Mansions. | 1. 5. 1905.

My dear Shorter,

I have received a letter from Greenwood, from which I fancy that he thinks I ought to have mentioned his name in relation to "Far from the Maddening Crowd", in the letter to the Spectator of last Saturday that was dragged from me by the odious slang-gossip in that book of Downey's—which if not more accurate in its account of other writers than in its account of me, is a highly imaginative work. The Daily News has made quite an oedipic riddle of the case; and it would be, I am sure, a satisfaction to Greenwood if you were to put a paragraph in your Literary Letter embodying what I have jotted down and enclose herewith (I get the facts from Greenwood's letter). Daily News paragraph is also enclosed. On second thoughts I think you should see G's letter, which please return.

Yours sincerely,
T. Hardy.

Text   Typed transcript Leeds.
from Greenwood: of 29 Apr 05 (typed transcript, Leeds).   *Maddening*: evidently a transcription error for 'Madding', repeated in letter of this date to Greenwood.   *Daily News*: a leading article in the *Daily News* of 29 Apr 1905 had asked how TH's and Greenwood's stories were to be reconciled.   *oedipic*: this form—assuming it to have been correctly transcribed—is not recorded in the *O.E.D.*   *your Literary Letter*: Shorter's regular literary page in each issue of the *Sphere*.   *enclose herewith*: accompanying this letter is a similarly typed transcript of what appears to be TH's draft of a possible paragraph for insertion in the *Sphere*; Shorter's account of the matter in his 13 May 1905 'Literary Letter' drew upon this but also upon other sources, including Greenwood's letter to him of 22 Apr 05 (typed transcript, Leeds).

To RAY ROCKMAN

1 Hyde Park Mansions | W. | 11: 5: '05

Dear Miss Rockman:

Why should you take this trouble. However, I will with pleasure come to your hotel at 6.30 Friday, when you can tell me what you have done about the theatre. As you are in the middle of your work I can easily go on to my club & meet you at the theatre afterwards. But that we can settle when I arrive.

You will find my wife, & probably myself, at home here any Saturday after 5—She will be glad to see you again.

Yours sincerely
T. Hardy.

Text MS. T. Trafton.
Rockman: Ray Rockman, American actress; she performed with Henry Irving, Sarah Bernhardt, etc., in New York, London, and Paris.   *this trouble*: it is not clear that anything more substantial was in question than securing seats for a particular theatrical performance.   *your work*: she was apparently involved in the season of French plays presented by Sarah Bernhardt (see II.291) at the Coronet Theatre, London, beginning 19 June 1905.   *see you again*: Miss Rockman visited Max Gate with the Whitefriars Club in 1901 (see above, letter of early July 01), and ELH had perhaps met her then.

To WILLIAM HEINEMANN

MAX GATE, | DORCHESTER. | 16: 7: 1905

Dear Mr Heinemann:
Will you kindly return to me the MS. of the Preface to Laurence Hope's last poems (which I was particularly pressed to write) & let me know as a mere matter of civility, why you did not print it?—seeing that, though worthless in itself, it would have helped the sale, if the prices paid me for a few lines of fugitive writing be any criterion, & was gratuitously contributed.

Yours truly
Thomas Hardy.

To avoid misapprehension I hereby withdraw all right to its publication, in another impression of the poems or elsewhere. T.H.

Text MS. Eton College.
Heinemann: William Heinemann, publisher; see above, letter of late July 26.   *Hope's last poems*: Laurence Hope, *Indian Love*, a vol. of poems pub. by Heinemann (London, 1905). For TH's admiration for Laurence Hope (i.e., Violet Nicolson) and his reaction to her suicide in 1904, see III.142–4 and Purdy, 309; the typescript of the unused preface, written at the urging of Blanche Crackanthorpe (see above, letter of 10 Apr 04), is in DCM.   *not print it?*: Heinemann's reply seems not to have survived.

To KATHARINE HARDY

[4 August 1905]

Programme for Friday, Sept 1.
(as at present understood)

1. Earliest party—(a supplementary one) about 160, conducted by Mr H. Pouncy of the Dorset Chronicle.
—From Bournemouth to Dorchester by special train
Lunch with Mayor & Corpn of Dorchr 12.30
Visit places of interest in D.
Call at Max Gate 1.45. Leave M.G. at 2 in carriages, through Lower Bockn, up B. Lane, to Top o' Hill: alight: walk up the village to heath —re-enter carriages Top o' Hill—drive on down Cuckoo Lane, P. Town, Bere, Wool.
Special train thence to Bournemouth.

2. Second or chief party—about 100.
   Bournemouth to Weymouth by special train
   Lunch with Mayor & Corpn of Weymouth.
   Train to Dorchester.
   Visit places in D.
   Reach Max Gate about 3. Tea.
   Leave M.G. at 3.45 on same route as previous party, but an hour later.

Text MS. (with envelope) Eton College.   *Date* From postmark.
Hardy: Katharine Hardy (see II.124), TH's younger sister; she was at this date still living in the cottage at Higher Bockhampton.   *Programme*: of the visit to Dorset by the members of the Institute of Journalists; see *LY*, 112–13.   *Pouncy*: Harry Pouncy (see III.247), journalist and local historian, on the staff of the *Dorset County Chronicle*.   *B. Lane*: Bockhampton Lane.   *the village*: Higher Bockhampton.   *P. Town*: Puddletown.

To EDWARD CLODD

Max Gate: | 14: 8: 1905

My dear Clodd:
   I think I can give myself the pleasure of accepting your kind invitation for Sept 16–18—, as I am intending to see Norwich Cathedral this autumn—& possibly Ely—so that I can work round to you by the date mentioned.
   But I hope there will be no demand upon me to appear in the Celebration —as I am not up to such things, & I shall, moreover, have been at work here on The Dynasts when I arrive, which will leave me in a complete state of unpreparedness. But your words are assuring on that point.
   I assume that you have been maddened by the London heats of the last month, with lucid intervals down at Aldeburgh.

Yours sincerely
T. Hardy.

P.S. If you should find yourself pressed for room I can, of course, get a chamber near. T.H.

Text MS. Eton College.
invitation: to Aldeburgh; see above, letter of 2 June 92.   *Norwich Cathedral*: TH did not in fact get there during the Aldeburgh trip; see III.180.   *the Celebration*: of the sesquicentenary of the birth at Aldeburgh of George Crabbe; see *LY*, 113–14.   *on The Dynasts*: TH finished the MS. of *The Dynasts*, Part Second, on 28 Sept 1905, shortly after his return from Aldeburgh.

To BLACKIE & SON

FROM THOS. HARDY, | MAX GATE, | DORCHESTER. | April 7. 1906

Dear Sirs:
   You have my full permission to print "The Going of the Battery" in the series you are planning. Please use as copy the poem as it appears in the Volume entitled "Poems of the Past & the Present," as the newspaper form was not quite correct.

Yours truly
T. Hardy.

Messrs Blackie & Son.

Text Facsimile (of correspondence card) Sotheby Catalogue, 4 June 1980, lot 1137.
Blackie & Son: the publishers; TH's 'The Going of the Battery' appeared in *Blackie's Model Readers, Book V* (London, [1906]).   *not quite correct*: TH had in fact omitted two stanzas from the original *Graphic* printing of the poem, 11 Nov 1899; see II.238.

To KATHARINE HARDY

[19 May 1906]

Woman's suffrage meeting—One woman rapped out: "We shall have more difficulty in getting the vote than you men had: we have committed the crime of being born woman". (Cheers from the men.)

Text MS. (picture postcard of Corfe Castle) David Holmes.   *Date* From postmark.
suffrage meeting: TH seems to have been present at the demonstration held in London the morning of 19 May by the Women's Social and Political Union, or at the afternoon meeting in Exeter Hall (followed by a mass meeting in Trafalgar Square) organized by the National Union of Women's Suffrage Societies.

To SIR HAROLD BOULTON

FROM THOS. HARDY, | MAX GATE, | DORCHESTER. | 20: 6: 06

Dear Sir:

I return the paper signed; & shall have pleasure in allowing my name to appear in the press as one of the signatories.

T.H.

Text MS. (correspondence card) Keats-Shelley Memorial Association.
Boulton: Sir Harold Edwin Boulton, Bt. (1859–1935), writer of songs, Hon. Secretary of the Keats–Shelley Memorial Association 1906–26.   *one of the signatories*: of a letter in *The Times*, 3 July 1906, appealing for funds for the purchase and maintenance of the house on the Piazza di Spagna, Rome, in which John Keats died.

To H. BERKELEY SCORE

FROM THOS. HARDY, | MAX GATE, | DORCHESTER. | Dec 7. 1906

Many thanks for "Poems Chiefly Lyrical", which I shall read with much pleasure.

Text MS. (postcard) T. Trafton.
Score: H. Berkeley Score, Dorset-born schoolteacher, author of school textbooks, and founder in 1892 of the short-lived Brotherhood of Poets and Verse Writers; TH wrote to him at Lathom Park School, Ormskirk, Lancashire.   *Chiefly Lyrical*": untraced and—as appears from a biographical note in Score, ed., *Dorset Poetry and Poets* (London, [1919]), 110—probably unpublished.

To VIOLET HUNT

FROM THOS. HARDY, | MAX GATE, | DORCHESTER. | 13: 1: '07

My dear Miss Hunt:

I feel almost sure that I have never said a word about receiving your kind gift of the Commonplace Woman—or of reading it. (I am reminded of this by seeing the title in a summary of the year's work in letters.). I read it shortly after it came, & I saw that your aim was to give a slice of real life, so to speak. But you seemed hampered by something—was it periodical publication?—& I confess that the story did not hold me like the first (much less probable) one. This, however, is no safe sign: the best work often requires longer time for digesting. Many thanks. With affectte regards

Yrs,
T.H.

Text   MS. (correspondence card, with envelope) Univ. of Kentucky.
Hunt: Isobel Violet Hunt (see II.109), novelist.   *the Commonplace Woman*: TH's slip (not necessarily inadvertent) for Hunt's novel *The Workaday Woman* (London, 1906).   *periodical publication?*: no serialization of the novel has been located.   *the first . . . one*: a copy of Hunt's previous novel, *Sooner or Later: The Story of an Ingenious Ingénue* (London, 1904) was in TH's library; though not her first novel, it was perhaps the first she sent TH.

To JOHN PURVES

(Max Gate: Dorchester.) | 20: 5: 1907

Dear Sir:

In reply to your request I have pleasure in giving you leave to print "A Christmas Ghost Story", "The Dead Drummer", & any other war poem of mine in your Anthology of South African Verse.

Yours very truly
Thomas Hardy.

John Purves, Esq.

Text   MS. (Athenaeum stationery) NLS.
Purves: John Purves (1877–1961), currently professor of English language and literature at Univ. of Pretoria, later reader in Italian at Edinburgh Univ.   *your Anthology*: *The South African Book of English Verse*, ed. by Purves (London, 1915); see V.2.

To [W. L. COURTNEY?]

THE ATHENAEUM, | PALL MALL. S.W. | 24: 5: 1907

My dear Sir:

I am flattered by your request that I should send another short poem. When I may be able to do is, however, doubtful, for I am up here till the latter part of July, & devoid of all writing power; while such short poems as I have in stock are locked up in a drawer in my house in Dorset. I will, nevertheless, not forget your letter.

Yours very truly
Thomas Hardy.

Text   MS. Lord Stockton.
Courtney: William Leonard Courtney (see V.109), editor of the *Fortnightly Review*; he had pub. TH's 'New Year's Eve' in his January 1907 issue and in October 1907 he rejected 'A Sunday Morning Tragedy' on the grounds that the *Fortnightly* was 'read in families' (see III.278).

To GEORGE VIERECK

THE ATHENAEUM, | PALL MALL. S.W. London. | 24: 5: 1907

Dear Sir:

I have received your letter & the kind present of your book of verse that accompanies it. I cannot do justice to reading it while I am here in town, but when I get back to the Country I shall be able to do so. The one or two poems that I have already looked at impress me much.

Yours truly
Thomas Hardy.

Text   MS. Univ. of Kentucky.
Viereck: George Sylvester Viereck (1884–1962), American author and editor.   *book of verse*: Viereck's *Nineveh and Other Poems* (London, 1907).

To ROBERT GILCHRIST

MAX GATE, | DORCHESTER. | 24: 10: 1907

Dear Mr Gilchrist:

I am sorry to tell you that I have been unsuccessful in my search for some MS. that would suit the new year's number of Alma Mater. Also that I am unable to write any special article for it, as I am just getting ready the Third Part of the Dynasts, & it leaves me no time, or rather no energy, for other writing. Believe me, with regrets,

Yours very truly
Thomas Hardy.

Text   MS. Aberdeen Univ.
Gilchrist: Robert Niven Gilchrist (1888–1973), currently a student at Aberdeen University, subsequently a university professor and senior civil servant in India.   *Alma Mater*: the university magazine, of which Gilchrist was the current editor; his request for a contribution was presumably prompted by TH's having received an honorary degree from Aberdeen in 1905 (see III.159ff. and above, letter of 5 Mar 05).   *getting ready* . . . *Dynasts*: TH had sent off the completed MS. of *The Dynasts*, Part Third (see III.277), but not corrected the proofs.

To JAMES MILNE

FROM THOS. HARDY, | MAX GATE, | DORCHESTER. | 15: 1: 08

Dear Mr Milne:

As you are so kind as to ask me, I send up the two or three details enclosed herewith, which I imagine cannot by any stretch of imagination be called the puff preliminary—a thing I should deprecate as you know.

Yours truly
T.H

Text   MS. (correspondence card) Eton College.
Milne: James Milne, journalist; see III.32.   *two or three details*: still accompanying this card on a separate sheet of paper is TH's pencilled MS. of a two-paragraph factual description of *The Dynasts*, Part Third (pub. 11 Feb 1908), which Milne included without attribution in the February 1908 number of the *Book Monthly*, of which he was editor.   *puff preliminary*: from Sheridan's *The Critic*, I. ii.

To ALFRED SWAFFIELD

Max Gate | Dorchester | 19: 2: 1908

Dear Sir:

I remember Mr Pretor's speaking to me about the Thackeray autograph letter; & it will give me pleasure to receive it here & keep it as a memento of him.

It has been a matter of much regret to me that I did not see him again, after the visit I paid him which turned out to be the last. My arrangement with him was that he should let me know how he was progressing, & that if he could not write himself he would get some one else to do so. The next thing I heard was of his death, & I suppose therefore that after I was there the acute st[age] came on rather rapidly.

Yours very truly
T. Hardy.

A. Swaffield Esq.

Text   Photocopy Dorset County Library.
Swaffield: Alfred Owen Swaffield (d. 1937, aged 85), of Wyke Regis, Dorset; he was a Senior Optime in the Cambridge mathematical tripos of 1875 and seems to have led thereafter a retired life devoted largely to yachting, reading, and higher mathematics.   *Pretor's*: Alfred Pretor (see III.45), classical scholar and author; he had recently died at Wyke Regis.   *Thackeray autograph letter*: a letter by the novelist William Makepeace Thackeray (see I.5) appears as lot 273 in the catalogue of the Hodgson sale of TH's library, 26 May 1938; it is not dated there but simply described as referring to a speech Thackeray had given at Harrow School.   *acute st[age]*: end of word evidently torn away in the untraced original.

To FREDERICK MACMILLAN

MAX GATE, | DORCHESTER. | April 26: 1908

Dear Mr Macmillan:

I return herewith the proof of the prospectus which I am glad to hear you are about to issue. It is ingeniously drawn up, & the selections from press-notices seem judiciously chosen.

As you are really an experienced critic (which some who print their criticisms are far from being) your personal opinion after reading the book through is highly assuring. I find, as you do, that if people once begin the drama they do not put it down, & they say at the end that if they had known it was a book which carried them on like a novel they would have read it sooner. The difficulty is to make them begin. I suppose it would not do to insert at the end of the quoted notices:

<u>Uncritical Public</u>.—"It carries you on like an exciting novel," though it has been said many times. (If you should think it worth doing, room could be made for it by omitting the last extract but one, from the Standard)

However please do as you think best.

I hope the air of the north is not too wintry for you, & am

Sincerely yours
Thomas Hardy.

Text MS. Eton College.
prospectus: an eight-page Macmillan & Co. advertising leaflet containing extracts from TH's
Preface to *The Dynasts*, Part First, quotations from the reviews of Parts First and Second (headed
'The Questioning Stage'), and further quotations from the early reviews of Part Third (headed
'The Verdict on Completion').   *Uncritical*: TH first wrote 'General'.   *an exciting novel,"*:
the prospectus does in fact carry in bold-faced type at the foot of its final page the statement, 'Many
readers who have begun the drama with some hesitation have afterwards assured the author that
they found it as exciting as a novel.'   *from the Standard)*: it was not in fact omitted, and reads,
'*The Dynasts* can scarcely be regarded as a great poem if we judge it by the exacting canons of art; it
is rather a great picture, alive with life and colour.'   *of the north*: apparently a humorous
allusion to the fact that the current unseasonable spell of cold winds and snowfalls had not spared
London and the south of England.

To WILLIAM WATKINS

MAX GATE, | DORCHESTER. | 14: 5: 1908

Dear Mr Watkins;

My thanks for your letter. I am glad that, as I hinted in my last note might be
advisable, the reading of my paper was put off. It is better suited to a meeting
than a dinner; moreover, in spite of the compliment you paid it (as I gather
from the D.C.C.) it was really written at a scrambling pace. I should like you to
let have it back before you typewrite it, to add & modify a few remarks. There
will be plenty of time for me to do this before the autumn.

Yours truly
T. Hardy.

Text MS. Adams.
Watkins: William Watkins (see III.129), secretary of the Society of Dorset Men in London.
your letter: apparently, though not certainly, that of 9 May 08 (DCM).   *paper was put off*:
TH's presidential address had not been read out at the Society's annual dinner, 11 May 1908; see
III.312.   *from the D.C.C.*: in the *Dorset County Chronicle*, 14 May 1908, Watkins was reported
as having referred to the address as 'a marvellous piece of writing'.   *let have*: TH, turning over
the page, omitted 'me' after 'let'.   *before the autumn*: when the Society's annual meeting would
be held; but see III.312.

To H. H. BRINDLEY

MAX GATE, | DORCHESTER. | 26: 7: 1908

Dear Mr Brindley:

I am delighted to have the reproduction of the Pickersgill sketch of
Wordsworth, & must thank you for sending it. It seems to me to convey an
expression that the finished picture lacks—the best expression of the poet's
face with which I am acquainted, being free from that starched & austere cast
which some of the portraits show.

With regard to the gutters & pipes of St John's that we looked at there can be
little doubt that the heads are original: possibly some of the old down-pipes
may have been renewed where worn out.

Wordsworth's shade must feel it as a satire that a side of his room should have
been removed to command a view of the cooking below: perhaps the cooks hear
hollow sighs of "O plain living & high thinking!" from above.

Yours sincerely
Thomas Hardy.

Text   MS. Eton College.
Brindley: Harold Hulme Brindley (1865–1944), zoologist and antiquarian, fellow of St. John's
College, Cambridge.   *Pickersgill sketch*: a red and black chalk drawing of William Wordsworth
by Henry William Pickersgill (1782–1875; *D.N.B.*), presented to St. John's in 1897; it is a study
for the famous Pickersgill portrait of Wordsworth, also belonging to the college.   *his room . . .*
cooking below: Wordsworth, as a sizar of St. John's, was given an undesirable room right over the
college kitchen; the floor was removed in 1893 to allow the height of the kitchen to be raised,
although a 'Wordsworth Room' with a modern floor has now been recreated.   *"O plain . . .*
thinking!": an allusion to the line 'Plain living and high thinking are no more' from Wordsworth's
sonnet, 'O friend! I know not which way I must look'.

To H. GREENHOUGH SMITH

MAX GATE, | DORCHESTER. | 31: 7: 1908.

Dear Sir:

The little tale I enclose herewith has been sent to me by a modest young
writer. As you will see, it is somewhat lurid & sensational, but not too much so
for the supposed date, & to my mind it is well told & striking. It has just
occurred to me that it would best suit the Strand Magazine & I therefore send it
on.

If you accept it will you kindly communicate with the writer, whose address
is given on the first page. If you do not, please return it to me.

Yours vy trly
Thomas Hardy.

Text   MS. Univ. of Kentucky.
Smith: Herbert Greenhough Smith (d. 1935), author and editor; although the *Strand Magazine*
carried the name of George Newnes (see I.242) on its cover, the editorial duties were in fact
performed by Smith 1891–1930.   *modest young writer*: Florence Dugdale (see above, letter of
4 Jan 26), later TH's second wife; the story, rejected by Smith, was resubmitted by TH to other
editors (see III.329) and is almost certainly to be identified with 'The Scholar's Wife', *Pall Mall*
Magazine, January 1909.   *the supposed date*: 'The Scholar's Wife' is set in sixteenth-century
Italy.

To JOHN LANE

MAX GATE, | DORCHESTER. | 6: 8: 1908

Dear Mr Lane:

I have received the picture of Poole harbour, & sincerely thank you for it, &
for the handsome frame it has been placed in: my slight assistance in choosing
the paintings was not worth so much.

I have been no long time in London this year, as you probably guess. Mr
Coutts said he thought of coming here this summer, but I hear nothing of him.

Vy truly yours
Thomas Hardy.

Text   MS. Univ. of Kentucky.
Lane: John Lane (see I.239), publisher.   *of Poole harbour*: the 16 Feb 1938 sale of Max Gate
effects included a painting of Poole Harbour, Dorset, attributed to 'Bond', perhaps to be identified
with William Joseph J. C. Bond (1833–1926), landscape and marine painter; the Harbour was
also a favourite subject of Frederick Whitehead's (see above, letter of 29 Apr 93).   *choosing the*
paintings: if for a book published by Lane, it has not been identified.   *Mr Coutts*: Francis
Burdett Thomas Money-Coutts (see III.65), poet; Lane was his publisher.

To FORD MADOX HUEFFER

Max Gate | 7: 11: 1908

Dear Mr Hueffer:

Your sub-editor's inquiry, by whom "A Sunday Morning Tragedy" has been copyrighted in America, reminds me that I have not copyrighted it at all,—the only copy of the ballad that has left my hands being the one sent to you. As I have in the past copyrighted many poems there by simultaneous publication I fancy the pirates may imagine this to be copyrighted also, & leave it alone. I will put up with losing what I might get by printing it there.

If, however, you think differently, & are printing other parts of the Review in America, will you do the same with my poem, copyrighting it in my name? It would be an easier plan than for me to do it independently—if, indeed, there is time now.

Yours vy truly
T. Hardy

Text MS. (with envelope) Yale.
Hueffer: Ford Madox Hueffer (see III.327), later Ford Madox Ford, novelist and critic; TH had sent him 'A Sunday Morning Tragedy' for pub. in the first issue of the *English Review* (see III.331). *sub-editor's*: Douglas Goldring (1887–1960), miscellaneous writer; see his *South Lodge: Reminiscences of Violet Hunt, Ford Madox Ford and the English Review Circle* (London, 1943), 15–16. *the one sent to you*: this MS. is now in the Huntington Library.

To WALTER BAWLER

FROM THOS. HARDY, | MAX GATE, | DORCHESTER. |
Friday. [20 November 1908]

I must congratulate you on your impersonation of the Miller, which in the opinion of good judges was very real & lifelike; also very amusing.

T.H.

Text MS. (correspondence card, with envelope) R. Greenland. *Date* From postmark.
Bawler: Walter Raymond Bawler (d. 1940, aged 78), Dorchester solicitor and amateur actor; he played Miller Loveday in the dramatization of *The Trumpet-Major* performed in Dorchester in November 1908. *good judges*: TH had not seen the performance himself; see III.357.

To H. O. LOCK

MAX GATE, | DORCHESTER. | Thursday. [11 March 1909?]

Dear Mr Lock:

I am sorry to say that this keen north-east wind has given me what I hope is not influenza, though enough to make it advisable that I should not come out to-night. I was hoping, too, to go to London, but think waiting the better policy. Thank you very sincerely for your kind invitation.

Truly yours
T. Hardy.

Text MS. Mrs. H. O. Lock. *Date* See below.
come out to-night: when Lock first invited him to meet Mr Ashe King, a visiting lecturer, on 11

March, TH replied that he expected to be out of town (see IV.11); it would appear that Lock, finding TH still at Max Gate, renewed his invitation the morning of the actual day. For the east wind on this date, see IV.12.

To WILLIAM ARCHER

MAX GATE, | DORCHESTER. | June 1. 1909

My dear Archer:
I have read a copy of the Petition for a site for a National Theatre, & the Report of the Executive Committee. It all seems reasonable & well thought out by those who have gone into the subject, though I can imagine magnificent plays which such an academic & municipal set of governours would absolutely refuse to have produced. However as I am not near enough to the centre of theatrical things to have a practical & definite opinion on any part of the scheme I must leave the Petition to be signed by those who are not so circumstanced.

Very truly yours
T. Hardy.

Text MS. British Theatre Association.
Petition for a site: in June 1908 the supporters of a National Theatre had joined with the Shakespeare Memorial Committee to mount a combined campaign for the creation of what was now called a Shakespeare National Theatre; on 15 June 1909 this joint committee presented to the London County Council a petition for the allocation of a site for such a theatre.   *Report* . . .
Committee: though Archer had presumably sent a separately printed copy of the report, TH could have read it in *The Times* of 23 Mar 1909.   *set of governours*: the original Archer–Barker proposals (see above, letter of 1 Nov 04) had been expanded to include, *inter alia*, nomination of governors by the British Academy, the universities of Edinburgh, Dublin, and Wales, and the cities of Manchester, Liverpool, Bristol, Glasgow, Birmingham, Leeds, Edinburgh, and Dublin. For TH's basic scepticism about the scheme, and about all theatrical presentations of Shakespeare's plays, see, e.g., III.313.

To CLEMENT SHORTER

FROM THOS. HARDY, | MAX GATE, | DORCHESTER. [3 June 1909]

My dear Shorter:
Best thanks for good wishes. The cold was simply influenza of ordinary type which has gone off now. Here the winter seems to have come back again.

Yours very truly
T.H.

Text MS. (correspondence card, with envelope) Case Western Reserve Univ.   *Date* From postmark.
good wishes: on TH's sixty-ninth birthday, 2 June.   *The cold*: see IV.25–6.

To GEORGE DEWAR

MAX GATE, | DORCHESTER. | 22: 9; '09

Dear Mr Dewar:
Many thanks. I remember that volume of Ralph Hodgson's, & the poem itself entitled "The Last Blackbird" from which it takes its title. It appealed to me because I hate blood-sport, & because, many years ago, I wrote some verses with similar feelings: I do not know if you ever met with them: they appeared

in "Poems of the Past & the Present" under the name of "The Mother Mourns."
However, nobody took any notice of the piece, so far as I am aware.

Yours sincerely
Thomas Hardy.

Text MS. BL.
Dewar: George Albemarle Bertie Dewar (see IV.139), currently on the staff of the *Saturday Review*, of which he was editor 1913–17.   *Many thanks*: Dewar's letter of 21 Sept 09 (DCM) gave TH permission to include in *Time's Laughingstocks* (London, 1909) the poem 'A Church Romance', first pub. in the *Saturday Review* 8 Sept 1906.   *takes its title*: Dewar had referred to *The Last Blackbird and Other Lines* (London, 1907), the first vol. pub. by the poet Ralph Edwin Hodgson (1871–1962; *D.N.B.*), frequent contributor to the *Saturday Review*; 'The Last Blackbird' itself is a poem of 37 quatrains.   *many years ago*: although 'The Mother Mourns' was first pub. in *Poems of the Past and the Present* in 1902, its central idea dated back at least to 1882; see *EL*, 213.

To FRANCES CORNFORD

MAX GATE, | DORCHESTER. | Jan. 13. 1910

Dear Mrs Cornford:

As your letter has only to-day reached me I am not sure whether you propose this week or next for your call. I shall be here to-morrow, & I believe the Thursday & Friday of next week. Your father's name is introduction sufficient, & I shall be pleased to see you.

Yours vy truly
T. Hardy.

Text MS. BL.
Cornford: Frances Crofts Cornford, *née* Darwin (1886–1960), poet; *D.N.B.* She married F. M. Cornford (see below, letter of 14 Dec 10) in 1909, and was staying with him at the Manor House, Broadwindsor, Dorset.   *your letter*: undated (DCM).   *Your father's name*: Francis Darwin (1848–1925), botanist, third son of Charles Darwin, the naturalist; *D.N.B.* Darwin wrote 30 Jan 10 (DCM) to thank TH for seeing his daughter and her husband.

To SIR ROBERT HUDSON

MAX GATE, | DORCHESTER. | July 21. 1910

Dear Sir Robert Hudson:

In spite of the avalanche of letters that you foresaw I must send a line of reply to yours now that I have got back here from our flat in London, & tell you how truly I thank you for your congratulations & good wishes.

Yes: that was a pleasant dinner. I have not seen "young" Clodd since, but hope to do so in the autumn.

I trust that if you ever come this way you will give me a call.

Sincerely yours
Thomas Hardy.

Text MS. (correspondence card) T. W. and V. Jesty.
Hudson: Sir Robert Arundell Hudson (see IV.112), secretary of the National Liberal Federation.   *avalanche of letters*: congratulating TH on his appointment to the Order of Merit; see IV.103ff.   *reply to yours*: of 11 July 10 (DCM).   *pleasant dinner . . . "young" Clodd*: Hudson had used these phrases when referring in his letter to a dinner given for Edward Clodd on his seventieth birthday; see IV.112.

To H. H. BRINDLEY

MAX GATE, | DORCHESTER. | 28 July 1910

Dear Mr Brindley:

I am late in answering your kind note of congratulation, but thank you none the less sincerely on that account. I am very glad to know that Cambridge friends are pleased.

Yours very truly,
Thomas Hardy.

Text   MS. (correspondence card) Eton College.
of congratulation: see letter of 21 July 10.

To WALTER BAWLER

Max Gate | Oct 6. [1910]

Many thanks for copy of Harmonized Carols.

T.H.

Text   MS. (postcard) R. Greenland.   *Date*   Year from postmark.
Harmonized Carols: *Three Carols Sung by the Mellstock Quire 1800–1840*, harmonized by the Dorchester organist and composer Frederick William Boyton Smith (see III.283); the carols were apparently not printed but prepared in several MS. copies for use in the November 1910 Dorchester production of *The Mellstock Quire* (based on TH's *Under the Greenwood Tree*), in which Bawler—drawing upon his skill as a violinist—played the part of Reuben Dewy.

To F. M. CORNFORD

MAX GATE, | DORCHESTER. | 14: 12: '10

Dear Mr Cornford:

I shall be home to-morrow afternoon, & Friday, unless anything sudden happens; so perhaps, in view of the bad weather, it will be your best plan to choose whichever of the 2 days is fine. We have not by any means forgotten you & Mrs Cornford, & the pleasant visit you paid us last time.

Very truly yours
T. Hardy.

Text   MS. (correspondence card, with envelope) BL.
Cornford: Francis Macdonald Cornford (1874–1943), classical scholar and author of *Microcosmographia Academica*; D.N.B.   *choose . . . fine*: the Cornfords were staying at Studland, near Wareham.   *Mrs Cornford . . . last time*: see above, letter of 13 Jan 10.

To AUSTIN LANE POOLE

FROM THOS. HARDY, | MAX GATE, | DORCHESTER. | 25: 4: '11

Dear Sir:

I am obliged by your interesting account of the Gloucestershire branch of the family I certainly had in my mind when writing "Tess" though I altered the name from a wish not to identify it with that of any real family. My disguise of "d'Urberville", however, was too thin—rather to my regret.

Yours truly
T.H.

Text   MS. (correspondence card, with envelope) BL.
Poole: Austin Lane Poole (1889–1963), historian, later president of St. John's College, Oxford. *the family*: the Turbervilles; in the absence of Poole's letter it is not clear what he was able to tell TH about the family's connection with Gloucestershire, but TH would already have known from John Hutchins, *The History and Antiquities of the County of Dorset* (see above, letter of late Nov 27), I.136, that the original Sir Pagan de Turberville (cf. *Tess of the d'Urbervilles* [Wessex edn.], 4) was in the retinue of Robert FitzHamon, later Earl of Gloucester.

To HENRY W. NEVINSON

MAX GATE, | DORCHESTER. | May 10: 1911

Dear Mr Nevinson:

Many thanks for your little book on Peace & War. I wish I had something of mine to send you, but I have not done much lately.

What you say is true. Civilization is a slow business. Perhaps nations will lead a reasonable life someday; but when!

Yours vy truly
T. Hardy.

Text   MS. (correspondence card) David Holmes.
Nevinson: Henry Woodd Nevinson (see III.223), journalist.   *little book*: his Conway Memorial Lecture, *Peace and War in the Balance* (London, 1911).   *What you say*: TH is referring to the lecture in general rather than to any particular passage.

To EDWARD CLODD

MAX GATE, | DORCHESTER. | 27: 5: 1911

My dear Clodd:

I learnt when it was too late that you were quite near me in Southampton Row on Thursday morning. I was just leaving, having caught a slight cold which, I foresaw, would make it useless to stay on. I shd have looked in upon you in the City if I had remained till the end of the week. I hear with pleasure that you are looking remarkably well.

No more London for me till after the timber is gone, & the huge disfigurements are a little obliterated.

Very sincerely
T.H.

Text   MS. (correspondence card) David Holmes. The MS. also carries a note in red ink from Clodd to C. K. Shorter, to whom the card was forwarded 30 May 11.
in Southampton Row: TH had evidently been staying at the West Central Hotel.   *timber . . . disfigurements*: a reference to the decorations and viewing stands being erected in preparation for the coronation of King George V.

To WILLIAM WATKINS

MAX GATE, | DORCHESTER. | 14: 11: '11

Dear Mr Watkins:

Many thanks for the tickets. I hope I may see you to-morrow evening at the performance.

I must congratulate you on your election to the Presidentship of the other Society.

There is a Dorset man in London to whom I should like to send a seat, if you have one left. *Any* part of the house will do.

Yrs

T. Hardy.

Text MS. (correspondence card) Lord Stockton.
the performance: TH's play *The Three Wayfarers* and A. H. Evans's dramatization of *The Distracted Preacher* were performed in Dorchester 15–16 Nov 1911; the tickets and seat mentioned, however, were presumably for the London performance, 27 Nov 1911. *other Society*: the Chartered Institute of Secretaries, of which Watkins was president 1911–12. *Dorset man*: TH's willingness to accept any available seat suggests that he might have had in mind ELH's nephew Gordon Gifford (see above, letter of 13 Jan 02), not born in Dorset but largely educated there and currently living in London.

To JOHN MEADE FALKNER

MAX GATE, | DORCHESTER. | Dec 17: 1911.

My dear Mr Falkner:

You may be sure that I did not find your letter too long, nor should I have done so if it had extended to five times as many pages. To get letters that can really be called such in the old sense is a pleasure I seldom experience nowadays—& other people could say the same, I imagine.

I am afraid you let your imagination exaggerate my habits of perseverance —seeing how limited my direct efforts have ever been towards achieving anything because it has value, in the ordinary sense, or for that matter in any sense. Indeed all my doings have been tendencies merely—just what I could not help doing even if they had brought poverty & ruin. And even as things are I have sacrificed thousands of pounds—tens of thousands I may say—in following them. No motors, no palatial hotels, no valuable collections of curios & objects of art for the scribbler of the sort of stuff that I write. But as Seneca said: It is all one not to desire & to have.

To make what you say true about pessimists—that a convinced pessimist could not feel any desire for literary activity, you must assume that he reckons by consequences & works for results. But there is such a thing as creative efforts in prose or verse becoming, or being innately, an irresistible propensity —such as smoking, drinking, gambling, etc., which is indulged for the pleasure of the indulgence itself. And the worst pessimist goes on writing with such an idiosyncrasy.

However, this is enough about myself. I am most sorry to hear that you have been suffering from insomnia. I think it must be caused by external affairs & is not inherent in you physically. Relax the strain, as you can readily do, come down to Weymouth, be absolutely idle in mind & body, & you will soon get rid of it, surely.

"Time's Laughingstocks" is, as you will have perceived after honouring me by reading it so carefully, a very mixed collection of utterances—written in all sorts of moods & circumstances, & at widely differing dates. I am glad that the volume appealed to you. Upon the whole I suppose from what people say that it contains a larger proportion of my best work—or at any rate characteristic work—than any other book I have published.

Yes: the vanity of life—the *cui bono?* is overwhelmingly borne in upon us with years. Yet I am rather surprised that such an active man as you should have become conscious of it yet. I was reading Ecclesiastes only this morning. What an extraordinary pronouncement it is! The latest of the decadents of our day (as people are pleased to term such) is not more advanced, more modern, than the writer of that book was.

I am pleased to hear that Nature appeals to you more & more. I fancy, though I am not sure, that I have lost some of my zest for it under the sense of the apparent undesireableness of the universe. True, its existence may not really be undesirable, but we can only judge with our means for judging.

The press-cutting you enclose is amusing—as if human qualities could be measured by units, as it were, like the power of a steam-engine! Trusting I may see you son

I am, sincerely yours
Thomas Hardy.

Text MS. DCM.
Falkner: John Meade Falkner (see III.336), author and antiquary.   *your letter*: of 8 Dec 11 (DCM); the text is incomplete, but the surviving pages mingle general reflections upon life with admiration of TH's achievement.   *as Seneca said*: the allusion is apparently to *Epistulae ad Lucilium*, no. 123.3.   *Laughingstocks*": pub. in December 1909; Falkner said that he had read it from cover to cover during a bout of insomnia.   cui bono?: i.e., to whose profit? From Cicero, *Pro Milone*, XII. xxxii.   *press-cutting*: it no longer accompanies this MS.   *son*: TH means 'soon'.

To THE REVD. HENRY HARDY

Max Gate | Dorchester [3 June 1912]

Many thanks for card and good wishes.

Yrs.
T.H.

Text MS. (postcard) Lilian Hamlyn.   *Date* Day and month from incomplete postmark, year noted on MS. by addressee.
Hardy: the Revd. Henry Hardy (see III.226), Anglican priest, TH's first cousin once removed.   *good wishes*: on TH's seventy-second birthday, 2 June 1912.

To CLEMENT SHORTER

MAX GATE, | DORCHESTER. | 8: 10: 1912

My dear Shorter:

I have not yet seen Meredith's Letters, but I don't want to tax you with sending me a copy, as I shall in the ordinary course get them from the *Times* book-club.

I don't suppose I shall be much in London this year, or at Aldeburgh at all, as I want to get this job of reading through proofs out of hand, though I wish half the volumes were consigned to oblivion instead of being reprinted—I mean those novels written in the past on conventional lines for magazine editors—"to keep base life afoot". However, there they are, unfortunately.

It was only influenza that was the matter with me—mild, but lingering.

Yours very truly,
Thomas Hardy.

P.S. I could not read quite all your letter, some words completely baffling me.
T.H.

Text MS. (with envelope) Rodney Legg.
Meredith's Letters: *Letters of George Meredith*, ed. W. M. Meredith (2 vols., London, 1912); Shorter sent them shortly afterwards (see IV.231). *reading through proofs*: for the Wessex Edition; see Purdy, 285–6. *"to . . . afoot"*: *King Lear*, II. iv. 215.

To MAY MORRIS

STRAFFORD HOUSE, | ALDEBURGH, | SUFFOLK. | April 26: 1913

Dear Miss Morris:

You have my ready permission to use the passage, which I return herewith. There has been a little delay in my reply owing to my being away from home.

Yours very truly
Thomas Hardy.

Text MS. BL.
Morris: May Morris (1863–1938), embroidery designer and editor of the collected works of her father, William Morris (see V.204). *the passage . . . herewith*: still accompanying this letter is a typescript copy of two paragraphs about the shearing barn from chap. 22 of TH's *Far from the Madding Crowd* (Wessex edn., 164–5), subsequently quoted in May Morris's introduction to vol. 18 of *The Collected Works of William Morris* (London, 1913). *away from home*: the address is that of Clodd's house on the sea front at Aldeburgh.

To THE REVD. H. M. BUTLER

MAX GATE, | DORCHESTER. | June 6. 1913

My dear Sir:

It is a great pleasure to me to receive from you such a kind letter of welcome to the Hall dinner on the 11th. But alas for a speech from me! I am a recluse, lately bereaved, & have not, so far as I can remember, been to a public dinner for years. So, though I feel your request to be an honour, perhaps one of the other & more distinguished men can respond to your toast?

Believe me,

Yours very truly,
Thomas Hardy.

The Rev. | The Master of Trinity.

Text MS. (mourning stationery) Trinity College, Cambridge.
Butler: the Revd. Henry Montagu Butler (1833–1918), headmaster of Harrow School 1860–85, master of Trinity College, Cambridge, 1886–1918; *D.N.B.*   *Hall dinner*: Butler (5 June 13, DCM) had invited TH to attend a dinner at Trinity on 11 June 1913, following the Senate House ceremony at which he was to receive from the Univ. of Cambridge the honorary degree of D.Litt.; see *LY*, 156–7.   *lately bereaved*: TH's wife, Emma Lavinia Hardy (see I.131), had died on 27 Nov 1912.   *your toast*: Butler asked TH to respond to the toast, 'The Recipients of Honorary Degrees', which he would himself be proposing.

To KATHARINE HARDY

Crown Hotel | Blandford. | Friday. [1 August 1913]

Am here with Mr Lane, the publisher. Think of motoring to Shaftesbury to-day, to Dorchester to-morrow. F. is at Max G. with Lilian.

T.H.

Text MS. (picture postcard of Crown Hotel and West Street, Blandford, pencil) Eton College.   *Date* From postmark.
with Mr Lane: TH and John Lane, the publisher, were seeking information about the painter Alfred Stevens (see IV.289, 290), who had been born in Blandford Forum.   *F.*: Florence Dugdale.   *Lilian*: ELH's niece Lilian Gifford; see IV.257.

To H. A. MARTIN

Max Gate, | Dorchester. | 9th. November 1913.

Dear Sir:

I return herewith the proof, marked with necessary corrections. The Synopsis of Scenes I think very well drawn up, and the views seem quite attractive.

I am much obliged for the tickets you enclose, and with regard to the matinées about which you enquire I should be glad to exchange two of the Wednesday evening tickets for two Thursday matinées, and two reserved tickets for Thursday for two *second* seats the same (Thursday) evening. The tickets are enclosed that the exchange may be made.

I fear I shall be unable to look in tomorrow (Monday) evening, as I have a slight cold.

Yours very truly,
T. Hardy.

P.S. If I cannot come on Monday evening and any question arises which Mr Tilley would like to discuss with me I shall be happy to see him on Monday afternoon or any morning that he likes to come to Max Gate. T.H.

Text MS. (typewritten) R. Greenland.
Martin: Henry Charles Austin Martin (see IV.57), auctioneer, Hon. Secretary of the Dorchester Debating and Dramatic Society. *the proof*: of the programme of the forthcoming Dorchester production of *The Woodlanders*, dramatized by A. H. Evans. *the views*: the programme included photographs of the Dorset countryside in which the action was set. second *seats*: reserved but unnumbered seats (as distinct from the reserved and numbered 'front seats'), perhaps intended for the Max Gate servants; TH had a cold (see IV.318, 319) and did not attend any of the performances himself. *Mr Tilley*: Thomas Henry Tilley (see IV.115–16), Dorchester alderman, stonemason, and producer for the Dorchester Debating and Dramatic Society.

To SIR COURTENAY ILBERT

MAX GATE, | DORCHESTER. | 15 Nov: 1914

Dear Sir Courtenay Ilbert:

My reply to your interesting letter will I fear be only of the vaguest kind, for I know of no work of fiction or drama that deals with the militia ballot of the Napoleonic time, though there are several I think that depict pressing for the Navy.

The effect upon the peasantry was I think rather to drive young men into the ranks of the Volunteers than into those of the regulars. A village would in those days have its company of volunteers, though so far as I remember the companies were mostly raised in towns only in the volunteer movement of 1860.

As to the "drawing", I remember hearing old people say that the common thing for a young man to do, if he were of the better class of villager who could afford it, was to find a substitute if the lot fell on him. The usual price paid the substitute was several pounds. Malingerers of course there were who could not afford to pay anything. One man in a village near here bound a pennypiece (one of the old copper ones) on to his knee "to poison his leg"—which the process effectually did, rendering him not only too lame to go soldiering but to do anything afterwards.

In the event of any form of conscription based on a ballot being introduced during the present war, a point would be whether substitution should be allowed or not.

I am delighted to find that you passed your boyhood in South Devon, that district having much charm for me. I am afraid it is almost too late, there or here, to find any traditions still surviving. I have known many old soldiers in the past who served in the Peninsula & at Waterloo, but they are all gone. I do not recall that one of them ever spoke of having enlisted to escape the ballot.

A system of conscription paying only half or two-thirds the bounty that would be paid on voluntary enlistment beforehand, would probably cause a rush for voluntary enlistment.

I am so sorry to be unable to give any valuable particulars, & am,

Sincerely yours
Thomas Hardy.

Text MS. A. D. C. Peterson.
Ilbert: Sir Courtenay Peregrine Ilbert (1841–1924), parliamentary draftsman, clerk of the House of Commons 1902–21; *D.N.B.* He may have written at the suggestion of H. H. Asquith (see above,

letter of 26 Mar 26), the prime minister, who had just thanked TH (11 Nov 14, DCM) for sending 'reminders' of methods of recruiting used in the past.　　*militia ballot*: recruitment of local military units by the drawing of lots; Ilbert, presumably anticipating the introduction of some form of conscription during the current war with Germany, asked TH (12 Nov 14, DCM) whether he knew of any literary works which threw light on the way the old Militia Ballot Acts had operated in practice and whether he recalled any local traditions of balloting that had survived into his own youth.　　*pressing for the Navy*: e.g., TH's own *The Trumpet-Major*; see above, letter of 25 Nov 04.　　*South Devon*: Ilbert was the eldest of the eight children of the Revd. Peregrine Ilbert, rector of Thurlestone, Devon, for more than fifty years.　　*& at Waterloo*: TH had, indeed, sought out such veterans of the Napoleonic Wars; see *EL*, 103, 139–40, etc.

To LUCY CLIFFORD

Max Gate | 11: 12: 1914

Dear Mrs Clifford:

I am glad to hear that the scenes from the Dynasts afforded you so much pleasure. Your own lively imagination helped the production largely, no doubt; though it is well done, as all agree. I have not been able to see it yet, except at an early rehearsal. Mr Granville Barker has done practically all, & the Prologue & Epilogue were written at his request.

I have read—not so closely as it deserved perhaps—the play you send in outline. I may as well be frank at starting, & say that I have not the vaguest idea of what effect it would have if written at length & staged. My ignorance in this respect is in accord with my having done nothing towards staging my own. To my eyes a play of anybody's from Shakespeare downwards is more vivid when read than when acted: so I am no good in such a question as this of yours.

Surely a manager is the one who knows best? But if you don't like the notion of showing it to a manager-friend I am inclined to suggest any literary friend who lives in London & often goes to plays & has therefore some power of divining the effect of this in presentation. "A woman's name"—if it were yours who have already produced plays—does not seem to be so dangerous to its consideration as you suppose.

As to the central conception—that the Krupps, or a woman-Krupp, might bring peace to the world by controlling its ordnance—it is naturally attractive in itself, especially to me; but as the theme of a practical drama which has to draw people to a theatre & make them pay: well, I am in the dark altogether.

By the way I should, if I were you, be careful to keep the plot & subject of the piece as much to yourself as possible.

I return the script, & hope it will reach you safely, & am

Sincerely yours
Thomas Hardy.

P.S. I am reminded by "Huntsman of Sheffield"—your character—that in Bulwer Lytton's novel The Last of the Barons, a poor man's invention of the steam engine is lost in a somewhat similar way, Though not sufficiently similar to affect you.

Text　MS. Mrs. A. M. Dilke.

from the Dynasts: the Granville Barker production; see V.51. Mrs. Clifford apparently went to the Kingsway Theatre on 4 December with her daughter, Ethel Dilke (author of two vols. of verse and wife of Fisher Wentworth Dilke), whose admiring letter to TH, dated 5 Dec 14, is in

DCM; Mrs. Clifford's own letter seems not to have survived.   *written . . . staged*: it does not appear to have been performed and was perhaps never completed.   *staging my own*: i.e., *The Dynasts*.   *already produced plays*: most recently *A Woman Alone*, performed at the Little Theatre in July 1914.   *the Krupps*: TH seems to be thinking both of the great German armaments firm and of its founder, Albert Krupp (1812–87).   *Lytton's*: Edward George Earle Lytton, first Baron Lytton (1802–73), novelist; *D.N.B.*   *somewhat similar way*: in the novel *The Last of the Barons* (London, 1843), set in the latter half of the fifteenth century, the poor man (Adam Warner) discovers the principle of the steam engine but is destroyed, and his invention suppressed, by the power of contemporary obscurantism and superstition embodied in the figure of Friar Bungey, the astrologer.   *Though*: TH signed his initials at the end of the postscript but then overwrote them, retaining the capital 'T', in order to add the last seven words.

To PERCY WITHERS

FROM THO. HARDY, | MAX GATE, | DORCHESTER. | 9 June: 1915

Dear Sir:

I have signed the application, & return it. I am not sure that the case is not one also for the Royal Literary Fund, being of a pressing &, I hope, temporary kind. Mr Edmund Gosse is one of the Committee of that Fund, & you might ask him, as I think he knows Mr Abercrombie, for whom I am deeply sorry.

Yours truly

T.H.

Text   MS. (postcard) Somerville College, Oxford.
Withers: Percy Withers (1867–1945), author and Oxford Univ. extension lecturer in English.   *the application*: Withers was organizing a formal application for a Civil List pension for Lascelles Abercrombie (1881–1938; *D.N.B.*), the poet and critic, on the grounds of his lack of income, his wife's serious illness, and the needs of their three young children; although a pension was not awarded, Abercrombie did receive a grant of £500 from the Royal Bounty Fund.   *not one also*: TH first wrote, 'not one rather'.   *Literary Fund*: see VI.74; TH evidently did not know that Abercrombie had been granted £100 by the Fund eight months previously.

To S. M. ELLIS

MAX GATE, | DORCHESTER. | 20th. May 1917.

Dear Mr Ellis:

I am sorry to say in reply to your inquiries that I can add very little on the subject of my first meeting with Meredith beyond what I said in the poem published in the Times a day or two after his death. I can however give the place and approximate date. It was in the latter part of 1868 or the beginning of 1869, and in a back room at Chapman and Hall's, in Piccadilly, opposite Sackville Street, a house now pulled down that stood on the site of the Institute of Painters,

Yours very truly,

Th: Hardy.

Text   MS. (typewritten) Eton College.
Ellis: Stewart Marsh Ellis (see IV.272), author. He drew upon this letter and that of 9 June 17 in his *George Meredith: His Life and Friends in Relation to His Work* (London, 1919), 244–5.   *in the Times*: 'G.M.', *The Times*, 22 May 1909—the day of Meredith's funeral.   *Institute of Painters*: more fully, the Royal Institute of Painters in Water Colours, at 195 Piccadilly.

To S. M. ELLIS

[9 June 1917]

Dear Mr Ellis:

I write for my husband to say in reply to your further inquiries that he is sorry he can find, after a search, no note of what Meredith said to him at their first interview in 1868 or 9. The gist of it he has often stated—that a novel—or first novel—should have a "plot"—& that, understanding from M.'s further remarks that he meant what is, or was, called a sensational plot, he wrote "Desperate Remedies"—a story quite foreign to his own instincts; and which therefore, oddly enough, owed its existence to Meredith.

Yours truly

Text MS. (pencil draft) DCM. *Date* From the typewritten letter, as signed and sent by FEH, in the Eton College collection.

To CLEMENT SHORTER

MAX GATE, | DORCHESTER. | Sunday 9: 3: 1919.

Dear Clement Shorter:

T. H. Bayly's Poems arrived this morning. I am afraid you took much trouble to find them—merely to indulge a sentimental fancy of mine, my mother having been accustomed to sing them when I was a child. I only meant that you should let me know of a copy, & I should feel more comfortable if you would let me pay for them. It does not matter that the two leaves are missing.

I hope you will have a cheerful time in America, though I do not envy you the journey. The change is not enough for the mileage—I mean in the literature. But you do not go for literary reasons.

Yours very truly
Thomas Hardy.

Text MS. (with envelope) Texas.
Bayly's Poems: Thomas Haynes Bayly, early nineteenth-century writer; see V.351 and *EL*, 17–18. *in America*: the visit lasted several months; see V.320.

To ARCHBISHOP JOHN BERNARD

MAX GATE, | DORCHESTER. | May 22: 1919

Dear Archbishop of Dublin:

I was glad to get your Psalter, & should have thanked you for it before, if my letter-writing had not been hindered by a bad cold.

The edition has several points of interest for me—partly because I am a great reader of the Psalms (preferring always the Coverdale version, except in a few instances)—& I value it.

I fancy from your introduction that I have hitherto been in error in supposing "tale" in "a tale that is told", to mean a number counted, as in the phrase "a tale of bricks" in Exodus, & that it really means an oft-told story.

Very truly yours
Thomas Hardy.

P.S. I am sending you a little publication of mine for what it may be worth.
Th.H.

Text   MS. Kildare Dobbs.
Bernard: the Right Revd. John Henry Bernard (see V.310), Archbishop of Dublin, later Provost
of Trinity College, Dublin; TH had met him at Lady St. Helier's (see above, letter of 7 May 26)
earlier in the month (see *LY*, 191).   *your Psalter*: Bernard's edn. of *The Psalter in Latin and
English* (London, 1911); it presents the St. Jerome and Coverdale (i.e., Book of Common Prayer)
versions of the psalms in parallel columns. TH's copy, presented by Bernard, is in the Purdy
collection.   *that is told"*: Psalms 90: 9; in his Introduction (xvii) Bernard identifies the source
of the phrase as Jerome's 'quasi sermonem'.   *in Exodus*: Exodus 5: 8, 18.   *publication of
mine*: TH's *Selected Poems* of 1917; the copy he sent Bernard is in the Purdy collection.

To ARCHIE WHITFIELD

[Early November 1919]

Dear Sir
   In reply to your letter I write for Mr Hardy, who is in bed with a chill, to say
that he cannot furnish you with any biographical details there being few more
than are given in "Who's Who" & similar handbooks. To your inquiry if Jude
the Obscure is autobiographical I have to answer that there is not a scrap of
personal detail in it, it having the least to do with his own life of all his books.
The rumour if it exists was started by idle press men some years ago. Speaking
generally there is more autobiography in a hundred lines of Mr Hardy's poetry
than in all the novels, though there are of course in the latter isolated incidents
which he may have witnessed or experienced. The handbook by Mr Harold
Child is as good a guide as any to Mr H's writings—

Text   MS. (pencil draft in FEH's hand) DCM.   *Date*   The 30 Oct 19 date assigned in *LY*,
196, was probably taken from the letter to which this replies.
Whitfield: Archie Stanton Whitfield, literary critic, currently at Lincoln College, Oxford; the
preface to his *Mrs Gaskell: Her Life and Work* (London, 1929) is dated from Japan.   *your
letter*: of 30 Oct 19 (DCM).   *write for Mr Hardy*: although this draft bears no trace of TH's
hand it has been accepted for inclusion on the basis of the statement in *LY*, 195, that it was written
'at his request'.   *Speaking . . . experienced*: Whitfield quoted this sentence in his *Thomas
Hardy the Artist, the Man and the Disciple of Destiny* (London, 1921).   *Child*: Harold
Hannyngton Child (see III.333); his *Thomas Hardy* was pub. in 1919 (see V.143).

To W. H. NORRIS

Dec 15. 1919

Dear Sir,
   In reply to your inquiry of February 14 I send the particulars you appear to
require. Mr Gordon Gifford is a relative of mine, & is the eldest son of Mrs
Charlotte Gifford deceased & her late husband Mr Walter Gifford. He is & has
been for many years an architectural draughtsman in the offices of the London
County Council.

Yours truly
T.H
(Justice of the Peace for Dorsetshire)

Text   MS. (pencil draft) DCM.
Norris: W. H. Norris, manager of the Accident Department, London Assurance Company.   *appear to require*: Gordon Gifford's mother had died and Norris wrote (14 Feb 19,
DCM) to ask if he was a proper person to receive an Administration Bond issued in his favour; the
apparent lateness of TH's reply is so uncharacteristic as to suggest—especially in the absence of
any word of apology—that 'Dec' is simply an error for 'Feb'. For Gifford himself, see above, letter
of 13 Jan 02.

To JOSEPH McCABE

February 18. 1920.

Dear Sir:

As Mr Hardy has a cold which makes writing trying to his eyes, I answer
your letter for him. He says he thinks he is rather an irrationalist than a
rationalist, on account of his inconsistencies. He has, in fact, declared as much
in prefaces to some of his poems where he explains his views as being mere
impressions that frequently change. Moreover, he thinks he could show that no
man is a rationalist, and that human actions are not ruled by reason at all in the
last resort. But this, of course, is outside the question. So that he cannot
honestly claim to belong to the honourable body you are including in your
dictionary, whom he admires for their straightforward sincerity and permanent convictions, though he does not quite think they can claim their title.

Yours very truly,
F. E. Hardy.

Text   Typed transcript (for inclusion in *Later Years*) DCM.
McCabe: Joseph Martin McCabe (1867–1955), rationalist author; *D.N.B.*   *trying to his eyes*:
the typescript first read, 'trying at his age'.   *answer . . . for him*: although there is no direct
evidence of TH's authorship of this letter, its inclusion in *LY*, 209–10, creates an overwhelming
presumption that it was indeed his work.   *your dictionary*: McCabe had wished to include TH
in his *A Biographical Dictionary of Modern Rationalists* (London, 1920). When the book appeared
Edward Clodd wrote to TH (9 Feb 21, DCM) to express outrage at the latter's absence from its
pages, although it is not clear whether Clodd, at the time he wrote, was aware that the omission
was at TH's own request.   *straightforward*: the typescript first read, 'straightforwardness'.

To HAMILTON FYFE

Max Gate, | Dorchester. | 11th. June 1921.

Dear Mr Fyfe:

I can say as much as the few words enclosed herewith on the proposed
"League of Thinkers". But having as yet only just turned to the matter they are
few, and I fear not of much service.

Yours truly,
Th: Hardy.

Text   MS. (typewritten) Eton College.
Fyfe: Henry Hamilton Fyfe (1869–1951), journalist and writer; *D.N.B.* He wrote 6 June 21
(DCM) from the office of the *New World* to solicit TH's public endorsement of the proposal for a
worldwide 'League of Thinkers' put forward in the May 1921 issue by Tolstoy's son, Leo Tolstoy,
Jr.   *enclosed herewith*: the MS. of TH's contribution, pub. in the July 1921 issue, no longer
accompanies this letter; a draft in his hand does, however, survive in DCM.

To JOHN PURVES

Max Gate, | Dorchester. | 21st. May 1922.

My dear Sir:

In reply to your request I enclose a few lines on Stevenson; which may appear to you, as they do to me, not worth printing. If however you and the Committee think otherwise please print them just as they stand.

Yours truly,
T. Hardy.

John Purves, Esq.

Text MS. (typewritten) NLS.
your request: of 18 May 22 (DCM).   *on Stevenson*: TH enclosed the typescript (NLS) of 'Robert Louis Stevenson', his brief contribution to *I Can Remember Robert Louis Stevenson*, ed. Rosaline Masson (Edinburgh, 1922). When Miss Masson (see VI.165) wrote 12 Apr 22 (DCM), TH for some reason failed to respond, but when she wrote again 25 May 22 (DCM) he apologized for having sent to Purves what was intended for her and for her book.   *and the Committee*: these words inserted in TH's hand; the Robert Louis Stevenson Club of Edinburgh had appointed a Book Sub-Committee to oversee the compilation and publication of *I Can Remember Robert Louis Stevenson*.

To J. H. FOWLER

MAX GATE, | DORCHESTER. | 19 January 1925

Dear Sir:

I have to thank you for the copy of the Introductions to the Indian edition of my novels, and to enclose some corrections that seemed to be required. I have found nothing to remark upon in the criticisms. It might be useful for you to read Hermann Lea's "Thomas Hardy's Wessex" (Macmillan), for guidance on the point of localities, if you write any more introductions.

I am sorry to say that I never met your friend Miss Meta Gaskell, who must have been a very appreciative reader.

Yours very truly,
T. Hardy.

J. H. Fowler Esq. | 16 Canynge Square | Clifton | Bristol.

ERRATA.

Biographical Note. page XIX. "Bockhampton, the Upper Mellstock of his novels". As to this and similar passages: no place mentioned under a fictitious name in the Wessex Novels is an exact portrait of any real place; but a more or less imaginary place, resembling some real one often, but with differences from it.

Same page: for 1858 read 1863.

Page XX. line 12: for "since that time", read "before and since that time."

Mayor of Casterbridge P. XVII. line 13: for "is in all" read, "is in many though not all."

Return of Native. p. XI. line 7 from bot., for "a wild tract", read "a combination of some wild tracts."

Page XVII line 9: for "is Weymouth", read, "is founded on Weymouth."

Trumpet Major. p XII line 2 from bot: dele "Kingston Russell near".
Page XVI. line 18: for "its real name is Upwey", read, "its basis is a composite
  of Sutton Pointz and Upwey."

Text   MS. (typewritten) Clifton College.
Fowler: John Henry Fowler (d. 1932), assistant master at Clifton College, editor of English texts
for use in schools, author of *The Novels of Thomas Hardy*, an English Association pamphlet of
1928.   *Indian edition*: Fowler (12 Dec 24, DCM) sent copies of the short introductions he had
written for Macmillan's forthcoming Indian edns. of *The Mayor of Casterbridge*, *Far from the
Madding Crowd*, *The Return of the Native*, and *The Trumpet-Major*.   *some corrections*: these
(set out on a separate sheet) appear to have arrived too late to be of immediate utility; Fowler (21
Jan 25, DCM) thanks TH for his trouble and promises to make the changes if the vols. are
reprinted.   *Meta Gaskell*: Margaret Emily (Meta) Gaskell (d. 1913, aged 76), second daughter
of Elizabeth Gaskell, the novelist; Fowler had referred to her as an admirer of TH's work both in
his letter and in his introduction to *Far from the Madding Crowd*.

Undated Letters and Fragments

To GEORGE MANVILLE FENN

[1882?]

Dear Mr. Fenn,

An accident has delayed for a day or two my reply to your letter. Any episode from "A Pair of Blue Eyes" that you think good enough for your purpose is at your service; the scene you mention would, I should think, be as good as any. I should tell you that the one volume edition contains the finally revised text.

I am so glad to perceive how successful your "Gleanings" have been hitherto, particularly, I think, in the country, where people take them, even if they possess the original works—to save themselves the trouble of using their own judgment, I suppose. The world gets indolent in its reading, and there seems now to be quite a demand for trained minds as pioneers.

I was not aware till now that *The Echo* critique was yours, and I take this late opportunity of expressing my sincere thanks for it. Indeed, if any fault could be found with your critiques at that time, it was that you were too kind.

Believe me, yours sincerely,
Thomas Hardy.

P.S. I hope you don't forget the birds in the whirl of your critical writings. I am expecting a big work from you some day embodying those tender essays on the humbler creatures that you seem to have a special gift for writing.

Text [Sir Arthur Spurgeon], *The Story of the House of Cassell* (London, 1922), 159. *Date* From internal evidence.
Fenn: George Manville Fenn (see I.78), novelist and editor.   *for your purpose*: i.e., for inclusion in the second vol. of Fenn's *Gleanings from Popular Authors, Grave and Gay* (London, 1883); the chosen extract from TH's *A Pair of Blue Eyes*, headed 'Love will Find out the Way', was taken from the cliff-episode in chap. 21 and spectacularly illustrated by W. J. Morgan. There is a copy in DCM, perhaps because it was in these pages that FEH first encountered TH's work.   *one volume edition*: i.e., that pub. by Henry S. King in 1877.   Echo *critique*: evidently of *A Pair of Blue Eyes*, although the only reference found (*Echo*, 4 July 1873) is a brief but positive comment ('clever and graceful story') on the final serial instalment in *Tinsley's Magazine*.   *tender essays*: see I.78.

To AN UNIDENTIFIED CORRESPONDENT

[1883?]

Persevering Sir,

When I have a spare month or six weeks in which to write out the documents you require I will not fail to send them. The autographs are less formidable, & here follows one.

Thomas Hardy,
again—
Thomas Hardy.
again again!
Thomas Hardy.

Text   MS. Berg.   *Date*   Estimate based on TH's handwriting.
Unidentified: the MS. is accompanied by an envelope annotated (not in TH's hand) 'Mr T.
Greig. | Morning Post'. The 'T' could perhaps be a 'J' and Greig consequently identified as James
Greig (d. 1941, aged 80), at one time art critic of the *Morning Post*, but there is no assurance that
the name on the envelope is that of the original autograph-seeker.

To AN UNIDENTIFIED CORRESPONDENT

[1885?]

if you think anything of this proposal.
   I am, dear Sir,

Faithfully yours
Thomas Hardy.

Text   MS. (fragment only) Historical Society of Pennsylvania.   *Date*   Entirely speculative,
based on the handwriting, the formality of the valediction (cf. I.138), and the likelihood that TH
was seeking a publisher for a novel or short story rather than for a poem.

To WALTER BESANT

[Spring 1886?]

My dear Besant,
   I shall not have the pleasure of being with you Friday—If there is to be a
dinner in the June month I shall be in town I believe.
   I have been asked by Mrs Everett, an acquaintance, to send one of the
enclosed programmes to any correspondent.

Sincerely yours
T. Hardy

Text   MS. P. C. Roscoe.   *Date*   See below.
dinner in the June month: the reference is evidently to the monthly dinners of the Rabelais Club, of
which Besant was a leading member, and it can at least be established (see I.147) that TH attended
the dinner on 6 June 1886.   *Mrs Everett*: Augusta Stewart Everett; see above, letter to her of 9
Sept 26.   *enclosed programmes*: their subject-matter remains unknown.

To AN UNIDENTIFIED CORRESPONDENT

[Autumn 1892?]

up. You hail from Chelsea, I surmise; though in my imagination you float
about Europe unhampered by addresses. For safety I send this through your
publishers. With best wishes I am

Yours sincerely
Thomas Hardy.

Text MS. (fragment only, mourning stationery) Gordon N. Ray.   *Date* Entirely speculative; TH used mourning stationery following the deaths of his father, July 1892, and his mother,
April 1904.
float about Europe: TH used a similar phrase when writing to Arthur Symons in September 1904
(see III.133), and it is possible that he is here responding to a gift of one of Symons's first books.

To WALTER BESANT

16, PELHAM CRESCENT, | SOUTH KENSINGTON. | Wednesday. 5.30 p.m.
[Spring 1894?]

My dear Besant:
  I have only this minute received your kind invitation. I am so sorry that I am
unable to accept owing to another engagement. With our kind regards to Mrs
Besant,
  I am,

Yours sincerely
Thomas Hardy.

Text MS. P. C. Roscoe.   *Date* TH stayed at this address late April–late July 1894 and
early April–late July 1896. For a possible specific date (23 May 94), see II.58.
Mrs Besant: Mary Garrett Besant, *née* Barham (d. 1904).

To AN UNIDENTIFIED CORRESPONDENT

THE ATHENAEUM, | PALL MALL. S.W. [1895?]

Mr Thomas Hardy believes that his height is five feet seven—not as you state
five feet eight.

Text MS. (correspondence card) Princeton.   *Date* TH's first dated use of this particular
Athenaeum letterhead appears to have been in May 1894.
as you state: the statement TH is correcting has not been identified.

To WILLIAM ROTHENSTEIN

MAX GATE, | DORCHESTER. | Tuesday. [1897?]

My dear Sir:
  I shall, I believe, be in London to-morrow (79 Harley St) & will come to
you, for the sitting I promised, Thursday morning at 11, unless you write to
say this is inconvenient, or I wire.

Yours,
T. Hardy.

Text MS. (correspondence card) Harvard.   *Date* See below.
Rothenstein: William Rothenstein (see II.149), painter, whom TH first met in 1897, sitting for
him that year and on several subsequent occasions.   *79 Harley St*: the address of Sir Francis
and Lady Jeune (see above, letter of 7 May 26); TH rarely stayed there after the mid-1890s and not
at all after the death of Lord St. Helier (as he had by then become) in 1905.

To ARTHUR SPURGEON

[Early July 1901]

particularly appropriate object of pilgrimage for the fraternity of White Friars —though I did not think of it at the time. That was an abbey of the order (Cistercians), their habit having been white, with a black scapular & hood.

Yours truly
Thomas Hardy.

Text MS. (fragment only) BL. *Date* See notes below.
Spurgeon: Arthur Spurgeon (see II.292), one of the secretaries of the Whitefriars Club, whose members had visited Dorset and Max Gate 29 June 1901; Spurgeon wrote 5 July 01 (DCM) to thank TH for his hospitality. *object of pilgrimage*: in the part of the letter now missing TH must have expressed regret that the visiting journalists had not included in their itinerary the abbey ruins at Cerne Abbas, a few miles N. of Dorchester.

To [JOHN MARSHALL LANG?]

[5 March 1905?]

I am impressed by its coming from Aberdeen, for though a stranger to that part of Scotland to a culpable extent I have always observed with admiration the exceptional characteristics of the northern University, which in its fostering encouragement of mental effort seems to cast an eye over these islands that is unprejudiced, unbiassed, and unsleeping.

Text Fragment, *LY*, 109. *Date* See III.160.
Lang: John Marshall Lang (see III.160), Principal of the University of Aberdeen; the paragraph apparently derives from a draft of TH's letter formally accepting the university's offer of an honorary degree.

To AN UNIDENTIFIED CORRESPONDENT

[March 1913?]

I thought I would have no letters forwarded. Hence this result amongst others.

I should like to see you once again informally. But I see few people nowadays.

Sincerely yours
Thomas Hardy.

Text MS. (fragment only) Cornell Univ. *Date* Entirely speculative; the melancholy tone is, however, strongly suggestive of the period following ELH's death. TH's visit to St. Juliot in early March 1913 (see IV.260) would fit in with his reference here to a recent period of absence.
once again informally: in view of this note of past intimacy it seems worth noting that Eliza Bright Nicholls, TH's *fiancée* in the 1860s, is said to have called to see him at about this time; see Millgate, 494.

To AN UNIDENTIFIED CORRESPONDENT

[September 1917?]

I wonder if you would like to read a novel I wrote of that part of Cornwall, in which I attempted to describe the scenery as it impressed me. I am sending a copy of it—which please don't take the trouble to acknowledge; & you will understand that I don't ask you to read such a prentice piece of work through as a story, but to glance at the scenes, because you are there amid them.

Yours sincerely
Thomas Hardy.

Text MS. (fragment only) David Holmes. *Date* See below.
a novel: *A Pair of Blue Eyes*. *that part*: TH first wrote 'that time', an obvious reference to the period of his courtship of his first wife and a strong indication that this letter dates from after her death. *there amid them*: TH was perhaps addressing Lady Stuart of Wortley, formerly Alice Stuart-Wortley (see II.22–3); Lord and Lady Stuart were accustomed to holiday in Tintagel, and TH met them there by accident during his last visit to St. Juliot in early September 1916 (see *LY*, 172). Lady Stuart's letter of 24 Sept 17 (DCM), written from Tintagel, describes a visit she had made to St. Juliot church that afternoon.

To EDWARD CLODD

MAX GATE, | DORCHESTER. [October 1917?]

My dear Clodd:
I wrote for the tickets, which was no trouble at all; & here they are. I hope you & Mrs Clodd will like the lecture.
I hope you both are keeping well. I hear that influenza is rampant in London.

Sincerely yours
T.H.

Text MS: (correspondence card) Leeds. *Date* See below.
Mrs Clodd: Clodd's second wife Phyllis, *née* Rope, whom he married in 1914; see V.81. *the lecture*: unidentified, but possibly Sir Henry Newbolt's Royal Society of Literature lecture on 'The Poetry of Thomas Hardy', delivered 17 Oct 1917 (see V.231).

To J. H. MORGAN

FROM TH. HARDY, | MAX GATE, | DORCHESTER. | Tuesday. [December 1919?]

Book arrived to-day. We mean to read it soon. You should not have troubled to get it. Many thanks.

T.H.

Text MS. (correspondence card) Berg. *Date* See below.
Morgan: John Hartman Morgan (see above, letter of 12 Jan 26); TH seems to have corresponded with him 1916–26. *Book*: not, apparently, one of Morgan's own books but very possibly —since Morgan had participated in the treaty negotiations at Versailles (see V.311)—John Maynard Keynes's *The Economic Consequences of the Peace*, pub. December 1919, a copy of which TH passed on to his neighbour Cecil Hanbury in January 1920 (see Hanbury to TH, 17 Jan 20, in DCM).

To ROBERT BRIDGES

[November 1925?]

verses, lately returned by the printer, & have picked out the pages I enclose that you may choose the best. One of them, & perhaps both, will I****

Best wishes to you & your house

Always truly yours
Thomas Hardy.

Text MS. (fragment only) Lord Bridges.   *Date* See below.
Bridges: Robert Seymour Bridges (see II.50), Poet Laureate since 1913. As the founder and principal officer of the Society for Pure English (see IV.305 and VI.125), Bridges had sought examples of TH's hand for facsimile reproduction in S.P.E. Tract no. xxiii, *English Handrwiting*, by Roger Fry and E. A. Lowe (Oxford, 1926).   *returned by the printer*: the reference is evidently to the MS. of *Human Shows*, pub. 20 Nov 1925, although the MS. of 'A Last Leaving' actually reproduced appears not to have been that sent to the printer; see Purdy, 246.   *Best . . . Hardy.*: this valediction and signature were superimposed upon the poem MS. in *English Handwriting*; the earlier portion of the letter has survived only because located on the other side of the excised segment.

To THE REVD. G. B. CRONSHAW

[Autumn 1926?]

Day, 1 Nov. But the flesh is weak in another sense than that usually meant, & I cannot get to you.

I will do the next best thing—be present in thought.

Kindest regards to all who may remember me.

Sincerely yours
Thomas Hardy.

Text MS. (fragment only) Queen's College, Oxford.   *Date* See below.
Day, 1 Nov.: All Saints' Day, and the date of one of the annual 'gaudies' at Queen's College specified in the founder's statutes.   *flesh is weak*: Matthew 26: 41.   *remember me*: an indication that this letter was probably written some time after TH's one visit to the college as an honorary fellow in June 1923.

CORRECTIONS AND AMPLIFICATIONS VOLUMES 1–6

All references are made by page and line numbers; in establishing the latter running heads have been ignored but all other lines of print (including the headings of letters) have been counted. The readings before the square brackets are those of the volumes as published; they should be replaced by the readings following the square brackets. Although changes in the location of documents have not been systematically recorded, it seems appropriate to note that the numerous letters to Smith, Elder in Volume One are all now in the National Library of Scotland.

Volume One

The changes marked with an asterisk were incorporated in the corrected second printing of this volume, 1979.

*xix.17	Harper & Brothers] Osgood, McIlvaine
*xx.14up	Congress;] Congress; University of London Library;
2.7–8	The Farm Street chapel was one of his many ecclesiastical buildings.] Only the spectacular high altar at Farm Street was in fact his work.
2.2up	"she zid a lot of others [be gone afore?]"] "he zid a lot of other voke guane up"
3.4	too] too,
3.8	Mrs. H. O. Lock] DCM
3.19	friend.] friend, and almost certainly Eliza Amey, aunt of the younger Eliza mentioned below.
3.20	unidentified.] almost certainly Eliza Amey of Dorchester, formerly a classmate of Mary Hardy's at the Salisbury Training College for teachers.
*9.2	time] time,
*9.25	MS.] MS. (with envelope) *Also at*: *35.15up, *38.12up, *38.3up, *42.16, *44.1, *44.14up, *44.2up, *45.12up, *47.13, *48.14, *48.26, *59.3, *60.7up, *61.1up, *62.9, *81.7up, *143.17, *160.12
18.13	72.] 72. *in reply*: Tinsley agreed to these terms 2 Aug 72 (DCM).
*23.13	stationery)] stationery, with envelope) *Also at*: *23.26, *24.13, *25.6
29.5up	*the matter*] *copy*: a copy in a copperplate hand (presumably TH's) of the beginning of the letter from Holt still accompanies this letter. *the matter*
51.11	magazine.] magazine; they had purchased the serial rights of TH's new novel 28 June 77 (copy, Univ. of Reading), apparently without seeing any of the MS.

60.16up	1878.] 1878. *your approbation*: Chatto & Windus (23 Sept 78; copy, Univ. of Reading) approved pub. 'any time after the middle of next month'.
64.10up	1870).] 1870). *representative of the family*: Mrs. Franklyn's daughter had married C. J. A. Rumbold (see above), a grandson of Sir Thomas.
71.4up	Arthur] Alfred
*80.2up	Princeton] Texas
91.3up	subsequently changed to 'Llanherne'.] the spelling 'Llanherne' seems to occur only in *EL*.
*92.14	through)] through, with envelope)
*94.4up	*Guyezdo*] *Gnyezdo*
*95.6	Guyezdo] Gnyezdo
96.1up	81.] 81. It seems likely that TH's correspondent was Henry Havelock Ellis; see I.118.
105.2up	30 Dec 81] 5 Jan 82
133.16–17up	Molyneux] Molyneux Herbert
*149.15up	find] finding
166.21	Scotland.] Scotland. *Lady Douglas*: Douglas's mother, Lady Mariquita Juana Petronila Scott-Douglas, the daughter of Don. Francisco Sanchez de Piña, of Gibraltar; Douglas abandoned the additional surname of Scott assumed by his grandfather.
*167.5	Added] Year added
172.18	*Mrs Procter's*] *Chrysanthemums . . . "Buffer"*: Paul had been reading the first instalment of TH's story 'The Waiting Supper', *Murray's Magazine*, January 1888; see *A Changed Man* (Wessex edn., 42). *Mrs Procter's*
176.3up	unidentified.] unidentified, but possibly Charlotte, daughter of Justin McCarthy (see II.162).
197.1up	1889.] 1889. *the incident*: Lockett, as a young journalist working for the *Dorset County Chronicle*, had once spoken to TH when he came 'to watch a fashionable wedding procession from our windows' (*Dorset County Chronicle*, 26 Jan 1928, 2).
*216.18	Locker] Locker's son (see note below)
217.6up	Fetherstonhaugh-Frampton] Fetherstonhaugh
*217.6up	Hall] House
222.11	Peachey] Pearcey
231.16	*Date*] *Data*
242.5up	Photocopy Purdy.] MS. Mrs. Norton Downs.
242.4up	*D.N.B.*] *D.N.B.* TH probably dealt, however, with H. Greenhough Smith; see VII.147.
244.7up	this work seems not to have been published.] later spoken of by Lockett as a short story published 'in some periodical' (*Dorset County Chronicle*, 26 Jan 1928, 2); the title appears to have resembled that of Henry James's earliest known

	story, 'A Tragedy of Error', *Continental Monthly*, February 1864.
266.16	women's suffrage.] presumably women's suffrage, although details of its activities have not been traced.
*273.9	DEL] DELAND
275.2up	officer.] officer and was drowned in the wreck of the ship he was commanding, H.M.S. *Cobra*, in September 1901.
277.13up	1892.] 1892. *Dorset by birth*: she was born Ellen Jerrard of Lyme Regis.
*287.6up	Dobson,] Dobson:
*288.1	Transcript (in the hand of Alban Dobson) Eton College.] MS. Univ. of London Library.
290.5	card)] card, mourning stationery)

Volume Two

viii.22	University of Leeds] University of Kentucky; University of Leeds
6.7up	Sir William Frederick Pollock, Bt., barrister and author; see I.126.] Sir Frederick Pollock, Bt. (1845–1927; *D.N.B.*), jurist, son of Sir William Frederick Pollock, Bt. (see I.126).
21.9	Eleanora] Eleonora
33.5	weare] we are
53.26	*Broderick*:] *Broderick*: correctly, Brodrick;
54.13	*Lyttleton*:] *Lyttleton*: correctly, Lyttelton;
54.14	Lyttleton] Lyttelton
70.9up	THE EDITOR OF THE *NORTHERN FIGARO*] ELLIOTT & FRY
71.2	*Northern*] *Elliott & Fry*: photographers, of 55 Baker Street, London. *Northern*
97.15	*the scene*] *Editor*: Ernest Bell (1851–1933), publisher, proprietor and editor of the *Animals' Friend* for many years. *the scene*
162.18up	servants.] servants. *Guildford Street*: correctly, Guilford Street, E. of Russell Square.
163.13up	*LY*, 66.] *LY*, 66. *S.K.*: South Kensington.
176.16	to Devon.] to the London area; later still he moved to Torquay, Devon.
225.1up	'contemptate'.] 'contemptate'. *edition described*: it seems not to have materialized.
226.19up	her 'Objections] her pro-suffrage 'Objections
238.16up	*Monthly*] *New Monthly*
249.13	HENRY] ADELAIDE
249.15	Mr.] Mrs
249.21	Typed transcript (from Goodspeed's, Boston) Purdy.] MS. Univ. of Kentucky.
249.22	*Allhusen*:] *Allhusen*: Adelaide Allhusen, *née* Vandeleur (d. 1936), aunt by marriage of

268.6up	Archaeological] Antiquarian
286.20	is a] is at

Volume Three

viii.24	Association;] Association; University of Kentucky;
9.1up	appears] appeared
41.13up	the occasion has not been identified.] to the Edinburgh Philosophical Institution.
59.22	weeks:] weeks;
79.5up	chap. 3] part two, chap. 3
90.13up	28 May] 21 May
103.6	182.] 182, or Browning's 'Childe Roland to the Dark Tower Came'.
138.17	illustrated.] illustrated. *Laughingstocks"*: subsequently collected as 'The Revisitation'.
142.5up	(DCM)] (Holmes)
143.10up	04.] 04. *The colonel*: i.e., the army officer who is the speaker of the poem.
154.16	Sladen, *my letter*: see Purdy, 301. see II.194] Sladen (see II.194), miscellaneous writer. *my letter*: the reference is apparently to TH's letter in the *Critic*, 10 Sept 1892; see Purdy, 301.
156.11up	some of these are cited by Pentin] Pentin gave a paper on these at the 21 Feb 1905 meeting of the Dorset Natural History and Antiquarian Field Club and cited some of them
181.4	Aldburgh] Aldeburgh
189.6up	forgotton] forgotten
197.11up	δνταστας] δυναστας
209.10up	Henry Irving.] Henry Brodribb Irving, elder son of Sir Henry Irving.
266.18	BL.] BL; envelope Berg.
300.18	Francis] Frederick
305.16	for you] for your
308.12up	of you] of your
309.11up	ask you] ask your
327.2	Max Gate, | Dorchester. | Aug. 2, 1908.] MAX GATE, | DORCHESTER. | Aug. 2. 1908.
327.4	object] objects
327.9	truly,] truly
327.11	Typed transcript (by Violet Hunt) Cornell Univ.] MS. Univ. of Kentucky.
329.16	almost certainly Florence Dugdale. If the story was in fact published, it must have been unsigned.] Florence Dugdale; the story was presumably her 'The Scholar's Wife' (see VII.147).
333.2	Country] County
340.12up	Mr] My

345.3up	presumably pub. in the *Bungalow*, of which no complete file appears to exist.] Judge's 'Portland Stone', *British Architect*, 20 Nov 1907.
354.19up	House] Hill
357.18	Henry Austin Charles] Henry Charles Austin

Volume Four

34.16up	playright] playwright
45.2	Clarke] Clark
47.18	grandfather] father
92.10up	Groove's] Grove's
100.12	MacCarthy] McCarthy
123.6	Library.] Library. *Date* Year from postmark.
152.5	Berg.] Berg; envelope apparently postmarked MY 4 11 also Berg.
174.10	HANDLEY] GEORGE EVANS
174.25–6	the Revd. Handley Carr Glyn Moule, Bishop of Durham since 1901; see I.70. TH had known him from childhood.] TH is evidently addressing the Revd. George Evans Moule (see I.84), recently returned to England following his resignation as Bishop of Mid-China.
178.21	search] searched
224.3up	Wilfred] Wilfrid
231.14up	George Meredith's grandfather] in fact, George Meredith's father
236.10up	BL.] BL; envelope Berg.
242.7	Taylor.] Taylor; envelope (postmarked DE 14 12) Berg.
316.16up	(transcript, DCM)] (DCM)
331.9	(transcript, DCM)] (DCM)

Volume Five

11.16	(transcript, DCM)] (DCM) *Also at*: 30.10up, 38.13up, 71.17, 87.18
21.4up	A. F. Pollard (1859–1944, literary scholar; *D.N.B.*)] Albert Frederick Pollard (1869–1948, historian; *D.N.B.*)
35.6up	John Francis] John Frederic
43.21	Buith] Builth Wells
56.6up	Boynton] Boyton
75.3	readable.] readable. *Dicken's*: FEH's error.
79.17	Bergonism] Bergsonism
81.4up	copies.] copies; the originals are in DCM.
82.1up	presumably the one manufactured and sold] evidently the one created by the sculptor William Carter Unwin, copies of which appear to have been sold
99.15–16up	transcript DCM)] DCM)
128.6up	Yale.] Yale; envelope Berg.
171.1up	ELH.] ELH; now in DCM.

179.9	*History*] *Tragedy*
216.14up	Guildford] Guilford
233.3up	'In Time] 'In the Time
261.4up	nolo] uolo
274.12	untraced.] untraced; see, however, the article on Came House in the *Dorset Year Book, 1924*, in which eleven portraits are listed.
275.12	Wilfred] Wilfrid
300.1up	Wilfred] Wilfrid
319.7	take] takes
320.5up	Holmes.] Holmes; envelope Berg.
349.3up	1869] 1862
357.12up	J.C., 330, 332,] J.C., 322, 330,

Volume Six

8.9up	perfomance] performance
23.1up	Kiss'.] Kiss'. In the catalogue of the sale of Max Gate effects, 16 Feb 1938, it was entitled 'A French Soldier embracing a dying German soldier on the Field of Battle'.
36.3–5up	Grace Amelia Morton Pitt (d. 1836), second wife of William Morton Pitt (1754–1836), owner of Kingston Maurward House, near Dorchester.] Lora Pitt, *née* Grey (d. 1750), second wife of George Pitt of Stratfield Say, Hampshire; see Hutchins, *History and Antiquities of the County of Dorset* (see VII.85), II.563n, 564, 566, etc. She was the heiress of the Grey family of Kingston Maurward House, in the parish of Stinsford, and well remembered for her many benefactions in the Dorchester area.
42.7up	it is not clear what (if any) particular passage TH had in mind.] from verse 8 of the Tate and Brady metrical version of Psalm 34 (adapted as hymn 290 of *Hymns Ancient and Modern*).
72.2	Brockhampton] Bockhampton
82.13	*Snelgroves*:] *Snelgroves*: correctly, Marshall & Snelgrove,
106.11–13up	possibly Capt. Robert Charles George Thwaites of the Royal Army Veterinary Corps, though the indicated relationship to Douglas has not been established.] probably the Revd. Nembhard Thwaites, vicar of Bothenhampton, Dorset; he had seen local service as an army chaplain during the recent war and had a Scottish wife.
121.8up	Adams.] Adams; envelope NYU.
123.8	such as] such a
134.11	Sample).] Sample); envelope Berg.
163.2up	Madern] Maddern
202.5up	BL.] BL; envelope Colby.
205.10	early] early,
205.18	Mary Jacobus.] (with envelope) DCM.

214.10up	by by] by
243.17	*New Adelphi*] *Adelphi*
245.2	*music for the songs*] *change the title*: as Boughton had suggested in his worried letter of 6 Apr 24 (copy, BL). *music for the songs*
276.6up	*the Agreement*] *your opinion*: as expressed in his letter of 26 Sept 24 (draft, BL). *the Agreement*
280.3up	Thomas Henry Tilley, the producer of the Hardy plays (see letter of 17 Nov 20), was a] E. W. Tilley, not the producer of the Hardy plays (the 'Mr Tilley' of TH's last paragraph), but a Dorchester
284.18	it] it to
284.23	*New Adelphi*] *Adelphi*
291.10up	Bovingdon] Bovington
303.1	BL.] BL; envelope Berg.
313.24	that] than
364.11up	works] words
374.12	evidently sent TH a copy] sent TH an inscribed copy (David Holmes)

INDEX OF RECIPIENTS
Volume Seven

Acland, John, 25
Aldrich, Charles, 112
Allhusen, Dorothy, 22, 27, 51, 84
Amery, L. S., 53
Archer, William, 136, 149
Ashley, the Hon. Jane, 115
Atkinson, Henry Tindal, 100

Barker, Ernest, 30, 50
Barker, Harley Granville, 25, 67, 85
Barker, Harley and Helen Granville, 54
Barrett, Wilson, 109, 109
Bates, Charles, 10
Bawler, Walter, 148, 151
Baxter, Lucy, 108
Beerbohm, Max, 133
Bell, Edward Price, 23
Bennet, the Revd. Norman, 34
Berkowitz, Walter J., 63
Bernard, Archbishop John, 160
Besant, Walter, 95, 99, 111, 166, 167
Blackie & Son, 141
Bone, Clement, 32
Boughton, Rutland, 33, 34, 35
Boulton, Sir Harold, 142
Bowen, John, 98
Bradish, Margaret, 12
Bridges, Robert, 170
Bright, R. Golding, 8, 22, 30, 36, 37, 58
Brindley, H. H., 146, 151
Bronson, Katherine, 106
Builder, the Editor of the, 133
Bullen, Florence, 82
Bulloch, J. M., 138
Butler, the Revd. H. M., 155

Cameron, N. O. M., 41
Carnarvon, Lord, 110, 110
Chatto & Windus, 90
Childs, C. Borlase, 71
Clifford, Lucy, 126, 127, 158
Clodd, Edward, 32, 70, 123, 131, 141, 152, 169
Cockerell, Sydney, 72
Collier, John, 93
Collins, Vere H., 36
Cornford, F. M., 151
Cornford, Frances, 150
Courtney, W. L., 143
Cowley, the Revd. H. G. B., 7, 9, 15

Crackanthorpe, Blanche, 135
Croft, W. D., 62
Cronshaw, the Revd. G. B., 88, 170

Dalton, Basil, 52
Denis, Lisbeth, 65
Dewar, George, 149
Dickinson, the Revd. J. H., 56
Douglas, Sir George, 70, 121
Drinkwater, John, 42, 47
Dron, T. M., 101, 112
Dugdale, Edward, Emma and Constance, 26

Edgcumbe, Sir Robert Pearce, 68
Edinburgh Philosophical Institution, 135
Ellis, Havelock, 113
Ellis, S. M., 159, 160
Ervine, St. John, 41, 43, 81
Everett, Augusta, 42

Falkner, John Meade, 153
Fenn, George Manville, 165
Field, Eugene, II, 23
Filleul, the Revd. S. E. V., 137
Flower, Archibald, 43
Flower, Newman, 60, 79
Forsyth-Major, O. H., 45
Foster, J. J., 114, 117, 127
Fowler, J. H., 163
Freund, A. W., 74
Frith, Miss, 95
Fyfe, Hamilton, 162

Galsworthy, John, 39, 42, 51
Gardiner, A. G., 130
Garland, Hamlin, 131
Gilchrist, Robert, 144
Godwin, J. T., 84
Gosse, (Sir) Edmund, 27, 33, 77, 81, 84, 89, 97, 103, 125
Greenwood, Frederick, 138
Guedalla, Philip, 39
Guest, Montague, 122

Halpérine-Kaminsky, E., 131
Hardy, the Revd. Henry, 154
Hardy, Katharine, 140, 142, 156
Harper & Brothers, 113, 118
Harrison, Mary, 119, 120

Heathcote, Thornhill, 97, 97, 98, 100
Heinemann, William, 140
Henley, W. E., 117
Herbert, Lady Winifred, 101
Herriot, George, 103
Higginson, Thomas Wentworth, 130
Hignett, John, 88
Hind, Arthur, 24
Hodges, Wilfrid, 26, 45
Holst, Gustav, 73
Holzmann, Maurice, 103, 104, 104, 105, 105
Houghton, Lord, 125
Hudson, Sir Robert, 150
Hueffer, Ford Madox, 148
Hueffer, Francis, 91
Hunt, Violet, 142
Hutchinson, John, 4
Hutchinson, Thomas, 111
Hutton, R. H., 101

Ilbert, Sir Courtenay, 157
Isbister, William, 92

Jarvis, C. W., 114
Jones, Henry Arthur, 13
Jones, J. Winter, 90

Keeble, Lady, 77, 82, 84
Kenyon, John, 68
Kinross, Albert, 134

Lacey, Charles, 62, 83
Lane, John, 147
Lang, John Marshall, 168
Laski, Harold, 24
Lasselin, Georges, 85
Lawrence, Harry, 67
Leake, Désirée, 129
Lee, H. W., 1
Linton, Eliza Lynn, 110
Lister-Kaye, Lady Beatrice, 132
Lock, H. O., 26, 28, 148
Longman, C. J., 106
Lytton, Lord, 107

McCabe, Joseph, 162
McCarthy, Justin, 107
Macer-Wright, Philip, 52
McKay, Roy, 21
Macmillan, Alexander, 91
Macmillan, Daniel, 31, 31
Macmillan, (Sir) Frederick, 1, 2, 6, 6, 8, 14,
   15, 28, 29, 35, 36, 46, 47, 48, 48, 57, 58,
   59, 59, 60, 63, 66, 69, 71, 71, 73, 75, 76,
   82, 86, 87, 145
Martin, H. A., 156
Maynard, Theodore, 18

Maxwell, William, 78, 80, 81
Medway, Frederick, 56
Meredith, W. M., 72, 79
Millay, Edna St. Vincent, 64
Milne, James, 144
Morgan, J. H., 3, 19, 169
Morris, May, 155
Moule, the Revd. G. H., 39
Moulton, Louise Chandler, 123

Napier, J. H., 129
Nevill, Lady Dorothy, 124
Nevinson, Henry W., 152
Newbolt, Sir Henry, 29, 55, 68
Nicholson, Sydney, 7
Norris, W. H., 161

Orr, Alexandra Sutherland, 93
Osgood, James, 117
Osgood, McIlvaine & Co., 119

Parker, W. H., 53
Parsons, J. D., 49
Pearsall, Robert, 43
Pinney, John, 14
Pinney, Lady, 5
Pollock, Walter, 93
Poole, Austin Lane, 151
Popham, Jane, 33
Powys, A. R., 17
Priestley, J. B., 38
Purves, John, 143, 163

Raad, the Revd. N. C., 74
Rice-Oxley, Sir Alfred, 50
Ridgeway, Philip, 19
Rockman, Ray, 139
Romer, Carol, 78
Rothenstein, William, 167

Salisbury, the Bishop of, 13
Salmon, Yvonne, 83
Sampson Low, Marston & Co., 94
Scarlet, John, 105
Score, H. Berkeley, 142
Sharp, William, 121
Shorter, Clement, 127, 132, 134, 135, 137,
   139, 149, 155, 160
Silver, Christine, 6
Sinclair, Upton, 69
Sladen, Douglas, 126
Slater, F. W., 16
Smallman, Percy, 11
Smith, H. Greenhough, 147
Sotheby & Co., 66
Spencer, Walter T., 134
Spurgeon, Arthur, 168

Squire, J. C., 10, 73
Stebbing, W., 46
Stopes, Marie, 16, 44
Swaffield, Alfred, 145
Symonds, A. G., 61
Symons, Arthur, 20

Tadema, Laurence Alma, 102, 128, 128, 129
Thorne, Doris, 87
Thring, G. Herbert, 4, 5, 11, 15, 21, 52, 55, 61

Unidentified Correspondents, 91, 109, 123, 165, 166, 166, 167, 168, 168
Untermeyer, Louis, 75

Viereck, George, 144

Walker, the Revd. E. M., 18
Watkins, William, 146, 153
Watson, Malcolm, 44
Watson, William, 118
Wells, H. G., 40, 49
Weltzien, Erich, 64
Whitehead, Frederick, 124, 125, 126
Whitfield, Archie, 161
Whyte, Frederic, 37
Wilmshurst, George, 95, 96
Wilson, Henry, 116
Wise, Thomas J., 12, 13, 58
Withers, Percy, 159

GENERAL INDEX
Compiled by Frank Dunn

The titles of Hardy's works are dispersed alphabetically throughout the index. All other works are indexed under their authors.

Sub-headings are arranged chronologically in the case of events, and alphabetically for buildings listed under towns and cities.

Under LONDON only churches, hotels, streets, and general references are given. Other specific buildings and institutions (e.g. British Museum), clubs, theatres, etc. appear alphabetically dispersed throughout.

Those footnotes which contain the main biographical details about a person are distinguished by an asterisk (e.g. i. 2 n.*).

Topical entries appear in bold-face (e.g. **architecture, interest in**).

'A.H., 1855–1912' (poem) iv. 215 ('the verses'), 216 n.

à Beckett, Patrick Abbott Forbes Winslow:
and Portland Garrison Gala Performance v. 131, 132 nn.
and Weymouth Garrison League Performance v. 168, 169 n.
letters to v. 131, 168

Abbey, Edwin Austin i. 115 n.*, 152 n., 269; ii. 286, 287 n., 304 n.
letters to i. 115, 128, 145, 148

Abbey, Mary Gertrude ii. 286 ('the Abbeys')

'Abbey Mason, The' (poem) ii. 197 n.; iv. 214 ('a poem'), 215 n., 326 ('a poem') and n.
MS. sold to J. P. Morgan iv. 208 and n.
pub. in *Harper's* iv. 208 and n., 254 and n.

Abbey Theatre company iv. 92 n., 95 n., 160 n.

Abbotsbury (Dorset) ii. 306; vii. 40 and n., 81 n.
St Catharine's Chapel iii. 337 and n., 346

Abbott, Edward i. 56 n.
letter to i. 56

Abbott, James Reymond de Montmorency iii. 23 n.*, 86, 126 n., 203, 240, 286 n., 354 and n.; iv. 262
Dorset sightseeing iii. 24, 25, 26, 82, 228
interest in organs iii. 25 and n., 89, 131
invited to Max Gate iii. 23, 100, 131, 240; iv. 263; vi. 272 n.
letters to iii. 23, 24, 25, 26, 87–8, 100, 126, 131, 144, 239; iv. 17, 51, 55, 171, 262, 279, 327; v. 27, 129, 172; vi. 272

Abercrombie, Lascelles iv. 225 n.; v. 68
Daily Herald article on TH v. 312, 313 n.
and 'Poets' Tribute' v. 326, 327 n.
monetary grants to vii. 159 and nn.
Thomas Hardy: A Critical Study iv. 225 and

n., 328 ('the last'), 329 n.; v. 68 n.
letters to v. 68, 312, 326

'Aberdeen' (poem) iii. 220 n.

Aberdeen v. 233 n., 281
Art Gallery vii. 138 n.

Aberdeen, University of iii. 220 n., 255 n., 278 and n.
TH as LL.D. of iii. 159, 161, 162, 165, 175, 279 n.; v. 233 n.; vii. 138 and n., 144 n., 168 and n.
Quatercentenary iii. 226
TH MS given to iv. 180, 181 n., 184, 186

Aberdeen University Press iii. 220 n.

'Absentmindedness in a Parish Choir' (story) iii. 319 ('story of mine') and n.; iv. 231 ('the story') and n.; v. 173 n.

'Absolute Explains, The' (poem) vi. 307, 311 ('the verses') and n.
pub. in *Nineteenth Century and After* vi. 308 n., 314 ('that poem') and n.

Academy i. 104 and n., 153; ii. 155 n., 205, 206 n., 214, 238 and n.; iii. 38, 39 n.; iv. 195 n.; vii. 119 n.
and *Well-Beloved* ii. 156 n., 160 and n.
TH's letter on Maeterlinck iii. 21 and n.
and Swinburne iv. 15, 16 n.

'According to the Mighty Working' (poem) vi. 218 and n.
pub. in *Athenaeum* v. 298 n., 301 ('proof'), 306, 307 n.; vi. 9 n., 18 ('short poem')

Acland, Arthur Herbert Dyke ii. 77 and n.

Acland, Captain John Edward iv. 123, 141 n.; vi. 226
as Curator of Dorset County Museum iii. 262, 293 and n.; iv. 184 ('a friend') and n., 190; v. 174; vi. 26
letters to iii. 262, 293, 340; iv. 76, 77, 80,

Acland, Captain John Edward (*cont.*)
119, 135, 190, 300; v. 174, 252; vi. 26;
vii. 25
Acland, Norah (Mrs J. Acland) iv. 123 n.
letter to iv. 123
Adams, A. Davies vi. 245 n.
Adams, Henry Brooks ii. 89, 90 n.*
Adams, William Davenport i. 134 n.
(ed.) *Songs from the Novelists* i. 134 n., 135
letter to i. 134
Adelboden iii. 196 and n.
Adelphi vi. 200 and n., 242, 243 n. (wrongly
New Adelphi), 284 n. (wrongly *New
Adelphi*)
Adey, William More iv. 306 n.
Adult ii. 160 n.
Aeschylus v. 246
Agamemnon iii. 197; vi. 256 and nn.
Affpuddle (Dorset) i. 142 n.
as 'East Egdon' ii. 255
Aflalo, Frederick G.:
(ed.) *Literary Year-Book, 1897* ii. 148
('Author's year book') and n.
'After the Visit' (poem):
pub. in *Spectator* iv. 112 n.
written to FEH v. 70 ('one to Florence'),
71 n.
'Afternoon service at Mellstock' (poem) vii. 9
Agate, James Evershed:
The Contemporary Theatre, 1925 vii. 26 n.
'Agnus, Orme' (John C. Higginbotham) iv.
205, 206 n.
'Ah, are you Digging on My Grave?' (poem):
pub. in *Saturday Review* iv. 288 n.
Aidé, Charles Hamilton ii. 26 n.
letters to ii. 26, 118
Ainley, Henry:
as Reader in *Dynasts* stage version v. 54 n.
Ainsworth, William Harrison:
Rookwood iv. 272 n.
Windsor Castle iv. 272 and n.
Air Pie: The Royal Air Force Annual v. 281 and
n.
Aitchison, John i. 92 and n.
Aix-les-Bains ii. 266 and n.; iii. 330; iv. 213
and n.
Alan's Wife (anon.) ii. 8 and n.
Albany (N.Y.), Bishop of ii. 92 n., 95
Albert, Prince Consort vi. 94, 95 n.
Albert John of Schleswig-Holstein, Prince ii.
26 ('Victor Albert') and n., 27
Aldeburgh (Suffolk) ii. 30 and n., 257; iv. 62
and n., 204, 257; v. 44
Whitsun gatherings at i. 237, 239 ('down
there') and n., 240 and n., 254, 255 n.; ii.
58 n., 75 n., 163, 217, 220 and n., 222,
287, 288 and n., 289; iii. 20, 59 and n.,

62 n., 122 and n., 196; iv. 21 and n., 25;
vii. 123 and n., 132 and n.
other visits to ii. 204; iii. 2, 20, 119, 172 n.;
iv. 29 n., 30, 40, 41 nn., 43 and n., 48 nn.,
49 and nn., 55 and n., 80 n., 81 n., 91 and
n., 112, 113, 114 nn., 119, 142 and nn.,
147, 148 n., 149 n., 150 and n., 151,
155 n., 176, 183 n., 185, 212, 214 n.,
258 n., 267, 268, 269, 270; vii. 141 and
nn., 155 n.
Crabbe celebration (1905) iii. 180 and n.,
182 n.; vii. 141 and n.
FED invited to iv. 35, 38, 39 and n., 41 n.
Aldeburgh, Leiston and Saxmundham Times
iv. 41 ('local paper'), 42 n.
Alden, Ada Foster (Mrs H. M. Alden) vi.
60 nn.
letter to vi. 60
Alden, Henry Mills i. 72 n.*; ii. 121 and n.; iv.
84 n.; vi. 60 and nn.
letters to i. 72, 180
'Alderworth':
original of ii. 255
Aldrich, Charles vii. 112 n.
letter to vii. 112
Aldrich, Thomas Bailey i. 102 n.*, 128
as editor of *Atlantic Monthly* i. 101 and n.,
103, 138 and n.
The Sisters' Tragedy i. 230 ('your volume')
and n.
letters to i. 101, 103, 138, 147, 230
Alexander, (Sir) George i. 284 n.*; ii. 148,
149 n.; v. 176, 177 n.
letter to i. 283
Alexander, John White i. 152 n., 153
letter to i. 152
Alexandra, Queen:
memorial to vii. 5 and n.
See also Wales, Princess of
Alexandra Club ii. 76 ('yr Club') and n., 78,
149, 150 n., 257, 261, 285, 286; iii. 318
('your Club'); iv. 31 and n.
'Alfredston':
Wantage as ii. 133
Alhambra Theatre iii. 213 and n.; v. 343 n.
'Alicia's Diary' (story) i. 162 ('promised
story'), 163 n.
Allbutt, Sir Thomas Clifford iii. 267 and n.*;
iv. 269 and n., 273; vi. 135 and n.
Allen, Ellen (Mrs Grant Allen) i. 277; ii.
234 n.; vii. 173
letter to ii. 234
Allen, Grant i. 277 n.*
on *Jude* ii. 106 n.
death ii. 234 and n., 235 n.
The British Barbarians ii. 106 and n.
The Lower Slopes ii. 58 and n.

Allen, Grant (cont.)
  The Woman Who Did ii. 68 ('your book'),
    69 n., 75 and n.
  letters to i. 277; ii. 58, 68, 74, 106
Allhusen, Adelaide ii. 38 and n.; vii. 173
  letter to ii. 249 (wrongly attributed to
    Henry)
Allhusen, Augustus Henry Eden i. 257 n.; ii.
    38 n., 249 n.*; iii. 4 n., 104 n., 196 and
    n.
  marriage to Dorothy Stanley ii. 119 n., 127
    n., 134 n.
  death vi. 324 and n.
  memorial to vii. 27 ('the room') and n.
  letter to ii. 249 (wrong attribution corrected
    at vii. 173)
Allhusen, Dorothea Elizabeth v. 241 ('your
    daughter') and n.; vi. 180, 181 n.,
    230 nn.; vii. 22 ('sweet child') and n., 27
  letter to vi. 230
Allhusen (formerly Stanley, q.v.), Dorothy ii.
    205, 206, 222; iii. 69 and n., 114 ('the
    girls') and n., 196, 267, 330; iv. 30, 268; v.
    27, 61; vi. 151, 152 n.; vii. 132 n.
  inscribed copies from TH iii. 1; iv. 316 ('the
    book'), 317 n.
  painted by Sargent iii. 265 ('the portrait')
    and n., 302 and n.
  gifts to TH iv. 197, 332; v. 20, 272
  visits *Dynasts* v. 57, 62, 63, 76
  wartime causes v. 57 n., 76, 100 n., 286 n.,
    310; vi. 23 ('experiences abroad') and n.
  at Max Gate v. 272 n.; vi. 180, 181 n.
  and appeal for Stoke Poges church vi. 206,
    207 n.
  A Book of Scents & Dishes vii. 51 ('the book')
    and n.
  letters to ii. 48, 119, 127, 134, 179, 191, 204,
    206, 219; iii. 1, 4, 8, 68, 104, 125, 202,
    208, 211, 215, 265, 270, 302, 312, 328; iv.
    96, 100, 197, 224, 247, 261, 316, 332; v. 8,
    20, 27, 57, 62, 76, 100, 240, 272, 286, 310,
    351; vi. 23, 59, 148, 151, 159, 206, 324;
    vii. 22, 27, 51, 84
Allhusen, Frederick Henry iv. 261 ('your
    friends') and n.
Allhusen, Henry Christian Stanley vii. 27 n.
Allhusen (later Congreve), Madeleine vi. 148
    and n.
  wedding vi. 159 and n., 163
Allhusen, Wilton ii. 38 and n.
*Allibone's Critical Dictionary of English Litera-
    ture* i. 189 n.
Allingham (formerly Paterson, q.v.), Helen i.
    74 n., 75 n., 181, 182 n.; iii. 218
  letters to i. 30, 73
Allingham, William i. 30 n.; iii. 218 and n.

Alma Mater (Aberdeen University magazine)
    iii. 220 and n.; vii. 144 and n.
Alma Tadema, Laurence vii. 102 n.
  proposed Italian translation of *Tess* vii.
    128–9 and n.
  Love's Martyr vii. 102 ('handsome book')
    and n.
  letters to vii. 102, 128–9
Alma-Tadema, (Sir) Lawrence i. 191, 192 n.*;
    ii. 20, 21 n.; vii. 102 n.
Almond, Arthur G. (Cambridge tailor) iv.
    273, 274 n., 301
Ambassadors Theatre vi. 367 n.
Ameen, Elin ii. 8 and n.
  'Befriad' ii. 8 n.
American Express Company v. 127 n.
American Play Company iii. 273 n.
American Poetry 1922: A Miscellany vi. 186
    and nn.
American Red Cross ii. 267 n.
Amery, Leopold Charles Maurice Stennett vii.
    53 nn.
  letter to vii. 53
Ames, Percy W. iv. 215 nn.
  letters to iv. 215, 216; v. 202
Ames, Winthrop:
  interest in producing *Tess* vi. 302 n., 312 n.,
    338 n., 353–4, 355, 357; vii. 8
(?)Amey, Eliza i. 2 ('Miss A.'), 3 n.; vii. 171
(?)Amey, Eliza (aunt of above) i. 2, 3 n. (un-
    identified, but see vii. 171)
'Among the Roman Gravemounds' (poem)
  pub. in *English Review* iv. 182 ('the poem')
    and n.
Amsteg (Switzerland) vii. 45, 46 n.
Amsterdam ii. 134
Amy (Max Gate servant) v. 61 and n.
'Ancient to Ancients, An' (poem) v. 319 n.; vi.
    160 and n.
  pub. in *Century Magazine* vi. 113 and n.,
    123 and n.
  in *Best Poems of 1922* vi. 183, 184 n.
'Ancient Earthworks at Casterbridge' (article)
    ii. 3 ('the article') and n., 35, 43
'And There Was a Great Calm' (poem) vi.
    46 n., 193 n.
Anderson, Graham vi. 355 n.
Anderson, Sherwood vi. 38 n.
Andrews, Arthur Robert iii. 1 n.
  letter to iii. 1
'Anet, Claude' (Jean Schopfer) vi. 174 and n.
'Anglebury':
  Wareham as iii. 359 n.
Anglo-Saxon Review ii. 271, 272 n.
Animal Defence and Anti-Vivisection League
    vi. 223 n.
animals, attitude towards i. 217; ii. 47, 97,

animals, attitude towards (*cont.*)
136, 157, 270, 272, 282; iii. 74, 82, 83, 85, 86, 90, 110, 137, 213, 231, 238, 333, 339, 341, 343, 347, 361; iv. 51, 90, 96, 132, 143, 174, 330; v. 1, 20, 30, 61, 71, 121, 277, 321, 340; vi. 9, 44, 82, 120, 144, 223, 243–4, 277, 278, 323; vii. 12, 51, 54

Animals' Friend ii. 97 n., 100 ('little periodical')
letter to ii. 97

Animals' Guardian ii. 199 n.; iv. 90 nn.

'Anna, Lady Baxby' (story) ii. 132

'Annie Laurie' (trad.) vii. 70, 71 n., 80 and n., 81 n.

'Anniversary Edition' iv. 308 n.; vi. 39, 40 n., 145 and n., 213

'Annotated edition' (proposed) iii. 16 and n.

'Anstey, F.' – *see* Guthrie, Thomas Anstey

Antell, John (cousin) i. 92 n.; iii. 74 n.; vii. 28 n.
letter to i. 92

Antell, John (uncle) i. 92 n., 232 n.

Antell (formerly Hand), Mary (aunt) i. 92 n., 232 n.

Antell, Mary Elizabeth ('Polly') (cousin) i. 232 and n., 237; v. 320 n.

Anthony, Joseph vi. 113 nn.
The Gang vi. 113 ('the novel') and n.
letter to vi. 113

Anti-Jacobin ii. 156 n.

Antommarchi, F.:
Mémoires vi. 105 and n.

Antrobus, Sir Edmund ii. 228, 229 n.

'Any little old Song' (poem) vi. 241, 275 n.

'Appeal to America on behalf of the Belgian Destitute, An' (poem) v. 76 ('the lines') and n.

Appletons' Journal i. 40, 41 n.

Arch, Joseph i. 118, 119 n.

Archaeological Review vii. 114 ('Review') and n.

Archer, William i. 228 n., 287 n.*; ii. 8 n., 139 n., 265; iv. 2 nn., 24 n.; v. 117 n.
copy of *Tess* sent to i. 287
criticism of *Life's Little Ironies* ii. 56 and n., 57 and n.
invited to Max Gate ii. 89
review of *Jude* ii. 104
and 70th birthday tribute to Ibsen ii. 187 n.
and *Wessex Poems* ii. 206, 207
interview with TH ii. 279 and nn., 280, 281; iii. 76 ('Conversation'), 77 n.
and *Dynasts* iii. 105 and n.
and 'Panthera' iv. 47 ('one a reviewer'), 48 n.
and scheme for national theatre vii. 136 and nn., 149 and nn.

'Pandering to Podsnap' ii. 90 ('an article') and n., 96 n.

Real Conversations iii. 77 n., 104 ('the book'), 105 nn.
letters to i. 287; ii. 8–9, 57, 89, 90, 96, 104, 206, 207, 279, 281; iii. 76, 84, 104, 107, 257; iv. 2, 23; vii. 136, 149

Architectural Association v. 116; vi. 187 n.
TH attends Conversazione i. 2, 3 nn.
'small prize' won by TH i. 4 and n.
TH's refusal of Hon. Membership vi. 186

architecture, interest in i. 1, 4, 95, 205, 220–1, 223, 225, 233; ii. 130, 141, 176, 178, 197, 278, 301; iii. 4, 35, 50, 54, 97, 224, 226, 235–6, 268, 283, 337, 346, 350; iv. 18–20, 56, 74, 78, 114, 122, 146, 261, 299, 326; v. 3, 171, 198; vi. 5, 15, 30, 36, 41, 71, 94, 122, 147, 176, 183, 206, 207, 226, 234; vii. 115–16, 133

Architecture Club vi. 147 ('Architectural') and nn., 183 ('A.C.') and nn.

Archiv für das Studium der neueren Sprachen ii. 39 n.

Ardilaun, Lady (Olivia Charlotte) ii. 19 and n.

Argosy vii. 59 and n.

Ariel Poems vii. 75 n.

Arlington Manor (Berks) (Jeune country home) ii. 34, 35 n., 74 n., 159, 173 n., 174, 208, 229, 232; iii. 2

Armitage, Edward iv. 207 and n.

Arnold, Matthew i. 70 and n., 117 n., 190; iv. 16 n.; vi. 102, 103 n., 327; vii. 22 n.
Essays in Criticism vi. 202 n.
'Tristram and Iseult' vi. 222 n.

Arnold, Samuel vi. 248 n.

Arnold, Lieut. Thomas Sarell v. 230 ('your nephew') and n.

Arnold, Major William Reginald iii. 283 n.
letter to iii. 283

art and artists, views on i. 1, 5, 25, 45, 73, 126, 150, 184, 185, 191; ii. 134, 255, 257, 286; iii. 56, 254; iv. 85, 151, 214; v. 303, 343

Art Journal ii. 295 n.; iii. 15 n.

Art for Schools Association i. 116–17

Art-World (projected journal) i. 202 ('painter's weekly'), 209 and n.

Arthur, Prince, of Connaught v. 30 n.

Arts and Crafts Exhibition Society v. 292 n.

Arts League of Service vi. 114 and n.

Arts Monthly i. 197 and n.

Ascham, Roger i. 282

Ashburton, Leonora, Lady ii. 144, 145 n.

Ashburton, Louisa, Lady ii. 35, 36 n., 145 n.

Ashley, Evelyn ii. 222 n.
letter to ii. 222

Ashley, Hon. Mrs Jane Frances i. 221 and n., 225; vii. 116
letter to vii. 115

Asquith, Herbert Henry (later Earl of Oxford

Asquith, Herbert Henry (cont.)
  and Asquith) iv. 287, 288 n.; v. 132 n.; vi. 262 n.; vii. 13 and n., 157 n.
  offer of knighthood to TH iii. 353 and n.
  sees *Dynasts* v. 59 n., 71
  letter to iii. 353
Asquith, Margot iii. 131 and n.; iv. 330, 331 n.; v. 59 and n.
Astell, Mrs Charles Edward ii. 204 and n.
Astor, Nancy Witcher Astor, Viscountess vi. 120 and n.
'At Casterbridge Fair' (poem) iv. 132 n.
  pub. in *Cornhill* iii. 7 ('my little rhyme') and n., 9 ('the proof')
'At the Entering of the New Year' (poem):
  pub. in *Athenaeum* vi. 51 and n., 57 ('poem of mine')
'At a House in Hampstead' (poem) vi. 43 ('sent off only one') and n., 82 ('Keats poem') and n.
'At an Inn' (poem) ii. 215, 216 n., 219
'At a Lunar Eclipse' (poem) v. 246
'At a Pause in a Country Dance' (poem) vi. 371 n.
'At the War Office After a Bloody Battle' (later 'At the War Office, London') (poem) ii. 241 and n.
  pub. in *Sphere* ii. 245
'At the Word "Farewell"' (poem) v. 250, 291 n.
Athelhampton Church (Dorset) v. 198 and n.
Athelhampton Hall (Dorset) ii. 86 and n., 201, 237 n., 238, 305 n.; iii. 138, 220 n.; v. 198 n.; vi. 140, 141 n., 275 and n.
Athenaeum i. 157 n., 258 and n.; iii. 38, 39 n.; iv. 185, 186 n.; v. 65 n., 180, 181 n.; vi. 43 and n.; vii. 26 n., 109 n.
  on *Desperate Remedies* i. 11, 12
  TH's obit. of Barnes in i. 153 nn., 157 n.; ii. 61 and n., 62; vii. 109 n.
  letter on Harper fair dealing i. 218, 219 nn., 223
  Kipling verse reply i. 219 n., 223 and n.
  TH disclaimer in iii. 48 n., 61 n.
  TH's obit. of 'Laurence Hope' in iii. 143 and n.
  revival of v. 297 ('first number'), 298 nn.
  'According to the Mighty Working' pub. in v. 298 n., 301, 306, 307 n.; vi. 9 n., 18 ('short poem')
  'The Maid of Keinton-Mandeville' pub. in vi. 12 ('some verses') and n.
  'At the Entering of the New Year' pub. in vi. 51 and n., 57 ('poem of mine') and n.
Athenaeum Club i. 270, 286; ii. 25, 76, 77 n., 82, 88, 269, 277; iii. 60, 62, 65, 88, 90, 127, 129 n., 310, 318, 321; iv. 9 and n., 23, 36, 79 and n., 82, 152, 153, 320; v. 92,
244; vi. 261, 262 n., 317 n.; vii. 122, 167 and n.
  TH's election to i. 234, 235 n.; vii. 110 and n.
Atkinson, Henry Tindal i. 111 n.*, 135 n.; vii. 98 n.
  letters to i. 111, 135; vii. 100
Atkinson, Louisa vii. 100 and n.
Atlantic Monthly ii. 96; iii. 332 n.; vii. 114 n., 131 nn.
  possible serialization in i. 29 and n., 32 and n., 67, 95, 138 n.
  serialization of *Two on a Tower* i. 95 n., 101–2, 103, 106 n., 138 n.
'Augustan Books of Modern Poetry' vi. 317 n.
Aus Fremden Zungen ii. 68 n.; iii. 222, 248
Austen, Jane v. 221, 222 n.; vi. 35 and n., 43
  as 'Wessex worthy' v. 337, 338 n.
Austerlitz, Battle of (1805) iv. 193 n.
Austin, Alfred i. 111 n.*, 258 n.; iv. 287 n.
  Lyrical Poems i. 238 ('your volume') and n.
  letters to i. 111, 238, 258
Austin, L. F. ii. 101 n.
Author ii. 237 n.
Authors, Society of – see Incorporated Society of Authors, Playwrights, and Composers
Authors' Cinematograph Agency iv. 289 n.
Authors' Club ii. 8 ('the Club') and n.; v. 130 n.
  dinner to Zola ii. 8 n., 34 n., 36 n.
Authors' Club of New York iii. 364
Authors' League of America vi. 195 n.
Authors' Syndicate i. 225 n., 241 n.; ii. 5 n., 9 ('a bureau') and n., 72 n.; vii. 111 ('scheme'), 112 n.
  Council of i. 261 and n.
  letters to i. 225; ii. 173
Autograph Edition iv. 217 ('edition in America') and n., 233 n., 244 ('American edition'), 254 ('this edition') and n., 308 n., 324 ('Wessex novels') and n.; v. 52 ('your Wessex edition') and n., 148, 259 ('recent edition')
'Autumn in My Lord's [King's Hintock] Park' (poem) iii. 235 ('the verses') and n., 236 ('shy-natured poem'), 242 ('lines of mine'); v. 134 ('the poem') and n.
  pub. in *Dorset Year Book* (as 'Autumn in the Park') v. 343 n.
Avebury (Wilts) vi. 314
Avenue Theatre ii. 139 n.
Aynard, Joseph iii. 71 n.
Ayrton, Mrs William Edward (Matilda Chaplin) iii. 89 and n.
'Ayscough, John' – see Bickerstaffe-Drew

Babbott, Frank L. iii. 326 n.

Baber, Sydney M. iv. 310 n.

Bacon, Sir Francis ii. 35, 36 n.

Baddeley, Angela vi. 336 and nn., 337, 339

Baddeley, Hermione vi. 336 and n., 337, 339, 340

Baddeley, Welbore St. Clair iv. 155 and n.

Bagber (Dorset) ii. 269 and n.

Bagot, Richard:
  and proposed Shakespeare memorial in Rome v. 217, 218 nn.
  letter to v. 217

Bainton, Revd George i. 169 nn.
  The Art of Authorship i. 169 n.
  letter to i. 168

Baldwin, Stanley vi. 357 n.; vii. 13 and n., 81 n., 84 n. ('Prime Minister')

Balestier, Charles Wolcott i. 223 and n.*, 224, 274 n.
  The Average Woman i. 274 ('stories') and n.

Balfour, Arthur James (later Earl) ii. 185 ('A.J.B.') and n.; iii. 131 n.; v. 99 and n.; vi. 33 n., 120 n.; vii. 3 and n., 121
  and former German colonies v. 283 and n.
  and presentation to Gosse vi. 44, 45 n.
  caricatured in Wells's *Men Like Gods* vi. 188 n.

Balfour, Colonel Eustace James Anthony iii. 211 and n.

Balfour, Major Kenneth Robert:
  and restoration of Stinsford church font v. 3, 4 n.

'Ballad Singer, The' (poem) v. 87

Balliol Players vi. 256 ('the company') and n.
  at Max Gate vi. 256 n.; vii. 29 ('undergraduates'), 30 n.

Bancroft, (Sir) Squire i. 212 and n.

Band of Hope v. 276, 277 n.

Bankes, Wynne Albert i. 205 and n.; iii. 4 n., 328 n.; iv. 241 and n.

Bankes, Florence iii. 328 and n. (?); iv. 241 and n.

Bantry, Lady ii. 27 and n.

Barclay, Sir Thomas iv. 327 n.

Bardolf Manor (Dorset) ii. 271 n.; iii. 123 n.; iv. 246 ('your house'), 247 n.

Bardolfston Hill (Dorset) vi. 131 n.

Barham, R. H.:
  Ingoldsby Legends iii. 39 n.

Baring, Maurice:
  and 'Poets' Tribute' v. 327 and n.
  letter to v. 327

Baring-Gould, Sabine:
  Songs of the West: Folk Songs of Devon and Cornwall iii. 247 and n., 283

Barker, Ernest vii. 31 n.
  letters to vii. 30, 50

Barker, Harley Granville iii. 257 and n.; iv. 100
  and nn.; v. 191; vi. 93, 135 and n., 298, 302 n., 312 n.; vii. 32 n.
  production of *Dynasts* v. 51 and n., 52–3, 55–6, 57, 58, 59–61, 62–3, 64–6, 69, 70, 74 and n., 78 and n., 87 and n., 94, 112, 131 and n., 349; vii. 158
  and *Queen of Cornwall* vi. 203 ('little thing'), 204 and n., 210, 219 ('a trifle') and n., 220 and nn.
  and *Tess* play vi. 339, 340, 344, 347 and n., 353, 354, 361, 362
  and scheme for national theatre vii. 136 n., 149 n.
  (with Helen G. B.) *Four Plays by . . . Quintero* vii. 86 n.
  Prefaces to Shakespeare vii. 85 ('Preface'), 86 n.
  The Exemplary Theatre vi. 123 ('new book'), 124 n.
  The Madras House vi. 367 and n., 373, 374 nn.; vii. 26 and n.
  Waste vii. 67 and n.
  letters to v. 51, 52, 53, 54–6, 58, 61, 62; vi. 123, 185, 203, 204, 218, 220, 248, 291, 310, 344, 347, 362, 367, 373; vii. 25, 54, 67, 85

Barker, Helen Granville vi. 93, 124 n.*, 135 n., 219 and n., 367 and n.; vii. 25, 26 n., 32 n., 86
  and *Tess* play vi. 361, 362
  Wives and Celebrities vii. 86 n.
  letter to vii. 54

Barker's (department store) ii. 82, 83 n.

Barnacot & Pearce (Taunton publishers) v. 227 ('Wessex Press'), 228 n.

Barnes, (Sir) Kenneth Ralph vi. 245 n.
  letter to vi. 245

Barnes, Lieut.-Colonel Raglan Wykeham iii. 167 ('Major Bankes') and n., 336 n.

Barnes, Mrs Raglan Wykeham iii. 335

Barnes, Revd William i. 120 n.*, 137, 157 n., 248 and n.; ii. 65 and n., 176 n.; iii. 39 n., 330 and n.; iv. 58 and n., 190, 226; v. 1
  Gosse meeting with i. 119–20, 156 ('bedroom scene'), 157 n., 158
  last illness i. 137 and n., 151, 153, 154
  memorial i. 154, 155 and n., 159 and n., 167; iii. 242 n., 243 n.; vii. 108, 109 n.
  TH's obit. of i. 154, 157 and n.; vii. 109 n.
  daughter's biography of i. 157, 158 n.; vii. 108 and n.
  DNB obit. of ii. 269 and n., 270
  poems set to music iii. 23 and n., 283
  TH's edition of poems (*Select Poems of William Barnes*) iii. 245, 292, 293 nn., 297, 301, 303, 304, 307, 311, 315, 316,

Barnes, Revd William (cont.)
    320, 322, 329, 334, 336,337–9, 340–1,
    342, 348, 351, 360; iv. 6 and n., 22,
    118, 119 n., 120; v. 181 n.; vi. 213, 237,
    238 n.
  TH's further selection of v. 181 and n., 187,
    219 ('dialect spelling'), 220 n., 230, 299
    n.
  Drinkwater's selection of poems vi. 237 and
    n.
  'Chris'mas Invitation' iii. 242 and n., 243
    and n.
  'Come' iii. 342 n.
  'The Fall' iii. 315, 338
  'The Geäte a-vallèn to' iii. 315 and n., 338
    and n., 339
  Glossary of the Dorset Dialect iii. 63 n.; iv.
    312 ('Barnes'), 313 n.; v. 168 n.
  'Joy passed by' iii. 339
  'Light or Shade' iii. 342 n.
  'Lullaby' iii. 342 n.
  'The Morning Moon' iii. 301, 315, 338
  Poems of Rural Life in Common English v.
    175 and n.
  Poems of Rural Life in the Dorset Dialect iii.
    245 and n., 283
    reviewed by TH i. 68 n., 281; ii. 61 and n.,
    62
    TH's selection from iii. 246, 292,
    293 nn., 297, 301, 303, 304
    MS at Dorset County Museum v. 175 and n.
  'Readen ov a Head-Stwone' iv. 120
  'Slow to Come' iii. 342 n.
  'White an' Blue' iii. 315, 338
  'The Wind at the Door' iii. 315, 338
  'Woak Hill' iii. 320, 322 n., 340, 341, 348,
    351 and n.
  letter to i. 119
Barnes, Revd William Miles i. 155 n.*, 217,
    233; ii. 67 n., 269; iv. 76
  and TH's selection of father's poems iii. 297
    ('poet's son') and n., 301, 315 and n., 336,
    337–8, 348
  his own selections iii. 338 n., 341 n.; vi. 237
    ('in aid of . . . school'), 238 n.
  letter to i. 155
Barnes Theatre (Surrey):
  production of *Tess* vi. 334 and n., 335–6,
    337, 338, 339, 340–2, 343–4, 345–6 and
    nn., 347, 348 and n., 349 and n., 350 and
    nn., 351, 352, 353 n., 359 ('the play'),
    361–2, 369 and n.; vii. 6 n.
  production of *Mayor of Casterbridge* vii.
    6 n., 19 n., 36 n.
Barnett, H. Walter iv. 55 n.
  photographs of TH iv. 54, 60 n., 225 and n.
  letter to iv. 54

Barrett, Wilson vii. 109 nn.
  letters to vii. 109
Barrie, (Sir) James Matthew i. 200 n.*; ii. 13;
    iii. 44 and n., 151, 156 n.; iv. 150, 256; v.
    220 n.; vi. 69 n., 86, 126, 281 and n., 357
  at Aldeburgh i. 237, 254, 255 n.
  suggests dramatization of 'The Three
    Strangers' ii. 7 and n.
  and protest against play censorship iii. 277
    and n.; iv. 200, 201 n., 202, 203
  TH's alleged promise to collaborate with iv.
    186 n.
  advice on music-hall fees iv. 193, 194
  knighthood iv. 276 and n., 278
  sees scenes from *Dynasts* v. 191, 193, 205
  at Max Gate v. 205; vi. 22
  as host to TH in London v. 222, 309, 313 n.
  death of adopted son vi. 89 n.
  and *Queen of Cornwall* vi. 220 and nn.
  and *Tess* play vi. 286, 299 n., 306, 339, 369
    and n.
  advice on agent vi. 299 n., 303, 369
  and scheme for national theatre vii. 136 n.
  The Admirable Crichton iii. 44 n.
  The Little Minister i. 247 and n.
  Quality Street iii. 44 n.
  Walker, London ii. 13, 14 n.
  letters to i. 200; ii. 7; iii. 277; iv. 193, 200,
    202, 276; v. 220, 236, 301; vi. 96, 138,
    298, 369
Barron, Louis ii. 165 n.
  proposed translation of *Tess* ii. 164, 167,
    170, 171, 218 and n.
  translation of *Mayor* iii. 225
'Barthélémon at Vauxhall' (poem) vi. 95 ('bad
    poem') and n.
Bartelot, Revd R. Grosvenor:
  and proposed memorial to Edward VII iv.
    138 and n.
  and ELH's death iv. 240 and n.
  (and A. M. Broadley) *Nelson's Hardy* iv. 7
    and n., 47 n., 272
  letters to iv. 138, 145, 240, 332
Barton, J. E. iv. 329 n.; v. 6 n.; vi. 141 nn.
Bashford, Major Lindsay iv. 81 n.
  letter to iv. 81
Basingstoke (Hants) ii. 163 and n., 165
Baskett, Samuel Russell (solicitor) iii. 334,
    335 n.
Baskett, Mrs S. R. iii. 334, 335 and n., 347
Bastow, Henry vi. 122 ('another pupil') and n.
Bat's Corner (Dorset) v. 40
Batcombe (Dorset) iv. 207 and n.
Bates, Charles H. vii. 10 n.
  letter to vii. 10
Bateson, Edith vi. 23 n. (expanded at vii. 176)
  letter to vi. 23

Bath, Hubert Charles vi. 239 and n.
The Wedding of Shon Maclean vi. 239 and n.
Bath i. 22 n.; iii. 40, 41, 330; iv. 145, 148 n.,
    243 and n., 319; v. 17 and n., 184
    Abbey iv. 146 n.
'Battle of Trafalgar, The' (segment of *Dynasts*)
    iv. 284
'Battle of Waterloo, The' (segment of *Dynasts*)
    iv. 284
Bawler, Walter Raymond vii. 148 n.
    letters to vii. 148, 151
Bax, Clifford vi. 114 n.
    Square Pegs vi. 114 ('little piece') and n.
    letter to vi. 114
Baxter, Lucy ('Leader Scott') i. 125 n., 158 n.*
    biography of father (Barnes) i. 157; vii. 108
        and n.
    TH's recollections of iii. 38, 39 and n., 40
        and n., 42
    letters to i. 157; vii. 108
Baxter, Samuel Thomas i. 158 n.; vii. 109 n.
Bayard, Thomas Francis ii. 149 and n.
Bayly, Thomas Haynes vii. 160
    'She wore a wreath of roses' v. 350, 351 n.
Bazalgette, Léon:
    proposed translation of *Life's Little Ironies*
        v. 3 and nn.
Beach, Thomas (portrait painter) v. 273,
    274 nn.
Beale, (?) Sophia ii. 283 and n.
Beament, William Oliver v. 5 n.
    letter to v. 4
Beaminster (Dorset) vi. 290 n.
    as 'Emminster' i. 274
    in *Tess* i. 274; iii. 147
Beatty, Alfred Chester vi. 42 n.
Bécquer, Gustavo Adolfo ii. 21 n.
Bedborough, George:
    letter to ii. 160
'Bedridden Peasant, The' (poem) iii. 219 n.
'Beeny Cliff' (poem) vi. 234 n.
Beer, Max iii. 248 n.
    letter to iii. 248
Beer (Devon) v. 116, 117 n.; vi. 88 and n., 312,
    351 n.
Beerbohm, (Sir) Max iii. 124 n.; iv. 91 n., 95 n.
    cartoon exhibition iv. 264 ('the show'),
        265 n., 267 ('exhibition') and n.
    on *Tess* vii. 133 n.
    letter to (?) vii. 133
Beesly, Edward Spencer iv. 220 nn.
    letter to iv. 220
Beeton & Co. (publishers) i. 266 n.
'Before and After Summer' (poem) v. 37
    pub. in *New Weekly* v. 6 n., 21 n., 30 n.
'Before Marching and After' (poem):
    tribute to Frank George v. 138 n.

Beith, John Hay ('Ian Hay') vi. 211 nn.
    letter to vi. 211
Belgravia :
    serialization of *Return of the Native* i. 50, 51
        and n., 52–3, 54–5, 57 n., 59 n., 60 and
        n.; vii. 90 n.
Bell, Arthur George i. 50 n.
Bell, Charles Frederic Moberly iv. 57 n.
    and women's suffrage iv. 107 and n.
    letters to iv. 56, 107
Bell, Edward Price v. 224 n.; vii. 23 n.
    World Chancelleries vii. 23 and nn.
    letters to v. 224; vii. 23
Bell, Ernest (editor of *Animals' Friend*) vii.
    173
    letter to ii. 97
Bell, Henry Glassford vii. 78
    Summer and Winter Hours vii. 78 n.
Bell, Henry Thomas Mackenzie iv. 33 n.
    Selected Poems vi. 109 and n.
    letters to iv. 33; vi. 109
Belmont, Battle of (1899) ii. 237, 258 and n.
Belmount Hall (Westmorland) ii. 215 n.
Benét, William Rose vii. 76 n.
'Benighted Travellers' (later 'The Honourable
    Laura,' q.v.) (story) i. 93 ('Christmas
    story') and nn., 97 and n.
    'resuscitation' of iii. 48 and n., 60, 61 n.
Benn, Ernest (publishers) vi. 317 n.
Bennet, Revd Norman Robert Ottiwell Gif-
    ford vii. 34 n.
    letter to vii. 34
Bennett, Andrew vi. 123 n.
    letters to vi. 123, 127
Bennett, Arnold v. 208 n.
    and manifesto on post-war peace v. 278 and n.
    Clayhanger iv. 172 and n., 177
    Hilda Lessways iv. 172 n., 177
    letter to v. 278
Benson, Arthur Christopher i. 280 n.; iv.
    227 n., 311; v. 26
    gift of TH portrait to Magdalene College iv.
        307, 308 n.
    presentation copy of *Satires of C* v. 60 n., 72,
        73 n.
    as master of Magdalene College v. 134 and
        n.; vi. 24 n., 194 n., 276 n., 331 n.
    mental illness vi. 24 and n., 193, 194 nn.
    death vi. 318 n., 331
    Le Cahier Jaune: Poems i. 280 and n.; vi.
        300, 301 n.
    The House of Menerdue vi. 318 ('new book')
        and n.
    Ode to Japan iii. 16 and n.
    Selected Poems vi. 300, 301 n.
    letters to i. 280; iii. 16; iv. 297, 307; v. 18,
        72; vi. 24, 193, 275, 300, 318

Benson, Edward White, Abp of Canterbury ii. 135 and n.
Bensusan, Samuel Levy v. 305 n.
  letter to v. 305
Bentley, George i. 50 n.*; ii. 113 n., 190
  letters to i. 50, 59
Bentley, Richard (1662–1742) vi. 254, 255 n.
Bentley, Richard (d. 1936) ii. 113 n.
  letter to ii. 113
Bentley, Richard & Son (publishers) i. 59 n.
Béranger, Pierre Jean de vii. 125 n.
Bere Heath (Dorset):
  as 'Egdon Heath' ii. 132
Bere Regis (Dorset) iv. 46 n.; vii. 115, 116 n.
  as 'King's-Bere' i. 274; ii. 133; vii. 122
  Turberville tombs in church ii. 32 n., 133
Beresford, Lord Charles William de la Poer ii. 22, 23 n.
Bergen, Francis v. 352 and n.
Berger, Adele iii. 222 n
Bergerat, Émile iv. 146 n.
  letter to iv. 146
Bergson, Henri vi. 259
  Creative Evolution v. 69, 70 n., 75 ('the book') and n., 78–79, 84, 85 n.
Berkowitz, Walter J. vii. 63 n.
  letter to vii. 63
Berlin vi. 161, 312 and n.
Bermondsey Book, The vi. 255, 256 n.; vii. 53 n.
Bernard, Right Revd John Henry, Abp of Dublin v. 309, 310 n.; vii. 161 nn.
  (ed.) *The Psalter in Latin and English* vii. 160, 161 n.
Bernard-Derosne, Charles i. 90 n.*
  translates TH works into French i. 90 and n., 105 and n., 108 and n.
  letters to i. 90, 108
Bernard-Derosne, Yorick i. 90 n.
Berne ii. 166
Bernhardt, Sarah ii. 291 n.; iii. 192
  letter to ii. 291
Berry, T. W.:
  Professions for Girls iv. 3 n
Besant, Geoffrey Barham vi. 195 n., 366 nn.
  letter to vi. 195
Besant, Mary Garrett (later Lady) vii. 167 n.
Besant, (Sir) Walter i. 63 n.*, 219 n., 220, 223, 231, 254; ii. 109 and n., 222, 246, 290 and n.; iii. 275; vii. 99 nn.
  and Society of Authors i. 128 n., 191 and n., 231; ii. 236, 237 n.; iii. 30 and n.; vi. 195 n.
  at Aldeburgh i. 237, 254, 255 n.; vii. 132 n.
  method of dramatizing iii. 74
  and Authors' Syndicate vii. 111 ('scheme'), 112 n.

All in a Garden Fair vii. 99 n.
The Ivory Gate i. 252 and n.
  letters to i. 63, 70, 162, 252; ii. 236, 244; vii. 95, 99, 111, 166, 167
Best, J. D. iv. 289 and n.
Bettany, George Thomas:
  Life of Darwin i. 174 and n.
'Between us now' (poem) vi. 257
Bexhill (Sussex) iii. 26
  Northfleet School iii. 27 n.
'Beyond the Last Lamp' (poem) v. 19 ('little poems') and n.
Bhompston Farm (Dorset) ii. 255 n.
  original of 'Blooms End' ii. 254; iii. 111 n.
Bible:
  request for Latin Vulgate iii. 33; vii. 134 and n.
Bible, quotations from:
  Acts vi. 11 n.
  Chronicles v. 300 n.
  Corinthians iii. 241, 251
  Daniel vi. 58 n.
  Ecclesiastes iii. 5 n.; vii. 154
  Exodus i. 283; vii. 160, 161 n.
  Galatians iv. 195 and n.
  Jeremiah v. 287 ('from Sheba'), 288 n.
  Job v. 315 and n.
  John v. 66 ('have written') and n.
  Judges ii. 241 n.
  Kings iii. 44 n.
  Luke v. 25 ('as Zacharias') and n.
  Matthew vi. 219 n.; vii. 170 n.
  Psalms: (1) iv. 283 and n.; (34) vii. 176; (51) vi. 186 n.; (88) vi. 30 n.; (90) iv. 94 n., vii. 160, 161 n.; (106) vi. 159 and n.; (115) v. 27 ('into silence') and n., vi. 189 n.; (126) iii. 88 n., v. 130 n.
  Samuel v. 300 n.; vi. 31 n.
  Song of Solomon iii. 53 n.
Bickerstaffe, Robert ii. 263 n.; vi. 134 n.
  letters to ii. 262; vi. 134
Bickerstaffe-Drew, Revd Francis Browning Drew ('John Ayscough') iii. 314 n.
  Dromina iv. 13 and n.
  Marotz iii. 314 n.
  letters to iii. 314; iv. 13
Bicknell, Ethel E. iii. 22 n.
  Praise of the Dog iii. 22 n.
  letter to iii. 22
bicycling i. 151, 186; ii. 106, 109, 179, 180, 181, 188, 197, 199, 201, 205, 222, 225, 226, 227, 229, 230, 234, 247, 253, 264, 270, 271, 302; iii. 20, 33, 40, 57, 82, 138, 224, 228, 229, 263, 270, 335, 344; iv. 32 n., 65; v. 30, 225, 283; vi. 18, 331
Bincombe Down (Dorset) iii. 176, 289
  in *Dynasts* iii. 138

Bincombe Down (*cont.*)
  in 'A Melancholy Hussar' ii. 131
  in *Trumpet-Major* v. 1 ('the Down') and n.
Bindon Abbey (Dorset):
  in *Tess* ii. 133
Bingham, Revd Charles William i. 51 n.
  letter to i. 51
Binyon, Laurence:
  An Englishwoman's Love-Letters ii. 277
    and n.
'Bird-catcher's Boy, The' (poem):
  pub. in *Sphere* iv. 236 n., 253 n.
'Bird-Scene at a Rural Dwelling, A' (poem):
  pub. in *Chambers's* vi. 263 ('little poem')
    and n., 266 ('little poem'), 267 ('the
    poem') and n.
Birdsmoorgate (Dorset) vii. 5 n.
Birmingham:
  Cathedral iv. 152 n.
  City Museum, as recipient of TH MS iv.
    178, 180, 181 n., 231; vii. 57
  University of iv. 190 and n.
Birrell, Augustine ii. 107 n., 274; iii. 198 and
    n.; iv. 49 and n.; vi. 18 n., 73
  re-elected as MP ii. 83 and n.*
  *Frederick Locker-Lampson: A Character
    Sketch* v. 287, 288 n.
Birrell, Eleanor Mary Bertha ii. 107 n., 111
    ('Mrs B.') and n.
  letter to ii. 107
Bishop, Sir Henry vi. 12 n.
Bishop's Waltham (Hants) iii. 327, 328 n., 329
Bizet, Alice Jacques iii. 213 ('the lady') and n.
Black, Clementina iii. 49 n.
Black, William i. 45 n.*, 101 n., 128 n., 219 n.,
    223, 269; v. 145 n.
  Macleod of Dare i. 65 ('last story'), 66 n., 67
    ('last story')
  letters to i. 45, 100, 225
Black's Guide to Dorset (ed. Moncrieff) ii. 146
    and n., 201
Black and White i. 217 n., 252 n.; ii. 181 n.,
    296 n.
Blackheath iv. 315, 316 n.
Blackie & Son (publishers) iii. 241 and n.
  letter to vii. 141
Blackie's Model Readers vii. 142 n.
Blackmore, Richard Doddridge i. 38 n.; v.
    145 n., 292
  Alice Lorraine i. 38 ('new book') and n.
  Christowell vii. 99 and n.
  Lorna Doone i. 37, 38 n.; vi. 155, 157 n.
  letters to i. 37, 39
Blackmore, Vale of (Dorset) iv. 156
Blackpool Magazine iv. 156 n.
Blackwell, (Sir) Basil vi. 139 n., 237 n., 373
    and n.

Blackwood, John i. 48 n., 169 and n.
  letters to i. 47, 49, 64
Blackwood, William i. 168 n.*, 169 n.; ii. 299
    n., 300 n.
  letters to i. 168, 169, 170, 171, 175, 259; ii.
    299
Blackwood's Edinburgh Magazine ii. 87 n.,
    105, 106; iii. 256 n.; vii. 92 n.
  Return of the Native offered to i. 49
  'Withered Arm' pub. in i. 168 and n., 169
    and n., 171, 172 n., 173
  on *Tess* i. 259 and n.
Blake, George vii. 58 n.
Blake, William iii. 304 and n.; vi. 110, 111 n.
  St Paul's memorial vii. 10 and nn.
  'Pity' v. 199 and n.
Blanchamp, Henry Frederick Ernest i. 230 n.
  letter to i. 230
Blanche, Jacques-Émile iii. 208 ('an artist') and
    n., 211, 302
  painting of TH iii. 208, 211 and n., 215, 265
    and n.; vi. 68, 69 n., 72 and n.
  copy of *Well-Beloved* sent to iii. 213
Blanche, Mme iii. 211, 213
Blandford (also as Blandford Forum) (Dorset)
    ii. 199; iv. 288, 289 n., 292; v. 20 and n.; vii.
    156 n.
Blathwayt, Raymond i. 252 n.*; ii. 40, 41 n.
  letter to i. 252
Blenheim, Battle of (1704) v. 80
Bliss, J. Howard vi. 35 n.
  letter to vi. 35
Blomfield, (Sir) Arthur William i. 2, 3 nn.*,
    4 n., 172; ii. 26 n., 141 n., 172 and n., 245
    and n., 256 n.; iv. 78; v. 14 and n.
  TH's working with i. 3 and n., 173 n.; ii.
    172 n.; iii. 194 and n.; iv. 70 n., 74 and n;
    vi. 177 n., 192, 261 n.; vii. 30, 43
  assistants and pupils vii. 43 and nn.
  letters to i. 172, 286
Blomfield, Lady ii. 256 and n.
Blomfield, Arthur Conran ii. 256 and n.
Blomfield, Revd Charles James vi. 192 ('the
    Bishop'), 193 n.
Blomfield, Charles James ii. 245 n., 256 and n.,
    286
  letter to ii. 245
'Blooms End':
  part-original of ii. 254; iii. 111 n.
'Blue Cross' charitable organization v. 194,
    195 n., 204
Blunden, Edmund vi. 39 n.
  *The Shepherd, and Other Poems of Peace
    and War* vi. 136 and n.
  The Waggoner, and Other Poems vi. 39
    and n.
  letters to vi. 39, 136

Blunt, Lady Anne:
  (trans.) *The Celebrated Stealing of the Mare*
    iv. 224 and n.
Blunt, Wilfrid Scawen iv. 224 n.; v. 275 n.,
  300 n.
Blyth, James, 1st Lord:
  gift of onions to TH v. 339
  letter to v. 339
Blyth, M. F. vii. 57 n.
Boccaccio, Giovanni:
  Olympia v. 146 ('interesting book') and n.
Bockhampton vi. 325 n. – *and see* Higher
  Bockhampton
Bodington, Revd Eric James vi. 182 n.
  lecture on TH vi. 182 and n., 184, 185 n.
  letters to vi. 182, 184
Boer War ii. 242, 246, 247, 248, 269, 277, 288
  impending ii. 229, 232
  troop departures ii. 233, 236, 269
  poems on ii. 236, 237, 241, 242, 277
  military engagements ii. 237, 241, 248
  last stages ii. 258, 259, 265, 280, 283, 293
  peace iii. 23 and n., 24 n., 32
Bognor (now Bognor Regis) (Sussex) vi. 110
  and n.
Bolton Weekly Journal i. 93 n.
Bonchurch (I. o. W.) iv. 192 and n.
Bond, William Joseph J. C. vii. 147 n.
Bone, Clement George vii. 32 n.
  letter to vii. 32
Bone, James vi. 235 n.
  The London Perambulator vi. 235 n.
  letter to vi. 234
Boni, A. & C. (publishers) vii. 70 n.
Bonnaire, Henri vi. 120, 121 n.
Bonnier, Charles:
  Milieux d'Art iii. 199 ('French publication')
    and n.
Book Buyer (New York) i. 260 n.
Book Monthly iii. 97 n., 125 and n.; vii. 144 n.
Book Notes vii. 27 n.
'Book War' (1906) iii. 233 ('the dispute'),
  234 n., 236 ('squabble')
Bookman, The i. 274 and n.; ii. 105, 106 n.,
  155 n., 233 n., 251 n., 296 n., 302 n.; iii.
  37, 38 n., 256 n.; v. 284 and n.
  map of Wessex in i. 256 and n., 275; ii. 60 n.
  portraits of TH in ii. 212 and n., 243 n.,
    296 n.
  Wessex Poems reviewed in ii. 212 n., 214
  article on TH in vi. 16 ('article thereon'),
    17 n.
Books: A Literary Supplement to the 'Daily
  Mail' iii. 232 ('halfpenny a week'), 233 n.,
  235 n., 236 and n., 252 and n., 262 n.
Boosey & Co. (music publishers) iii. 126, 127 n.
Borrow, George iv. 170 n., 273 and n.

Borsa, Mario iii. 56, 57 n.
Bosanquet, Dorothy Mary Cautley vi. 87 n.
  letter to vi. 86
Boscastle (Cornwall) ii. 65 and n., 70; iv. 260;
  v. 176, 271
Boucher, Léon i. 45 n., 108 n.
Boughton, George Henry i. 115 n., 269 and n.
Boughton, Rutland vi. 225 n.
  musical setting of *Queen of Cornwall* vi. 225
    and n., 234 and n., 236–7, 239 and nn.,
    244, 245 nn., 249–50, 257 and nn., 265 n.,
    271 and n., 272, 273–4, 276, 321 and n.,
    360 and n.; vii. 33 and n., 34, 35 n.
  at Max Gate vi. 234 and n., 257 n.
  Alkestis vi. 236 and n.
  The Immortal Hour vi. 225 n., 236 and n.
  letters to vi. 225, 232, 234, 237, 239, 244,
    249–50, 257, 271, 273, 276, 360; vii. 33,
    34, 35
Boulge (Suffolk) ii. 288 and n., 289
Boulter, Revd Sidney ii. 301 n.; iii. 47 n., 115
  letters to ii. 301; iii. 47, 50
Boulton, Sir Harold Edwin vii. 142 n.
  letter to vii. 142
Bournemouth i. 126; ii. 248, 266, 277; iii. 281;
  iv. 177; vi. 275; vii. 77 ('B.') and n.
  as 'Sandbourne' i. 274; ii. 132
  proposed production of *Tess* vi. 295 and n.,
    297
  performance of *Queen of Cornwall* vi. 295 n.,
    321 and nn.
Bournemouth Poetry Society vi. 127
  ('Centre'), 128 n., 150 n.
Bowen, Henry Chandler i. 132 n., 220 n.; vii.
  99 n.
  letter to i. 219
Bowen, John Eliot i. 132 n., 220 n.
  letters to i. 132, 137, 141; vii. 98
Bowker, Richard Rogers (Harper's London
  rep.) i. 75 ('young commissioner') and n.,
  77 n.*, 83 n., 112 n.; vii. 16 and n.
  letters to i. 77–8, 79, 80–83, 84, 85, 86–8,
    89, 91, 93, 94, 106
Bowman, William G. vi. 131
  letters to vi. 130, 143
Braddon, Mary Elizabeth i. 51 n.; vi. 319
Bradish, Margaret Julia vii. 12 n.
  letter to vii. 12
Bradley, Andrew Cecil iii. 363 and n. (?); iv.
  46, 47 nn.; vii. 86 and n.
Bradpole (Dorset):
  Holy Trinity Church iv. 68 ('Church bells')
    and n.
Bramlins (film agents) vi. 73, 74 nn.
Brangwyn, (Sir) Frank iv. 207 n.
Brawne, Fanny v. 248 n.
Brennecke, Ernest vi. 145 n.

Brennecke, Ernest (cont.)
(ed.) *Life and Art* (of TH) vi. 319 and n., 322 and nn., 323
The Life of Thomas Hardy vi. 304 n. ('biography'), 317 ('Life') and n., 318–19, 322 n., 325
Thomas Hardy's Universe: A Study of a Poet's Mind vi. 207 ('typoscript'), 208 n., 225 and n., 259, 260 nn., 283, 284 n., 317 and n., 319
letters to vi. 207, 225, 259, 283
Brett, George Platt iii. 91 and n.
Bridges, Robert Seymour ii. 50 and n.*, 85; iv. 287, 288 n.; vi. 275 ('Poet Laureate') and n.
and 'Poets' Tribute' v. 327 and n.
and Society for Pure English v. 333 and n.; vi. 125 and nn.
on free verse vi. 165 and n.
letters to v. 327, 333; vi. 125, 165; vii. 170
Bridport (Dorset) i. 151, 152 n.; iv. 224 and n.; v. 238
as 'Port Bredy' ii. 132; iii. 147 ('scene of "Fellow Townsmen"')
Bridport News iii. 300 and n.
Bright, Reginald Golding (theatrical agent) ii. 102 n.; vi. 339, 368, 369, 370
and 'Three Wayfarers' iii. 272 and n., 273 n.; iv. 193 and n.
and *Tess* vi. 299 n., 368; vii. 72 n.
letters to iii. 272, 273; iv. 12, 72, 155, 194, 323; vi. 303, 305, 330, 335, 337, 340–1, 344, 345, 349, 352–4, 357, 364, 365, 366, 367, 368, 369, 372, 374; vii. 8, 22, 30, 36, 37, 58
Brighton i. 260; ii. 72, 73, 118 and n., 119, 122; iii. 46, 55; iv. 172 and n.; v. 71, 72 n., 277 n.
Morton's Hotel i. 31 and n.
Royal York Hotel v. 277
Brindley, Harold Hulme vii. 147 n.
letters to vii. 146, 151
Bristol ii. 197, 278
Cathedral iv. 146 n.
Bristol, University of:
conferring of Honorary D. Litt. degree vi. 316 and n., 326, 331, 332
British Academy v. 119 and n., 174 n.
and destroyed Library of Louvain v. 119 and n., 126
British Actors' Film Company v. 254 and n.
British Archaeological Association iii. 262 and n.
British Architect vii. 175
British Broadcasting Corporation vi. 223, 224 n.; vii. 6 and n., 21 n.

British and Foreign Blind Association iv. 285 n.
British Museum i. 59 and n., 133, 134, 145 n., 224; iii. 209, 212, 249 and n., 253, 261, 289 and n.
TH MSS given to iv. 178 and n., 184, 192, 199, 200; vi. 34; vii. 66
Elgin Room vii. 89 and n.
application for Reader's Ticket vii. 90 and n.
British Quarterly Review i. 89 and n., 96 and n.
Broadbent, Henry vi. 360 n.
letter to vi. 360
Broadbent, Muriel v. 106 n.
Broadlands (Hants) iv. 175 n.
Broadley, Alexander Meyrick iii. 199 n.*; iv. 295 n.; v. 34 n., 238 and n.
lecture on Napoleon iii. 286 and n., 292 and n., 293 ('the lecture'), 294 n.
and *Dynasts III* iii. 296, 299 and n.
Chats on Autographs iv. 144 n.
Doctor Johnson and Mrs Thrale iv. 60, 61 n., 144 n.
Napoleon in Caricature iv. 88 nn., 144 n.
The Three Dorset Captains at Trafalgar iv. 8 n.
(and R. G. Bartelot) *Nelson's Hardy: His Life, Letters and Friends* iv. 7 and n., 47 n., 272
(and H. F. B. Wheeler) *Napoleon and the Invasion of England* iii. 285 and n., 286
letters to iii. 199, 285–6, 289, 292, 296, 299, 306, 360, 361; iv. 7, 60, 68, 88, 144, 313, 331; v. 34
Broadmayne (Dorset) v. 31 and n., 329 n.
Broadway (Glos) i. 151, 152 nn.
Brock, C. E. v. 343 n.
Brodrick, Lady Hilda ii. 18 ('H.B.') (?) and n., 53 and n., 258 and n.
Brodrick, Muriel (later Lady Tweedmouth) ii. 258 ('their girl') and n.
Brodrick, William St John (later Viscount Midleton) ii. 258 and n.; iii. 42 n., 196 and n.
wedding iii. 46, 48, 49
Brodrick, Mrs W. St John (formerly Madeleine Stanley, q.v., and later Viscountess Midleton) iii. 42 n., 65, 114 ('the girls') and n., 196, 202
Bronson, Katherine Colman vii. 106 nn.
letter to vii. 106
Brontë, Charlotte:
Jane Eyre vi. 156
Brooke, Rupert iv. 301 n., 307 n.
Brotherhood of Poets and Verse Writers vii. 142 n.

Broughton, John Cam Hobhouse, Lord:
  Recollections of a Long Life iv. 40 ('Remi-
  niscences'), 41 n.
Broughton, Rhoda ii. 81 n.
  letter to ii. 81
Brown, Albert Curtis (literary agent) iii.
  101 n.; v. 106 and n.; vi. 310, 354, 357
  letter to iii. 101
Brown (Curtis), Ltd v. 103, 104 n.; vi. 48,
  49 n., 108, 196 n., 302 n., 353
  letter to vi. 302
Brown, Horatio:
  John Addington Symonds: A Biography ii.
  123 and n.
Brown, Revd Richard Howel v. 9 ('the vicar')
  and n.
Brown, Thomas Edward:
  Collected Poems ii. 270 and n.
Browne, Charles John Cornish v. 273 ('friends
  of ours'), 274 n.
Browne, Martha:
  hanging of iii. 195 and n.; vi. 75, 77 n.; vii. 5
  and n., 46 and n.
Browne, Sir Thomas:
  Urn Burial ii. 25 and n.
Browning, Oscar vi. 105 n.
  'Napoleon' vi. 105 and n.
  letter to vi. 105
Browning, Robert i. 133; ii. 293; iii. 252; iv. 4
  and n.; v. 211 and n.; vi. 148, 166 and n.;
  vii. 106 n., 174
  Wessex Tales sent to i. 175, 176 n.
  quoted in *Tess* and *Jude* i. 182; iii. 133
  and n.
  rejected marriage proposal ii. 144, 145 n.
  as literary puzzle ii. 216
  casuistry of iii. 41
  'Abt Vogler' vi. 239 n.
  'The Last Ride Together' v. 247 n.
  *Letters of Robert Browning and Elizabeth
  Barrett Barrett 1845–1846* ii. 277 and n.
  'Memorabilia' vi. 101 ('well-known lines')
  and n.
  *Pocket Volume of Selections from the Poetical
  Works* v. 133 and n.
  Poetical Works iv. 4 n.; vi. 164 n.
  The Ring and the Book iv. 4 and n.
  'The Statue and the Bust' iii. 94 n.
  'A Toccata of Galuppi's' v. 149, 150 n., 183
  'The Worst of It' ii. 126 ('never the worse'),
  127 n.
  letter to i. 175
Bruckmann, F. (Munich publisher) vi. 249
  and n.
Bruges ii. 130
Brussels ii. 130, 131, 133 n., 134, 135; iv. 306,
  307 n.

Brunius, August Georg vi. 6 n., 7 ('Swedish
  gentleman')
'Brush' (Henniker dog) vi. 120 and n.
Bryan (George) & Co. (Oxford printing firm)
  and 'Wessex novels' picture postcards iii.
  101, 103, 109 n., 110, 112 n.
  letters to iii. 101, 103, 110
Bryan, Marie Theresa iv. 256 and n.
Bryanston House (Dorset) ii. 199 n.
Bryce, James, Viscount v. 119 and n., 251, 263
  and Shakespeare Tercentenary v. 33, 34 n.
  letter to v. 33
Bryce, Lloyd Stephens ii. 96 n.
  letter to ii. 95
Bryer, William (Dorchester mayor) iv. 147
Brymer, Revd John George iv. 74 ('present
  owner') and n., 78 and n.
Brymer, Lieut.-Colonel William Ernest iv. 74
  ('late owner') and n.
  elected MP for South Dorset i. 236 n.; ii.
  270, 271 n.
Buchan, John v. 87 n.; vi. 130; vii. 29 and n.
  invites TH to visit GHQ in France v. 220
  and n.; vi. 107 n.
  A History of the Great War vi. 106 ('valuable
  book'), 107 n., 127 ('third volume') and
  n., 152 and n.
  letters to v. 220; vi. 106, 127, 152
Buchanan, Robert i. 279 n.
  'The Wedding of Shon Maclean' vi. 239
  and n.
Buckle, George Earle ii. 53 and n.*, 159 n.,
  298 n.; iv. 150
  letter to ii. 297
'Budmouth Dears' (song) v. 87
  in *Dynasts* iii. 299 and n., 320 ('song') and
  nn.; v. 56 and n., 131 ('enclosed'), 132 n.
'Budmouth Regis':
  Weymouth as ii. 131
Bugler (later Woodhall), Augusta Noreen vi.
  295 ('her sister'), 296 n.
Bugler (later Toms), Diana vi. 290 ('the baby')
  and n.
Bugler, Capt. Ernest Frank vi. 290 n., 297,
  340
Bugler, Gertrude vi. 251 n., 269 n., 336 n.
  as Marty iv. 327, 328 n.; vi. 299 n., 338
  and n.
  as Eustacia vi. 46 n., 67 n. 290 n., 300 n.
  as Tess vi. 279, 288, 290 n., 291 and n., 292,
  295, 296, 297, 298–9, 338, 340 and n., 342
  and n., 359 ('leading lady'), 360 n.
  inscribed copies of *Tess* and *Return* vi.
  290 n.
  decision not to play Tess in London vi. 308
  and n., 310
  letters to vi. 290, 291, 297, 308

Bugler's (Dorchester confectioners) iv. 115, 116 n., 327 ('a baker here'), 328 n.; vi. 299 n.
Builder ii. 268 n.; vii. 133 and n.
Buist, Walter Scott ii. 128 and n.
Bullen, Arthur Henry iii. 176 n.
 'Stratford Town' edn of Shakespeare iii. 176 and n.
Bullen, Florence vii. 83 n.
 letter to vii. 82
Buller, Lady Audrey ii. 199 and n.
Buller, General Sir Redvers Henry ii. 53 and n.*, 84 n., 199, 233 n., 241 and n.
Bulloch, John Malcolm iii. 160 nn., 254, 255 n., 332 n.
 assistant editor *Sphere* iii. 160 n., 250 n.
 as dramatic critic iii. 249–50
 as *Graphic* editor v. 233 n., 281 n.
 letters to iii. 159, 249–50, 332; iv. 59; v. 233, 280; vii. 138
Bullock, Lady Victoria vii. 86 n.
Bungalow iii. 345 nn. (corrected at vii. 175)
Bunker, J. A. i. 2, 3 nn.
Bunting, Percy William i. 121 n.*, 208 n.; ii. 126 n.
 letters to i. 121, 123–4, 207, 236
Bunyan, John:
Pilgrim's Progress vi. 299
'Buonaparty' (song):
 in *Dynasts* iii. 355, 358 and n.; v. 56 and n.
Burden, Frank (murderer) iii. 23 n.
Burford (Oxen) v. 176 ('the Bull') and n.
Burford Bridge (Surrey) ii. 82 n.
Burgas, Clemente Fernández vi. 367 ('Spanish gentleman') and nn.
Burghclere, Lady iii. 214, 215 n.
'Burghers, The' (poem) iii. 137
Burne-Jones, Sir Edward vi. 227 n.
Burnett, Frances Hodgson:
 A Lady [Woman] of Quality ii. 219 and n.
Burney, Frances vi. 1, 2 n.
Burns, John Elliot v. 87 and n., 99 n.
Burns, Robert iii. 297; iv. 15, 16 n.; vi. 276 n.
 'Bonnie Peg' v. 90 n.
Burr, Frederick vi. 72 ('Barr') and n.
Burton Bradstock (Dorset) v. 253 and nn.
Bury, John Bagnell iv. 47, 48 n., 155 n.*; v. 117 n.; vi. 80 n.
 and magic iv. 154
 at Aldeburgh iv. 113, 114 n., 155 n.
 at Max Gate v. 158
 Romances of Chivalry on Greek Soil iv. 154, 155 n.
 letter to iv. 154
Bury, Mrs J. B. (Jane Bury) iv. 113, 114 n.; v. 158 and n.
Busch, Adolphina vi. 115 n.
Busse, Dr Kurt vi. 196 n.

Butler, Charles McArthur v. 116, 117 n.
Butler, Revd Henry Montagu vii. 156 n.
 letter to vii. 155
Butler, Nicholas Murray vi. 147 n.
 letter to vi. 146
Butler, Samuel (1612–80):
 Hudibras i. 92 and n.
Butler, Samuel (1835–1902) iv. 185, 186 n.; v. 351 n.
Butterworth, Walter iv. 178, 179 n.
'By the Century's Deathbed' (later 'The Darkling Thrush', q.v.) (poem) iii. 79 n.
'By Mellstock [later 'Henstridge'] Cross at the Year's End' (poem):
 pub. in *Fortnightly Review* v. 340 ('short poem') and n.
Byron, Lord i. 262; ii. 24 n., 144; iv. 40, 41 n.; vi. 106
 proposed commemoration in Westminster Abbey vi. 262 and nn.
 Bride of Abydos v. 47 n.
 Cain vi. 268 and n.
 Childe Harold's Pilgrimage ii. 169; iii. 285 n.; v. 28 and n., 75 and n.
 English Bards and Scotch Reviewers vi. 110, 111 n.

Caddy, Walter William (gardener) vi. 278, 279 and n.
Caesar, George Julius Adelmare vi. 141 n.
 letter to vi. 141
Caesar, Julius:
 Commentaries on the Civil War vi. 3, 4 n.
'Caged Thrush, The' (poem) v. 240
Caine, (Sir) Thomas Henry Hall iii. 151 and n.
 and mean age for highest intellectual development v. 246, 247 n.
 and 'national cinema film' scenario v. 264 and nn.
 The Christian ii. 180 and n.
 (with W. Barrett) *The Ben-my-Chree* vii. 109 n.
 letters to v. 246, 264
Caird, Alice Mona Henryson i. 193 n., 207, 208 n.
Calais:
 ELH in iii. 85, 86, 89, 90, 95, 333, 334 and n., 339, 341
'Call to National Service, A' (poem) vi. 149
 pub. in *Times* v. 206 and n.
Cambridge, George, Duke of i. 6
Cambridge i. 81 n., 82; ii. 209, 268; iii. 224, 324; iv. 213 n., 321 and n.; v. 27 and n., 28
 Fitzwilliam Museum iv. 178 n., 180, 181 n., 210 and n.; v. 317 n.; vi. 227 n.
 John portrait of TH presented to vi. 231 n.

Cambridge Magazine v. 194 n., 224 and n., 256 n.
  attacked for publishing survey of foreign press v. 208 n.
Cambridge Review v. 79 n.
Cambridge University v. 30 and n.; vi. 21, 327
  abandonment of plans for attending i. 7 and n.
  delayed hon. degree from i. 7 n.; iv. 210, 213 ('Cambridge doings') and n., 214 ('the memorial'), 215 n., 259, 269, 270 n., 273, 275, 278 n., 280, 291 n., 313 ('last June') and n.; vi. 21 and n.; vii. 156 n.
  Slade Professorship of Fine Art ii. 12, 13 n., 15
  Milton Tercentenary iii. 324 n., 325 n.
  'The Elysians' v. 4, 5 n.
  Chair of French v. 273 and n.
  Magdalene College iv. 297, 331 n.; vi. 194 n., 275
    TH as hon. fellow of iv. 291, 300, 302 n., 308, 309 n., 314, 316; v. 7 ('with you') and n., 18 n., 26; vi. 24 n., 194 n., 276 n.
    portrait of TH for iv. 307, 308 n.
    Pepys commemoration v. 7 and n., 9
    and TH's second marriage v. 18
    Benson as master v. 134 and n.; vi. 24 n., 194 n., 276 n., 331 n.
    80th birthday wishes to TH vi. 24
  St John's College vi. 119 and n.
    'Porte-Latin' feast v. 25 and n., 27, 28
    Wordsworth at vii. 146, 147 nn.
  Trinity College vii. 27 n., 156 n.
Cambridge University Musical Society v. 351 n.
Camden, William:
Remaines iii. 177 and n.
Cameron, N. O. M. vii. 41 n., 62 and n.
  letter to vii. 41
Campbell, Mrs Patrick ii. 30, 31 n., 125 n., 269
  and *Tess* dramatization ii. 76, 77 n., 81, 82 n., 109, 128, 148, 150, 151 n., 209–10
  as Juliet ii. 100 and n.
  in Dorchester ii. 107 and n.
  in *The Joy of Living* iii. 67 ('opening play') and n.
  letters to ii. 81, 107, 128, 150
Campbell, Thomas vi. 314 n.
Canadian Bookman v. 305 and n.
Canadian National Exhibition (Toronto 1924) vi. 263, 264 n.
Canby, Henry Seidel vii. 76 n.
Canfield, Cass (publisher) vii. 16 and n.
Cannan, Charles iii. 297 n., 338 nn., 349 n.
  letters to iii. 337–9, 340–1, 342, 348, 351

Canonbie (Dumfries) v. 90 n., 91
Canterbury ii. 226; iii. 224
Cape, Jonathan (publisher) vi. 183
Carlyle, Thomas ii. 184; iii. 217 and n., 238; v. 229, 230 n.
  Frederick the Great vii. 54 n.
Carmen up to Data (Gaiety burlesque) i. 231 n. (corrected at vii. 172)
Carnarvon, Henry Howard Molyneux Herbert, 4th Earl of i. 128 n., 133 n.; vii. 102 n.
  letter to vii. 110
Carnarvon, Elisabeth Catharine, Lady i. 132, 133 n.; vii. 102 and n.
Carnegie, Andrew iii. 220 and n.
Carr, J. W. Comyns:
  collaboration over dramatization of *Far from the Madding Crowd* i. 99, 105 and n., 100, 103 n., 105 n.; iv. 27 n., 80, 81 n.; vii. 95 n.
  letter to i. 105
Carr, Philip Alfred Vansittart Comyns iv. 27 n.
  letter to iv. 27
'Carrier, The' (poem) vi. 241; vii. 75
Carson, Sir Edward Henry (later Baron) ii. 258 ('Solr Genl') and n.
Carter, Capt. G. V. iv. 58 ('the owner'), 59 n.
Cartillo, J. Pius vi. 34 n.
Cartwright, Charles Morley iii. 298 n.
  proposed dramatization of *Mayor of Casterbridge* iii. 297, 298 n., 351 n.; iv. 149 ('the dramatizer') and n.
  letters to iii. 297, 350
Case (Dorchester bookseller) ii. 272, 273 n.; vii. 124
Case, Beatrice – *see* Whitehead, Beatrice
Casement, Sir Roger v. 154 n.
  petition for reprieve v. 154 n., 167 n.
Cassell, John (publisher) vii. 60 and n.
Cassell & Co. (publishers) i. 78 n.; iv. 83 n.; v. 227, 229, 343 n.; vii. 35, 36, 59
  and film rights v. 257
  projected nature work vi. 173 and n.
  Flower's purchase of vii. 60 and n.
  The Story of the House of Cassell vi. 109 ('the book') and n.
Cassell's Family Magazine ii. 169 and n.
Cassell's Saturday Journal i. 266 nn.
Cassell's Winter Annual v. 343 n.; vi. 90 n.
Casson, (Sir) Lewis vi. 284, 285 n., 296, 306 and n.
'Casterbridge':
  Dorchester as i. 274; ii. 131
'Castle De Stancy':
  Dunster Castle as ii. 133
Catholic World vii. 18 and n.
Catling, Thomas i. 246 n.

Cattistock Church (Dorset) iii. 264 n.

Catullus v. 261 and n.

Cave, Sir Lewis William i. 247 and n.

Cave Hole, Portland (Dorset) v. 31

Cecil, Lord Eustace Brownlow Henry iii. 315 n.

Cecil, Lord Robert v. 271 and n.

censorship, views on ii. 90, 125, 143, 219; iii. 25, 278; iv. 53, 63, 167, 200, 202, 207

Century Magazine i. 152 n.; ii. 13, 14 and n.; iv. 128 n.; v. 319 n.; vi. 241

'An Ancient to Ancients' pub. in vi. 113 and n., 118, 123 and n.

Cerne Abbas (Dorset) ii. 270; v. 123 n.; vi. 355 n.

Abbey ii. 268 and n., 270; vii. 133 and n., 168 n.

Cerne Giant (Dorset) vi. 355 and n.

Chalfont St Giles (Bucks):

Milton's cottage v. 95 n.

Chamberlain, Arthur Neville v. 206 and n.

Chamberlain, Sir Austen vi. 322 n.

Chamberlain, Joseph i. 119 nn.; ii. 22, 23 n.; iii. 95 n.

Chambers, Charles Edward Stuart (publisher) iv. 9 n.; vi. 261 n.

letters to iv. 9, 13; vi. 261, 263, 266, 267

Chambers, William vi. 263 n.

Chambers, W. & R. (publishers) vi. 263 n.

Chambers's Cyclopaedia of English Literature vi. 267 and n.

Chambers's Journal iv. 13 and n.

'How I Built Myself a House' pub. in iii. 260; iv. 9 and n., 69, 70 n.; v. 94 ('architectural sketch'), 95 n.; vi. 261 ('first appearance') and n., 263 ('form of receipt') and nn., 267

'A Bird-Scene' pub. in vi. 263 and n., 266 ('little poem'), 267 ('with the poem')

Chancellor (Dublin photographer) ii. 34 and n., 35, 40, 41 n.

Chang the Chinese Giant i. 6, 7 n.

'Changed Man, A' (story) ii. 239 n. ('this story'); iv. 57 n., 297, 298

pub. in *Sphere* ii. 246 ('the story') and n.; vii. 132 n.

serial rights iii. 29

film rights v. 97

Changed Man, A (stories) i. 285 n.; ii. 3 n., 6 n., 34 n., 192 n.; iii. 291 n.; iv. 199 n., 305 n., 315 ('stories'), 316 n.; v. 22 ('old tales') and n.; vi. 143 n., 167 n., 368

publication ii. 231 n.; iv. 293 n., 313 n.

preparation iv. 254 ('such a volume'), 265 ('short stories'), 297 ('short stories') and n., 300 ('short stories'), 302 ('short stories'), 303, 304

Prefatory Note iv. 303 and n., 325

American edn iv. 298 and n., 299, 303, 306, 308

Wessex Edn iv. 302 n., 329 and nn.; v. 36 and n., 232

frontispiece to iv. 302 ('new vol.') and n., 304 ('photographs')

presentation copies iv. 315 ('the book') and n., 316 and n., 323 ('the book') and n.

in Tauchnitz series iv. 317 and n., 321 and n., 325 n.

proposed Braille transcription iv. 321 and n.

French translation of stories from v. 24 ('lady translator') and n.

Uniform Edn v. 132

Pocket Edn v. 301 n.

Canadian rights vi. 65, 81

'Channel Firing' (poem):

pub. in *Fortnightly* v. 26 and n., 30 n.

Channing, Mary vi. 256 n.

Chapbook vi. 179 ('March number') and n.

'Chapel Organist, The' (poem) vi. 122 and n.

Chapman, Frederic ii. 290 n.

letter to ii. 290

Chapman, John i. 118 n.

letter to i. 118

Chapman, Robert William iii. 297 n., 338 n., 340

letters to iii. 297, 301, 304, 307, 311, 315, 320, 322, 334, 336

Chapman and Hall (publishers) ii. 299 n.; iv. 130; vii. 159

Chapman's Magazine ii. 169 and n., 190, 192, 194 ('C's), 196 n.

Chappell (music publisher) ii. 124

Charborough House (Dorset):

as 'Welland House' ii. 133

Charlecote Park (Warws) iii. 271 and n.

Charles II v. 269 n.

Charles (Max Gate servant) iii. 86

Charles Scribner's Sons – *see* Scribner's Sons, Charles

Charlotte, Queen vi. 1, 2 nn.

Charminster (Dorset) iii. 4 n.

Charrington, Charles ii. 9 n.

in *Three Wayfarers* ii. 15

letters to ii. 9, 15, 268, 271

Chartered Institute of Secretaries vii. 153 ('other Society') and n.

Chase, Lewis Nathaniel iv. 152 n., 166 n.; v. 213 n.

at Max Gate iv. 166 n.; v. 25 n.

gifts of fruit to TH iv. 166; v. 25

Poe and His Poetry v. 25 and n.

letters to iv. 166; v. 25, 212

'Chaseborough':
Cranborne as vii. 122
Chatterton, Thomas ii. 278 and n.
Chatto, Andrew ii. 57, 58 n.; iii. 15
Chatto & Windus (publishers) vii. 90 n., 172
and *Under the Greenwood Tree* copyright iii. 13, 15; iv. 162; vi. 214 n.
letters to i. 50, 57, 60; vii. 90
Cheesewright, Floretta v. 214 ('distant cousin'), 215 n.
Cheesewright, John Francis v. 214, 215 n., 230 ('on the West front')
Cheetham, F. H.:
Louis Napoleon and the Genesis of the Second Empire iii. 330 n., 363 ('Napoleon book')
Cheltenham (Glos) ii. 197
Chesterton, Gilbert Keith iii. 73 n.
and 'Poets' Tribute' v. 333 and n.
TH's epitaph on v. 333 n.
Magic iv. 324 n.
letter to v. 333
Chew, Samuel Claggett vi. 105 n.
Swinburne v. 251 and n.
Thomas Hardy: Poet and Novelist v. 251 n., 259 ('your criticisms'); vi. 153–7
letters to v. 251, 259; vi. 153
Cheyne, Revd Thomas Kelly iv. 47, 48 n.; vi. 374 and nn.
Chicago Daily News v. 224 n.; vii. 23 nn.
Chichester (Sussex) vi. 110
Cathedral iv. 51 n.
Child, Harold Hannyngton iii. 333 nn.
invited to Max Gate iii. 332, 347 ('a Times man'), 349, 355, 356; v. 95, 143; vi. 16
seeks information for book on TH v. 94, 95 n.
death of wife v. 290 ('bereavement'), 291 n.
and *Moments of Vision* v. 290, 294
Bookman article on TH vi. 16, 17 n., 20
articles on TH's poetry vi. 101 and n.
and Dorchester production of *Queen of Cornwall* vi. 221, 222 nn.
on *Tess* play vi. 342 n.
Thomas Hardy v. 143 ('little book') and n., 302 ('little book') and n.; vi. 16 ('little book'), 17 n., 101 ('former book') and n.; vii. 161 and n.
TH's corrections to vi. 292–4
The Yellow Rock and Other Poems of Love v. 350 ('the book') and n.
letters to iii. 332, 349, 355–6; v. 94, 95, 143, 290, 294, 302, 350; vi. 16, 20, 45, 101, 221, 285, 292, 338, 340
Children of the Hour (projected periodical) ii. 138 and n.

letter to Editor ii. 138
'Children and Sir Nameless, The' (poem) vi. 118 n., 122 n.
pub. in *Nash's and Pall Mall Magazine* vi. 121 n.
Childs, Annie i. 222 and n.
Childs, Christopher i. 222 n.; vi. 28 ('maternal ancestor')
Childs, Christopher (great-great-uncle) v. 216 and n.
Childs, Dr Christopher (Weymouth physician) v. 216 and n.; vi. 317 n.; vii. 72 ('your father') and n.
Childs, Christopher Borlase Macrae vi. 317 n., 322 nn.; vii. 72 n.
letters to vi. 317, 322; vii. 71
Childs, John Frederick vi. 317 ('your uncle') and n.
Ching (formerly Gifford), Edith (ELH's cousin) iv. 311 and n.; v. 12 and n.
Chislehurst (Kent):
Luson House, Camden Wood iv. 212, 213 n.
Chiswick Press iii. 16 n., 314 n.; iv. 233 n.; v. 322 n.; vi. 115 n.
Cholmondeley, Marcia (Pitt) iv. 20 n.
Chosen Poems of Thomas Hardy:
revised version of *Selected Poems* vii. 59 and nn., 75 and n., 76 and n., 82 and n.
Christie, Augustus Langham i. 131 n.
Christie, Mary Elizabeth i. 117 n.
letter to i. 116
Christie, Lady Rosamond i. 131 and n.
Christie's:
Red Cross sales v. 86 n., 93 ('the sale') and n., 100, 105, 243, 244 n., 252 n.
'Christmas in the Elgin Room' (poem):
pub. in *Times* vii. 89 ('verses') and n.
'Christmas Ghost Story, A' (poem) ii. 242 ('a few lines'), 243 n.; vii. 143
'Christminster':
Oxford as iii. 226 n.; vii. 41, 42 n.
Christy, Gerald iii. 362, 363 n.; iv. 1 n.
letter to iv. 1
Church of England Temperance Society iv. 322 n.; v. 276, 277 n.
Church Missionary Society ii. 219 n.
'Church Romance, A' (poem) iii. 223 ('short MS.'), 226 ('the sonnet'); iv. 264; vi. 149; vii. 150 n.
pub. in *Saturday Review* iii. 223 n., 226 n., 235 ('that Sonnet') and n.; vii. 150 n.
'Church and the Wedding, The' (poem):
pub. in *Chapbook* vi. 179 ('very poor thing') and n., 180 ('the poem') and n., 185 ('proof') and n.

Churchill, Elizabeth (Max Gate parlourmaid) iii. 63 n., 69 ('Bessie'), 82, 83, 85, 90, 151 n.
    letters to iii. 62, 64
Churchill, Lord Randolph ii. 53 and n.
Churchill, Lady Randolph ii. 272 n.; vi. 93 and n; vii. 121
Churchill, Sarah v. 38 n.
Churchill, (Sir) Winston Leonard Spencer v. 38 and n., 99 n.
Churchill, Mrs Winston (Clementine Hozier) v. 38 and n.
Cicero:
    Pro Milone vii. 154 n.
Circulating Libraries' Association iv. 63 n., 64 n.
Cires-lès-Mello (France) v. 286 and n.
City of London Electric Lighting Co. i. 254
City of London Pickwick Club vi. 159 n.
Civic Arts Association v. 146 and n.
Civil List iii. 362 and n., 363; iv. 53 n., 113 n.; v. 223 n.; vi. 228 n.; vii. 159 n.
Clairmonte, Mary Chavelita ('George Egerton') ii. 47, 48 and n.*; iii. 272 n.
    and *Jude* ii. 102 and n.
    Keynotes ii. 48 and n., 52, 102
    letter to ii. 102
Clarendon Press iii. 245 n., 292, 297 n., 303, 338 n.
    letter to iii. 326
Clark, Barrett H. (and Maxim Lieber):
    (ed.) *Great Short Stories of the World* vi. 372 n.
Clark, R. & R. (printers) ii. 46 n.; iii. 278 n.; iv. 45 n.; vi. 6 and n., 40, 41 n.; vii. 6 and n., 78 n.
    letter to vi. 371
Clarke, Charles Allen iv. 156 n.
    letter to iv. 156
Clarke, Sir Edward iii. 39 n., 40 n.; v. 247 n.
Clarke, John (Keats's schoolmaster) vi. 313 n.
Claybury Asylum (Essex) v. 320 n.
Clayton, Arthur Essex (Dorchester accountant) v. 184 n.
    letter to v. 183
Clifford, (Sir) Hugh iii. 33 and n.; iv. 120, 121 n.
Clifford, Lady (Mrs Henry de la Pasture) iv. 120 ('the lady'), 121 n.
Clifford, Sophia Lucy (Mrs W. K. Clifford) ii. 109 and n.*; iv. 34 n.; v. 117 n.; vii. 127 n.
    as playwright vii. 158, 159 nn.
    Mrs Keith's Crime vi. 166 ('much discussed book') and nn., 167 n.
    A Wild Proxy v. 11 ('little book') and n.
    A Woman Alone vii. 159 n.

letters to iv. 34, 104, 251, 274; v. 11; vi. 166, 199; vii. 126-7, 158
Clifford, William Kingdon i. 262 and n.; ii. 109 n.
Clive, Edward E. vii. 37, 38 n.
'Clock of the Years, The' (poem) v. 291 n.
Clodd, Arnold iii. 155 n., 319 n.
Clodd, Arthur iii. 155 n.; iv. 267 n.
Clodd, Edward i. 237 n.*, 241; ii. 30 n., 122; iii. 66, 67, 72, 92 n., 132, 172 n., 204 nn.; iv. 80 n., 81 n., 151, 167 and n., 229 n., 270, 279, 280 n.; v. 29, 50; vi. 216; vii. 122 n., 162 n.
    Whitsun gatherings at Aldeburgh i. 237, 239 ('down there') and n., 240 and n., 254; ii. 58 n., 75 and n., 163, 217, 220 n., 222, 287, 288, 289; iii. 59 and n., 122 and n., 196; iv. 21 and n., 25; vii. 123 and n., 132 and n.
    defence of *Life's Little Ironies* ii. 56 and n.
    and *Jude* ii. 92
    invited to Max Gate ii. 234, 263; iii. 146, 155 n.; iv. 120, 121, 279, 280 and n., 282
    birthday wishes to ii. 263 and n.; iv. 222 and n., 283; v. 107, 108 n., 113 and n., 314, 315 n.; vi. 253; vii. 70
    gifts to TH iii. 22, 287
    as Secretary of London Joint Stock Bank iii. 23 n., 287 n.; iv. 39 n.; v. 81 n., 139 n.
    TH poems sent to iii. 94; iv. 63; v. 65 n.
    and *Dynasts* iii. 116, 196, 298 and n.
    and death of TH's mother iii. 119
    foreign travel iii. 155 and n., 166 and n., 197 and n., 202; iv. 91 and nn.
    and Crabbe celebration iii. 180 and n., 182 n.
    death of son iii. 319 and n.
    death of cousin iv. 9 ('Clodd's loss'), 12 ('sad loss') and n.
    accompanies FED to *Tess* opera iv. 32 and n., 36
    mishap on Alde mud iv. 41, 42 n., 219 and n.
    and 'Panthera' iv. 47 ('Rationalist reviewer'), 48 n., 49; v. 132
    and Aldeburgh photographs iv. 49 and n.
    70th and subsequent birthday wishes to TH iv. 91, 219; v. 107, 163, 265, 308; vi. 31, 253; vii. 70
    his own 70th birthday iv. 98, 99 n., 101 and n., 112 ('the dinner'); vii. 150 ('dinner') and n.
    attends *Mellstock Quire* iv. 130
    TH MS given to iv. 179 n., 186 n., 207, 208 n.
    attends *Far from the Madding Crowd* iv. 51 n., 62
    attends *Distracted Preacher* and *Three Wayfarers* iv. 194 and n.

Clodd, Edward (cont.)
attends *Trumpet-Major* iv. 239 ('the play')
birthday gift of books to iv. 281, 282
meets TH's brother and sisters iv. 287 n.
attends *Woodlanders* iv. 323, 327 ('the play')
portrait fund v. 22 and n.
Gissing's letters to v. 26 and n.
financial advice sought v. 80
second marriage v. 81 n.
articles on spiritualism vi. 31 and nn.
and state of religion vi. 222, 223 n.; vii. 32 and n.
Animism: The Seed of Religion iii. 196, 197 n.
Gibbon and Christianity v. 152 and n.
Pioneers of Evolution from Thales to Huxley ii. 143 ('your book') and n.
The Question: 'If a Man Die, Shall He Live Again?' v. 207 ('book in hand'), 247; vi. 8, 9 n.
The Story of the Alphabet ii. 257 and n.
Thomas Henry Huxley iii. 2 ('Huxley book'), 5
Tom Tit Tot ii. 202
letters to i. 236, 238, 254, 257; ii. 29, 54, 56, 75, 92, 136, 143, 163, 168, 202, 204, 217, 234, 255, 257, 263, 281, 290; iii. 1, 5, 20, 22, 59, 94, 116, 119, 122, 146, 152, 154, 180, 196, 202, 205, 241, 244, 287, 298, 311, 330, 244; iv. 12, 21, 25, 29, 32, 35, 38, 42, 49, 55, 62, 63, 91, 98, 103, 112, 113, 118, 120–1, 128, 130, 142, 147, 150, 169, 175, 176, 185, 194, 204, 207, 212, 219, 222, 229, 233, 236, 239, 257–8, 264, 267, 268, 280, 283, 310, 323, 327; v. 9, 26, 42, 44, 50, 64, 80, 107, 113, 139, 152, 163, 207, 247, 265, 308, 314; vi. 8, 31, 36, 56, 141, 202, 215, 222, 253; vii. 70, 123, 131, 141, 152, 169
Clodd, Eliza (first Mrs E. Clodd) v. 81 n.
Clodd, Phyllis (second Mrs E. Clodd) v. 81 n., 152; vii. 169 and n.
Clodd, Susan ii. 204
Co-operative Publishing Society of Prague vii. 52
Coal Strike (1921) vi. 79, 80 nn., 82 n.
Coblentz ii. 293 and n.
Cobra, HMS vii. 173
Cochrane, George vi. 140, 141 n.
Cock, Revd Albert A. vi. 63 nn., 322 nn.
letters to vi. 62, 321, 326
Cockerell, (Sir) Christopher v. 218 and n.; vi. 349, 350 n.
Cockerell, Kate (Lady) iv. 221, 222, 224, 285; v. 201 n.*, 351 and n.
at Max Gate iv. 280 n., 282 n.
inscribed copy of *Changed Man* to iv. 315 ('the book') and n.

ill health v. 155, 157, 158 n., 199, 201 n., 216
ELH's Bath chair offered to v. 157, 158, 167 and n.
makes nightcap for TH v. 199, 200, 201 n.
letters to iv. 333; v. 200
Cockerell, (Sir) Sydney Carlyle iv. 178 n.*; v. 26 and n., 150 n., 288, 290, 291 n., 295 n., 300; vi. 72 n., 202 n., 253 n., 266 n., 319 n., 327; vii. 72 nn.
and distribution of TH manuscripts iv. 178, 180–1, 184, 185, 186 n., 192, 193, 199 ('librarian friend') and n., 230
birthday wishes to TH iv. 218; v. 216 and n.
invited to Max Gate iv. 221, 235 n., 279; v. 41, 143, 154, 199
and Cambridge honorary degree for TH iv. 269, 273, 275
at Max Gate iv. 280 n., 282 n.; v. 41 n., 147 n., 155 n., 193, 195
and *Dynasts* errata iv. 285 and n.
sends *Memoir* of Thomas Hardy, radical politician iv. 325 ('this memoir') and nn.
on Mistral v. 23 n.
as one of TH's literary executors v. 45 and n., 46 n., 147 and n., 169 ('a friend')
and 'Song of the Soldiers' v. 48
and binding of TH MSS v. 120 and n.
TH books sent to v. 123 and n., 124 and n., 256 and n.
at *Wessex Scenes from Dynasts* v. 193, 195
and 'New Year's Eve in War Time' v. 199
corrections to *Selected Poems* v. 199 and n.
corrections for Wessex Edn v. 316 and n.
and *Late Lyrics* vi. 116–17, 119, 121–2, 124
and proofs of *Human Shows* vi. 307 ('coming volume'), 349, 350 n., 358
The Gorleston Psalter iv. 214 ('reproduction'), 215 nn.
Psalter and Hours . . . [of] Isabelle of France iv. 259 and n.
letters to iv. 178, 180, 184, 186, 189, 192, 193, 210, 213, 214, 218, 221, 222, 224, 235, 259, 269, 273, 275, 279, 281, 285, 301, 314, 325, 333; v. 9, 23, 25, 26, 41, 45, 48, 50, 73, 120, 123–4, 134, 135, 138, 147, 154, 157–8, 167, 178, 199, 203, 216, 218, 256, 275, 294, 300, 316, 326, 346, 350; vi. 1, 42, 114, 116–17, 119, 121–2, 124, 128, 191, 226, 274, 277, 307, 349, 358; vii. 72
Colbourne, Maurice v. 348 n., 349 n.
letter to v. 347
Coldingham (or Goldingham), Miss:
letter to iii. 25
Coldstream Guards ii. 145 n.; iii. 56 n., 95 n.; v. 134 n.
in Boer War ii. 229, 230 n., 233 n., 236 n., 237, 238 n., 241 n.

Coleridge, Ernest Hartley iii. 347 ('of Coleridge') and n.
Coleridge, John Duke Coleridge, 1st Lord i. 242 and n.
Coleridge, Samuel Taylor v. 21 and n.
poems pub. in *Morning Post* v. 209 and n.
'Fears in Solitude' v. 202, 203 n.
Collected Poems iv. 4 n.; vi. 39, 149, 189 n., 190
one-vol. edn v. 299, 301 n., 312 and n., 313, 316 and n.; vi. 2 n., 4 n., 14, 23 n., 196 n.
frontispiece for v. 312 and n.
Murry review of v. 341 and n.
corrections to v. 342 and n.; vi. 2 n., 4
American pub. vi. 22 ('the poems'), 23 n., 105, 214; vii. 46, 47 and n.
thin-paper issue vi. 104, 105 n., 164 and n., 195, 196 n., 206
expanded edn vi. 164 and n., 169 and n., 170, 177, 195
Colles, William Morris (literary agent) i. 225 n., 241 n.*; ii. 2 n.; iii. 145 n.; vi. 123 n.; vii. 112 n.
letters to i. 240, 246, 254, 261; ii. 2, 5, 7, 9, 13, 22, 32, 54, 72, 97, 121, 136, 207, 241; iii. 49, 129, 145, 189, 191, 324; iv. 11, 131; v. 22; vi. 37, 123, 179
Collier, John v. 23 n.
illustrates *Trumpet-Major* serial i. 66, 67 n.; ii. 109 n.; vii. 93 and nn.
letter to vii. 93
Collier, Peter Fenelon ii. 295, 296 n.
Collier, William Frederick ii. 6
Tales and Sayings of William Robert Hicks, of Bodmin ii. 6 and n.
Collier's Weekly ii. 295, 296 n.; v. 195 and n.
Collingwood, Vice-Admiral Cuthbert iii. 114 and n.
Collins, John Churton i. 155 n., 157 n.
Collins, Mrs J. C. (Pauline Mary):
petition for Civil List pension iii. 362 and n., 363
Collins, J. W. D. (bank official) v. 127 n.
letter to v. 127
Collins, Lottie vii. 121, 122 n.
Collins, (Sir) Stephen iii. 322, 323 n.; vii. 83, 84 n.
Collins, Mrs Stephen iii. 323 ('Mrs C.') and n.
Collins, Vere Henry Gratz (publisher) iv. 145 n.; vi. 73 n., 139 n.
Talks with Thomas Hardy at Max Gate, 1920–1922 iv. 145 n.; vi. 139 n.
(ed.) *Poems of War and Battle* iv. 145 ('your anthology') and n.
letters to iv. 145; vi. 73, 138–9, 142, 144, 190, 285; vii. 36

Collins, William Wilkie vi. 156, 157 n.
proposed memorial to i. 210
Collins, William, Sons & Co. (publishers) iii. 249 n.
Colman, George the younger:
The Mountaineers vi. 248 n.
Colony Press of New York vi. 268 n.
Colton, Charles Caleb:
Lacon, or Many Things in Few Words vii. 52 and n.
Columbia University vi. 147 nn.
Columbus Album i. 263 and n.
Colvin, (Sir) Sidney iii. 56 n.; iv. 291
at Max Gate iv. 285, 286 n., 291 n.
John Keats: His Life and Poetry, His Friends, Critics, and After-Fame v. 31 n., 90 and n., 248 and n., 253, 254 n.; vi. 203 n.
letters to iv. 285; v. 31, 40, 62, 90; vi. 268
Colvin, Lady (Frances Fetherstonhaugh) iv. 285, 286 n.
death vi. 268 and n.
Colyton (Devon) iv. 286 and n.
Comben, Robert Stone (mayor of Weymouth) v. 245 n.
letter to v. 244
Comedy Theatre ii. 90 n., 219 n.
'Comet at Yell'ham, The' (poem) iv. 54 ('my little poem') and n.
Comfy (Max Gate cat) iii. 86, 341, 342 n., 343, 347
death iii. 361; iv. 51
Coming Citizen, The (projected newspaper) iii. 360 and nn.
'Committee-Man of "The Terror", A' (story) ii. 101 ('short story') and n., 126 n., 129 ('the tale') and n., 139 ('my story'); iv. 298
pub. in *Illustrated London News* ii. 129 n., 142 ('little story') and n.
French translations iii. 290 ('the story'), 291 n.; v. 33 n.
Common Cause, The iii. 360 n.
'Compassion' (poem) vi. 293
pub. in *Times* vi. 243, 244 n., 256 n.
Compton, Fay vi. 336 and n., 337, 339
Comstock, Harriet T.:
Janet of the Dunes v. 24 and n.
Condell, Henry vii. 49 and n.
Condor, Josiah vi. 11 ('Conder') and n.
Congreve, (Sir) Geoffrey Cecil vi. 148 and n.
Congreve, William i. 179; vii. 38, 39 n.
Coniston (Lancs) ii. 201, 202
Conrad, Joseph iii. 203 n.; vi. 282 and n.
Heart of Darkness iii. 148 n.
(and Hueffer) *Romance* vi. 157 n.
Conservative Club ii. 20; iii. 216

Constable & Co., Archibald (publishers):
and Library Edn of Fielding's novels ii. 195 n., 196, 200 n.
letter to ii. 195
Constantinople:
Santa Sophia, v. 296 and nn.
Contemporary Review i. 121 n., 207, 208 n., 236 and n., 260; ii. 125, 189 n.
'Convergence of the Twain, The' (poem):
pub. in *Fortnightly* iv. 216 ('some lines') and n., 222
American edn iv. 223 and n., 225, 226 and nn., 228; v. 7 n., 161 n.
Conybeare, Charles Augustus Vansittart ii. 83 and n.
Cook, John Douglas iv. 288 ('Cooke') and n.
Coolidge, Calvin vii. 23 and n.
Coombe (Oxon) vi. 231 and n.
Coombs, Edwin H. ii. 181 n.
letter to ii. 181
Coote, Revd Herbert Chidley v. 277 and n.
Copinger, Walter Arthur:
The Law of Copyright in Works of Literature and Art i. 108 n.
Copley Theatre Company vii. 37, 38 n.
'Copying Architecture in an Old Minster' (poem) i. 95 n.
Copyright Act (1911) v. 4 and n.
Copyright Act (American) i. 222 and n.
Copyright Association i. 36 and n.
Corbie Ridge (France) v. 201 and n.
Corelli, Marie iii. 151 and n.
Corfe Castle (Dorset) ii. 251
as 'Corvsgate Castle' ii. 132
Cornford, Frances Crofts vii. 150 n., 151
letter to vii. 150
Cornford, Francis Macdonald vii. 150 n., 151 n.
letter to vii. 151
Cornhill i. 53 and n., 75, 148 n.; ii. 140, 276, 277 and n.; iii. 149 and n., 170 n., 203 and n., 251, 274 n.; iv. 13 and n., 48 and n., 114 and n., 256, 257 nn.; v. 324 n.
serialization of *Far from the Madding Crowd* i. 22 n., 23 and n., 24–5, 27 and nn., 28, 29 n., 30 nn.; ii. 294; iv. 9 n., 256, 257 n.; v. 244 n.; vi. 255 n.; vii. 138, 139 n.
serialization of *Hand of Ethelberta* i. 35 and nn., 38 and n., 41 n., 42, 43; iv. 9 n.; v. 244 n.
'Souls of the Slain' pub. in ii. 249 and n., 251, 253 and n., 266; v. 244 n.
'At Casterbridge Fair' pub. in iii. 7 n., 9 ('the proof')
'Trampwoman's Tragedy' declined by iii. 59 and n., 75 n., 278 n.

'Noble Lady's Tale' pub. in iii. 153 and n., 159
'Spring Call' pub. in iii. 203 n.; v. 24 n.
'Memories of Church Restoration' pub. in iii. 215, 216 n.
'Let Me Enjoy' pub. in iv. 8 ('my little song'), 9 n.
Jubilee number (1909) iv. 66
Trumpet-Major declined by vii. 92 n.
Cornwall, Duchy of:
lease of land for building Max Gate i. 73 and n.; vii. 95–7, 98, 100
purchase of Max Gate site i. 135 nn.; ii. 66, 67 n.; vii. 103–5
letters to officials of i. 135; ii. 66–7; vii. 95–6, 97, 98, 100, 103–5
Coronet Theatre ii. 239 n.; vii. 133 n.
'Corvsgate Castle':
Corfe Castle as ii. 132
Cosmopolis ii. 99 ('new magazine') and n., 104
Cosmopolitan i. 266, 267 n.
Cotton, James Sutherland i. 104 n.
letters to i. 104, 153
Council of Justice to Animals iv. 143 and n., 176; v. 20; vi. 44, 45 n.
Country Life ii. 295 n.; vi. 80 and n., 83 nn., 234, 235
'Country Wedding, The' (formerly 'The Fiddler's Story') (poem) v. 322 n.
pub. in *Cassell's Winter Annual* v. 343 n.; vi. 90 n.
Court Journal iii. 133 n., 185 and n., 190 and n.
Court Theatre – *see* Royal Court Theatre
Courthope, W. J. i. 111 n.
Courtney, William Leonard iii. 139 n.; iv. 216 n.; v. 109 and n.*
rejection of 'A Sunday Morning Tragedy' iii. 278 ('poem of mine') and n., 331 ('returned it') and n.; vii. 143 n.
letter to vii. 143
Cousin, D. R. v. 297 n.
Covent Garden Opera House i. 2; iii. 57 n., 204 n.; iv. 198 n.
production of *Tess* opera iv. 25, 30 and n., 31–2, 33, 35, 36, 100 n., 103 and n., 230; vi. 350 nn.
Titanic matinée iv. 216 n., 226 n.
Coward, Mrs Christiana (Bockhampton postmistress) iii. 166 n.
Cowley, Abraham v. 48 n.
Cowley, Revd Henry Guise Beatson:
and ELH's funeral iv. 237, 238 and n.
and restoration of Stinsford church font v. 3, 41
and recasting of Stinsford bells vii. 7, 8 n., 9 and n., 15, 16 nn.

Cowley, Revd Henry Guise Beatson (*cont.*)
  letters to iv. 237, 266, 268; v. 3, 180, 297; vi. 46, 107, 298; vii. 7, 9, 15
Cowley, Ethel Florence (Mrs H. G. B. Cowley) iv. 296 n.; v. 4, 281 n.; vi. 36 n., 298
  birthday presents to TH vi. 135, 198
  letters to iv. 296; v. 281; vi. 36, 41, 71, 135, 198
Crabbe, George ii. 222; iii. 59 and n.; iv. 114 n.
  150th anniversary celebration iii. 180 and n., 182 n.; vii. 141 and n.
  1914 Commemoration v. 34 n.
  as influence on TH v. 294 and n.
  The Borough iii. 59 n.
Crackanthorpe, Blanche Alethea ii. 108, 109 n.*; iii. 92 n., 321; iv. 89 and n., 92, 153; v. 349 n.; vii. 140 n.
  masked ball ii. 111, 112; iii. 265
  letters to iii. 91; vi. 8; vii. 135
Crackanthorpe, Hubert Montague iv. 89 n.
Crackanthorpe, Montague Hughes ii. 109 n.; iii. 265; iv. 89 ('Mr C') and n.
Craigie, Pearl Mary Teresa ('John Oliver Hobbes') ii. 10, 11 n., 36 ('Mrs C.') and n., 89 and n., 157, 160 n.*, 185 and n., 258; iii. 104 ('Mrs C's talk'), 105 n.
  and *Jude* ii. 100 and n.
  and *Well-Beloved* ii. 160
  death iii. 221 and n., 224, 239
  publication of correspondence iii. 239 and n.; iv. 151 and n.
  memorial to iii. 323 and n.
  A Repentance ii. 217 ('new little play') and n.
  letters to ii. 160, 217
Craigie, Reginald Walpole ii. 90 n.
Craik, George Lillie i. 131, 132 n.
Cramb, John Adam:
  Germany and England v. 50 ('Cramb's book'), 51 n.
Cranborne (Dorset):
  as 'Chaseborough' vii. 122
Cranborne Chase:
  in *Tess* ii. 133 ('Cranbourne')
Cranborne Manor (Dorset) v. 338 n.
Crashaw, Richard i. 114
Crawford, F. Marion:
  A Cigarette Maker's Romance iii. 105, 106 n.
Crawford, David Alexander Edward Lindsay, 27th Earl of v. 296 and n.
Crawford, Oswald John Frederick ii. 8 n., 73
  second marriage iii. 35 and n.
  The Sin of Princess Eladane iii. 93 ('the book') and n.
  Two Masques iii. 34, 35 n.
  letters to ii. 8; iii. 34, 93
Crawfurd, Mrs Oswald (Margaret Ford) ii. 73

Crawfurd, Mrs Oswald (Lita Browne) iii. 35 n.
Creevey, Thomas iii. 95 and n.
Creighton, Mandell, Bp of London ii. 280 ('Right Reverend') and n.; v. 248 n.
Crewe, Frances ii. 43 and n.
Crewe, Hungerford, 3rd Lord ii. 47 ('your uncle'), 48 n.
Crewe, Robert, Earl of (formerly Robert Offley Ashburton Crewe-Milnes, 2nd Lord Houghton, q.v.; later Marquess of Crewe, q.v.) ii. 79 n., 111 n., 142 ('her brother'), 208 n., 216 n., 219 ('yr brother'), 228 and n., 270 and n.; iv. 61 ('your brother') and n., 256, 257 n.
  illness ii. 235 and n., 236
  accident iv. 143 and n.
  presentation copy of *Satires of C* v. 60 n.
  letters to ii. 2, 79, 235
Crewe, Robert Offley Ashburton Crewe-Milnes, Marquess of (formerly Lord Houghton, then Earl of Crewe, qq.v.) vi. 44, 45 n.
Crewe, Lady (Lady Peggy Primrose) ii. 216 n.; vi. 93, 94 n.
Crewe Hall (Cheshire) ii. 29 and n., 123 n., 141, 142, 208, 215, 277
Crichton-Browne, Sir James iii. 267 and n.
Crickmay, George Rackstrow (Weymouth architect) i. 10 n., 15 n.; vii. 115, 116 n.
Crickmay, Harry W. (Weymouth architect) vi. 171 and n.
Crickmay & Son (architects) ii. 178, 179 n.
Cripplegate Institute iv. 55, 58, 59, 125, 129, 194 n., 323, 325
Criterion Theatre iv. 98 n.
Critic (New York) i. 103 ('literary reviews'), 104 nn.; ii. 127 n., 296 n.
criticism, sensitivity to i. 12, 89, 145, 154, 156, 159, 214, 215, 250, 252–3, 255, 257, 259, 264, 265, 267–8; ii. 56, 57, 93, 94, 96, 97–8, 99, 103, 104, 105, 106, 126, 154–5, 156–7, 159; iii. 98, 99, 104, 106, 112, 114, 266, 308; iv. 5, 28, 33; v. 183, 250, 346; vi. 116, 121, 122, 132 n., 177
Croft, W. D. vii. 62 nn.
  letter to vii. 62
Croft, William i. 6 and n.
Crome, John iv. 110 n.
Cronje, Piet Arnoldus ii. 248, 249 n.
Cronshaw, Revd George Bernard vi. 172 n.
  letters to vi. 172; vii. 88, 170
Croppy (Max Gate cat) ii. 270, 271 n., 272
Cross, Wilbur Lucius vi. 20 n.
  letter to vi. 20
'Cross in Hand' (Dorset) ii. 32, 33 n., 275 ('the Stone') and n.; iii. 177, 189
Crowe, William v. 269 and n.

'Cry of the Homeless' (poem) v. 117 ('enclosed page'), 118 n.

Cunnington, Edward (antiquary) ii. 43 ('local man') and n.; iv. 203 n.

Cunnington, Edward B. Howard iv. 203 n.
letter to iv. 203

Curle, James:
A *Roman Frontier Post and Its People* iv. 255 ('beautiful book'), 256 n.
letter to iv. 255

Curtis, Charles Henry (Dorchester mayor) iv. 290 and n.

Curtis, Daniel iii. 68 and n.

Curtis, Mrs Daniel iii. 68 and n.

Curzon, George Nathaniel (later Marquess Curzon of Kedleston) i. 273 n.*; ii. 53 and n., 54 and n., 82, 89 n., 90 n.; iii. 314 n., 318 and n., 323 n., 327; v. 109 and n., 296 n.
copies of *Dynasts* sent to iii. 313
70th birthday wishes to TH iv. 93, 94 ('Ld C.'), 95 n.
opposition to suffrage movement iv. 106, 107
Persia and the Persian Question i. 272 ('monumental work'), 273 n.
letters to i. 272; iv. 93

Cutler, William Henry:
setting of Psalm 126 iii. 88 and n.; v. 129 ('Cutler'), 130 n.

'Cynic's Epitaph' (poem):
pub. in *London Mercury* vi. 337 n.

Daddy Hole Plain (Devon) v. 17, 18 n.

Daily Chronicle i. 250 and n.; ii. 84 and n., 102 n., 193 n., 227, 228 and n., 229 and n., 234, 235 n.; iii. 97 and n., 157 n., 216 n., 357; iv. 45 and n., 117 and n., 169 and n., 174 n., 175 n.; v. 81 n.; vii. 73 n.
W. Archer letters and articles in ii. 56 and n., 57 and n., 104 n., 207 and n.
'The Departure' pub. in ii. 233 n., 238
and 'Sixpenny Dickens' iv. 118 and n.
and *Tess* play vi. 350 n., 359 ('deliberate lie')

Daily Express v. 20, 21 n.; vi. 178 n.

Daily Graphic iii. 144 n., 296 and n.; vi. 31 and n.

Daily Herald v. 88 and n., 312, 313 n.

Daily Mail ii. 252, 283; iii. 48, 207 ('D.M.') and n.; iv. 45, 81 and n.; v. 10 n.
Literary Supplement iii. 232, 233 n., 235 n., 236 and n., 252 and n., 262 n.
TH's recommendation of FED to iii. 261
letter to Editor ii. 252

Daily Mirror iii. 357; v. 342 n.

Daily News i. 99 n., 201, 214 and n., 215, 248 n.; iii. 51 and n., 306, 307 nn., 310 n., 357; iv. 45, 234, 235 nn.; v. 43, 44 and n.; vi. 31 and n., 350 n.; vii. 139 and n.
and Meredith's 80th birthday iii. 295 n.
on TH's MSS and dramatic plans iv. 185, 186 n.
'The Pity of It' quoted in v. 215 n.

Daily Paper iii. 105 and n.

Daily Telegraph vi. 245 nn.

Daisy (Max Gate servant) iii. 335, 336 n., 340; iv. 85, 87

Dalton, Basil Imlay vii. 52 n.
letter to vii. 52

Dalton, Frederick Thomas ii. 248 n., 262 n.
letter to ii. 262

Daly, Augustin i. 213 n.; ii. 19
opening of theatre ii. 11, 17 and n.
letters to i. 213; ii. 17, 21, 81, 82

Daly's Theatre ii. 11, 12 n., 17 n.

'Dame of Athelhall, The' (poem) ii. 305 ('the story') and n.; iii. 138

Damer, Colonel George Lionel Dawson iii. 344 n.

Damerham (near Salisbury) vi. 5 n.

'Dance at the Phoenix, The' (poem) ii. 209, 283; iii. 137, 240 n.; v. 246

Danielson, Henry:
bibliography of TH v. 147 and n., 154, 170 and n., 175 n.
letter to v. 170

D'Annunzio, Gabriele:
The Virgin of the Rocks ii. 265 and n.

Dardanelles v. 101 n., 120, 125, 134, 154 n.

'Darkling Thrush, The' (poem) ii. 305 n.; iii. 79 ('lines on a thrush') and n., 219 n.; iv. 151, 256 n.; v. 259 n.; vi. 33, 149

Darmesteter, James i. 231, 232 n.

Darmesteter, Mme (*née* Agnes Mary Frances Robinson, later Mme Duclaux, qq.v.) i. 231, 232 n.

Dartmoor v. 214, 231, 274, 276

Dartmouth, Earl of i. 119 n.

Dartmouth (Devon) v. 17

Darwin, Charles:
Origin of Species iv. 63

Darwin, Erasmus:
The Loves of the Plants ii. 156 n.

Darwin, Francis iv. 30 n.; vii. 150 n.

Davidson, John iv. 25 and n.

Davies, Michael Llewelyn vi. 89 n., 138 n.

Davies, William Henry iv. 337 n.
'The Kingfisher' v. 337 and n.
letter to v. 337

Davis, George (Dorchester alderman) iv. 76, 77 n.

Davray, Henry ii. 267 n., 274 n.*
and translations of TH's novels ii. 267, 273, 278 ('*Mercure de France*'), 279 n.

Davray, Henry *(cont.)*
letter to ii. 273
De Casseres, Benjamin iii. 38 n.
articles by iii. 37; v. 5 and n.
The Shadow-Eater v. 160 and n.
letters to iii. 37; v. 5, 160
de Lafontaine, Alfred C. ii. 86 n., 201 ('our neighbour'), 202 n., 237 n., 238, 305 n.; iii. 220 n.; vi. 141 n.
letters to ii. 305; iii. 220, 317; iv. 56, 121; v. 198
De la Mare, Constance Elfrida vi. 202 n.
De la Mare, Walter John iv. 307 n.; vi. 113, 228 n., 247 n.
and *Dynasts* v. 284 and n.
and 'Poets' Tribute' v. 330, 331 n.
at Max Gate vi. 92 and n., 93
and protest against Irish policy vi. 94, 95 n.
'The Listeners' v. 310 n.
Memoirs of a Midget vi. 92 ('a novel'), 97 ('the book'), 98 nn.
'Seaton's Aunt' vi. 201, 202 n.
The Veil, and Other Poems vi. 108 ('your poems'), 109 n., 110 ('new poems')
(ed., with Thomas Quayle) *Readings* vi. 373 ('Anthology') and n.
letters to v. 284, 310, 330; vi. 94, 97, 108, 201
De la Pasture, Mrs Henry (Lady Clifford) iv. 120 ('the lady'), 121 n.
De Lautour, Mary Thérèse vi. 128 n.
letter to vi. 127
De Valera, Eamon vi. 100 n.
De Vere, Aubrey Thomas i. 151, 152 n.
'Dead and the Living One, The' (poem) v. 138 ('other poem') and n.
pub. in *Sphere* v. 128 and n., 129 n., 150 n.
pub. in *World* v. 150 n.
'Dead Drummer, The' (retitled 'Drummer Hodge', q.v.) (poem) ii. 236 n., 242 ('little poem'), 243 n.; v. 2 and n.; vii. 143
pub. in *Literature* ii. 238 and n.
'Dead Quire, The' (poem) iv. 67 and n.; vi. 149; vii. 9
Deane, Thomas Newenham iv. 60 and n.
'Dear, The' (poem) iii. 21 ('little poem') and n.
'Death of Regret, The' (poem) iv. 66 ('lines on . . . cat') 67 n.
Debenham, Ernest Ridley v. 144 nn.; vi. 69 nn.
'December Rain-Scene, A' (poem):
pub. in *Fortnightly Review* vi. 106 and n., 110, 111 n.
Deighton, E. Lonsdale:
(comp.) *British Legion Album* vi. 218 and n.
letter to vi. 218

Delabole (Cornwall) v. 128 and n.
Delacre, Jules vi. 357 ('the Manager'), 358 n., 365; vii. 8 ('Belgian manager'), 9 n.
Deland, Lorin Fuller i. 273 and nn.
Deland, Margaret Wade Campbell i. 273 n.
John Ward, Preacher i. 273 and n.
letter to i. 273
Delhi iii. 41, 42 n.
Denchworth (Berks) i. 5 n.
Mary H as teacher at i. 4 n.
Denis, Lisbeth vii. 65 n.
letter to vii. 65
Denis, Maurice vii. 65 nn.
Denison, Revd Edward vi. 194 ('one of them') and n.
Dennett, Solomon (Superintendent of Dorchester Police) iv. 113 n.
letter to iv. 113
Dent, Edward Joseph:
musical setting of 'The Oxen' vi. 43 and n.
Dent, Joseph Malaby:
(comp.) *English Short Stories* vi. 97 and n., 99 and n.
'Departure, The' (later 'Embarcation,' q.v.) (poem) ii. 233 nn., 238; vi. 192 n.
Derbyshire (troop-ship) vii. 51 n.
d'Erlanger, Baron Frédéric:
and production of *Tess* opera iii. 204 n.; iv. 2 n., 30, 31, 35, 36, 103 n., 230 and n.; vi. 350 and nn.
letters to iii. 204; iv. 35, 230; vi. 350
Derriman, Captain G. L. iii. 213 n.
Desperate Remedies (novel) ii. 32, 33 n.; iii. 149 n., 260; v. 205 and n.; vi. 129 n., 166 ('own similar case'), 167 n., 254
publication of i. 10 and n., 11; vii. 37
reviews of i. 11 ('a late novel'), 12, 13; iv. 159 n., 161
publisher's account for i. 13, 15, 16 n.
American publication i. 27 and n., 28, 29 n., 111 and n.
TH's reluctance to re-publish i. 129, 274, 286 n.
'New Edn' i. 185, 186 and n.; vii. 37 n.
'Popular Edn' i. 286 and n.; vii. 37 n.
copyright of ii. 51 and n., 58
in Colonial Library ii. 60, 63
'Wessex Novels' edn ii. 63
film rights v. 335
'Destiny and a Blue Cloak' (story) i. 31 and n.
Detroit Post i. 130 n.; ii. 34 n.
Devizes (Wilts):
town-criers' contest (1912) iv. 203 and n.
Dewar, George Albemarle Bertie iv. 139 n.; vii. 150 nn.
as editor of *Saturday Review* iv. 288; v. 68 and n., 72 n.

Dewar, George (cont.)
  as editor of *Nineteenth Century and After* vi.
    231, 232 n.
  The Leaning Spire iv. 139 ('book of stories')
    and n.
  letters to iv. 139, 288; v. 68; vi. 231; vii. 149
'D'Exideuil, Pierre' (G. Lasselin) vii. 85 nn.
Dial vi. 47 and nn., 77
Dial Press vi. 316 n.
dialect, interest in i. 172, 181, 277, 279; ii.
  46, 168, 214, 299; iii. 22, 32, 41, 42, 63,
  69–70, 124, 170, 297, 304, 307, 333, 335,
  363; iv. 15, 183, 207, 214, 312; v. 155, 167,
  291; vi. 74, 75–7; vii. 8, 68 and n.
Dickens, Catherine vi. 229 and n.
Dickens, Charles vi. 158, 159 n., 229 and n.
  Kitton edn of ii. 301 and n.
  compared with Hugo iii. 81
  'Sixpenny' Dickens iv. 118 and n.
  Testimonial Stamps iv. 118 and n.
  David Copperfield v. 74
  Dombey & Son v. 74
  Great Expectations ii. 155 ('Mr Wemmick'),
    156 n.
  Martin Chuzzlewit ii. 155 ('young woman'),
    156 n.; v. 74
  Old Curiosity Shop v. 74
  Pickwick Papers v. 74
Dickins, Arthur F.:
  Poems and Songs iv. 172 and n.
  letter to iv. 172
Dickinson, F. (fine art dealer) v. 229 n.
Dickinson, Revd John Harold iv. 262 n., 276 n.
  and TH's second marriage v. 15
  80th birthday wishes to TH vi. 29
  Records of St Juliot and Lesnewth vii. 56,
    57 n.
  letters to iv. 261, 275, 299; v. 15, 81, 171,
    177; vii. 56
Dickinson, Goldsworthy Lowes vi. 26 nn.
  The Magic Flute: A Fantasia vi. 63, 64 n.
  letters to vi. 26, 63
Dickinson, Miss L. M. (sister of Revd J.H.D.)
  iv. 261, 262 n.; v. 15; vii. 57 n.
Dicksee, (Sir) Frank i. 75 n.
Dictionary of National Biography (*DNB*) ii.
  269 n., 270; iv. 233 n.
Dieppe iii. 270
'Difference, The' (poem) v. 38 ('very small
  poem') and n.
Digby, Lady (wife of 9th Lord) ii. 144, 145 n.
Dilke, Ethel vii. 158 n.
Dinant ii. 130
Disraeli, Benjamin i. 36 n.; iii. 199 and n.
'Distracted Preacher, The' (story) i. 204 n.; ii.
  54; iv. 97, 165 n., 182, 188, 284; vi. 156
  dramatization of iv. 147 and nn., 178 n., 182,

183 n., 186, 187 and n., 189, 190, 191 n.
  Dorchester performances iv. 177, 178 n.,
    179–80, 182, 183 n., 187, 189, 191 and n.;
    vii. 153 n.
  London performance iv. 194 n.
  proposed film of vi. 6 and n., 7, 165 n.
  reprinted in *Argosy* vii. 59, 60 n.
'Division, The' (poem) iv. 132 and n., 151 n.,
  211 ('my verses') and n.
Dix, Revd Cyril Poynder iii. 346 n.
Dixon, G. E.:
  letter to ii. 219
Dobson, Austin i. 37 n., 288 n.*; iii. 232,
  233 n., 283, 320 n.; iv. 287 n.
  copy of *Tess* sent to i. 287
  and 'Poets' Tribute' v. 334
  'In Memoriam' iv. 90 ('a few verses') and n.
  letters to i. 287; iii. 320; iv. 90, 110; v. 334
'Doctor's Legend, The' i. 219 ('short story'),
  220 n.
Dodd, Francis H.:
  portrait of TH vii. 63 and n.
Dodd & Livingston (American publishers)
  v. 7 n.
Dodderidge, George (churchwarden) v. 24 n.
  letter to v. 24
Dodge, Louise Preston i. 153 n.
Doeg, William Henry iii. 60 nn.
  letters to iii. 60, 188, 310
Dolman, Frederick i. 290 n.; ii. 44 ('that inter-
  viewer'), 45 n.
  letter to i. 289
Dolmetsch, Eugene Arnold v. 7 and n.
'Donaghadee' (poem) vi. 270 ('few lines') and
  n., 351 and n.
Donaghadee (Co. Down) vi. 270 and n.
Donald, (Sir) Robert iii. 313 n.
  letter to iii. 313
Donaldson, Revd St Clair George Alfred vi.
  194 ('Bp. of Salisbury') and n.; vii. 14 n.
  letter to vii. 13
Donaldson, Revd Stuart Alexander iv. 315
  as Master of Magdalene College, Cambridge
    iv. 260 n., 291, 308, 314, 315 n.; v. 26 and
    n., 134 n.; vi. 194 n.
  as Vice-Chancellor of Cambridge Univ. iv.
    260 n., 269, 270 n.
  resignation from Vice-Chancellorship iv.
    311, 312 n., 321 n.
  death v. 134 n.
  letters to iv. 259, 291, 308, 311, 314; v. 7
Donaldson, Lady Albinia (wife of Revd
  S.A.D.) iv. 291 and n., 297, 308, 314; v. 7
  and n.
Donne, John iii. 326 and n.; vi. 155
Dorchester, Joseph Damer, 1st Earl of iii. 156
  and n.; iv. 58 and n.

Dorchester (Dorset) i. 119 and n.; ii. 43, 146, 199, 272, 284, 285 n., 295, 298 and n.; vi. 114 n., 155, 168 and n.; vii. 3 n., 26
postmasters i. 4 and n.
TH's purchase of building plot i. 73 and n., 105, 135; vii. 95–7, 98, 100, 103–5
Barnes memorial i. 155 and n.; vii. 108, 109 n.
as 'Casterbridge' i. 274; ii. 131
restoration of old street-names ii. 4 and n.; iii. 17, 19; iv. 76–7, 80 and n., 135; v. 102
TH as JP for ii. 50 ('the other') and n., 291 and n.; iii. 18 n.; v. 267 and n.
bank failure ii. 159, 176
TH's contribution to guide-book to iii. 17 and n., 19, 28
sewage system iii. 130, 132, 179 n., 234 and n.
measles epidemic iii. 158 and n.
Trafalgar centenary iii. 185 and n.
new school buildings iii. 207
visit of Society of Dorset Men in London iii. 212 and n.
'Ye Merrie Maie Fayre' (1908) iii. 294 and n., 317 n.
University extension lectures iii. 326; iv. 11 n.
Freedom presented to TH iv. 128 ('little function') and n., 129, 130 ('my speech') and n., 141 ('last autumn') and n.
mayors of iv. 147 and nn.
and humane slaughtering v. 20; vi. 178 and n.
soldiers billeted in v. 41, 42, 43 and n., 90, 91
German prisoners in v. 42 and n., 43, 44, 46, 57, 71, 203, 204
Patriotic Concert v. 63 and n.
entertainment for soldiers' children v. 73 and n.
Temperance meeting v. 84, 85 n.
effects of war v. 132, 271, 283
art painting-room v. 135 and n.
'Kut-Fund Day' events (1916) v. 168, 169 n.
performance of scenes from *Far from the Madding Crowd* v. 342 n.
TH's schooldays in vi. 3, 4 n.; vii. 45 n., 46
hangings at vi. 75, 77 n.; vii. 46
Bazaar for Hospital funds opened by TH vi. 98 and n.
Prince of Wales's visit vi. 204–5
'bloody assize' vii. 17 n.
All Saints' Church iii. 35 ('the church') and n.
Antelope Hotel iii. 267, 269, 285, 347, 356

Came House ii. 38 n.; v. 273, 274 n.; vii. 39 ('a house') and n.
Cemetery iii. 137
Colliton House iii. 137
Conquer Barrow iv. 234 and n.
County Asylum iii. 333 and n.; iv. 123 n.
County School vi. 174, 175 n.
Grove House iv. 241 n.
Handel House iii. 79 n., 344 n.
High West Street iii. 137
    former theatre vi. 248 n.
    (No. 24) iii. 167 n.
    (No. 51) ii. 163 n., 227 n.; iii. 290 and n. letting of iii. 29, 36, 78 and n., 158 and n., 167 and n. sale of iii. 336 n.
    (No. 54) iii. 24 n., 100 n.; (?) iv. 172
Holy Trinity Church iii. 283 n.
Isaac Last's Academy for Young Gentlemen vi. 3, 4 n.
Isaac Last's British School ii. 237 n.
Judge Jeffreys' Lodgings vii. 17 and n.
King's Arms Hotel i. 119; ii. 107 n.; iii. 336; iv. 165; v. 266; vi. 132 n.
Loud's Mill vii. 105 and n.
Max Gate – *see separate entry*
National School iii. 119 n.
Obelisk iv. 80 and n.
Octagon iv. 80 and n.
Phoenix Inn iii. 137
Post Office war memorial tablet vi. 38 and n., 44 and nn., 51, 52 n.
St Mary's Church v. 342 n.
St Peter's Church ii. 176 n.; iii. 242 n., 332 and n.; iv. 238 nn.
    Barnes statue outside i. 155 n.; iii. 242 n., 243 n.; vii. 108, 109 n.
Shire Hall Lane i. 119 n., 120 ('our new house'); vii. 98 and n.
Somerleigh Court ii. 4 n.; iv. 261
South Court iv. 189 n., 286 n.; vi. 43 and n.
South Street (No. 10):
    as original of Henchard's house iii. 109 and n.
Syward Road vii. 105 n.
Town Hall iii. 281 nn., 292 n., 300 and n., 317; iv. 141 and n.
Town Pump iv. 80 n., 300
Trinity Church iii. 226 n.
Twelve-Men Way iv. 136 and n.
Dorchester Agricultural Society iv. 42 n.
Dorchester Corporation iii. 179 and n., 180 n.; vii. 17
Dorchester Debating and Dramatic Society (later Hardy Players) iv. 116 n., 149 n.; v. 227, 284 ('Dorset Dramatic Society'); vi. 191 n., 329; vii. 19 n.

Dorchester Debating Society (cont.)
performances of *Trumpet-Major* iii. 300 and n., 332, 333 n., 349, 350 n., 356 and nn., 357; iv. 236 and n., 239, 244 and n., 245 n., 250 ('the play'); vii. 148 n.
performance of *Far from the Madding Crowd* iv. 22 n., 57 and n.
performances of *Mellstock Quire* iv. 125–6, 127, 129, 130; vii. 151 n.
performances of *Distracted Preacher* and *Three Wayfarers* iv. 177, 178 n., 179–80, 182, 183 n., 187, 189, 191 and n., 194 and n.; vii. 153 n.
performance of *Woodlanders* iv. 292 n.; v. 3 n.; vi. 265, 266 n.; vii. 156, 157 n.
performance of *Wessex Scenes from The Dynasts* v. 149, 150 and n., 162 and nn., 165 and n., 166 and n., 176, 182 nn., 184, 186 and n., 187 n., 188 ('the play') and n., 189, 191 and n., 193, 194, 195 n.
performances of *Return of the Native* v. 285 n.; vi. 45, 46 and n., 47, 52, 57
Christmas entertainment at Max Gate vi. 57
performances of *Queen of Cornwall* vi. 203 and n., 208, 209 and n., 211, 219 and n., 220 and nn., 221–2, 223, 224 n., 237 and n.
performance of scenes from *Far from the Madding Crowd* vi. 250, 251 n., 268 ('the performance'), 269 n.
performances of *Tess* vi. 269 and n., 279 and n., 284, 285–6, 287, 289 ('the play'), 291 ('the play') and n., 294 and n., 295, 296, 297, 298 n., 306
Dorchester Grammar School ii. 79 n., 174 n., 227 n.; iv. 314 and n.; vii. 45 n., 85 n.
TH as Governor iv. 3 and n., 252, 253 and n.; v. 208; vi. 174, 175 n., 375 and n.
Governors' meetings iv. 55, 149, 225, 315
TH's refusal of invitation to distribute prizes v. 101
rebuilding vi. 174, 175 n.; vii. 61 and nn., 68, 69 n., 72 n.
stone-laying ceremony vii. 61 and n., 68, 72 n.
'Dorchester Hornpipe' iii. 283 n.; iv. 125
Dorchester Lecture Society i. 121
Dorchester Old Grammarians' Club:
TH retires as vice-president vii. 45 and n.
Doré, Gustave i. 63 and n.
Dorking (Surrey) iv. 26 and n.
Dorset:
TH as JP for ii. 50 and n., 291 and n.; iii. 62 and n., 78 and n., 81, 82 n., 84 and n., 85, 153 n.; vi. 174, 175 n.
Dorset, Clerk of the Peace for:
letter to ii. 291

Dorset Assizes iv. 278 n.
TH as Grand Juror at iii. 18 and n., 23 and nn.; iv. 232 n.
Dorset County Chronicle (sometimes *Dorset Chronicle*) i. 180, 217 n.; ii. 4 n., 53 and n., 101 n., 273 n., 284, 285 n.; iii. 185 n., 247 n., 293 n., 299 n., 315 n., 317 and n., 335 ('D.C.C.'), 336 n.; iv. 20 n., 147 n., 198 n.; v. 42, 43 n., 96 n., 198 and n., 227, 250 n., 269; vi. 191 n., 228 n., 237, 248 n.; vii. 62 and n., 101 n., 112, 124 n., 146 ('D.C.C.') and n., 172
TH's obit. of sister Mary i. 4 n.; v. 136 n.
TH's marriage announced in i. 31 and n.
and Barnes memorial i. 155 and n.
and 'tale' about Max Gate purchase ii. 67 and n.
'The Going of the Battery' pub. in ii. 237 and n.
TH's recollections of 'Leader Scott' pub. in iii. 38, 39 nn.
Moule verses in iii. 115, 116 n.
Dynasts II sent to iii. 195 and n.
Barnes poems in iii. 342
notice of ELH's pictures iii. 343, 344 n.
back numbers returned by TH v. 210 and n.; vii. 62
Dorset County Council:
elections (1889) i. 180 and n., 187 and n.
Dorset County Library vii. 32, 33 n.
request for complete set of TH's writings iv. 116, 117, 119
Dorset County Hospital vi. 169
Dorset County Museum i. 121 n.; iii. 228, 262 and n.; iv. 38; v. 279 and n.; vi. 33; vii. 17, 33 and n.
TH elected to Council of i. 185 and n., 252 n.
TH's gift of books to iii. 293
TH's gift of MSS to iv. 179 n., 184 and n., 190
Barnes MSS at v. 174, 175 n.
TH as Vice-President of v. 252
doorkeeper as alleged source of gossip vii. 25 and n.
Dorset County Nursing Association vi. 250, 251 nn.
Dorset Daily Echo vii. 27 n., 28 and n.
Dorset Daily News vi. 188 n.
Dorset Men in London, Society of – *see* Society of Dorset Men in London
Dorset Natural History and Antiquarian Field Club i. 195, 196 n.; ii. 138 n., 268 n.; iii. 247 n.; iv. 123, 183 n., 308; v. 102 n., 198 n.; vi. 226, 249 nn.; vii. 100 ('the club') and n., 174
meeting at Pilsdon Pen i. 136 and n.; iv. 119, 120 n.; v. 111, 112 n., 167

Dorset Natural History Club (cont.)
  visit to Wool iii. 209, 210 n.
  publication of Barnes poems iii. 297 and n.
  TH elected Hon. Member iii. 311, 314, 315
  visit to excavation of Maumbury Rings iii.
    335 ('at the Amphitheatre'), 336 n.
  visit to Milton Abbey iv. 58 and nn.
Dorset Red Cross v. 339 n.
Dorset Regiment (also as Dorsetshire) iii.
    283 n.
  known as 'Green Linnets' iii. 74
  Pouncy lecture on v. 42 and n.
  in Great War v. 85 and n., 168 and n., 240,
    241 n.
  'Comforts Fund' v. 63 n., 169 n., 241 n., 243
    and n.
Dorset & South-Western Counties of England
  Sugar Beet & Beet-Sugar Development
  Association vi. 188 n.
Dorset Volunteer Rangers v. 274 n.
'Dorsetshire Labourer, The' (article) iii. 10
    n.
  pub. in *Longman's* i. 107 n., 119 n.; iii. 9;
    iv. 178
  MS given to Dorset County Museum iv.
    179 n.
Dostoievsky, Feodor:
  Poor Folk ii. 42 n.
Doubleday, Frank Nelson ii. 240 n.
Doubleday & McClure (publishers) ii. 240
    and n.
Doughty, Charles:
  Wanderings in Arabia iv. 187 and n., 189
Douglas, Francis John Scott i. 166 n.; v. 136,
    137 n., 248 n.
Douglas, Sir George Brisbane i. 166 n.*, 243;
    ii. 20, 21 n., 28, 64 n., 100, 122; iii. 42,
    181; iv. 256 n.; v. 1; vi. 18; vii. 135 n.
  at Max Gate ii. 91
  and *Jude* ii. 105
  and *Well-Beloved* ii. 154, 161
  interest in Spanish literature v. 303, 304 n.,
    324 and nn., 342
  and Goethe v. 303, 323, 324 n.
  Diversions of a Country Gentleman iii. 22
    and n.
  A History of the Border Counties ii. 70 n., 210
    ('County history') and n.
  Life of Major-General Wauchope iii. 66 n.,
    130
  New Border Tales i. 247 and n.
  The Pleasure Seeker (probably later *Diver-
    sions of a Country Gentleman*, q.v.) ii. 64
    and n., 98 and n., 105 ('excellent title')
  Poems of a Country Gentleman i. 183 n.; ii.
    161 n., 182
  'Unfortunate Shepherdess' ii. 105, 106 n.
  (ed.) *Love-Songs of Robert Burns* vii. 122
    ('your Burns') and n.
  (ed.) *Scottish Minor Poets from the Age of
    Ramsay to David Gray* i. 247 n.
  (ed. with G. Ramsay) *The Panmure Papers*
    iii. 143 n.
  letters to i. 165, 182, 242, 246, 249, 285; ii.
    63, 70, 91, 98, 100, 105, 154, 161, 163,
    166, 182, 188, 210, 243, 251, 255, 282,
    289, 303; iii. 22, 40, 48, 62, 66, 81, 130,
    143, 172, 175, 216; iv. 40, 111, 245, 300,
    312; v. 12, 88, 91, 136, 247, 262, 303, 323;
    vi. 106, 203, 228; vii. 70, 121
Douglas, Lady (mother of Sir George) – *see*
  Scott-Douglas, Lady Mariquita Juana
  Petronila
Douglas, George Francis Valentine Scott v.
  248 ('Francis's boy') and n., 303 ('your
  nephew'), 304 n., 324 ('nephew') and n.;
  vi. 203 ('nephew') and n.
Douglas, James:
  on fictionalized biography iv. 234–5
  letter to iv. 234
Douglas, Mary Helena Henrietta (sister of Sir
  George) iii. 81, 82 n.; v. 136, 137 n.; vi.
  229 n.; vii. 70, 71 n.
Douglas, Richard (laird of Fingland) vii. 70,
  71 n., 80
Dover ii. 129, 130 n.; iii. 82, 83 n., 85, 95
Dowden, Edward:
  The Life of Percy Bysshe Shelley ii. 125 and
    n., 169 and n.; iii. 86, 87 n.
Dowie, Ménie Muriel ii. 87
  Gallia ii. 87 and n.
  A Girl in the Karpathians ii. 87 and n.
'Down Wessex Way' (previously 'The Spring
  Call', q.v.) (poem):
  pub. in *Society of Dorset Men in London
    Year-book* v. 23, 24 n.
Downey, Edmund (publisher) i. 129 n.
  Twenty Years Ago vii. 138 ('Downey's
    book'), 139 n.
Downey, W. & D. (photographers) vii. 127
'Downfall of Paris, The' (military march) iii.
  240 and n.
Doyle, (Sir) Arthur Conan ii. 184, 185 n.
  petition for Casement reprieve v. 167 n.
Drake, William A. vi. 6 and nn.
Drama Society iv. 180 and n.
Drayton, Michael:
  Complete Works iii. 133 and n.
  Polyolbion iii. 133
Dreiser, Theodore vi. 38 n., 268 n.
Dresser, John ii. 76 n.
Drew, Walter (Dorchester head postmaster)
  vi. 44 n.
  letter to vi. 44

Dreyfus, Captain Alfred ii. 223 and n., 229, 230 n., 231 n.
Drinkwater, Albert Edwin v. 59 n.*
and *Dynasts* production v. 54, 59, 63, 65, 78, 96, 112, 346 n.; vi. 219 n.
and suggested filming of *Dynasts* production v. 63 and n., 130–1, 133, 257, 258 n., 335 and n.
production of scenes from *Dynasts* for OUDS v. 346 and n., 347
letters to v. 59, 63, 65, 78, 112, 130, 346
Drinkwater, Daisy vi. 273 n.
Drinkwater, John iv. 34 n.*, 307 n.; v. 132 n., 303 n.; vi. 57 and n.
and *Moments of Vision* v. 258 and n.
invited to Max Gate v. 258 and n.
and 'Poets' Tribute' v. 351
dramatization of *Mayor of Casterbridge* vii. 19 and n., 35, 36, 38, 42 n.
Abraham Lincoln v. 281 ('Play') and n.; vi. 311 n.
A Book for Bookmen vii. 47, 48 n.
Cophetua iv. 193 n.
From an Unknown Isle vi. 273 ('forthcoming poems') and n., 286
'The Loom of the Poets' iv. 67 ('the Sonnets') and n.
Lyrical and Other Poems iv. 34 and n.
Mary Stuart vi. 160, 161 n.
Preludes vi. 165 ('little book') and n.
Rebellion v. 96 n.
Swords and Ploughshares v. 96 n.
Tides v. 235 and n.
'To Thomas Hardy' vi. 328 ('the poem') and n.
(comp.) *An Anthology of English Verse* vi. 160 ('volume of poetry') and n.
(ed.) *Twentieth-Century Poetry* vii. 76 ('his book') and n.
(ed.) *Twenty Poems in Common English* (Barnes) vi. 237 and n.
(comp.) *The Way of Poetry* v. 278 ('anthology') and n.
letters to iv. 34, 67, 193; v. 96, 235, 258, 278, 281, 351; vi. 160, 165, 237, 273, 286, 328; vii. 42, 47
Dron, Thomas Middleton vii. 101 nn., 112 n.
letters to vii. 101, 112
'Drummer Hodge' (formerly 'The Dead Drummer,' q.v.) (poem) ii. 238 n.
pub. in South African anthology v. 2 and n.; vii. 143 and n.
Drummond, William iii. 267 n.
Du Bos, Charles vii. 85 n.
Du Maurier, George Louis Palmella Busson i. 71 n.*, 269; ii. 135 and n.; iv. 158, 159 n.; v. 145 n.

illustrates *Hand of Ethelberta* i. 71 n.; iv. 43
illustrates *Laodicean* i. 71 n., 74–5, 76, 79, 80 and nn., 91
working methods i. 74
letters to i. 71, 76
Dublin vii. 125 n.
Easter rising (1916) v. 154 n., 158 and n., 159 ('this event'), 160 n., 167 n.
University College iii. 310 n.
'Duchess of Hamptonshire, The' (story) iv. 175 and n.
Duckworth, Gerald (publisher) vi. 166 n.
Duckworth, H. C. i. 228 n.
Duclaux, Agnes Mary Frances (*née* Robinson, later Mme Darmesteter, qq.v.) vii. 65 and n.
Duclaux, Professor Émile vii. 65 n.
Dudley, Anita:
and *Royal Artillery War Commemoration Book* v. 352, 353 n.
letter to v. 352
Dudley (Worcs):
war memorial inscription vi. 357 and n.
'Duel, The' (poem) vi. 96
Duff, Charles Gordon ii. 256 n.
Duff, Mary ii. 256 and n., 267
Duffield, William i. 2 n.
Duffin, Henry Charles:
Thomas Hardy: A Study of the Wessex Novels v. 156 ('your book'), 157 n., 172 n.
letter to v. 156
Dugdale, Alice Frances ii. 27, 28 n.
Dugdale, Constance (sister of FED) iv. 103 n., 296 n.; v. 101; vi. 32 and n., 89, 90 n.
holidays with TH and FED iv. 148 n., 150 n., 157 n.
birthday wishes to TH v. 107, 163 and n.
at Max Gate vi. 135 and n., 254
letters to iv. 103; v. 100, 102, 107, 120, 163; vi. 328; vii. 26
Dugdale, Edward (father of FED) iii. 261 n.; iv. 157 n., 246; vi. 32
at FED's marriage to TH v. 9, 10
and photograph of FEH v. 33 and n.
letters to v. 33; vi. 178; vii. 26
Dugdale, Mrs E. (Emma Taylor, mother of FED) iv. 246 n., 277 n.; vi. 313 ('wife's mother') and n.
at Max Gate v. 33
illness vi. 32, 35 ('Florence's mother')
letters to iv. 246, 277, 333; v. 135; vi. 32, 89, 253; vii. 26
Dugdale, Eva (FED's sister) iv. 296 n.; v. 325; vi. 1 ('my sister-in-law') and n., 57 ('F's sister') and n., 81, 205
Dugdale, Florence Emily (FED) (later F. E. Hardy, q.v.) iii. 205 n.; iv. 16 n., 49 n., 83 n., 95 ('young cousin'), 106, 132, 143,

Dugdale, Florence Emily (cont.)
146 n., 177, 204, 205 n., 211, 215, 223 n., 258 nn., 262 n., 302 and n., 315
possible first visit to Max Gate iii. 179 and n., 193
research for *Dynasts* iii. 249 n., 253, 261
literary work iii. 249 and n., 261 and n., 274 and n.; iv. 13 and n., 23 n., 43 ('her MS') and n., 45, 98, 114 and n., 117 and n.; v. 8, 15, 137; vii. 147 and n.
recommended to publishers by TH iii. 261–2, 274, 329 ('the author') and n.; iv. 13 and n., 117 and n.; vii. 147 and n.
family's Dorset origins iii. 261 and n., 274; iv. 46 and n.; v. 13 and nn., 14
as typist iii. 261, 262; iv. 271 and n.
on staff of *Standard* iv. 23 n., 98
attends *Tess* opera iv. 32 and n.
ill-health iv. 35, 38, 39, 257, 258 n., 260, 330
invited to Aldeburgh iv. 35, 38, 39 and n., 41 n.
at Aldeburgh iv. 39 n., 41 n., 42 n., 43 n., 55 n., 62 and n., 80 n., 91 n., 112, 113, 114 n., 142 and n., 147, 149 n., 176 ('my young friend') and n., 212, 214 n., 219 n., 267, 268, 270; v. 15 n.
attends *Far from the Madding Crowd* iv. 51 n., 62
cathedral tours with TH iv. 51 n., 148 n., 150
lecture on TH's books iv. 62 and n.
'taken up' by ELH iv. 92 n., 121 n., 130 n., 165 n.; v. 15, 17, 18, 19, 156, 177
in Peterborough with TH iv. 98 n.
article on TH at seventy iv. 98, 99 n.
portrait by Mary Hardy iv. 112 and n.; v. 135 and n.
at Max Gate iv. 121, 122 n., 128, 129 ('a friend'), 239, 244, 280 n.
portrait by Strang iv. 122 and n.; v. 12 and n.
attends *Mellstock Quire* iv. 130
TH's birthday gift to iv. 136 and n.
in Lake District with TH iv. 157 n.
secretary and friend to Mrs Henniker iv. 212 and n., 267, 268; v. 11 n., 38
and ELH's death iv. 239, 244
at Max Gate after ELH's death iv. 244, 280 n., 310, 330; vii. 156
The Adventures of Mr. Prickle-back iv. 43 n.
'The Apotheosis of the Minx' iv. 13 n.
'Blue Jimmy the Horse-stealer' iv. 114
Country Life iii. 249 ('children's stories') and n.
Cousin Christine iii. 249 n.
In Lucy's Garden v. 137 n.
Old Time Tales iii. 249 n.

'The Scholar's Wife' iv. 13 n.; vii. 147 n., 174
'Trafalgar! How Nelson's Death Inspired the Tailor' iv. 45 ('the sketch') and n., 117 ('topical sketch') and n., 118
letters to iii. 179, 193, 249, 253; iv. 15, 45, 58, 136, 171, 195, 212, 232, 255, 260, 270
Dugdale, Margaret (FED's sister, later Soundy, q.v.) v. 101 ('M.')
at FED's marriage to TH v. 9 and n., 10
marriage to Reginald Soundy v. 203 and n., 205
Duke, Thomas Crooks (farmer) iii. 84 and n.
'Duke's Reappearance, The' (story) iv. 298
pub. in *Saturday Review* ii. 139 n.; iv. 178
MS given to Clodd iv. 179 n., 186 n., 207 ('promised Manuscript'), 208 n.
Duke and Co. (Dorchester auctioneers) vi. 128, 129 n.
Dumas, Alexandre *père* vi. 156, 157 n.
Duneka, Francis A. (publisher) iv. 254 n.
and proposed *Tess* film iv. 265 and n.; v. 265
and *A Changed Man* iv. 265, 298, 299, 303, 308
letters to iv. 254, 265, 303, 308; v. 52
Dunkin, E. i. 96 n.
Dunn, Clement C. (Dorchester hotel-keeper) iii. 356 and n.
Dunn, James Nicol ii. 175 n.; iii. 155 n.
and W. E. Henley Memorial iii. 106
letters to ii. 174, 275, 298; iii. 106, 155
Dunsany, Lord:
The Glittering Gate iv. 95 n.
Dunster Castle (Somerset):
as 'Castle De Stancy' ii. 133
Durdle Door (Dorset) v. 31, 40
Durham iv. 51
'During Wind and Rain' (poem) vi. 96
'Durnover moor':
original of ii. 131
Durrant, Wilfred S. iv. 28 n.
letter to iv. 28
Durrant's (press-cutting agency) ii. 77, 78 n.
Duse, Eleonora ii. 20, 21 n.
interest in playing Tess vii. 129 and nn.
Dynasts, The (poetic drama) iii. 41 n., 176, 221, 225, 294 n., 313; v. 4, 5, 42, 153, 251, 284 and n.; vi. 54, 188, 260 n.; vii. 37 and n.
choice of title iii. 102, 197
philosophy of iii. 106, 113, 195 n., 207, 255, 351; v. 69–70; vi. 99
topographical backgrounds iii. 138
omission of promised list of authorities iii. 310 and n.; iv. 64 and n.
critical reception iii. 352; iv. 5, 37, 44 and n., 52, 53 nn.; v. 36; vii. 146 nn.

Dynasts, The (cont.)

treatment of Napoleon in iv. 88 and n.; vi. 105 and nn., 161; vii. 83

MS given to British Museum iv. 178 and n., 192, 200; vi. 34

errata in iv. 285 and n.; v. 323; vi. 85; vii. 29, 30 n., 31 and n., 66 and n.

songs in v. 56 and nn., 58, 63

suggested filming of v. 63 and n., 130–1 and nn., 257, 258 n., 335 and n.

verses on v. 88 and n.

extracts in *Selected Poems* v. 133 and n.

dialect words in v. 136

first idea of v. 246

extracts in anthologies vi. 83 and n., 316 and n., 373 n.

proposed German translations iii. 308, 309 n.; vi. 249 and n.

French translation of segments vii. 83 and n.

prospectus for vii. 145, 146 n.

EDITIONS:

American iv. 171 and n.; vi. 105, 214

Mellstock v. 39

one-vol. iv. 3–4, 5, 6 and n., 7 n., 10, 11, 64 and n., 118 and n., 130 and n., 228 and n., 232 n.; v. 299, 316 n., 323 n.; vi. 186 and n., 189; vii. 63 n.

Pocket iv. 4 n.; vi. 235 and n., 236, 283 n., 316

thin-paper vi. 104, 105 n.

three-vol. limited and signed vii. 14 and n., 15 and n., 29, 30 n., 31 and n., 63 and n., 66 and n., 71 and n., 86 and n.

Wessex iv. 228 and n.; vii. 31

PRODUCTIONS:

amateur, of scenes from iii. 294 n., 311, 317; v. 149, 150 and n., 162 ('pro-gramme') and nn., 165 and n., 166 and n., 176, 182 nn., 184, 186 n., 187 n., 188 ('the play') and n., 189, 191 and n., 193, 194, 195 nn., 346 and n., 347–9, 351 and n.; vi. 5, 8, 9, 30, 323 n.

professional London v. 51 and n., 52, 53–6, 57, 58, 59–61, 62–3, 64–6, 68, 69, 70, 74 and n., 76, 78, 87 and n., 94, 95 n., 96, 131 and n., 349; vi. 219 n.; vii. 158 and n.

broadcast reading vii. 6 and n.

Dynasts, The: Part First iii. 112, 169, 256, 289, 310 n.; iv. 116, 169 n., 193 n.

writing and proofreading of iii. 35 ('a MS.') and n., 81 n., 82 ('play in blank verse'), 83 n., 85; iv. 215 n.; vii. 135 n., 137 and n.

agreement with Macmillan iii. 76, 77, 80 and n., 91

production and publication of iii. 75–7, 85, 90, 91 and nn.

American copyright iii. 76 and n., 77, 91, 93, 277; iv. 171 n.

critical reception iii. 98–9, 100, 102, 104, 106, 107 and n., 112, 113, 126 and n., 309 and n.

setting to music of 'The Night of Trafalgar' iii. 100, 126, 127 n.

Commons debate in iii. 105 and n., 113

presentation copies iii. 108 and n., 125

'broaching the Admiral' scene iii. 114 and n., 124

revision of iii. 126 and n., 182 and n., 188 and n.

facsimile of MS pages iii. 178 and n.

misprint in iii. 188 and n.

Preface to iii. 204 and n.

in Wessex Edn iv. 228 n.

in Mellstock Edn vi. 7

Pitt's speech in vii. 83 and n.

Dynasts, The: Part Second iii. 135, 187, 256, 277 n.; iv. 137 n., 139 n.; v. 168, 304 n.; vi. 55 n.

writing of iii. 133, 143

completion of iii. 182, 183, 185, 186; vii. 141 and n.

critical reception iii. 183 n., 197–9, 200, 204, 206

publication iii. 195 and n.

presentation copies iii. 195, 196, 202

in Wessex Edn iv. 228 n.

error in vi. 307, 308 n.

Dynasts, The: Part Third iii. 240 n., 286, 327; iv. 88 and n., 145 n.; vi. 55 n., 203 and n., 328 n.

writing of iii. 133, 197, 218, 233, 255, 267, 269 n., 270 ('Napoleonic drama'), 274, 275, 276

research for iii. 209, 249, 253, 261

completion of iii. 277, 287, 289; vii. 144 and n.

American edn iii. 277 and n., 290

ball-room scene iii. 284, 285 n.

publication iii. 290, 294, 295, 296, 297 n., 306 n.

critical reception iii. 296, 298, 300, 304–5, 316, 349

'Budmouth Dears' song iii. 299 and n., 320 ('song') and nn., 355, 358 and n.; v. 56 and n., 87

in Wessex Edn iv. 228 and n.

MS of closing chorus v. 244 n.

Earl Marshal – *see* Norfolk, Duke of

Early Life of Thomas Hardy (prose) v. 332 n.

'East-End Curate, An' (poem):

pub. in *London Mercury* vi. 242 n., 277 n.

East and West v. 98, 99 n.

East, (Sir) Alfred ii. 286, 287 n., 292 and nn.
'East Egdon':
    original of ii. 255, 303
'East Endelstow':
    Lesnewth as vi. 29
East Stour (Dorset) ii. 99 n.
Eastlake, Sir Charles Lock v. 216 and n.
Eastleigh (Hants) ii. 28 and n.
Echo vii. 165 and n.
Echo de Paris ii. 218
Eden, George Rodney, Bp of Wakefield ii. 219 and n.
Edgcumbe, Frances Pearce i. 243 n.
Edgcumbe, (Sir) Robert Pearce i. 180 n.*, 217 n., 227, 228 n.; ii. 4 n., 51 n.; iv. 115 n., 261 ('friend of mine') and n.; v. 271 nn.
    contests South Dorset constituency i. 231, 233–4, 235, 236 and n., 272 and n.; vii. 124 n.
    recommends TH as JP for Dorset ii. 50
    knighthood ii. 66 and n.
    and bank failure ii. 159 n., 176 and n.
    letters to i. 180, 185, 187, 233–4, 235, 236, 243; ii. 4, 50, 66, 72, 138, 175; iv. 115, 251; v. 270; vi. 28, 175; vii. 68
Edinburgh:
    St Giles's Cathedral iv. 51
    Stevenson memorial vii. 130 n.
Edinburgh Philosophical Institution vii. 135 n., 174
    letter to vii. 135
Edinburgh Review i. 149 n., 267 ('E.R.'), 268 n., 279; ii. 303 n.; v. 75 n., 246 n., 261 n., 267
Edis (later Galsworthy), Olive:
    TH photographed by iv. 330 ('young lady'), 331 n.; v. 9, 10 n.
Edmonds, Dr Florence Mary v. 349 and n.
education, views on i. 116–17; iii. 311; vi. 62, 321, 326
Education Bill (1896) ii. 124 and n.
Educational Book Company v. 172, 173 n.
Educational Review (Madras) vi. 307 n.
Edward VII iv. 111 and n.
    accession ii. 280 n., 291 n.
    coronation ii. 20 n., 21, 22, 25, 26 and n., 43
    death iv. 78 n., 87, 88 n., 89, 90 n., 230 and n.; vi. 350 n.
    proposed memorial to iv. 138 and n.
    See also Wales, Prince of
'Egdon Heath' ii. 93 and n.; vii. 73
    map of i. 61; iv. 137 and n.
    originals of ii. 74, 132, 302, 303; iv. 137
    association with Lear iii. 177 and n.
Egerton, Caledon Philip iv. 242 and n.
Egerton, Caroline Blanche iii. 357 n.

'Egerton, George' – *see* Clairmonte, Mary Chavelita
Eggesford House (Devon) i. 131; vii. 102 and n.
Einstein, Albert v. 353 and n.; vi. 173 and n.
'Ejected Member's Wife, The' (later 'The Rejected Member's Wife') (poem) iii. 196 and n.
Eldon, John Scott, 1st Earl of vi. 1, 2n.
Eldridge, Joseph i. 272 nn.
    letter to i. 272
Eldridge, Pope & Co. (Dorchester brewers) i. 100 n.; vi. 168 and nn.
Electric Furnace Company v. 338 n.
Elgar, Sir Edward William:
    proposed collaboration with TH iv. 291 and nn.
    letter to iv. 291
Eliot, George i. 195, 200, 299, 300 n.; vi. 155
    Daniel Deronda vi. 156, 157 n.
Eliot, Richard ffolliott i. 285 and n.
Eliot, Mrs Richard i. 285 n.
    letter to i. 285
Eliot & Pearce (bankers) ii. 159 and n.
Elizabeth the Queen Mother (as Duchess of York) vi. 348 and n.
Elliot, Hugh vi. 9 n.
Elliot, Rosamond Fogg iii. 128 ('pretty child') and n.
Elliott & Fry (photographers) i. 270; ii. 7, 42, 70, 71 n.; iii. 281; vii. 127
    letter to ii. 70 (incorrectly attributed to 'Editor of *Northern Figaro*')
Ellis (pupil of architect Hicks) i. 1, 2 n.
Ellis, Henry Havelock i. 118 n.
    'The Ancestry of Genius' vii. 114 n.
    The New Spirit vii. 113, 114 n.
    (?) *Sexual Inversion in Women* ii. 83 ('Pamphlet') and n.
    Sonnets, with Folk Songs from the Spanish vi. 320 and n.
    'Thomas Hardy's Novels' i. 117; vii. 113 ('the review'), 114 n.
    letters to i. (? 96 – *see* vii. 172), 117; ii. 83; vi. 320; vii. 113
Ellis, Stewart Marsh iv. 272 nn., 278 ('cousin of Meredith's') and n., 292, 295
    George Meredith: His Life and Friends in Relation to His Work v. 236 and n.; vii. 159 n.
    letters to iv. 272, 292, 295; v. 236; vii. 159–60
Ellsworth, William Webster vii. 73, 74 n.
Elton, Godfrey vii. 79 n.
Eltville (Germany) ii. 84
Ely (Cambs) iii. 224; iv. 213 n., 273

'Elysians, The' (Cambridge society):
TH as hon. member v. 4, 5 n.
'Embarcation' (formerly 'The Departure',
q.v.) (poem) ii. 233 n.; iv. 145 and n.; vi.
44 n.
Embley House (Hants) iv. 175 n.
Emily (Max Gate maid) ii. 5 and n.
'Emmeline, or Passion versus Principle' (story)
i. 132 n.
'Emminster':
Beaminster as i. 274
Empire Marketing Board vii. 53 and n.
Empress Club iii. 159 and n.
Encyclopaedia Britannica i. 88 n.; ii. 267 n.
Enfield (Middlesex) iv. 46 n., 246 n., 258 n.,
315
St Andrew's Boys' School iii. 261 n.
St Andrew's Girls' School iv. 103 n.
St Paul's Literary Society iv. 62 n.
marriage of FED and TH at v. 9 and n.
FEH visits to family at v. 61 n., 150 n., 203,
277, 320
old Palace vi. 178 and n.
Clarke school vi. 313 and n.
Enfield Gazette and Observer vi. 178 n.
English Academy of Letters:
proposed iv. 75 and n., 107 and n.
English Association iii. 237 and n.; iv. 47 n.,
276 n., 278 n.; vi. 125, 158 n.
English Drama Society iii. 253 n.
English Folk Dance Society:
Journal vii. 62 n.
News vii. 41 n., 62 n.
English Illustrated Magazine i. 245 n.; ii.
41 n., 45 and n., 49 n., 55 n., 72 n.,
140 n.; vii. 127 and n.
'Interlopers at the Knap' pub. in i. 125 and
n.; vii. 100
'On the Western Circuit' pub. in i. 243 and
n., 251 n.
'Ancient Earthworks at Casterbridge' pub.
in ii. 34 and n., 43 and n.
English Players vii. 9 n.
English Race, The vi. 50 nn.
English Review iii. 193 and n., 327 ('such a
magazine') and n.; iv. 71 and n., 232 and
n.; vi. 220 n.; vii. 3 and n.
'Sunday Morning Tragedy' pub. in iii. 331
('the poem') and n., 354 ('the ballad') and
n.; iv. 7 n.; vii. 148 and n.
'Two Rosalinds' and 'Reminiscences of a
Dancing Man' pub. in iv. 8 ('two poems')
and n.
'A Singer Asleep' pub. in iv. 79 and n., 81,
178 ('some lines')
Spectator attack on iv. 158–9, 161 and n.,
167

boycott by W. H. Smith iv. 167 and n.
'Among the Roman Gravemounds' pub. in
iv. 182 ('the poem') and n.
'The Place on the Map' pub. in iv. 289 ('the
verses') and n., 295
Ensor, Thomas Henry (Dorchester auctioneer) iv. 76, 77 n.
'Enter a Dragoon' ii. 238 ('little story') and n.,
246 ('short stories') and n.; iv. 57 n., 298
pub. in *Harper's Magazine* ii. 276 ('short
story') and n., 277 ('soldier story') and
n.
'Epitaph on a Pessimist' (poem) vii. 4 n.
pub. in *London Mercury* vi. 337 n., 359
('epigram'), 360 and nn.
Epps, Mrs George Napoleon (Gosse's mother-
in-law) i. 224 n.
Erichsen, Dr Hugo i. 128 n.
Methods of Authors i. 128 n.
letter to i. 128
Ervine, Leonora Mary vi. 306 and n.
Ervine, St John Greer vi. 85 n.
presentation of Keats first edn to TH vi. 84,
85 n., 88, 90 and nn., 100 and n.
letter on Ulster and Sinn Fein vi. 100
('sturdy letter') and n.
projected rewriting of *Tess* play vi. 306 and
n., 309 and n., 310, 311–12
praise of *Tess* production vi. 350, 351 n.
attempted dramatization of *Jude* vii. 19 and
n., 38, 41, 42 n.
The Lady of Belmont vi. 233 and n.
Parnell vi. 312 ('your book') and n., 332
The Ship vi. 132, 133 n.
Some Impressions of My Elders vi. 187,
188 n.
The Wayward Man vii. 81 and n.
letters to vi. 84, 88, 90, 100, 132, 187, 233,
270, 306, 309, 311, 332, 350; vii. 43, 81
Escott, Thomas Hay Sweet i. 130 n.
letter to i. 130
Esler, Erminda Rentoul:
The Way They Loved at Grimpat ii. 85
and n.
Eton College Chronicle vi. 138 n.
Eugenics Education Society iv. 89 n.
Euripides v. 246; vi. 221
Alcestis vi. 236 n.
The Bacchae v. 330 n.
Hippolytus vii. 29
The Trojan Women v. 343 n.
Eutropius:
Breviarum Historiae Romanae vi. 3, 4 n.
Evans, Alfred Herbert v. 227
dramatization of *Trumpet-Major* iii. 300 n.,
332, 333 n., 335, 351 n., 356 n.; iv. 22 and
n., 236

Evans, Alfred Herbert (cont.)
dramatization of *Far from the Madding Crowd* iv. 22 and n., 46 and n., 59
dramatization of *Under the Greenwood Tree* iv. 116 n., 124–6, 127, 128, 129, 130; v. 241 n.
dramatization of 'The Distracted Preacher' iv. 147 and nn., 178 n., 189 ('a chemist') and n., 191; vii. 153 n.
proposed dramatization of *Mayor of Casterbridge* iv. 149 and n.
dramatization of *Woodlanders* iv. 292 ('play') and n., 323 and n., 325; v. 2, 3 n.; vii. 157 n.
letters to iv. 22, 46, 124–5, 126, 127, 149; vi. 265
Evans, (?) Caradoc iii. 258 and n.
Evans, Laura Eliza (Mrs A. H. Evans):
as Bathsheba iv. 58 and n., 59, 60 n., 61 n.
Evans, Maurice iii. 333 n.; iv. 22 n.; vi. 265, 266 n.
'Evelyn G. of Christminster' (poem) vi. 52 n., 151 ('dear Evelyn') and n.
Evening News iv. 194 n.; v. 83 n., 257 n.; vi. 224 n.
Evening Standard iv. 98, 99 n.
Everett, Augusta Stewart vii. 42 nn., 166 and n.
letter to vii. 42
Everett, Revd Henry vii. 42 n.
Everett, Herbert vii. 42 n.
Every Saturday:
serialization of *Far from the Madding Crowd* i. 29 nn., 32 and n.
Everyman's Library vi. 97 n., 99, 181 and n.
Ewart, Lady Evelyn ii. 144, 145 n.
Ewart, Wilfred Herbert Gore vi. 252 and nn.
Ewbank, Eileen vi. 284, 285 n.
Ewer, W. N. v. 88 n.
Examiner i. 41 and nn.
Exeter ii. 197, 199, 201
Cathedral iv. 168, 262
Royal Albert Memorial College (later University College of the South West of England) vi. 62, 63 n.
School of Art iv. 266 n.

Fabre, Ferdinand ii. 188 ('F.F.'), 189 n.
'Faintheart in a Railway Train' (formerly 'A Glimpse from the Train') (poem) v. 330 n.
Fairholme, Edward George vi. 244 n.
letter to vi. 243
Falkner, John Meade iii. 335 ('Faulkner'), 336 n., 340; vii. 154 n.
The Nebuly Coat iii. 87 ('new novel') and n.
letter to vii. 153
Falkner, Mrs J. M. iii. 335, 340

family and local background i. 89; iii. 119, 186, 234, 260; iv. 46, 72, 110, 188; v. 13; vi. 4, 154, 182 and n., 184–5; vii. 84, 85 n.
Famous History of the Queen of Cornwall, The – see *Queen of Cornwall*
Famous Players Film Company:
film of *Tess* iv. 265 n., 278, 279 n., 303 nn., 305 ('Film Company'), 309, 310 and n., 327 ('film company'), 329 and n.; v. 254 n., 308 n.
Far from the Madding Crowd (novel) i. 18 n., 38, 69 ('the book') and n.; v. 334
terms for i. 22–3, 24
illustrations i. 25 and n., 30 and n.; iii. 218
Bathsheba as imperfect woman i. 33
critical reception i. 34, 41 and n., 122 n.; ii. 294 and n.
copies as gifts i. 243 and n.; ii. 69; v. 212 n.
reprinted extracts ii. 37; iii. 22 n., 221 and n.; vii. 155 n.
copyright of ii. 37 n.
inscribed copies ii. 68 and n.; iv. 75 n.; v. 123 and n.; vi. 55, 56 n.
background and originals of places ii. 131, 230, 294; iii. 97 n.; iv. 10, 18 and nn., 56 n., 58, 74, 222 n.
'work of a youngish hand' ii. 294 and n.
spelling of 'felon' (whitlow) iii. 41 and n.
as example of fact imitating fiction iii. 48, 49 n.
picture postcards based on iii. 168, 169 n.
Turpin reference iv. 272 and n.
binding of fragments of first draft v. 120 n.
discovery and sale of MS v. 243, 244 n., 252 and n., 268, 269 n.
ending of vi. 155 ('supposed drowning'), 157 n.
DRAMATIZATIONS:
i. 99 and n., 100 and n., 103 n., 105 and n.; iii. 247 ('play of mine') and n., 260, 280 ('dramatic scenes'), 281 nn., 297, 298 n.; iv. 22 and n., 27 n., 46 and n., 51 and n., 55, 57 and n., 58 and n., 59, 60 n., 61 and n., 62, 80, 81 n.; v. 58 n., 342 n.; vi. 251 n., 268 ('the performance'), 269 n.; vii. 95 nn.
EDITIONS:
American i. 29 and n., 30, 32 and n., 34, 35 n.
Colonial ii. 63 and n.
first (two-vol.) i. 32 and n., 256
Indian vi. 177 and n.; vii. 164 n.
one-vol. i. 43, 45 and n., 48 and nn., 58
sixpenny ii. 282 and n.; iii. 14 n.; iv. 18 n.
Tauchnitz i. 43 and n., 55 and n.
three-and-sixpenny (Uniform) iii. 27, 218

Far from the Madding Crowd (cont.)
 Wessex iv. 185 ('second one') and n., 186,
  209 n., 272 n.; v. 123
 FILM VERSIONS:
  v. 111 n., 131 n., 133 and n.; vi. 42 and
   nn., 164, 165 n.
  proposed iv. 322 ('the offer') and n., 324,
   329, 330; v. 103
 SERIALIZATIONS:
  i. 22 n., 23 and n., 24–5, 27 and nn., 28,
   29 n., 30 nn., 32 and n.; ii. 294; iv. 9 n.,
   256, 257 n.; v. 244 n.; vi. 255 n.; vii.
   138, 139 and nn.
 TRANSLATIONS:
  Czech vi. 324 and n.; vii. 11
  French ii. 273, 274 n.; vi. 108 and n.;
   projected i. 105 and n., 108
  German projected i. 43 and n.
  Scandinavian v. 345 and n.; vi. 15
Farnborough (Hants) iii. 327
Farquharson, Robert:
 *In and Out of Parliament: Reminiscences of
  a Varied Life* iv. 157 n.
Fasque (Kincardine) ii. 37, 38 n.
Father Christmas (children's annual) i. 50 n.,
 52
Faulkner, C. W. & Co. (publishers) vi. 240
 and nn.
Fawcett, Edward Douglas:
 Divine Imagining vi. 98–9
 letter to vi. 98
Fawcett, Millicent Garrett i. 264 nn.
 and women's suffrage iii. 238, 239 n.
 letters to i. 263; iii. 238
Fawley (Berks):
 as 'Marygreen' ii. 133
Feacey, Jem (Dorchester architect) iii. 50 n.
Fédération britannique des comités de l'alli-
 ance française vi. 305 and n.
Felixstowe (Suffolk) iv. 223 n.
'Fellow-Townsmen' (story) ii. 33 and n.; iii.
 151; iv. 97
 payment for i. 72 and n.
 original of 'Port Bredy' in ii. 132; iii. 147
Felpham (Sussex) vi. 110 and n., 111 n., 120
 and n.
Fenn, George Manville i. 78 n.; vi. 109 n.
 *Gleanings from Popular Authors, Grave and
  Gay* vii. 165 and n.
 letters to i. 78; vii. 165
Fergusson of Craigdarroch vii. 71 n., 80
Fernandez, Ramon vii. 85 n.
Ferrey, Benjamin (architect) iii. 35 and n.
Fetherstonhaugh, Teresa Charlotte i. 217 and
 n. (corrected at vii. 172); ii. 4 n.*; iii. 335,
 336 n.
 letters to ii. 4; iii. 123; iv. 274

Fetherstonhaugh-Frampton family i. 242 and
 n.; v. 144 n.
Fetherstonhaugh-Frampton, Louisa iii. 335
 ('Mrs Frampton'), 336 n.; iv. 274 ('Mrs
 Frampton')
Feuerbach, Ludwig Andreas iii. 244 and n.
'Few Crusted Characters, A' (story) ii. 131
 draft of (as 'Wessex Folk') iv. 287 and n.; vii.
 113 n.
Ffooks, Edward Archdall iii. 18 n.
 letters to iii. 18, 78; v. 208
Ffrangçon-Davies, Gwen:
 as Tess vi. 343 and n., 345, 346 n., 351,
  352 n., 361–2
 at Max Gate vi. 344 n., 346 n., 351
 letters to vi. 343, 361
fiction, views on i. 5, 7, 33, 190, 195, 196,
 250, 257; ii. 68, 234; iii. 147, 183–4, 258; iv.
 234–5
'Fiddler of the Reels, The' i. 289 ('short story')
 and n.; ii. 13 ('my little story'), 14 n.
'Fiddler's Story, The' (later 'The Country
 Wedding', q.v.) (poem) v. 322 and n.; vi.
 90 n.
Field, Roscoe & Co. (solicitors) vi. 143 and n.
Field, Eugene vii. 23 ('your father's'), 24 n.
Field, Eugene, II vii. 24 n.
 letter to vii. 23
Field Place (Sussex):
 proposed Shelley memorial v. 28 and nn.
Fielding, Henry ii. 99; vi. 58 and n., 156
 as local novelist ii. 195, 196
 Library Edition of ii. 195 n., 196, 200
 Tom Jones ii. 195 ('Molly') and n., 200
  ('Molly'), 203 n., 294 n.
Fight for Right movement v. 208 n.
'Figure in the Scene, The' (poem) vi. 96
Filleul, Revd Samuel Edward Valpy iii. 35 n.,
 185 n.; iv. 76, 77 n.
 letters to iii. 35, 131, 132, 293; v. 182; vii.
 137
Filleul, Mrs S. E. V. (Mary Jane Bashall) iv.
 322 n.
 letter to iv. 322
Filmer, A. E. vi. 343 and n., 344, 346, 348, 361
Finance Bill (1909) iv. 62 n.
Findon (Sussex) vi. 111 n.
'Fire at Tranter Sweatley's, The' (poem) i. 39
 ('the ballad'), 40 ('the ballad') and n.,
 41 n.; ii. 61 ('original ballad') and n., 209;
 iv. 312, 313 n.; v. 249 n.
 pub. in *Gentleman's Magazine* ii. 61 ('the
  magazine') and n.
'First Countess of Wessex, The' (story) i. 180
 ('Christmas story') and n., 196 ('Christmas story') and n.; iii. 190 and n.; v. 134;
 vii. 113 n.

'*First Countess of Wessex, The*' (cont.)
    illustrations for i. 181 ('Christmas story'), 182 n., 186 n., 187 n.
First Edition and Book Collector vi. 263 and n.
First World War – *see* Great War
Fisher, Dr Frederick Bazley ii. 272, 273 n.; iv. 301 n.; vi. 13 nn.
    letters to vi. 12, 15
Fisher, Mrs F. B. ii. 300 n.; iv. 301 n.
    letters to ii. 300; iv. 301
Fisher, W. A. i. 226 n.
    letter to i. 226
Fisher, (?) William James ii. 102 n.
    letter to ii. 102
Fiske, Harrison Grey ii. 110 and n.*; v. 83, 84 n., 263 n.; vii. 133 and n.
Fiske, Minnie Maddern ii. 110 n.
    as Tess ii. 110, 111 n., 151 n., 152, 157, 167 and n., 186, 239 n.; iv. 265 n.; v. 84 n.; vi. 163 n.; vii. 133 n.
FitzGerald, Edward ii. 54, 55 n., 288 and n., 289
Fitzgerald, Sir Gerald ii. 17 n., 21 n.
Fitzgerald, Lady ii. 19 n., 20 ('your sister'), 21 n., 122
    death iii. 32, 33 n.
Fitzgerald, Gerald v. 193 ('Gerrie') and n., 283 ('your nephew'), 340 and n.
Fitzmaurice-Kelly, James v. 306 n.
    letter to v. 306
Flecker, James Elroy iv. 307 n.
Fletcher, John Gould:
    'The Black Rock' vi. 20 ('Fletcher's poem') and n.
Flood, William Henry Grattan v. 29 n.
    letter to v. 29
Florence i. 158 n., 164; iii. 187; vii. 109 n.
Flower, Archibald Dennis vii. 44 nn.
    letter to vii. 43
Flower, Newman ii. 164 n.*; iv. 83 n., 164 n.; v. 227 ('Cassells'), 228 n., 229, 257 ('Cassell's'), 258 n.; vi. 131, 230 n., 231 n.; vii. 59, 80 n.
    as editor of *Dorset Men in London Year-book* v. 23, 24 n., 49, 229, 343 n.
    and serialization of *Mayor of Casterbridge* vii. 35, 36, 37 n., 59
    purchase of Cassell's vii. 60 and n.
    Crucifixion v. 202 n.
    (ed.) *History of the Great War* v. 202 n.
    letters to ii. 164; iv. 83, 164; v. 23, 49, 202, 229, 342; vi. 90, 128, 173, 230; vii. 60, 79
Floyer, Georgina Charlotte iii. 69 n.
Foley, Admiral the Hon. F. A. C. i. 243 n.
folk-lore, interest in ii. 54, 136, 189; iii. 47, 93; v. 111, 136; vi. 251–2, 365; vii. 41 n., 62

Folk-Lore ii. 204 n.; (?) iv. 236, 237 n.; v. 136 and n.; vi. 365 ('another periodical') and n.
Folk-Lore Society i. 160 and n., 199 n.; ii. 136 n.; iv. 236 ('the Club'), 237 n.; v. 284, 285 n.
Fontmell Magna (Dorset) ii. 164 n.
Foote, George William iv. 97 n.
    letter to iv. 96
Foote, Samuel:
    The Liar ii. 155, 156 n.
'For Conscience' Sake' (story)
    pub. in *Fortnightly* i. 230 ('my story') and n.; vii. 116 n.
    MS given to Manchester Univ. Library iv. 178 n.
Forbes-Robertson, Ian ii. 210 n.
    letter to ii. 209
Forbes-Robertson, Sir Johnston ii. 83 n.*; vi. 339
    and *Tess* dramatization ii. 77 n, 82 ('the play'), 114 n., 209 ('your brother'), 210; iii. 107 ('a manager') and n.; vi. 288 and n.; vii. 129 n.
    as Romeo ii. 100 and n.
    letter to vi. 288
Forbes-Robertson, Lady (Gertrude Elliott) vi. 288 and n.
Ford, Ford Madox (formerly Hueffer, q.v.):
    and Irish situation vi. 53 and nn.
    and *Transatlantic Review* vi. 217 ('publication'), 218 n.
    letters to vi. 53, 217, 220
Ford, John iv. 159 and n.
Ford, S. Gertrude v. 223 n.
Ford Abbey (Dorset) vi. 87 and n.
Fordington (Dorset) i. 70 and n., 73, 135 and n.; v. 271 n.
    cholera epidemic v. 315, 316 n.
Fordington St George church (Dorset) iii. 47 n.
    restoration ii. 301 and n.; iii. 50 and n., 51 n., 54, 138 and n., 235; iv. 146 and n.; v. 33 n.
    Moule burials at iii. 115, 116 n.
    schools iii. 299 n.
    Easter offering v. 24, 25 n.
    'Fancy Fair' v. 33 ('bazaar') and n.
    Band of Hope v. 276, 277 n.
Fordington moor (Dorset):
    as 'Durnover moor' ii. 131
Foreign Office iv. 150, 151 n., 153 n.
Forrest, E. Topham vi. 181 and n.
Forrest, (Sir) George William David Starck iii. 268 n.; vi. 315 nn.
    Cities of India iii. 267
    A History of the Indian Mutiny, Reviewed

Forrest, (Sir) George William (cont.)
  and Illustrated from Original Documents
  iv. 232 (*'magnum opus'*) and n.
  letters to iii. 267; vi. 315
Forsyth-Major, Major O. H. vii. 46 n.
  letter to vii. 45
Fortescue, (Sir) John William iv. 108 n.; v.
  266, 267 n., 288
  letters to iv. 108, 181
Fortescue, Winifred v. 266, 267 n., 288
Fortnightly Review i. 130 and n., 144 and n.,
  156, 157 and n., 158, 260; ii. 160 and n.;
  iii. 109 n., 174 n., 212 and n.; iv. 28 and
  n., 278
  'For Conscience' Sake' pub. in i. 230 n.; vii.
  116 n.
  'The Midnight Baptism' pub. in i. 232 and
  nn., 233, 249 n.
  attack on *Jude* ii. 123
  'The Revisitation' pub. as 'Time's
  Laughingstocks' in iii. 117 n., 135
  ('romantic poem') and n., 151
  'New Year's Eve' pub. in iii. 242 ('verses of
  mine'), 244 ('New Years' fantasy') and n.;
  vii. 143 n.
  'Sunday Morning Tragedy' rejected by iii.
  278 ('poem of mine') and n., 287 ('a bal-
  lad'); vii. 143 n.
  'Satires of Circumstance' pub. in iv. 143 and
  n., 151; v. 260, 261 n., 314
  'The Sacrilege' pub. in iv. 177 ('another
  ballad'), 178 n.
  'God's Funeral' pub. in iv. 205 n., 287 n.
  'Convergence of the Twain' pub. in iv. 216
  ('some lines') and n., 222
  'Channel Firing' pub. in v. 26 and n., 30
  and n.
  'The Pity of It' pub. in v. 86 ('sonnet'),
  87 n.
  'To Shakespeare After Three Hundred
  Years' pub. in v. 160, 161 n.
  'By Mellstock Church at the Year's End'
  pub. in v. 340 and n.
  'A December Rain-Scene' pub. in vi. 106
  and n., 110, 111 n.
Forum (New York) i. 168 n., 276, 277 n.; ii.
  106 n.; v. 5 n.; vii. 121 and n.
  'Profitable Reading of Fiction' pub. in i. 168
  and n.; vii. 121 n.
Foss, Hubert James vi. 334, 335 nn.
  Seven Poems by Thomas Hardy vi. 334,
  335 n., 338 ('Song-Cycle'), 339 n.
Foster, Ernest i. 266 n.
  letter to i. 266
Foster, Joshua James i. 160 n.*; v. 229
  and collection of paintings of Wessex scenes
  ii. 74, 78

seeks advice on Dorset publishers v. 227,
  229
seeks membership of Society of Authors v.
  337 and n.
*Samuel Cooper and the English Miniature
  Painters of the XVII. Century* v. 180,
  181 n., 229, 231
Wessex Worthies v. 227 ('the volume'), 228
  n., 229, 230 n., 338 n.; vi. 40 n., 58
  ('handsome book'); vii. 128 n.
  letters to i. 160, 198; ii. 74, 78; v. 180, 227,
  229, 231, 273, 337; vi. 40, 58, 176; vii.
  114, 117, 127
Foster, Captain Richard Bayntum, R. N. ii.
  230 and n.
Foster & Braithwaite (investment brokers) ii. 5
  and n., 109 ('F. & B.')
Foster Brown Co. Ltd (booksellers) vi. 64, 65
  and n., 66 and nn.
Fournier, August:
  Napoleon I: A Biography iv. 173, 174 nn.
Fournier-Pargoire, Jeanne vi. 77 n., 328 ('the
  translator'), 329 n.
Fowey (Cornwall) iv. 227 n.; v. 151 n., 193
Fowler, Ethel Louisa vi. 11 n.
Fowler, John Henry vi. 177 n., 307 n.; vii.
  164 nn.
  letter to vii. 163
Fowler, (Sir) Robert Nicholas (Lord Mayor of
  London) i. 128 n.
  letter to i. 128
Fox, Charles James ii. 43, 44 n.
Fox-Pitt, Sir George ii. 252 n.
Fox-Pitt, Lionel Charles Lane v. 125 and
  n.
Fox-Strangways, Lady Mary Theresa v. 184
  ('your sweet daughter'), 186 n., 187 n., 193;
  vi. 7
Fox-Strangways, Lady Susan Sarah Louisa v.
  109 n.
Frampton Court (Dorset) ii. 230 n.
France, Anatole iii. 53 and n., 330 and n.; iv.
  326, 327 n.; vi. 106 n.
  Histoire Comique iv. 17 and n.
Francillon, Robert Edward:
  grants from Royal Literary Fund iv. 256,
  257 n.; v. 275 and n.
  Zelda's Fortune iv. 256 ('a story'), 257 n.
Franco-British Exhibition (1908) iii. 323 and
  n., 327
Franklyn, Annie S. i. 64 n.; vii. 172
  letter to i. 64
Fraser, Sir William Augustus:
  The Waterloo Ball iii. 284, 285 n.
Fraser's Magazine i. 107 n.
Frazer, (Lady) Elisabeth Johanna iii. 172
  and n.

Frazer, (Sir) James George ii. 136 n., 288 and n.*, 289; iii. 172 and n.; vii. 1 n.
  at Aldeburgh iv. 114 n.
  The Golden Bough ii. 288 and n.
Frederick William I of Prussia vi. 167 n.
Free Review ii. 115 n., 116, 117, 118, 120, 123 n., 124 and n., 138 n.
Freeman vi. 38 and n.
Freeman, Edward Augustus iv. 288 and n.
Freeman, John:
  and 'Poets' Tribute' v. 347 and n.
  letter to v. 347
Freer, Revd Arthur Savile Beresford ii. 113 n.
  letter to ii. 113
Freethinker iv. 96, 97 nn.
Freund, Adolf Walter vii. 74 n.
  letter to vii. 74
Frew, Revd Robert iv. 47 ('two others'), 48 n., 91 and n., 114
'Friends Beyond' (poem) ii. 209; iii. 137; v. 246; vi. 149, 285
Fripp, Sir Alfred Downing vi. 349, 350 n.
Frith, Walter i. 247 n.
  letter to i. 247
Frith, William Powell i. 126 n., 129 n.*, 145 n., 150; iii. 106 and n., 145; iv. 249 n.
  Derby Day i. 183 and n.
  My Autobiography and Reminiscences i. 183 and n.
  letters to i. 129, 183
Frith, Mrs W. P.:
  letter to i. 150
Frith, Miss (daughter of W. P. Frith):
  letter to vii. 95
Frome Valley:
  in *Tess* ii. 133
Frome Whitfield House (Dorset) iv. 241 n.
Froom Hill (Dorset) v. 201, 329
Frost, Robert vi. 38 n.
Frowde, Henry (publisher) iii. 246 and nn.; v. 137 n.
Fry, Roger:
  (and E. A. Lowe) *English Handwriting* vii. 170 n.
Fryer, Bertram vi. 224 n.
Fryston (Yorks) ii. 23 and n., 84
Funk & Wagnalls Co.:
  New Standard Dictionary of the English Language iv. 258 and n., 313
  letter to iv. 313
Furley, J. S. v. 82 n.
  letter to v. 82
Furniss, Harry i. 238 nn.
  letter to i. 238
Fyfe, Henry Hamilton vii. 162 n.
  letter to vii. 162
Fyfe, James Hamilton i. 31 and n.

Fyler, Samuel William ii. 55 n.
Fyler, Mrs ii. 76

Gaiety Theatre i. 231 and n.; vii. 121, 122 n.
Gale (later Harvey), Alice ('Dolly') iv. 243 ('the servant'), 244 n.
Gallimard, Gaston vi. 73 and n.
Gallipoli v. 120, 121, 122, 124, 154 and n., 230
Galpin, Stanley Ingram iv. 179 n.; vi. 159 n.
  letters to iv. 179; vi. 158
Galsworthy, Ada Pearson vi. 71 nn., 93
Galsworthy, Edwin John iv. 331 n.
Galsworthy, John iii. 202 n.*; iv. 331 n.; v. 214, 215 n.; vi. 18 n., 126 and n.
  and censorship of plays iv. 53 n.
  and protest against use of aircraft in war iv. 161, 162 nn., 164
  and *Dynasts* v. 153 and n.
  notion of existence v. 156 and n.
  dedicates *Beyond* to TH v. 221 and n., 224 ('new book')
  refusal of knighthood v. 241 and n.
  as *Reveille* editor v. 275, 276 n.
  at Max Gate vi. 18, 19 n., 93
  stage schemes vi. 103, 104 n.
  as P.E.N. Club President vi. 107 n., 192 n.
  visit to South Africa vii. 51 and n.
  Beyond v. 221 ('dedication') and n., 224 ('new book'), 226 ('the book')
  Five Tales v. 274 ('book of stories') and n., 275, 276 nn.
  The Freelands v. 119 ('new book') and n.
  In Chancery vi. 70 ('new book'), 71 n.
  The Man of Property iii. 201, 202 n., 225; iv. 162 and n.
  A Sheaf v. 182 ('the book') and n.
  The Silver Spoon vii. 39 ('the book') and n., 42 ('the book'), 43 n.
  The Skin Game vi. 18, 19 n.
  Tatterdemalion vi. 18, 19 n.
  To Let vi. 103 ('this last one'), 104 nn.
  The White Monkey vi. 283 and n.
  letters to iii. 201; iv. 161, 164; v. 119, 153, 156, 182, 221, 224, 226, 241, 274, 275; vi. 18, 70, 103, 192, 283; vii. 39, 42, 51
'Garden Seat, The' (poem) vi. 118
Gardiner, Alfred George iii. 307 nn.; vi. 329 n.
  Prophets, Priests, and Kings iii. 307 n.
  'Thomas Hardy: A Character Study' iii. 306 ('character study'), 307 n., 308 ('your Article')
  letters to iii. 306, 308; v. 43; vi. 329; vii. 130
Gardiner, Henry Balfour iii. 99 n.
  setting to music of 'Stranger's Song' iii. 99 and n.
  projected opera from 'Three Strangers' iv. 1, 2 n.

Gardiner, Henry Balfour (*cont.*)
  letters to iii. 99, 358; iv. 1
Gardiner, William iii. 49 n.
Gardner, Rodway v. 10 n.
Garland, Hamlin vi. 205 n.
  letters to vi. 205; vii. 131
Garnett, Edward iii. 148 nn.
  A Censured Play: The Breaking Point iii. 278
    and n.
  letters to iii. 147, 278
Garnett, Olivia ii. 290, 291, 298
Garnett, Richard ii. 290 n.
  invited to Max Gate ii. 291, 297
  *Idylls and Epigrams, Chiefly from the Greek
    Anthology* ii. 298 and n.
  *William Shakespeare, Pedagogue and
    Poacher* iii. 149, 150 n.
  (with Edmund Gosse) *English Literature:
    An Illustrated Record* iii. 98, 99 n.
  letters to ii. 290, 291, 298, 299; iii. 149
Garrick Theatre ii. 303 n.
  production of *Tess* vi. 349 n., 374 and n.
Garvin, James Louis iii. 164 ('the Ed'), 166 n.;
  iv. 199 n.
  letters to iii. 166, 168, 183; iv. 199
Gascon, HMS ii. 236 and n.
Gaskell, Margaret Emily (Meta) vii. 163,
  164 n.
Gaston, E. P. iv. 258 n.
  letter to iv. 258
Gauntlett, Henry John vi. 89, 90 n.
Gautier, Théophile iv. 146 and n.
Geach, Joseph (monumental mason) iv. 275,
  276 n.
General Elections (1885) i. 137 n.; (1892) vii.
  123, 124 nn.; (1895) ii. 80 n., 83 and n.;
  (1906) iii. 196 and n., 198 and n.; (1910) iv.
  129 n.; (1924) vi. 279 and n., 283 and n.
General Strike (1926) vii. 22 and n., 23, 30
Geneva ii. 167, 168–9; vi. 173, 174 n.
Genge, Dixon and Jameson (Dorchester
  drapers) ii. 276 and n.
Genoa:
  Palazzo Doria iii. 4 and n.
Gentleman's Magazine i. 40 n.; ii. 61 n.
Gentlewoman, The vii. 137
'Geographical Knowledge' (poem) iii. 166
  ('little poem')
  pub. in *Outlook* iii. 164 ('short piece') and n.;
    iv. 199 ('some verses') and n.
George III:
  at Weymouth i. 83, 98, 178; iii. 285, 289; iv.
    294, 295 n.; v. 183, 184 n., 244; vi. 1,
    2 nn., 171 n.
  reviews held by iii. 289
  hillside figure of iii. 359; vi. 355 and n.
George IV iii. 287

George V iv. 108 ('his Majesty')
  TH's refusal to write poem on Coronation of
    iv. 134 and n.
  TH's absence from Coronation of iv. 134 n.,
    141 and n., 143
  Coronation iv. 152, 153, 156, 157 ('Thurs-
    day next') and n., 160, 168, 169 n.; vii.
    152 n.
  exchange of birthday wishes with TH vi. 21,
    22 n.
  See also Wales, Prince of; York, Duke of
George VI (as Duke of York) vi. 348 and n.
George, Angelina (second cousin) v. 120 ('His
  mother') and n., 121, 215 n.
George, Bertha (distant cousin) v. 121 n.
George, Cecil (distant cousin) v. 120 n.
George, Charles (distant cousin) v. 120 n.
George, Ernest:
  as president of RIBA iv. 78 n.
  letter to iv. 78
George, Frank William (distant cousin) v. 85
  and n., 115 and n.
  death in action v. 120–1, 122–3, 124, 125
    ('lost one dear friend'), 133, 154 ('killed
    there') and n., 230
  poem in memory of v. 138 n.
George, Kathleen (distant cousin) v. 121 n.
George, William v. 120 n.
Georges-Bazile, Cecil iii. 226 n.
  translates 'An Imaginative Woman' iii.
    226 n.; v. 234 and n.
'Ghost of the Past, The' (poem) v. 212
Gibbon, Charles iv. 77, 78 and n.
Gibbon, Mrs Charles iv. 77
Gibbon, Edward ii. 167; v. 152 and nn.
  Decline and Fall of the Roman Empire v. 152
    ('chapters') and n.
Gibran, Kahlil vii. 21 n.
Gibson, W. Milne ii. 71 n.
Gibson, Wilfrid Wilson:
  Krindlesyke vi. 169 n.
Giffen, Robert Lawrence v. 307 and n.
Gifford, C. H.:
  *History of the Wars Occasioned by the
    French Revolution* i. 103, 104 n.
Gifford, Charles Edwin (ELH's cousin) ii. 16,
  17 n.; v. 338 and n.; vi. 120 and n.
  and ELH's death iv. 237 n.
  illness iv. 284 and n., 315
  move to West Byfleet v. 338 ('little nearer')
    and n., 344
  'Recollections of a Naval Secretary' vi. 26,
    27 n., 51, 52 n.
  letters to iv. 237, 283, 284; v. 124, 126, 338;
    vi. 26, 51
Gifford, Charlotte (ELH's sister-in-law) ii.
  245 n.

Gifford, Revd Edwin Hamilton (ELH's uncle) i. 31 and n.*; ii. 17 n., 68 n., 245 and n.; iii. 89 ('your uncle') and n., 146 ('her uncle'); v. 35 and n.; vi. 29 n.

Gifford, Effie (Mrs Charles E. Gifford) ii. 17 n.

Gifford, Emlin (Mrs George Gifford) vi. 26 ('excellent mother'), 27 n., 100 ('wife's aunt') and n.

Gifford, Emma Farman (ELH's mother): death i. 253 n., 280

Gifford (later Hardy, q.v.), Emma Lavinia i. 13 n., 22 n., 48 n.; vi. 155, 263 n., 281 n. wedding i. 31 and n., 131 n. early years at St Juliot iv. 260, 299, 328; vi. 29 and n.

Gifford, Evelyn Hamilton (ELH's cousin) v. 189 n., 215; vi. 29 *Selected Poems* sent to v. 188, 189 n. death vi. 29 n., 51, 151 and n. letters to v. 188; vi. 8

Gifford, George (ELH's uncle) ii. 17 n.; v. 12 ('your father') and n.; vi. 27 n.

Gifford, Gordon (ELH's nephew) ii. 218 n.*, 233 n., 236 ('Em's nephew'), 257, 268 n.; iv. 299 ('relative') and n.; v. 32, 34; vii. 153 ('Dorset man') and n. as architectural pupil ii. 245 ('my nephew') and n., 256, 257, 286 n.; vii. 133 n., 161 at Max Gate v. 27 and n. invited to *Dynasts* v. 68 position with L.C.C. v. 179; vi. 180, 181 n.; vii. 161 letters to v. 27, 34, 43, 68, 179

Gifford, Helen (ELH's second cousin) v. 127 ('youngest daughter') teaching career v. 344; vi. 34 and n., 51, 52 n., 182 n. letters to v. 344; vi. 34, 181

Gifford, John Attersoll (ELH's father) i. 131 n.; v. 32, 110 death i. 215 and n.

Gifford, Kate (ELH's cousin) iv. 284 ('your sister') and n.; v. 177 ('of my late wife's') and n. presentation copy of *Satires of C* v. 64 letters to v. 11, 64

Gifford, Léonie (ELH's second cousin) iv. 283 and n., 284; v. 124 ('Miss Gifford'), 125 n., 338; vi. 27 n. letter to iv. 315

Gifford, Lilian (ELH's niece) ii. 257 and n.; v. 27 n., 179 at Max Gate ii. 270 ('our niece'), 271, 272, 276; iv. 239 ('Mrs Hardy's niece') and n.; v. 69 and n.

at Royal Academy reception iii. 67 ('young relative'), 69 on holiday with ELH iii. 83 and n., 84, 85, 89, 90, 141 n. at Max Gate after ELH's death iv. 239 ('Mrs Hardy's niece'), 244, 250, 257, 260; vii. 156 later visits iv. 310 ('my niece') and n., 327 ('my niece'), 330 ('my niece'); v. 129 ('my niece'), 130 n. mental illness v. 320 n.

Gifford, Margaret (Daisy) (ELH's cousin) vi. 29 and n., 59 n., 201 n. letters to vi. 59, 151

Gifford, Margaret Symons Jeune (Mrs E. H. Gifford) ii. 17 n.; v. 35 ('my late wife's aunt') and n., 64 n., 127; vi. 5 n., 29 n., 201 n. letter to vi. 29

Gifford, Mary Attersoll (ELH's great-grandmother) v. 125 n.

Gifford, Nathaniel (ELH's great-uncle) v. 213, 214 n.

Gifford, Richard Ireland (ELH's grandfather) v. 124, 125 n.

Gifford, Mrs Richard Ireland (Helen Davie, ELH's grandmother) v. 32, 110

Gifford, Walter Edwin (ELH's brother) i. 31 and n.*; ii. 245, 256 n., 276 n.; iii. 61 n., 125 n. death iii. 141 and n., 142, 143

Gifford, Walter Stanley (ELH's second cousin) v. 124 ('your son'), 125 n., 127 ('your son'), 338 ('your son's') and n.; vi. 52 n.

Giggleswick School vi. 105 n.

Gilchrist, Robert Niven vii. 144 n. letter to vii. 144

Gilder, Jeannette Leonard ii. 127 n. and *Jude* ii. 103 and n., 126 letter to ii. 126

Gilder, Richard Watson ii. 127 n., 167 n. letter to ii. 167

Giles, Peter vi. 21 n. letter to vi. 21

Gili, Gustavo v. 208, 209 n.; vi. 33 ('another Spanish publisher')

Gillette, William: (and H. C. Duckworth) *All the Comforts of Home* i. 227 ('a comedy'), 228 n.

Gillon, Lieutenant Stair Agnew v. 91, 92 n.

Girl Guide Association vii. 58 and n.

Gissing, George Robert i. 149 n.; ii. 187 *Mayor of Casterbridge* sent to i. 166 at Max Gate ii. 86, 87 n., 235 n. fictionalized biography of iv. 234, 235 n. *Demos* i. 149 n. *Isabel Clarendon* i. 149 and n.

Gissing, George (cont.)
  Letters to Edward Clodd v. 26 and n.
  The Unclassed i. 149 n.
  letters to i. 149, 166, 193; ii. 86, 235
Gladstone, Sir John Robert ii. 38 n.
Gladstone, William Ewart i. 248 n.; ii. 135 n.;
  vi. 289, 290 n.
  resignation ii. 52 and n.
  death ii. 193 n., 194
  statue of ii. 265
  and Home Rule v. 38; vii. 124 n.
Gladstone, Mrs W. E. ii. 54 n.
Glamorgan v. 291 and n.
Glasgow:
  Royalty Theatre iv. 12 n., 155 n.
Glasgow Herald iv. 90 and n.
Glasgow News iv. 41, 42 n.
Glasgow University Liberal Club:
  invitation to TH to stand for Lord Rec-
    torship ii. 119, 122
Glastonbury (Somerset) ii. 179; iii. 135, 174
  and n.
  in 'Trampwoman's Tragedy' iii. 146
  Festival vi. 225 n., 236 nn., 244, 245 n.,
    265 n., 270, 271 and n., 274 n., 360 and
    n.; vii. 35 n.
Glen Dye (Kincardine) ii. 229, 230 n.
'Glimpse from the Train, A' (later 'Faintheart
  in a Railway Train') (poem):
  pub. in London Mercury v. 330 n.
Globe i. 214, 215 and n.; ii. 20, 21 n.
Globe Publishing Company vi. 227 and n., 345
  and n., 347, 358 and n.
Globe Theatre i. 227, 228 n.; vii. 132 n.
Gloucester ii. 197 and n.
Goddard, John Styles iii. 38 and n.
'G.M.' (poem) iv. 24 ('few lines'), 25 n.; v. 236
  ('the poem') and n.
'G.M.: A Reminiscence' (article) vii. 79 ('few
  pages') and n.
'God's Education' (poem) vi. 54 ('His Edu-
  cation'), 55 n.
'God's Funeral' (poem) iv. 204
  pub. in Fortnightly iv. 205 n., 287 n.
Godfrey, Sir Dan vi. 321 nn.
  letter to vi. 321
Godmanstone (Dorset):
  Manor House i. 217 and n.
Godoy, Manuel de v. 303 ('Prince of Peace')
  304 n.
Godwin, John Thomas (Dorchester shop-
  keeper) iv. 120 and n.; v. 82 n.; vi. 248
  and n.; vii. 85 n.
  letter to vii. 84
Godwin, Mrs William (Mary Jane Clairmont)
  iii. 86, 90
Goethe, Johann Wolfgang von v. 303, 304 n.,

323, 324 nn.; vii. 36
'Going of the Battery, The' (poem):
  pub. in Graphic ii. 236 n., 237 ('enclosed
    lines'), 238
  anthologized vi. 11 n.; vii. 141, 142 n.
'Going and Staying' (poem):
  pub. in London Mercury v. 322 ('little
    poem') and n., 330 n.
Golden Cap (Dorset) vi. 14 n.
Golden Hind, The (journal) vi. 114 n.
Goldingham, Miss (Dorchester schoolteacher)
  iii. 25 n.
Goldman, Agnes Mary iii. 164 n.
  letter to iii. 164
Goldman, Charles Sydney iii. 164 n.
Goldman, Edwin E. iv. 311 n.
Goldman, Lorna iv. 310, 311 n.
Goldring, Douglas vii. 148 ('sub-editor's')
  and n.
Gollancz, (Sir) Israel iii. 175 n.; v. 34 n.
  (ed.) A Book of Homage to Shakespeare v.
    129 and n., 145 and n.
  (ed.) Olympia (Boccaccio) v. 146 n.
  (trans.) 1616–1916 (Jochumsson) v. 197
    ('Icelandic poem') and n.
  letters to iii. 174; v. 128, 145–6, 197
Gollop, George Tilley i. 188 ('your loss'),
  189 n.; vii. 33 n.
  reminiscence of v. 1 ('your father') and n.;
    vi. 160 ('your father') and n., 161 ('Dorset
    man')
Gollop, Thomas v. 1 n.
Good Housekeeping :
  'Weathers' pub. in vi. 121 n.
Good Words i. 65 ('the magazine'), 66 n.; vii.
  99 nn.
  serialization of Trumpet-Major i. 66, 67 and
    n., 83; vi. 333 and nn.; vii. 92 and nn.,
    93 n., 99 n.
Goodden, Revd Robert Blundell iii. 326 n.
  letters to iii. 326, 335
Gordon, Alfred v. 305 and n.
Gordon, John iii. 332 n.
Gorst, Harold E. ii. 262 n.
  letter to ii. 262
Gorst, Hilda i. 289 n.
  letter to i. 289
Gorst, Sir John Eldon i. 289 n.
Goschen, George Joachim (later Viscount) i.
  223 and n.
Gosse, (Sir) Edmund William i. 110 n.*, 115
  n., 154, 192 n., 231; ii. 17 n., 65 n., 286;
  iii. 3, 31, 137 and nn., 206, 316; iv. 49, 86,
  109 n., 166 n., 202, 203 n., 256, 257 n.; v.
  20, 21 n., 176, 237; vi. 128 n., 176, 247 n.,
  275, 276 n.; vii. 48 n., 84 nn., 159
  and Two on a Tower i. 110, 114, 122 n.

Gosse, (Sir) Edmund (cont.)

meeting with Barnes i. 119–120, 156 ('bed-room scene'), 157 n., 158

at Max Gate i. 151, 152 nn.; iii. 138, 144 n.; iv. 191, 227 and n., 239 n.; vii. 103 and n.

quoted in *Woodlanders* i. 153 and n.; iii. 11 and n.; v. 222 and n.

Collins attack on i. 154 ('article you speak of'), 155 n.

reviews *Woodlanders* i. 164 n.

ancestors i. 224

translation of *Hedda Gabler* i. 227, 228 n. 233 and n.

copy of *Tess* sent to i. 288 and n.

and *Jude* ii. 93, 94 n., 99, 104–5; iv. 33

praise of *Well-Beloved* ii. 152, 153, and n., 158, 159 and n.

and 70th birthday tribute to Meredith ii. 184–6, 187 ('our late fizz') and n.

and similar tribute to Ibsen ii. 187 n.

and Library Edn of Fielding ii. 195 n., 196, 200

and *Wessex Poems* ii. 208 n., 214 and n., 216

and 'Century of French Romance' series ii. 230 ('your undertaking'), 231 n.

and *Poems of the Past and the Present* ii. 305 and n.

controversy with Clarke iii. 39 and n.

praise of 'Trampwoman's Tragedy' iii. 83 and n., 84

and *Dynasts* iii. 98, 102, 198, 302

as House of Lords Librarian iii. 131 n., 141, 198 and n., 214 n.; iv. 33 n.; v. 35 n., 46 ('official position'), 47 n.

cycling iii. 138, 141 ('bruises') and n.

and protest against proposed Shakespeare Memorial iii. 156 n.

foreign holidays iii. 187 and nn.; iv. 33 and n., 86, 93, 306

as editor of *Books* iii. 232, 233 n., 235, 236, 252 and n.

gifts to TH iii. 243, 326 ('the Donne') and n.

on TH's pessimism iii. 37 n.; iv. 65; v. 256 n.

and censorship iv. 63

Time's Laughingstocks sent to iv. 63 ('a book'), 65

and proposed English Academy of Letters iv. 75 and n.

and Hedgcock's book on TH iv. 157 and n., 165

made CB iv. 220 ('honour'), 221 n.

DNB article on Swinburne iv. 233 and n.

and ELH's death iv. 242

TH MSS given to iv. 281, 287 and n.

and manifesto on war aims v. 46, 47 n.

presentation copy of *Satires of C* v. 60 n., 66 n.

sees *Dynasts* v. 65 ('the play')

and Red Cross Sale of books and MSS v. 93 and n., 143 n., 144, 145 n., 149 n., 200

as presumptive literary executor to TH v. 148 n.

copy of *Moments of Vision* sent to v. 234 ('the book') and n.

questions for review of TH lyrical poems v. 245–6, 249 and n., 253, 260 ('this you send me'), 261 nn., 267

birthday wishes to TH v. 266, 309; vi. 19 n., 197 and n.

reads lessons at church service v. 288 and n.

70th birthday testimonial v. 306 and n., 324, 325 n., 340 n.

and 'Poets' Tribute' v. 329

at Weymouth vi. 1, 3, 4 n., 10

presentation of portrait bust to vi. 44, 45 nn., 47, 57 n., 69 and n.

proposed presentation of portrait to TH vi. 68–9, 72 and n.

and *Late Lyrics* vi. 131 ('kind review') and n., 132 n.

as *Sunday Times* reviewer vi. 197 and n., 328, 329 n.; vii. 27 and n., 77 and n.

knighthood vi. 328 ('honour'), 329 n.

broadcast vii. 33 and n.

alarming illness vii. 77 and n.

assists J. M. Murry vii. 81 and nn.

Biographical Notes on the Writings of Robert Louis Stevenson iii. 314 and n.

Critical Kit-Kats i. 152 n.; ii. 152 and n.

Father and Son: A Study of Two Tempera-ments iii. 282 ('autobiography') and nn.; iv. 157 and n.

Firdausi in Exile and Other Poems i. 137 ('book') and n.; ii. 208 and n.

From Shakespeare to Pope i. 155 n.

'The Future of English Poetry' iv. 276 ('your lecture') and n., 278 ('your lecture') and n.

Gray i. 110 and n.

Inter Arma: Being Essays Written in Time of War v. 164 ('E.G.'s essays') and n.

Jeremy Taylor iii. 102, 103 n.

Life of William Congreve i. 179 and n.

Life of Algernon Charles Swinburne v. 66 n., 211 and n., 215, 231, 232 n., 261 and nn.

'Mr. Hardy's Lyrical Poems' v. 246 n., 249 n., 261 n.

'The Napoleonic Wars in English Poetry' v. 75 ('the article') and n.

On Viol and Flute ii. 208 and n.

Raleigh i. 150 and n.

The Secret of Narcisse i. 288 and n.

Seventeenth Century Studies: A Contribu-tion to the History of English Poetry i. 122 and n.

Gosse, (Sir) Edmund (cont.)
  Some Diversions of a Man of Letters v. 261 n.
  'To Our Dead' v. 71 ('Gosse's poem') and n.
  Two Pioneers of Romanticism: Joseph and Thomas Warton v. 140 ('your paper') and n.
  'Two Points of View' i. 153 ('quote you'); iii. 11 ('the lines') and n.; v. 222 and nn., 329 ('liked so long') and n.
  (with R. Garnett) *English Literature: An Illustrated Record* iii. 98, 99 n.
  (ed., with T. J. Wise) *Letters of Algernon Charles Swinburne* v. 77 n.
  letters to i. 110, 113, 114, 120, 122, 137, 144, 150–2, 153, 154, 156, 159, 163, 164, 166–7, 173, 179, 181, 185, 217–18, 224, 253, 255, 270–1, 288; ii. 17, 24, 28, 56, 80, 82, 93, 99, 104, 114, 152, 153, 156, 158, 159, 160–1, 165, 184–6, 187, 188, 191, 195, 196, 200, 207, 213, 216, 221, 222, 230–1, 233, 244, 247, 259, 282, 284, 287, 300, 305; iii. 11, 39, 52, 68, 83, 98, 102, 124, 127, 131, 138, 141, 144, 153, 155, 175, 187, 193, 198, 205, 214, 218, 232, 235, 236, 242, 243, 244, 252, 256, 262, 282, 302, 314, 326; iv. 22, 33, 37, 63, 65, 75, 93, 99, 100, 103, 129, 152, 157, 176, 191, 196, 220, 227, 233, 242, 276, 277, 279, 281, 287, 292, 306; v. 10, 35, 46, 60, 65, 75, 77, 93, 132, 140, 143, 144, 149, 190, 200, 211, 234, 237, 245, 249, 253, 254, 256, 258, 260–1, 266, 303, 309, 324, 329; vi. 1, 3, 68, 72, 115, 131, 197, 328; vii. 27, 33, 77, 81, 84, 89, 97, 103, 125
Gosse, Ellen (later Lady) i. 151, 167, 217; ii. 191, 305; iii. 3, 316; iv. 33; v. 86, 93, 306; vi. 1, 10
  death of mother i. 224 ('her sorrow') and n.
  illness iii. 218
  and ELH's death iv. 238, 242
  letters to iv. 238; v. 108
Gosse, Philip iii. 324, 525 and n.; iv. 292 and n.; v. 35 and n.
  war service v. 140 and n., 149 and n., 191
  Memoirs of a Camp-Follower v. 150 n.
Gosse, Mrs Philip (Gertrude Agnes Hay) iii. 325 n.; iv. 292 n.
Gosse, Philip Henry i. 110 nn.*, 115 n., 181 and n.
  death i. 179 and n.
  zoological work in Weymouth vi. 3, 4
  The Romance of Natural History i. 179
Gosse, Sylvia ii. 286, 287 n.; iv. 93 n.; vi. 131 and n.
Gosse, Teresa (Tessa) i. 167 and n.; iv. 93 n.
Gover, William iii. 328 n.; iv. 74 n.
  letter to iii. 328

Gowans, Adam Luke iii. 140 n.
  (ed.) *Lyric Masterpieces by Living Authors* iii. 139 ('volume of lyrics'), 140 n.
  (comp.) *The Ways of God* iii. 232 and n.; iv. 146 and n.
  letters to iii. 140, 232; iv. 146
Gower, George Granville Leveson iii. 200 n.
  letter to iii. 200
Gowring, Dr Benjamin William Nettlefold iv. 246 ('a doctor') and n., 260 and n.; v. 8 and n.; vi. 114 ('the doctor'), 115 n.
Graham, Derrick (Clodd's grandson) v. 207 and n.
Graham, Edith (Clodd's daughter):
  inscribed copy of *Pair of Blue Eyes* sent to iv. 43 and n., 44 n.
  letter to iv. 43
Graham, Robert Bontine Cunninghame ii. 211 n.
  and *Trumpet-Major* iii. 169 and n.
  letters to ii. 211; iii. 169; iv. 22
Graham, Stephen vi. 252 nn.
  Life and Last Words of Wilfred Ewart vi. 252 n.
  letter to vi. 252
Grahame, Elspeth iii. 270 n.
  letter to iii. 270
Grahame, Kenneth ii. 187 n.
Grahame, W. Francis iii. 142 n., 144 n.
Granby, Lady (wife of Henry John Brimley Manners, Marquess of Granby, later 8th Duke of Rutland) ii. 89, 90 n.*; iii. 211 and n.
Grand, Sarah (Mrs Frances Elizabeth Mac-Fall) ii. 12 n., 33 and n., 286
  The Heavenly Twins ii. 12 and n., 18 n.
Grant, James:
  The Scottish Cavalier vii. 70, 71 n., 80
Granville-Barker, Harley – see Barker, Harley Granville
Granville-Barker, Helen – see Barker, Helen Granville
Graphic i. 78 and n., 170, 188, 189; ii. 303 n.; iii. 136 and n.; v. 233, 281 n.
  publication of 'Romantic Adventures of a Milkmaid' i. 115 ('the story') and nn., 189 n., 284
  serialization of *Mayor of Casterbridge* i. 139 ('a story') and n., 141 ('story's conclusion'), 143; vii. 102 and n.
  publication of 'A Group of Noble Dames' i. 189 and n., 202 n., 209 n., 210 ('Christmas number'), 215–16, 222
  serialization of *Tess* i. 202–4, 207 and n., 225 ('the story'), 226 and nn., 228, 229, 230 n., 245, 268; vi. 362 ('in 1891'), 363 n.; vii. 118 n.

Graphic (cont.)
French edn of Christmas 1890 number (*Noël*) i. 205 n.
21st anniversary dinner i. 222 n.
'The Going of the Battery' pub. in ii. 236 ('verse of mine') and n., 237 ('enclosed lines') and n., 238; vii. 142 n.
portrait of TH's mother in iii. 119 and n., 120, 121
'The Darkling Thrush' ('By the Century's Deathbed') pub. in iii. 79 n.
photograph of TH in iv. 54, 59, 60 n.
'The Peace Peal (After Years of Silence)' pub. in v. 313 n.
'Grave by the Handpost, The' (story) ii. 171 ('the story') and n., 181 n.; iv. 298, 323
Graves, Robert vi. 35 ('poet and his wife'), 90 n.
Graves, Mrs Robert (Nancy Nicholson) vi. 35
Gray, Harold St George iii. 335 n.; iv. 141 n.
letters to iv. 141, 309
Gray, James vi. 204 n.
Gray, Thomas ii. 222, 257; vi. 313; vii. 78
Poetical Works v. 272 and nn.
'Great Hintock':
Melbury Osmond as i. 163 (wrongly 'Little Hintock'), 164
'Great Hintock Court':
Melbury House as ii. 132
Great War v. 57, 67, 80, 101, 119, 218, 219 n., 240, 351 n.; vi. 45, 275
outbreak of v. 41 ('the present') and n.
billeting of troops v. 41, 42 and n., 43 and n., 90
German threat to Paris v. 44
British writers' manifesto on war aims v. 46–7
German prisoners v. 42, 43, 57, 71, 91, 203, 204
TH's letters on German bombardment of Rheims v. 58 n.
conscription v. 69, 70 n.; vii. 158 n.
poems of v. 71
German air raids v. 81 and n., 107 and n., 114, 124, 154, 155 n., 176, 177 n., 232 and n., 249, 254 n.
possible duration v. 72, 78, 86
German responsibility v. 86
Italian entry into v. 99 and n.
TH pessimism over v. 119, 120, 123, 133, 142, 149, 163, 177, 187, 189, 191, 232, 234, 236, 247, 265, 271
personal losses v. 120–1, 122–3, 124, 125, 133, 137, 154, 165 n., 188 and n., 211 n., 214, 215 n., 230, 235, 271
'blackout' regulations v. 130 n., 132 ('after dark') and n., 154

Ireland and v. 154 n., 158 and n., 159, 160 n.
petrol restrictions v. 168, 225
caution against extravagant memorials v. 176
National Service v. 206
German advance in Russia v. 218, 219 n., 230 and n.
invitation to GHQ France declined by TH v. 220; vi. 107 n.
submarine menace v. 249
future of German colonies v. 283 and n.
Armistice v. 285 and n., 303
memorial service for fallen authors v. 288 n.
peace treaty v. 311 and n., 315, 317 and n.; vii. 169 n.
Green, Charles i. 181, 182 n.
Green, Herbert vii. 43 and n.
Green, Matthew iv. 159 n.
Greenberg (American publisher) vi. 284 n., 318
Greenhill, (Sir) Alfred George i. 66 ('member of the Mess') and n., 71 n.* (corrected at vii. 172), 98 n.; iii. 128 n., 323 and n.; iv. 185, 186 n.
letters to i. 71, 88
'Greenhill Fair':
original of ii. 131, 230, 294
Green-Hill Pond (Dorset) iv. 183 and n., 188
Greenwood, Frederick vii. 139 and nn.
75th birthday dinner iii. 165 and n.; vii. 138 ('that dinner'), 139 n.
and *Far from the Madding Crowd* vii. 138–9 and nn.
letter to vii. 138
Gregory, Isabella Augusta, Lady iii. 127 n.
and *Dynasts* iv. 37
Seven Short Plays iv. 37 ('the plays') and n.
The Workhouse Ward iv. 92 n.
letters to iii. 27, 129; iv. 36, 91, 95, 113
Gregory, Odin vi. 268 n.
Cain vi. 268 and n.
Caius Gracchus vi. 268 n.
Jesus vi. 268 n.
letter to vi. 268
(?) Greig, James vii. 166 n.
Grein, Jack Thomas i. 195 n.
dramatization of *Woodlanders* i. 195 and n., 211 n.; vii. 114 n.
proposal for British 'Théâtre Libre' i. 213 ('your enterprise') and n.
letters to i. 195, 213
Grenfell, Alice:
letter to i. 266
Grey, Sir Edward (later Viscount Grey of Fallodon):
on causes of Great War v. 86, 87 n.

Gribble, Vivien (Mrs Doyle Jones):
  illustrated edition of *Tess* vi. 292 and n., 294
    and n., 295; vii. 1, 2 n., 46
Grierson, (Sir) Herbert John Clifford iii.
  161 n.
  letters to iii. 161, 165
Griffin, Bernard (Weymouth photographer)
  iii. 357 and n.; iv. 225
Griffin, Florence (Max Gate servant) iii. 322,
  323 n.
Grimsditch, Herbert Borthwick vi. 365 n.
  *Character and Environment in the Novels
    of Thomas Hardy* vi. 364 ('your book'),
    365 n.
  letter to vi. 364
Grosart, Revd Alexander Balloch i. 174 n.
  letter to i. 174
Grosvenor Literary Agency vii. 72 n.
Grouchy, Emmanuel Marquis de vii. 20 and n.
Group of Noble Dames, A (stories) i. 93 n.; ii.
  63; iii. 10, 11 n.; 48 n., 60, 190 n., 250;
  iv. 134 n.; vi. 371; vii. 117, 118 n.
  reception of i. 239, 241, 245
  MS given to Library of Congress iv. 181 and
    n., 193
  American film rights v. 97
  Canadian rights vi. 81, 88
  originals of places in ii. 131, 132; iv. 170 n.,
    175 and nn.; v. 134
  EDITIONS:
    first (one-vol.) i. 230 ('the book'), 231 n.,
      237 n., 238, 239 n.; vii. 113 n.
    Tauchnitz i. 248, 249 n.
    Wessex iv. 220 n.
  SERIALIZATIONS:
    in *Graphic* i. 189 and n., 198 ('the story')
      and n., 201 ('short one'), 202 n., 207 n.,
      209 n., 210 ('Christmas number'),
      215–16, 222 n.; vii. 113 n.
    in *Harper's Weekly* i. 207 n., 209 ('Christ-
      mas story') and n.; vii. 113 n.
  TRANSLATIONS:
    French i. 205 and n.; vi. 108
    German iii. 101 and n.
    Swedish vi. 15
Grove, Agnes Geraldine (later Lady) ii. 87 n.,
  92 n.*, 248; iii. 55, 214, 274; iv. 111 n.
  illness ii. 169, 180, 192; iii. 196
  literary efforts ii. 180, 189, 190, 192, 194,
    196, 226, 247, 251, 253 and nn.; iii. 53,
    and n., 108 ('leap into journalism'),
    109 n., 266, 268, 269, 271, 272, 274 n.,
    284, 327, 328 n., 345, 354; iv. 3 and n., 82,
    83, 88–9
  dedicates book to TH iii. 268–9
  on *Time's Laughingstocks* iv. 67
  death of mother iv. 94, 95 n.

  and ELH's death iv. 246
  and TH's second marriage v. 13
  The Human Woman iii. 327, 328 n., 345 ('the
    book') and n., 354
  On Fads iv. 82, 83 n., 84 n., 89 n., 92 ('the
    book') and n.
  'Reply' to article 'Why Women do not Want
    the Ballot' ii. 91, 92 and n., 95–6, 101
  The Social Fetich iii. 266 ('the book') and n.,
    268–9, 271 ('first sheet'), 272 ('them all'),
    274 n., 284
  'What children should be told' ii. 101, 114,
    115, 116, 117, 120 and n., 123 and n., 124
    and n., 137 ('the Essay'), 138 n., 139
    ('proof of article'), 140 n., 141, 142 n., 145
    ('the article')
  letters to ii. 91, 92, 96, 101, 114–15, 116,
    117, 118, 120, 123, 124, 125, 128, 137,
    139, 142, 145, 153, 180, 189–90, 192, 194,
    196, 226, 230, 247, 251, 253; iii. 53, 108,
    257, 266, 268–9, 271, 272, 284, 327, 329,
    345, 354; iv. 3, 36, 67, 82, 83–4, 88, 92,
    94, 111, 246; v. 13; vi. 151, 162
Grove, Archibald ii. 2 and n.
Grove, Sir Coleridge ii. 229, 230 n.
Grove, George vii. 92 n.
Grove, Honor iv. 36 n.
Grove, Oenone iv. 36 n.
Grove, Sir Walter ii. 145 n.; iv. 36 ('Sir W.')
  and n.
Groves, Major Herbert John vi. 1 ('managing
  director'), 2 n.
Gruyer, Paul:
  Napoléon, roi de l'île d'Elbe iii. 219 and n.
Grylls, Miss (dressmaker) i. 227, 228 n.
Guardian ii. 98 and n.; iv. 28, 29 n., 226; v. 34
  and n.
Guedalla, Philip vii. 39 n.
  The Second Empire vii. 39 ('the book') and n.
  letter to vii. 39
Guest, Ivor Churchill (later 1st Viscount
  Wimborne) ii. 248, 249 n.
Guest, Montague John vii. 122 n.
  letter to vii. 122
Guildhall School of Music vi. 57, 59
Guilford, Francis North, 1st Lord:
  *A Narrative of Some Passages in or Relating
    to the Long Parliament* v. 216 n.
Guppy, (?) Robert (Long Bredy carpenter) ii.
  221, 222 n.
Gurdon, Lady Eveline Camilla ii. 30 and n.
Guthrie, Thomas Anstey ('F. Anstey') ii.
  123 n.
  Vice Versâ vii. 99 and n.
  letter to ii. 123
Guyot, Raymond:
  Napoleon vii. 54 and n.

Gwynn, Stephen Lucius ii. 291 n., 299 and n.
Gwynne, Nell iii. 316 and n.

Haase & Son (publishers) vi. 227 and n.
Hachette (publishers) ii. 170 n., 177, 218 n., 273; vi. 62 n.
Hackwood (near Basingstoke) iii. 313, 318 n., 327
Hadden, Maude ii. 136 n.
    letter to ii. 135
Hadley, Patrick:
    Scene from Thomas Hardy's 'The Wood-landers' vi. 338 n.
Haggard, (Sir) Henry Rider i. 233 and n., 235 n.*; vi. 370 and n.
    death of son i. 235 and n.
    Eric Brighteyes i. 235 and n.
    The Mahatma and the Hare: A Dream Story iv. 191, 192 n.
    Rural England iii. 10 n.
    letters to i. 235; iii. 9, 150; iv. 105, 191, 298
Hague, The ii. 134
Hake, Thomas v. 97 n.
Haldane, Richard Burdon (later Viscount) iii. 198 and n.; iv. 49 and n., 154, 292 n.
Hale, William Bayard iii. 316 n.
    letter to iii. 316
Hales, John Wesley i. 278 n.
    letter to i. 277
Halesworth (Suffolk) iv. 270 and n.
Hall, Hammond iii. 144 n.
    letter to iii. 143
Hallam, Arthur ii. 24 n.
Halley's comet iv. 54 and n., 60 and n.
Halpérine-Kaminsky, Ely vii. 131 n.
    Le Rôle de l'art d'après Tolstoi vii. 131 and n.
    letter to vii. 131
Hambro, Colonel i. 231, 232 n.
Hamilton, Geoffrey iii. 201 n.
Hamilton, John Arthur:
    The MS. in a Red Box iii. 72 and n.
Hamilton and Brandon, Nina Mary Bonita Douglas-Hamilton, Duchess of vi. 144 n.
    letters to vi. 144, 223, 323
Hamilton-Spencer-Smith, Revd Spencer Compton ii. 83 ('Spencer Smith') and n.
Hammerton, John Alexander vi. 371 nn.
Hammett, William (Tolpuddle builder) v. 198 and n.
Hammond, J. L. and Barbara:
    The Village Labourer, 1760–1832 iv. 206 ('the book') and n.
Hammond, William (Dorchester jobmaster) v. 110, 111 n.
Hampshire Independent vi. 39 and n.
Hanbury, Caroline vi. 135 ('the baby') and n.
Hanbury, Cecil v. 35 and n., 127, 287, 316,

340; vi. 1, 110, 115, 131, 135; vii. 169 n.
Hanbury, Dorothy (Mrs Cecil H.) v. 35 and n., 127, 186, 187 n., 188 n., 189, 225 and n., 237 n., 287, 316, 338 ('his daughter'), 339 nn., 340; vi. 1 and n., 93, 94 n., 110, 115, 131, 135
    letters to v. 188, 273
Hanbury, Louisa (Mrs John Capel H.) ii. 41, 42 n.
Hanbury, Sir Thomas v. 127 and n.
Hand, Elizabeth (maternal grandmother) iii. 124 ('her mother') and n.
Hand, George (maternal grandfather) iii. 124 ('her father') and n.
Hand of Ethelberta, The (novel) iv. 319; vii. 65 and n.
    writing of i. 35, 37, 41 and n.
    sub-title objected to i. 37 and n.
    illustrated by Du Maurier i. 71 n.; ii. 135 n.; iv. 43
    originals of places in ii. 132
    discovery of part MS v. 243, 244 n.
    'London portions' vi. 154
    dramatization vi. 310–11
    EDITIONS:
        American i. 42 n.
        first i. 44 and nn.
        one-vol. i. 47 and n., 58; vii. 95 n.
        Tauchnitz i. 43 n.
    SERIALIZATIONS:
        in *Cornhill* i. 35 and nn., 38 and n., 41 n., 42, 43; iv. 9 n.; v. 244 n.
        in *New York Times* i. 44 and n., 138 n., 140 n.
Hankey, Revd Basil v. 20 nn.
Hankey, Meg (Mrs B. Hankey):
    and humane slaughtering v. 20
    letter to v. 20
Hankin, St John:
    The Last of the De Mullins iv. 2 ('the play') and n.
Hannah, James (Dorchester undertaker) iv. 238 n.
    letter to iv. 238
Hannan, Charles iii. 106 n.
    offer to dramatize *Two on a Tower* iii. 92 and n., 105, 107, 111
    letters to iii. 92, 111
Hannay, Colonel (later Brig.-General) Cathcart Christian v. 85 and n., 122
Hanson, Sir Charles Augustin (Lord Mayor of London) v. 273 n.
    letter to v. 273
'Hap' (poem) iii. 232
    French version vi. 181, 182 n.
Harcourt, Elizabeth (wife of Sir William) v. 160, 161 n.

Harcourt, Lewis, 1st Viscount ('Lulu') vi. 120 and n.

Harcourt, Sir William George Granville Venables Vernon ii. 83 and n.

Harding, Henry iii. 241 n.; vi. 228 n.
  Dorset: A Reading-book for Schools iii. 240, 241 n.
  letter to iii. 240

Hardinge, Sir Henry, 1st Viscount iv. 137 n.

Hardinge, Henry Charles Maurice iv. 137 n.
  Strangers Within the Gates iv. 137 n.
  letter to iv. 137

Hardy, Albert Augustus (second cousin) v. 151 n.
  letter to v. 151

Hardy, Alfred John (impostor) vii. 67 and nn.

Hardy, Augustus (cousin) iv. 95 ('your father'), 96 n.; vi. 56 n.
  death v. 151

Hardy, Mrs Augustus (Mary Ann Lee) iv. 188 ('your mother's') and n.

Hardy, Basil Augustus (distant cousin) vi. 55, 56 n.

Hardy, Charles Meech (second cousin) iii. 290 n.; iv. 305 n.
  letter to iii. 290

Hardy (formerly Gifford, q.v.), Emma Lavinia (first wife) i. 106 n., 131 n.*, 134, 144, 146, 149, 150, 217, 242, 243; ii. 32, 37, 70, 125, 152, 189, 191, 198, 204, 206, 281, 294, 295, 299 n., 302, 303; iii. 60, 78, 106, 108, 146, 210, 239 n., 253, 259; iv. 129, 130 n., 155; vii. 125
  wedding i. 31 and n., 131 n.
  honeymoon i. 31 n., 32 n., 35 n.; iii. 21 n.
  ill-health i. 82, 223, 237, 263, 264, 265; ii. 95, 110, 111, 112, 117, 192; iii. 23, 41, 53, 62, 64, 68, 203, 299, 302, 303, 305, 312, 316, 318, 319, 328; iv. 102, 105, 106, 165; v. 157, 158; vii. 122
  and Barnes's death i. 153
  Italian tour i. 158 n., 163; iv. 213 n.; vii. 46 n., 109 n.
  girlhood reading i. 179, 242
  and Max Gate pets i. 217, 218
  death of mother i. 253 n., 280
  supplies facts for article on herself i. 289, 290 n.
  in Ireland ii. 10 n., 11 n.; vii. 125
  her sight ii. 53; iii. 324
  and London flats ii. 73, 76–8, 280, 282
  bicycling ii. 106, 109, 128, 130 and n., 136, 169, 174, 176, 181, 227, 256
  investments ii. 109
  and anti-vivisection ii. 148 n., 157
  in Switzerland ii. 166, 167, 168–9

tending of dying sister ii. 271, 272, 273, 274, 276
  as hostess iii. 31, 133, 138, 143, 225, 269, 355; iv. 92 and n., 94, 95, 96, 98, 116, 255 n.; vii. 100, 140
  Pretor book dedicated to iii. 45 n.
  and James's *Wings of the Dove* iii. 55
  at Dover iii. 82, 85, 95
  in France iii. 84, 85, 86, 87, 88, 90, 91, 95, 333, 334, 335, 339, 341, 343, 347, 350; vii. 95 n.
  death of brother iii. 141, 142, 143
  dissuaded from London visits iii. 321, 322–3, 324; iv. 31, 105
  as artist iii. 343 ('your pictures'), 344 n.; v. 171 ('sketch') and n.
  strained relations with TH iv. 21 ('domestic circumstances') and n., 239, 243, 247
  interest in women's suffrage iv. 21 n., 106 n.
  friendship with FED iv. 92 n., 121 n., 130 n., 165 n.; v. 15, 17, 18, 19, 156, 177
  Thursday 'At Homes' in London iv. 92 and n., 93, 94, 95, 96, 98, 100
  attempts at publication iv. 121 n.
  death iv. 237, 243, 246, 248, 249, 250, 259, 298; v. 331 n., 340; vii. 156 n.
  funeral iv. 237–8, 240–1, 242, 244
  TH's thanks for condolences on death of iv. 238–52, 254–5
  instability iv. 243 ('painful delusions'), 247 ('peculiar'), 255 ('hallucination'), 260 ('mentally'); v. 16, 19, 64
  diaries iv. 255 n.
  early agnosticism iv. 260
  tombstone iv. 262 and n., 263 and n., 264 and n., 266, 268, 269 n., 270; v. 294, 336
  St Juliot memorial to iv. 275, 276 n., 283, 299; v. 64, 156, 176, 177, 179, 271
  prototype of heroine of *Pair of Blue Eyes* iv. 288; v. 95 n.; vi. 3 n.
  early years at St Juliot iv. 299, 328; vi. 29 and n.
  family graves iv. 311 and n.; v. 32 and n., 34, 110, 124
  TH's remorse over v. 37
  poems relating to v. 64 and n., 70, 246
  TH's memories of v. 266, 267 n., 287
  application for British Museum reading ticket vii. 90 n.
  Some Recollections v. 64 ('memoranda') and n.
  letters to i. 131, 132, 215, 221–2, 223, 227, 230–3, 269, 287; ii. 5, 27, 52–4, 55, 72, 76–8, 82, 89, 108–9, 112, 149, 255–7, 270, 272, 276, 284, 285–6; iii. 3, 61, 65, 68, 82, 83, 85, 86, 88–90, 318, 321,

Hardy, *Emma Lavinia* (*cont.*)
  322–4, 325, 333, 334, 335, 339, 341, 343,
  347, 359; iv. 30, 81, 84–6, 105, 106, 153
Hardy (formerly Dugdale, q.v.), Florence
  Emily (second wife) v. 226, 227, 232, 235,
  247 n., 248 n., 268, 271 n., 273, 274, 287,
  331; vi. 92, 124 n., 176, 177 n., 201, 203;
  vii. 8, 10, 17 n., 22, 27, 29 n., 46, 72 n.,
  80 n., 81 n., 84 n., 165 n.
  marriage v. 8 and n., 9–20, 38, 81 and n.
  honeymoon v. 17, 21
  interest in gardening v. 17, 30, 215; vi. 139
  charitable and public activities v. 33 and n.,
    276, 277 n., 339 n., 340; vii. 32
  as TH's amanuensis and reader v. 52 n., 162,
    164, 174, 178, 191, 219, 253, 259, 275,
    280, 293, 294, 298, 305, 311, 343, 346; vi.
    17 n., 34, 91 n., 94, 96, 97, 114, 126,
    138–41, 142, 143, 144, 145–7, 149, 153–
    8, 163, 169, 188, 197, 207, 216, 218, 220,
    240, 243, 245, 250, 254, 264–5, 268, 269,
    304, 310, 355 and n., 359; vii. 4 n., 11
    ('E.F.') and n., 19, 38, 39, 46, 55, 67,
    80 n., 83, 85, 87, 160, 161, 162
  at *Dynasts* first night v. 57 and n., 62, 63
    and n.
  visits to Enfield v. 61 ('your journey') and n.,
    203, 320; vi. 32 and n.
  poem written to v. 70, 71 n.
  Lea photograph of v. 83 n., 104
  nasal operation v. 99, 100, 101, 102 n., 104,
    105, 106, 107, 110
  private printings of TH poems v. 138 and n.,
    203 and n., 204 n., 322 and n.; vi. 112 n.,
    114, 115 n.
  as hostess v. 143, 155, 159, 233; vi. 140,
    234 n., 256; vii. 73
  as one of TH's literary executors v. 147,
    148 n., 169
  as book reviewer v. 150 n., 165, 166 n., 215
    and n., 283 and n.; vi. 7
  ill-health v. 155, 158 n., 212 and n., 219 n.,
    221; vi. 114, 115, 116, 117, 119, 325,
    326 n., 367; vii. 77
  intention to apply for Society of Authors
    membership v. 169
  said to be compiling TH bibliography v. 175
    and n.
  attends *Mellstock Quire* v. 249, 250 n.
  cycle rides with TH v. 283
  secret composition of 'Life and Work of TH'
    v. 331 ('what she is doing'), 332 n.
  at Hunt Ball vi. 1
  at Oxford performance of *Dynasts* vi. 5 and
    n., 8, 9, 51
  at Weymouth vi. 22
  use of telephone vi. 56
  dislike of Blanche portrait of TH vi. 69 n.,
    72 n.
  extraction of teeth vi. 81, 82 n.
  letter about squirrels vi. 110, 111 n.
  and question of slaughterhouses vi. 178
    and n.
  and neck operation vi. 197, 198 n., 272 and
    n., 274 and n., 275, 277 and nn., 278–80
  at *Saint Joan* vi. 253 and n.
  at *Queen of Cornwall* opera vi. 321 and n.
  The Book of Baby Beasts v. 276, 277 n.
  The Book of Baby Birds v. 276, 277 n.
  letters to v. 7, 61, 101, 102, 104, 108, 110,
    276, 320, 325; vi. 38, 81, 135, 278, 280
Hardy, Frederick John (cousin) i. 124 ('F.H.')
  and n.
Hardy, Henry ('Harry') (brother) i. 1 n., 3, 4,
  31 n.*; ii. 4 and n., 76, 77 n., 193, 221; iii.
  252 ('my brother'); iv. 31, 72 ('my
  brother'), 87, 105, 148 ('H.') and n.,
  157 n., 269 ('H.'); v. 104 ('H.'), 300
  ('my brother'); vi. 205 ('H.') and n., 279
  ('H.'), 280
  cycling holiday with TH ii. 197 ('we') and n.
  alterations to Max Gate iii. 333 ('H.'), 334 n.
  cathedral tours with TH iv. 51 n., 148 n.,
    150
  Cornish tour with TH iv. 260 ('H.') and n.
  at Talbothays iv. 287 and n.; v. 71 n., 320;
    vi. 205 n., 280
  at TH's second marriage v. 9, 10
  illness v. 138 and n.
  letters to i. 31, 59, 73; v. 36
Hardy, Revd Henry (cousin) iii. 226 n.; iv.
  96 n.; vi. 56
  letters to iii. 226; iv. 95, 188; vi. 55; vii. 154
Hardy, James (uncle) v. 151 n.
Hardy, Jemima (mother) i. 60; ii. 139; iv. 206
  and n.; v. 92, 269; vi. 16, 84 and n., 252;
  vii. 160
  birthplace ii. 139 n., 164 n.
  ancestry ii. 139; iv. 72, 110
  in old age iii. 79, 84, 115, 119, 120, 123; iv.
    40; v. 216, 248
  portraits by Mary H. iii. 116 ('oil painting')
    and n., 118, 119 n., 120, 121, 122, 125 and
    n., 196; v. 137; vii. 137 n.
  death iii. 118, 119, 120, 121, 122, 125 n.; iv.
    40; vii. 135, 167 n.
  letter to i. 163
Hardy, John le (ancestor) iii. 235
Hardy, John (g.g.grandfather) iv. 37 n.
Hardy, John (uncle) ii. 124 n.
Hardy, John (Royal Marine pensioner) vii.
  67 n.
Hardy, Katharine ('Kate') ('Kitty') (sister) i.
  1 n., 4; ii. 124 n.; iv. 168, (?) 239 ('my

Hardy, Katharine (cont.)
    sister'); v. 61 ('K.'), 104 ('K.'), 300 ('my
    sister'), 320 n.; vi. 279 ('K.'), 280
    cycling ii. 193; iii. 224
    at Talbothays iv. 287 and n.; v. 71 n.
    and Mary's illness v. 8
    letters to ii. 124, 140, 162, 166, 172, 192,
      193, 220, 221; iii. 44, 152, 181, 207, 310;
      iv. 41, 79, 148, 214, 223, 269, 331; v. 17;
      vi. 204; vii. 140, 142, 156
Hardy, Mary (*née* Head) (grandmother) iii.
    124 n.; v. 269, 270 n.
Hardy, Mary (sister) i. 1 n.*; ii. 172 and n.,
    221; iii. 207 ('M.'); iv. 326
    at Salisbury Training College i. 2 n., 4 n.
    drawing prize i. 4 and n.
    as teacher at Denchworth i. 4 n.
    TH's obit. of i. 4 n.; v. 136 n.
    on TH's honorary degree from Cambridge
      i. 7 n.
    oil painting of mother iii. 116 and n., 118,
      119 n., 120, 121, 122, 190, 196; v. 137;
      vii. 137 n.
    pencil sketch of mother iii. 125 n.
    portrait of TH iii. 252 n., 306 n.
      as frontispiece to one-vol. *Dynasts* iv.
        7 n., 10, 11 and n., 13
    poor health iii. 293 n.; iv. 239 n.; v. 8 and n.,
      135 and n.
    portrait of FED iv. 112 ('to my sister') and
      n., 202 ('my sister'); v. 135 and n.
    at Talbothays iv. 287 and n.; v. 71 n.
    final illness and death v. 8 and n., 135 and n.,
      154 n.
    TH's thanks for condolences on death of v.
      135, 136, 137, 138, 142
    tombstone v. 161 and n., 180
    letters to i. 1–7, 237; ii. 140; iii. 44, 123, 125,
      152, 201, 243; iv. 214, 269, 331; v. 116
Hardy, Thomas (grandfather) iii. 329 n.; iv.
    183, 184 n.; v. 203, 204 n., 297 and n.
Hardy, Thomas (father) i. 6, 70; iii. 40 n.,
    240 n.; iv. 19 ('one who assisted'), 20 n.,
    206, 325, 327; v. 269; vi. 3, 4 n.
    London visit i. 2
    'last of old master-masons' i. 89
    illness i. 271 ('near relative') and nn., 276,
      277 ('dying relative'), 278, 285; vii. 123 n.
    death i. 276 n., 278, 279, 280, 285; ii. 1 n., 27
      and n.; vii. 167 n.
    memorial service leaflet i. 279, 280 n.
    and music iii. 240 n., 264 and n.; iv. 180 n.;
      vi. 191 and nn.; vii. 7 n.
    ancestry iv. 72; vi. 184 n.
    compilation 'Tunes for the Violin' iv. 180 n.
Hardy, Thomas (author of 'Two Roses') i. 107
    and n.; vii. 97 n.

Hardy, Thomas (politician and bootmaker) iv.
    325 ('another T.H.') and n.
Hardy, Thomas (violent namesake) iii. 23 n.
Hardy, Thomas Bush (painter) v. 300
    ('T.H.'), 301 n.
Hardy, Sir Thomas Masterman iii. 170 and n.,
    186, 234, 260 n.; iv. 7, 8 n.; vi. 4
    Portsmouth lodging iv. 47 n., 231 ('Capt.
      T.H.'), 272
Hardy Players – *see* Dorchester Debating and
    Dramatic Society
Hardye (or Hardy), Thomas (founder of
    Dorchester Grammar School) iv. 3 and n.;
    vii. 85 n.
Hare, (Sir) John i. 103 and n.; vii. 131, 132 n.
Harford, Revd John Battersby vi. 67 n.
    (with F. C. Macdonald) *Handley Carr Glyn
    Moule, Bishop of Durham* vi. 67 and n.
    letter to vi. 67
Harland, Henry ii. 47, 48 n.
Harmsworth London Magazine iii. 67 n.
Harmsworth's [Children's] Encyclopaedia vi.
    69 and n.
Harnham, East and West (Wilts) ii. 172 and n.
Harper, Charles G.:
    *The Hardy Country: Literary Landmarks of
    the Wessex Novels* iii. 151 and n.; vii.
    24 n.
    Wessex iv. 310 ('Wessex book') and n.
Harper, Fletcher i. 76 n.
Harper, George McLean vi. 356 n.
    William Wordsworth vi. 356 and n.
    letter to vi. 356
Harper, Joseph Henry i. 76 nn.*; ii. 1 n., 44,
    45 n.; iii. 60 n.; vii. 118, 119
    *The House of Harper: A Century of Pub-
    lishing in Franklin Square* iv. 210 and n.
    letters to i. 76; ii. 1; iii. 59–60
Harper & Brothers (publishers) i. 29 n., 51,
    54 n., 112 n., 141, 143, 162, 203 and n.,
    209; ii. 42 n., 47 and n., 55 n., 146, 231 n.;
    iii. 53 n., 96; iv. 198, 200 n., 210; v. 175
    and n.; vii. 87 and nn.
    London representatives of – *see* Bowker,
    R. R.; McIlvaine, C. W.
    publish *A Laodicean* i. 94 and n.
    'fairness of dealing' i. 218, 219; iii. 12
    financial difficulties ii. 240 and n., 243, 244,
      246, 250 n.; iii. 6 n., 7, 33
    and sixpenny edn of *Tess* and *Far from the
    Madding Crowd* ii. 263, 265, 282 and n.;
    iii. 246
    agreement for cheap uniform edn ii. 295,
      296 n.
    expiry of contracts iii. 5–6, 7–8, 11, 12, 13,
      28, 30
    transfer of TH works to Macmillan iii. 12,

Harper & Brothers (*cont.*)
   13, 15–16, 27 and n., 28, 32, 91 and n.; iv.
   7 and n., 118 n.
and *Jude* ii. 103 and nn.
and *Tess* dramatization ii. 109–10, 111–12,
   121, 122 n., 151 n., 239
and *Well-Beloved* ii. 141 n., 205; iii. 28; vii.
   119 and n.
and *Wessex Poems* ii. 205
and *Life's Little Ironies* ii. 225
and *Dynasts* iv. 171 and n.; v. 52
and Autograph Edn iv. 217 ('edition in
   America') and n., 233 n., 254 ('this
   edition'), 308 n., 324 ('Wessex novels')
   and n.; v. 52 n., 259
and film version of *Tess* iv. 277, 278, 279 n.,
   303; v. 97, 98, 262, 263 nn., 265
and *A Changed Man* iv. 298 and n., 299, 303,
   305 n., 306; vi. 167 and n.
and Wessex Edn iv. 308 n.; vi. 39, 83
copyright agreements and film-rights v.
   97–8, 148, 149, 262, 263 nn., 265, 307
   and nn., 313; vi. 21 n., 65, 66 and nn.,
   80–81, 83 and n., 87–8, 89, 213
and 'Wessex Novels' edn v. 255 ('Harper
   one') and n.
and Canadian market vi. 65, 66 and n.,
   80–81, 83 and n.
and 'Anniversary' edn vi. 145 and n., 213
letters to i. 54, 58, 63, 72, 74–5, 112, 207; ii.
   103, 109, 111, 121, 205, 225, 239, 250,
   295; iv. 299; vii. 113, 118
Harper's Bazar:
   serialization of *The Woodlanders* i. 138 n.,
   157 n.
   serialization of *Tess* i. 196 n., 207 and n.,
   275 n.; vii. 113 n.
Harper's Christmas (annual) i. 106 n., 112 n.
Harper's Monthly Magazine – see *Harper's
   New Monthly Magazine*
Harper's New Monthly Magazine i. 72 n.,
   152 n., 156 n., 266, 267 n.; ii. 121 n.,
   304 n.; iv. 84 nn.
   serialization of *Return of the Native* i. 54 n.
   serialization of *Laodicean* i. 64 n., 72 and n.,
   73, 75–7, 79, 80–81, 82–3, 84, 85, 86–9,
   91, 93, 94; vii. 94 n.
   'First Countess of Wessex' pub. in i. 180 n.,
   186 n.; vii. 113 n.
   'Wessex Folk' pub. in i. 182 n.; iv. 287 n.,
   292; vii. 113 n., 116 n.
   serialization of *Jude* ii. 46 n., 68, 69 n., 70,
   94 n., 105; vi. 60 ('views differed') and n.
   'Enter a Dragoon' pub. in ii. 238 n., 246, 276
   and n., 277 ('soldier story') and n.
   'Abbey Mason' pub. in iv. 208 and n., 254 n.,
   326 ('a poem') and n.

Harper's Weekly i. 58 n., 72 n., 93 n., 97 n.,
   140 n., 251 n.; ii. 103 ('*Weekly*') and n.,
   187 n.; iii. 75 n., 80; vii. 130 and n.
   serialization of *Mayor of Casterbridge* i.
   143
   'Group of Noble Dames' pub. in i. 207 n.,
   209 ('Christmas story') and n.; vii. 113 n.
   'Noble Lady's Story' pub. in iii. 153 n.
Harraden, Beatrice ii. 199 and n.
   Ships that Pass in the Night ii. 199 n.
Harris, A. H. (Dorchester seedsman) ii. 54
   and n.
Harris, Frank iv. 159 n.
Harris, James Rendel v. 263 nn.
   letter to v. 263
Harrison, Austin iii. 193 and n.; iv. 71 n.,
   91 n., 94
   as editor of *English Review* iv. 71, 79, 87,
   91 n., 158–9, 161, 167, 182, 289, 295
   letters to iv. 71, 87, 90, 158, 161, 167, 182,
   289, 295; vi. 179
Harrison, Bernard iv. 79 ('your other son')
   and n.
Harrison, Constance Cary ii. 121 n., 122
   ('great American authoress'), 123 n.
   letter to ii. 121
Harrison, Ethel ii. 286 ('Mrs H.'), 294, 296; iii.
   305; v. 180 and n.
   illness ii. 297 and n.; iv. 94 and n.
   letter to iv. 332
Harrison, Frederic i. 134 n.*, 137; ii. 184,
   185 n., 286, 287 n.; iii. 46 n., 53 and n.,
   193, 196; iv. 89 ('Fredk H.'); v. 193; vii.
   121
   Wessex Tales sent to i. 176
   and *Far from the Madding Crowd* ii. 294
   and n.
   invited to Max Gate ii. 294, 296
   and *Dynasts* iii. 98, 99, 304
   foreign travel iv. 79 and n.
   birthday wishes to TH iv. 94, 218
   and ELH's death iv. 243
   and TH's second marriage v. 16
   and Home Rule referendum v. 21 and n.
   and Henry James article ('drivel') v. 21 n.
   affected by Great War v. 43, 44 n.
   90th birthday address to vi. 102 ('address')
   and nn.
   adverse review of *Moments of Vision* vi.
   130 n.
   death vi. 179
   *Memories and Thoughts. Men – Books –
   Cities – Art* iii. 230
   National and Social Problems iii. 304 ('&
   Socialism'), 305 n.
   Nicephorus: A Tragedy of New Rome iii. 191,
   192 n.

Harrison, Frederic (cont.)
'A Pedantic Nuisance' iii. 186 ('article of yours') and n.
The Positive Evaluation of Religion iv. 319 and n., 320
Theophano: The Crusade of the Tenth Century iii. 99 ('your romance of fact'), 100 n.
(ed.) *New Calendar of Great Men* i. 251 and n.
letters to i. 133, 176, 251; ii. 294, 296; iii. 46, 98, 99, 186, 191, 230, 304; iv. 79, 94, 218, 243, 319; v. 16, 21, 269; vi. 130
Harrison, Frederick (Forbes-Robertson's partner) ii. 114 n.
proposed London production of *Tess* vi. 295, 296 n., 297, 298, 308 and n., 310
letter to vi. 295
Harrison, Jane Ellen iv. 30 n., 47 ('lady of light & leading'), 48 n.; v. 208 n.
Harrison, Revd Lionel Gordon v. 253 n.
letter to v. 253
Harrison, Mary St Leger ('Lucas Malet') i. 264 n.; vii. 120 nn., 121
Colonel Enderby's Wife vii. 119, 120 n.
The History of Sir Richard Calmady ii. 303 and n.
Mrs Lorimer vii. 119, 120 n.
The Wages of Sin i. 264; vii. 120 ('a novel') and n.
letters to vii. 119–20
Harsent, Rose Anne (Peasenhall murder victim) iii. 49 n.
Harte, Francis Bret i. 122 n.
invited to lecture at Dorchester i. 121
letter to i. 121
Harvey, George Brinton McClellan iii. 8 and n.*, 71, 72 n., 75 n.; v. 46 n., 83 n.
letter to v. 46
Harvey, William Thomas ii. 221 n.
letter to ii. 220
Harzburg iv. 177 and n.
Hassall, Arthur:
A Handbook of European History, 476–1861, Chronologically Arranged iii. 141, 142 n.
Hatfield (Herts) iv. 206 n.; vii. 108 n.
Hatherell, William ii. 94 n.
letter to ii. 94
'Haunting Fingers' (poem):
pub. in *New Republic* vi. 112 and n.
in *Late Lyrics* vi. 112 n.
in 'Two Phantasies' vi. 115 n.
'Havenpool':
Poole as ii. 132
Havens, Raymond Dexter iv. 234 n.
letter to iv. 233
Haweis, Revd Hugh Reginald ii. 37 n.; v. 349 n.
Haweis, Mary ii. 37 n.*, 154 n.; v. 349 n.

'Lecturettes' ii. 59
letters to ii. 36, 59
Hawes, Lady Millicent vi. 373 nn.
That Fool of a Woman vi. 372 ('remarkable novel'), 373 n.
letter to vi. 372
Hawker, Ethel iv. 61 ('girl of this county') and n.; v. 162 n.
Hawker, Revd Robert Stephen iv. 326, 327 n., 328; vii. 47, 48 n.
Cornish Ballads & Other Poems iv. 328 ('a book') and n.
Hawkhurst (Kent) iv. 94 and n.
Hawkins, (Sir) Anthony Hope – *see* Hope, Anthony
Hawkins, Mrs Anthony Hope (later Lady) (Elizabeth Somerville Sheldon) iii. 69 n.
Hawthornden Prize vi. 86 n.
Hawthorne, Julian i. 157 n.
Hay, James Macdougall v. 226 n., 228
'Haydn, Owen' iv. 138
Souvenir iv. 138 ('poems') and n.
Hayley, William vi. 110, 111 n.
Hayling Island (Hants) iii. 224, 225 n.
Haymarket Theatre iv. 100 n.; vi. 296 n., 297, 303, 308
Hayne, Mary Ann ii. 194 and n.
Hayne, Robert (Dorchester JP) iv. 76, 77 n.
Hazlitt, William:
Sketches and Essays iii. 23 n.
'He Abjures Love' (poem) vi. 54
'He Revisits His First School' (poem) v. 291 n.
Head, Henry vi. 95 n., 96 ('your husband'), 129 n., 272 n., 349, 350 n.; vii. 5 n.
letters to vi. 129, 272, 276
Head, Ruth vi. 95 n., 272 and n., 349, 350 n.
(comp.) *Pages from Thomas Hardy* iv. 83 n.; vi. 92 ('anthology'), 93 n., 95 ('a selection'), 96, 129 and nn., 133, 137 n., (?) 170 n.
Pictures and Other Passages from Henry James vi. 92, 93 n.
letters to vi. 95, 96, 129
health, concern with i. 190, 211, 231; ii. 25, 83, 84, 122, 190, 191, 192, 197, 224, 226, 231, 271, 302; iii. 90, 242, 252, 253; iv. 104, 111, 141, 171, 298; v. 113, 277, 324; vi. 13, 114, 216, 218, 222, 270; vii. 13, 53, 89, 94, 117
bladder inflammation i. 81, 82, 84, 87, 88, 89, 90; ii. 25; v. 237; vi. 115, 119, 123, 127, 128, 131, 137, 142, 148
colds and coughs i. 2, 177, 237, 285, 289; ii. 11, 69, 97, 116, 117, 118, 219, 221, 238, 283; iii. 5, 95, 165, 172, 232, 240, 243, 248, 312, 355, 363; iv. 9, 66, 68, 73, 91, 128, 138, 154, 155, 157, 158, 210, 318,

319, 320, 322, 323, 325, 327; v. 2, 60, 64, 65, 68, 76, 138, 139, 140, 142, 144, 145, 146, 151, 194, 195, 200, 237, 253, 338, 339; vi. 30, 42, 43, 113, 166, 180, 182, 185, 196, 198, 200, 281, 314, 320, 326; vii. 8, 77, 152, 156, 160, 161, 162

diarrhoea iv. 100, 101, 218; v. 93; vi. 215

dyspepsia ii. 149, 153; iv. 9; v. 138

eye trouble ii. 224, 227, 265, 293; iii. 5, 8, 43; v. 35, 174, 309, 311; vi. 248

eyesight, failing v. 314; vi. 90, 91, 97, 117, 134, 136, 148, 149, 151, 187, 189, 191, 194, 197, 199, 200, 234, 244, 256, 260, 265, 286, 288, 299, 302, 307, 313, 332; vii. 19, 39, 54, 70, 87

headaches i. 133, 232, 233, 236, 264; ii. 109, 149, 184, 238, 248

influenza i. 63, 208, 209, 236, 240; ii. 48, 219, 227, 287, 288, 302; iii. 2, 20, 104, 126, 205, 206, 273, 356, 361; iv. 22, 25, 26, 29, 94, 97, 115, 325; vi. 315; vii. 148, 149, 155

lumbago vi. 363; vii. 29

neuralgia i. 236; ii. 47, 240, 272; iii. 40, 42, 106, 238, 240

rheumatism ii. 116, 128, 153; iii. 51, 53, 55, 65; v. 33, 65, 234; vi. 30, 175, 230, 248

toothache ii. 256; iii. 40, 257, 259; iv. 36

varicose veins iv. 265, 267, 268, 269, 272, 276, 284; v. 30

Hearth and Home i. 266 and n.

Hearts Insurgent – see *Jude the Obscure*

Heath, Frank Roland iii. 176 n.
   Dorset iii. 175 ('your little guide'), 176 n.
   (with Sidney Heath) *Dorchester* (*Dorset*) *and its Surroundings* iii. 182 ('the proof') and n., 188
   letters to iii. 175, 182, 188

Heath, Frederick W. vii. 53 and n.

Heath, Sidney iv. 79 n.
   The South Devon and Dorset Coast iv. 79 and n.
   letter to iv. 79

Heathcote, Thornhill Bradford vii. 97 nn.
   letters to vii. 97, 98, 100

Hedgcock, Frank Arthur iv. 37 and n., 109 nn.; vi. 146 n.
   proposed translation of *Under the Greenwood Tree* iv. 162 and n.
   at Birmingham University iv. 190 and n.
   David Garrick et ses amis français iv. 152 n.
   'Reminiscences of Thomas Hardy' iv. 109 n.
   Thomas Hardy, penseur et artiste iv. 37 n., 152 n., 157 ('his book') and nn., 162 ('your essay'), 165 ('critical essay') and n.; vi. 138 ('Hedgcock's book'), 140, 142 and n., 145–6, 156

letters to iv. 109, 152, 162, 165, 190; vi. 145

Heinemann, William (publisher) i. 274 n.*; ii. 51 n., 60, 231 n.; vi. 372 n.
   criticisms of *Tess* i. 273
   publication of *Desperate Remedies* vii. 37 and n.
   failure to print Laurence Hope preface vii. 140
   letters to i. 273, 286; ii. 51; vii. 140

Heming, John vii. 49 and n.

Henderson, Alice Corbin vi. 183 n.

Henderson, Thomas F. iii. 297 n.

Henley, William Ernest i. 214 n.; iii. 57 and n.; vii. 118 n.
   Memorial Committee iii. 106
   accepts 'Saturday Night in Arcady' vii. 118 n.
   (and R. L. Stevenson) *Macaire* ii. 270 n.
   (and T. F. Henderson) (ed.) *The Poetry of Robert Burns* iii. 297 and n.
   letters to i. 214, 216, 229; vii. 117

Henniker (Henniker-Major), Major-General Arthur Henry ii. 3 n., 11 n., 32, 145 n., 230 n.; iii. 56 nn., 120, 135 n., 184, 185, 207 n.; iv. 316, 331 n.; vi. 52 and n.
   limited literary interests ii. 108
   on manoeuvres ii. 198, 199; iii. 74, 75 n.
   sporting trophies ii. 227 and n.
   in South Africa during Boer War ii. 233 and n., 236 n., 241 n., 246, 248, 253, 258 and n., 265, 269, 283, 287, 293
   photograph requested by TH ii. 236, 238
   return from S. Africa iii. 32, 39, 66
   later career iii. 95 n.
   death iv. 211 ('cheerful now?') and n.
   TH's poem in memory of iv. 215 ('the verses'), 216 n.
   letters to ii. 233; iii. 206

Henniker, Florence Ellen Hungerford ii. 3 and n., 11 n.*, 57, 59 ('my friend') and n., 77, 79, 82, 100, 102 n., 108, 138 n., 142, 165, 174, 286; iii. 66, 327; iv. 92, 212 and n., 213 n., 322 ('literary friend') and n.; v. 132 and n., 133 n., 186, 219 n., 252 n.; vi. 51, 81, 177 n., 319, 320 n.; vii. 125 n.
   study of architecture ii. 11, 13, 16, 23
   as author and translator ii. 13, 14, 18, 20, 21 n., 29, 30, 33, 34, 35–6, 37–41, 43, 44, 46, 55, 62, 71–2, 87, 113, 122, 134, 137, 139, 140, 148, 161, 169, 195, 197, 201, 203, 205, 212, 215, 218, 225, 227, 245, 252, 264; iii. 42, 47, 151, 159, 181, 190, 214, 275; iv. 143 and n., 151, 154, 177, 210–11; v. 115 n., 176, 177 n., 215 and n.; vii. 127
   collaboration with TH ii. 26, 30, 31, 35–6, 37–41, 43, 62, 71–2

Henniker, Florence Ellen (*cont.*)
  gift of inkstand to TH ii. 30, 31, 32
  gift of photographs to TH ii. 34, 35, 40
  gift of *A Shropshire Lad* to TH iii. 46
  health iii. 181, 184, 206 ('second infliction'), 207 n., 212, 214; v. 214; vi. 44, 45 n.
  presentation copies from TH iii. 196, 206; iv. 316 n.; v. 70
  and slaughter-house reform iv. 168, 170
  'G. Worlingworth' pseudonym iv. 177 and n.; v. 115 n., 176
  attends 'Hardy plays' iv. 191 and n., 244
  death of husband iv. 211 ('cheerful now?') and n.
  birthday wishes to TH iv. 218; v. 266, 309
  and ELH's death iv. 243
  at Southwold iv. 267, 268, 269 n., 272 n., 300
  and TH's second marriage v. 19 and n.
  invited to Max Gate v. 30
  on Barrie v. 205 n.
  in Dorchester v. 266, 267 n.; vi. 132 and n.
  at Weymouth vi. 21, 22, 33 n., 35
  Arthur Henniker: A Little Book for His Friends iv. 216 ('little book') and n.
  'At the Crossing' ii. 139 n.
  'Bad and Worthless' ii. 44 ('type-written story'), 45 ('military sketch') and nn., 49 ('story') and n.
  Bid Me Good-bye ii. 3 and n.
  'A Brand of Discord' ii. 122, 123 n., 140
  'A Bunch of Cowslips' iii. 190 n.
  Contrasts ii. 197, 246 n.; iii. 47 ('16 stories') and n., 57 and nn.
  The Courage of Silence iii. 151 ('your play') and n., 159 ('that play'), 181 ('the play')
  'Desire' (later 'The Spectre of the Real', q.v.) ii. 30, 31 n., 33, 36, 38
  'A Faithful Failure' ii. 264, 265
  Foiled ii. 18 and n., 228, 229 n.
  'His Best Novel' iii. 190 n., 214 ('your little story'), 215 n.
  'His Excellency' ii. 29 and n., 30, 31 n.
  'In the Infirmary' ii. 87 and n.
  In Scarlet and Grey ii. 72 n., 87 n., 113 n., 135 n.
  'Lady Gilian' ii. 245
  'The Lonely House on the Moor' ii. 203 ('*Speaker* story')
  'The Man Who Waited' ii. 169 n.
  'Mrs Livesey' ii. 169 n.
  Our Fatal Shadows iii. 275 and n.
  Outlines ii. 29 ('the collection') and n., 39 ('the volume') and n., 41 ('the book') and n., 43 ('our two volumes'), 44 ('the book') and n., 55 and nn.
  'A Page from a Vicar's History' ii. 71 ('the

  little story'), 87 and n.; vii. 127 ('little tale') and n.
  'Past Mending' ii. 252 ('little story'), 253 n.
  Second Fiddle iv. 132 n., 143 ('that novel') and n., 151 ('your novel'), 210 ('new novel')
  Sir George ii. 13, 14 n.
  Sowing the Sand ii. 148 ('1 vol. story') and n., 161 ('your novel'), 162 n., 195 ('story') and n., 201
  'The Spectre of the Real' (originally 'Desire', q.v.) ii. 31 n., 32 n., 39 ('the story'), 41 n., 42 ('little work') and n., 43, 62 n., 135 n., 137; iii. 189
  'A Statesman's Love-Lapse' ii. 29 and n.
  'A Successful Intrusion' ii. 113
  'Three Corporals' ii. 205, 212, 215
  letters to ii. 10, 11, 13, 16, 18–19, 20, 22–4, 25–6, 27, 29, 30, 31, 32, 34, 35, 37–41, 43–5, 47, 83–5, 86–7, 94, 99, 110, 122, 130, 134, 137, 138, 140, 144, 148, 150, 157, 161, 168, 195, 197, 198–9, 201, 203, 205, 209, 211, 215, 218, 224, 226–8, 229, 232, 236, 237, 240, 245, 248, 252, 257, 264, 269, 277, 279, 283, 287–8, 293; iii. 32, 39, 42, 46, 55, 57, 74, 94, 113, 120, 134, 150, 159, 180, 184, 189, 196, 206, 212, 214, 224, 242, 267, 275, 287, 316, 361; iv. 24, 34, 61, 66, 132, 143, 150, 154, 168, 176, 210, 215, 218, 243, 316, 330; v. 10, 19, 29, 37, 70, 86, 99, 114, 116, 121, 165, 176, 177, 192, 204, 214, 249, 266, 282, 287, 309, 339; vi. 9, 21, 33, 35, 44, 56, 82, 93, 110, 119, 132
Henning, Frances Amelia iv. 241 n.
  letter to iv. 240
Henschel, Lillian June Bailey ii. 68 n.
  letter to ii. 67
'Her Death and After' (poem) ii. 209, 283; iii. 137
'Her Reproach' (poem) v. 246
Herbert, Lady Winifred Anne Henrietta Christine i. 132, 133 n.; vii. 102 nn.
  letter to vii. 101
Hereford Cathedral iv. 149 n., 152 n.
Herkomer, (Sir) Hubert von ii. 143 n.; iii. 123, 124 n.
  illustrations to *Tess* i. 255 and n.
  portrait of TH iii. 322, 323 and n., 324, 325, 359; v. 86 and n., 252 n.; vi. 68
  as film-maker iv. 322 and n.; v. 104 n.
Herkomer, Siegfried von iv. 322 n., 329, 330; v. 103, 104 n., 106, 133
Herkomer Film Company iv. 322 and n., 324 and n.; v. 103, 104 n., 106
Herriot, George (Duchy of Cornwall official) i. 135 and n., 231; ii. 67 n.; vii. 96 n., 97 n.,

Herriot, George (cont.)
103 n.*, 104 n.
letters to ii. 66–7; vii. 103
Herschell, Farrer Herschell, Lord ii. 53 ('Ld Chancellor') and n.
Hester (Max Gate servant) v. 61 and n.
Hewlett, Maurice Henry ii. 291 and n.; iv. 28 n., 29 nn., 111
and *Late Lyrics* vi. 162, 163 n.
letters to iv. 27, 28–9
Heywood, C. iii. 139 and n.
Hiatt, Charles Wall i. 177 n.
letter to i. 177
Hibbert Journal v. 323, 324 n.
Hibbs, George iv. 46 n.
Hickman, Dr Sophia Frances iii. 81 ('that case') and n.
Hicks, Revd James vi. 27 n., 111 n.
Hicks, John (Dorchester architect) iv. 20 n.; v. 198 n.; vi. 27 n., 111 n.
TH as pupil of i. 2 n.; ii. 177 n.; iv. 20 n.; v. 198 and n., 253 and n.
Hicks, John George vi. 27 nn.
letter to vi. 27
Hicks, (Sir) Seymour:
Blue-Bell in Fairyland iii. 4 n.
Hicks, William Searle vi. 27 n., 111 n., 139 n.
Hicks Beach, Lady Lucy ii. 258 and n.
Hicks Beach, Sir Michael Edward ii. 258 and n.
Higbee, Frank D. ii. 267 n.
letter to ii. 267
Higginbotham, John C. ('Orme Agnus') iv. 205, 206 n.
Higginbottom, Frederick James v. 206 n.
letter to v. 206
Higginson, Thomas Wentworth vii. 130 nn.
The Procession of the Flowers vii. 130 and n.
letter to vii. 130
High Stoy (Dorset) ii. 70 n.
Higher Bockhampton (Dorset) ii. 255 n.; iii. 79 n. ('Upper'); iv. 96 n.
TH's birthplace i. 8 n.; ii. 255 n.; iii. 290 n.; iv. 286 and n., 296 n.; v. 304 n.; vi. 185 ('old homestead') and n.; vii. 137 ('mother's house') and n.
Far from Madding Crowd finished at i. 27 ('here')
as 'Mellstock' i. 126 and n.
death of Jemima H at iii. 118 n.
erroneous description of Hardy home iii. 119 ('tiny cottage')
tripper nuisance iii. 145, 146
Reading-Room vi. 325 n.
'Highways and Byways' series vi. 278 and n.; vii. 24
Hignett, John Marcus vii. 88 n.

letter to vii. 88
Hilfield St Nicholas (Dorset) v. 324 n.
Hill, Revd Charles Rowland Haydock iii. 294 n., 311
letter to iii. 294
Hill, Mrs Charles Rowland iii. 84 and n., 294, 335
Hill, Mrs Frank Harrison (Jane Dalzell Finlay) i. 65 n.
letter to i. 65
Hill, Vernon iv. 328 and n.; vi. 140, 141 nn.
Hills & Rowney (Dorchester picture frame manufacturers) v. 31 and n.
Hind, Arthur Mayger vii. 24 nn.
letter to vii. 24
Hind, Charles Lewis ii. 155 n.; iii. 189, 190 and n.; vi. 256 n.
letters to ii. 155; vi. 255
Hinkley, Rufus H. (publisher) iv. 165 n.
proposed *de luxe* edn of TH works iv. 124 n., 160 and nn., 163, 165, 171 and n., 182, 195–6, 198, 217
at Max Gate iv. 163 and n., 165 n.
letter to iv. 165
Hinstock (Hants) iv. 34, 35 n.
Hirschmann, Anna ii. 86 ('Anna') and n.; v. 99 n., 309 ('Anna'), 340 ('Anna's'); vi. 22 ('Anna'), 35 ('Anna')
Hirst (spelt Hurst by TH), Major John vi. 135 and n.
Hirst, Kathleen vi. 135 and n., 221, 222 n.
'His Country' (poem) vi. 218
Hoare, Sir Henry Hugh Arthur iv. 75 n.; v. 36 n., 38, 104
80th birthday gift to TH vi. 24
letters to v. 211, 235; vi. 24
Hoare, Lady (Alda Weston) iv. 75 n.; v. 21 and n., 36 n., 38; v. 104
and slaughter-house reform iv. 168
and ELH's death iv. 241
and TH's second marriage v. 13
literary tastes v. 74
birthday gifts to TH v. 216, 268, 311; vi. 24
letters to iv. 75, 195, 241; v. 13, 26, 57, 74, 141, 211, 216, 235, 268, 311; vi. 29, 134, 355
Hoare, Henry Colt Arthur iv. 195 n.; v. 57 and n., 141 n.
death in action v. 211 n., 235 and n.
'Hobbes, John Oliver' – *see* Craigie, Pearl Mary Teresa
Hobbes, Thomas:
Leviathan, TH's purchase of first edn for 6*d* iii. 40
Hodder & Stoughton (publishers) v. 137 ('his firm') and n.

Hodge, Harold iii. 223 n.; iv. 91 n.
  letter to iii. 223
Hodges, Wilfrid Francis (Dorchester wine merchant and mayor) iv. 314 n.
  letters to iv. 314; vii. 26, 45
Hodgson, Ralph Edwin vii. 150 n.
  The Last Blackbird vii. 149, 150 n.
Hodgson, William Earl ii. 264 n.
  letters to ii. 264, 271
Hoffman, Harold v. 135 n.
Hogarth, William iii. 334 and n.
Hogarth Press vi. 255 and n.
Hogg, James ('Ettrick shepherd') ii. 210
Hogg, James (editor) i. 107 n., 109 n.
  letters to i. 107, 109
Hoghton, Major-General David vi. 308 n.
Holder, Revd Caddell i. 13 n.; iv. 275, 276 n., 328; v. 288 n.; vi. 13 n., 15, 27 ('my brother-in-law') and n.; vii. 47 ('relative of mine'), 48 n.
Holder, Helen (Mrs Caddell H) (ELH's sister) ii. 271 n., 276 n.; iv. 328; vi. 15, 27
Holder, Colonel Cecil vi. 13 and n., 16 n.
Holiday Fund for City Children:
  matinée for i. 213 and n., 214 and n., 215
Holland, Archie K. v. 250 n.
Holland, Clive (Charles James Hankinson) ii. 177 n.*, 233 n., 302 n.; iii. 34 n.
  at Max Gate ii. 292; iii. 55
  scheme for abridging TH novels iv. 54
  Old and New Japan iii. 276 n.
  Things Seen in Egypt iii. 276 n.
  'Thomas Hardy, and the Land of Wessex' iii. 178 ('your article') and n., 190 ('the Wessex article')
  Wessex iii. 147 n., 194 ('the sheets') and n., 195; vi. 145 ('past book') and n.
  letters to ii. 177, 201, 233, 292, 296; iii. 34, 55, 152, 174, 176, 178, 186, 188, 194–5, 197, 276; iv. 20, 54, 96, 104, 205; vi. 206
Holland, Robert iii. 53 ('shopkeeper of Dorchester') and n.
Holmes, Harry vi. 68 and n.
Holmes, Harry Nicholls vi. 68 n.
Holmes, Oliver Wendell i. 144 ('O.W.H.')
  at Rabelais dinner i. 147
Holst, Gustav Theodore iii. 73 n.; iv. 52 n.; vii. 73 n.
  setting to music of TH poems iv. 52 and n., 69 and n.
  at Max Gate vii. 73 and n.
  Egdon Heath vii. 73 and n.
  Six songs for baritone and piano iv. 52 n., 69 n.
  letters to iv. 52, 69; vii. 73
Holt, Henry i. 27 n., 58 n.
  as TH's first American publisher i. 27 n., 28,

40; vi. 81 and n.
  letters to i. 27, 30, 32, 34, 40, 42, 44, 140
Holt, Henry & Co. (publishers) i. 27 n., 35 n., 58, 116
  misunderstanding over *Far from the Madding Crowd* i. 28–9, 30, 32
  letter to i. 111
Holzmann, Maurice vii. 104 n.
  letters to vii. 103–5
Home-Reading Magazine vi. 101 n.
Homer v. 246
Homer, Eleanor Christine Wood iv. 247 n.; v. 2 n.
  letter to v. 1
Homer, Eliza Wood ii. 271 and n.; iii. 123 n.; iv. 247 n.; v. 2 n.
  letters to iii. 122; iv. 246, 307, 332
Homer, George Wood ii. 271 and n.; iii. 123 and n.; iv. 247 n.; v. 2 n.
'Homes of All Nations' exhibition (1911) iv. 145 and n.
Hone, Joseph Maunsell vi. 121 n., 122 n., 132 n.
'Honourable Laura, The' (formerly 'Benighted Travellers', q.v.) (story) i. 93 ('Christmas story') and n.; iii. 48 ('another title') and n.; iv. 175 n.
honours, attitude to and reception of i. 7 nn.; ii. 66, 79, 119, 122, 181; iii. 158, 159, 161, 162, 165, 186, 311, 314, 315, 326, 349, 353, 364; iv. 3, 27, 28–9, 33, 49–50, 59, 64, 75, 102, 103, 104, 105, 107, 108, 109–12, 115, 119, 129, 130, 141, 145, 210, 213, 215, 216, 236, 259, 269, 273, 291, 308, 314, 316, 330; v. 4, 82, 178, 191, 206, 208, 218, 252; vi. 11, 21, 30, 50, 62, 91, 106, 107, 123, 127, 147, 167, 170, 172, 174, 186, 214–15, 267, 316, 321, 326–7, 330, 331, 332, 375
Hooper, Charles E. ii. 223 n.
  letter to ii. 223
Hope, Anthony (Anthony Hope Hawkins) ii. 246 and n., 258; iii. 8 n.*
  at Aldeburgh ii. 287, 288, 289
  and Society of Authors iii. 8 and n.; vi. 18 n.
  marriage iii. 69 and n.
  and manifesto on war aims v. 47 n.; vi. 18 n.
  The Girl in the Car ii. 87 and n.
  letter to vi. 17
'Hope, Laurence' (Violet Nicolson) iii. 142 and nn.
  suicide iii. 142, 143, 144 n.; vii. 140 n.
  Indian Love, TH preface to vii. 135 n. ('poems'), 140 ('last poems') and n.
Hopkins, Arthur i. 53 n.
  illustrations to *Return of the Native* serialization i. 52–3, 54–5, 59
  letters to i. 52, 54, 59

Hopkins, Gerard Manley i. 53 n.
Hopkins, Robert Thurston vii. 26, 27 nn., 28 and nn.
Hopwood, Admiral Ronald Arthur vi. 4 n.
  letter to vi. 4
Horace:
  quoted in *Tess* i. 282
  Odes iii. 303 n.; iv. 275 n.
Horder, Percy Richard Morley iv. 18 nn.
  letters to iv. 17, 58
Hornby, Charles Harry St John v. 148 n.
Hornsey Players vi. 266 n.
Horrocks, Jeremiah i. 97, 98 n.
Horsley, Victor Alexander Haden ii. 124 and n.
Horton, William Thomas iv. 10 nn.
  letter to iv. 10
Houghton, Arthur Villiers vi. 158 n.
  letter to vi. 157
Houghton, Claude vi. 125 n.
  Judas vi. 125 and n.
  letter to vi. 125
Houghton, Richard Monckton Milnes, 1st Lord i. 96 and n., 118 n.*, 128 n., 228 and n.; ii. 23 and n., 24 n., 81 n.; vi. 166 and n.
  Poetical Works ii. 23, 34 and n.
  letters to i. 118, 134
Houghton, Robert Offley Ashburton Crewe-Milnes, 2nd Lord (later Earl, then Marquess of Crewe, qq.v.) ii. 3 n.*, 11 n., 31 ('your brother') and n., 71 n.
  created earl ii. 79 and n.
  Gleanings from Béranger vii. 125 ('charming volume') and n.
  Stray Verses ii. 2, 3 n.
  letter to vii. 125
Houghton, H. O. & Co. (publishers) i. 32 n.
Houghton, Mifflin & Co. (publishers) i. 95 n., 102, 106 and n.; vii. 76 and n.
  letter to i. 109
Houghton, Osgood & Co. (publishers) i. 67 n.
  letter to i. 67
Hounsell, Thomas (Dorchester stonemason) v. 198
Hounsell, Walter John Bowditch (Dorchester stonemason) iv. 262 n.; v. 198 ('present one')
  and ELH's tombstone iv. 262 and n., 263 and n., 264 and n., 266 ('the mason'), 270
  and Mary H's tombstone v. 161 and n., 180
  letters to iv. 262, 263, 264, 270; v. 161, 180, 294, 316
'House of Hospitalities, The' (poem):
  pub. in *New Quarterly* iii. 295 n., 354 n.; iv. 1 n.
House of Lords iv. 99, 100 n.
  Gosse as librarian to iii. 131 n., 141, 198 and

n., 214 n.; iv. 33 n.; v. 35 n., 46 ('official position'), 47 n.
  and Finance Bill (1909) iv. 62 n.
  and Parliament Bill (1910) iv. 86 and n., 129 n.
Household, The:
  serialization of 'Our Exploits at West Poley' i. 116 n., 140, 141 n.
Housman, A. E. iii. 73 n.; iv. 202, 203 n., 275, 307 and n., 321 nn.; vi. 281 and n.
  presentation copy of *Satires of C* v. 60 n.
  A Shropshire Lad ii. 204 n.; iii. 46, 47 n.
  letter to iv. 320
Housman, Laurence iii. 71 n., 73 n.
  Sabrina Warham: the Story of Her Youth iii. 134 and n.
  letters to iii. 71, 73, 134
How, William Walsham, Bp of Wakefield:
  burning of *Jude* ii. 125 and n., 143 ('second class prelate'), 219; iv. 29 n.
'How I Built Myself a House' (article):
  pub. in *Chambers's Journal* iv. 9 n., 69, 70 n.; v. 94, 95 n.; vi. 261 and n., 263 and n., 267
  reprinted in *Review of Reviews* vi. 263 and n.
Howe, Percival Presland:
  J. M. Synge: A Critical Study iv. 225 and n.
Howe, William Thomas Hildrup vi. 70 n.
  letter to vi. 70
Howells, Mildred iv. 102 n.
Howells, William Dean i. 110 and n.*, 119 n., 155 n., 156 n.; ii. 103; iii. 122 n., 318, 319 n.; iv. 102 nn.; vii. 98 n., 131 and n.
  praise of *Mayor of Casterbridge* i. 156
  The World of Chance i. 266 ('your novel'), 267 n.
  letters to i. 156, 266; iv. 102
Howth Castle ii. 29 and n.
Hrůša, Josef:
  Czech translation of *Jude* vii. 52 n.
Hudson, Edward vi. 83 n.
  letter to vi. 83
Hudson, Sir Robert Arundell iv. 112 and n.; vii. 150 nn.
  letter to vii. 150
Huebsch, B. W. (publisher) iv. 131 n.; vi. 38 n.
  letter to vi. 38
Hueffer, Ford Madox (later Ford Madox Ford, q.v.) iv. 30 n.
  as editor of *English Review* iii. 327 ('such a magazine') and n., 354 ('the editor') and n.; iv. 7, 8; vii. 148
  and ELH's death iv. 248
  Antwerp v. 72 ('verses') and n.
  (and Conrad) *Romance* vi. 157 n.

Hueffer, Ford Madox (*cont.*)
  letters to iii. 327, 331; iv. 7, 8, 97, 160, 248;
    v. 72; vii. 148
Hueffer, Francis i. 57 n.; iii. 327 n.
  letters to i. 57; vii. 91
Hugo, Victor iii. 81; vii. 14 and n.
Hull, Beatrice iii. 281 and n.
Hullah, John:
  (comp.) *The Song Book. Words and Tunes
    from the Best Poets and Musicians* iii. 247
    and n.
Human Shows (poems) vi. 230 n., 270 n., 275
  n., 348 nn., 350 n., 358 ('the Poems') and
  n., 364 n., 373 n.; vii. 2, 75, 170 n.
  former title (*Poems Imaginative and In-
    cidental*) vi. 341 and n., 347
  publication vi. 363 n., 368 ('volumes of
    poems'), 369 nn.
  corrections to vi. 371 and n.
  American edn vii. 2 and n., 46
Humanitarian ii. 137, 142 and n., 145, 226 n.;
  iv. 90 and n., 96, 97 n.
Humanitarian League ii. 136 n.; v. 240 and
  n.
Humperdinck, Engelbert iv. 205 n.
'Hundred Years Since, A' (poem):
  pub. in *North American Review* v. 46 n., 69
    ('some verses') and n.
Hunt, Gladys Holman iii. 214 n.
  letter to iii. 214
Hunt, Isobel Violet ii. 108, 109 n.*; iii. 128 n.,
  257; iii. 29 n.
  Sooner or Later vii. 143 n.
  White Rose of Weary Leaf iii. 300 ('your new
    book'), 301 n.
  The Workaday Woman (called *Common-
    place Woman* by TH) vii. 142, 143 n.
  letters to iii. 127, 165, 257, 300, 319; vii. 142
Hunt, Leigh v. 90 and n.
Hunt, Marion Edith (Mrs W. Holman Hunt)
  iii. 248 n.
  letter to iii. 248
Hunt, William Holman i. 134 and n.; iii. 205
  and nn.
  80th birthday iii. 248 and n.
Hunter, Colin ii. 16 n.
  letter to ii. 16
'Husband's View, The' (poem) iv. 67
Hutchins, John:
  *History and Antiquities of the County of
    Dorset* i. 51 n., 224 and n.; iii. 337 and n.;
    iv. 18 n., 147 and n., 221 n., 297 n.; v.
    13 n., 31, 134 and n., 238, 253; vi. 71 and
    n., 172; vii. 85 and n., 152 n., 176
Hutchinson, John H. vii. 4 nn.
  letter to vii. 4
Hutchinson, Thomas vii. 111 n.

*Ballades and Other Rhymes of a Country
  Bookworm* vii. 111 ('genial poems') and n.
  letter to vii. 111
Hutchinson & Co. (publishers) ii. 38, 39 n.,
  41, 44, 45 n.; iii. 271 n.; vi. 366 n.
  letter to iii. 271
Hutton, Charlotte (Mrs E. Hutton) iii. 199
  and n.
Hutton, Edward iii. 199 and n.
Hutton, John i. 61 ('a critic') and n.
  review of *Desperate Remedies* i. 12 ('one of
    the editors') and n.; iv. 161 n.
  review of *Pair of Blue Eyes* i. 21 n., 22 n.
Hutton, Richard Holt:
  and *Spectator* i. 21 n., 178 n.; vii. 101 n.
  letters to i. 178; vii. 101
Huxley, Thomas Henry i. 96 and n.*, 276,
  287; ii. 75 and n.
  Clodd's book on iii. 2, 5
  on Westminster Abbey iv. 23 and n., 26
  'Agnosticism' iii. 5 n.
Huxtable, Henry Anthony (Dorchester solici-
  tor) iv. 42 n.; v. 244
  letters to iv. 42, 294
Huxtable, Mrs H. A. iii. 340 and n.
Hyatt, Alfred H. iii. 205 n.
  (comp.) *The Pocket Thomas Hardy* iii. 205
    ('little book'), 206 n., 242 ('a little book'),
    243 n.; iv. 83 n.
Hymns Ancient and Modern :
  'Old 113th' iv. 327 and n.
Hyndman, Henry Mayers, v. 270 and n.; vii. 1
  and nn.
Hyndman, Rosalind v. 270 n.; vii. 1 and n.
Hyndman Club and Institute vii. 1 and n.

'I Look into My Glass' (poem) ii. 208 n.
'I Met a Man' (poem) vi. 218 n.
'I travel as a phantom now' (poem) vi. 245
'I was not he' (poem) vi. 118
Ibsen, Henrik ii. 10, 13
  70th birthday tribute to ii. 187 n.
  Hedda Gabler (trans. Gosse) i. 228 n., 233
    and n.
  Little Eyolf ii. 139 ('Ibsen play') and n.
  The Master Builder ii. 14 n.
  The Wild Duck vi. 367
Ideas iii. 246 n.
ideas and philosophy i. 174, 190, 260, 261–
  2; ii. 25, 143, 156; iii. 5, 37, 53, 98, 99, 102,
  106, 113, 117, 207, 231, 244, 255, 298, 308,
  329, 351; iv. 37; v. 50, 69–70, 78–9, 84, 121,
  153, 156, 353; vi. 48, 52, 54, 98–9, 259; vii.
  153, 162
Idler ii. 210
Ilbert, Sir Courtenay Peregrine v. 61 and n.;
  vii. 157 n., 158 n.

Ilbert, Sir Courtenay Peregrine (cont.)
  letter to vii. 157
Ilbert, Revd Peregrine vii. 158 n.
Ilchester, Elizabeth Horner, Lady (wife of 1st Earl) v. 134 n.
Ilchester, Giles Stephen Holland Fox-Strangways, 6th Earl of iii. 337 and n.; iv. 191, 323; vi. 22
  in Great War v. 134 and n., 166
  Henry Fox, First Lord Holland, His Family and Relations vi. 7 ('the book') and n., 10
Ilchester, Lady (Helen Mary Theresa Fox-Strangways) (wife of 6th Earl) iv. 191 n., 330; v. 8 ('Birdie') and n., 166, 176, 177 n., 186 nn., 193, 283, 309 ('Birdie'), 340; vi. 10, 22, 69 n.
  and *Changed Man* iv. 323 ('the book') and n.
  at Max Gate v. 266
  letters to iv. 191, 254, 323; v. 135, 184, 186; vi. 7
Ilchester, Henry Edward Fox-Strangways, 5th Earl of i. 105; ii. 139 and n.; iii. 185
  and 'First Countess of Wessex' iii. 190 and n.
Ilchester, Land Steward to Earl of:
  letter to i. 105
Ilchester, Mary Eleanor Anne, Dowager Lady (widow of 5th Earl) v. 108, 109 n.
Ilfracombe (Devon) iv. 168
Illica, Luigi iii. 56 ('writer of the libretto'), 57 n.
Illustrated London News i. 53 nn., 60 and n., 245 and n.; ii. 68 n.; vi. 134 n.; vii. 127 n.
  'The Son's Veto' pub. in i. 232 n.
  serialization of *Pursuit of the Well-Beloved* i. 245 n., 283, 284 and n.; ii. 152 n.
  'Master John Horseleigh, Knight' pub. in ii. 6 n., 8 ('little sketch'), 19 ('the story')
  'A Committee-Man of "The Terror"' pub. in ii. 101 ('short story') and n., 126 ('the story') and n., 129 n., 137 ('little sketch'), 142 ('little story') and n.
  'What the Shepherd Saw' pub. in iv. 293 n.
Ilsley, Samuel Marshall ii. 218 n.
  By the Western Sea ii. 218 and n.
  letter to ii. 218
'Imaginative Woman, An' (story) ii. 6 n., 32 n.; iii. 225
  fee for ii. 5 ('a story'), 7 ('a 6000-word story')
  deletion from ii. 48, 49 n.
  French translation of iii. 226 n.; v. 234 and n.
  MS given to Aberdeen University iv. 180, 181 n., 184, 186
Imperial Conference (1911) iv. 151 n.
Imperial Institute ii. 163
Imperial Yeomanry ii. 247, 249 n.

'In the Evening' (poem) vi. 230 ('hasty tribute') and n.
'In Her Precincts' v. 225 ('a poem') and n.
'In Time of "the Breaking of Nations"' (poem) v. 286 n.; vi. 136, 183 n.
  pub. in *Saturday Review* v. 144 n.
  private printing of v. 144 and n.
  MS sold for Red Cross v. 145 n., 158
'In Time of Wars and Tumults' (poem):
  pub. in *Sphere* v. 233 n.
'In a Wood' (poem) ii. 209
Incorporated Society of Authors, Playwrights, and Composers i. 191 n., 231; ii. 5 n., 9 n., 13, 236 ('the Society'), 237 n.; iii. 7, 8 nn., 30 n., 111; v. 4 n., 226, 337; vi. 195 and n., 324 n.; vii. 112 n.
  dinners i. 128 and n., 177 and n., 178, 191 and n., 192, 193 and nn., 194, 197; vi. 211 and n.; vii. 95
  'conferences' i. 162 n.
  and 'Book War' iii. 233, 234 n.
  TH's reluctance to accept presidency iv. 27–9; v. 190 n.
  TH as president iv. 29 and n., 33, 34 n., 40 n., 53 n., 73 n., 103 n., 133 n.; v. 119 n., 190 n., 191, 192 n.; vi. 17 n., 37, 195 n., 212; vii. 55 n.
  and censorship iv. 53, 64 n.
  and destroyed Library of Louvain v. 119 and n., 126
  congratulates H. James on OM and naturalization v. 126 and n., 141 and nn.
  advice on copyright of deceased authors v. 155, 164, 169 and n.
  and Charity Books v. 189–90, 191
  as literary executors vi. 17 and n.
  deputation and address on TH's 80th birthday vi. 18, 21, 36 n., 37 and n.
  and Alexandra Memorial vii. 5 and n.
  See also Besant, Walter; Sprigge, Samuel S.; Thring, George H.
Incorporated Stage Society ii. 269, 271 n.
Independent (New York) i. 132, 137, 138, 141 and n.; ii. 197, 198 n., 205, 265 n.; vii. 98
  'Emmeline, or Passion versus Principle' pub. in i. 132 n.; vii. 99 n.
  'The Doctor's Legend' pub. in i. 219 ('short story'), 220 n.
  on purchase of land for Max Gate ii. 66 ('tale'), 67 n.
Independent, The (projected magazine) ii. 6 and n.
Independent Review iii. 168
Independent Theatre i. 195 n., 213 n.
Indergand, Rosine vii. 45, 46 n.
Indian Mutiny iv. 232

'Indiscretion in the Life of an Heiress, An' (story) iv. 306
  pub. in *New Quarterly* i. 57 ('the story') and n., 61 n.; iv. 306 n.; vii. 91 ('the story') and n.
  American publication i. 58 and n.
Inge, Very Revd William Ralph vi. 36
  Outspoken Essays vi. 36 n.
Inglis, Ethel (Mrs H.A.) v. 115 n., 193
Inglis, Colonel Henry Alves v. 115 and n.
Ingpen, Roger vi. 101 nn., 202 n.
  gift of Shelley's *Epipsychidion* to TH vi. 148 and n.
  letters to vi. 100, 148
Innes, A. Mitchell vi. 85 ('Bedford gentleman'), 86 n.
Insel-Verlag (Leipzig publisher) vii. 74 n.
Institute of Journalists iii. 34 n.
  visit to Dorset and Max Gate iii. 176, 177 n.; vii. 140–1
  annual dinner (1906) iii. 197 and n.
Inter-Allied Commission of Control vi. 31 n., 79 ('Berlin business'), 80 n.
Interlaken ii. 166, 168
'Interlopers at the Knap' (story) iv. 164 and n.; vii. 100 ('little story') and n.
  pub. in *English Illustrated* i. 125 ('a story') and n.
International Anti-Vivisection and Animal Protection Congress (London 1909) iv. 34, 35 n.
International Arbitration League iv. 162 n.
International Congress on Motion Picture Arts (1923) vi. 194 and n.
International Exhibitions (1851) vi. 95 n.; (1862) i. 1, 2 n.; vi. 95 n.
International Magazine Co. vi. 121 n., 241 n.
International Monthly ii. 300 and n.
International Parliamentary Union iii. 217 n.
International Story Company vi. 165 nn.
International Woman Suffrage Alliance iv. 21 n.
Iowa State Historical Department vii. 112 n.
Ireland, Richard v. 125 n.
Irish Home Rule v. 29, 38 and n.; vii. 124 n.
Irish Peace Agreement (1921) vi. 111 n.
Irving, (Sir) Henry i. 105 n., 227; ii. 147; iii. 185 n., 259 n.; iv. 26
  farewell performance ii. 22, 23 n., 27
  as Coriolanus ii. 285 n.
  letter to i. 104
Irving, Henry Brodribb iii. 209 n.
Isbister, William (publisher) i. 66 n.; vi. 333 and n.
  letters to i. 66; vii. 92
'Isle of Slingers' ii. 152, 155
  Portland as ii. 152 n.

Ismay, James Hainsworth vi. 247 n.
  letter to vi. 247
Iwerne Minster (Dorset) vi. 248 n.
Iyer, N. R. Harihara vi. 306 ('Indian schoolmaster'), 307 n.

Jacks, Lawrence Pearsall:
  Mad Shepherds, and Other Human Studies iv. 111 and n.
Jackson, Thomas G. v. 296 n.
Jacob family (Lower Bockhampton) vi. 71, 72 n.
James (Max Gate gardener) ii. 271 and n.
James, Henry i. 147, 287; ii. 148, 161 n.; iii. 90 and n., 127 n., 184, 325; vi. 92, 93 n., 275, 276 n.; vii. 106 n., 172
  'appreciation' of Gissing ii. 187 and n.
  in protest to *Spectator* iv. 158, 159 n.
  protest v. play censorship iv. 202, 203 n.
  illnesses iv. 281 and n.; v. 140 and n., 141
  naturalization v. 126 and n., 141
  appointment to Order of Merit v. 126 n., 141 and n.
  Notes on Novelists v. 130 and n.
  The Wings of the Dove iii. 55, 56 n.
  'The Younger Generation' v. 21 and n.
  letters to v. 117, 141
James, Montague Rhodes iv. 320 ('Vice-Chancellor's'), 321 n.
  as Provost of Eton v. 280 ('undertaking') and n.
  Ghost-stories of an Antiquary iv. 320, 321 n.
  More Ghost Stories of an Antiquary iv. 320, 321 n.
  letter to v. 280
Jane (Max Gate servant) iii. 333, 334 n., 340, 347
Jarvis, C. W. i. 195 nn., 213 n.
  dramatization of *Woodlanders* i. 195 and n., 196, 210, 212; vii. 114 n.
  letters to i. 195, 210, 212; vii. 114
Jefferies, Richard:
  Amaryllis at the Fair iii. 147 ('the book'), 148 nn.
Jeffrey, Francis v. 174 and n.
Jeffreys, George, Lord vii. 17 and n.
Jelf, Richard William vii. 30, 31 n.
Jennings, Louis John i. 31 n.
  letter to i. 31
Jerome, Jerome Klapka ii. 50 n.
  letters to ii. 50, 62
Jerrold, Walter Copeland iii. 219 n.
  (ed.) *The Book of Living Poets* iii. 219 n.
  letter to iii. 219
Jersey (C.I.):
  Hardy ancestors in iii. 235; iv. 188; v. 118; vi. 182 and n., 184

Jersey Morning News vi. 182 and n.

Jeune, Christian Francis Seaforth iii. 3 and n., 114
  death iii. 135 and n., 167

Jeune, Sir Francis Henry (later Baron St Helier, q.v.) i. 144 n., 227, 234 n.*; ii. 23 n., 27, 74 n., 110, 137, 156 ('the President') and n., 207, 229; iii. 2 n.; vi. 166 n.; vii. 121, 122 n.
  letter to i. 234

Jeune, John Frederic Symons vi. 35 n., 127, 140 n., 164 n.*, 166, 188 n., 237, 273, 338; vi. 29, 93, 110, 115
  invited to Max Gate v. 225
  books inscribed by TH for v. 259, 261 n.
  gift of Gosse's *Swinburne* to TH v. 261 and nn.
  letters to v. 164, 188, 225, 259, 261

Jeune, Mary (later Lady, then Lady St Helier, q.v.) i. 133, 144 n.*, 213, 215, 256; ii. 2 and n., 17 n., 35, 72, 73, 79 n., 84, 109, 119, 137, 149, 174 n., 205, 208, 220 n., 229 ('M.J.'), 242, 256 n.; iii. 2 n., 3 ('Lady J.'), 114; vi. 166 n.
  copy of *Mayor of Casterbridge* sent to i. 143
  as hostess i. 166, 222 and n., 223, 224, 227, 262, 269, 270, 272, 289 n.; ii. 16, 18, 22, 25, 26, 27, 34, 36, 47, 52–3, 74, 83, 112; iii. 3, 65, 66 ('friends in Harley Street') and n.
  Holiday Fund for City Children i. 213 n., 214 and n., 215
  as journalist i. 234, 235 n.; ii. 40, 41 n., 69 and n., 169, 237
  defence of *Life's Little Ironies* ii. 56 and nn.
  and *Tess* dramatization ii. 110, 111
  and Woman's Exhibition ii. 254 n.
  Memories of Fifty Years ii. 69 n.
  letters to i. 143; ii. 56, 97, 111, 112, 116, 147, 148, 156, 159, 171, 173, 186, 206, 237

Jewett, Sarah:
  The Country of the Pointed Firs iii. 148 n.

Jewish Board of Deputies vi. 63 n.

'Jezreel' (poem) v. 281, 282
  pub. in *Times* v. 281 n.

'Jingle on the Times, A' (poem) v. 322 n.

Jochumsson, Matthias:
  1616–1916 v. 197 ('Icelandic poem') and n.

Jockey Club ii. 228 n.

John (Max Gate 'man') ii. 76, 77 and n.

John, Augustus v. 221, 222 n.; vi. 150 n.
  portrait of TH vi. 231 n., 247 ('the portrait'), 248 n.

John, Sir William Goscombe vi. 45 n.

John o' London's Weekly vi. 346 n.
  serialization of *Tess* vi. 356 and nn., 363 ('the Cheque') and nn.; vii. 35 and n.

series of TH poems vii. 57, 58 n., 60, 76

Johnson, Alfred C. i. 45 n.

Johnson, Austen H. v. 346, 347 n.

Johnson, Lionel Pigot ii. 122, 206 n.
  and *Wessex Poems* ii. 212
  The Art of Thomas Hardy i. 239 n., 275 n., 284, 285 n.; ii. 20 n., 61 n., 62 n., 64, 101 n., 115 n.; iii. 70 ('Johnson's Book'), 71 n.; iv. 328 ('Johnson's book') and nn.; v. 5 ('Johnson's book'), 6 n.; vi. 140 and n., 141 n., 145, 207; vii. 134 and n., 137
  letter to ii. 212

Johnson, Dr Samuel iv. 60

Jones, Mrs Doyle – *see* Gribble, Vivien

Jones, Frederick Warner (dental surgeon) v. 110, 111 nn.

Jones, Professor Henry iv. 62 n.
  letter to iv. 62

Jones, Henry Arthur ii. 30, 31 n.*, 149, 150 n.
  and Society of Authors iv. 53 and n.
  and play censorship iv. 53 and n.
  and *Tess* play vi. 351
  misunderstanding over National Theatre vii. 13 and n., 136 n.
  ill-health vii. 13 and n., 87, 88 n.
  public recognition sought for vii. 87, 88 n.
  The Case of Rebellious Susan iv. 98 and n.; vi. 351, 352 n.
  The Dancing Girl vii. 122 n.
  The Masqueraders ii. 58 and n.
  The Tempter ii. 30, 31 and n.
  letters to ii. 31, 58, 113, 147; iii. 209; iv. 53, 98; vi. 351; vii. 13

Jones, J. B. iv. 64 n.

Jones, John Winter vii. 90 n.
  letter to vii. 90

Jonson, Ben vii. 49 and n.

Jose, John v. 81 and n.

Journal des Débats iii. 290 ('des Débats'), 291 n.; iv. 52, 53 n.
  serialization of *Tess* ii. 164 and n., 165, 273
  'Tragedy of Two Ambitions' and 'Tony Kytes' pub. in ii. 224 and n., 225 ('short stories')

Journal of Education i. 117 n.; v. 196 and n.

Jowett, Benjamin iii. 133, 134 n.

Joyce, James vi. 90 n.

Joyce, Thomas Heath ii. 303 and n.; iii. 119 n.
  letter to iii. 119

Jude the Obscure (novel) ii. 87 and n., 173; iv. 167 n.; vii. 48 and n.
  part prototype of Jude i. 92 n.
  writing of ii. 32 ('the next long story'), 33 n., 38 ('coming long story') and n., 42 ('the story') and n., 47 ('the long story'), 63 ('serial story'), 68 ('story . . . for Harpers'), 69 n., 70, 102

Jude the Obscure (cont.)

  background and originals of places ii. 86, 87,
    132, 133; iii. 226 n.
  and 'marriage question' ii. 92, 93, 97, 98, 99;
    iii. 144
  'grimy' features of ii. 93, 94 n., 105
  'Jude at the Milestone' illus. ii. 94 and n.
  pig-killing scene ii. 94, 95 n., 97, 100, 136;
    iv. 170 n.
  corrections to ii. 98, 100, 183 and n.; iii. 27
  Bishop's burning of ii. 125, 219; iv. 28, 29 n.
  dialect in ii. 168 n.; iii. 124 and n.
  quotations in iii. 133 and n.; vi. 101 and n.,
    202 n.
  film rights v. 97, 254 and n., 335
  alleged autobiography vi. 16, 154, 208
  Canadian rights vi. 65, 81, 87, 88
  CRITICAL RECEPTION:
    ii. 92–5, 96, 97–9, 100, 103 and nn.,
      104–5, 106, 110, 111 n., 122, 123 and
      n., 125, 126, 219; iii. 43 ('book of
      mine'), 44 n., 133 n.; iv. 28, 29 n., 33;
      vii. 128 and n.
  DRAMATIZATIONS:
    Ervine attempted vii. 19 and n., 38, 41,
      42 n.
    French proposed vi. 173, 174 n.
  EDITIONS:
    American ii. 103 and nn.; iv. 299, 300 n.
    Colonial ii. 88 and nn.
    first ii. 90 ('the book') and n., 91 and n.,
      92–4
    Wessex iv. 171 and n., 209 and n., 214
    'Wessex Novels' ii. 69 n.
  SERIALIZATION:
    ii. 46 and n., 55 n., 68, 69, 90 n., 101 and
      n., 105, 106
  TRANSLATIONS:
    Czech vii. 52 and n., 55, 61
    French ii. 164, 171, 175, 177, 273, 274 n.,
      282 n.; iii. 228 n.; vi. 64, 65 n.
    German iii. 56, 222 and nn., 248
    Spanish proposed v. 278, 279 and n.
Judge, Max iii. 345 nn.
  letter to iii. 345
Jullien, Jean v. 178 n.
  letter to v. 178
Junior Carlton Club i. 171, 172 n.
Jutland, Battle of (1916) v. 163 ('naval battle')
  and n., 164 n.
Juvenal:
  Satires vii. 136 and n.

Kahle, (?) Bernard iv. 73 and n.
Kamenka, Alexandre vi. 196 n.
'King's Soliloquy, A' (poem) vi. 149
Kant, Immanuel v. 50, 51 n.

Kardo-Sysoeva, V. ii. 121 n.
Karrakis, Samuel vi. 311 n.
  letter to vi. 310
Kauser, Alice v. 83, 84 nn., 98 n.
Kean, Edmund iii. 19, 20 n.; vi. 248 and n.
Kean, Howard vi. 248 ('boy at his back') and n.
Keary, Charles F. ii. 29 n.
  The Two Lancrofts ii. 29, 40
Keates, William:
  supposed original of Reuben Dewy v. 31 n.
Keats, John i. 264; ii. 300; v. 90; vi. 203, 262
  and n.
  grave of i. 163 and n.
  possible Dorset visit v. 31 and n., 40 n.
  Colvin's *Life* of v. 31 n., 90 and n., 248 and
    n., 253, 254 n.; vi. 203 n.
  Lamia first edn presented to TH vi. 84,
    85 n., 88, 90 and nn., 100 and n.
  Lowell's *Life* of vi. 229, 230 n., 313 and nn.
Keats-Shelley Memorial Association iii.
  200 n.; vii. 142 n.
Keats-Shelley Memorial Fund iii. 200 and n.,
  249 n.
Keeble, Sir Frederick William vii. 77 n., 84 n.
Keeble, Lady (formerly Lillah McCarthy,
  q.v.) vii. 77 nn., 82 n., 84 n.
  letters to vii. 77, 82, 84
Keene, Charles Samuel i. 66 and n.; v. 145 n.
Kegan Paul, Trench, Trübner, & Co.
  (publishers):
  edn of Barnes's poems iii. 292, 293 n., 297,
    301, 302 n., 307, 336, 338, 340, 341 n.,
    342 and n., 348, 349 n., 351 n.; vi. 237
  See also Paul, Charles Kegan
Kelmscott Press iv. 178 n., 179 n.
Kelso i. 243
Kendal, (Dame) Madge i. 101 and n.
Kendal, William Hunter i. 101 n., 103 ('K.')
  and n.
Kennard, Anne (Nina H. Kennard) ii. 27
  and n.
Kennedy, Arthur John Clark vi. 331 n.
  Winter Nights vi. 331 and n.
  letter to vi. 331
Kennedy, Hugh Arthur:
  dramatization of *Tess* ii. 239 and n.; vii. 133
    and n.
Kensal Green Cemetery i. 269 n.
Kensington (now Victoria and Albert)
  Museum i. 1, 2 n.
Kensington Parish Church iii. 325 n.
Kent, Victoria of Saxe-Coburg, Duchess of vi.
  84 and n.
Kent, Rockwell v. 319 and n.; vi. 113 n.
Kenyon, Sir Frederic George iv. 192 and n.
Kenyon, John Samuel vii. 68 nn.
  letter to vii. 68

Ker, W. P.:
   Epic and Romance ii. 160
Kernahan, Coulson v. 219 n.; vi. 370 ('a study'), 371 n.
   In Good Company v. 219 ('pleasant book') and n.
   letter to v. 219
Kerr, Elias William (mayor of Dorchester) iii. 17 n.
   letter to iii. 17
Kerrison, Lady vi. 132 n.
Ketteringham, H. vi. 359 n.
   letter to vi. 359
Key, Revd Samuel Whittell iii. 110 n.
   letter to iii. 110
Keynes, John Maynard:
   The Economic Consequences of the Peace vii. 169 n.
Kibbey, Albert vii. 25 and n.
Kidd, Revd Beresford James vi. 55 ('his successor'), 56 n.
Kiddleywinkempoops (Max Gate cat) (also known as Trot) i. 217
Kiedrich (? Kiedrecht) ii. 87
Kinden, Charles William iii. 340 and n.
Kinden, William vii. 56 n.
Kinden, Mrs William iv. 113 and n.; vii. 56 n.
Kindersley, Edward Leigh ii. 53 and n.
King, Henry (Brighton lodging-house keeper) ii. 118 n.
King, Henry S. (publisher) i. 45 n., 48 n.; vii. 165 n.
King, R. Ashe iv. 11 and n.; vii. 148 n.
'King's Bere':
   Bere Regis as i. 274; ii. 133; vii. 122
King's College (London):
   French class at i. 6; vii. 30, 31 n.
   annual dinner vii. 50, 51 n.
King's Own Scottish Borderers v. 90, 91
King's Theatre, Hammersmith iii. 151 n.
Kingdon, H. Napier ii. 226 ('preparatory school'), 227 n.
Kingman, Francis (dairyman) ii. 272, 273 n.
Kingsley, Charles i. 186 and n., 264 n.
Kingston Lacy (Dorset) ii. 230 and n.
Kingston Maurward (Dorset) ii. 179 n.; vi. 110
Kingston Maurward House (Dorset) v. 35 and n., 125, 127, 177 n., 225 and nn., 288 n., 326 n.; vi. 4 n., 135 n.
   'In Her Precincts' associated with v. 225 ('a poem') and n.
   previous owners v. 225 and n.
Kingston Russell House (Dorset) vi. 294 and n., 297
Kingsway Theatre:
   Dynasts prod. at v. 51 ('your theatre') and

n., 57 and n., 59, 60, 62, 63, 64–5, 68, 69, 70, 112, 130, 131 n.; vii. 158 n.
Kinloch-Cooke, Clement ii. 8 n.
   letter to ii. 7
(?) Kinross, Albert vii. 134 n.
   letter to vii. 134
Kipling, John Lockwood i. 233
Kipling, Rudyard i. 232, 233; ii. 44, 185 and n.; iii. 90 and n.; iv. 150, 151 n.; v. 173 n., 304; vi. 262 n., 370 n.
   search for Dorset home ii. 181 and n.
   awarded Nobel Prize for Literature iii. 288 and n.
   'Bombay' edn v. 36, 37 n.
   'The Brushwood Boy' iv. 154 ('modern story'), 155 n.
   The Courting of Dinah Shadd and Other Stories i. 219 n.
   'Recessional' iii. 11 n.
   'The Rhyme of the Three Captains' i. 219 n., 223 ('a ballad')
   'They' iv. 303 and n.
   Traffics and Discoveries iv. 303 n.
Kirby, J. W. vi. 352 n.
Kitchener, Field Marshal Lord v. 50 n., 164 n.
Kitsey (Max Gate cat) iii. 333, 334 n., 335, 339, 340, 343
   death iv. 132 and n.
Kitton, Frederic George ii. 301 n.
   edn of Dickens ii. 301 and n.
   edn of Thackeray iii. 2 and n.
   letters to ii. 301; iii. 2
Knapp, William iii. 286 and n.
Knebworth (Herts) vii. 107, 108 n.
Knight, Joseph Philip v. 350, 351 n.
Knight, William Angus i. 21 and n.
Knopf, Alfred A. (publisher) vi. 202 n.
'Knollsea':
   Swanage as ii. 132
Knollys, Francis (later Viscount) i. 98 n.
   letter to i. 98
Knowles, Sir James Thomas iii. 117 n.
   letters to iii. 117–18
Koczwara, František:
   The Battle of Prague v. 352, 353 n.
Kruger, Stephanus Johannes Paulus ii. 248, 249 n.
Krupp, Alfred vii. 158, 159 n.
Kubelik, Jan ii. 285 n., 288
Kubin, Alfred vii. 74 n.
Kuo Yu Shou vii. 79, 80 nn.
Kut-el-Amara, siege of (1916) v. 168 and n.
Kuypers, Dom A. B.:
   (ed.) *The Prayer Book of Aedeluald the Bishop, commonly called The Book of Cerne* ii. 268 and n.

La Haye Sainte vii. 20 n.
Lacey, Charles ii. 237 n.
  letters to ii. 237; v. 210; vi. 228; vii. 62, 83
'Lacking Sense, The' (poem) iii. 137
Ladies' Home Journal i. 290 n.
'Lady Icenway, The' (story) iv. 175 n.
'Lady Mottisfont' (story) iv. 175 nn., 220 n.
'Lady Penelope, The' (story) ii. 131
Lady's Realm ii. 196 and n.
Lafayette (Dublin photographer) ii. 40, 41 n.
Laffan, William Mackay i. 112 and n., 269
Lamb, Charles vii. 22 n., 86 and n.
Lamb, Henry vi. 150 n.
Lambert, E. Frank iv. 132 and n.
Lancaster, Charles William i. 98 n.
Land & Water v. 187 and n., 226 n.
Landor, Walter Savage:
  *An Address to the Fellows of Trinity College,
    Oxford on the Alarm of Invasion* v. 203 n.
Lane, Edgar Alfred (Dorchester musician):
  sets Barnes poems to music iii. 23 and n.
  rents house from TH iii. 23 n., 29 and n., 36,
    78, 158, 167 and n.
  sets 'Song of the Soldiers' to music v. 48, 49
    and n., 58 n., 63
  letters to iii. 23, 29, 36, 78, 158, 167; v. 48,
    63
Lane, John (publisher) i. 239 n.*; ii. 197 and
    n., 198, 304 n.; iii. 65, 135, 174 n., 267,
    285; vii. 48 n., 137, 147 nn., 156 and
    n.
  bibliography of TH's first edns i. 239 and n.,
    256, 281; ii. 19, 20 n.; iii. 70, 71 n.; iv.
    98 n.; vii. 134 and n.
  and publication of Sudermann novel iv. 131
    and n., 133 and n.
  projected book on Alfred Stevens iv. 288,
    289 n., 290, 292
  death vi. 308, 309 n.
  letters to i. 239, 256, 270, 275, 276, 278, 280,
    281, 284; ii. 19, 49, 50, 51, 61–2, 65; iii.
    52, 64, 70, 72, 174, 318, 330, 362, 363; iv.
    53, 97, 131, 228, 288, 290, 326, 328; v. 5;
    vi. 25, 140; vii. 147
Lane, Mrs John (Annie Eichberg) ii. 197 ('lady
    he is to marry'), 198 n.; iii. 64, 65, 136,
    267
  Kitwyk iii. 52 and n.
  'Toothpowder or Gunpowder' iii. 174 and n.
  letter to vi. 308
Lang, Andrew i. 146 n.; vi. 370 n.; vii. 111 n.
  on *Tess* i. 257 and n.; ii. 62 and n.
  letter to i. 146
Lang, John Marshall iii. 160 and n., 161, 278
  (?) letter to vii. 168
Langbridge, Revd Frederick iii. 203 n.
  letter to iii. 203

Langdon-Davies, John vi. 163 n.
  letter to vi. 163
Lange, Wilhelm i. 43 and n.
Langton Matravers (Dorset) iii. 261 n.
Lanhydrock (Cornwall) vi. 29, 30 n.
Lanivet (Cornwall) v. 246 n.
Lanoire, Maurice iv. 53 n.
  on *Dynasts* iv. 52, 53 nn.
  letter to iv. 52
Lansade, Magdelaine de:
  translates stories from *A Changed Man* v. 24,
    33 and n.
Lansbury, George v. 88 n.
Laodicean, A (novel) vi. 15 and n., 214 n.
  projected German translation i. 98 and n.
  critical reception i. 100 n.; ii. 25; vii. 93,
    94 n.
  alleged plagiarism in i. 103 and n.
  composition ii. 23, 25; v. 237
  original of Castle De Stancy ii. 133
  EDITIONS:
    American i. 94 and n.
    first (three-vol.) i. 94 and n., 97 ('my
      story') and n.
    one-vol. edn ii. 23 n.
    Tauchnitz i. 82 and n., 102 and n.
  SERIALIZATIONS:
    in *Harper's New Monthly Magazine* i.
      64 n., 72 and n., 73, 76–7, 79, 80–1,
      82–3, 84, 85, 86–9, 91, 93, 94; vii. 94 n.
    Du Maurier illustrations i. 71 n., 72, 73–
      5, 76, 77, 79, 80 and n.; ii. 135 n.
    Australian i. 75 and n., 91 and n.
Larbaud, Valery iii. 352 n.
  letter to iii. 351
Larner, Miss A. A. ('Guss') iv. 9 ('Clodd's
    loss'), 12 ('your sad loss') and n.
Lascelles, Lord Henry George Charles (later
    6th Earl of Harewood) vi. 120 n.
Laski, Harold Joseph vii. 25 nn.
  letter to vii. 24
Lasselin, Georges vii. 85 nn.
  *Le Couple humain dans l'oeuvre de Thomas
    Hardy* vii. 85 n.
  letter to vii. 85
Last, Isaac Glandfield (Dorchester school-
    master) ii. 237 n.; vi. 3, 4 n.
'Last Leaf, The' (poem) vi. 241
  pub. in *Nash's and Pall Mall* vi. 242 n.
'Last Leaving, A' (poem) vii. 170 n.
Late Lyrics and Earlier (poems) vi. 101 n.,
    112 n., 151 n., 152, 153 n., 179 ('the
    volume') and n., 218 n.; vii. 54 n.
  preparation of vi. 104 ('other poems'), 108
    ('new poems'), 115 ('stray verses'), 116–
    19, 121–2, 124, 130
  publication vi. 105 n., 112 n., 113 ('print

Late Lyrics and Earlier (*cont.*)
them') and n., 118, 119 n., 128, 129 n., 131 ('the book') and n., 132 and n., 133 and n.
'Apology' vi. 116–18, 138, 162, 223 n.
critical reception vi. 137 nn., 162 ('Poems'), 163 n., 177 n.
included in *Collected Poems* vi. 164 and n., 170
corrections to Wessex Edn vi. 361 n.; vii. 2 and n., 3 and n., 8
Later Years of Thomas Hardy (prose) v. 332 n., 345 n.
Latey, John Lash i. 53 n.
letter to i. 53
Latimer (customs-officer) iv. 190
Launceston (Cornwall) v. 124, 125 n., 177
Laurie, Annie vii. 70, 71 n., 80
Lausanne ii. 167, 168; v. 152
Lawrence, Harry Tom (police superintendent) vii. 67 nn.
letter to vii. 67
Lawrence, Thomas Edward ('Lawrence of Arabia') vi. 291 and n.; vii. 51 ('Another friend') and n.
Lawson, Sir Edward Levy- ii. 53 and n.
Lawson, Victor Fremont vii. 23 and n.
Lawton, Frederick iii. 212 n.
Le Gallienne, Richard Thomas ii. 115 n.
George Meredith: Some Characteristics i. 239 n.
Prose Fancies ii. 125 ('your little book') and n.
Retrospective Reviews ii. 115 and n.
letters to ii. 115, 125
Lea, Hermann ii. 232 n.*, 279 n.; v. 51 n., 61; vi. 38 n., 226
photographs of TH iii. 33 and n., 97 n., 140, 160; iv. 293 and n.; v. 312 and n.
and 'Wessex novels' picture postcards iii. 109 and n., 112 and n., 160, 164 and n., 168
photograph of portrait of TH's mother iii. 116, 118, 120, 122
invited to Max Gate iii. 116, 149, 160; iv. 148, 169, 179, 226
'little story' iii. 122 and n.
choice of house name iii. 200 and n.
photographs of TH's portrait iii. 252, 254
photographic frontispieces for Wessex Edn iv. 204 n., 205 and n., 220 and n., 302 and n., 303, 304; v. 304
as occupant of TH's birthplace iv. 286 n., 296 n.
photographs of Max Gate iv. 293 and n.
photographs for Autograph Edn iv. 324 and n.
photograph of FEH v. 83 n., 104

takes TH on car drives v. 116 and n.
A Handbook to the Wessex Country of Thomas Hardy's Novels and Poems iii. 138 n., 140, 146 ('the MS.'), 149 ('your tours'), 170 ('little book'), 171–2, 173; iv. 135 and n., 136 and n., 137
'Some Dorset Superstitions' iii. 264 ('witch stories'), 265 nn.
Thomas Hardy's Wessex iv. 164 n., 169 ('notes'), 173 ('the book'), 179 ('typoscript'), 223 ('Guide book') and n., 263 ('typoscript') and n., 264 ('guide book'), 280 ('Guide Book') and n., 286 and nn., 293 and n., 294 and nn., 295 ('guide book'); v. 94, 95; vi. 78 ('T.H.'s W.') and n., 163, 278 ('your volume') and n., 281 and n.; vii. 2 ('Mr Lea's book'), 3 n., 24, 163
'Wessex Witches, Witchery, and Witchcraft' iii. 47 and n.
letters to ii. 232, 294; iii. 32, 33, 47, 109, 111, 112, 116, 118, 120, 122, 137, 140–1, 145–6, 148, 149, 160, 164, 168, 170, 171, 173, 200, 252, 254, 264; iv. 138, 140, 148, 164, 169, 173, 175, 179, 205, 206, 220, 223, 226, 263, 264, 280, 286, 293, 294, 295, 302, 304; v. 83; vi. 278, 281
'Leader of Fashion, A' (poem):
pub. in *Adelphi* vi. 200 n.
League of Nations v. 288; vi. 247
'League of Thinkers' (proposed) vii. 162 and n.
League of Youth vi. 52 n.
Leake, Désirée Mary vii. 129 n.
letter to vii. 129
Leathes, Stanley Mordaunt v. 141 n.
and Charity Books v. 192 n.
letter to v. 191
Lecture Agency, Ltd. iii. 362, 363 n.; v. 18 n.
lecturing, attitude to i. 143; ii. 36; iii. 211, 215; v. 130, 352; vii. 135
Lee, Henry William vii. 1 n.
letter to vii. 1
Lee, John T. (architect):
as former colleague of TH i. 3 n., 4 and n., 5, 6 n.; v. 14 and n.; vii. 43 and n.
Lee, (Sir) Sidney iii. 237 n., 317; vi. 255
letters to iii. 237; iv. 46
'Lee, Vernon' (Violet Paget) iii. 177, 178 n.
'Of Hardy and Meredith' iii. 178 n.
Lee-on-Solent (Hants) ii. 271 n.
Leeds Mercury iii. 85 n.
Lees, Sir Elliott iii. 347 and n.
Lefèvre, Frédéric vi. 163 n., 304, 305 n.
Leftwich, Ralph Winnington iii. 358 n.
A Shakespeare Commemoration for London iii. 358 and n.

Leftwich, Ralph (cont.)
letter to iii. 357
'Legend of the Year Eighteen Hundred and
Four, A' (later 'A Tradition of Eighteen
Hundred and Four', q.v.) (story):
pub. in *Harper's Christmas* i. 106 n., 112
and n.
Legitimation League ii. 160 and n.
Leicester, Revd William Henry vi. 28 n.
Leighton, Clare vii. 87 ('lady you mention')
and n.
Leighton, Frederic, 1st Lord:
funeral ii. 108, 109 and n.
'Leipzig' (poem) v. 246
illustration for iii. 61, 62 n., 100 and n.
Leipzig, Battle of (1813):
in *Dynasts* ii. 233 and n.; vi. 161
Lemperly, Paul iv. 70 n.; vi. 328 n.
letters to iv. 69; vi. 327
Lenz, Maximilian:
Napoleon: a Biographical Study iii. 271
and n.
Leslie, Lady Constance Wilhelmina Frances
iii. 344 and n., 363; iv. 227 n.
letter to iv. 226
Leslie, Revd Edward Charles iii. 344 and n.;
iv. 202 n.; v. 72 n.
letter to v. 71
Leslie, Mrs E. C. (Margaret Moule) iii. 344
and n.; iv. 202 and n.; v. 72 n.
Leslie, Fred vii. 121, 122 n.
(co-author) *Cinderellen Up Too Late* vii.
122 nn.
Lesnewth (Cornwall) vi. 29, 30 n., 258
as 'East Endelstow' vi. 29
'Let Me Enjoy' (poem) iv. 67; v. 259 n.; vi. 149
pub. in *Cornhill* iv. 8 ('my little song'), 9 n.
Letters on the War (pamphlet) v. 58 n.
'Levelled Churchyard, The' (poem) iii. 227 n.
Levine, Isaac:
sets 'To Life' to music iv. 139, 166, 167 n.
letters to iv. 139, 166
Lewis, (Sir) George Henry i. 100 and n.; ii.
146 n.
Lewis, Lady (Elizabeth) ii. 146 n.; iii. 49 and
n.; iv. 153 and n.
Lewis, M. G.:
'The Banks of Allan Water' i. 18 n.
Library Review i. 260 n., 265 and n.
Lichfield Cathedral iv. 148 n., 152 n.
Lieber, Maxim vi. 372 n.
Liège ii. 130
'Life and Work of Thomas Hardy, The' (prose)
v. 332 n.
Life's Little Ironies (stories) i. 106 n., 217 n.;
ii. 38 n., 45 ('my proofs'), 46 n., 53 n.,
55 n., 115 n.; iii. 226 n., 319 n.; vi. 251,

252 n.; vii. 76 n., 126 ('my book') and
n.
publication of ii. 43 ('our two volumes'), 44
and n., 45 n., 47 and n., 48, 51, 52 and n.
American edns ii. 44, 45 n., 47 and n., 225
controversy over ii. 56 and nn., 59 n.
proposed translations ii. 120, 121 n.; v. 3 and
n.; vi. 325 and n.
originals of places in ii. 132
French translation of stories from ii. 178,
211, 224 and n., 225, 278; iii. 213
'Wessex Novels' edn iii. 11 n.
MSS given to Manchester iv. 178, 181 and
n., 184
American film rights v. 97
Canadian rights vi. 81, 88
Lily (Max Gate maid) v. 325, 326 n.
Lincoln iii. 224; v. 95 and n.
Lind-af-Hageby, Lizzy:
(and Leisa K. Schartau) *The Shambles of
Science: Extracts from Two Students of
Physiology* iii. 74, 75 n.
Lindsay, Ruby iii. 211 and n.
'Lines' (poem) v. 249 n.
Ling, Ernest Lorenzo (mayor of Dorchester)
vi. 171 n.
letters to vi. 171, 199
Ling, Henry (Dorchester printer) v. 227,
228 n.
Linton, Eliza Lynn ii. 73 and n.
essays on 'woman question' vii. 111 ('in the
S.R.') and n.
letters to ii. 73; vii. 110
Linton, William James ii. 73 n.
Lippincott Co., J. B. i. 66 n.
letters to i. 65, 97
Lippincott's Magazine i. 65, 66 n.
Lister-Kaye, Lady Beatrice-Adeline vii. 132 n.
letter to vii. 132
Literary Theatre Society iii. 209 n.
Literary World i. 56 and nn., 265 n., 267
Literary Year-Book, 1897 (ed. Aflalo) ii. 148
and n.
Literature ii. 214 and n., 217 n., 223 n., 238,
247, 248 n., 262, 293 and n., 299
Little, Lady Guendolen ii. 19 and n., 22
Little, James Stanley i. 177 n.
and Shelley Memorial v. 28 and nn.
letters to i. 177, 178, 260, 265, 267, 268, 278;
v. 28, 98
'Little Hintock' ii. 132; vii. 24
Little Theatre iv. 324 n., 325; vii. 159 n.
Littlecote House (Wilts) vi. 314 and n.
Litwinski, Dr Leon v. 207 nn.
letter to v. 206
Liverpool:
TH invited to literary dinner iv. 64

Living Nature (proposed Cassell publication) vi. 173 and n.

Llanelwedd (Builth) v. 43 n.

Lloyd's Weekly Newspaper i. 246 n.

local history and traditions, interest in i. 51, 121, 204, 224; ii. 4; iii. 17, 18–20, 28, 48, 93, 124, 156, 195, 241, 264, 285, 286, 289, 359; iv. 76, 77, 80, 135–6, 147, 154, 186, 190, 206; v. 102, 183–4, 244, 269; vi. 131, 171

Locarno, Pact of (1925) vii. 3 n.

Lock, Arthur Cuthbert v. 165 n.

Lock, Arthur Henry (Dorchester solicitor) i. 73 and n.; ii. 272, 273 n.; iii. 245 n.; v. 16 n.

Lock, Benjamin Fossett v. 165 and n.; vi. 364 and n.

Lock, Emma (Mrs A. C. Lock) iv. 241 n.; v. 16 and n., 142 ('your mother'), 143 n.
    letter to iv. 241

Lock, Eveline Mary (later Mrs Ryle Swift) iii. 356 n.; v. 143 n.

Lock, Francis (Dorchester postmaster) i. 4 and n.

Lock, Francis William i. 3 and n.

Lock, Henry Osmond (Dorchester solicitor) iii. 356 n.; iv. 11 n.*, 241 and n.; vii. 148 n.
    and TH's second marriage v. 16
    war service v. 142 and n.
    letters to iv. 11; v. 16, 142; vii. 26, 28, 148

Lock, Joseph Marvin (Dorchester butcher and coal merchant) iv. 76, 77 n.

Lock, Reginald (Dorchester butcher and coal merchant) iv. 76, 77 n.

Lock, Revd Walter iii. 245 and n.; vi. 55 ('former Warden of Keble'), 56 n.
    Personal Religion vi. 363 ('booklet'), 364 n.
    letter to vi. 363

Lock, Reed, and Lock (Dorchester solicitors) iii. 167 and n.; vi. 143 n.

Locke, William John ii. 182 n.
    The Morals of Marcus Ordeyne iii. 174 and n.
    letter to ii. 182

Locker, Arthur (editor of *Graphic*) i. 115 n., 216 n. (see correction at vii. 172)
    letters to i. 115, 170, 173, 188, 189–90, 198, 201, 202–4, 205, 209–10, 215, 229

Locker (later Locker-Lampson), Frederick i. 69 n., 115 n.; v. 287, 288 n.
    'The Old Stonemason' i. 69
    'Rotten Row' i. 69 and n.
    letter to i. 69

Locker, William Algernon i. 215 ('your son's'), 216 ('your son') and nn. (corrected at vii. 172), 226 n.*, 228 n.
    letters to i. 225, 228

Lockett, William George i. 197 n.; ii. 101 n.; vii. 172
    'Marguerite' ii. 101
    Tragedy of Errors i. 244 and n.; vii. 172
    letters to i. 197, 212, 244, 281; ii. 101, 253

Lockwood, Sir Frank ii. 53 and n.

Lodge, Sir Oliver Joseph v. 191 n.
    Raymond; or, Life and Death v. 191 and n., 192

Lodge, Thomas i. 122

Logan, Alice v. 276, 277 n.

London:
    smallpox epidemic (1902) iii. 9 and n.
    influenza epidemic (1908) iii. 305, 306
    heat wave (1911) iv. 167, 168 n., 172
    air raids during Great War v. 107 n., 114, 124, 176, 232 and n, 249, 254 n.
    public execution of pirates vii. 46 and n.
    preparation for George V's coronation vii. 152 ('timber') and n.
    Abercorn Place, Maida Vale (No. 13) ii. 245 n., 256 ('Maida Vale') and n.; iii. 61 and n., 89, 90, 125 and n., 126 ('up here'), 127 n.; v. 111
    Adelphi Terrace v. 231 and n., 237
        (No. 8) Blomfield office at i. 3 ('new office'), 4 n.; iii. 194 and n.; v. 221 and n., 302 n.; vi. 176, 177 n., 192; vii. 30
    Artillery Mansions, Victoria Street iv. 82
    Arundel Terrace (No. 1), Upper Tooting, i. 79, 82 n.; v. 237
        move to i. 55 n., 56; v. 91 n.
        removal from i. 90, 91, 92; vii. 90
    Ashley Gardens (No. 90) ii. 76 and n.; iv. 85 and n.; vii. 128 n. ('a flat')
    Bedford Place (No. 14), Russell Square i. 145 n.
    Bertolini's Hotel vii. 12 ('Bartolini's'), 13
    Blomfield Court (No. 47), Maida Vale iv. 84–7, 89 ('this flat'), 92, 93, 96 ('a flat'), 97, 98, 102, 105 ('at the flat') and n., 111, 115 ('flat in Maida Vale')
    Bolingbroke Grove (No. 1) i. 53 n.
    Buckingham Gate iv. 82
    Burlington House iii. 65 n.; iv. 151 n.
    Campden Hill iii. 354 and n.
    Campden Hill Road iii. 354 n. (corrected vii. 175)
        (No. 5) i. 165 n.; vii. 50 n., 107 n. *See also* South Lodge
    Celbridge Place (No. 4), Westbourne Park i. 16 n., 24, 31
    Chapel Place (No. 5), Cavendish Square vii. 113, 114 n.
    Charing Cross area, proposed new layout vi. 176 and n.
    Cheyne Gardens (No. 8) iii. 126 and n.

London (cont.)
Cheyne Walk v. 349 n.
Clarence Place (No. 3), Kilburn i. 1 n.
Dorset Street (No. 22 A) v. 211 n.
Earl's Court:
    Woman's Exhibition (1900) ii. 246 ('the
        Exhibition'), 254 and n.
Edwardes Square, Kensington iv. 38 and n.
Farm Street Chapel i. 1 ('Roman Catholic
    Chapel'), 2 n.; vii. 171
Fitzroy Square vi. 281 n.
Gaiety Restaurant iv. 32 n.
Grafton Galleries ii. 171 n.
Great Russell Street (No. 56) i. 134 n.
Grosvenor Place (No. 25) vi. 12 and n.
Hamilton Terrace (No. 70), St John's Wood
    ii. 7 n., 8, 52 and n.; v. 111
Harley Street (No. 79) (Jeunes' house) i.
    261, 262 n., 271 n.; iii. 3, 211 and n.,
    316; vi. 59 and n.; vii. 167 n.
Hertford House ii. 19 and n.
Holland House v. 109 and n.
Hotel Russell v. 92, 93, 137
House of Lords Terrace iii. 131 n.
Hyde Park Mansions (No. 1) iii. 164 n., 166,
    168, 169, 172, 175, 176, 202 and n.,
    203, 208, 251, 254, 263, 321 and n.
Kensington Gore (No. 15) v. 121, 122 n.
Kingsley Hotel ii. 284
Leicester Galleries iii. 173 n.; iv. 265 n.
Mandeville Place (No. 12) i. 234 and n., 235;
    vii. 117 n.
Margaret Street (No. 61) i. 45 n.
Marlborough Place, St John's Wood iii. 259
    and n.
Midland Temperance Hotel ii. 162
Monmouth Road (No. 20), Bayswater i.
    192 n.
Mont Blanc restaurant iii. 279 and n.
Montague Street (No. 23) i. 144; (No. 29) i.
    127 n., 133
New Burlington Street i. 59 and n.
Newton Hall, Fetter Lane i. 134 and n.; vi.
    180 and n.
Newton Road (No. 18), Paddington i. 35 n.,
    36 n.
Old Hummums Hotel, Covent Garden i. 1,
    2 n.
Oxford Terrace (No. 27) ii. 287 and n.,
    289
Pelham Crescent (No. 16) ii. 55 and nn., 76,
    114 and n.; vii. 50 and n., 129 ('used to
    have') and n., 167 and n.
Portland Place iii. 316; v. 108, 109 n.
Quex Road (No. 15), W. Hampstead iv. 82
St Giles Cripplegate vii. 137 n.
St Martin's-in-the-Fields vi. 192, 193 n.

St Martin's Place (No. 8), Charing Cross i.
    3 n.
St Mary's Church, Kilburn i. 1
St Peter's Church, Eaton Square iii. 3 n.
St Peter's Church, Paddington:
    TH married at i. 31 n.
Savoy Hotel iv. 327 n.
Shirley's temperance hotel ii. 284, 285 n.
South Kensington Museum (now Victoria
    and Albert) ii. 55 ('S.K.M.') and n.,
    163; iii. 253; iv. 207 ('S. K. Museum')
    and n.
South Lodge (80 Campden Hill Road) iii.
    128 n.; vii. 148 n.
Stafford House iii. 224, 225 n., 239
    Keats–Shelley exhibition iii. 249 and n.
Stratford Place (No. 13) (Henniker home)
    ii. 202 and n.; iii. 74, 267, 275; v. 30
    and n.
Sussex Place (No. 3) (Henniker home) vi. 10
Temple Church iv. 103 and n.
Thurloe Square iii. 175 and n.
Tufnell Park iv. 32 n.
Upper Bedford Place (No. 28) i. 148 n.
Upper Phillimore Place (No. 5) i. 176 n.
Warwick Crescent (No. 19) v. 211 n.
Waterloo Place (Smith, Elder offices) i. 148
    and n.
West Central Hotel i. 222, 269; ii. 109
    ('W.C.H.') and n., 261, 284, 285,
    286 n.; iii. 88 and n., 310, 316 ('little
    hotel'), 318 ('W. C. Hotel') and n., 321,
    322, 324; iv. 31 ('W.C.H.') and n.; v.
    34; vi. 279 and n.; vii. 152 n.
Westbourne Park Villas (No. 16) i. 7 n.; v.
    211 nn.
Whitehall Court iv. 82
Wimpole Street (No. 37) i. 223 n., 227, 270,
    271 n.
Wynnstay Gardens, Kensington (No. 9) ii.
    192, 193 and n.; (No. 20) ii. 220 and n.,
    221; vii. 50 and n., 131
London Anti-vivisection Society ii. 199 n.; iv.
    90 n.
London Assurance Company vii. 162 n.
London County Council vi. 180, 181 nn.; vii.
    161
London Joint Stock Bank:
    Clodd as Secretary iii. 23 n., 287 n.; iv.
    39 n.; v. 81 n., 139 n.
London Library iii. 186 and n.
London Mercury v. 322 ('this project') and n.,
    338 ('first number'); vi. 121 ('the review')
    and n., 147 n., 165 and n., 202 n., 281 and
    n., 311 and n., 336
    'Going and Staying' pub. in v. 322 ('little
    poem') and n., 330 n.

London Mercury (*cont.*)
'Glimpse from the Train' pub. in v. 330 n.
'The Woman I Met' pub. in vi. 50
'Voices from Things Growing' pub. in vi. 106 and n., 109 and n., 110, 113
'Reprints' vi. 137 and n., 160
'On the Portrait of a Woman about to be Hanged' pub. in vi. 178 n.
'Waiting Both' and 'An East-End Curate' pub. in vi. 242 n., 277 n.
'Cynic's Epitaph' and 'Epitaph on a Pessimist' pub. in vi. 337 n., 340 ('another Epitaph'), 359 ('epigram'), 360 n.
London Pavilion vii. 122 n.
London Quarterly iii. 201 and n.
London Society vii. 50 n.
London Society :
contribution signed 'Thomas Hardy' i. 107 and n., 108
Londonderry, Charles Stewart Vane-Tempest-Stewart, 6th Marquess of ii. 258; iii. 3 ('Lord L.')
Londonderry, Lady (Theresa, widow of 6th Marquess) ii. 22 ('her sister'), 23 n., 52 ('Lady Ly'), 100, 169, 258; iii. 3 ('Lady L.'); v. 266 ('her mother')
Londonderry, Lady (Edith Chaplin, wife of 7th Marquess) v. 166 and n.
Londonderry House iii. 3
Long, Colonel Charles J. ii. 241 and n.
Long, Ray vi. 241 n.
Longfellow, Henry Wadsworth:
'Travels by the Fireside' v. 151 ('poem') and n.
Longman, Charles James (publisher) i. 107 and n., 168 n.; vi. 370 nn.
letters to vi. 370; vii. 106
Longman, Frederick George (Dorchester printer and bookseller) iii. 82, 299, 300 nn.; v. 227, 228 n.
Longman's (publishers) v. 2 and n.
Longman's Magazine i. 107 n., 114 n., 116 n., 119, 140 n., 168 n., 181 n.; ii. 134, 135 n.; iii. 233; vii. 106 n.
'Dorsetshire Labourer' pub. in i. 107 n., 119 and n.; iii. 9; iv. 178
'Withered Arm' rejected by i. 168 n.; vii. 106 n.
'Longpuddle':
originals of ii. 131
Longstreet, Augustus Baldwin:
Georgia Scenes i. 103, 104
Loomis, Roger Sherman vi. 209 n., 232 n.
(trans.) *The Romance of Tristram and Ysolt* vi. 209 ('the book') and n.
letters to vi. 209, 232
Loos, Battle of (1915) v. 133 n.

'Lorna the Second' (poem) iv. 307 n.
'Lost Pyx, The' (poem) ii. 33 n., 305 n.; iii. 93, 94 n., 189
pub. in *Sphere* ii. 275 ('the legend') and n.; iii. 189 n.
Lotus (Clodd's boat) iv. 99 ('Lotos') and n.
Lotus II iv. 219 ('new yacht') and n.
Louis Napoleon (later Napoleon III) iii. 330 and n., 344, 363; vii. 39 and n.
Louvain (Belgium):
destroyed Library of v. 119 and nn., 126
Love, John:
The New Weymouth Guide, or Useful Pocket Companion iii. 359 and n.
Loveday, Thomas vi. 316 n.
letters to vi. 316, 326, 331, 332
Lovelace, Ralph Gordon Noel King Milbanke, 2nd Earl of iv. 40, 41 n.
Loves of the Triangles, The (anon.) ii. 155, 156 n.
Lowe, E. A. vii. 170 n.
Lowell, Amy vi. 38 n., 186 nn., 201; vii. 64 n.
at Max Gate v. 67 and n.
Can Grande's Castle v. 292 ('new book'), 293 n.
John Keats vi. 229 ('Keats book'), 230 n., 313 and nn.
'The Rosebud Wall-paper' vi. 230 and n.
'The Swans' vi. 186 and n.
Sword Blades and Poppy Seed v. 67 and n.
letters to v. 67, 292; vi. 186, 229, 313
Lowell, James Russell i. 80 n.*, 156, 157 n., 177 n., 192 and n.
and proposed Anglo-U.S. copyright treaty i. 79
letter to i. 79
Lowestoft (Suffolk) iii. 242
Lowndes, Frederic Sawrey Archibald iv. 109 n.
letter to iv. 109
Lowndes, Marie Adelaide Belloc iv. 30 n., 89, 109 and n.
Lubbock, Alice, Lady ii. 192 and n.
Lubbock, Sir John ii. 192 n.
Lucas, Edward Verrall v. 252 n.
'At the Pines' v. 157 ('account of his interview'), 158 n.
(ed.) *The Book of the Queen's Dolls' House Library* vi. 193 and n.
(comp.) *The Open Road* ii. 227 ('little book'), 228 ('little book') and n.
letter to v. 252
Lucas, Mrs L. Maud vi. 371 n.
letter to vi. 371
Lucretius:
De Rerum Natura ii. 143 ('Munro's

Lucretius (cont.)
  translation') and n.; iii. 287 and n.; iv. 209
    and n.; v. 233 n.
Lucy, Lady (of Charlecote) iii. 150 and n.
Lucy, (?) Emily Anne ii. 286 ('the Lucys')
Lucy, (?) (Sir) Henry William ii. 286, 287 n.
Ludlow Castle (Salop) ii. 27
Lulham, Edwin Percy Habberton iii. 191 n.
  photographic 'studies' of Tess iv. 134 and n.
  Devices and Desires iii. 190, 191 and n.
  The Other Side of Silence v. 115 and n.
  letters to iii. 191; iv. 134; v. 115
'Lulstead Cove':
  Lulworth Cove as ii. 132
Lulworth, East (Dorset):
  church ii. 175, 176–7
Lulworth Cove iii. 224; iv. 281, 282 n.; v. 31,
    40
  as 'Lulstead Cove' ii. 132
Lutyens, Sir Edwin vi. 136 n.
Lyceum Club iii. 270 n.; iv. 32 and n., 46 n.,
    70 n., 98; vi. 38 and n.
Lyceum Theatre i. 214 and n., 215; ii. 23 n.,
    114 n., 285 n.
Lyme Park (Cheshire) v. 140 n.
Lyme Regis (Dorset) v. 338 n.; vi. 33, 34
'Lyme Regis' (psalm-tune) iii. 285
Lynd, Robert Wilson v. 44 n.; vi. 85 n.
  and *Moments of Vision* v. 318, 319 n.
  Old and New Masters v. 318, 319 n.
  letters to v. 318, 319
Lynmouth (Devon) iv. 168, 169 n.
Lyric Theatre ii. 21 n.; iii. 209 n.
Lyscombe (Dorset) ii. 72 and n.
Lyttelton, Katharine ii. 53 ('Mrs Lyttleton'),
    54 n., 55
Lyttelton, Neville Gerald ii. 53 ('Col. L.'),
    54 n.
Lytton, Edward George Earle Lytton Bulwer-
    Lytton, 1st Baron i. 240 and n.; iii. 250; v.
    292
  The Last of the Barons vii. 158, 159 n.
  Pelham i. 6, 7 n.
Lytton, Edward Robert Bulwer-Lytton, 1st
    Earl of ('Owen Meredith') i. 240 n.
  After Paradise; or, Legends of Exile vii. 107
    ('new volume'), 108 n.
  letters to i. 239; vii. 107

Maartens, Maarten (Joost van der Poorten
    Schwartz) ii. 13, 14 n.; iii. 44 n.
  Harmen Pols, Peasant iv. 126, 127 n.
  letters to iii. 43; iv. 126, 252
MacAlister, George Ian (architect) v. 116,
    117 n.
Macaulay, Thomas Babington, 1st Baron vi. 7
    and n.

Macbeth-Raeburn, Henry Raeburn ii. 65 n.
  as illustrator of 'Wessex Novels' edn ii. 65
    and nn., 70 and n.; iii. 36 n.
  letters to ii. 64, 65, 69
McCabe, Joseph Martin vii. 162 n.
  *Biographical Dictionary of Modern
    Rationalists* vii. 162 n.
  letter to vii. 162
McCall's Magazine:
  'The Midnight Revel' pub. in vi. 271 and nn.
McCarthy, (?) Charlotte vii. 172
  letter to i. 176
MacCarthy, (Sir) Desmond iii. 24 n., 69 n.,
    126 and n., 203 n.*, 217 n.; iv. 327 n.
  recommended by TH to *Outlook* iii. 168
    and n.
  cycling with TH iii. 228; iv. 65
  as editor of *New Quarterly* iii. 276 and n.,
    294, 295 n., 353, 354 n.; iv. 1 and n.
  in protest against play censorship iv. 202,
    203
  letters to iii. 203, 217, 228, 240, 276, 294,
    353; iv. 1, 65, 203
MacCarthy, Lady (Mary Warre-Cornish) iii.
    217 n., 228; iv. 65, 327 n.
McCarthy, Justin ii. 162 n.*, 218, 219 n.,
    225 n.
  Reminiscences ii. 226, 227 and n., 228 n.
  letters to ii. 162; vii. 107
McCarthy, Lillah (later Lady Keeble, q.v.) iv.
    100 nn., 186 n.; v. 112; vi. 124 n.
  letter to iv. 99
MacCarthy, Louise ('Isa') Joanne Wilhelmine
    iii. 69 n., 88 and n., 89, 126 n.
  letters to iii. 69, 121, 152
MacCarthy, Michael iii. 276 ('the baby') and
    n.; vi. 272 n.
McClure, Samuel Sidney i. 217 n.; ii. 240 n.
  letter to i. 216
MacColl, Dugald Sutherland v. 114 n.
MacColl, Norman i. 153 n., 154, 193 n.
  letters to i. 153, 193, 194, 258; iii. 3
McCutcheon, George Barr iv. 222 ('your cor-
    respondent'), 227 n.
Macdonald, Frederick Charles vi. 67 n.
MacDonald, James Ramsay vii. 13 and n.
Macdonald, Lydia (Mrs P. W. Macdonald) iv.
    123 n.
  letter to iv. 123
Macdonald, Dr Peter William iii. 255 nn.; iv.
    123 n.
  letter to iii. 254
Macdonell, Annie ii. 212 n., 213 n.
  Thomas Hardy ii. 64 and n., 101 n.
McDowall, Arthur v. 246 n., 248 n.*
  at Max Gate v. 245 ('Oxford man of letters'),
    246 n., 248 n.

McDowall, Arthur (*cont.*)
  Thomas Hardy: A Critical Study v. 248 n.
  letters to v. 248, 306, 329; vi. 314
McDowall, Mrs A. v. 248 n.
Macer-Wright, Philip vii. 53 n.
  letter to vii. 52
McEwan, John iv. 258 n.
Mach, Zdenek vi. 143 n.
Machen, Arthur iv. 194 n.
  seeks TH's reminiscences for *Evening News*
    v. 257 and n.
  letters to iv. 194; v. 257
McIlvaine, Clarence W. (publisher) i. 219 n.,
    269 and n.; ii. 37, 38 n., 41, 47 n.*, 63 and
    n., 64, 65, 149, 150 n.; iv. 217
  and lapse of contracts with TH iii. 5–6, 8,
    10, 12
  and Morgan purchase of TH MSS iv. 199
    and n., 200, 205, 208, 219
  death iv. 254 and n.
  letters to ii. 47, 69, 71; iii. 5–6, 10; iv. 199,
    200, 205, 208, 219
McIlvaine, Mrs Clarence W. ii. 149
Macilwaine, Herbert Charles v. 130 n.
  letter to v. 130
Mackail, Clare v. 174 ('your daughter') and n.,
    196
Mackail, John William v. 174 n.
  inscribed copy of *Selected Poems* v. 195
    ('little book'), 196 n.
  Bentley's Milton vi. 254 ('the lecture'),
    255 n.
  Life of William Morris v. 203, 204 n.
  The Pilgrim's Progress vi. 299 ('little Bunyan
    book'), 300 n.
  (ed.) *Select Epigrams from the Greek Anthol-
    ogy* vii. 4
  Shakespeare After Three Hundred Years v.
    173, 174 n.
  letters to v. 173, 195; vi. 254, 299
McKay, (Revd) Roy vii. 21 n.
  letter to vii. 21
McKinnel, Norman vi. 337, 338 n., 339
Maclachlan, Angus iv. 132 n.
  'At Casterbridge Fair' iv. 132 ('Sing Ballad-
    singer') and n., 202 and n.
  letters to iv. 132, 202
(?) McLachlan, Thomas Hope iv. 202 n.
McLennan, John F. vii. 135 n.
Macleod, Very Revd Donald i. 66 and n.; vi.
    333 and nn.
McLintock-Bunbury, William ii. 248 ('Bun-
    bury'), 249 n.
Macmillan & Co. (publishers) i. 132 n.; iii. 90,
    228 n., 278 n.; v. 80
  inclusion of TH's works in Colonial Library
    i. 146 and n., 148 and n., 162, 175 n.; ii.

57, 58 n., 59 and n., 60, 63 and n., 88, 158,
    240 n., 263; iii. 11, 13
  publish *Woodlanders* i. 161–2, 164, 180
    and n.
  publish *Wessex Tales* i. 174 and n., 175 and
    n., 180 and n.
  one-vol. edns i. 180 and n., 195
  dispute with ii. 12 and n., 13, 14–15, 22, 39
  and transfer of TH works from Harper ii.
    240 and n., 243; iii. 11–14, 15–16, 27 and
    n., 28, 31; iv. 7 ('our agreement') and n.,
    118 n.
  and Wessex Edn iii. 16 n.; iv. 160 n., 161 n.,
    184–5, 201, 208; v. 94
  Uniform (3s 6d) edn iii. 27, 29 n., 32, 36 and
    nn., 77, 94 n., 96, 121 ('cheaper edition')
    and n.; iv. 116 and n., 271; v. 132, 133 n.
  Pocket Edn iii. 217 and nn., 221 and n., 226,
    227, 229, 230, 246, 275 n.; iv. 4 n.; vi.
    227 n.
  edn (1868) of Barnes's poems iii. 301, 303,
    304, 336, 338
  Selected Poems v. 133 and n., 148 n., 152 n.,
    161 and n., 171, 176, 192, 286; vi. 14 n.,
    40, 41 n., 96, 97 n.; vii. 59, 75
  and Mellstock Edn v. 321
  Indian edns vi. 177 and n.; vii. 164 n.
  new agreement with TH vi. 210 and n.,
    211–14
  prospectus for *Dynasts* vii. 145, 146 n.
  letters to i. 11, 13, 174, 286; ii. 12, 14, 15,
    240, 243; iii. 31, 77, 195, 202, 216, 230,
    233, 300, 355; iv. 8, 60, 106, 116, 154,
    184, 186, 208; v. 79, 169, 223, 321, 323,
    328; vi. 2, 210, 211, 215
Macmillan Co. of Canada vi. 264 n.
Macmillan, Alexander (publisher) i. 8 n.*,
    132 n.; ii. 58 n.; iv. 306; vii. 92 n.
  death ii. 108
  letters to i. 7–8; vii. 91
Macmillan, Daniel de Mendi (publisher) iii.
    294 ('your son's') and n.; vi. 212 n.
  and Wessex Edn iv. 201, 203–4; vii. 31
  letters to vi. 66; vii. 31
Macmillan, Lady Dorothy vi. 67 n.
Macmillan, Douglas vi. 365 n.
  letter to vi. 365
Macmillan, (Sir) Frederick Orridge i. 132 n.*,
    139 n.; ii. 12 and n., 58 n.; iii. 90, 218,
    246 n., 322; iv. 256 n.
  and transfer of TH works from Harper iii.
    11–14, 15–16, 27 and n., 28
  on TH's keen eye iii. 31 n.
  and restriction on use of 'Wessex' iii. 102 n.
  and Pocket Edn iii. 217 and nn., 218 n., 221
    and n., 227 and n., 246, 274; v. 301 n.; vi.
    283 n.

Macmillan, (Sir) Frederick (cont.)
  and one-vol. *Dynasts* iv. 3–4, 6, 118 n., 130;
    v. 299, 301 n.
  and one-vol. *Collected Poems* iv. 4 and n.,
    116, 117; v. 299, 301 n., 342; vi. 164, 177,
    195
  knighthood iv. 64 n.
  and proposed *édition de luxe* iv. 123–4, 160
    and nn., 162–3, 182, 195–6, 198 and n.;
    v. 123, 312 n.
  and film rights and proposed films iv. 140
    and n., 142, 143 n., 277, 278, 302, 303 n.,
    305, 309, 310, 322, 324, 329; v. 83, 84 n.,
    97, 103, 106, 111, 131, 133 and n., 255,
    257, 262, 265, 307 and nn., 313, 331, 334,
    335 nn., 337; vi. 42, 72–3, 152, 153 nn.,
    158, 164, 165 nn., 172 and n., 195, 196 n.,
    198, 202 and n., 368, 369 and n., 370
  and Wessex Edn iv. 184, 198 and n., 209,
    217, 228 ('definitive edition'), 230, 329; v.
    132, 299, 301 n., 304, 306; vi. 39, 358,
    361; vii. 2 n., 8, 48 and n.
  negotiations with Tauchnitz iv. 317 and n.,
    318, 321 and n., 324, 325
  and Mellstock Edn v. 36 ('limited edition'),
    37 n., 39, 312, 313, 342; vi. 20, 104, 105 n.
  sees *Dynasts* v. 60 and n.
  and *Selected Poems* v. 133, 148 and n., 149,
    152, 161; vi. 40, 41 n.; vii. 59 n., 75 and
    n., 76 n., 82 and n.
  and *Moments of Vision* v. 223 ('the Poems')
    and n., 232, 234, 259, 260 n.
  and Spanish translations v. 279 and n.; vi.
    108 and n.
  proposed price increases for TH books v.
    342 and n.
  and Scandinavian translations v. 345 and n.;
    vi. 19, 41 n., 227 and n.
  and reprint and anthology permissions vi. 6
    and n., 39, 40 and n., 92, 99, 177 and n.,
    179 and n., 181 and n., 183, 184 n., 187
    and n., 193 and n., 241 and nn., 260 and
    n., 316, 317 n., 366 and n., 371 n., 373 and
    n.; vii. 6 n., 28, 29, 36, 47 and n., 57,
    58 n., 59 and n., 69 n., 74 n., 76 n., 87
    and n.
  and American publication vi. 21, 22, 23 n.;
    vii. 47 and n., 87
  and Russian translations vi. 48, 49 n.
  and French translations vi. 64, 65, 73 and n.
  and Canadian publication vi. 64, 65, 66 nn.,
    81 and n., 83, 87, 88–9
  and *Late Lyrics and Earlier* vi. 105 nn., 108
    ('new poems'), 112 ('new poems'), 117–
    19, 129 n., 130, 133, 152, 153 n.
  and cheap Indian edns of TH novels vi. 177
    and n.

  and proposed German translation vi. 195,
    196 n., 249 and n.
  and *Queen of Cornwall* vi. 208 ('one-act
    play'), 209, 210, 211, 216, 217, 219, 223,
    236, 238, 272 and n.
  new agreement with TH vi. 210 and n.,
    211–14
  and Net Book Agreement vi. 264 and n.
  and royalty accounts vi. 272 and n., 358 and
    n.; vii. 57 and n.
  and illustrated *Tess* vi. 292 and n., 294 and
    n.; vii. 1, 2 n., 3 n., 6, 14 and n., 15 and n.,
    30 n., 46, 47 n.
  and limited, signed edn of *Dynasts* vii. 14
    and n., 29, 30 n., 63 and n., 66 and n.,
    71 n., 86 and n.
  and new edn of *Selected Poems* (*Chosen
    Poems*) vii. 59 n., 75 and n., 76 n., 82
    and n.
  and one-vol. edn of TH short stories vii. 76
    and n.
  letters to i. 131, 138, 140, 146, 147, 161, 164,
    175, 180; ii. 57, 59, 60, 63, 88, 158, 263;
    iii. 11, 12, 15, 27–8, 30, 36, 56, 75–6, 77,
    80, 85, 90, 100, 112, 126, 139, 182, 213,
    217, 221, 227, 228, 245–6, 274, 277, 303,
    308, 313; iv. 3, 6, 10, 11, 13, 42, 43, 44,
    47, 48, 64, 101, 117, 123–4, 130, 137, 140,
    142, 160, 162–3, 171, 182, 192, 195, 198,
    209, 217, 228, 230, 231, 256, 277, 278,
    289, 297, 298, 302–3, 304, 305, 306, 309,
    310, 317, 318, 321, 322, 324, 325, 329; v.
    24, 32, 33, 36, 39, 59, 83, 97, 103, 106,
    111, 131, 132, 148–9, 152, 161, 173, 208,
    223, 232, 234, 240, 255, 257, 259, 262,
    265, 278–9, 286, 299, 301, 304–5, 306,
    307, 312, 313, 331, 334, 337, 342, 345; vi.
    6, 7, 19, 20, 22, 39, 40, 41–2, 48, 64–5, 72,
    73, 80, 83, 87, 88–9, 92, 99, 104, 108, 112,
    117–18, 120, 129, 130, 133, 152, 158, 164,
    167, 168, 170, 172, 177, 179, 181, 183,
    187, 193, 195, 198, 202, 208, 209–10,
    211–14, 216, 217, 219, 223, 227, 235–6,
    238, 241, 249, 260, 264, 270, 272, 283,
    289, 292, 294, 304, 306, 312, 316, 317,
    318, 325, 345, 347, 348, 358, 361, 366,
    368, 370, 371, 373; vii. 1–2, 6, 8, 14, 15,
    28, 29, 35, 36, 46–7, 48, 57–8, 59, 60, 63,
    66, 69, 71, 73, 75, 76, 82, 86–7, 145
Macmillan, George Augustin (publisher) ii.
    108 n.*; iii. 100 n.; iv. 17 n., 48 n.; v. 60;
    vii. 29, 30 n., 92 n.
  and proposed film of *Tess* iv. 140 and n.
  letters to ii. 108; iii. 105, 178, 205, 264, 299;
    iv. 13–14, 26, 66, 69, 140; v. 2, 3, 40, 41,
    222, 284; vi. 13, 14, 33, 68, 69, 78, 169,
    189, 240, 243, 263, 334, 338, 341

Macmillan, (Lady) Georgiana iii. 321 and n., 322, 324; vii. 58 and n.

Macmillan, Harold (later Lord Stockton) vi. 67 n., 212 n., 271 n., 345 n., 358 n.
  letters to vi. 72, 85, 271, 273, 343

Macmillan, Helen Artie (Mrs M. C. Macmillan) vi. 67 n.
  letter to vi. 67

Macmillan, Malcolm Kingsley (publisher) i. 12 n., 13 n.
  letter to i. 12

Macmillan, Maurice (later Viscount Macmillan) vi. 67 n.

Macmillan, Maurice Crawford (publisher) ii. 243 n.; iii. 261 n.*; iv. 17 n., 48, 231 n.; v. 60 and n., 113 nn.; vi. 67 n., 363 nn.; vii. 35 n.
  and film rights v. 254
  letters to iii. 261, 294; iv. 17, 293; v. 112, 113, 114, 170, 172, 210, 254; vi. 11, 356, 363

Macmillan, William E. F. iv. 271 n.
  letter to iv. 271

Macmillan's Magazine i. 132 n., 141 ('magazine I write in here'), 202 n.; iii. 16 n.; vii. 92 n.
  serialization of *Woodlanders* i. 131 ('the novel'), 138 and n., 139 and n., 140, 141, 143, 144 n., 148, 149, 153 and n., 161

Macnamara, Francis vi. 150 nn.
  letter to vi. 149

Macquoid, Katharine Sarah i. 33 n.*, 39 and n., 125
  letter to i. 33

Macquoid, Thomas Robert i. 39 n.
  Examples of Architectural Art in Italy and Spain i. 125 n.
  letters to i. 39, 125, 245

McTaggart, John McTaggart Ellis v. 25 and n.; vi. 308 and n.
  The Nature of Existence v. 353 ('Magnum Opus') and n.
  The Relation of Time and Eternity iii. 329 and n.
  Some Dogmas of Religion iii. 207, 208 n.
  letters to iii. 207, 329; v. 353

Maeterlinck, Maurice:
  The Buried Temple iii. 21 n.
  Monna Vanna (banning of) iii. 25 n.

Magnus, Dr Edwin vi. 196 n.

Magrath, Revd John Richard (provost of Queen's College) vi. 201 and n.

'Maid of Keinton-Mandeville, The' (poem):
  pub. in *Athenaeum* vi. 12 ('some verses') and n.

Maiden Castle (Dorset) ii. 34 n., 35, 247 n., 305, 306 n.; iv. 302 and n., 304 ('photographs') and n., 305; vii. 43 and n.

Maiden Newton (Dorset) iv. 323
  White Horse Inn ii. 178–9

Mainz ii. 293 and n.

Maitland, F. W. iii. 238 n.
  Life and Letters of Leslie Stephen iii. 176 n., 237, 242; v. 76 ('Maitland's book'), 77 n.
  letter to iii. 237

Maitland, R. E. Fuller iv. 307, 308

Major, Ethel Homer (Dorchester amateur actress) vi. 296 and n.

Malden, Walter James v. 321 n.
  letter to v. 321

'Malet, Lucas' – *see* Harrison, Mary St Leger

Malmaison vi. 328 and n.

Malory, Sir Thomas vi. 293
  Morte d'Arthur vi. 294 n.

'Man, A' (poem) iii. 137

'Man he Killed, The' (poem) vi. 149
  pub. in *Sphere* iii. 35 ('some verses'), 36 n., 42 ('the verses')

Manaton (Devon) iv. 162 n.; v. 154 n., 215 n., 225 n.; vi. 104 n.

Manchester, Consuelo, Duchess of ii. 43, 44 n., 52 ('M.'); vii. 132 n.

Manchester:
  public libraries' 50th anniversary iii. 54, 55 n.
  TH MSS presented to libraries iv. 178 and n., 179 n., 181
  Pouncy lecture at v. 18 and n.

Manchester *Courier* iii. 155 n.

Manchester Guardian v. 258 and n.; vii. 21 and n.
  TH's letters on German bombardment of Rheims v. 58 n.

Manchester, Wessex Society of – *see* Wessex Society of Manchester and District

Manners, Lady Marjorie iii. 211 and n.

Manners, Lady Violet iii. 211 and n.

Mansel, George Morton iv. 22 and n.

Mansel, John Delalynde ii. 252 n.

Mansel, Margaret iv. 241 n.

Mansel, Susan iv. 241 n.

Mansfield, Kathleen vi. 184 ('your loss') and n., 241 n.

Mansion House ii. 18 n.; iii. 361

Maquarie, Arthur iv. 215 n.; v. 179 n.
  letters to v. 179, 209

Maquarie, Mary Lintner iv. 215 and n.

Marbury, Elisabeth iii. 273 and n.; v. 255, 257

'March of the Loyal Burton Bradstock Volunteers' (song) iii. 292 n.

'Marchioness of Stonehenge, The' (story):
  dramatic possibilities i. 240 and n.; iii. 250
  setting of iv. 170 n., 175, 220 n.

Marcus Aurelius i. 236 and n.

Margueritte, Ève-Paul vi. 62 n.
Marie Louise, Princess vi. 136 n.
 and Queen's Dolls' House library vi. 136 and
  nn., 149, 193
 letters to vi. 136, 149
Marienbad ii. 85, 86, 87
'Market Girl, The (Country Song)' (poem) iii.
 73 n.
Markie (Marky) (Max Gate cat) iii. 82, 83 and
 n., 85, 86, 333, 334 n., 335, 339, 341, 343;
 iv. 51
Marks, Lionel Simeon iii. 263 n.; iv. 102 and
 n.
'Marlott':
 Marnhull as ii. 132; vii. 122
Marlowe, Julia iii. 295 ('Julia') and n.
Marlowe, Thomas ii. 252 n.
Marnhull (Dorset) iii. 222 and n.; iv. 229,
 230 n.
 as 'Marlott' ii. 132; vii. 122
marriage, views on ii. 92, 93, 94, 97–8, 99,
 104; iii. 144; iv. 177; v. 19; vi. 156
Marsh, Clara v. 320 n.
Marsh, (Sir) Edward ii. 161 n.
 'Little Book' v. 285 ('your book'), 286 n.
 (ed.) *Georgian Poetry 1916–1917* v. 236 and
  n., 242 n.
 (ed.) *Georgian Poetry 1918–1919* v. 285
  ('new volume'), 286
 letter to v. 285
Marshall's Elm (nr. Glastonbury) iii. 138
Marshall, Archibald iii. 262 n.
 letter to iii. 261
Marshall, Beatrice iv. 131 n.
Marshall, Hugh John Cole vi. 74 nn., 330 n.,
 375 n.
 letters to vi. 74, 330, 374
Marshall (wrongly spelt 'Marshal' by TH) &
 Snelgrove vi. 81, 82 n.
Marston, Edward (publisher) i. 171 n.; ii. 2 n.
 letters to i. 171; ii. 1, 37
Marston, Robert Bright i. 171 n.; vi. 17 n.
 letter to vi. 17
Martin, Basil Kingsley vi. 276 ('bye-fellow')
 and n.
Martin, Lady Christian Norah vi. 135 and n.
Martin, Sir George Clement iii. 89 and n.
Martin, Revd George Currie vi. 215 n., 254 n.
 letters to vi. 214, 254
Martin, Henry Charles Austin (Dorchester
 auctioneer) iii. 357 n.; iv. 57 nn.; v. 162
 and n., 186, 187 n., 188, 250 n.; vi. 46,
 219, 222
 letters to iii. 357; iv. 57, 146, 179, 187; vii.
  156
Martin, Julia Augusta Pitney ii. 26 n., 179
 and n.

(?) Martin, Capt. W. F. vi. 106 ('neighbour')
 and n.
Martínez-Amador, Emilio v. 209 n.
Martinstown (Dorset) iii. 234
 alternative name of Winterborne St Martin
  iii. 235 n.; v. 4 n.
 font at v. 4; vi. 36
Martyn, Sir William vi. 275 n.
Marvell, Andrew iv. 175 n.
Mary, Queen:
 Dolls' House vi. 136 and n., 149 and n.,
  193
 See also Wales, Princess of; York, Duchess
  of
Mary, Princess (later Princess Royal) vi. 89,
 90 n.
 wedding vi. 120 ('yesterday's wedding')
  and n.
'Marygreen':
 Fawley as ii. 133
Masefield, John iv. 301 n.; v. 199; vi. 228 n.
 presentation copy of *Satires of C* v. 60 n.
 at *Dynasts* first night v. 63 n.
 at Max Gate vi. 93, 103
 visit from TH vi. 200, 201 n., 202
 stages *Queen of Cornwall* vi. 287 and n., 303
  and n.
 Ballads and Poems iv. 189 and n.
 Collected Poems vi. 189 n., 190
 The Everlasting Mercy iv. 189 ('you send')
  and n.; v. 123 and n.
 King Cole, and Other Poems vi. 200 and n.
 The Old Front Line v. 199 n.
 Sard Harker vi. 287 and n.
 Sonnets and Poems v. 178 and n.
 letters to iv. 189; v. 178; vi. 174, 189, 190,
  200, 287, 303
Mason-Manheim, Madeline:
 Hill Fragments vii. 20 ('poems'), 21 n.
Massingham, Harold John:
 and statement on 'The Plumage Trade' v.
  317, 318 nn.
Massingham, Henry William i. 250 n.*; ii.
 193 n.; iii. 258 n.
 letters to i. 250; ii. 193; iii. 258; v. 317
Masson, Rosaline vi. 165 n.
 (ed.) *I Can Remember Robert Louis
  Stevenson* vi. 165 ('R.L.S. book'), 166 n.;
  vii. 163 nn.
 letter to vi. 165
Master Films, Ltd v. 334 ('the Company'), 335
 and n., 337
'Master John Horseleigh, Knight' (story) iv.
 298
 pub. in *Illustrated London News* ii. 6 n., 8 ('a
  little sketch') and n., 19 ('the story')
 use of 'bastard' in ii. 6 and n.

Masterman, Charles Frederick Gurney v. 47 n.
and manifesto on war aims v. 46, 47 n.
Masters, Edgar Lee:
Spoon River Anthology v. 314 ('your book')
and nn.
letter to v. 314
Masters, Captain Joseph i. 38 n.
Mate, Frederick Skinner (mayor of Bourne-
mouth) vi. 295 n., 297, 321 n.
letter to vi. 295
Mate, W. & Sons (Poole publishers) v. 227,
228 n.
Mathews (Elkin), and John Lane v. 147 and n.
Matterhorn ii. 168 and n., 169
Matthews (Max Gate gardener) ii. 5 and n., 54
Matthews, A. E. v. 254 n.
Matthews, James Brander i. 119 n.
letter to i. 119
Maud, Constance Elizabeth:
(trans.) *Memoirs of Mistral* v. 23 and n.
Maude, Aylmer ii. 225 n.
Maugham, W. Somerset iii. 71 n.
Maumbury Rings (Dorchester) iii. 241 n., 335
('the Amphitheatre') and n., 336 n., 340,
343, 344 n.; iv. 141 n.; vi. 256 and n.; vii.
43
Maupassant, Guy de vii. 82, 83 n.
Maurward family v. 225 and n.
Max Gate (Dorchester) i. 134 n., 147 n., 235,
284 n.; ii. 60 n., 290; iii. 74, 312, 323
and n.; v. 139 and nn.; vi. 155 ('outskirts'); vii. 107, 111 ('little house here')
purchase of land for building of i. 73 and n.,
105, 135; ii. 66, 67 n.; vii. 95–7, 98, 100,
103–5
conveyance of freehold i. 135 and n.
maintenance i. 201; iii. 325; iv. 257, 265,
268, 270, 279; vi. 16
Latin pun on i. 217 and n.
pets i. 217 and n., 218; ii. 270, 271 n., 272,
283; iii. 82, 83, 85, 86, 90, 137 and n., 291,
333, 335, 339, 341, 343, 347, 361; iv. 51
and n., 132; v. 8 and n., 30, 61 and n., 71,
101, 121, 193, 201, 277, 320, 329, 340; vi.
9, 22, 38, 82, 120, 253, 277, 278, 279
('W.'); vii. 51 and n., 54
domestic staff i. 232; ii. 5 and n., 54, 73 and
n., 76, 77 and n., 162 n., 193, 194, 221,
271 and n.; iii. 31, 63 n., 82, 83, 85, 86,
90, 151, 322, 323 n., 325, 333, 334 n., 335,
336 n., 340, 347; iv. 85, 87 and n., 243; v.
61 and n., 108, 109 n., 325; vi. 10, 92, 124
and n.; vii. 27
garden at i. 246; iii. 63, 84; v. 203, 204
extensions and alterations to ii. 33, 60 n., 64,
70 n., 77 n., 221, 222 n.; iii. 325, 332, 333,
334 n., 335, 339, 341, 343, 347, 349, 351

Whitefriars Club visit ii. 281, 290 and n.,
291, 292 and n., 293, 297 and n.; vii.
140 n., 168 and n.
sundial at ii. 299 and n.
lent to Moule iii. 63 n., 78
affected by sewage works iii. 130, 131, 132
'Pets' Cemetery' iii. 137 and n., 361 and n.;
iv. 132 n.; vii. 54 and n.
Institute of Journalists visit iii. 176, 177 n.;
vii. 141
bird life iii. 336; v. 192, 212, 250, 283
young apple-stealers at iv. 113 and n., 274
difficulty of photographing iv. 293 and n.
Romano-British remains iv. 309 and n.; v.
247 and n.; vii. 100 n., 114 and n.
ELH's last garden party at v. 266, 267 n.,
288
rosebush planted by ELH v. 287
telephone installed v. 291 n.; vi. 1, 56, 210 n.
dependence on lamps and candles v. 338
post-box at gate vi. 1 and n., 82 n.
Society of Authors visit to vi. 18 ('a deputation'), 37
construction of side-walk on Wareham Road
vi. 171 and n.
Balliol Players at vi. 256 and nn.; vii. 29,
30 n.
Tess performed at vi. 372 ('down here')
and n.
Maxwell, (?) Lieutenant B. B. v. 90 and n, 91
Maxwell, Gerald iii. 133 n.; vi. 320 n.
By Right Divine iv. 197 and n.
The Star Makers vi. 320 n.
letters to iii. 132, 185; iv. 197; vi. 319
Maxwell, Sir Herbert:
(ed.) *The Creevey Papers* iii. 95 and n.
Maxwell, (?) 2nd Lieutenant R. v. 90 and n.,
91
Maxwell, William (printer) vii. 78 nn.
letters to vii. 78, 80, 81
Maynard, Theodore vii. 18 nn.
letter to vii. 18
Mayne Down (Dorset) iii. 289
Mayo, C. H.:
*The Municipal Records of the Borough of
Dorchester Dorset* iv. 188 and n.
Mayor of Casterbridge, The (novel) ii. 180 n.;
iii. 148 n.; iv. 8; v. 210 n.; vi. 159,
160 n., 188; vii. 100 n.
presentation copies i. 143, 146, 166
critical and public reception i. 144 ('the
story'), 145 and n., 146, 149 ('the
book'), 156 and n., 159
remaindered stock of i. 160 and n.
background and originals of places ii. 131,
132; iii. 109 and n.; iv. 10; vii. 43 and n.
as example of fact imitating fiction iii. 48

Mayor of Casterbridge, The (*cont.*)
  picture postcards based on iii. 112 n.
  title-changes iii. 218 and n.
  wife-sale in iii. 241
  MS given to Dorset County Museum iv. 184
    and n., 190
  line from Scottish song in v. 90 and n., 91
  possible American piracy v. 298 n.
  DRAMATIZATIONS:
    Drinkwater's vii. 6 n., 19 and n., 35, 36
      and n., 38, 42 and nn., 44 ('the play'),
      45 n.
    proposed i. 146; iii. 297, 298 n., 351 ('the
      play') and n.
  EDITIONS:
    Colonial i. 146, 148 and n.
    first (two-vol.) i. 142 and n., 143
    Indian vi. 177 and n.; vii. 163, 164 n.
    Wessex vi. 64
  FILM VERSIONS AND RIGHTS:
    iv. 324; v. 335; vi. 72 ('agreement'), 73 n.,
      78 and nn., 93 and n., 164, 165 n., 369
      and n.
  SERIALIZATIONS:
    American i. 143
    Graphic i. 139 ('a story') and n., 141
      ('story's conclusion'), 143; vii. 102
      and n.
    T. P.'s Weekly vii. 35 and n., 36, 37 n., 59
  TRANSLATIONS:
    Czech proposed vi. 297 and n., 304
    French iii. 95, 225; vi. 61, 62 n., 64, 65,
      66 n., 73 and n., 75
Medici Society vi. 39, 40 and nn., 41 n.
Medico-Psychological Association iii. 255 n.,
  267 ('dinner')
Medway, Frederick vii. 56 nn.
  letter to vii. 56
'Melancholy Hussar, The' (story) i. 178 ('your
  story'), 285; ii. 121 n., 173; iv. 271; v.
  173 n.
  syndicated publication i. 179 n., 201 and n.,
    204, 285 n.; ii. 143, 144 n.
  scene of execution in ii. 131
Melbury House (Dorset) i. 182 ('the mansion')
  and n., 187 ('the spot') and n.; ii. 139 n.;
  iii. 235 and n., 242 ('Ilchester's park'); iv.
  191 and n., 323 n.; v. 109 and n., 134, 166,
  176, 266; vi. 84 n.
  as 'Great Hintock Court' ii. 132; v. 134
Melbury Osmond (Dorset) ii. 139 n.; iii.
  235 n.; iv. 110 n., 164 and n.; v. 267 n.;
  vi. 252, 317 n.
  as 'Great Hintock' i. 163 and n. (wrongly
    'Little Hintock'), 164
  as birthplace of TH's mother ii. 139 n.; iv.
    164 n.; vi. 252 n.

'Melchester':
  Salisbury as ii. 132, 172 n.
'Melcombe' (psalm-tune) iii. 285
'Mellstock':
  Higher Bockhampton as i. 126 and n.
'Mellstock Church' ii. 141
  Stinsford Church as ii. 140; iv. 264; vii. 9
Mellstock Edition v. 36 ('limited edition'), 37
  and n., 39, 45, 100 and n., 305 n., 312 and
  nn., 313, 321; vi. 3 n., 20, 104, 105 n., 112
  and n.; vii. 58 n.
  corrections for v. 313, 314 n., 316 n., 342; vi.
    6, 26
  proof-reading of verse-volumes vi. 6, 7,
    22 n., 26
  omission of classification of volumes vi. 49
    and n.
Mellstock Quire, The (play) (dramatized ver-
  sion of *Under the Greenwood Tree*) iv.
  116 n., 124
  Dorchester performances iv. 125–6, 127; v.
    240 ('a play'), 241 n., 243 n., 248 and n.,
    249, 250 nn.; vii. 151 n.
  London performance iv. 125, 128 and n.,
    129, 130
Memling, Hans ii. 134
'Memories of Church Restoration' (lecture) iii.
  211 ('my lecture') and n., 215 ('the Lecture'), 216 n., 224 ('my paper'); iv. 20 n.
Men of the Time (annual) i. 96
'Men Who March Away' (poem) (formerly
  'Song of the Soldiers', q.v.) v. 47 n., 56,
  63, 105 and n., 264, 289 n.; vi. 149, 246;
  vii. 23
  in *Satires of Circumstance* v. 52 and n.,
    211 n.; vi. 6
  set to music v. 63
  MS sold for Red Cross v. 105
  in American anthologies v. 211 n.; vi. 6
  moved to *Moments of Vision* v. 305 n.
Mercure de France ii. 274 nn., 278, 282 and n.
'Mere Interlude, A' (story) iii. 66, 67 n.; vii.
  59 n.
Meredith, Augustus (father of G. Meredith)
  iv. 47 and n., 231 and n. (erroneous identi-
  fications corrected at vii. 175), 272 n.
Meredith, George i. 147, 287; ii. 43 n., 87 n.,
  213 n., 300; iii. 25 n., 138, 165 and n.,
  175, 219 n.; iv. 47 n., 229 and n., 231 n.;
  v. 145 n., 236; vi. 126 and nn., 266; vii. 27
  and n.
  70th birthday tribute to ii. 184–6, 187 n.
  health iii. 117 and n., 175 and n., 187
  and TH's pessimism iii. 187 and n.
  death iv. 23 n., 24
  refused Abbey burial iv. 23 n., 26
  Abbey memorial service iv. 23 and n., 24, 25

TH's poem on iv. 24, 25 n.; v. 236 and n.; vii. 159 and n.
TH's opinion of iv. 24; vii. 38
as President of Society of Authors iv. 27, 28 and n., 29 n.
and 'Poor Man and the Lady' iv. 130, 306; vi. 254 ('first novel') and n.
TH's centenary article on vii. 72 ('your father') and n., 78 and n., 79 and n.
TH's first meeting with vii. 159, 160
The Egoist iv. 24, 25 n.
'Odes in Contribution to the Song of French History' vi. 156, 157 n.
Meredith, William Maxse vii. 72 n., 78, 79 n.
(ed.) *Letters of George Meredith* iv. 229 and n., 231 and n.; vii. 155 and n.
letters to vii. 72, 79
Merevale Hall (Warws) ii. 28, 37
Merit, Order of iv. 111 and n.
TH's appointment to iii. 353 n.; iv. 103 and n., 104, 105, 107, 108, 109, 110, 111, 112, 119; vii. 150 n.
TH's portrait as member of iv. 108, 116, 122 n.
Merrell, Sarah Lawrence Penny vii. 16 n.
Merriman, Hugh Seton:
Flotsam ii. 134, 135 n.
The Sowers ii. 134, 135 n.
Merry England i. 115 ('the new magazine'), 116 n.
'Merrymaking in Question, A' (poem):
pub. in *Sphere* v. 160 ('two poems'), 161 n.
Mers, J. T.:
A History of European Thought in the Nineteenth Century v. 81 n.
Metcalf, Lorettus Sutton i. 168 n.
letter to i. 168
Metcalfe, Revd Alfred iii. 115, 116 n.
and ELH's funeral iv. 238 and n.
testimonial to iv. 238 and n.
letter to iv. 238
Metcalfe, Sir Theophilus John i. 267 n.
Metcalfe, Lady i. 267 n.
letter to i. 267
Methuen, Sir Algernon Methuen Marshall vi. 85 n.
(comp.) *An Anthology of Modern Verse* vi. 85 ('charming book') and n.
letter to vi. 85
Methuen (publishers) vi. 64, 65 n., 83 and n.
Metro (later Metro-Goldwyn) Pictures Corporation v. 308 n., 331 ('American Company') and n.; vi. 152, 153 n., 163 n. ('Goldwyn Pictures')
Metropolitan Asylums Board iii. 9 n.
Meugens, Nancy R. E. i. 50 n.
letters to i. 50, 51, 52, 55

Mew, Charlotte v. 275 n.; vi. 113, 114 n.
and 'Poets' Tribute' v. 336
at Max Gate v. 336 n.
Civil List pension vi. 228 n.
letters to v. 336; vi. 228
Meynell, (Sir) Francis vi. 316 n.
Meynell, Violet:
(ed.) *Friends of a Lifetime: Letters to Sydney Carlyle Cockerell* v. 41 n., 275 n.
Meynell, Wilfred i. 116 n.
letters to i. 115; iv. 47
Mickle, William Julius vi. 229 n., 266 and n., 267 and n.; vii. 78, 79 nn.
Middleton, John Henry ii. 13 n.
Midleton, Lady (formerly Madeleine Stanley, then Mrs St John Brodrick, qq.v.) iv. 272 and n.
'Midnight Baptism, The' (story) (episode omitted from serial version of *Tess*):
pub. in *Fortnightly Review* i. 232 ('sketch') and n., 233 ('story') and n., 249
'Midnight Revel, The' (later 'The Paphian Ball') (poem) vi. 270 ('fairly good one')
pub. in *McCall's* vi. 271 and nn.
Milan:
Cathedral iii. 4
Mill, John Stuart ii. 86
On the Subjection of Women ii. 86 n., 87
Millar, H. R. ii. 62 n.
Millay, Edna St Vincent vi. 186 and n.
The King's Henchman vii. 64 and n.
letter to vii. 64
Miller, Sir Charles John Hubert ii. 238 and n.
Miller, George (labourer) iii. 49 n.
Miller, Revd John Aaron iii. 27 n.
letter to iii. 26
Miller, W. Addis vii. 135 n.
Millet, F. D. i. 152 n.
Millet, Jean François iii. 49
Milman, Lieut.-General George Bryan ii. 13, 14 n., 45
Milman, Lena (Angelena Frances) ii. 14 and n., 20, 22, 25 n.*
exchange of photographs with TH ii. 28, 33, 41, 45
as translator ii. 42 and n.
letters to ii. 24, 28, 33, 41, 45
Milne, James:
literary editor of *Daily Chronicle* ii. 227 ('representative'), 228 n.; iii. 32 n., 97 n., 216 nn.; iv. 169 n.
editor of *Book Monthly* iii. 97 n.; vii. 144 n.
editor of *Graphic* v. 313 n.
letters to iii. 32, 97, 216; iv. 117, 118; v. 313; vii. 144
Milne, W. O. vii. 43 and n.
Milner, Alfred Milner, Viscount vi. 10 n., 63 n.

Milner (Henniker dog) v. 340 and n.; vi. 9,
  10 n., 44
Milnes-Gaskell, Lady Catherine ii. 27
  ('Catty'), 28 n., 30 ('her sister') and n.
Milnes-Gaskell, Charles George ii. 28 n.
Milton, John:
  tercentenary iii. 324 n., 325 n., 361
  unveiling of statue vii. 137 n.
  Lycidas iv. 301 n.
  Paradise Lost vi. 254, 255 n.
Milton, Meyrick vi. 42 and n.
Milton Abbas (Dorset) iii. 156 n.; iv. 58 n.
  doggerel rhymes iii. 156 and n.
Milton Abbey (Dorset) iii. 156 and nn.; iv. 57,
  58 nn.
Mind iii. 207, 208 n., 329
Minehead (Somerset) iv. 168
Ministering Children's League vi. 90 n.
Minterne, Conjuror iii. 264; iv. 206, 207 n.
Minterne (Dorset) ii. 30, 70 n., 132
Minterne Parva (Dorset) i. 163 and n.
  barn at vii. 24 and n.
Minto, William i. 41 n.
  letter to i. 41
'Minute before Meeting, The' (poem) vi. 257
Mistral, Frédéric v. 23 and n.
Mistress of the Farm, The (play) (dramatized
  version of *Far from the Madding Crowd*) i.
  99 and n.
  Pinero's alleged plagiarism of i. 100, 101 nn.,
    103 and nn.
Mitchell, Edgar A. vi. 39 n.
  letter to vi. 39
Mitchell, Revd Henry i. 278 n.
  letters to i. 278, 279
Mivart, St George Jackson vi. 162, 163 n.
Molloy, Joseph Fitzgerald i. 133 and n.
  Court Life Below Stairs i. 133 n.
'Moments of Vision' (poem):
  MS sold for Red Cross v. 244 ('two poems')
    and n.
Moments of Vision (poems) v. 223 ('parcel') and
  n., 225 n., 227 ('little book') and n., 237
  ('the poems'), 238 n., 246, 251, 259, 286,
  316 n.; vi. 96, 104, 218 n.; vii. 35
  Wessex Edn v. 95 n., 234 n., 255, 291 n.,
    299, 301 n., 304, 305 and n., 306
  publication v. 223 n., 232 ('the book') and n.
  presentation copies v. 232, 234
  corrections to v. 234, 260, 286, 290, 291 n.,
    294
  critical reception v. 250 and n., 253, 258,
    290, 294, 318; vi. 130 n., 246 n.
  proposed French translation v. 259, 260 n.
  Pocket Edn v. 291 n., 301 n.
Monck, Nugent:
  The Hour iii. 253 n.

Moncrieff, Ascott Robert Hope:
  (ed.) *Black's Guide to Dorset* ii. 146 and n.,
    201
  letter to ii. 146
Monet, Claude, i. 191
money, attitude to i. 232; ii. 5, 76, 77, 109,
  112, 113, 270; iii. 20, 29, 249, 321, 322, 333,
  339; iv. 31, 82, 84, 86–7, 230; v. 80, 272; vi.
  9 n.; vii. 1, 15, 30, 57, 58, 59, 76, 93, 117, 120
Money-Coutts (later Coutts-Nevill, then Lord
  Latymer), Francis Burdett Thomas iii.
  64, 65 n., 135, 267, 347 ('Mr Coutts'); vii.
  147 and n.
  The Poet's Charter, or the Book of Job iii. 64,
    65 n.
Monro, David Binning iii. 90 ('Vice Chancellor') and n.
Monro, Harold iv. 307 n.
  and 'Poets' Tribute' v. 332
  as editor of *Chapbook* vi. 179 and n.
  Real Property vi. 126 and n.
  letters to v. 332; vi. 126, 137, 179, 180, 185
Monroe, Harriet vi. 183 n.
  (ed. with A. C. Henderson) *The New Poetry*
    vi. 183 ('Proof') and n.
  letter to vi. 183
Mons, retreat from (1914) v. 189 and n.
Montacute House (Somerset) iii. 74, 75 n.
Montagu, Basil v. 90 n.
Monthly Review iii. 21 and n., 112, 295 n.
Moore, George ii. 42 and n.; iv. 133 n.; v.
  303 n.
  hostility to TH vi. 242, 243 nn., 246
  Confessions of a Young Man vi. 155, 157 n.
  Conversations in Ebury Street vi. 242 ('book
    of his'), 243 n., 247 n., 284 ('Moore's
    book') and n.
  Esther Waters ii. 56 n.; v. 183 n.
  letter to iv. 133
Moore, James Carrick:
  *The Life of Lieutenant-General Sir John
    Moore, K.B.* iv. 139 n.
Moore, Sir John iv. 137, 139 and n.
Moore, Thomas Sturge:
  and 'Poets' Tribute' v. 335 and n.
  letter to v. 335
Mordell, Albert:
  Dante and Other Waning Classics v. 163,
    164 n.
  letter to v. 163
Moreton Heath (Dorset):
  as 'Egdon Heath' ii. 132
Moreton House (Dorset) i. 217 n. (corrected at
  vii. 172); ii. 4 n.; v. 144 and n.
Morgan, Charles Langbridge:
  and OUDS production of *Dynasts* v. 348–9;
    vi. 4–5, 8, 323 ('the play') and n.

Morgan, Charles Langbridge (*cont.*)
  My Name Is Legion vi. 323 ('the book') and n.
  letters to v. 348; vi. 4, 5, 323
Morgan, John Hartman iii. 94 and n. (?); v.
    187 n.; vii. 169 n.
  journalism v. 187 and n., 226 and n.; vii. 3
    and n.
  at Max Gate v. 248 ('friend of ours') and n.
  on Inter-Allied Commission of Control vi.
    31 n., 79 ('Berlin business'), 80 n., 160
    ('friend of ours')
  nominated for Nobel Peace Prize vi. 267
    and n.
  Gentlemen at Arms v. 260 n.
  John, Viscount Morley vi. 260 ('dedicn.') and
    n., 289, 290 nn.
  'The Personality of Lord Morley' vi. 233 and
    n., 247 ('second article') and n.
  The Present State of Germany vi. 233,
    234 n., 267 n.
  letters to v. 187, 226, 260, 311; vi. 30, 79,
    161, 233, 247, 260, 267, 289; vii. 3, 19,
    169
Morgan, John Pierpont iv. 186 n.
  purchase of TH MSS iv. 199 and n., 200,
    208 and n., 219
Morgan, Sidney vi. 78 nn.
  letter to vi. 78
Morgan, W. J. vii. 165 n.
Morison, James Cotter i. 147 and n., 173 and n.
  The Service of Man i. 173 and n.
Morley, George iii. 251 n.
  A Bunch of Blue Ribbons iii. 251 and n.
  letters to iii. 251, 259
Morley, Henry:
  Of English Literature in the Reign of Victoria
    i. 102 and n.
Morley, John (later Viscount) i. 8 n., 13 n.,
    119 n.*, 176; ii. 53, 54 n., 77 and n., 184;
    iii. 198 and n., 316, 317 n., 345; iv. 27,
    28 n., 288; vi. 79, 80 n., 233 n., 247, 289,
    290 nn.
  sent 'Dorsetshire Labourer' i. 119 and n.
  and *Poor Man and the Lady* iv. 130, 306
  resignation at outbreak of war v. 87 and n.,
    99 and n.
  Recollections vi. 289 ('reminiscences'),
    290 n.
  letters to i. 118, 136
Morning Chronicle v. 269
Morning Leader iii. 15 n., 227 n.; iv. 2 n., 24 n.
Morning Post ii. 175 n., 275 ('M.P.') and n.,
    276; iii. 155 n.; iv. 130 n., 157 and n.; v.
    208 n., 209 and n.; vi. 52 and n.
  on *Desperate Remedies* i. 11, 12
Morrell, Lady Ottoline Violet Anne vi. 275 nn.
  letter to vi. 274

Morris, Sir Lewis ii. 36 and n.; iii. 3
Morris, May vii. 155 n.
  letter to vii. 155
Morris, William iv. 178 n., 179 n.; v. 203,
    204 nn.; vii. 155 n.
Morris and Killanin, Michael Morris, Lord ii.
    53 and n.
Morris and Killanin, Lady ii. 54 and n.
Morrison, Walter i. 290 n.
  letter to i. 290
Morsbach, Dr Lorenz vii. 64, 65 n.
Mortimer, James vii. 67 and n.
Mortola, La (Ventimiglia) vi. 115 and n.
Morton, W. E. ii. 193 n.
Morwenstow (Cornwall) iv. 327 n., 328; vii.
    47, 48 n.
Moss (Max Gate dog) i. 217 and n., 218
Moss, Mary iii. 331 ('American friend'),
    332 n., 342, 343
'Mother Mourns, The' (poem) vii. 150 and
    n.
Motley, John Lothrop i. 184 n.
Moule, Revd Arthur Christopher vi. 191,
    192 nn.
Moule, Mrs A. C. vi. 191, 192 n.
Moule, Arthur Evans i. 244 n.
  New China and Old i. 243, 244 n.
  letters to i. 243; iii. 78, 114
Moule, Charles Walter i. 70, 84 n.*, 278 and
    n.; ii. 44 ('old acquaintance'), 45 n., 157
    ('a Cambridge Don') and n.; iii. 325 and
    n.; v. 271; vi. 87 ('his fellowship') and n.,
    124 n.
  copy of *Greenwood Tree* sent to i. 84
  and ELH's death iv. 249
  death vi. 86 ('dear father'), 87 n.
  letter to i. 84
Moule, Revd Frederick John ii. 276 and n.
Moule, Revd George Evans i. 84 n.
  letter to iv. 174 (correctly identified at vii.
    175)
Moule, Revd George Herbert vi. 5 n.; vii.
    40 nn.
  letters to vi. 5; vii. 39
Moule, Revd Handley Carr Glyn i. 70 n.; ii.
    248 ('a religious man'), 249 n.; iii. 114
    ('Bp. of Durham'), 117 ('Bp. of
    Durham'); iv. 174 n.
  Life of vi. 67 and n.
  Apollo at Pherae v. 315, 316 n.
  Dorchester Poems i. 84 n.
  Memories of a Vicarage iv. 326 and n.; v.
    315 n.
  letters to i. 70; iv. 174 (erroneous identifi-
    cation, corrected at vii. 175), 326; v. 315
Moule, Revd Henry i. 2 n., 70 n.*, 244 n.; ii.
    248 ('old parson'), 249 n., 301 n.; iii. 115

Moule, Revd Henry (cont.)
('your father'); v. 315 ('Vicar of Fordington') and n.
death i. 70; v. 316 n.
as part prototype of Revd Mr Clare in *Tess*
vii. 40
Moule, Henry Charles Cautley vi. 124 ('a musician') and n.
Moule, Henry John iii. 273 ('little boy') and n.
Moule, Henry Joseph i. 121 and n.*, 205 and
n., 278 ('my neighbour'); ii. 259, 260 n.;
iii. 25 n., 273 n.
Max Gate lent to iii. 63 n., 78
death iii. 114, 117 ('old friend'), 123; iv. 119,
120 n.
funeral iii. 115
Dorchester Antiquities iii. 176 n.; iv. 309
('book of his') and n.
Moule, Horatio (Horace) Mosley i. 1
('H.M.M.'), 2 n.*, 4, 7 and n., 8, 10 ('my
friend') and n., 70 n., 121, 278 n.; vi. 124
and n.
reviews *Desperate Remedies* i. 13 n.
reviews *Greenwood Tree* i. 17 and n., 19 n.
suicide i. 22 n.
verses by iii. 115, 116 n.
TH's last meeting with v. 27 n.
'Ave Maria' vi. 137 ('the poem') and n., 160
('the poem')
Moule, John Frederick iii. 273 nn.
letter to iii. 272
Moule, Margaret ii. 276 and n.
Moule, Mary Dora (Mrs C. Moule) vi. 86,
87 n.
Moule, Mary Mullett (Mrs Henry Moule) vii.
40 and n.
Moule, Revd Walter vii. 40 n.
Moult, Thomas vi. 184 n.
(ed.) *Best Poems of 1922* vi. 183, 184 n.
Moulton, Ellen Louise Chandler i. 194 n.*; ii.
19 and n., 20, 86; iii. 65 and n.; v. 219 and
n.
At the Wind's Will: Lyrics and Sonnets ii.
266 ('the poems') and n.
*In the Garden of Dreams: Lyrics and Son-
nets* i. 208 and n.
Miss Gyre from Boston, and Others i. 194
('the book') and n.
letters to i. 194, 208, 241, 280, 288; ii. 79,
127, 265; vii. 123
Moulton, John Fletcher ii. 79 n., 80 n., 107,
108, 181 ('your father'), 187 ('father'), 254
Moulton, William U. (publisher) i. 194 n.
Moultrie, Revd John:
(ed.) *Poetical Works of Thomas Gray* v. 272
and n.
Mount Batten, Colonel John iii. 322, 323 n.

Mourey, Gabriel v. 259, 260 n.
Mowbray, Morris i. 265 n.
Mozart, Wolfgang Amadeus v. 237, 238 n.
Mudie's Library iv. 63, 64 n.; vii. 99 and n.
Mullins, Edwin Roscoe ii. 176
statue of Barnes i. 167 and n.; vii. 109 n.
Mundy, Harriott Georgiane ii. 179 n.
letter to ii. 179
Munro, David Alexander iii. 72 n., 75 n.*
letter to iii. 75
Munro, George (publisher) i. 284, 285 n.
Munro, Hugh Andrew Johnstone ii. 143 and
n.; iii. 287 n.
Murger, Henry:
Les Nuits d'hiver vi. 331 n.
Murray, David Christie vi. 330 and n.
Murray, George Gilbert Aimé iv. 29 n., 263; v.
47 n., 208 n.; vi. 239
protest against play censorship iv. 202,
203 n.
Alcestis v. 236 and n.
The Bacchae v. 330 and n.
*The Story of Nefrekepta, from a Demotic
Papyrus* iv. 144 and nn.
The Trojan Women v. 343 and n.
letters to iv. 144; v. 330
Murray, James iii. 161, 163 n.; vii. 138 and n.
Murray, Sir James Augustus Henry iii. 70 n.;
iv. 214, 215 n.
Oxford English Dictionary iii. 70 n.; v. 97
and n.
letters to iii. 69; iv. 312
Murray, John (publisher) i. 268 n.; ii. 229 n.
letter to ii. 229
Murray, Marion Christie vi. 330 ('widow')
and n.
*Murray's Handbook for Residents and
Travellers in Wilts and Dorset* (ed. Windle)
ii. 133 n., 135, 229 and n.
*Murray's Handbook for Travellers in France.
Part I* iii. 334 ('guide book') and n.
Murray's Magazine i. 170, 268 n.
Tess rejected by i. 202 n., 268
Murry, John Middleton v. 298 n., 308 and n.;
vi. 241 n.; vii. 89 ('J.M.M.') and n.
as editor of *Athenaeum* v. 297 ('of a review'),
298 nn., 301, 341; vi. 9, 12, 18, 43, 51
review of *Collected Poems* v. 341
death of wife (K. Mansfield) vi. 184 and n.
as editor of *Adelphi* vi. 200 and n., 242,
243 n.
attack on Moore vi. 242, 243 n., 284 and n.
financial difficulties vii. 81 and nn., 84
and nn.
Cinnamon and Angelica vi. 43 and n., 51
The Evolution of an Intellectual vi. 2 ('the
book')

Murry, John Middleton (cont.)
  Poems v. 318 and n.
  'To TH' v. 336 ('verses') and n.
  letters to v. 297–8, 301, 318, 336, 341; vi. 2,
    9, 12, 18, 25, 42, 51, 184, 200, 242, 246
Murry, Violet vii. 81 ('his wife') and n., 89
  and n.
music, interest in i. 192, 198–9; ii. 9, 124,
    283, 285, 288; iii. 23, 38, 73, 99, 100, 131,
    144, 240, 247, 283, 285, 286, 288, 299, 320,
    328, 347, 355, 358; iv. 51, 52, 69, 126, 132,
    139, 166, 179, 183, 327; v. 49, 50, 56, 129,
    288, 350; vi. 2, 79, 89, 124, 159, 191, 225,
    234, 239, 249, 264–5; vii. 106
'Mute Opinion' (poem) vi. 149
Mutford (Dorchester plumber) iii. 64
'My Cicely' (poem) iii. 137, 362
'My Love's gone a-fighting' (song):
  in *Dynasts* v. 56 and n.

Napier, J. Harold vii. 130 n.
  letter to vii. 129
Naples iii. 204 n.
Napoleon iii. 271, 289; iv. 173, 193 n.; v. 326
    and n.; vii. 19, 20 and n., 54
  in *Dynasts* iv. 88 and n.; vi. 105 and nn.,
    161; vii. 83
Napoleon III – *see* Louis Napoleon (later
  Napoleon III)
Napolitano, Mrs iv. 166
Nares, Owen v. 254 n.
Nash (Eveleigh) & Grayson (publishers) vi.
  166 n.
Nash's and Pall Mall Magazine vi. 120
  TH poems pub. in vi. 121 n., 242 n.
Nation iii. 258 n.; iv. 2 and nn., 15, 16 n.; v.
    318, 319 n.
  'Sunday Morning Tragedy' rejected by iii.
    287 ('a ballad')
Nation (New York) i. 103 and n., 104 n.
Nation and Athenaeum vi. 196 and n., 314 n.
National Agricultural Labourers' Union i.
  119 n.
National Club ii. 17 n.; iii. 153 n., 155 ('din-
  ner'); v. 132 n.
National Council for Adult Suffrage:
  invitation to membership refused by TH v.
    186
National Home-Reading Union vi. 101 n.
National Observer i. 229 ('N.O.') and n., 234
  'Saturday Night in Arcady' pub. in i. 247
    ('sketch') and n., 249 ('sketch') and nn.;
    iii. 274 ('episode from the story'), 275 n.;
    vii. 117, 118 n.
National Review i. 111 ('the magazine') and n.,
    271 n.; ii. 140; iii. 41
  on *Tess* i. 258

National Secular Society iv. 97 n.
National Service, Ministry of v. 206 and n.
National Theatre, proposed vii. 13 n., 136 and
    nn., 149 and nn.
National Union of Women's Suffrage Societies
    iii. 360 nn.; iv. 21 n.; vii. 142 n.
National War Aims Committee v. 264 n.
'Nature's Questioning' (poem) vi. 54
'Near Lanivet, 1872' (poem) v. 250 ('At
    Lanivet'), 295, 341 ('white clothed form');
    vi. 96
  association with ELH v. 246
Needham, Joseph:
  (ed.) *Science, Religion and Reality* vii. 3
    and n.
Neel, Philippe vi. 73 n.
Neighbour, Gerald M. iv. 289 and n.
Nelson, Harold iv. 331 n.
Nelson, Horatio, Viscount iii. 114, 182 n.
Nelson, Horatio Nelson, 3rd Earl i. 2 n.
'Nether Moynton':
  Ower Moigne as ii. 132
Netherhampton House, Salisbury vi. 91,
    92 n.
Netherton Hall (Devon) vii. 32 n.
Netley Hospital (Hants) v. 166 and n.
Neuchâtel ii. 166
Nevill, Lady Dorothy ii. 53 and n., 201, 277;
    vii. 124 nn.
  letter to vii. 124
Nevinson, Henry Woodd iii. 223 n., 229 nn.,
    363 n.
  at Max Gate iii. 223; iv. 39
  organizer of petitions iii. 363 and n.; iv. 39
    and n., 154 and n.
  as war correspondent v. 154 and n.
  Peace and War in the Balance vii. 152 and n.
  letters to iii. 223, 228, 253, 363; iv. 39; v.
    154; vii. 152
New, Edmund H. ii. 256 n., 302 and n.
New Adelphi (corrected to *Adelphi* at vii. 177)
    vi. 243 n., 284 n.
New Age iv. 266 n.
New Century ii. 140 n., 153, 154 n.
New Orphanage (unidentified) ii. 242
New Quarterly iii. 276 ('new magazine') and
    n.
  'House of Hospitalities' pub. in iii. 295 n.,
    354 n.; iv. 1 n.
New Quarterly Magazine i. 67 ('the maga-
    zine'); vii. 94 n.
  'An Indiscretion in the Life of an Heiress'
    pub. in i. 57 ('the story') and n., 60 ('my
    contribution'), 61 n.; iv. 306 n.; vii. 91
    ('the story') and n.
  TH's review of Barnes's poems in i. 68 n.,
    281; ii. 61 n.

New Quarterly Magazine (*cont.*)
'The Distracted Preacher' pub. in ii. 54 and n.
New Republic:
'Haunting Fingers' pub. in vi. 112 and n.
New Review i. 257 and n.; ii. 2 n., 62 n., 115, 117
New Saturday ii. 134, 135 n.
New Statesman v. 96 and n., 158 n.
New Sussex Hospital for Women and Children v. 349 n.
New Theatre iii. 67
New Weekly:
TH poems pub. in v. 6 and n., 20, 21 and nn., 22 and n., 30 n.
wartime closure v. 53 and n.
New World vii. 162 n.
'New Year's Eve' (poem) v. 212; vi. 54
pub. in *Fortnightly* iii. 242 ('verses of mine'), 244 ('New Year's Fantasy') and n.; vii. 143 n.
'New Year's Eve in War Time, A' (poem):
pub. in *Sphere* v. 193, 195 ('proofs') and n., 199 and n.
New York:
production of *Tess* ii. 111 n., 147 and n., 150, 151 nn., 152 and n., 156, 157, 162, 167 and n., 186
New York Herald vii. 16 n.
New York Journal ii. 154
New York Theatre Guild vi. 353, 354 and n., 357
New York Times i. 31 and n.; v. 76 n.; vi. 38 n.
serialization of *Hand of Ethelberta* i. 44 and n., 138 n., 140 n.
New York Times Magazine vii. 28 and n.
New York Times Review of Books iv. 173 ('N.Y. Times'), 174 n.; vi. 145 n.
New York Times Saturday Review ii. 297 n.; iii. 266 n.
New York Tribune i. 192 and nn.
New York World iii. 259; v. 150 n.; vi. 102 n.; vii. 16
and *Jude* ii. 103 and n., 126
Newbiggin Hall (Westmorland) iii. 265
Newbolt, (Sir) Henry John iii. 21 n.; iv. 6 nn., 232 n.; vi. 57 and n., 143; vii. 169 n.
and *Dynasts* iii. 112, 195; iv. 5
invited to Max Gate iv. 125, 127, 129, 216, 217 n.; vi. 246; vii. 29, 68
at Dorchester performance of *Mellstock Quire* iv. 125, 127
and presentation of R.S.L. medal to TH iv. 216, 217, 218 n.
lecture on TH v. 230, 231 n.
and 'Poets' Tribute' v. 328

proposed anthology of short stories vii. 28 and n., 29 and n.
Collected Poems, 1897–1907 iv. 108 and n.
'Drake's Drum' v. 231 n.
A New Study of English Poetry v. 238 ('your lectures'), 239 n.
Poems New and Old iv. 254 and n.
Studies Green and Gray vii. 55 and n.
Tales of the Great War v. 189 ('the book') and n.
(comp.) *An English Anthology of Prose and Poetry* vi. 91 ('job of yours'), 92 n., 102–3; vi. 245 ('your previous book'), 246 n.
(comp.) *The Tide of Time in English Poetry* vi. 245 ('book you are preparing'), 246 n., 326, 327 n.
(comp.) *The Year of Trafalgar* iii. 154 ('your collection') and n.
letters to iii. 21, 104, 112, 154, 195, 233; iv. 5, 107–8, 125, 127, 129, 216, 217, 254; v. 189, 230, 238, 289, 328; vi. 30, 52, 91, 102, 245–6, 326, 330; vii. 29, 55, 68
Newbury (Berks) ii. 234
Newcombe, Bertha ii. 244 and n.
Newington Steam Trawling Co.:
letter to vi. 352
Newnes, (Sir) George i. 242 n.; vii. 147 n.
letter to i. 242
Newnes, George (publishers) vi. 356 and n.; vii. 47 and n.
Newquay (Cornwall) v. 271; vii. 69 and n.
Newton, Ernest v. 116 ('well-known architect'), 117 n.
Ney, Marshal vii. 20 and n.
Nichol, John:
Tables of European History, Literature, and Art, from A.D. 200 to 1882 iii. 141, 142 n.
Nicholls, Eliza Bright vi. 111 n.; vii. 168 n.
Nichols, Robert v. 242
and 'Poets' Tribute' v. 332
Ardours and Endurances v. 242 n., 319 n.
'Fulfilment' v. 242, 332 n.
letter to v. 332
Nicholson, Sydney Hugo vii. 7 n.
letter to vii. 7
Nicodemus, Gospel of iv. 120, 121 n.
Nicoll, (Sir) William Robertson i. 244 and n.*, 274 n.; ii. 60 n.; v. 80 and n., 137 and n.
letter to ii. 60
Nicolson, Lieut.-General Malcolm Hassels iii. 142 and n., 143
Nicolson, Violet – *see* 'Hope, Laurence'
Nietzsche, Friedrich Wilhelm v. 50, 51 n.
'Night of Questionings, A' (poem) vi. 241
'Night of Trafalgar, The' (song) iii. 154 and n.
setting to music of iii. 100, 126, 127 n.; v. 56
replica of MS vi. 34, 35 n.

Nimmo, James Valence ii. 119 n.
  letter to ii. 119
Nineteenth Century iii. 47 n., 117 and n., 118
  ('XIXth'), 186 n.
Nineteenth Century and After:
  'Xenophanes, the Monist of Colophon' pub.
    in vi. 231 ('the poem'), 232 n., 293
  'The Absolute Explains' pub. in vi. 308 n.,
    314 ('that poem') and n.
  'G.M.: A Reminiscence' pub. in vii. 72 n.,
    78 and n., 79 and n.
Niven, Revd George Cecil vi. 163 ('old
  fashioned rector') (?), 163 n., 279
'No Bell-Ringing' (poem):
  pub. in *Sphere* vi. 303 n.
Nobel Prize for Literature (1921) vi. 106 ('the
  prize') and n.
Nobel Prize for Peace (1924) vi. 267 and n.
'Noble Lady's Tale, The' (poem) iii. 153
  ('Romance in verse') and n., 159 and n.
Noble, Celia Saxton iii. 265 and n.
Noel, Roden Berkeley Wriothesley i. 165 n.,
  260 n.
  A Little Child's Monument i. 264, 265 and
    n.
  A Modern Faust i. 265 and n.
  letters to i. 165, 259, 261, 264, 265, 267, 271,
    279
Nonesuch Press vi. 316 and n.
Nordau, Max:
  Conventional Lies of Our Civilization ii. 83
    and n.
Nordysk Forlag vi. 78, 80, 81 n.
Norfolk, Henry Fitz-Alan Howard, 15th Duke
  of iv. 141 n.
  letter to iv. 141
Norfolk, Horatio Edward:
  Gleanings in Graveyards vi. 82 n.
(?) Norreys, Rose vii. 121 ('Miss Norris'),
  122 n.
Norris, John ii. 46 n.
  letter to ii. 46
Norris, W. H. vii. 162 n.
  letter to vii. 161
Norris, William Edward i. 270, 271 n.; vii. 125
  and n.
North American Review ii. 92 n., 96 n., 102 n.,
  173 n.; iii. 71, 72 n.
  'Trampwoman's Tragedy' pub. in iii. 75 n.,
    82 ('the other'), 83 and n., 84, 87 and n.,
    88; iv. 4 ('one of these') and n.
  'A Hundred Years Since' pub. in v. 46
    ('shape of verse') and n., 69 ('some verses')
    and n.
  letters to editors of iii. 71; v. 69
North American Review Co.:
  letter to iii. 87

North Dorset Conservative Association vi.
  288 n.
Northcliffe, Alfred Charles William Harms-
  worth, Viscount:
  interest in TH's books v. 282 and nn.
  letter to v. 282
Northern Figaro ii. 70, 71 n.
  letter to ii. 70 (erroneous identification, cor-
    rected at vii. 173)
Norwich Cathedral vii. 141 and n.
'Nothing Matters Much' (poem) vi. 364
  ('brother Fossett') and n.
Nouvelle Revue Française vi. 282 and n.
Nouvelles Littéraires vi. 163 n., 305 nn.
Novel Review i. 277 n.
Novello & Co. (music publishers) vi. 191 n.
Noyes, Alfred iii. 296 n.
  reviews of TH works iii. 296; vi. 224 and n.
  and 'Poets' Tribute' v. 331 and n.
  on TH's 'philosophy' vi. 52 and n., 53–5
  'Bacchus and the Pirates' iv. 9 ('Noyes's
    contribution') and n.
  letters to iii. 296; v. 331; vi. 52, 53, 59, 196,
    224
Nuremberg i. 167 n.

'O Jan, O Jan, O Jan' (folk-piece) vi. 191 and
  n., 219 n., 245, 293
O'Brien, Lady Susan (*née* Strangways) iii.
  159 n.; vi. 46 n.
O'Brien, William v. 109 n.; vi. 46 n.
O'Connor, Elizabeth Paschal ii. 139 ('Mrs
  T.P.')
O'Connor, Thomas Power ii. 53 and n.*, 139
  and n.; iv. 71 n.
  letter to iv. 71
O'Rourke, May v. 270 ('unknown young
  lady'), 271 nn.
  as occasional secretary v. 271 n.; vi. 259,
    260 n., 278, 279 n.; vii. 4 n., 24 n., 26 n.,
    36 n., 56
Oaker's Wood House (Dorset) iii. 123 and n.
Oakeshott, (Sir) Walter Fraser vi. 256 n.
  letter to vi. 256
Observer iii. 193; v. 247 n., 295 n.; vi. 137 and
  n., 350, 351 n.
Octaves dinners i. 218 and n.
'Often When Warring' (poem) vi. 23 and n.,
  218
  pub. in *Sphere* v. 233 n.
Ogden, Charles Kay v. 208 n.
  and support for *Cambridge Magazine* v.
    207, 208 n.
  letter to v. 207
Old, Robert George (blacksmith) iv. 260
  and n.
Oliphant, Francis Wilson i. 107 n.

Oliphant, Margaret Oliphant Wilson i. 107
n.*, 133; ii. 87 n., 105 ('rival novelist'),
106 n.
letter to i. 107
Oliver, Revd John ii. 5 n.
letters to ii. 4; iv. 138
Oliver, Vere Langford vi. 226 and n.
Olivier, Sir Sydney v. 152 ('Chairman') and n.
Ollendorff, Paul (publisher) ii. 178 n., 273,
274 n.
Omar Khayyám Club ii. 288 n., 289
dinners ii. 75 and n., 78, 80 ('your guest'),
81 n., 82 and n., 274; iii. 104, 113 n.; iv.
12 and n.
'On the Application of Coloured Bricks and
Terra Cotta to Modern Architecture' (essay)
ii. 24 and n.; vi. 187 n.
'On the Portrait of a Woman about to be
Hanged' (poem) vi. 178 n.
'On Sturminster Foot-Bridge' (poem) v. 318
'On the Western Circuit' (story) ii. 52 n.; iv.
318 n.
pub. in *English Illustrated* i. 243 ('short
story') and n., 251 ('the story') and n.
original scene of ii. 132, 172 n.
MS given to Manchester Public Library iv.
178 n.
'One We Knew' (poem):
pub. in *Harper's Weekly* iii. 75 ('other
poem') and n., 80 ('poem on old times')
pub. in *Tatler* iii. 81 n., 82 ('the poem'), 92
('the poem') and n., 136 n.
Open Air Theatre Society iv. 301 and n.
Oppenheim, Charles Augustus i. 126 n.
Oppenheim, Isabelle i. 126 n.
and *Dynasts* iii. 106
letters to i. 125, 145; iii. 106, 134, 144
Organist and Choirmaster iii. 178 and n.
Orr, Alexandra Sutherland i. 68 n.; vii. 94 n.
letter to vii. 93
Ortelius:
Theatrum Orbis Terrarum v. 41 ('atlas')
and n.
Osborne, Samuel Duffield iii. 364 n.
letter to iii. 364
Osbourne, Lloyd vii. 26 n.
Osgood, James Ripley (publisher) i. 180,
182 n.*, 222 and n., 230, 258; ii. 16 n.,
47 n.; iii. 6
death i. 268, 269 and n.; vii. 117 n.
letters to i. 181, 196, 211, 218–19, 220; vii.
117
Osgood, James R. & Co. (publishers) i. 29 and
n., 32 and n.
Osgood, McIlvaine & Co. (publishers) i.
219 n.; ii. 12 n., 47 n., 51 n., 55 and n.,
88, 240 n.; iv. 161 n.; v. 133 n.

pub. *A Group of Noble Dames* i. 230 ('the
book'), 231 n.; iii. 11 n.; vii. 119 n.
pub. *Tess* i. 268 ('next door neighbour')
and n.
and 'Wessex Novels' edn ii. 60 n., 63 and n.,
65 n., 69 and n., 71, 76 n., 201 n.; iii.
11 nn., 36 n., 91 n., 96, 275 n.; iv. 43 n.,
44 n., 116 n., 124 n., 199 n.; vi. 35 n.
and *Tess* dramatization ii. 110, 111
and *Well-Beloved* ii. 141 n.; iv. 60 n.; vii.
119 and n.
TH's seven-year contract with iii. 5 ('our
agreement'), 6 n., 7, 11, 13
merger with Harper iii. 6 n., 33
Osmington (Dorset) iv. 190; vi. 355 n.
Ostend ii. 130
Ottery St Mary (Devon) i. 242 n.
Otway, Thomas ii. 246
Venice Preserved ii. 246 n.
'Ouida' (Marie Louise de la Ramée) iii. 105,
106 n.
Ould, Herman vii. 80 n.
Our Dumb Friends' League v. 195 n.
'Our Exploits at West Poley' (story):
serialization i. 116 ('the story') and n., 123,
126 ('the story'), 127 n., 141 n., 158
('short story')
Outlook iii. 168 and n., 183 n.; vi. 33 and n.
review of *Wessex Poems* ii. 212, 213 n., 214
'Geographical Knowledge' pub. in iii. 164
and n., 166 n.; iv. 199 and n.
'Overcombe':
original of ii. 131; iii. 285; iv. 123
Ovid v. 231, 232 n.
Owen, Arthur Synge vi. 363, 364 n.
Owen, Catharine ii. 30 ('her elder sister'),
31 n., 147 n., 201 n. ('her sister'), 202
('those Americans'), 203 n., 215 n.; iii.
108 ('your sister'); iv. 243 ('some callers'),
244 n., 245 n.
letter to iv. 244
Owen, Revd George Vale:
The Life beyond the Veil vi. 31 n.
Owen, Rebekah ii. 3 and n., 30 ('young American lady'), 31 n., 32 ('American friend'),
147 n.*; iv. 243 ('some callers'), 244 n.,
245 n.
at New York *Tess* dramatization ii. 152
in Lake District ii. 201, 202 ('those Americans'), 203 n., 215 n., 259
and *Wessex Poems* ii. 214
inscribed copies of TH works iii. 108 and n.,
148 ('your book'), 149 n.
conversion to Roman Catholicism iii. 344
and ELH's death iv. 243 ('some callers'),
244 n., 245 n.
reference from TH v. 127

Owen, Rebekah (*cont.*)
  letters to ii. 146, 152, 201, 203, 214, 259,
    273; iii. 106, 148, 284; iv. 244
Ower Moigne (Dorset):
  as 'Nether Moynton' ii. 132
'Oxen, The' (poem) ii. 189 n.; v. 278; vi. 51,
  136
  MS sold for Red Cross v. 145 n.
  reprints of vi. 34, 35 n., 240 ('print the card')
    and n.; vii. 58 n.
  musical setting vi. 42, 43 n.
Oxford i. 5; ii. 16, 174 n.; iii. 225; vii. 121,
  122 n.
  as 'Christminster' iii. 226 n.; vii. 41, 42 n.
Oxford Book of English Verse vi. 104
Oxford and Cambridge Club vi. 370 n.
Oxford Magazine iii. 126 and n.
Oxford University i. 37 and n.
  offer of honorary degree to Swinburne iv.
    15, 16 n.
  Museum jubilee iv. 54, 60
  honorary degree for TH v. 351 n.; vi. 5 n., 8
    ('congratulations'), 9 n., 30, 55
  Bodleian Library iv. 180, 181 n., 184
  Keble College vi. 364 n.
  Queen's College:
    TH elected hon. fellow of vi. 167 ('the
      distinction'), 168 n., 170 ('it came') and
      n., 172 n.; vii. 18 n.
    invitations to college feasts vi. 172 and n.;
      vii. 88 and n., 170 and n.
    TH visits vi. 201 and n., 202, 203; vii.
      170 n.
    TH's gift of portrait-etching vii. 18 and n.
Oxford University Dramatic Society:
  production of scenes from *Dynasts* v. 346
    and n., 347–9, 351 and n.; vi. 5, 8, 9, 30,
    323 n.
Oxford University Extension Delegacy iii. 326
  n.; iv. 11 n.
Oxford University Press iii. 246; iv. 145; vi. 73
  and nn., 285, 334, 335 n., 339 n.; vii. 69 and
  n. *See also* Clarendon Press

P., A.N.T.A.:
  Theories: Studies from a Modern Woman ii.
    117 and n.
Page, Walter Hines v. 109 and n.
  letters to v. 109, 165
Page, Mrs W. H. v. 165 and n.
Pageant of Youth (1921) vi. 89, 90 n.
Pain, Barry:
  'The Kaiser and God' v. 46 n.
Pair of Blue Eyes, A (novel) ii. 63; v. 95; vi. 61,
  64, 181; vii. 165 and nn., 169 n.
  writing of i. 14 ('another'), 16 ('3 vol
    novel'), 17 ('the MS.')

  tentative title i. 17, 18 n.
  illustrations i. 18 and nn.; ii. 65 and n.
  payment for i. 20, 23 n.
  presentation copies i. 26, 161 and n.; ii.
    297 n.; iv. 209 and n.
  as operatic subject iv. 291
  film version of scene from v. 24 n.
  history of MS v. 147 and n.
  BACKGROUND AND ORIGINALS OF
  PLACES:
    i. 167; iv. 139, 210; vi. 27, 29, 154, 155;
      vii. 168 ('a novel')
    heroine based on ELH iv. 288; v. 95 n.;
      vi. 3 n., 155
    original of Stephen Smith in vi. 110, 138,
      139 n., 140 n., 154
    autobiographical element vi. 154, 155,
      157 n.
  CRITICAL RECEPTION:
    i. 21, 22 and nn.; v. 282; vi. 157 n.
    praised by Tennyson and Patmore ii. 296;
      iv. 288, 291; v. 282
  EDITIONS:
    American i. 27 n., 28
    first (three-vol.) i. 21; v. 168 and n.
    Mellstock v. 313, 314, 316, 342; vi. 3 n., 6
    one-vol. i. 43, 45 and n., 48 and n.
    Wessex iv. 209 and n.
    'Wessex Novels' ii. 65 and n.
  SERIALIZATION:
    i. 17–19, 20, 21; v. 147
  TRANSLATIONS:
    French vii. 11
    Spanish v. 209 n., 342, 345; vi. 33, 61,
      62 n.
Palgrave, Francis Turner i. 155 and n.
  (comp.) *Golden Treasury of English Lyrics*
    ii. 208
Pall Mall Gazette i. 22 n., 156, 157 n.; ii. 98
  and n.
  Archer's attack on Gosse in i. 227, 228 n.
Pall Mall Magazine ii. 264, 265 n.; iii. 178 n.,
  190 and n.; iv. 13 and n., 199 and n.
  'An Imaginative Woman' pub. in ii. 6 n., 7,
    22 ('P.M.M. story') and n., 32 n., 49 n.
  Archer interview with TH in ii. 279 ('the
    copy') and n.
  photographs of TH in ii. 279 and n.; iii. 33
    and n.
Palmer, Arnold vii. 26 n., 32 n.
Palmer, Cecil v. 281 n.
  (comp.) *The Thomas Hardy Calendar* v. 32
    and nn., 281 n.
  letter to v. 281
Palmer, John v. 68 n.
Palmerston, Lord i. 6; vi. 276
  funeral of i. 5; iii. 143; vii. 7, 43 n.

Panmure, Fox Maule, 2nd Lord iii. 143 n.
'Panthera' (poem) iv. 45 n., 47 ('legendary one'), 48 nn., 114; v. 139
Panton, James (Dorchester brewer) i. 144, 145 n.; iv. 249 and n.; vi. 98 and n.
Panton, Jane Ellen i. 126 and n., 145 n.; iv. 249 n.
  letters to i. 144; iv. 249; vi. 98
Paris i. 114; iii. 84, 89 n., 265 n.; iv. 72, 73 n., 306, 307 n.; v. 44; vi. 310 and n.
  TH's honeymoon in i. 32 n., 35 n.; iii. 21 and n.
  TH revisits (1882) vii. 95 and n.
Paris Exhibition (1900) ii. 257 and n.
Parker, Louis Napoleon iii. 136 n.
  letters to iii. 135, 298
Parker, Walter H. vii. 54 n.
  letter to vii. 53
Parliament Bill crisis iii. 353 n.; iv. 86 and n.
Parnell, Charles Stewart v. 29
Parnell, Katharine:
  Charles Stewart Parnell, His Love Story and Political Life v. 29 and n.
Parratt, Arthur M. vi. 287 n.
  letter to vi. 286
Parry, A. Ivor vi. 187 ('troublesome anthologist') and nn.
Parsons, Alfred William i. 115 n., 181, 182 n., 186 n.*, 187; ii. 78 n.
  illustrates 'First Countess of Wessex' i. 182 n., 186 n., 187 n.
  letters to i. 186, 187; iv. 109, 245, 264
Parsons, Charles (Dorchester postmaster) i. 4 and n.
Parsons, John Denham vii. 49 nn.
  letter to vii. 49
Parton, Mrs Eugenie v. 222
Pasco, E. iii. 94 n., 154
  letters to iii. 93, 124
Pasco, Rear-Admiral John iii. 94 n., 124 n., 154
Pasquier, J. A. i. 18 n.
Passchendaele, Battle of (1917) v. 230 n.
Pater, Walter ii. 17 n.
Paterson (later Allingham, q.v.), Helen i. 30 n.
  illustrates *Far from the Madding Crowd* i. 25 n., 30 and n.
Pathé Frères Cinema Co. iv. 289 and nn.
Patmore, Coventry Kersey Dighton i. 156, 157 nn., 158
  praise of *Pair of Blue Eyes* iv. 288, 291
  Principle in Art i. 208 ('little volume') and n.
  letters to i. 157, 208
Patten, Harry (Portland bank manager) iv. 306 n.
Patterson, Charlotte Helene vii. 71 n.
Paul, Charles Kegan (publisher) i. 48 n., 58 n.*, 68 nn., 95 n., 154 and n.; ii. 128 n.

essay on 'Mr Hardy's Novels' i. 89 and n., 96 n.
  letters to i. 57, 67, 89, 145, 172; ii. 127
  See also Kegan Paul, Trench, Trübner, & Co.
Paul-Margueritte, Ève iii. 139 n.
Payn, James i. 148 n.; iv. 9 and n.
  letter to i. 148
Payne, Police Constable iv. 113 n.
Peabody, Josephine Preston (Mrs Lionel Marks) iii. 263 n.
  The Singing Man: A Book of Songs and Shadows iv. 201 and n.
  letters to iii. 263; iv. 102, 201
'Peace Peal, The, (After Years of Silence)' (poem):
  pub. in *Graphic* v. 313 n.
Pearce, Clara Jane ii. 138 and n.
Pearce, Isabel ii. 51 n.
  letter to ii. 50
Pearce, Philip vi. 288 n.
  letter to vi. 287
Pearce, Thomas Alfred (Dorchester accountant) iv. 76 and n.
Pearcey (corrected from 'Peachey' at vii. 172), Mary Eleanor i. 222 and n.
Pearsall, Robert vii. 43 nn.
  letter to vii. 43
Pearson, Karl i. 263 n.
  The New University for London i. 263 n.
  letters to i. 263, 272, 276
'Peasant's Confession, The' (poem) ii. 207 and n., 211; vii. 19, 20 n.
Peasenhall (Suffolk):
  murder iii. 48, 49 n.
Peaty, Frank Walter Henville (mayor of Weymouth) vi. 261 n., 295
  letter to vi. 260
Peel, Julia Beatrice ii. 22, 23 n.
Peirce, Walter iv. 40 n.
  letter to iv. 40
Pembroke, George Robert Charles Herbert, 13th Earl of ii. 53 ('her husband'), 54 n., 55 and n.
Pembroke, Lady ii. 53, 54 n., 55
P.E.N. Club vi. 107 n., 192 ('the Club') and nn.; vii. 79, 80 n.
  letter to secretary vi. 107
Penderel-Brodhurst, James George Joseph ii. 171 n.
  letter to ii. 171
Pendleton, Charlotte ii. 261 n.
  letter to ii. 261
Penn Mutual Life Insurance Co. of Philadelphia ii. 219 n.
Pennell, Joseph iii. 245 n.
  letter to iii. 244

Pennie, John Fitzgerald vi. 58 and n.
The Tale of a Modern Genius; or, the Miseries of Parnassus i. 111 and n.
Pentin, Revd Herbert iii. 156 nn., 278 n., 315 n.
'Dorset Children's Doggerel Rhymes' v. 279 and n.
(and T. Perkins) *Memorials of Old Dorset* iii. 265 n.
letters to iii. 156, 278, 314; iv. 57; v. 279
People's Palace i. 210 and n.
Pepys, Samuel:
Cambridge commemoration v. 7 and n., 9
Perkins, Alfred More vi. 258 n.
Perkins, Revd Frederick vi. 258 n.
Perkins, Revd Thomas ii. 199 and n., 202, 227, 255 n.*; iii. 223, 250, 251 n.; iv. 90
as photographer ii. 254, 255 n., 265, 279 n.; iii. 101 and n., 109 and n., 110, 111 and n., 112 n.
and protection of ancient buildings iii. 50, 51 n., 54 and n.
(and H. Pentin) *Memorials of Old Dorset* iii. 265 n.
letters to ii. 254; iii. 54, 97
Perkins, Revd William Henry vi. 258 n.
letter to vi. 258
Péronne (France) v. 310, 311 n.
Perrett, Wilfrid iii. 177 n.
The Story of King Lear from Geoffrey of Monmouth to Shakespeare iii. 177 ('book on King Lear') and n.
letter to iii. 177
Perrins, Charles William Dyson iv. 214, 215 n.
Perry Mason & Co. (publishers) i. 116 n.
letters to i. 116, 123, 126
pessimism, alleged i. 190, 262; ii. 141, 215; iii. 187, 231, 306, 308; v. 182, 278, 309; vi. 51, 54, 55, 245, 329 n.
Peterborough (Cambs) iv. 98 n.
Cathedral ii. 141 and n.
Petrie, (Sir) Flinders ii. 222 and n.; vii. 132 n.
Phalange, La iii. 351, 352 n.
'Phantom Horsewoman, The' (poem) v. 212
Phelps, Samuel v. 174 and n., 195, 196 n.
Phelps, William Henry ii. 239 n.
Words for the Wind: A Book of Prose-Points ii. 239 and n.
letter to ii. 239
Phelps, William Lyon v. 352 nn.
letter to v. 352
Philips, Katherine iii. 102 ('Orinda'), 103 n.
Phillips, Stephen ii. 188; iii. 73 n.
Paolo and Francesca ii. 243 and n., 246 ('play')
Poems ii. 188 n.
Phillpotts, Eden ii. 181 n.; v. 214, 231; vi. 143

Cheat-the-boys vi. 238 ('Devon story') and n.
The Iscariot iv. 207 and n.
Old Delabole v. 128 and nn.
Old Plymouth v. 128
Orphan Dinah v. 57 ('your book'), 58 n.
The Secret Woman iv. 200 ('the play'), 201 n., 202 ('the play')
letters to ii. 180; iv. 207; v. 17, 122, 128; vi. 57, 238
philosophy – *see* ideas and philosophy
Philpot, Glyn v. 242 n.; vi. 69 and n.
Phipps, Paul iii. 288 n.
'Photograph, The' (poem) vi. 96
Pickersgill, Henry William vii. 146, 147 n.
Pike, Laurence Warburton ii. 238 and n., 265 n., 266 and n.
Pilsdon Pen (Dorset) i. 136 n.; iv. 119 ('Hill'); v. 111, 112 n., 167; vi. 14 n.
'Pine-Planters, The' (poem) iii. 41 ('some lines')
pub. in *Cornhill* iii. 42 n.
Pinero, (Sir) Arthur Wing ii. 19 and n., 20 n.; vii. 136 n.
and proposed Shakespeare Memorial iii. 156 n., 157
and TH's second marriage v. 14
The Benefit of the Doubt ii. 90 ('the play') and n.
The Gay Lord Quex ii. 219 ('successful play') and n.; vii. 132 n.
Iris ii. 303 and n.
Playgoers v. 14 ('one of yours') and n.
The Second Mrs Tanqueray ii. 43 and n.
The Squire i. 99 and n., 100 and n., 101 n., 103 n., 104 n.; ii. 19, 20 n.; vii. 95 n.
letters to iii. 157; iv. 247; v. 14
'Pink Frock, The' (poem) v. 250 and n.
Pinker, James Brand iii. 29 and n., 281 and n.
letter to iii. 29
Pinney, Lady Hester vi. 375 n.; vii. 5 n.
letter to vii. 5
Pinney, John vii. 375 n.
letters to vi. 375; vii. 14
Pinney, Major-General Sir Reginald John vi. 375 n.; vii. 5 n.
Pitoëff, Georges vi. 365, 366 n.
Pitt, George vi. 41 and n.
Pitt, Grace Amelia Morton (erroneous identification, corrected at vii. 176) vi. 36 and n.
Pitt, Lora (wrongly identified as Grace Amelia) vi. 36 and n., 71; vii. 176
Pitt, William iii. 41; iv. 120; vi. 1, 2 n., 259, 260 n.; vii. 83 and n.
Pitt-Rivers, Alexander Edward Lane Fox- ii. 270 ('Lady Grove's brother') and n.
Pitt-Rivers, Alice ii. 87 ('the hostess') and n.; iv. 82, 83 n., 94, 95 n.

Pitt-Rivers, General Augustus Henry Lane Fox- ii. 84, 85 n., 228, 270 n.; iv. 95 n.
Pittsburgh Institute iii. 220 n.
    letter to iii. 220
'Pity of It, The' (poem) v. 215 and n.
    pub. in *Fortnightly* v. 86 ('sonnet'), 87 n.
Pixie (Max Gate cat) iii. 86, 90
'Place on the Map, The' (poem):
    pub. in *English Review* iv. 289, 295
plagiarism, imputed i. 103–4 and nn.
Platt, William ii. 123 and n.
Playhouse Theatre iii. 250 n.
Plummer, Henry iii. 55 n.
Plymouth (Devon) iv. 257, 260; v. 230, 231 n., 271; vi. 58
    Gifford family graves iv. 311 and n.; v. 30, 32 and nn., 34, 110, 124
    ELH's childhood in iv. 327
    proposed Anglo-American University v. 263 and n.
    TH MSS presented to Public Library vi. 58 n.
Plymouth School of Art:
    letter to Committee of iii. 103
Pocket Edition iii. 217 and nn., 218 n., 221 and n., 226, 227 and nn., 229, 230, 246, 274 ('the 2/6'), 275 n., 283 n.; iv. 4 n., 271 n.; v. 291 n., 301 n.; vi. 227 n., 235 and n., 236, 238, 283 n.; vii. 48 and n., 58 n.
Pocock, Constance v. 277 and n., 325
Pocock, Constantine v. 325, 326 n.
Poe, Edgar Allan ii. 303 and n.; v. 25
'Poems of 1912–13' v. 35 ('some poems') and n., 64 and n., 70 ('those in memory of Emma')
Poems of the Past and the Present ii. 168 n., 232 n.; iii. 13, 24, 30, 93, 94, 140, 189, 217, 260; v. 254 n.; vi. 101 n., 181; vii. 141, 150 and n.
    preparation of ii. 282 ('volume of poems') and n., 293 ('the poems') and nn., 298 ('that MS.') and n., 300 ('the volume') and n.
    possible setting to music of lyrics in iii. 73
    topographical backgrounds iii. 137
    MS given to Bodleian iv. 180
    Canadian rights vi. 65
    EDITIONS:
        Collected Poems iv. 4 n., 10, 14 and n., 17 and n.
        first ii. 295 ('Poems'), 296 n., 300 ('the volume'), 303 ('Poems'), 304 ('my own volume') and n., 305 ('poems') and nn.; iii. 5 n.
        Pocket iii. 217 and n., 227 n., 283 n.
        Uniform (3s.6d.) iii. 29 n., 94 and n.
poetry, views on i. 122, 182, 241; ii. 214; iii.

105, 114, 133, 199, 221, 258; iv. 113, 300, 301 n., 307; v. 75, 215, 275, 292, 330, 345; vi. 77, 138, 165, 186, 229; vii. 36
Poetry and Drama iv. 307 and n., 330; v. 87 n.
'Poets' Tribute' (for TH's 79th birthday) v. 326 and n., 327 and nn., 328–9, 330–1, 332–4, 335–6, 337, 338 n., 339, 340 ('three and forty'), 344 and n., 347, 351
Poldon (Polden) Hills (Somerset) iii. 83
politics, attitude to i. 6, 119, 121, 123–4, 180, 231, 233–4, 236, 248, 272; ii. 52, 83, 135, 270; iii. 46, 79, 95, 190, 196, 304; iv. 62, 86, 129; v. 38, 99, 159, 160; vi. 37, 53, 71, 79, 94, 95 n., 102, 110, 246, 247
Pollard, Albert Frederick v. 21 n. (correctly identified at vii. 175)
Pollock, Sir Frederick v. 208 n.; vi. 170 n.; vii. 3 and n., 173
    letters to ii. 6 (correctly identified at vii. 173); vi. 170
Pollock, Walter Herries i. 121 nn.*, 145 n., 252 and n.; vi. 370 n.
    letters to i. 121; vii. 93
Pollock, Sir William Frederick i. 126 n.; ii. 6 n. (erroneous identification, corrected at vii. 173)
    letter to i. 126
Pollock, Lady i. 126 n.
    letter to i. 126
Poncet, Marcel vii. 65 and n.
Pond, Major James Burton iii. 281 n.
Pond, Miss vi. 45, 46 n.
Ponsonby, Sir Henry Frederick i. 83 n.
    letter to i. 83
Ponting, Charles Edwin iii. 346 ('the architect's') and n.
Poole, Austin Lane vii. 152 n.
    letter to vii. 151
Poole, Henry vii. 10 n.
Poole, John:
    Paul Pry v. 297 n.
Poole, Stanley Edward Lane- i. 184 n.
    letter to i. 184
Poole (Dorset) i. 114, 115 n.; vii. 147 and n.
    as 'Havenpool' ii. 132
Poor Man and the Lady, The (unpub. novel) i. 12 n.; iv. 23 n.
    offered to publishers i. 7–10; iii. 277 ('first MS.') and n.; iv. 130, 306; vi. 155 ('latter part of 1868'), 157 n., 254 ('first novel') and n.
Pope, Alexander:
    The Dunciad v. 75 n.
    Epistle to Lord Bathurst vi. 340 n.
    Epistle to Dr Arbuthnot vii. 108 n.
Pope, Alfred (Dorchester brewer) i. 100 n.*, 170 n.; iv. 55 n., 76; v. 102 n., 103 n.

Pope, Alfred (*cont.*)
lecture on 'Dorset Dew-ponds' iv. 183 and n.
and ELH's death iv. 240
paper on 'Dorchester Walks' v. 102 n., 198 and n.
sons' military service v. 102 and n., 104, 133 and n., 270 and n.
A Book of Remembrance v. 102 n., 270 ('the book') and n., 287 ('Biographies') and n., 290 ('through it') and n., 295 n., 296 ('them') and nn.
The Walks and Avenues of Dorchester v. 198 and n.
letters to i. 100, 170; iii. 130, 189; iv. 55, 149, 183, 188, 197, 213, 224, 225, 240, 315; v. 101, 133, 198, 267, 270, 287, 290, 295, 296, 302, 310; vi. 43, 168, 174
Pope, Mrs Alfred (Elizabeth Mary Whiting) iv. 286 n.; v. 104; vi. 43 and n.
letter to iv. 286
Pope, Lieut. Cyril v. 104 ('prisoner son') and n.
Pope, Lieut.-Colonel Edward Alexander v. 302 ('your son') and n.
Pope, 2nd Lieut. Percy Paris:
death on active service v. 133 ('missing son') and n., 188 ('the soldier') and n.
Popham, Jane Susanna v. 1 n.; vi. 160 n.
'On Egdon He'th' v. 1 ('your verses') and n.
letters to v. 1; vi. 159; vii. 33
Poplar Farm (near Newbury) iii. 288 n., 318; iv. 273 n.
'Port Bredy':
Bridport as ii. 132; iii. 147 ('scene of "Fellow Townsmen"')
Portesham (Dorset) iii. 234 (spelt 'Portisham'); vi. 128, 129 nn.
Portland, Sir William John Arthur Charles James Cavendish-Bentinck, 6th Duke of vii. 5 and n.
Portland (Dorset) ii. 152 n., 153
as background of *Well-Beloved* i. 249 n.; ii. 133, 152 n.; vii. 45 n.
during Great War v. 42, 132 n., 249
stone vi. 234, 235 and n.
proposed local museum vii. 44, 45 n.
Portland Bill (Dorset) ii. 266; iii. 137; vii. 17 n.
Portland Roads (Dorset) v. 71 and n.
Portmore (Ireland) iii. 102, 103 n.
Porto-Riche, Georges de:
Bonheur manqué, carnet d'un amoureux iii. 109, 110 n.
Théâtre d'Amour iii. 109, 110 n.
letter to iii. 109
Porto-Riche, Mme de (Lise Lunel):
proposed dramatization of *Tess* iii. 109, 110 n.

'Portraits, The' (poem) vi. 241
pub. in *Nash's and Pall Mall* vi. 242 n.
Portsmouth, Newton Wallop, 5th Earl of i. 128 n., 131 and n.*, 153 n.
Portsmouth, Eveline Countess of i. 127, 128 n.*, 131, 132, 153 n., 263; ii. 302 n.; vi. 155 ('society Countess'), 157 n.
letter to ii. 301
Portsmouth iv. 47 n., 231, 272
Positivist Society i. 134 n.; ii. 46 n., 53; vi. 180 n.
Poulton, Edward Bagnall vi. 252 n.
letter to vi. 251
Pouncy, Harry iii. 247 n.*, 286; iv. 76, 147 n., 304 and n., 308; vi. 171 and n., 224 n., 240 n., 251 n.; vii. 140, 141 n.
'Hours in Hardyland' presentation iii. 279 ('the performance'), 281 n., 281, 299 ('the lecture') and n.; v. 58 n.
assisted by TH iii. 247, 281, 359, 362; iv. 1; v. 18 and n., 42 and n.
'The Pulpit Rock' iv. 170 and n.
letters to iii. 247, 279, 281, 299, 317, 359, 362; iv. 147, 170, 322; v. 18, 42, 58; vi. 224
Pouncy, Thomas (Dorchester saddler and amateur actor) v. 3 n.; vi. 296 and n.
Pouncy, Walter (Dorchester photographer):
TH portrait as post-card v. 243 and n.
letter to v. 243
Pound, Ezra Loomis vi. 47 n.
gift of inscribed volumes to TH vi. 49 and n., 77
'Homage to Sextus Propertius' vi. 77, 78 n.
Hugh Selwyn Mauberley vi. 49 n., 77 ('H.S.M.'), 78 n.
Quia Pauper Amavi vi. 49 n., 78 n.
letters to vi. 47, 49, 77
Poundbury Camp (Dorset) iii. 109 and n.
Pourbus family ii. 134
Powell, G. H.:
'Satires of Circumstance' parodied by v. 314 and n.
Powys, Albert Reginald v. 296 nn.; vi. 206, 226 n.
letters to vi. 207, 226; vii. 17
Powys, Llewellyn iv. 266 n.; vi. 230 n.
'Death' iv. 266 ('essay') and n.
letter to iv. 266
Practical Junior Photographer ii. 255 n.; iii. 111
Pratt, Harriett Ann iv. 250 n.
letter to iv. 250
Press Club ii. 220, 221 n.
Preston, Harriet Waters i. 153 and n.*; ii. 13 ('a lady-critic'), 14 and n.

Pretor, Alfred iii. 25 and n., 26, 45 n.*, 84 and
  n., 112 ('Fellow') and n.; vii. 145 and n.
  Ronald and I iii. 45 n.
  letter to iii. 45
Price, Jane iv. 308 and n.
Prideaux, Charles Sydney (Dorchester dentist
  and antiquarian) ii. 163 n., 227 ('dentist-
  tenant') and n.; iii. 347, 348 n.; iv. 141 n.
  letter to ii. 163
Pridham, John Alexander vi. 251 nn.
  letter to vi. 250
Priestley, John Boynton:
  Figures in Modern Literature vi. 281 ('kind
    gift') and nn.
  George Meredith vii. 27 and n., 38 and n.
  letters to vi. 281; vii. 38
Primrose, Lady Peggy (later Lady Crewe) ii.
  215 ('Rosebery's daughters'), 216 n.
Princess Alice, s.s. i. 59, 60 n.
Princess's Theatre vii. 109 n.
Printers' Pension, Almshouse and Orphan
  Asylum Corporation iii. 178 n.
Printers' Pie iii. 178 n.
Prior, Matthew iii. 283 and n.
privacy, views on and concern for i. 89; ii.
  279, 280, 281, 296; iii. 146, 282; vi. 16, 113,
  126, 163, 206; vii. 16, 20, 25
Procter, Anne i. 114 n.*, 172 and n.; v. 90; vi.
  148 and n., 315 and n.
  letter to i. 114
Procter, Bryan Waller i. 114 n.
'Profitable Reading of Fiction, The' i. 172
  ('essay') and n.; ii. 106 n.; iv. 235 n.
  pub. in *Forum* i. 168 and n.; vii. 121 n.
Progress Film Company vi. 72, 73 n., 74 n.,
  78 n., 165 n., 369 n.
Prothero, George Walter iv. 6 n., 47, 48 and n.
Psychical Research Society i. 260 and n.
Public Trustee Office vi. 17 n.
Publishers' Association iv. 63 ('the pub-
  lishers'), 64 n.
Publishers' Weekly iii. 191 and n.
Puddlehinton (Dorset):
  as 'Longpuddle' ii. 131
Puddletown (Dorset) i. 92 n.; ii. 244 n.; iii.
  74 n.; iv. 305 n.
  as 'Weatherbury' ii. 131, 238 n.; iii. 97 n.; iv.
    10, 56 n., 74, 222 n.
  Goddard's chapel iii. 38 and n.
  Ilsington House vi. 251 n., 269 n.
  St Mary's Church iii. 97 and n., 328 and n.;
    iv. 56 and n., 73–4, 78 and n., 114 and n.,
    121, 144 and n., 222 n., 264; vi. 275 and n.
Puddletown Heath (Dorset):
  as 'Egdon Heath' ii. 132
  fire on iii. 171 and n.
Puddletrenthide (Dorset):

  as 'Longpuddle' ii. 131
Pugin, Augustus Welby Northmore i. 1, 2 n.
  (corrected at vii. 171)
Punch i. 6, 7 n., 74, 75
  'Satires of Circumstance' parodied in v. 314
    and n.
Pucknowle Manor (Dorset) iv. 22 ('Punc-
  knoll') and n.
Purcell, Henry:
  The Fairy Queen v. 351 and n.
Purchase, Francis (Dorchester mayor) iv. 147
Pursuit of the Well-Beloved, The (former title
  of *The Well-Beloved*, q.v.) (novel) i.
  204 n., 266 ('slight sketch'), 267 n.; iii. 71
  and n.; vii. 119 and n.
  serialization in *Illustrated London News* i.
    245 n., 283, 284 and n.
  writing of i. 249 ('the story'), 253 and n., 254
    and n., 255, 256 n.; vii. 118 ('syndicate
    story') and n.
  background i. 249 n.
  possible dramatization i. 283
Purves, John vii. 143 n.
  (ed.) *The South African Book of English
    Verse* v. 2 n.; vii. 143 and n.
  letters to vii. 143, 163
Putnam, George Haven iv. 156 n.*; vi. 253
  and n.
  letter to iv. 156
Putnam, Mrs G. H. (Emily Jane Smith) iv.
  153, 156 and n.
Putnam, George Herbert iv. 193 n.
Putnam's (G.P.) Sons (publishers) vi. 252 and
  n., 253
Putney:
  Newnes Public Library iv. 179 n.
  Swinburne's home at The Pines v. 77, 78 n.
'Puzzled Game-Birds, The' (poem) ii. 232 and
  n.; v. 240
Pyddle Valley (Dorset) iii. 234

Quarterly Review ii. 135 n.; iv. 5, 6 nn. 47,
  48 n., 167 and n.; vi. 8, 9 n., 233 and n.,
  247 and n.
  attack on Gosse i. 154, 155 n., 156
  attack on *Tess* i. 264, 265 and n., 268
Quatre Bras, Battle of (1815) v. 218, 219 n.
Quayle, Thomas vi. 373 n.
Queen ii. 238, 239 n.
Queen of Cornwall, The (poetic drama) iv. 4 n.;
  v. 179 n.; vi. 203 ('little thing') and n.,
  204 ('the play') and n., 208, 210, 215,
  216, 217, 229, 232, 233 nn., 293, 304
  Hardy Players' production of vi. 135 n., 203
    and n., 208, 209 and n., 211, 219 ('com-
    ing to see') and n., 220 and nn., 221–2,
    223, 224 n., 237 and n.

Queen of Cornwall, The (cont.)
  musical setting vi. 225 and n., 234 and nn., 236–7, 239 and n., 244, 245 and nn., 249–50, 257 and nn., 265 and n., 269, 271 and n., 272, 273–4, 276, 295 n., 321 and n., 360 and n.; vii. 33, 34 and nn., 35
  MS at Toronto Exhibition (1924) vi. 263, 264 n., 273 and n.
  Masefield production of vi. 287 and n., 303 and n.
  possible stage and film productions vi. 303, 305; vii. 19
  EDITIONS:
    first vi. 208 n., 209 and nn., 211, 219, 221, 223
    Pocket vi. 235 and n., 238, 304 and n., 306, 312
    second vi. 233 nn., 243 and n., 250 n.; vii. 71
    Wessex vi. 361 n.; vii. 8
Queensberry, Lady ii. 122, 123, 128, 251, 252 n.
Quennell, Charles Henry Bourne vi. 80, 83 n.
  letter to vi. 80
'Question of Marriage, A' (poem) ii. 145 n.
Quiller-Couch, Sir Arthur Thomas v. 199, 208 n., 273 n.
  discussion of war poetry iii. 51 and nn.
  preference for Moore's *Esther Waters* over *Tess* v. 183 n.
  lecture on TH's poetry v. 256 and n.
  and 'Poets' Tribute' v. 328, 329 n.
  Adventures in Criticism v. 183 n.
  On the Art of Writing v. 150 ('handsome book'), 151 n.
  'The Sacred Way' v. 193, 194 n.
  (ed.) *Oxford Book of English Verse 1250–1900* ii. 277 and n.
  (ed.) *Oxford Book of Victorian Verse* iv. 227 and n.
  (comp.) *The Pilgrims' Way: A Little Scrip of Good Counsel for Travellers* iii. 221 n.
  letters to iii. 51, 221; iv. 227; v. 150, 183, 193, 295, 328; vi. 327
Quiller-Couch, Bevil v. 183 ('your son') and n., 295 ('your loss') and n.
Quilter, Harry i. 179 nn., 201
  disappointment over professorship ii. 13 n., 15
  letters to i. 178, 210; ii. 12, 15

Raad, Revd Nicholas Charles vii. 74 n.
  Life and Love: Sonnets vii. 74 ('sonnets') and n.
  letter to vii. 74
Rabelais Club i. 63 and n., 70 n., 73, 97, 98, 106 and n., 147; vii. 93 n., 99 and n., 166 n.

Racedown Lodge (Dorset) v. 167, 168 n., 338 n.; vi. 375 n.
Rail Strike (1924) vi. 234 and n.
Rains, Claude vi. 245 n.
Raleigh, (Sir) Walter Alexander iii. 245 n., 304 n., 322 n.; vi. 5, 9, 10 n.
  Wordsworth iii. 245 and n.
  letters to iii. 245, 292
Ralston, William Ralston Shedden- i. 95 n.
  letter to i. 94
Ramsay, Allan:
  Scots Songs vii. 80 n.
Ramsay, Sir George Dalhousie iii. 143 n.
Raper, Robert William ii. 89 ('man from Oxford'), 90 n.
'Rash Bride, The' (poem) iv. 322
Rationalist Press Association v. 22 n., 23 n.
  Hon. Associateship declined by TH ii. 223; v. 22, 23 n.
  Annual and Ethical Review v. 117 and n.
Rawle, Richard, Bp of Trinidad vii. 57 n.
Rawle, William vii. 57 and n.
Rawlins, Revd Thomas S. F. i. 4 n.
Rayleigh, John William Strutt, 3rd Lord v. 273 and n.
Raymond, Walter i. 248 n.; ii. 65 n.
  recital of Barnes's poems i. 248 and n.
  letter to i. 248
Rayner, John L. v. 162 n.
  letter to v. 162
Read, John iv. 207 n.
  Conjuror Lintern iv. 206, 207 n.
  Wold Ways A-gwain iv. 207 ('the volume') and n.; v. 39, 40 n.
  letters to iv. 206; v. 39
Reade, Charles vi. 156, 157 n.
Reader iii. 223 n.
Reading:
  University College vii. 83 and n.
Red Cross v. 188 n., 340 n.
  sale of MSS and books for v. 86 n., 93 ('the sale') and n., 100, 105, 143 n., 144, 145 n., 149 ('gratuitous work') and n., 154, 158, 159, 191 n., 200, 243, 244 and n., 252 n.; vi. 34, 35 n.
  performance of *Dynasts* scenes for v. 150, 162, 166, 182 and nn., 189 n., 191 and n., 193
Redclyffe, E. v. 272 n.
Redesdale, Algernon Bertram Freeman-Mitford, 1st Lord v. 191 and n.
  Memories v. 137 and n., 138
Rees, Leonard vi. 19 n.*, 128 n.
  as editor of *Sunday Times* vi. 19, 150, 162 n., 218 and n.
  letters to vi. 19, 150, 162, 218

Rees's *Chambers's Cyclopaedia, or Universal Dictionary of the Arts & Sciences* iii. 70 and n.

Reeve, Christina Georgina i. 149 n.*, 195, 279 ('editor's wife') and n.; v. 1 n.; vi. 159, 160 n.
letters to i. 148, 188

Reeve, Henry i. 149 n., 267 ('E.R. editor')

Reform Bill (1832) v. 210 and n.

Regent's Park Open-air Theatre iv. 301 n.

Rehan, Ada i. 213 and n.*, 214, 215; ii. 12 n., 22
as the Shrew ii. 11, 17 n., 18, 19, 20
as Helena in *Midsummer Night's Dream* ii. 81 n.

Reid, Forrest iii. 291 n.
letter to iii. 291

Reid, Stuart Johnson ii. 1, 2 n., 3 n.
letter to ii. 3

Reid, Thomas Wemyss i. 228 n.
Life, Letters, and Friendships of Richard Monckton Milnes, First Lord Houghton i. 228 and n.
letter to i. 228

Reid, Whitelaw i. 192 ('Reed') and n.; iii. 279 n.

Reigate Priory (Surrey) ii. 89 n.

Reinhardt, Max iv. 198 n., 205 n.

'Rejected Member's Wife, The' (poem) iii. 196 n.

religion, attitude towards i. 259; ii. 143; iii. 5, 157; iv. 174, 319; vii. 21, 32

religious observance, views on i. 1, 6, 70, 136, 269, 287; iii. 273; iv. 260; vi. 162, 222

'Remembrance' (poem) iii. 75 n.

'Reminiscences of a Dancing-Man' (poem):
pub. in *English Review* iv. 8 ('the shorter') and n.

Return of the Native, The (novel) i. 65 ('the book') and n., 73 and n., 190, 191 n.; ii. 70; iii. 47 n., 70 and n., 177 n.; iv. 8; v. 298 n.; vi. 290 n.
writing of i. 47 and n., 48 and n., 49 and n.
offered to Blackwood i. 47, 48 n., 49
offered to *Temple Bar* i. 50
illustrations to i. 51, 52–3, 54–5, 59 and n.
supposed scene as frontispiece i. 61 and n.; iv. 137
protests at Rumbold story in i. 64 and n.; iv. 229, 230 n.
background and originals of places ii. 74, 132, 254–5, 302, 303; iii. 111 n., 173
disposition of MS iii. 309, 310 n., 319
mumming play in v. 284, 285 n.; vi. 45, 46 n., 47, 57, 134 and n., 232 n.
preservation of unities vi. 221

DRAMATIZATION:
v. 285 n.; vi. 45, 46 and n., 47, 52 ('the play'), 57, 59, 66 n., 67 n., 134 n.

EDITIONS:
Braille v. 268 and n.
first (three-vol.) i. 60 and n., 61, 62
Indian vi. 177 and n.; vii. 163, 164 n.
limited illustrated vii. 87
Tauchnitz iv. 8 n.
Wessex iv. 208, 212

FILM RIGHTS:
vi. 172 and n., 195, 196 n., 198, 202 and n.

SERIALIZATIONS:
American i. 54 n.
Belgravia i. 50, 51 and n., 52–3, 54–5, 57 n., 59 n., 60 and n.

TRANSLATIONS:
Czech vi. 251 and n., 261, 314 and n.
French vi. 61, 62 n., 64

Reveille:
'Whitewashed Wall' pub. in v. 275 ('humble lines'), 276 n.

Review of Reviews vi. 263 and n.

Review of the Week ii. 235, 237, 260 ('series') and nn.

'Revisitation, The' (poem) iii. 117 ('short poem'), 118 ('the lines'); v. 283 and n.; vii. 174
pub. in *Fortnightly Review* iii. 117 n., 135 ('romantic poem') and n.

Revue des Deux Mondes i. 45 and n., 108 and n.; iii. 224, 225 n., 309 and n.

Revue Hebdomadaire vii. 65 and n., 83 n., 85 and n.

Revue Nouvelle vii. 65 n., 83 nn.

Revue de Paris iii. 70, 71 n.

Revue politique et littéraire v. 234 n.

Rew Manor (Dorset) i. 217 ('Rew'); vii. 116 n.

Reynolds, Sir Joshua i. 185 ('your ancestor')

Rheims:
German bombardment of cathedral v. 58 n.

Rhys, Ernest Percival ii. 60 n.
as editor of Everyman's Library vi. 97 nn., 181 nn.
letters to ii. 60; iv. 308; vi. 97

Riccardi Press vi. 40 n., 41 n.

Rice-Oxley, Sir Alfred James vii. 50 n.
letter to vii. 50

Richards, Francis Thomas Grant (publisher) ii. 204 n.; iii. 22 n., 47 n.
letter to ii. 204

Richards, John Morgan iii. 239 n.; iv. 151 n.
letter to iii. 239

Richardson, Henry Handel:
Maurice Guest iv. 24, 25 n.

Richardson, J. E. ii. 172 and n.

Richardson, Nelson Moore:
    and Dorset Natural History and Antiquarian
        Field Club ii. 268 n.; iii. 210 n., 311 and
        n.; iv. 249 n.; v. 28 and nn.; vi. 249 n.
    letters to ii. 268; iii. 209, 311, 315; iv. 249; v.
        28, 118; vi. 248
Riches, T. H. vi. 231 n.
Richmond Hill (Surrey) ii. 290; iii. 176 and n.,
    318
Rickett, Arthur Compton iv. 222 n.
    The Vagabond in Literature iii. 234 and n.
    (and T. Hake) *Life and Letters of Theodore
        Watts-Dunton* v. 96, 97 n.
    letters to iii. 234; iv. 221; v. 96
Rideing, William Henry i. 159 n.; ii. 21 n.
    (ed.) *The Boyhood of Living Authors* i. 158
        ('the subject'), 159 n.
    letters to i. 158, 212; ii. 21, 80
Ridgeway, Rt Revd Frederick Edward, Bishop
    of Salisbury v. 276 ('the Bishop'), 277 n.,
    309 ('our Bishop'), 315 ('our bishop'), 338,
    339 ('the Bishop')
Ridgeway, Philip vi. 334 n.; vii. 19 nn., 38
    production of *Tess* vi. 334 and n., 335–6,
        337, 338, 339, 340–2, 343–4, 345–6 and
        n., 348, 349, 350 and nn., 351, 353–4,
        355 n., 357, 361, 362, 369, 372, 374; vii.
        30 and n., 58 and n.
    production of *Mayor of Casterbridge* vii.
        19 n., 42 n.
    letters to vi. 334, 336, 339, 342, 343, 346,
        348; vii. 19
Ridgeway Hill (Dorset) iii. 82
Ridley, Rosamond, Viscountess v. 35 and n.
Riggs, Jane (Max Gate cook) ii. 162 (?); v. 108,
    109 n.
Riggs, William Henry (labourer) iii. 84 and nn.
Riley, William Edward (architect) v. 179
    and n.
Ritchie, Anne Isabella Thackeray i. 177 n.*; ii.
    38 and n., 89, 90 n.; iv. 256
    Miss Angel iv. 257 n.
    Mrs Dymond i. 132 n.
    letter to i. 177
Ritchie, Richmond Thackeray Willoughby ii.
    89, 90 n.
Rivière, Jacques vi. 282 n.
    letter to vi. 282
'Robert Louis Stevenson' (brief article) vii. 163
    and n.
Robert Louis Stevenson Club vi. 106 n.; vii.
    163 n.
    TH's refusal of hon. life membership vi.
        214, 215 n.
Roberts, A. Llewellyn ii. 57 n.; iv. 78 n.; v.
    226 n.
    letters to ii. 57; iv. 77; v. 226, 228

Roberts, Morley iii. 204 n.
    and *Dynasts* iii. 204
    The Prey of the Strongest iii. 204 ('your new
        book') and n.
    The Private Life of Henry Maitland iv. 234,
        235 n.
    letter to iii. 204
Roberts, Richard Ellis iii. 256 n.
    letter to iii. 256
Robertson, David Allan v. 251 n.
    letter to v. 250
Robertson, Sir George Scott ii. 287, 288 and n.
Robertson, John Mackinnon iii. 85 and n.
Robespierre iii. 291
Robins, Elizabeth ii. 108, 109 n.; v. 349 n.
    letters to iii. 128, 129; v. 349
Robinson, Agnes Mary Frances (later Mme
    Darmesteter, then Duclaux, qq.v.) i. 165 n.,
    193 n.
Robinson, John Richard i. 248 n.
    letter to i. 248
Robinson, Mabel i. 193 n.
Robson and Sons (printers) i. 18 and n.
Rockman, Ray vii. 140 n.
    letter to vii. 139
Rodd, Sir James Rennell vi. 262 n.
    letter to vi. 262
Röhm, C. E. vi. 325 and n.
Rolland, Madeleine ii. 145 n.; vii. 40 n.
    translations of *Tess* ii. 145, 164, 165, 170,
        171, 218 n., 273, 278, 282 n.; iii. 96; vi.
        33 n., 61, 62 n., 64, 75–7
    offer to translate *Jude* ii. 164, 171, 175, 177;
        vi. 65 n.
    translation of stories from *Life's Little
        Ironies* ii. 178, 211, 224, 225, 278
    invited to Max Gate ii. 224; iii. 49; vi. 32
    translation of *Mayor of Casterbridge* iii. 95,
        225; vi. 61, 62 n., 64, 65, 73
    visit to Max Gate iii. 269 ('Parisian visitor')
        and n., 291 n.; iv. 255 n.
    translation of 'A Committee-Man of "The
        Terror"' iii. 290 ('the story'), 291 n.
    and possible translation of TH poems vi. 61,
        62 n., 75
    letters to ii. 145, 164, 167, 170, 171, 173,
        175, 177, 211, 218, 224, 278; iii. 49, 95,
        225, 290; iv. 72, 112, 255; vi. 32, 61, 74,
        173, 228
Rolland, Marie vi. 32, 33 n.
Rolland, Romain vi. 32, 33 n.; vii. 39, 40 n.
    Millet iii. 49 and n.
Rolls, Ann i. 4 and n.
Rolls, Charles Stewart iv. 105 and n.
Rolls, William (farmer) i. 4 n.
Roma June Bureau, Ltd vi. 172 n.
'Roman Gravemounds, The' (poem) iv. 132 n.

'Romantic Adventures of a Milkmaid, The' (story) i. 189; ii. 3 and n.; vii. 87
    published in *Graphic* i. 115 ('the story') and nn., 189 n., 284
    collected in *A Changed Man* i. 285 n.; iv. 299, 329 n.; vi. 143 n.
    Seaside Library edn i. 285 n.; ii. 118 n.
    MS purchased by J. Pierpont Morgan iv. 199 and n., 200
    in Tauchnitz series iv. 321 and n.
    scene of vi. 13
    Czech translation vi. 143 and n.
    possibility of filming vi. 165 n., 367, 368 and n., 369, 370
Rome i. 163; v. 16; vi. 185 and n.
    Keats and Shelley graves and memorials i. 163 and n.; ii. 300; iii. 200 n.; vi. 276 n.; vii. 142 n.
    proposed Shakespeare memorial v. 217, 218 nn.
'Rome: At the Pyramid of Cestius near the Graves of Shelley and Keats' (poem) ii. 300 ('a poem') and n.; vi. 101 n.
Romer, Carrol vii. 78 n., 79 n.
    letter to vii. 78
Romsey (Hants) ii. 226
Roscoe, Sir Henry Enfield i. 276 and n.
Rose, James iii. 235 n.
    letters to iii. 234, 260
Rosebery, Archibald Philip Primrose, 5th Earl of ii. 215
    resignation from Liberal leadership ii. 135 and n.
    and title of *Dynasts* iii. 197
Rosenbaum, Herr (German translator) iii. 101
Ross, Alexander Galt v. 306 n.
Ross, Robert Baldwin:
    memorial to v. 77 and n.
Rossetti, Dante Gabriel iii. 229 n.; iv. 184 n.; v. 349 n.
Rossetti, William Michael iii. 229 and n.
Rostand, Edmond:
    L'Aiglon ii. 251 and n.
Rothenstein, Alice Mary (later Lady) ii. 266; iii. 98 n.; iv. 70 n.
    letters to iii. 98, 208; iv. 70
Rothenstein, (Sir) William iii. 193 n.; iv. 206 n., 229 n.
    portrait drawings of TH ii. 149, 150, 260; iii. 54 and n., 63 and n., 67 n., 98 and n.; v. 144 and n., 146; vii. 167
    invited to Max Gate ii. 266; iv. 229; v. 91
    birthday wishes to TH iv. 219; vi. 28
    English Portraits ii. 187 n.
    Goya ii. 266 and n.
    Six Portraits of Sir Rabindranath Tagore v. 146 ('book of drawings') and n.

Twenty-four Portraits v. 144 n.; vi. 49 ('book of portraits'), 50 n., 52, 53 n.
    letters to ii. 149, 150, 187, 260, 266; iii. 54, 63, 67, 193; iv. 206, 219, 228; v. 91, 144, 146; vi. 28, 49
Rouen:
    TH's honeymoon in i. 32 n., 35 n.
Routledge (publishers) iv. 133, 134 n., 135
Rowe, Nicholas vi. 100 n.
    The Tragedy of Jane Shore vi. 100 and n.
Rowton, Montagu William Lowry Corry, Lord ii. 53, 54 n.
Royal Academy i. 172, 173 n., 201 n.; ii. 16, 18, 257
    annual dinners iv. 149, 150, 151 n. (1911); v. 26 n. (1914), 301, 302 n. (1919)
    annual receptions iii. 67 ('*soiree*'), 68 n., 69 (1903), 256, 257 n. (1907)
    Private Views, Summer Exhibitions ii. 191 n. (1898), 255 and n. (1900), 286 and n. (1901); iv. 85, 86 n. (1910), 213 n. (1912); v. 158, 159 and n. (1916), 303, 304 n. (1919); vi. 197 and n. (1923); vii. 124 and n., 126 n. (1893)
    Summer Exhibitions iii. 254 (1907); iv. 76 and n. (1909); v. 214 and nn. (1917)
    Winter Exhibitions i. 126 (1884), 184, 185 (1889); ii. 216 n. (1899); iii. 2 (1902), 56 and n. (1903), 152 ('the card') and n. (1904)
Royal Academy of Dramatic Art vi. 244, 245 and n.
Royal Agricultural Hall iv. 145 n.
Royal Blind School and Asylum v. 268 and n.
Royal Bounty Fund vii. 159 n.
Royal Court Theatre iii. 127 n., 258 n.; iv. 92 and n., 95, 137 n., 160
Royal Institute of British Architects ii. 182 and nn.; iv. 78 n.; v. 116, 117 n.
    TH wins silver medal of i. 4 and n.; ii. 24 n., 182 n.; v. 117 n.; vi. 187 and n.
    Town Planning Conference (1910) iv. 78 and n.
    TH elected Hon. Fellow v. 117 n.; vi. 15
Royal Institute of Painters in Water Colours vii. 159 and n.
Royal Literary Fund iii. 349; iv. 77, 256, 257 nn.; v. 226 n., 228, 275 and n.; vi. 74 and nn., 330 n., 375 nn.; vii. 81 nn., 159 and n.
Royal Navy vii. 56 and n.
Royal Observatory, Greenwich:
    application to visit i. 96
Royal Society:
    Conversazione (1903) iii. 65 and n.
    dinner (1905) iii. 190 and n.

Royal Society of Arts:
   The Preservation of Ancient Cottages vii.
      62 n.
Royal Society of British Architects:
   TH as Hon. Fellow of vi. 11, 15 and n.
Royal Society of Literature iv. 234 ('R.S.L.');
      v. 231 n., 239 n.; vi. 135 ('R.S.L.') and n.,
      367 n.; vii. 169 n.
   Academic Committee of iv. 107 and n., 176
      and n.
   award of gold medal to TH iv. 213 ('that
      honour'), 215 and n., 216 ('that medal'),
      217 ('engagement'), 218 n.
   TH appointed to Entente Committee v. 179,
      202 and n., 210 n.
   proposed Imperial Oriental Press v. 209
   TH elected Vice-President vi. 91 and n.
   letter to v. 256
Royal Society of Painter-Etchers iv. 75, 76 n.
Royal Society for the Prevention of Cruelty to
      Animals vi. 244 nn., 293; vii. 12 n.
   letter to iii. 213
Royal Society of St George vi. 50 ('popular
      Society') and n.
Royal Wessex Society (proposed) vi. 131 n.,
      144 n.
Royat-les-Bains iii. 265 n., 267, 270
Royle, John (Lord Mayor of Manchester) iii.
      55 n.
   letter to iii. 54
Roz, Firmin ii. 274 n., 282 n.; iii. 225 n., 228 n.
   letter to iii. 227
Ruan Minor (Cornwall) iii. 133 n.
Rubens, Peter Paul ii. 134
Ruff, Howard iv. 50 n.
   letter to vi. 50
Rumbold, C. J. A. i. 64 n.; vii. 172
Rumbold, Charles Edmund Arden Law i.
      64 n.; iii. 290 n.; iv. 230 nn.; v. 125 n.
   letters to iii. 290, 295; iv. 229; v. 125
Rumbold, Sir Thomas i. 64 and n.; iii. 290 n.;
      iv. 229 ('great grandfather'), 230 nn.; vii.
      172
Runeberg, Nino v. 345 n.
Rushmore (Dorset) ii. 85 n., 86, 87, 90 nn.; iii.
      269
Rushy Pond (Dorset) iv. 183 and n.
Ruskin, John i. 117 n.
   Modern Painters i. 1
   *The Nature of Gothic: A Chapter of The
      Stones of Venice* iv. 178, 179 n.
Russell, John, 1st Earl i. 6
Russell, Ada v. 67 and n.
Russell, George William ('AE'):
   and 'Poets' Tribute' v. 339
   letter to v. 339
Russell (photographers) iii. 93

Russkaia mysl':
   translation of *Tess* in i. 283 nn., 288 and n.;
      ii. 42 n.
Russkaia Vedomosti ii. 121 n.
Russo–Japanese War iii. 135 ('present war')
      and n.
Rutland, Henry John, 8th Duke of v. 272
      and n.
Rye (Sussex):
   Lamb House vi. 275 ('the house'), 276 n.,
      300 ('seaside house'), 301 n., 318

Sachs, Howard J. (book collector) vi. 217
      and n.
Sackbut vi. 43 n.
Sackville, Lionel Edward Sackville-West, 3rd
      Baron vi. 170 n.
Sackville, Josephine Victoria Sackville-West,
      Lady vi. 169 nn., 170 nn.
   letter to vi. 169
Sackville-West, Victoria ('Vita'):
   The Heir: A Love Story vi. 170 ('the story')
      and n.
'Sacrilege, The' (poem):
   pub. in *Fortnightly* iv. 177 ('another bal-
      lad'), 178 n.
St Albans, Grace, Duchess of iii. 316 and n.
St Andrews, University of:
   hon. degree conferred on TH vi. 123 and n.,
      127 and n.
St Bartholomew's Hospital v. 341 ('Barts') and
      n., 342 nn.
St Conger's Barrow (Dorset) vi. 131 n.
St Cross, Hospital of (near Winchester) ii. 245
      and n.
'Saint George,' Play of v. 285 n.; vi. 219 n., 232
      and n., 293
St Helier, Baron (formerly Sir Francis Jeune,
      q.v.) v. 35 n.
   death iii. 167 and n.
St Helier, Mary, Lady (formerly Jeune, q.v.)
      iii. 167 and n., 288, 316, 318; iv. 30, 105,
      261 ('your mum') and n.; v. 288, 309; vi.
      23 ('your mother'), 181 n., 206 n.; vii. 1 n.
   as hostess iv. 105, 106; v. 30, 35, 38, 108,
      114, 116, 117 n., 118, 132
   invited to *Dynasts* first night v. 57, 62, 63
   social work v. 93 n., 196 and n.; vi. 181 n.
   at Max Gate vi. 206 n.
   Memories of Fifty Years iv. 61 n.
   letters to iii. 167; iv. 195, 219, 258, 265, 272;
      v. 92, 93, 105, 196, 222, 325; vi. 180
St James's Budget ii. 171 nn.
St James's Gazette i. 100 and n., 118, 119 n.,
      274; ii. 94 n., 158 n., 159 n.
St James's Theatre i. 99, 101 n., 103 n.; ii.
      58 n., 147 n., 149; iii. 250 n.

St John, Florence i. 231 n.
St Juliot (Cornwall) ii. 65 n.; v. 15, 16, 316 n.; vi. 27 and n.; vii. 47, 169 n.
  TH at Rectory i. 13 and n.
  TH's visit to, after ELH's death iv. 257, 260 and n.; vii. 168 n.
  ELH's early years at iv. 260, 299, 328; vi. 29 and n.
  TH's first visit and meeting with ELH at iv. 260 n.; v. 16 n., 128 n.
  visit with FEH v. 163 n.
  union of parish with Lesnewth vi. 29, 258
St Juliot Church iv. 260, 261, 262 n.; vi. 258; vii. 57 and n., 169 n.
  memorial to ELH iv. 275, 276 n., 283, 299; v. 64, 156, 176, 177, 179, 271
  oak screen iv. 276 n., 299
  TH's sketches of v. 81 and n.
  ELH sketch of v. 171, 177
  repair and restoration vi. 27, 28 n., 258, 262
St Martin's Review vi. 192, 193 nn.
St Martin's Theatre vi. 19 n.
St Paul's Cathedral iii. 4, 86, 88, 126; iv. 51, 55, 189 n.
  organ iii. 89, 130, 131
  Blake memorial vii. 10 and nn.
Saintsbury, George i. 147 ('Saturday man') and n.*, 255 ('G.S.') and n.
Sale (Cheshire) i. 143 ('your town') and n.
Saleeby, Caleb William v. 70 n.; vi. 260 n., 332 n.
  'Longest Price of War' lecture v. 69, 70 n., 84 and n.
  and *Dynasts* v. 69, 75 n.
  addresses Dorchester Temperance meeting v. 84, 85 n., 92, 96 n.
  at Max Gate v. 84, 92
  Modern Surgery and Its Making v. 96 ('surgical one') and n.
  The Progress of Eugenics v. 96 n.
  letters to v. 69, 75, 78, 84, 92, 96, 107, 237; vi. 332
Salisbury, James Gascoyne Cecil, 4th Marquess of iii. 131 n.
Salisbury, Robert Cecil, 1st Earl of v. 337, 338 n.
Salisbury i. 1, 2 n., 52; ii. 172 and nn., 173, 199, 226, 234; vi. 32, 33 n., 92; vii. 130, 131 n.
  as 'Melchester' ii. 132, 172 n.
  Cathedral i. 1, 5; ii. 172; vi. 30, 191 and n.
  Cathedral Hotel iv. 285 ('that hotel') and n.
  St Thomas's church i. 1, 2 n.
  Training College i. 2 n., 4 n.; ii. 172 ('"Kings House"') and n.
Salisbury Plain ii. 230; vi. 92
Salmon, Yvonne M. vi. 305 nn.

translation of *Dynasts* segments vii. 83 and nn.
  letters to vi. 304; vii. 83
Salt, Henry Stephens iv. 209 n.
  (trans.) *Treasures of Lucretius* iv. 209 and n.
  letter to iv. 209
Sampson, John:
  (ed.) *The Lyrical Poems of William Blake* iii. 304 n.
Sampson, Low, Marston & Co. (publishers) i. 98 n.; ii. 1, 2 n., 3 n., 4 n., 296 n.
  pub. *Two on a Tower* i. 109 n., 115 n.
  purchase stock of *Mayor of Casterbridge* i. 160 and n.
  pub. cheap one-vol. edn of TH's novels i. 171 n., 195, 243 n.; vii. 94, 95 n.
  expiry of rights ii. 37 n., 59, 60, 63 n.
  purchase stock of *Hand of Ethelberta* vii. 95 n.
  letters to i. 109; ii. 63; vii. 94
'San Sebastian' (poem) v. 246
'Sandbourne':
  Bournemouth as i. 274; ii. 132
Sandercock, Mr (St Juliot sexton) vi. 263 n.
Sandercock, Mrs vi. 262, 263 n.
Sandhurst, William Mansfield, Viscount:
  letter to v. 341
Sappho ii. 84, 158
Sarah Ann (Max Gate servant) ii. 193, 194, 221 ('S.A.')
Sardou, Victorien iii. 181 and n.
Sargent, John Singer i. 152 n., 191; iii. 265 and n., 302 and n.; v. 303, 304 n.
Sassoon, Siegfried Loraine v. 201 n., 214, 312; vi. 90 n., 120, 140 ('literary friend'), 141 n., 316 n.; vii. 25 ('S.S.') and n.
  war service v. 171 ('your nephew') and n., 213 and n., 236 n.
  at Max Gate v. 286 n., 326 and n.; vi. 93
  American lecture tour vi. 3 ('your journey') and n., 48 and nn.
  'At the Grave of Henry Vaughan' vi. 311 ('the sonnet') and n.
  Counter-Attack and Other Poems v. 272 and n.
  The Daffodil Murderer v. 123 and n.
  Lingual Exercises for Advanced Vocabularians vi. 320 and n.
  The Old Huntsman and Other Poems v. 201 ('book of poems') and n., 213, 215 ('S's book'), 236 n.
  'The Passing Show' vi. 3 ('the poem') and n.
  Picture Show v. 317 and n.
  Siegfried's Journey v. 242 n.
  'To any Dead Officer' v. 224, 272
  'To Victory' v. 142 ('verses by "S.S."') and n.

Sassoon, Siegfried Loraine (cont.)
'Two Hundred Years After' v. 201 ('about Corbie Ridge') and n.
letters to v. 201, 213, 224, 236, 242, 272, 317; vi. 3, 100, 112, 137, 311, 318, 320
Satires of Circumstance (poems) iv. 293 n.; v. 38 n., 77 n., 113, 211 n., 259; vi. 6
'Satires of Circumstance' pub. in *Fortnightly* iv. 143 and n., 151; v. 260, 261 n., 314 and n.
book pub. v. 22 ('the volume') and n., 35 n., 59 ('the book'), 60 nn., 79, 80, 84
preparation of v. 39, 40 ('the poems'), 41, 45, 52 ('new volume') and n.
American market v. 59, 60 n.
presentation copies v. 59, 60 n., 64, 65 n., 66 n., 68, 70, 80 and n.
section relating to ELH v. 64 and n., 70
critical reception v. 68 ('review of the poems') and n., 70, 72, 73 n.
in Wessex Edn v. 95 n., 255, 299, 301 n., 304, 305 and n., 306 and n.; vi. 14, 39
'Saturday Night in Arcady' (story) (episode omitted from serial version of *Tess*):
pub. in *National Observer* i. 247 ('sketch') and n., 249 and n.; iii. 274, 275 n.; vii. 117, 118 n.
Saturday Review i. 2, 3 n., 17 n., 19 and n., 121 and n., 145 n., 147 n., 155 n., 164 n., 247 and n.; ii. 110, 111 n., 139, 153 n., 180 and n., 214, 215 n., 267 and n.; iii. 59 and n., 169 and n., 230 and n.; iv. 91 n., 288 and nn.; v. 68 n.; vii. 111 ('S.R.') and n., 133 nn.
review of *Desperate Remedies* i. 13 and n.
review of *Mayor of Casterbridge* i. 145 n., 146, 159 ('my last novel') and n.
attack on *Tess* i. 252 and n., 253, 254, 255 and n., 256 n., 258
'Duke's Reappearance' pub. in ii. 139 n.; iv. 178
'A Church Romance' pub. in ii. 223 n., 226 n., 235 and n.; vii. 150 n.
'Ah, are you Digging on My Grave?' pub. in iv. 288 ('verses') and n.
'In Time of "the Breaking of Nations"' pub. in v. 144 n.
hostile review of TH's poetry v. 346, 347 n.
Savage Club iii. 208 and n.
Savernake Forest (Wilts) ii. 36
Savile Club i. 86 ('the club') and n., 113, 119 n., 252 n.; ii. 47, 49 and n., 56, 82, 146, 149, 161, 162, 234, 250, 255, 256, 284, 285; iii. 193 and n., 203 and n., 214, 294 n.; vi. 370 n.; vii. 98 n., 121, 123 n.
TH's membership of i. 57 ('the Club'), 59, 66, 75, 76, 77, 78, 86 n., 94, 105, 113, 127,

128, 144, 145, 147, 170, 185, 232, 235, 252, 253, 270, 275; iii. 210 and n., 294; iv. 156
Savoy ii. 90 ('the magazine') and n., 120
Savoy Theatre iii. 257, 258 n.
Saxelby, F. Outwin:
(comp.) *A Thomas Hardy Dictionary* iv. 133 ('the work') and n., 135, 172 ('forthcoming book'); vii. 2, 3 n., 24 n.
letters to iv. 133, 135, 172
Saxmundham (Suffolk) iv. 270; vii. 132 and n.
Scarborough (Yorks) iv. 300, 301 n.
Scarlet, John vii. 106 n.
letter to vii. 105
Schartau, Leisa K. iii. 75 n.
Schenck, Elliott ii. 261 and n.
Schopenhauer, Artur iii. 351, 352 n.; iv. 37 and n.; v. 50, 51 n.; vi. 259, 260 nn.
'Schreckhorn, The' (poem) v. 76 ('lines . . . of your father'), 77 nn.
Schuster, Sir Claud:
and manifesto on war aims v. 47 and n.
letter to v. 47
Schwalbach (Germany) ii. 293 and n.
Schwartz, Ada van der Poorten iv. 127 n.
Schwartz, Joost van der Poorten – see Maartens, Maarten
Score, H. Berkeley vii. 142 n.
Poems Chiefly Lyrical vii. 142 and n.
Scots Observer i. 214 ('S.O.') and n.
re-named *National Observer* (q.v.) i. 229 and n.
Scott, Alicia, Lady John vii. 80 and n.
Scott, Catharine Amy Dawson vi. 107 n., 179 and n.
Scott, Cyril iii. 127 n.; v. 56 and n.
Scott, Sir George Gilbert iii. 50; vi. 30 and n.
Scott, Sir John Murray vi. 169 n.
'Scott, Leader' – see Baxter, Lucy
Scott, Marjorie Dawson vi. 107 n.
letter to vi. 107
Scott, Robert Forsyth v. 25 n.
Scott, Sir Walter ii. 200; iii. 16 and n., 214; iv. 54, 276; v. 74; vi. 156
The Bride of Lammermoor ii. 206
Guy Mannering iv. 325 n.
The Lay of the Last Minstrel iii. 260 n.
Scott-Douglas, Lady Mariquita Juana Petronila (referred to as Lady Douglas) i. 166; iv. 40; v. 92, 248 and n.; vii. 172
death v. 262
Scott-James, Rolfe Arnold iii. 310 n.
as *New Weekly* editor v. 6 and n., 20, 21, 22
Personality in Literature v. 6 ('book of essays') and n.
letters to iii. 310; v. 6, 20, 22, 53
Scottish Repertory Theatre iv. 12 n.

Scribner's Magazine i. 289 and n.; ii. 13; vi. 356 and n.

Scribner's Sons, Charles (publishers) i. 260 n., 262 and n.

letters to i. 260, 289

Scripture, Professor Edward Wheeler vii. 36 n.

Scudamore, Joyce Maud vi. 38 and n.

Sea Town (Dorset) v. 277 and n., 325, 326 n.

Seaman, Sir Owen v. 47 n., 220 n.

Searle, W. F. D. Townley (bookseller and author) iv. 237 nn., 301 n.

letters to iv. 236, 301

Seaside Library i. 285 n.; ii. 118 n.

Seaton (Devon) v. 116 and n.

Seccombe, Thomas ii. 269 n.; iii. 279 n.; v. 5, 6 n.

letters to ii. 269; iii. 279

Secker, Martin iv. 225 nn.

letter to iv. 225

Secker & Warburg (publishers) iv. 225 n.

Sedgehill Manor (Wilts) ii. 247 n.

Seely, Major-General John Edward Bernard vi. 63 n.

Selected Poems of Thomas Hardy v. 113 ('little volume') and n., 148 ('little book') and n., 149 and n., 152 and n., 176, 183 ('selection'), 188 ('little book'), 189 n., 196 and n., 204, 212, 245, 286

publication v. 133 n.; 161 n., 183 n.; vi. 14 n., 40, 41 n., 97 n.

vignette of TH for title-page v. 161 and n., 169–71, 172, 343

American publication v. 175 and n.

presentation copies v. 188 ('little book'), 189 n., 192, 194 ('little selection'), 195 ('little book'), 196 n., 197 n., 200 n.

principle of selection v. 255 and n.; vi. 96

revised version as *Chosen Poems* vii. 59 and nn., 75 and n., 76 and n., 82 and n.

'Selfsame Song, The' (poem) vi. 118

Seltzer, Thomas iv. 131 n.

Selwyn and Blount (publishers) vi. 101 n.

Seneca vii. 153

Epistulae ad Lucilium vii. 154 n.

'Serjeant's Song, The' (song) iii. 73 and n.; v. 87, 88 n.

Holst's setting of iv. 69 n.

Foss's setting of vi. 334

Seton, Ernest Thompson:

'The Trail of the Sandhill Stag' iii. 118 and n. ;

Sette of Odd Volumes i. 270 and n., 285 n.; ii. 65 n.

Severn, Joseph v. 31 and n., 40 and n.

Seymour, Herbert John iii. 136 n.

letter to iii. 136

Shaftesbury (Dorset) iii. 135, 270; iv. 156; vii. 74 n.

as 'Shaston' i. 274; ii. 87, 132, 133; vii. 74 n.

Shakespeare, Ann iii. 150 and n.

Shakespeare, Susannah v. 174 n.

Shakespeare, William iii. 150, 271 n., 313; v. 173–4; vii. 86 and n.

quoted in *Tess* i. 283

proposed Memorial in London iii. 155, 156 nn., 157 and n., 174; iv. 27 and n.

'Stratford Town' edn iii. 176 and n.

Tercentenary Commemoration v. 33, 34 n., 128, 129 nn.

proposed Memorial in Rome v. 217, 218 nn.

authorship questioned vii. 49 and nn.

King Lear vii. 86 ('terrible play') and n.

Romeo and Juliet ii. 100 and n.

quotations from:

Antony and Cleopatra v. 325 n.

As You Like It vi. 219 n.

Coriolanus ii. 285 and n.

Hamlet v. 44, 247 n.; vi. 77 n.

Henry IV, Part One vi. 55 n., 273 n.

Henry V iii. 102 ('Piece out'), 103 n., 113 ('Pieced out') and n.

King Lear iii. 102 ('Dark Tower'), 103 n.; vii. 155 n.

Macbeth v. 174, 235 n., 301 n.; vi. 196 n., 220 n.; vii. 39 n.

Merchant of Venice i. 110 n.

Midsummer Night's Dream ii. 81 n., 82 ('the play'); vi. 243 n.

Othello iii. 209 and n., 210; v. 173, 195, 196 n.

Pericles ii. 210

The Tempest i. 278 n.

Twelfth Night iv. 307 n.

Winter's Tale vii. 3 n.

Shakespeare Head Press iii. 176 n.

Shakespeare Memorial Committee iii. 174, 175 n.; vii. 149 n.

Shannon, Charles Haslewood iii. 129, 130 n.

Shansfield, William Newton iii. 299 and n.; vi. 215, 217 n.

letter to vi. 216.

Shapcote, Sarah (ELH's cousin) iv. 311 and n.

Sharp, Cecil:

setting of songs for *Dynasts* v. 56 n.

The Country Dance Book vi. 191 n.

Sharp, Evelyn:

and women's suffrage iii. 210 n.; v. 186 and n.

letters to iii. 210, 269; v. 186

Sharp, William ('Fiona Macleod') i. 277 n.*; ii. 271 and n.; iii. 2 and n.; vi. 236 and n.; vii. 121 n.

letters to i. 276; vii. 121

Sharpe, Revd George Brereton v. 43 ('my uncle's brother') and n.

Sharpe, John Brereton (uncle) iv. 58 and n.; v. 43 n.

Sharpe, Martha (aunt) iv. 58 ('handsome aunt') and n.; v. 43 n.

'Shaston':
Shaftesbury as i. 274; ii. 87, 132, 133; vii. 74 n.

Shaw, Charlotte Frances v. 158 and n.; vi. 306 and n.

Shaw, George Bernard ii. 138 n.; iii. 256 n.; iv. 203 n., 235 n.; vi. 126 and n.; vii. 1 n.
at Max Gate v. 158
Saint Joan vi. 253 and n., 367 and n.
You Never Can Tell vi. 155 ('in a play'), 157 n.

Shaw, P. (fellow lodger in Kilburn) i. 1 ('P.S.'), 2 and n., 3 and n., 4 ('P.S.') and n.

Shaylor, Joseph iv. 50 n.
letter to iv. 49

Shelley, Harriet iv. 168, 169 n.

Shelley, Mary ii. 169; iii. 86, 90; vi 282 and n.

Shelley, Percy Bysshe ii. 23, 24 n., 169, 200, 300; iii. 86, 90; iv. 15, 168, 169 n.; vi. 100, 262 and n., 282
Memorial Fund i. 278, 279 n.; v. 28 and nn.
TH's admiration for ii. 144
Adonais vi. 276 n.
Epipsychidion ii. 23, 25, 26 n.; vi. 101 nn., 148 and n.
Hellas ii. 157 and n.
The Necessity of Atheism ii. 125 ('book') and n.

'Shelley's Skylark' (poem) vi. 101 n.

Sheppard, Revd Hugh Richard Lawrie ('Dick') vi. 193 nn.
letter to vi. 192

Sherborne (Dorset) ii. 70; iv. 227 n.; vi. 94 and nn.
as 'Sherton-Abbas' ii. 132
Pageant (1905) iii. 135, 136 and n.

Sherborne Journal i. 51

Sheridan, Algernon Thomas Brinsley i. 184 n., 270; ii. 141 n., 230 and n., 256 n., 272, 275 n.; vi. 282 and n.

Sheridan, Mary (Mrs A. T. B. Sheridan) i. 184 n.*, 270; ii. 230 and n., 256 n., 267, 272, 275 n.; iii. 64 n., 334, 335; iv. 241, 330; v. 109
on 'negative Christmases' ii. 141, 142
death v. 271 and n.
letters to i. 184, 191, 245; ii. 274; iii. 63; iv. 155, 239, 317, 318; v. 137

Sheridan, Richard Brinsley vi. 282 ('R.B.S.') and n.
The Critic vii. 144 and n.
'How oft Louisa' i. 192 and n.
The Rivals vii. 109 n.

The School for Scandal ii. 43, 44 n.; iv. 185 ('Piper's twins'), 186 n.

Sheridan, Wilfred v. 137 n.

Sherman, Stuart P. vi. 126 n.

Sherren, James (surgeon) vi. 272 n., 277 n.

Sherren, Wilkinson ii. 268 n.
A Rustic Dreamer, and Other Stories iii. 43 ('your type-written romance') and n.
The Wessex of Romance ii. 268 n.; iii. 14 and n., 22 n., 224 n., 317 ('of Sherren's') and n.
letters to ii. 268; iii. 43, 224

Sherren & Son (Weymouth printers) i. 121 n.

'Sherton-Abbas':
Sherborne as ii. 132

Shinohara, K. iv. 271 n.
letter to iv. 271

Shipley, Howard Maynard iii. 58 n.
letter to iii. 58

Shipton Gorge (Dorset) v. 253 n.

Shirley, Miss (tenant of Hardy property, Dorchester) ii. 82, 83 n.; iii. 87 and n.

Shirley, W. F. ii. 285 n.

Shockerwick House (near Bath) iv. 169 and n.

Shoreham (Sussex) iv. 316 and n., 331 n.; v. 11 n., 30 ('little orchard') and n., 38 n.

Short Stories of Thomas Hardy vii. 76 and n.

Shorter, Annie Doris (*née* Banfield) vi. 45 and n., 253

Shorter, Clement King i. 245 n.*; ii. 122, 281 n., 289; iii. 92 n., 159, 160 n., 180 n.; iv. 41, 42 n.; v. 158 n., 194, 247 and n., 294 and n., 314 n.; vi. 16, 253; vii. 152 n.
as editor of *Illustrated London News* ii. 6 n., 8, 68 and n., 101, 126 and n., 129, 187; vi. 134 ('as Editor') and n.
as editor of *English Illustrated Magazine* ii. 34, 35, 43 ('the editor') and n., 44, 45, 46, 49 and n., 71; vii. 127
as editor of *Sketch* ii. 42 and n., 43 n., 55, 59, 101, 213
marriage ii. 126 and n.
as editor of *Sphere* ii. 240 n., 246, 266 n., 275, 297 n.; iii. 24, 30 n., 35 ('some verses'), 36 n., 118, 119 n., 166 and n., 219 and n., 250, 257 n., 306 n., 329; iv. 41 and n., 71 ('that article'), 72 n., 167 n., 170 nn., 236, 253 and n., 328; v. 15 and n., 122 and n., 128, 129, 150, 160, 166, 195, 284 n., 320; vi. 302; vii. 32 n., 132, 134, 137
as editor of *Tatler* ii. 292, 293; iii. 81 n., 82 ('the poem'), 136 n., 194, 329; vii. 134 and n.
'Literary Letters' in *Sphere* ii. 297 n.; iii. 119 n., 166 n., 219 n., 257 n.; iv. 41 and n., 72 n., 167 and n., 170 nn.; v. 15 n., 29

Shorter, Clement King (cont.)
    and n., 122 n., 175 n., 320 and n.; vi. 263
      and n.; vii. 32 n., 139 and n.
    and 'Changed Man' copyright iii. 29
    and 'Benighted Travellers' republication iii.
      48 n., 60, 61 n.
    offer to have TH's MSS professionally
      bound iii. 81 n., 303 n., 309, 313 ('them'),
      319; iv. 207
    invited to Max Gate iii. 146; iv. 282; v. 159
    foreign travels iii. 296, 297 n.; iv. 275 n.; v.
      320 and n.; vii. 160 and n.
    proposed complimentary dinner to TH iv.
      41, 49–51
    at Aldeburgh iv. 142 nn., 148 n., 149 n., 151,
      214 n., 260
    illness iv. 167; vii. 32 and n.
    and RL Fund iv. 256, 257 n., 275
    at Max Gate iv. 280 n., 282 n., 287 n.; v. 266
      ('one visitor') and n.
    and birthday gift of books to Clodd iv. 281,
      282, 283 n.
    meets TH's brother and sisters iv. 287 and n.
    private printings of TH material v. 47 and
      n., 49, 58 and n., 144 n., 150 and n., 159,
      160 n.
    and petition for Casement reprieve v. 167
      ('the paper') and n.
    death of wife v. 195 n., 242 and nn., 320 n.
    second marriage vi. 45 and n.
    letters to i. 245, 262; ii. 6, 11, 34, 35, 42, 45,
      46, 55, 59, 68, 71, 75, 78, 101, 117, 126,
      129, 151, 173, 191, 198, 213, 239, 240,
      246, 254, 265, 266, 274, 275, 285, 289,
      292, 293, 297, 303; iii. 4, 18, 24, 29–30,
      35, 48, 60, 66, 67, 80, 82, 92, 113, 118,
      132, 136, 165, 166, 172, 180, 191, 194,
      208, 211, 219, 229–30, 250, 256, 259, 266,
      296, 303, 306, 309, 313, 319, 329; iv. 9,
      21, 23, 41, 50, 70, 71, 101, 134, 149, 151,
      153, 167–8, 173, 189, 210, 231, 236, 241,
      253, 256, 260, 274, 281, 282, 296; v. 15,
      29, 47, 49–50, 58, 75, 80, 88, 92, 112, 116,
      122, 128, 129, 138, 144, 150, 159, 160,
      167, 195, 207, 218, 242, 275, 320; vi. 10,
      134, 214, 302; vii. 127, 132, 134, 135, 137,
      139, 149, 155, 160
Shorter (formerly Sigerson, q.v.), Dora ii.
    266, 289, 293; iii. 66 and n.; iv. 275; v.
    159, 160 n., 160
    at Aldeburgh iv. 142 n., 151, 214 n., 260
    at Max Gate iv. 282 and n., 287 n.
    meets TH's brother and sisters iv. 287 and n.
    illness and death v. 194, 195 and n., 209,
      219, 242 and nn., 320 n.
    Collected Poems iii. 319 ('poems') and n.
    New Poems iv. 236 and n.

The Sad Years v. 283 ('Mrs Shorter's
    poems') and n.
'The Three Fates' iv. 242 n.
*The Woman Who Went to Hell, and Other
    Ballads and Lyrics* iii. 18 ('volume of
    poems') and n.
    letter to iv. 287
Shorthouse, Joseph Henry:
    John Inglesant vii. 99 and n.
Shotover Papers (Oxford) i. 37 and n.
Shrewsbury, Theresa, Dowager Countess of ii.
    16, 17 n., 18, 19
'Sick Battle-God, The' (poem) iii. 51 ('The
    Sick God'), 217
Sidmouth (Devon) iii. 242
Sienkiewicz, Henryk v. 206, 207 n.
Sigerson (later Shorter, q.v.), Dora ii. 126 n.
Silver, Christine vi. 374 n.
    as Tess vi. 374 n.; vii. 6 n.
    letter to vii. 6
Simmons, Edward George (murderer) iii.
    23 n.
Simpson, John William vi. 15 nn.
    letter to vi. 15
Sinclair, May (Mary) Amelia St Clair iii.
    332 n.*, 340; iv. 32 n., 38 n.
    cycle ride to Weymouth with TH iii. 342,
      343, 344 and n.; iv. 32 n.
    and women's suffrage iv. 39 n.
    The Creators: A Comedy iv. 128 and nn.
    letters to iii. 331, 342; iv. 31, 38, 45, 92, 101,
      108, 128
Sinclair, Upton Beall vii. 70 n.
    Oil! vii. 69, 70 n.
    letter to vii. 69
'Sing Ballad-singer' (poem) iv. 132 and n.
Singer, G. Astor ii. 120 n.
'Singer Asleep, A' (poem) iv. 79 ('monody
    on Swinburne'), 81 ('my poem') and n;
    v. 66 ('Swinburne one') and n., 251 and
    n.
    pub. in *English Review* iv. 79 n., 178 ('lines
      on Swinburne's death')
    MS of iv. 178, 179 n., 184 ('Swinburne
      poem'), 192, 282
'Sitting on the Bridge' (poem) v. 250
Sketch i. 245 n.; ii. 42 n., 43 and n., 55 and n.,
    59, 101 and n., 151 n., 213 and n., 296 n.
Sladen, Douglas Brooke Wheelton ii. 194 n.,
    239 n.; vii. 126 n.
    *The Admiral: A Romance of Nelson in the
      Year of the Nile* ii. 194 ('a novel') and n.
    letters to ii. 194, 238; iii. 154; vii. 126
Slater, Frederick William (Harper's London
    rep.) v. 175 n.*, 262, 263 nn. 265, 307 and
    n.; vi. 145 nn., 152, 153 nn., 167 n.
    letters to v. 175; vi. 145; vii. 16

Slater, John vi. 11 n.
  letter to vi. 11
'Sleep Walker, The' (poem) v. 212
'Slow Nature, The' (poem) ii. 209
Small, William i. 75 n., 181, 182 n.
Smalley, George Washburn i. 192 and n.
Smalley, Phoebe i. 192 and n.
Smallman, Percy vii. 11 n.
  letter to vii. 11
Smedley, Anne Constance iii. 270 and n.
  interview with TH iii. 270 n.; iv. 70 and n.,
  71
Smedmore (Dorset) ii. 251, 252 n.
Smellie, James (mayor of Dudley) vi. 357 n.
  letter to vi. 357
Smerdon, Edgar Wilmot vi. 46 n., 221 ('local
  doctor'), 222 n., 286 ('Angel Clare') and n.
Smith, Alan Wyldbore i. 275 ('your nephew')
  and n.; vii. 173
Smith, Alice Christiana iv. 242 ('your sister')
  and n.
Smith, Arthur Lapthorn:
  *How to be Useful and Happy from Sixty to
  Ninety* vi. 140, 141 n.
Smith, Blanche (later Mrs C. P. Egerton) i.
  46 n.; iv. 242 n.
Smith, Emily Geneviève i. 26 n.; vii. 66 and n.
  letters to i. 26
Smith, Evangeline Frances i. 46 n.; iii. 357 n.;
  iv. 110 n.; v. 135 n.
  story commented on i. 45, 46 n.
  letters to i. 45, 259, 275; iv. 110, 242
Smith, Flora Bosworth iv. 311 n.
  letter to iv. 310
Smith, Frederick William Boyton (Dorchester
  composer) ii. 283 and n.; v. 56 n.
  harmonized carols vii. 151 and n.
Smith, George (publisher) i. 35 n.; vii. 138,
  139 n.
  letters to i. 35–6, 43, 47, 48, 141–2
Smith, George Murray (publisher) i. 127 n.,
  133, 146
  letter to i. 127
Smith, H. W. iii. 295 n.
  letter to iii. 295
Smith, Herbert Greenhough vii. 147 n., 172
  letter to vii. 147
Smith, Isabel (Mrs R. J. Smith) v. 161, 162 n.
  discovery of TH MSS v. 243, 244 nn.
  letter to v. 243
Smith, Revd John Alexander ii. 272 n.
  letter to ii. 272
Smith, John Bryce (artists' colourman) iv. 122
  and n.
Smith, J. C.:
  (ed.) *A Book of Modern Verse* vi. 285 n.
Smith, Logan Pearsall iv. 305 n.
  letters to iv. 305, 318
Smith, Nowell Charles vi. 94 nn.
  letter to vi. 94
Smith, Reginald Bosworth i. 26 ('Mr B.S.')
  and n*, 275 n.; vii. 66 and n.
  illness and death iii. 334, 335, 344, 347
  letter to iii. 197
Smith, Reginald John (publisher and editor) ii.
  249 n.*; iii. 268; v. 161, 162 n., 243, 244 n.
  declines 'Trampwoman's Tragedy' iii. 59 n.,
  278 n.
  letters to ii. 249, 251, 276; iii. 7, 9, 41, 58,
  147, 149, 153, 169, 170, 215, 251, 274; iv.
  8, 48, 66, 102, 114
Smith, Revd Reginald Southwell i. 26 nn.,
  46 n.; iii. 357 nn.
Smith, Revd Sydney vi. 333 nn.
  letter to vi. 333
Smith, T. Roger (architect) i. 16 n., 50 and
  n.*; vi. 11 and n.
Smith, Elder & Co. (publishers) i. 9 n., 90,
  127 n., 148 nn.; ii. 249 n.; iii. 266 n.,
  274 n.; iv. 320 n.; v. 133 and n.; vii. 90
  ('my publishers') and n., 95 n.
  concern over American arrangements i.
  28–9, 30
  pub. *Return of the Native* i. 60 and nn., 61,
  62
  pub. *Trumpet-Major* i. 78, 81, 92
  pub. *Mayor of Casterbridge* i. 142 n., 143
  letters to i. 8–9, 22–3, 24, 25, 27, 28–9, 30,
  32, 35, 38, 41–2, 43, 44, 45, 48, 58, 60,
  61–2, 78, 81, 92, 143, 160
Smith, W. H. & Son ii. 56 n.; v. 299
  boycott of *English Review* iv. 167 and n.
Smithard, W. iii. 157 n.
'Snow in the Suburbs' (poem) vii. 75
Snowdove (Max Gate cat) iii. 82, 86, 137 ('one
  of our little animals') and n.
Sobieniowski, Floryan vi. 241 n.
  letter to vi. 240
Social Democratic Federation vii. 1 nn.
Société des Films Albatros vi. 195, 196 n., 198,
  202 n.
Société des Gens de Lettres vi. 121
  TH elected hon. member v. 178
Society of Architects v. 116, 117
Society of Authors – *see* Incorporated Society
  of Authors, Playwrights and Composers
Society of Dorset Men in London iii. 129 and
  n., 159 and n., 248, 283, 323 nn.; iv. 119,
  120 n., 179 and n., 224 n.; v. 194; vi.
  159 n.; vii. 17
  TH as vice-president iii. 158
  visit to Dorchester iii. 212 and n.
  TH as president iii. 248 n., 285 n., 288, 312;
  iv. 59 and n.; vi. 234

Society of Dorset Men in London (*cont.*)
  and Dorset psalm-tunes iii. 285 and n., 288
  Year-book of iii. 285 n.; iv. 164 n., 170 n.,
    179 nn.; v. 23, 24 nn., 49, 215 n., 229, 343
    and n.; vi. 230 n., 235 and n.
  TH's unread Address to iii. 312 and nn.; vii.
    146 and nn.
  Far from Madding Crowd performed before
    iv. 46 and n., 51 and n., 55, 58 and nn., 59,
    61 and n., 62
  performance of *Mellstock Quire* iv. 129
  song sung at meetings of iv. 179 and n.
  performances of *Woodlanders* iv. 325, 327
    ('the play'), 328 n.
  performance of *Return of the Native* vi. 57,
    59
Society of Noviomagus i. 106 n.
Society for the Protection of Ancient Buildings
    i. 95 and n.; ii. 67 n., 141 n.; iii. 35 n.,
    283, 284 n., 337; vi. 178, 206
  and Stratton Church i. 205 and n., 220, 221,
    233; vii. 116 n.
  and Fordington Church iii. 50, 51 n., 236
  TH's lecture for iii. 211 and n., 215, 224;
    iv. 20 n.
  and Puddletown Church iv. 74, 114 n., 122
  and Sta Sophia, Constantinople v. 296
    and n.
  letters to Secretary of ii. 235; v. 296 – *see
    also* Powys, Albert Reginald; Turner,
    Thackeray
Society for the Protection of Animals ii. 97 n.
Society for Pure English iv. 305 ('the Society')
    and n., 319 n.; v. 333 ('S.P.E.') and n.; vi.
    125 ('S.P.E.') and nn.; vii. 170 n.
Solly, Henry:
  These Eighty Years ii. 298 and n.
'Some Romano-British Relics Found at Max
    Gate, Dorchester' (paper) iv. 309 ('the
    paper') and n.; v. 249 n.; vii. 100 n.
Somerset, Lady Henry ii. 89 n.
Somerset and Dorset Notes & Queries v. 167,
    168 n.
Somme, Battles of (1916) v. 177 n., 187 n.,
    311 n.
'Son's Portrait, The' (poem) vi. 241
'Son's Veto, The' (story) i. 232 ('its scene in
    London') and n.; vi. 99
'Song of Hope' (poem) vi. 149
'Song to an Old Burden' (poem) vii. 75
'Song of the Soldiers' (later 'Men Who March
    Away,' q.v.) (poem) v. 48 ('the song', 'the
    verses') and n., 301 and n.
  pub. in *Times* v. 47, 56
  private printing of v. 47 and n., 49
  set to music v. 48 ('use it'), 49 and n., 50, 56,
    58 and n.

'Song of the Soldiers' Wives' (poem) ii. 277; vi.
    11 n.
  pub. in *Morning Post* ii. 275 ('effusion'), 298
Sophocles v. 246
  Oedipus Rex iv. 198 n.
Sotheby & Co. (auctioneers) vii. 66 n.
  letter to vii. 66
Sotheran's (booksellers) v. 261 and n.
'Souls of the Slain, The' (poem) ii. 249 ('en-
    closed lines'), 250 ('enclosed poem') and
    n., 253 ('visionary verses') and n., 305 n.;
    iii. 137; vi. 11 n., 149, 260 n.
  pub. in *Cornhill* ii. 249 n., 251 ('revise') and
    n., 266; v. 244 n.
  MS of v. 244 and n.
Soundy (formerly Dugdale, q.v.), Margaret v.
    217; vi. 70 n., 89 and n.
  wedding present v. 212 and n.
  birth of son v. 283 ('little boy') and n.
  letters to v. 212, 217
Soundy, Reginald Henry v. 204 n., 205
    ('young Lieutenant') and n., 215 ('F's sister's
    husband'), 217 and n., 283 ('flying man'); vi.
    90 n.
Soundy, Thomas Dugdale v. 283 ('little boy')
    and n.; vi. 70 n.
South, Robert i. 282
South Dorset constituency i. 272
  by-election (1891) i. 231, 233 n., 235, 236
    and n.
South Dorset Liberal Association i. 272 n.
South Perrott (Dorset) church iii. 283, 284 n.
Southampton ii. 226, 233 nn., 235, 236, 269
  University College vi. 63 n., 322 n.
Southern Irish Loyalists' Relief Association vi.
    152 n.
Southern Times iii. 179, 180 n.
Southerndown (Glamorgan) v. 291 n.
Southey, Robert:
  The Doctor iii. 1 ('words of S') and n.
Southwold (Suffolk) iv. 155 and n., 267,
    268–9, 278, 300
  church iv. 269 and n.
Souvestre, Marie v. 344 n.
Sowter, Ven. Francis Briggs i. 225 and n.
Spa (Belgium) ii. 135
Sparks, James (uncle) i. 2 n.
Sparks, James (second cousin) ii. 188 n.; iii.
    38 n., 70 n.; vi. 331 n.
  medallion by iii. 72
  TH's recommendation of iii. 103; iv. 266 n.
  invited to Max Gate iv. 305
  sketch of Gifford headstone v. 213, 214 n.
  exhibits at Royal Academy v. 214 and n.
  letters to ii. 188; iii. 70, 72, 73; iv. 266, 305;
    v. 213
Sparks, Maria (aunt) i. 2 n.; iii. 38 n.

Sparks (later Duffield), Martha Mary (cousin) i. 1, 2 n.

Sparks, Nathaniel (cousin) ii. 188 n.; iii. 38 n.; vi. 331 n.
  supplies TH with cello iii. 38 and n.
  letters to iii. 38, 264

Sparks, Nathaniel junior ii. 188 n.; iii. 38 n.; iv. 76 n.; vi. 331 n.
  TH's testimonial to iii. 263
  letters to ii. 188; iii. 45, 263; iv. 75

Spasskaia, Vera i. 283 n.
  translates *Tess* into Russian i. 281, 283 nn., 288 and nn.; ii. 42 n.
  letters to i. 281, 288

Speaker i. 218 n.; ii. 52 and n., 139 and n., 203; iii. 200, 201 n., 217 and n.; v. 183 n.

Spearing, Rosetta Grace vi. 374, 375 nn.

Spectator i. 178 and nn.; iii. 196 and n., 203 n. 227 and n.; vi. 246 n., 332 and n.; vii 101 nn., 138, 139
  on *Desperate Remedies* i. 11, 12; iv. 158 ('April 22'), 159 n., 161
  on *Pair of Blue Eyes* i. 21 and n., 22 and n.
  on *Woodlanders* i. 178 and n.
  on *Tess* i. 255 and n.
  on 'Sunday Morning Tragedy' iv. 29 n.
  'After the Visit' pub. in iv. 112 n.
  attack on *English Review* iv. 158–9, 161 and n., 167
  and *Late Lyrics* vi. 177 ('mean notice') and n.

'Spectre of the Real, The' (story) – *see under* Henniker

Speed, John iv. 185 and n.

Speed, Lancelot i. 235 n.

Spencer, Herbert ii. 184, 185 n.; iii. 244 and n.; iv. 23 and n., 26 and n.; v. 275
  Portrait Fund ii. 142, 143 n.
  First Principles ii. 24, 25 n.; v. 156
  System of Synthetic Philosophy ii. 143 n.

Spencer, Walter T. (bookseller) iii. 33 n.; v. 136 and n.
  letters to iii. 33; vii. 134

Spender, E. Harold vi. 102 nn.
  letter to vi. 102

Spender, John Alfred iii. 178 n.; v. 223 n.
  letter to iii. 177

Spenser, Edmund:
  The Fairy Queen i. 191

Speyer, Charles Anthony:
  musical setting of 'When I set out for Lyonnesse' v. 288, 289 nn.; vi. 14 and n., 43 n.
  and 'Tristram's Song' vi. 264, 265 nn.
  letters to v. 288; vi. 14, 264

Sphere i. 245 n.; ii. 266 n., 278, 297 n.; iii. 24 n., 160 n., 166 and n., 219 and n., 249, 250 and n., 251 n., 257 n., 297 n.; iv. 41 and n., 72 n., 167 n., 170 and n.; v. 122 n., 274 and n.; vi. 160 n.; vii. 32 and n., 134, 137 and n.
  'At the War Office After a Bloody Battle' pub. in ii. 240 ('poem') and n., 241 n., 245
  'A Changed Man' pub. in ii. 246 ('story') and n.; iii. 30 n.; vii. 132 n.
  'The Lost Pyx' pub. in ii. 275 ('legend') and n., 276; iii. 189 n.
  'The Man He Killed' pub. in iii. 35 ('some verses'), 36 n., 42 ('the verses')
  'Benighted Travellers' pub. in iii. 48 n.
  portrait of TH's mother in iii. 118, 119 n., 122, 123
  portrait of TH in iii. 306 and n.
  'Bird-catcher's Boy' pub. in iv. 236 n., 253 n.
  'To Meet, or Otherwise' pub. in iv. 253 n., 330 ('few verses'), 331 n.
  photographs of FEH in v. 15 n.
  'The Dead and the Living One' pub. in v. 128 and n., 150 n.
  FEH as reviewer for v. 150 n., 166 n., 215 n.
  'The Wound' and 'A Merrymaking in Question' pub. in v. 160 ('two poems'), 161 n.
  erroneous report of FEH bibliography of TH v. 175 and n.
  'A New Year's Eve in War Time' pub. in v. 193, 195 ('proofs') and n., 199
  'Often When Warring' and 'In Time of Wars and Tumults' pub. in v. 233 n.
  'Valenciennes' pub. in v. 284 n.
  'No Bell-Ringing' pub. in vi. 303 n.
  first issue vii. 132 n.

Spicer-Simson, Theodore vi. 70 n.
  bronze medallion of TH vi. 70, 91 and n., 126 n.
  Men of Letters of the British Isles vi. 126 ('book you mention') and n.
  letters to vi. 91, 126

Spithead:
  naval review (1911) iv. 168 n.

Sprague, Edward iv. 123 n.

Sprigge, Samuel Squire i. 191 n.
  letters to i. 191, 192–3

'Spring Call, The' (later 'Down Wessex Way,' q.v.) (poem) iv. 256 n.; v. 88 n.
  pub. in *Cornhill* iii. 203 n.; v. 24 n.

Spring-Rice, Revd Aubrey i. 151, 152 n.

Springfield Republican ii. 213 n.

Springwood Park (Roxburgh) i. 166 and n.

Sproul, George D. (publisher) ii. 301 and n.; iii. 2 and n.

Spurgeon, (Sir) Arthur ii. 281 and n., 292 n.; vi. 109 n.
  letters to ii. 292; vi. 109; vii. 168

'Spy' (Sir Leslie Ward):
  cartoon of TH vii. 42 ('Caricature') and n.

'Squire Petrick's Lady' (story) vi. 371, 372 n.
Squire, Eileen vii. 10 n.
Squire, John Collings v. 312
  as editor of *London Mercury* v. 322 and nn., 330 and n., 338; vi. 50, 109 n., 121, 122, 137 and n., 178 and n., 242, 277 and n., 336
  and 'Poets' Tribute' v. 330 and n.
  broadcast on TH vi. 252, 253 n., 254 n.
  American Poems and Others vi. 199 ('book of poems') and n.
  Poems in One Volume vii. 10 ('your poems') and n.
  'The Stockyard' vi. 137 and n., 199 and n.; vii. 10
  'To a Bull-dog' vi. 86 and n.
  (ed.) *A Book of Women's Verse* vi. 113 ('Women Poets') and n.
  letters to v. 322, 330, 338; vi. 25, 50, 86, 113, 137, 147, 178, 183, 199, 242, 252, 277, 307, 336, 340, 359; vii. 10, 73
Stage Society ii. 269, 270 n., 271; iii. 358
Stainer, Sir John ii. 283 and n.
Stainsby, Henry iv. 285 n.
  letter to iv. 284
Stair Hole (Dorset) v. 40
Standard iv. 23 and nn., 98, 99 n., 226
  on *Dynasts* vii. 146 n.
Standard Stories vi. 366 and n.
Stanhope, Lady Hester iv. 139 and n.
Stanley of Alderley, Edward John, 2nd Lord ii. 87 n.; iv. 95 n.
Stanley, Colonel John Constantine i. 144 n., 257 n.
Stanley, Madeleine Cecilia Carlyle (later Mrs St John Brodrick, then Lady Midleton, qq.v.) i. 269 n.; ii. 48 and n., 52 ('Lady J.'s girls') and n., 112, 149, 229, 258 n.; iii. 3, 4
  as photographer ii. 2 and n.
  marriage iii. 42 and n., 46, 48, 49
  letter to i. 268
Stanley, Maude i. 227, 228 n.
Stanley (later Allhusen, q.v.), Osma Mary Dorothy i. 257 n.*; ii. 38 n., 48 n., 52 ('Lady J.'s girls') and n.
  engagement to Henry Allhusen ii. 119
  TH's wedding present to ii. 127
  letter to i. 256
Stanmore, Arthur Hamilton-Gordon, Lord: *Life of Lord Aberdeen* ii. 3, 4 n.
Stanway (Glos) vi. 96 n.
Statham, Henry Heathcote vii. 133 n.
  letter to vii. 133
Stavordale, Giles Fox-Strangways Holland, Lord:
  marriage iii. 3, 4

Stavordale, Helen Vane-Tempest Stewart, Lady:
  marriage iii. 3, 4
Stead, William Thomas iv. 211 n.
  suggests organized visits to historic shrines ii. 10 and n.
  Hymns That Have Helped ii. 139 and n.
  letter to ii. 10
Stebbing, William iv. 273 n.*
  legacy to TH vii. 46 and n.
  Five Centuries of English Verse: Impressions iv. 273 and n.
  Greek Epigrams vii. 4
  Virgil & Lucretius v. 232 ('book of Translations'), 233 n.
  letters to iv. 273; v. 232
Stebbing, William P. D. vii. 46 n.
  letter to vii. 46
Steel, Flora Annie:
  On the Face of the Waters ii. 144 ('novel'), 145 n.
Steele, Marshall:
  (comp.) *The One & All Reciter* iii. 319 and n.
Steinmetz, Andrew:
  The Gaming Table: Its Votaries and Victims i. 64 and n.; iii. 70 and n.
Stephen, Sir James FitzJames iv. 288 and n.
Stephen, (Sir) Leslie i. 23 nn., 27 n.*, 47, 148 n., 177 n.; ii. 223 n.; iii. 117 and n., 237; iv. 128, 256, 288 and n.; v. 145 n., 229, 230 n.; vi. 196 n.; vii. 86
  accepts *Far from the Madding Crowd* for *Cornhill* i. 23 nn., 27 n.; vi. 255 n.; vii. 138, 139 n.
  solicits *Hand of Ethelberta* i. 35 n., 37 and n.
  on 'Withered Arm' i. 173 n.
  and 70th birthday tribute to Meredith ii. 184, 185
  on 'Browning's Casuistry' iii. 41 and n.
  Maitland's *Life* of iii. 176 n., 237, 242; v. 76, 77 n.
  TH's sonnet on v. 76, 77 nn.
  declines *Trumpet-Major* for *Cornhill* vii. 92 n.
  Some Early Impressions vi. 255 and n.
  letters to i. 27, 28, 37
Stephen, Thoby iii. 237 and n.
Stephens, James:
  and 'Poets' Tribute' v. 332, 333 n.
  letter to v. 332
Stereoscopic Co. vii. 128
Sterne, Laurence:
  A Sentimental Journey iii. 86, 87 n.
Stevens, Alfred (artist) iv. 228 and n.; v. 114 n.; vii. 156 n.
  projected book on iv. 288, 289 n., 290, 292

Stevens, B. F., & Brown (library and literary agents):
  and special printing of 'Convergence of the Twain' iv. 223 n.; v. 160, 161 n.
  inquiry over American pub. of *Three Wayfarers* v. 6
  letter to v. 6
Stevens, C. L. McCluer iii. 245, 246 n.
Stevens, Edwin John (Dorchester civil servant) iv. 190 n.; v. 66 n.; vi. 171 nn.
  letters to iv. 190; vi. 171
Stevens, Henry (American bookseller) i. 95 n., 101, 106 n., 138
  letters to i. 95, 106
Stevens, William (artist) iv. 290, 292
Stevenson, Robert Louis i. 147 n., 167 and n.; ii. 198; iii. 314; v. 214; vi. 26 and n., 106 ('writer you celebrate') and n., 268 n.
  considers dramatizing *Mayor of Casterbridge* i. 146
  at Max Gate v. 215 n.
  Memorial to vii. 129, 130 nn.
  Letters . . . to his Family and Friends iii. 55, 56 n.
  (and W. E. Henley) *Macaire* ii. 270 n.
  letter to i. 146
Stewart, Robert iv. 176, 177 n.
Stickland, Emma iv. 244 n.
  letter to iv. 244
Stickland, Revd Robert Pattison iii. 264 n.; iv. 244
  letter to iii. 263
Stièvenard, Léonce vii. 30, 31 n.
Stinsford (Dorset) v. 316; vi. 1, 33; vii. 33 and n.
  parish register vi. 107 and n.
Stinsford Church (Dorset) v. 46 n., 272 n., 297 and n.; vi. 71 and n., 298 n.
  memorial service to TH's father i. 280 n.
  as 'Mellstock Church' ii. 140; iv. 264; vii. 9
  restoration iii. 346, 350; iv. 15 ('the church'), 16, 18–20
  ELH buried at iv. 237, 238 and n., 262 and n., 263 and n., 264 and n., 266, 268, 269 n., 270; v. 294, 336
  restoration of old font v. 3–4; vi. 36 and n., 41, 71 and n.
  Mary H. buried at v. 135 n., 161 and n., 180
  Maurward family graves v. 225
  Hardy family graves v. 316; vi. 57 and n., 276 n.
  recasting of bells vii. 7, 8 nn., 9 and nn., 15, 16 nn.
  quire vii. 7 n., 9 and n.
Stinsford Hill (Dorset) i. 105
Stinsford House iv. 296 and n.; v. 253 ('house described'), 254 n.; vi. 59 and n.

Stirling, Edward vii. 8, 9 n.
Stoddard, Lorimer:
  dramatization of *Tess* ii. 112 n., 239 n.; iv. 80; v. 263 and n.; vii. 133 n.
Stoke Court (Stoke Poges) ii. 220 n., 222, 257 n., 258; iii. 104 n., 215 n.; iv. 96 n.; v. 241 n., 272 ('your grounds') and n.; vi. 148 and n.; vii. 131, 132 n.
Stoke Poges ii. 205, 220 n., 222; iii. 270; v. 272 n.
  church ii. 222, 257 n.; iii. 215 n., 265; vi. 206 and nn., 207
Stoker, Bram i. 105 n.; iii. 259 n.
  letter to iii. 258
Stokes, Francis Griffin i. 37 n.
  letter to i. 37
Stokoe, Miss (owner of Montague Street lodgings) i. 133 and n.
Stone, Revd Edward Daniel v. 194, 195 n.
  Dorica v. 194 ('poems'), 195 n.
Stone, Henry (architect):
  as former colleague of TH v. 14 and n.
  letter to v. 14
Stone, Joseph (Dorchester solicitor) v. 195 nn.
Stone, Lucia Catherine Boswell:
  Memories and Traditions v. 209 and n.
Stone, Walter George Boswell iv. 119, 120 n.; v. 194, 195
Stone, W. M. v. 268 n.
  letter to v. 268
Stonehenge ii. 228, 229 and n.
  in *Tess* ii. 132, 228
  appeal for vii. 73 and n.
Stoneleigh Court (Dorset) i. 227 ('P. Edgcumbe's'), 228 n.
Stopes, Marie Charlotte Carmichael vii. 17 n.
  Vectia vii. 16 ('your play'), 17 n.
  letters to vii. 16, 44
Štorch-Marien, Dr vii. 11 ('Dr Marven') and n.
Stourhead (Wilts) iv. 75 n., 241; v. 36, 38
  tower v. 26 and n., 36 and n., 235 and n.
Strachey, Giles Lytton vi. 84 n., 130
  Queen Victoria vi. 84 and n., 94, 95 n., 98 and n., 109 n.
  letter to vi. 84
Strachey, John St Loe iv. 112 n.
  letter to iv. 112
Straight, Sir Douglas ii. 49 n.
  letter to ii. 48
Strand Magazine i. 242 n.; vii. 147 and n.
  Dickens Stamp scheme iv. 118 and n.
Strang, William i. 275, 276 and n., 278, 280, 284 n.*
  portrait-etching of TH i. 275 ('the etching') and n., 284 and n., 285 n.; vi. 68, 69 n., 140, 141 n.; vii. 18 and n., 137

Strang, William (cont.)
portrait of TH for OM iv. 108, 116, 122 n., 210 and n.
invited to Max Gate iv. 116, 122, 280 n.
portrait of FED iv. 122 and n.; v. 12 and n.
etching of TH for Mellstock Edn v. 312 and n.
letters to i. 284; iv. 116, 122, 250; v. 12
Strange, Harman Daniel v. 291 n.
letter to v. 291
'Stranger's Song, The' (poem):
setting to music of iii. 99 and n.
Stratford-on-Avon ii. 128, 129 n., 161
Shakespeare Memorial Theatre proposal iii. 310 and n., 313; iv. 27 n.
theatre rebuilding vii. 13 and n., 43, 44 n.
Stratton (Dorset):
rebuilding of church i. 205, 220, 225, 233; vii. 115, 116 n.
Strauss, Richard ii. 163 n.
Streatfield, T. E. C. vii. 43 and n.
Street, George Edmund vii. 115, 116 n.
Street (George) & Co. (publishers) i. 91 n.
Strong, Walter Ansel vii. 23 and n.
Strutt, Joseph vi. 122 and n.
Stuart-Wortley, Alice (later Lady Stuart of Wortley) ii. 22, 23 n.; vii. 169 n.
Stucley, Gladys (formerly Bankes) iii. 4 n.
Stucley, Hugh Nicholas Granville iii. 4 n.
Sturgeon, Mary C.:
Studies of Contemporary Poets v. 328 and n.
Sturgis, Howard Overing i. 245 n.
Tim i. 245
Sturgis, Julian Russell i. 184 and n.; (?) ii. 9 and n.
Sturgis, Marie (Riette) iii. 218 ('Mrs S.'), 219 n.
Sturminster Newton (Dorset) i. 52; ii. 269 n.; iii. 222 and n.; vi. 155
Riverside Villa i. 45 n., 47 n.
move from i. 56; vii. 90, 91 n.
style, views on i. 168; iii. 102, 237; iv. 89
Suart, Evelyn (later Lady Harcourt) iv. 52 ('Smart') and n.
Sudermann, Hermann:
Das Hohe-lied (*The Song of Songs*) iv. 131 and n., 133 ('the book') and n., 228 ('novel'), 289
The Joy of Living iii. 67 n.
Sullivan, Sir Arthur ii. 283 and n.
'Summer Schemes' (poem) vi. 118
'Sunday Morning Tragedy, A' (poem) vii. 148
rejected by *Fortnightly* and *Nation* iii. 278 ('poem of mine') and n., 287 ('a ballad'), 354; vii. 143 n.
pub. in *English Review* iii. 331 ('the poem') and n., 354 ('the ballad') and n.; iv. 7 n.

criticized by *Spectator* iv. 28 ('another'), 29 n.
MS in Huntington Library vii. 148 n.
Sunday Times vi. 197 and n., 321 n., 328 n., 329 n., vii. 27 n., 77 and n.
and TH's 80th birthday vi. 19 nn.
centenary vi. 150 and n., 162 n.
and TH's 83rd birthday vi. 196, 197 nn.
Armistice Day issue (1923) vi. 218 and n.
See also Rees, Leonard
'Superstitious Man's Story, The' (story) ii. 55 n.; vi. 251
Surbiton (Surrey):
St David's Villa, Hook Road i. 32 and n., 35 n.
Sutro, Alfred ii. 250 n.
John Glayde's Honour iii. 249, 250 n.
letter to ii. 250
Sutro, Esther ii. 250 n.; v. 61 and n.
Sutton (Surrey):
Marie Souvestre School vi. 34 n., 182 n.
Sutton Poyntz (Dorset) iii. 359 and n.
as 'Overcombe' ii. 131; iii. 285; iv. 123
Suvla Bay v. 122, 123 n.
Svenska Andelsförlaget vi. 15 n.
Swaffield, Alfred Owen vii. 145 n.
letter to vii. 145
'Swan-knolls' (Dorset) vi. 131
Swanage (Dorset) iii. 260; v. 31
West End Cottage i. 88 n.
as 'Knollsea' ii. 132
opening of Children's Hospital v. 338, 339 and n., 341
Sweet, Blanche vi. 153 n.
Swetman, Christopher iv. 208 n.; vi. 317 n.
Swetman, Grace iv. 208 n.
Swetman, Leonard iv. 208 n.
Swetman, John (great-grandfather) v. 216 n.
Swetman, Maria (*née* Childs) (great-grandmother) v. 216 n.
Swift, Ryle v. 143 n.
Swinburne, Algernon Charles i. 165 n.; ii. 26 n., 184, 216 nn., 304 and n.; iii. 25 n., 175, 268; iv. 23, 26, 287; v. 77, 90, 96, 157, 232 and n., 261 n.; vi. 189
copy of *Woodlanders* sent to i. 165
quoted in *Tess* i. 282
praise of *Jude* ii. 92, 93; vi. 226
and *Well-Beloved* ii. 158
his 'special favourites' in *Wessex Poems* ii. 209; v. 246
and *Dynasts* iii. 114, 124; v. 251
obituaries of iv. 15, 16 nn.
TH's admiration of iv. 15, 24, 25, 79 and n.
TH's 'monody' on iv. 79 and n., 81 ('my poem') and n., 111, 178, 179 n., 184, 192, 282 and n.; v. 66 and n., 251 and n.

Swinburne, Algernon Charles (*cont.*)
  Gosse on iv. 233 and n.; v. 66 n., 77 and nn.,
    211 and n., 215, 231, 232 n., 261 and nn.
  'Anactoria' ii. 159 n.; iv. 16 n.
  Atalanta in Calydon iv. 63, 64 n.
  'Faustine' iv. 159 and n.
  Poems and Ballads ii. 26 and n., 40, 159 n.;
    iv. 16 and n., 25 n., 63, 64 n., 93; v. 260 n.
  'The Transvaal. October 9, 1899' ii. 232
    ('sonnet') and n., 235 n.
  Tristram of Lyonesse vi. 222 n., 226, 227 n.
  letters to i. 165; ii. 158
Swinburne, Admiral Charles Henry iii. 114
  and n.
Swinburne-Hanham, John Castleman vi.
  375 n.
  letter to vi. 375
Swinley, Ion vi. 346 n.
Swire, Elizabeth (Mrs John Hardy) (g-g-
  grandmother) iv. 37 n.
Sydling St Nicolas (Dorset) ii. 306 n.; iii.
  15 n., 64 n.
Sydney *Mail* i. 75 n.
Symes, C. F. (Dorchester mayor) iv. 147 n.
Symonds, Arthur George (Dorchester solicitor
  and Town Clerk) iii. 344 n.; iv. 76 and n.,
  253 n.
  letters to iv. 234, 252, 253; vii. 61
Symonds, Giles (Dorchester solicitor and
  Town Clerk) i. 231, 232 n.; iii. 157 n.; v.
  194, 195 n.
Symonds, Henry (Dorchester solicitor and
  Town Clerk) iii. 157 n., 158 n., 344 n.
  letters to iii. 18–19, 28, 157
Symonds, John Addington i. 191 n., 265 and n.
  letter to i. 190
Symondsbury (Dorset) iv. 120 and n.; v. 238,
  269
Symons, Arthur William ii. 90 n.*, 273, 274 n.,
  299; iii. 143
  invited to Max Gate ii. 263, 267; iii. 31,
    133
  presentation copies sent to iii. 125, 133 and
    n., 198, 305
  country cottage iii. 222 and n., 226 and n.,
    305
  nervous breakdown iii. 344, 352, 353 n.; v.
    80 and n.
  portrait painted by Augustus John v. 221,
    222 n.
  unwelcome visit to Max Gate vii. 29 n.
  Cleopatra in Judaea iii. 253 ('the play')
    and n.
  Figures of Several Centuries v. 197 and n.
  The Fool of the World and Other Poems iii.
    231
  Images of Good and Evil ii. 258–9

An Introduction to the Study of Browning iii.
  252, 253 n.
'The Life and Adventures of Lucy New-
  come' v. 105 ('pages you sent'), 106 n.
Lyrics iii. 58 ('little book') and n.
Plays, Acting, and Music iii. 125 ('book of
  yours'), 126 n.
Spiritual Adventures iii. 183–4, 222 and n.
The Symbolist Movement in Literature ii.
  258 n.
Tristan and Iseult iii. 295 n.
(comp.) *A Sixteenth Century Anthology* iii.
  133 ('book of old verse') and n.
letters to ii. 90, 120, 258, 263, 267; iii. 21,
  25, 31, 58, 125, 133, 142, 176, 183, 198,
  209, 210, 222, 226, 230, 231, 241, 252,
  295, 305; iv. 248; v. 48, 105, 197, 221,
  304; vi. 67; vii. 20
Symons, Rhoda Bowser (Mrs A. W. Symons)
  iii. 21 and n., 31, 58, 353 n.
  seeks part in *Dynasts* v. 54 and n.
  letters to iii. 352; v. 54
Synge, John Millington iv. 225 and n.
  The Playboy of the Western World iv. 92 n.,
    95 n., 160 n.
Syrett, Netta iv. 46 nn.
  letter to iv. 45

Tabley, John Byrne Leicester Warren, 3rd
  Lord ii. 77 and n.
Tagore, Sir Rabindranath v. 146 n.
  Gitanjali iv. 285 and n.; v. 146 ('poem')
    and n.
Taine, Hippolyte Adolphe i. 191
Talbot, Robert Randall iii. 179, 180 n.
  letter to iii. 179
'Talbothays dairy':
  scene of ii. 133
Talbothays Lodge (Dorset) v. 102, 104,
  105 n., 325; vi. 38
  as home of TH's brother and sisters iv. 287
    and n.; v. 71 n., 103 n., 320; vi. 38 n.,
    205 n., 280
Tarrant Keynston (Keyneston) (Dorset) iv.
  221 and n.
Tate, Nahum, and Nicholas Brady vii. 176
Tate Gallery v. 159 and n., 181 n.
Tatler ii. 292 and n.; iii. 118, 194 and n., 299
  and n.; vii. 134 and n.
  'Wives in the Sere' pub. in ii. 293 ('the lines')
    and n.
  'One We Knew' pub. in iii. 81 n., 136 n.
Tauchnitz, Christian Bernhard:
  publication of TH's novels i. 43 and n., 55
    and n., 82 and n., 102 and n., 248, 249 n.,
    281, 283 n.; iii. 222; iv. 8 n., 317 and n.,
    318, 321 and n., 324, 325

Tauchnitz, Christian Bernhard (cont.)
  and *Tess* ii. 74, 145, 146 n.
  and *Changed Man* iv. 317 and n., 321 and n.,
    324, 325 n.
  letter to i. 102
Tauchnitz jun., Freiherr von i. 82 n.
Taylor, Alphonse Warington v. 134 n., 139 n.
Taylor, Edith (FED's mother's cousin) iv.
    174 n.
  letter to iv. 174
Taylor, Florence (FED's mother's cousin) iv.
    175 n.
Taylor, Jeremy i. 282
  Holy Living and Dying iii. 102, 103 n.
Taylor, John (Keats's first publisher) vi. 313
    and n.
Taylor, Margaret (FED's great-aunt) iv. 175 n.
Taylor, Mary Ann (original 'Trampwoman')
    iii. 83
Tearle, Godfrey v. 254 n.
Teck, Francis, Duke of ii. 27
Teck, Princess Mary Adelaide, Duchess of ii.
    22, 23 n., 27
Teck, Princess Mary of – *see* York, Duchess of
Teignmouth (Devon):
  TH and FEH 'honeymoon' trip to v. 17 and n.
Tempest, (Dame) Marie vi. 337, 338 n., 339
Temple Bar i. 50; ii. 113 and n., 189, 190,
    283 n.
'Temporary the All, The' (poem) iii. 44 n.; vi.
    149
Tennyson, Alfred Lord i. 96 and n.; ii. 24 and
    n., 293; vii. 10 and n.
  quoted in *Tess* i. 282
  funeral i. 286, 287 and n., 289
  praise of *Pair of Blue Eyes* ii. 296; iv. 288,
    291; v. 282
  one-vol. edn of works iv. 4 and n.; vi. 189
    and n.
  as President of Society of Authors iv. 27, 28,
    29 n.
  Becket ii. 23 n.
  Idylls of the King vi. 22 n.
  In Memoriam ii. 24 n.; iii. 258 n.; iv. 5
  'Locksley Hall' v. 293; vi. 313 n.
  'Morte d'Arthur' vii. 69 n.
  letter to iii. 349
Tennyson, Hallam, 2nd Lord iii. 349 n.
  Alfred Lord Tennyson: A Memoir ii. 183
    and n.
Ternan, Ellen Lawless vi. 229 and n.
Terrer, F. Climent vi. 108 n.
Terriss, Ellaline iii. 4 n.
Terry, (Dame) Ellen i. 191, 227; ii. 149; vii.
    121, 122 n.
  desire to play Tess ii. 147
Terry, Marion v. 145 n.

Terry's Theatre ii. 9 n., 16 n.; iv. 80, 181 n.
Tess of the d'Urbervilles (novel) i. 238 n.; ii. 4,
    13, 14, 16, 189 n.; iii. 39 n.; iv. 207 n.;
    vi. 177 and n., 373 n.; vii. 37 n., 126 n.
  suggested titles i. 194 and n., 196, 197
  cancellation of Tillotson agreement i. 201 n.,
    204 n.
  illustrations i. 207 and n., 209 ('my serial
    story'), 255 and n.; iii. 36 n.
  separate pub. of 'Midnight Baptism' i.
    232 n., 249 n., 257; ii. 8 and n., 9, 272
    and n.; iii. 246 and n.
  separate pub. of 'Saturday Night in Arcady'
    i. 247, 249; iii. 274
  question of Tess's 'purity' i. 267; iv. 62
  verse quotations in i. 281–3
  presentation copies i. 287; vi. 290 n.
  Clare as 'accessory' to Alec's murder i. 290
    and n.
  bull-and-fiddle episode ii. 6 n.
  compared with Zola's *Nana* ii. 36 n.
  unlikelihood of Tess's sentence ii. 62 and n.
  legend of phantom coach iii. 93, 94 n.
  photographic 'studies' of Tess iii. 107; vi.
    288 and n.
  MS given to British Museum iv. 178 and n.,
    192, 199, 200
  compared with *Esther Waters* v. 183 n.
  Canadian market vi. 65, 66, 80, 87, 88
  reference to 'strange birds' vii. 34 and n.
  BACKGROUND AND ORIGINALS OF
    PLACES:
    i. 273, 274, 286, 287 n.; ii. 19, 23, 30, 32,
      132, 133, 228 and n.; iii. 147, 171 and
      n., 209, 210 n.; iv. 10, 156; vi. 371 n.;
      vii. 122, 123 n., 151, 152 n.
    prototypes of characters i. 51 n.; ii. 248,
      258; vi. 75; vii. 40
    writing of true place-names in Mrs
      Henniker's copy ii. 19, 23
    physical model for Tess ii. 265 n.; v.
      97 n.; vi. 75, 77 n.
  CRITICAL RECEPTION:
    i. 249, 250 and n., 251 and n., 254, 255
      and n., 257, 258, 259, 263, 264, 265,
      268, 273, 277, 279, 281, 289; iv. 233 n.
    German review ii. 39 and n.
    Quarterly attack i. 264, 265, 268
    Saturday Review attack i. 252 and n.,
      253, 254, 255 and n., 256 n., 258
  DRAMATIZATIONS:
    ii. 77 n., 81, 82 n., 85, 103, 104, 109–10,
      111–12, 114 n., 121, 122 n., 128, 147–
      52, 156, 157, 162, 167 and n., 186, 209,
      239, 241, 291; iii. 107, 109, 110 n., 203,
      260; iv. 80, 99, 100 n.; v. 263 n.; vi. 269
      and n., 278, 279 and n., 288, 289, 293,

Tess of the d'Urbervilles (cont.)
330; vii. 8, 9 n., 17, 83, 128, 129 n., 133 and n.
Barnes Theatre production vi. 334 and n., 335–6, 337, 338, 339, 340–2, 343–4, 345–6 and nn., 347, 348 and n., 349 and n., 350 and nn., 351, 352, 353 n., 359 ('the play'), 361–2, 369 and n.; vii. 6 n., 22 n.
new scene vi. 361, 362 n., 366
possible production abroad vi. 344, 346, 347 n., 349, 352–5, 357, 365, 366, 367 n., 369; vii. 36, 37, 58
transference to West End vi. 349 and n., 361, 374 and n.
private performance at Max Gate vi. 372 ('down here') and n.
tour of vii. 6 n., 22 n., 30 ('fees') and n., 58 n.
Bournemouth proposed production vi. 295 and n., 297
French proposed iii. 107, 109, 110 n.
Hardy Players' production vi. 269 and n., 279 and n., 284, 285–6, 287, 289 ('the play'), 291 ('the play') and n., 294 and n., 295, 296, 297, 298 n., 302, 342 n.
Italian proposed translation vii. 129 and n.
London proposed productions vi. 291, 295–6, 297, 298–9, 303, 308 and n., 310
projected rewriting of vi. 306 and n., 309 and n., 310, 311–12
EDITIONS:
American i. 275 ('abridged') and n.; vii. 118 ('this story') and n., 119 and n.
de luxe vii. 1, 2 n.
'fifth' (one-vol.) i. 284, 288 nn.
first (three-vol.) i. 247, 248, 253, 254, 255, 268
illustrated and signed vi. 292 and n., 294 and n.; vii. 1, 2 nn., 6 ('the sheets') and n., 14 and n., 15 and n., 29, 30 n., 46, 47 n.
sixpenny ii. 263, 265, 282; iii. 14 n., 246
Tauchnitz i. 281, 283 n.; ii. 74
three-and-sixpenny (Uniform) iii. 27, 36 and n.
Wessex iii. 275 n.; iv. 185, 186, 204 and n., 209 n., 271 n.; v. 245; vi. 62 n.
'Wessex Novels' ii. 69, 71, 145 ('London edition'), 146 n., 201 n.; iii. 36 and n.
FILM VERSIONS AND RIGHTS:
iv. 140 and nn., 142, 265 and n., 277, 278, 279 n., 302, 303, 305 ('their film') and n., 309, 310 and n., 312, 327; v. 97, 98, 254 and n., 262, 263 and nn., 265, 307 and nn., 308 n., 313, 334; vi. 152, 153 n., 163, 164, 165, 284 n.

OPERATIC VERSIONS:
Italian iii. 56, 57 n., 204 and nn.; iv. 2 and n., 25, 99, 100 n., 103 n.
London production iv. 25, 30 and n., 31–2, 33, 35, 36, 38, 100 n., 103 n., 230 and n.; vi. 350 and nn.
projected ii. 261 and n.
SERIALIZATIONS:
American i. 196 n., 207 and n., 209, 275 n.
Graphic i. 202–4, 207 and n., 212 and n., 225 ('the story'), 226 and nn., 228, 229, 230 n., 245, 268; vi. 362 ('in 1891'), 363 n.
John o' London's vi. 356 and n., 363 and nn.
Tillotson proposed i. 163 n., 187 and n., 188 ('the novel'), 194, 197, 200, 201 n., 204 n.
TRANSLATIONS:
Czech vii. 11 and n., 15
French ii. 145, 164, 165, 167, 170, 171, 218 and n., 273, 278, 282 n., 291; iii. 56, 96; vi. 33 n., 61, 62 nn., 75–7
German ii. 68 and n.; iii. 56, 222 n.
Russian i. 281, 283 nn., 288 and n.; ii. 42 ('my last novel') and n.; iii. 57
Thackeray, William Makepeace i. 16; iii. 2, 279
TH's praise of i. 5
autograph letter given to TH vii. 145 and n.
The Book of Snobs ii. 17 n.
Vanity Fair i. 5, 274; ii. 294 n.; iii. 228 and n.
Yellowplush Papers vi. 86 n.
Thames Tunnel i. 2, 3
theatre, interest in i. 99, 100, 103, 104, 105, 213, 214–5, 227, 231, 233, 240; ii. 11, 13–14, 15, 16 n., 17, 18, 20, 21, 43, 52, 81, 82, 100, 104, 109–12, 113, 121, 128, 147, 148, 149, 150, 152, 162, 167, 186, 209, 225, 239, 241, 261, 269, 283, 285, 291; iii. 67, 204, 250, 272, 280, 313, 349, 356, 357, 361; iv. 2, 12, 27, 30–32, 33, 35, 36, 58, 59, 99, 125–6, 127, 129, 189, 194; v. 57, 59–60, 62, 64–5, 70, 346–9; vi. 5, 8, 9, 30, 45, 46, 47, 52, 124, 219–22, 232, 250, 256, 265, 269, 279, 280, 284–6, 287, 288–9, 291, 292, 293, 294–6, 297, 298–9, 302, 303, 305, 306, 308, 309–12, 334, 335–6, 337–55, 357, 359, 360, 361–2, 365, 366, 369; vii. 8, 16, 30, 36, 37, 41, 42, 87, 109, 121, 122 n., 128, 129, 131, 132 n., 136 and nn., 139, 140 n., 149, 153 and n.
Theatre Royal, Drury Lane vii. 43, 44 nn.
'Then and Now' (poem) v. 264
Theobald, Lewis v. 75 n.
Thiers, Louis Adolphe vii. 19
Histoire du Consulat et de l'Empire de Napoléon vii. 20 n.

'Thieves Who Couldn't Help Sneezing, The' (story) i. 50 n.

Thomas-a-Didymus v. 300, 301 n.

Thomas, Brandon:
Charley's Aunt v. 144, 145 n.

Thomas, Edward iv. 307 n.
(comp.) *This England: An Anthology from Her Writers* v. 87 ('your selection'), 88 n.
letter to v. 87

Thomas, William Luson i. 215, 216 and n.
dinner to i. 222 and n.

Thomas, William Moy i. 36 n.
letters to i. 36, 99, 103, 108, 196, 214

Thomas Hardy (trawler) vi. 352 n.

Thompson, Revd E. J. vi. 317 n.

Thompson, Edith Jessie vi. 178 n.

Thompson, Sir Henry i. 218 n.*; ii. 22, 23 n., 27, 191 n.
letters to i. 218; ii. 191

Thompson (later Grogan), Lady iii. 164, 168 n.

Thomson, Elspeth (later Mrs Kenneth Grahame) ii. 107 ('your sister') and n., 108 ('her sister'), 181 ('your sister'), 187 n.
valentine from ii. 186
letter to ii. 186

Thomson, George William:
TH photograph sent to iii. 72

Thomson, James v. 140 and n.

Thomson, Winifred Hope ii. 79 n.*; iii. 270 n.
portrait of TH ii. 78 ('the picture'), 79 n., 80, 85, 107, 108, 109, 117, 165 ('object of art'), 174, 212, 242, 243 n., 246, 247 n., 252, 254 and n., 260 n.; iii. 252 n., 306 and nn.; v. 86 and n.; vi. 68, 69 n.
'Jezebel' painting ii. 107
gift of TH letters to Red Cross v. 86, 252 and n.
letters to ii. 78, 80, 85, 106, 108, 117, 165, 174, 181, 212, 242, 246, 252, 260–1; iv. 115; v. 86

Thorndike, (Dame) Sybil vi. 285 n.
interest in producing *Tess* vi. 284, 288, 291, 295–6, 306 n., 308, 310 and n., 311, 312
letter to vi. 284

Thorne, Jenny Doris vii. 88 n.
letter to vii. 87

Thorne, Edwin v. 244 n.

Thornhill, Constance Emily ii. 112, 113 n., 122, 198, 228 n.

Thornhill, Mary Cecilia ii. 112, 113 n., 122, 198, 228, 236; iii. 267

Thornhill, Sir Thomas ii. 113 n.

Thornhill, Thomas ii. 113 n.

Thornton, Emily Mary Bineta (later Mrs W. H. F. Weber):
TH's wedding gift to iii. 37 and n.
letter to iii. 37

Thornton, R. Douglas ii. 82, 83 n.; iii. 37 n.

Thornycroft, Agatha (later Lady) ii. 265; iii. 137 n.
as physical model for Tess ii. 265 n.; v. 97 n.
and scientific alphabet v. 97
letter to v. 97

Thornycroft, Oliver v. 97 ('your son') and n.; vi. 231 ('your son')

Thornycroft, Thomas vi. 48

Thornycroft, (Sir) William Hamo ii. 265 n.; iii. 137 n.*; v. 217 n., 224
cycle ride with TH ii. 264
sees *Dynasts* v. 74 n.
bust of TH v. 82, 83 n., 88 and n., 90, 93, 104, 106, 108, 114, 115 and n., 158, 159, 170, 171, 343; vi. 69 and n.
'Kiss' group v. 159 and n., 181 n.
proposed new layout of Charing Cross area vi. 176 and n.
war memorial vi. 176, 177 n.
letters to iii. 137, 138; v. 74, 82, 88, 90, 93, 95, 106, 114, 115, 142, 159, 171, 176, 181, 214, 217, 231, 343; vi. 47, 176, 231, 268

'Thoughts of Phena' (poem) iii. 227 n.

Thrale, Hester iv. 60

'Three Strangers, The' (story) i. 114 n., 134, 140 n.; iii. 151, 233, 264 n.; iv. 181, 271, 284; vi. 99 and n.; v. 28 and n., 29; vii. 47
dramatization – see *Three Wayfarers*
setting to music of 'Stranger's Song' iii. 99 and n.
proposed operas from iii. 358 n.; iv. 1, 2 n.; vi. 239 n.
MS given to Cockerell iv. 178 and n.; v. 256 n.

Three Wayfarers (TH's dramatization of 'Three Strangers') ii. 7 and n., 9, 10 ('scrap of a play'), 11 n., 268; iii. 260, 272, 273; iv. 2 n., 146; v. 6, 7 n., 256 and n.; vi. 293, 294 n., 363; vii. 19
first London performance ii. 9 n., 10, 15, 16 n., 61; iii. 272 n., 358; iv. 80, 147 n., 181 and n.
Stage Society performances ii. 269, 270 n., 271; iii. 358
Scottish Repertory Theatre performances iv. 12 and n., 72, 155 n.
Dorchester performances iv. 147 n., 178 ('a play here'), 179–80, 183 n., 187 n., 189, 191 and n.; vii. 153 n.
'College Hornpipe' in iv. 179, 180 n., 183
hangman's song in iv. 179, 180 n.
requests to perform iv. 180, 181, 193, 194
later London performances iv. 183 n., 194 and n., 323 ('the performance'), 324 n.
performance at Keble College vi. 364 n.

Thring, George Herbert iii. 8 nn.; v. 54
  as Secretary of Society of Authors iii. 8 nn.;
    v. 54, 55 n.; vi. 36, 37, 271, 273; vii. 4, 5,
    11, 33 and n., 52, 55, 61
  letters to iii. 7; iv. 40, 73, 80; v. 4, 119, 126,
    155, 164, 169, 189, 298; vi. 37, 143, 194,
    251, 261, 297, 304, 314, 323, 324; vii. 4, 5,
    11, 15, 21, 52, 55, 61
Thwaites, (?) Revd Nembhard vii. 176
Thwaites, (?) Capt. Robert Charles George vi.
  106 and n.; vii. 176
Thyen, George i. 90 n.
  letters to i. 90, 91
Tigan, Miss (typist) ii. 39, 41 n.
Tilby, A. Wyatt:
  'The New Literary Criticism' vi. 33 n.
Tile Club i. 106 and n.
Tillett, Alfred W.:
  Spencer's Synthetic Philosophy v. 79 n.
Tilley, Miss A. (Dorchester amateur actress)
  iii. 356 n.
Tilley, E. W. vi. 280 (wrongly identified as
  T. H. Tilley); vii. 177
Tilley, Thomas Henry (Dorchester mayor and
  amateur actor) iii. 356 n.; iv. 115 n.*; v.
  3 n.; vi. 209 n., 220, 250, 251 n., 279 and
  n., 280 and n.; vii. 156, 157 n.
  dramatization of *Return of the Native* vi. 45,
    46, 47, 52
  and production of *Tess* vi. 279 and n., 280
    (erroneous identification, corrected at vii.
    177)
  letters to iv. 115, 183, 186, 188, 292; v. 2,
    162, 165; vi. 46, 66, 269, 329
Tillotson, William Frederic i. 188 and n.
Tillotson, Mrs W. F.:
  letter to i. 188
Tillotson & Son (Tillotson's Newspaper
  Fiction Bureau) i. 93 n., 188 n.; iii. 48, 66;
  vii. 118 n.
  proposed serialization of *Tess* i. 163 n.,
    187 n., 194, 197, 200, 201 n., 204 n.
  syndication of 'Melancholy Hussar' i. 179 n.,
    201 n., 204, 285 n.; ii. 143, 144 n.; vii.
    112 n.
  letters to i. 93, 162, 187, 194, 197, 200, 201,
    204, 249, 253, 255
Tilly-Whim caves (Dorset) v. 31
'Time's Laughingstocks, A Summer Romance'
  (later 'The Revisitation', q.v.) (poem) iii.
  135 n., 138, 143, 151
  MS given to Fitzwilliam Museum iv. 180
Time's Laughingstocks (poems) iii. 331 n.; iv.
  65, 67 n., 116, 117, 132, 154, 171 and n.,
  172, 264 n., 284; v. 87; vi. 54, 55 n.,
  278 n.; vii. 150 n., 154 and n.
  preparation of iv. 4 ('print them') and n., 6

  ('separate form'), 7 n., 35 ('fugitive
    poems') and n., 42
  choice of title iv. 26 and n., 61
  revision of copy iv. 42, 43 and n., 44, 47–8
  publication iv. 42 n., 52 ('new poems of
    mine'), 61 and n., 62 ('new poems'), 63
  proofreading of iv. 46, 47 n., 49
  inscribed copies iv. 63, 64 n.; vii. 83 and n.
  critical reception iv. 65, 67, 73 ('the
    volume')
  reprinting iv. 66 and n., 69 and n.
  in Wessex Edn iv. 228 n., 264 ('new edn.')
  in Mellstock Edn vi. 20
Times, The i. 149, 179, 244, 279 n.; ii. 1 and n.,
  107 n., 186 n., 232 and n., 235 n., 238 n.,
  239 n., 241 n., 247, 270 and n.; iii. 9 n., 39
  and nn., 40 n., 127, 128 n., 156 n., 165 n.,
  187 and n., 193 n., 262 n., 325 and n.,
  343; iv. 15, 16 n., 26 and n., 74 and n.,
  90 n., 94 and n., 106 and n., 107 n.,
  130 n., 174 n., 175 and n.; v. 21 and n.,
  65 n., 142 and n., 166 and n., 248 and
  n., 272 and n., 325 n., 343 n.; vi. 110,
  131 n., 231 n., 252 n., 262 and n., 298 n.,
  319 n., 338 and n., 342 and n.; vii. 72 n.,
  73 and n., 94, 95 n.
  and *Well-Beloved* ii. 159 and n.
  'V.R. 1819–1901' pub. in ii. 280 ('some
    lines') and n.
  censorship protests in iii. 25 n.; iv. 63 and n.
  Trumpet-Major performance noticed in iii.
    333 and n., 357
  'G.M.' (on Meredith) pub. in iv. 24 ('lines of
    verse'), 25 n.; vii. 159 and n.
  Christmas Gift Book Supplement (1909)
    iv. 57 and n.
  TH's letter on performing animals iv. 330,
    331 n.; v. 2 n.
  war poems v. 45, 46 n., 47 n., 48
  authors' manifesto on war aims in v. 47 n.
  'Song of the Soldiers' pub. in v. 47 n., 56, 58
  'Call to National Service' pub. in v. 206
    and n.
  'Jezreel' pub. in v. 281 n.
  Armistice Day supplement (1920) vi. 45,
    46 n.
  and *Queen of Cornwall* vi. 221, 222 n.
  'In the Evening' pub. in vi. 230 and n.
  'Compassion' pub. in vi. 243, 244 n., 256
    and n.
  'Christmas in the Elgin Room' pub. in vii. 89
    ('verses') and n.
Times Book Club iii. 234 nn., 236; iv. 232,
  233 n.; vii. 155
Times Literary Supplement iii. 298 n.; v.
  280 n., 301 n.; vi. 7 and n., 79, 80 n., 184
  and n., 221, 222 n.

Times Literary Supplement (*cont.*)
  and *Dynasts* iii. 98 and n., 99, 107 n.
  Henry James article in v. 21 and n.
  'curious blunder' vi. 190 and n.
'Timing Her' (poem) v. 250 ('the "Lalage" one') and n.
Tincleton Heath (Dorset) iii. 138
  as original of 'Egdon Heath' ii. 74, 132
Tinsley, Edward i. 9 n.
Tinsley, William:
  as TH's first publisher i. 9 n., 10, 11, 13–22, 23 n., 24, 33; vii. 138
  purchase of *Greenwood Tree* copyright i. 16, 34 and n.; iv. 162
  letters to i. 10, 11, 13, 15–22, 23, 24, 25, 33, 34, 39
Tinsley Brothers (publishers) i. 9 n., 129 n.; ii. 58 n.
  pub. *Desperate Remedies* i. 10 and n., 11
  letters to i. 9–10
Tinsleys' Magazine i. 17, 22, 23
  Pair of Blue Eyes pub. in i. 17–19, 20, 21; v. 147; vii. 165 n.
Tintagel (Cornwall) iv. 260; v. 176, 177, 179; vi. 229 n.; vii. 169 n.
  Castle vi. 281 and n.
Tip (Max Gate cat) ii. 270, 271 n., 272
Tissot, James Joseph Jacques ii. 234 and n.
Titanic, s.s. iv. 211 and n.
  TH's poem on iv. 216 and nn., 222, 223 n., 225, 226 and nn., 228
  matinée in aid of disaster fund iv. 216 and n.
Tite, William i. 4 n.
Titmarsh Club iii. 279 and n.
Titterington, Ellen Elizabeth ('Nelly') (parlour maid) vi. 279 and n.
Tiverton (Devon) vi. 13, 16 n.
'To C.F.H.' (poem) vi. 135 n.
'To Life' (poem):
  set to music iv. 139, 166, 167 n.
'To Lizbie Browne' (poem) ii. 305 n.
'To Meet, or Otherwise' (poem) v. 212, 259 n.
  pub. in *Sphere* iv. 253 n., 330 ('few verses'), 331 n.
  in *Satires of C* v. 87
'To the Moon' (poem) vi. 96
'To my Father's Violin' (poem) vi. 55
'To Please His Wife' (story):
  terms for i. 216 ('the story'), 217 n.
  original scene of ii. 132
'To Shakespeare After Three Hundred Years' (poem) vii. 44 ('verses to Shakespeare') and n., 49 and n.
  pub. in *Book of Homage to Shakespeare* v. 129 n., 145 and n., 146 ('my lines')
  private printing of v. 159, 160 n.
  reprinted in *Fortnightly* v. 160, 161 n.

'To Sincerity' (poem) ii. 262 ('scrap of verse') and n.
'To the Unknown God' (poem) iii. 232
To-Day ii. 43 n., 62 and n.
Toller Porcorum (Dorset) ii. 67 n.
Toller Whelme (Dorset) iii. 234; vii. 85 n.
Tolstoy, Count Leo iii. 127
  80th birthday iii. 303, 304 n., 320 n.
  'Bethink Yourselves' iii. 128 n.
  Fruits of Culture iii. 128 n.
  Resurrection iii. 57 and n.
  What is Art? ii. 225 and n.
Tolstoy, Leo jun. vii. 162 n.
Tomlinson, Henry Major vii. 24, 25 n.
Toms, Diana (*née* Bugler) vi. 290 ('the baby') and n.
Tomson, Arthur i. 199 nn.*, 201 n.; ii. 295 n.; iii. 15 n., 64 n.
  Many Waters iii. 128 ('new book') and n.
  letters to ii. 295, 305; iii. 14, 17, 64, 128
'Tomson, Graham R.' – *see* Tomson, Rosamund
Tomson, Rosamund ('Graham R. Tomson') i. 192, 193 nn, 199 n.*; ii. 24 ('an enfranchised woman') and n., 67 n., 295 n.
  idea of 'painter's weekly' i. 202, 209 and n.
  A Summer Night and Other Poems i. 248 ('pair of volumes'), 249 nn.
  (ed.) *Concerning Cats: A Book of Poems by Many Authors* i. 248, 249 n.
  Selections from the Greek Anthology i. 199 ('little book') and n., 201
  letters to i. 199, 200, 202, 206, 209, 248
Tonerspuddle (Dorset) v. 174 and n.
'Tony Kytes' (story) vi. 99
  French translation of ii. 211, 224 n.
'Too Late, Beloved!' (former title of *Tess of the d'Urbervilles*, q.v.) i. 196, 197 n., 200
  cancellation of agreement i. 201 n.
Toole, John Lawrence ii. 14 and n.
Toole's Theatre ii. 14 n.
Torquay (Devon) ii. 197, 266; v. 17, 18 n.
Town Planning Conference (1910) iv. 78 n.
Townly & Bonniwell (Surbiton warehousemen) i. 36 n.
  letter to i. 36
Toynbee, Paget Jackson vi. 313 and n.
T.P.'s Weekly iii. 270 n.; iv. 70, 71 and n.
  serialization of *Mayor of Casterbridge* vii. 35, 36, 37 n., 59
'Tradition of Eighteen Hundred and Four, A' (formerly 'A Legend of the Year Eighteen Hundred and Four', q.v.) (story) i. 106 n.; ii. 278; v. 326 n.
Trafalgar, Battle of (1805) iii. 94 n., 170 n.
  in *Dynasts* iii. 170, 359 and n.
  centenary iii. 170 n., 182, 183, 185 and n.

'Tragedy of Two Ambitions, A' (story) i. 183 ('short story') and n.; ii. 38 and n.; vi. 156 ('drowning person'), 157 nn.; vii. 110 ('little story') and n.
  pub. in *Universal Review* i. 178 ('ending tragically'), 179 ('cold-blooded murder') and n.; vii. 110 ('little story'), 111 n.
  French translation of ii. 211, 224 n.
  background iii. 146
  MS given to John Rylands Library iv. 178 n.
  German translation of vi. 189, 190 n.
Traill, Henry Duff ii. 222 ('Trail'), 223 n., 248 and n., 262 n.
'Trampwoman's Tragedy, A' (poem) iii. 58 ('ballad form'), 135, 247 ('one of mine') and n.; iv. 79 n.; v. 212, 319
  declined by *Cornhill* iii. 59 and n., 75 n., 278 and n.; iv. 79
  pub. in *North American Review* iii. 75 and n., 83 and n., 84, 87, 88; iv. 4 n.
  original title iii. 75 n.
  background iii. 138, 146
  FEH's privately printed pamphlet of v. 203 and n.
Transatlantic Review vi. 218 n., 220 and n.
'Tranter Sweatley' (poem) ii. 209
Traquair, Ramsay v. 305 n.
Tree, (Sir) Herbert Beerbohm i. 212 and n.
Treitschke, Heinrich von v. 50, 51 n.
Trench, Herbert:
  Deirdre Wed, and Other Poems iii. 51 n.
  Napoleon v. 326 n.
Trevelyan, George Macaulay iv. 150 and n.
  and *Dynasts* iii. 200, 201 n.
  letter to iii. 200
Trevelyan, R. C. vi. 256 n.
Trevelyan, Revd W. B.:
  Prayers for Church and Nation vi. 33, 34 n.
Treves, Sir Frederick iii. 53 n.*, 159, 267; v. 105 and n.; vi. 128 n., 173, 174 n., 227, 230 n., 281 n.
  Highways and Byways in Dorset iii. 216 ('about Dorset') and n., 223
Treves, Lady (Anne Elizabeth) iii. 267; vi. 231 n.
Treves, William (Dorchester shopkeeper) iii. 53 and n.
Trevis (Max Gate gardener) iii. 322, 323 n.; iv. 87, 113
Trevor, Austin vi. 346 n.
Trimble, Larry v. 111 n.
Trist, Sidney G. ii. 199 and n.*, 202; iv. 90 n.
  letter to iv. 90
Trollope, Anthony v. 145 n.
  Barchester Towers i. 5, 6

Trot (Max Gate cat) (also known as Kiddleywinkempoops) i. 217 and n.
Trübner, Nicholas (publisher) i. 102 and n.
Trübner & Co. (publishers) i. 102 n., 104, 106 nn.
  letter to i. 106
Trumpet-Major, The (novel) i. 59 ('a new story') and n., 64 ('next time') and n., 125, 134; ii. 70; iii. 169, 294 ('T.M.') and n.; iv. 284; vi. 160 n., 257, 373 n.; vii. 56
  TH's research for i. 51 n., 59 n.; iii. 286, 289 and n.
  offered to magazines i. 65–7; vii. 91 ('the story'), 92 n.
  illustrations i. 66, 67 n.; ii. 109 n.; vii. 93 and n.
  copy sent to Queen Victoria i. 83; iv. 182
  copy sent to Prince of Wales i. 98 and n.
  alleged plagiarism in drill scene i. 103, 104
  'Sergeant's Song' from iii. 73 and n.
  TH's opposition to acting edition iii. 299, 300 n.
  hieroglyphic portrait of Napoleon described in iv. 88 and n.
  MS in Royal Library, Windsor iv. 182 and n.
  possible film version v. 83, 84 n., 335
  use of 'Patagonians' in vi. 167 and n.
  press-gang scene vii. 137 and n., 158 n.
  BACKGROUND AND ORIGINALS OF PLACES:
    i. 83, 98; ii. 30, 31 n., 131, 173; iii. 285, 289; iv. 123, 197 n.; v. 1 and n.; vi. 159, 160 ('T.M.')
    part-original for Anne vi. 315
  DRAMATIZATIONS:
    dramatized scene iii. 294 and n.
    Evans dramatization iii. 300 and n., 332, 333 nn, 351 n.; iv. 22 and n.; vii. 148 n.
    Dorchester amateur performances iii. 300 and n., 332, 333 nn., 335, 349, 350 n., 356 and n., 357; iv. 236 and n., 239 ('the play'), 244 and n., 245 n., 250 ('the play')
  EDITIONS:
    first (three-vol.) i. 78, 81, 92; vii. 93 and n.
    Indian vi. 177 and n.; vii. 164 and n.
    one-vol. i. 98 and n.
    Pocket iii. 285 ('a copy'), 286 ('poor little reprint') and n.
  SERIALIZATION:
    i. 66, 67 and n., 83; vi. 333 and nn.; vii. 92 nn., 93 n., 99 n.
  TRANSLATION:
    French i. 90 and n., 108

'Tryst at an Ancient Earthwork, A' (story) i. 130 n.; ii. 34 n.
  model for antiquary in ii. 43 ('local man') and n.; iv. 203 n.
Tucker, W. L. iii. 142 n.
  letter to iii. 142
Tugela, Battle of (1899) ii. 241 and n.
Tuohy, James M. vi. 102 n.
  letter to vi. 102
Turbervile, Sir Pagan de vii. 152 n.
Turberville family iii. 93, 209; vii. 152 n.
Turgenev ('Tourguèneff', 'Turgeneff'), Ivan Sergeevich, i. 94, 95 n.; ii. 198
  Liza (A Nest of Gentlefolk) i. 94, 95 n.
Turner, Alfred v. 257 and n.
Turner, Charles Tennyson ii. 208 and n.
Turner, Florence v. 111 n.
Turner, Herbert Hall iv. 60 n.
Turner, Hugh Thackeray i. 205 n.*; ii. 67 n.; iii. 35 n., 284 n.; v. 296 n.; vii. 116 n.
  and Puddletown Church iii. 97 n.; iv. 74 n., 78 n., 114, 144 and n.
  letters to i. 205, 220–1, 223, 225, 233; ii. 67, 175, 176, 178; iii. 283, 337, 346; iv. 73, 78, 114, 122
Turner, J. M. W. vi. 161
Turner, (?) John Sidney ii. 116 and n.
Turner, Reginald iv. 95 n.
  letter to iv. 95
Turner, Walter James Redfern v. 312, 313 n.; vi. 3 and n.
  (ed.) *Great Names* vi. 316 n.
Turner Film Company v. 111 and n., 113 n., 131 n., 133 n.; vi. 42 and nn.
Turnerspuddle (Dorset) i. 142 and n.; v. 174 n.
Turnworth (Dorset) ii. 199 n., 227
Turpin, Dick iv. 272 and n.
Tussaud, John Theodore iii. 92 and nn.; v. 101
Tussaud's Waxworks Exhibition iii. 92 n.
Tweedie, Colonel John Lannoy vi. 38 and n.
'Two Fantasies' (poem) vi. 114, 115 nn.
'Two Houses, The' (poem) vi. 101 and n., 183 n.
  pub. in *Dial* vi. 47 n.
'Two Rosalinds, The' (poem):
  pub. in *English Review* iv. 8 n.
'Two Roses' (poem falsely attributed to TH) i. 107 and n., 108 ('ungrammatical verses'), 109 and n.
Two on a Tower (novel) i. 130; ii. 125 and n.; iii. 160, 229; vi. 35, 44, 45 n.
  serialization i. 95 ('complete story') and n., 101 ('serial story'), 102 n., 103, 106 n., 109, 114, 138 n.
  research for i. 96 n., 97 ('the story'), 98 n.
  English copyright of i. 106 nn.
  first (three-vol.) edn i. 109 and n.

copy sent to Gosse i. 110, 114, 122 n.
  role of science in i. 110
  reception of i. 110, 114
  one-vol. edn i. 115 n.
  originals of places in ii. 133
  dialect in ii. 168 n.; iii. 42, 43 n.
  French translation ii. 273
  scheme for dramatization iii. 92 and n., 105, 107, 111
Tynan, Katharine ii. 55 n.
Tyndale, Walter:
  water-colours of 'Thomas Hardy's Country' iii. 147 n., 148, 173 and nn., 181, 194 n.; vi. 145 n.
  letters to iii. 146, 173, 181
Tyrrell, R. Y. ii. 123 n.

Udal, John Symonds i. 136 n.; iv. 120 n.; v. 109
  at Field Club meeting i. 136 n.; iv. 119; v. 111, 167
  at Max Gate iv. 248, 249 n.
  interest in dialect v. 167, 168 n.
  signed copies of TH first edns v. 167, 172, 194
  collection of play-bills v. 194, 204, 209
  and Dorset Mummers' Play v. 284, 285 and n.
  awarded Mansel-Pleydell Medal vi. 248 ('the prize'), 249 n.
  'Christmas Mummers in Dorsetshire' v. 285 n.
  Dorsetshire Folklore v. 111, 112 n., 238, 285 n.
  Marriage, and Other Poems v. 274 ('your poems'), 275 n.
  letters to i. 136, 195; iv. 119, 248; v. 111, 136, 167, 172, 194, 204, 205, 209, 238, 268, 274, 284–5
Umbria, s.s. ii. 1 n.
'Unborn, The' (poem) vi. 54
Under the Greenwood Tree (novel) ii. 140 n.; iii. 178 and n., 260, 329 n.; vi. 103 n.; vii. 21, 68 n.
  offered to publishers i. 11, 13, 16; vi. 254 and n.
  Christmas party scene i. 12 and n.
  sale of copyright i. 16, 18 n., 33, 34 and n.; ii. 144 n.; iv. 162 n.
  publication i. 17 and n., 19, 20; vii. 132
  American publication i. 27 n., 28
  new edn i. 39
  inscribed copies i. 84 and n.; iii. 37 and n.
  originals of places in i. 126; iii. 145
  'King Arthur' ballad quoted in i. 199 n.; v. 29 n.
  dialect words in i. 277, 278 n.; v. 136

Under the Greenwood Tree (cont.)
  transfer of copyright ii. 57, 58 n.; iii. 13, 15; vi. 214 n.
  'rising moon' error iii. 79 and n.
  dramatization as *The Mellstock Quire* (q.v.) iv. 116 n.
  French translations iv. 162 and n. (proposed); vi. 61, 62 n., 64
  'originals' of characters in v. 31 n., 297 and n. in Wessex Edn v. 136
unidentified correspondents i. 56, 96, 98, 101, 127, 130, 136, 149, 189, 204, 211, 244, 261, 271, 274; ii. 3, 76, 120, 146, 154, 182, 200, 242, 274, 296; iii. 12, 40, 66, 93, 108, 201, 277; iv. 77, 145; v. 24, 36, 201, 345; vi. 48; vii. 91, 109, 123, 165–6, 167, 168
Uniform Edition (Macmillan) iii. 27 ('3/6 edn'), 29 n., 36 ('new edition') and nn.; iv. 116 ('3s/6d edition') and n., 124 ('our edition') and n., 161 n., 271 n.; v. 132 ('3s./6d. edition'), 133 n., 299 ('3/6'), 301 n.; vi. 83; vii. 48 and n., 57
United Services Museum vii. 93 ('U.S.M.') and n.
Universal Magazine ii. 253
Universal Review i. 179 nn., 201 n.
  'Tragedy of Two Ambitions' pub. in i. 178 ('ending tragically'), 179 ('cold-blooded murder') and n.; vii. 110 ('little story'), 111 n.
University College of the South West of England, Exeter vi. 62, 63 n.
Untermeyer, Louis vi. 158 n.
  (comp.) *Modern British Poetry* vi. 158 and n., 333; vii. 75 and n.
  letters to vi. 158, 333; vii. 75
Unwin, Thomas Fisher (publisher) ii. 144 n.*; iii. 173 n., 194 n.; vi. 260 n., 317 n., 319
  letters to ii. 143; iv. 290
Unwin, Mrs T. Fisher (Jane Cobden) iii. 173 n.
  The Hungry Forties iii. 173 and n.
  The Land Hunger iv. 290 and n.
  letters to iii. 173, 206
Unwin, William Carter vii. 175
Unwin, William Cawthorne i. 98 n.
  The Elements of Machine Design i. 97 ('the book'), 98 n.
  letter to i. 97
Up-Cerne (Dorset) ii. 30, 32, 38; vi. 132 n.
Up-Sydling (Dorset) iii. 234, 260
Upper Bockhampton – *see* Higher Bockhampton
Upwey (Dorset) i. 199 ('Upway'); ii. 270, 271, 306; iv. 123 and nn.
  as 'Overcombe' ii. 285
  'dungeon' vii. 137 and n.

Vachell, Horace Annesley:
  Her Son iii. 249, 250 n.
'Vagrant's Song' (poem) vi. 241
  pub. in *Nash's and Pall Mall* vi. 242 n.
'Valenciennes' (poem):
  pub. in *Sphere* v. 284 n.
Valentin, Hugo Maurice:
  and Swedish translations vi. 14, 19
Vane-Tempest-Stewart, Lady Helen Mary (later Lady Ilchester) ii. 258 ('Birdie') and n.
Vanhomrigh, Esther ('Vanessa') ii. 29 n.
Vanity Fair:
  'Spy' cartoon of TH vii. 42 and n.
Vaudeville Theatre i. 233 n.; iii. 4
Vaughan, Eleanor Mary vi. 82 and n.
Vaughan, Henry v. 194 and n.; vi. 311 n.
Vedrenne, John E. iii. 257 and n.
Veley, Margaret i. 53 n.
  For Percival ascribed to TH i. 53 and n.
Venables, Revd E. Malcolm v. 276 n.
  letter to v. 276
Venice iii. 68 and n.; vii. 106 and n.
Venture, The: An Annual of Art and Literature iii. 71 and n., 73 and n.
Verdun v. 194 n.
Verhaeren, Emile v. 206, 207 n.
Vernon, H. M. and K. D.:
  A History of the Oxford Museum iv. 54 n., 60
Verrall, Arthur Woollgar iv. 214, 215 n., 221
  The 'Choephori' of Aeschylus iv. 215 n.
Versailles, Treaty of (1919) v. 311 and n.; vii. 169 n.
Vesuvius, Mount:
  eruption (1906) iii. 204 and n.
Victoria, Queen:
  accepts copy of *Trumpet-Major* i. 83; iv. 182
  Golden Jubilee i. 165 and n.
  Diamond Jubilee ii. 154, 171 n.
  visit to Ireland ii. 252 and n.
  death ii. 280 n., 291 n.
  TH poem on ii. 280 ('lines') and nn., 297; vi. 149
  'a most uninteresting woman' vi. 84 and n.
Victoria and Albert Museum ii. 55 n., 220 n.
Victoria Memorial iv. 150, 151 n.
Viereck, George Sylvester vii. 144 n.
  Nineveh and Other Poems vii. 144 ('book of verse') and n.
  letter to vii. 144
Vinall, Charles George i. 95 n.
  letter to i. 95
Vincent, Leon Henry ii. 213 n.
  The Bibliotaph and Other People ii. 213 and n.
  letter to ii. 213
Vincent, Louis:
  and proposed film of *Tess* iv. 140 and nn.

Vineyard, The v. 1 and n.
Virgil v. 233
  Aeneid iv. 281, 282 n.; vii. 66 n.
Virgin, James T. (Dorchester banker) iii. 347, 348 n.
Vitagraph Company v. 263 n.
Vočadlo, Dr Otakar vi. 324 n.
Vogue, La ii. 223 nn.
  letter to editor of ii. 223
'Voices in a Churchyard' (poem) vii. 9
'Voices from Things Growing' (poem) vi. 121 n.
  pub. in *London Mercury* vi. 106 and n., 109 and n., 110, 113 ('Mercury poem')
  in 'Two Phantasies' pamphlet vi. 115 n.
Vollmoeller, Carl Gustav:
  The Miracle iv. 204, 205 n.
Vorwärts iii. 248 n.
Voss, Harold Lionel (chauffeur) vi. 279 and n., 280 and n.; vii. 280 n.
'V.R. 1819–1901' (poem) ii. 280 ('lines . . . about the Queen') and nn., 297; vi. 149
Vymětal, L. vi. 251 n.

Waddon Vale (Dorset) iii. 137
Wagner, Richard vi. 293
  Tristan und Isolde vi. 294 n.
Wagstaff, William Henry vi. 91 n.
  letter to vi. 91
'Wagtail and Baby' (poem) v. 240
'Waiting Both' (poem) vii. 73, 75, 76 n.
  pub. in *London Mercury* vi. 242 n., 277 n.
'Waiting Supper, The' (story) i. 170 ('short sketch') and n.; iv. 297, 299; vii. 172
  German translation vii. 74 and n.
Wakely, Samuel iii. 286 and n.
Waldy, Frances Helen i. 142 n.
  Bonnie Editha Coplestone i. 142 n.
  letter to i. 142
Wales, Prince of (later Edward VII, q.v.) i. 6; ii. 66, 67 n.
  wedding of i. 3, 4 n.
  copy of *Trumpet-Major* presented to i. 98 and n.
Wales, Princess of (later Queen Alexandra, q.v.):
  wedding of i. 3, 4 n.
Wales, Edward, Prince of (later Edward VIII):
  visit to Dorchester vi. 204–5; vii. 56 and n.
Walker, Revd Edward Mewburn vi. 168 n., 201 n.; vii. 18 nn.
  letters to vi. 167; vii. 18
Walker, (Sir) Emery iv. 259 n.
Walker, Francis C. vi. 260 n.
Walker, Revd J. ii. 125
Walker, Sophie ii. 141 and n.

Walker, William Hall (later Lord Wavertree) ii. 141 n.
Walkley, Arthur Bingham iii. 107, 151
  and *Dynasts* iii. 98 ('Times review') and n., 99, 107 n., 113 ('*Times* dramatic critic')
Wallace, William Vincent:
  Lurline i. 2, 3 n.
Waller, Edmund v. 350 n.
Wallop, Lady Dorothea i. 132
Wallop, Lady Eveline Camilla i. 132, 161 and n.
Wallop (later Watney), Lady Margaret i. 132, 133, 161 n.*, 224 and n., 227
  presented with *Pair of Blue Eyes* i. 161 and n.
  letters to i. 161, 172
Walpole, Horace i. 64 and n.; ii. 43, 44 n.; iv. 229
Walpole, (Sir) Hugh iv. 152 n.
Walton, Sydney v. 305 n.
Wantage (Berks):
  as 'Alfredston' ii. 133
war, attitude towards ii. 229, 232, 248, 277; iii. 51, 135; iv. 161; v. 41, 43
  See also Boer War; Great War
'Warborne':
  Wimborne as ii. 133
Ward, Artemus (Charles Farrar Browne) v. 44 and n.
Ward, Helen iii. 360 n.
  letter to iii. 360
Ward, Mrs Humphry i. 263 n.*; iii. 233, 234 n.; v. 220; vi. 12 and n.
  visits French battlefields v. 299 and n.
  The Coryston Family iv. 320 and n.
  Fields of Victory v. 299 n.
  The Marriage of William Ashe iii. 163 ('the novel') and nn.
  Robert Elsmere i. 176, (?) 191 ('the book'), 192 n.
  letters to i. 263; iii. 163; iv. 320
Ward, Osbert (publisher) i. 129 n.
Ward, Revd Stanhope Edgar:
  The Ivory Mouse: A Book of Fairy Tales iv. 3 n.
  letter to iv. 3
Ward, Thomas Humphry iii. 90 and n.; iv. 320
  (ed.) *The English Poets: Selections with Critical Introductions by Various Writers* iii. 85, 86 n.; v. 181 n., 187, 230 ('Barnes pages'), 299 n.; vi. 237, 238 n.
  letters to v. 181, 187, 219, 230, 298; vi. 12
Ward & Downey (publishers) i. 129 n.
  re-publish *Desperate Remedies* i. 185, 186 and n.; vii. 37 and n.
  letters to i. 129, 135, 185, 186

Wareham (Dorset) iii. 64 n., 261 n., 343, 344;
iv. 46 n., 310
as 'Anglebury' iii. 359 n.
Dugdale associations v. 13 and n.
'Wareham' (psalm-tune) iii. 285, 286 and n.
Wareing, Alfred iv. 12 n.
Waring, J. B. i. 125 n.
Warne, Frederick & Co. (publishers) ii. 37
Warner, Sir George Frederic iv. 178 and n.
Warre-Cornish, Francis Warre iv. 327 ('friends
at Eton') and n.
Warren, Revd Dawson:
The Journal of a British Chaplain in Paris iv.
331 and n.
Warren, Thomas Henry iv. 54 n.
and Halley's comet iv. 54 and n., 60
letters to iv. 54, 60
Warrender, Julian Margaret Maitland i. 237 n.
letter to i. 237
Warton, Thomas:
History of English Poetry v. 140 and n.
Warwick Trading Company iv. 142, 143 n.
Washington (D.C.):
TH MSS given to Library of Congress iv.
181 and n., 193
Waterloo, Battle of (1815) ii. 211; v. 80, 220 n.;
vii. 19, 20 n.
battlefield ii. 135; vii. 20 and n.
in *Dynasts* iii. 298; iv. 88; v. 55; vii. 19
Waterston Manor (Dorset) iv. 17 ('Lower
Waterson House')
original of Bathsheba's house iv. 10, 18 and
nn., 58
Watford (Herts) i. 144
Watkins, William iii. 129 n.*; vi. 200 ('a
friend'), (?) 269 ('City broker') and n.
as secretary of Society of Dorset Men in
London iii. 129 and n., 158 n., 312 nn.,
322, 323 n.; iv. 58, 119, 120 n.; vi. 201 n.,
235; vii. 17 and n., 146 nn.
letters to iii. 128, 158, 212, 248, 312; iv. 54,
59; vii. 146, 153
Watney, Vernon i. 224 and n.
Watson, Annie Carr (ELH's cousin):
and Gifford graves v. 32, 34, 110
letters to v. 32, 109
Watson, Ellen Elizabeth (Mrs R. G. Watson)
v. 32 ('your mother') and n.
Watson, Helen Charlotte (ELH's relative) v.
110
Watson, Helena (ELH's cousin) v. 110 ('your
sister') and n.
Watson, Henry Brereton Marriott i. 199 n.
Watson, Malcolm vii. 44 n.
letter to vii. 44
Watson, Robert Gifford (ELH's cousin) v.
32 n.

Watson, (Sir) William ii. 280; iii. 267
petition for ii. 49 and n., 50
hostility to *vers libre* v. 192, 193 n.
and 'Poets' Tribute' v. 334
on TH's use of 'scientific words' vii. 118,
119 n.
*Ode on the Day of the Coronation of King
Edward VII* iii. 26 and n.
Poems vii. 118, 119 n.
Retrogression and Other Poems v. 193 n.
Sable and Purple, with Other Poems iv. 98 n.
*The Superhuman Antagonists and Other
Poems* v. 228 n.
'To America, Concerning England' v. 83
and n.
'The Unreconciled' v. 228 ('the poem')
and n.
Wordsworth's Grave, and Other Poems i. 241
and n.
letters to i. 241; iii. 26; iv. 247; v. 83, 222,
228, 334; vii. 118
Watt, Alexander Pollock (literary agent) i. 113
n.*; ii. 37, 38 n., 41, 43 and n.; iv. 124,
317, 318 and n.; vii. 112 and n., 120 n.
letters to i. 113, 243, 251
Watt, Alexander Strahan (literary agent) vi.
118 n., 241 n., 270, 271 n., 313 n.
Watt, Theodore iii. 220 n.
letter to iii. 220
Watts, Charles Albert v. 22 n.
letters to v. 22, 117
Watts, George Frederic iii. 152 n.
Watts, Isaac:
'There is a land of pure delight' iii. 144 and
n.; vi. 197 n.
Watts-Dunton, Walter Theodore ii. 216 n.*;
iv. 170 n.
essay on poetry ii. 216
and Swinburne ii. 216 n.; v. 78 n., 96, 157
biography of v. 96, 97 n.
Aylwin ii. 216
Christmas at the Mermaid ii. 304 and nn.
letters to ii. 216, 304; iv. 170, 251; v. 14
Watts-Dunton, Mrs T. (Clara Reich) iv. 251
Watts-Hughes, Mrs:
Home for Destitute Boys ii. 107 n.
Wauchope, Major-General Andrew Gilbert iii.
66 and n., 81, 130 and n.
Waugh, Arthur ii. 299 n.
letter to iii. 14
'Weary Walker, The' (poem):
pub. in *Bermondsey Book* vi. 256 n.
'Weatherbury' ii. 238
original of ii. 131, 238 n.; iii. 97 n.; iv. 10,
56 n.
'Weathers' (poem) vi. 118, 285
pub. in *Good Housekeeping* vi. 121 n.

Webb, A. P.:
  A Bibliography of the Works of Thomas Hardy v. 175 n.
Webb, Mary Gladys vi. 153 n.
  Seven for a Secret vi. 153 ('your novel') and n.
  letter to vi. 153
Webb, Philip v. 134 n.
Weber, Captain (later Colonel) William Hermann Frank iii. 37 n.; vi. 325 n.
  letter to vi. 325
Weber, Mrs W. H. F. (Emily Mary Bineta Thornton) iii. 37 n.
Wedgwood, Frances Julia vii. 101 n.
Wedmore, (Sir) Frederick ii. 64 and n., 84; iii. 190; iv. 301 n., 322, 323 n.
  Brenda Walks v. 165 ('Wedmore's book'), 166 n.
  The Collapse of the Penitent ii. 265 ('story') and n.
Wedmore, Millicent iv. 331 n.
  Chiefly of Heroes iv. 330 ('poems'), 331 n.
Weekly Comedy i. 195 n., 213 n.; iii. 356 n.; vi. 124 n.
Weekly Dispatch v. 162 n.; vi. 278, 279 n.
Weisse Ritter Verlag, Der (German publishers) vi. 190 n.
'Well-Beloved, The' (poem) ii. 305 n.
Well-Beloved, The (novel) (originally *The Pursuit of the Well-Beloved*, q.v.) i. 204 n.; ii. 154; iii. 13, 14 n., 71 n., 190, 213, 222; vi. 235 n.
  original scene of ii. 133; vii. 45 n.
  publication of ii. 140, 141 n., 144, 147 ('my new story') and n., 151 n., 152, 153, 205; vii. 119 n.
  earlier serialization ii. 152 n., 206
  reception of ii. 152, 153 and n., 154, 155–7, 158–60, 161, 169; iii. 190
  Colonial Library edn ii. 158
  suggestion for plot of ii. 169
  Macmillan 3s 6d (Uniform) edn iii. 28, 29; iv. 60 and n.
  French translation iii. 139 and n.
  American film rights v. 97, 335
  Spanish translation vi. 34 n., 108 n.
  Canadian rights vi. 65, 81
'Welland House':
  original of ii. 133
Wellesley, Lady Dorothy vi. 307 n.
Wells, Amy Catherine v. 282 n.
  letter to v. 282
Wells, Herbert George ii. 111 n.; vi. 128 n.
  at Max Gate v. 293 and n.
  Joan and Peter v. 280 and n.
  Marriage iv. 232, 233 n.
  Men Like Gods vi. 188 ('the book') and n.

  The New Machiavelli iv. 177, 178 n.
  The Undying Fire: A Contemporary Novel v. 308 ('the book') and nn.
  The World of William Clissold vii. 40 ('new book'), 41 n., 49, 50 n.
  letters to v. 280, 293, 308; vi. 188; vii. 40, 49
Wells, John T. iii. 79 ('music seller') and n.
Wells, Thomas Bucklin (publisher) iv. 84 nn.
  letter to iv. 84
Wells (Somerset) ii. 179; iii. 135
  in 'Tragedy of Two Ambitions' iii. 146
Wellspring, John sen. and jun. (Dorchester builders) iv. 20 n.; v. 198 and n.
Wellwood, Samuel (publisher) iii. 264 and n.
Weltzien, Dr Erich vii. 63 and n., 64 nn.
  letter to vii. 64
Wengern Alp ii. 168
Wenlock Abbey (Salop) ii. 27, 28 n.
Wessex (Wessie) (Max Gate dog) v. 8 and n., 61 and n., 101, 201 ('our dog'), 277, 320, 329 and n., 340; vi. 38 ('Wess'), 82, 277, 278, 279 ('W.')
  character v. 30, 71, 121, 193; vi. 9, 22, 120, 253
  put to sleep vii. 50 ('Our poor dog'), 51 n., 54 and n.
Wessex iii. 12; iv. 156; vi. 12
  first use of name, in fiction i. 171
  exclusive right to name i. 171; iii. 36, 101, 102 n., 103
  maps of i. 256, 275; iii. 16 n., 103, 221 and n.; iv. 137, 182 and n., 184, 204, 329, 330 n.; v. 312; vi. 69
  relation to real places i. 273, 274; ii. 74, 131–4, 135, 254–5; iii. 101, 137–8, 146–7, 171, 172, 359 n.; iv. 10, 137, 164 and n., 175 and nn., 220 and n., 264 and n. *See also individual novels*
  paintings of ii. 74 and n., 78 and n.; iii. 147 n., 148, 173 and n., 181
  books on ii. 135 n., 302; iii. 14 and nn., 16 and n., 22 and n., 138 n., 140 ('hand-book'), 141, 146 ('the MS.'), 147 n., 149 ('your tours'), 151 ('Harper') and n., 170 ('little book'), 171–2, 194 ('the sheets'), 195; iv. 135, 136 and n., 137, 173 ('the book'), 179 ('typoscript'), 223 ('Guide book') and n., 263 ('typoscript') and n., 280 ('Guide book'), 286 nn., 293 nn., 294, 295 and n.; v. 94, 95 ('Lea's book')
  not 'wholly Leopardian' ii. 213 n.
  not 'intrinsically romantic' ii. 297 n.
  picture postcards of iii. 101, 103, 109 n., 110, 112 ('to six') and n., 160 ('sets') and n., 164 and n., 168
  association of Lear with iii. 177 and n.
  pottery iv. 120 and n.

Wessex, University of (proposed) vi. 62, 321, 322 nn., 326–7 and nn.
proposal for Thomas Hardy Chair vi. 321, 322 n., 327 and n., 330
Wessex Edition i. 249 n.; iii. 16 n., 218 n., 226 n., 275 n.; iv. 4 n., 223 n., 264 ('new edn.'), 293, 294 and n., 297 ('prose series') and n., 302 n., 308 and n.; v. 2 n., 36 and n., 37 n., 94, 95 n., 113, 123, 132, 232, 234 n., 245, 253, 254, 259 ('recent edition'), 291 n., 299, 301 n., 304, 306 ('this edition'); vi. 62 n., 64, 66, 112, 181, 358, 361 and n.; vii. 2 and n., 8, 58 n.
preparation of iv. 160 ('for correction') and n., 161 n., 171 and nn., 184, 198, 201 and n., 203–4, 205 and n., 208–9, 211 ('proofs'), 212, 213, 214 ('new series'), 216 ('proofs'), 221 ('reprint'), 224 ('proofs'), 225 ('edition . . . in process'), 227 ('definitive edition'), 228 ('definitive edition') and n., 229 ('proofs') and n., 231 and n., 236 ('proofs'), 329 and nn.
royalties on iv. 185, 198; vi. 13, 14 n.
choice of title iv. 198 and n.
frontispieces to iv. 203, 204 n., 205 and n., 220 and n., 302 and n., 304, 305
corrections in iv. 271 and n.; v. 316 n.; vi. 13, 14 and n.; vii. 31 and n.
text used for Mellstock Edn v. 39, 45
American version v. 52 and n., 148; vi. 23 n., 39, 40 n. *See also* Autograph Edition
gift of complete set to Cockerell v. 124 and n.
dialect most correct in v. 136
prefaces v. 254, 258 and nn.; vii. 48 and n., 49 n., 76
classification of volumes vi. 49 n.
'Wessex Folk' (alternative title of 'A Few Crusted Characters'):
draft MS given to Gosse iv. 281 ('manuscript'), 287 and n.
pub. in *Harper's* iv. 287 n., 292; vii. 113 n., 116 n.
Wessex Life (projected magazine) vi. 131 and n., 143, 144 nn., 150 ('another "Wessex" periodical') and n.
'Wessex Novels' edition ii. 60 n., 63 and n., 65 n., 69 and n., 71, 76 n., 85 n., 91 ('a proof-sheet') and n., 101 n., 127 n., 140 n., 146 n., 201 n., 254 ('last edn.'), 255 n.; iii. 10 ('present green volumes'), 11 n., 91 n., 121 ('best edition in appearance') and n., 275 n.; iv. 43 n., 44 n., 116 n., 124 n., 137 n., 199 ('our set') and n.; v. 255 n.; vi. 35 n.
frontispieces to ii. 65 and n., 70 and n.; iii. 36 and nn.

map in iv. 137 and n.
See also Uniform Edition
Wessex Poems ii. 206 ('volume of verses'), 207 ('book of mine'), 212 n., 219, 251, 283 ('Poems') and n.; iii. 13, 260, 362; iv. 284; v. 88 n., 246, 249; vii. 20 n.
preparation of ii. 198 ('little matters') and n., 199 ('mysterious occupation') and n., 202 ('verses of mine'), 203, 204 ('the poems') and n., 214, 216
illustrations to ii. 199 n., 202, 203, 205, 217; iii. 13, 36 n.; vii. 57
'Leipzig' drawing iii. 61, 62 n., 100
reception of ii. 207, 208, 211, 212, 213 and nn., 214 and nn., 215, 216, 217
Swinburne's favourite poems in ii. 209 and n.
'local' character of ii. 210
use of 'old English words' in ii. 214; iv. 318
possible setting to music of lyrics from iii. 73
topographical backgrounds iii. 137
MS given to Birmingham Museum iv. 180, 231; vii. 57
Canadian rights vi. 65, 81
EDITIONS:
American ii. 205 and n.; iii. 30
first ii. 204 n.
Mellstock vi. 20; vii. 58 n.
one-vol. collected iv. 4 n., 10, 14 n., 17 and n.
Pocket iii. 217 and n., 227 and n., 283 n.; vii. 58 n.
Uniform iii. 28, 29 n., 62 n.
Wessex iv. 231 and n.; vi. 181; vii. 57, 58 n.
Wessex Press v. 227, 228 n.
Wessex Review vi. 128 n., 149, 150 nn.
Wessex Saddleback Pig Society:
TH as first Hon. Member v. 321 and n., 340
Wessex Society of Manchester and District iii. 1, 142
TH as first President ii. 181; iii. 1 n., 362
Wessex Tales (stories) i. 178 and n., 204 n.; ii. 33 n., 54, 63; iii. 225, 226 n., 233; iv. 97, 182, 183 n., 284; vi. 6, 64; vii. 65 and n., 76 n.
first (two-vol.) edn i. 174 and n., 175 and n., 177
copies sent to Browning and Harrison i. 175, 176
one-vol. edn i. 180 and n.
American edn i. 184 ('flimsy one') and nn.
misunderstanding over copyright of ii. 12 and n., 14–15, 22
originals of places in ii. 132
episodes of hanging v. 270 n.

West, George Herbert:
Gothic Architecture in England and France
iv. 151, 152 n.
West, Rebecca (Cicily Isabel Andrews) v. 293
('the lady')
The Return of the Soldier v. 293 and n.
West Bay (Dorset) iii. 53 and n.
West Briton, The vi. 28 and n.
West Stafford (Dorset) i. 259 n.; iii. 357 nn.
Western Weekly Mercury vi. 28 and n.
Westgate-on-Sea (Kent) ii. 224, 225 n., 226,
227 n.
Westminster Abbey iii. 88 n., 89; iv. 23 and n.
Palmerston funeral i. 5; iii. 143; vii. 7
Meredith memorial service iv. 22, 23 n., 24,
25
coronation of George V iv. 141, 143, 160
rejection of Byron memorial vi. 262 and nn.
Special Choir vii. 7 and n.
Westminster Gazette ii. 8 and n., 9 and n., 57
and n.; iii. 177, 178 nn.; iv. 14 and n.,
15 n., 242 and n.; vii. 26, 27 n., 28 and n.,
52, 53 n.
interview with TH in ii. 44, 45 n.
'Christmas Ghost-Story' pub. in ii. 242 ('few
lines'), 243 n.
Westminster Hospital vi. 215, 216 ('your
letter'), 217 n.
Westminster Review i. 117, 118 and nn.; ii.
115, 137, 140; vii. 113, 114 n.
and *Moments of Vision* v. 250 and nn.
Weston, John (London landlord) ii. 287 n.
Weston, Montague C. (Dorchester solicitor) i.
133 and n.
Weyhill (Hants):
as 'Weydon Priors' ii. 132
Weymouth (Dorset) i. 79 n., 110 n., 178; ii.
193 ('W.'), 264, 303; iii. 24, 25, 112,
135, 234, 235, 262 n., 281, 306, 330,
335; iv. 176, 177, 228, 239, 279 n.; v.
118 n., 193, 293 and n.; vi. 21, 22, 35,
87, 155, 188, 201
TH as architect in i. 10 n., 15 n.
scene of *Trumpet-Major* i. 83, 98; iii. 285,
289; v. 184 n.
George III's visits i. 83, 98, 178; iii. 285,
289; iv. 294, 295 n.; v. 183, 184 n., 244;
vi. 1, 2 nn.
'Records' of i. 121
as setting of 'A Committee-Man of "The
Terror"' ii. 129
as 'Budmouth Regis' ii. 131
cycle ride to iii. 342, 343, 344
meeting of 'Back Sea' and 'Front Sea' iii. 359
Canadian teachers' visit iv. 294, 295 n.
performance of *Woodlanders* iv. 327 ('the
company'), 328 n.

soldiers at v. 41, 42, 43, 129, 283
performance of scenes from *Dynasts* v. 149,
150 and n., 162 ('programme') and nn.,
166 and n.
Gosse connection with vi. 3, 4 n., 10
Tess performances vi. 291, 292, 294 and n.,
295, 296, 297, 298 n.
delegation to Weymouth (Mass.) vii. 11
and n.
Mayor performance vii. 42 and n., 44, 45 n.
Burdon Hotel vi. 93
Gloucester Hotel iii. 138; vi. 10
George III residence iv. 144 and n., 294,
295 n.; vi. 1, 2 nn., 171 n.
proposed plaque for iv. 294, 295 n.; v. 184
and n., 185, 244; vi. 171 and n.
Royal Hospital v. 132 nn.
Royal Hotel v. 293 n.; vi. 33 n., 93
Weymouth College iii. 27 and n.
Weymouth Garrison League v. 169 n.
Wharton, Edith iii. 67 n.
A Backward Glance v. 118 n.
(ed.) *The Book of the Homeless* v. 118 nn.
letter to v. 118
Wharton, Henry Thornton:
Sappho ii. 84 and n., 158, 159 n.
'What the Shepherd Saw' (story) iv. 293 and
n., 296 n.; vi. 314 n.
French translation v. 33 n.
MS fragment sold for Red Cross v. 145 n.
Wheeler (Weymouth photographer) i. 260 n.;
ii. 3
Wheeler, W. Reginald:
(comp.) *A Book of Verse of the Great War* v.
301 ('anthology') and n.
'When Dead' (poem) vii. 75
'When I set out for Lyonnesse' (poem) v. 70,
87, 250, 255 and n.; vi. 136, 234 n., 285
American popularity v. 199, 212
TH's favourite lyric v. 204
musical setting v. 288, 289 n.; vi. 2, 14 and
n., 43 and n.
'When Lawyers Strive' (poem) v. 87
Whetham, William Cecil Dampier v. 324 and
n.; vi. 349, 350 n.
Whibley, Charles i. 214 n.
Whistler, James Abbott McNeill iii. 245 n.
proposed memorials to iii. 244, 262 n.
Whitaker's Almanack v. 163 and n.
Whitcomb Church (Dorset) iv. 226, 227 n.
White, Gleeson:
(ed.) *Ballades and Rondeaus, Chants Royal,
Sestinas, Villanelles, & c.* ii. 23 ('book of
ballads'), 24 nn., 227, 228 n.
White's Club i. 64 and n.
Whitefriars Club ii. 281 n.; iii. 276 and n., 299;
iv. 42 n.; vi. 217 n.

Whitefriars Club (*cont.*)
  at Max Gate ii. 281, 290 and n., 291, 292
    and nn., 293, 297 and n.; vii. 140 n., 168
    and n.
  proposed complimentary dinner to TH iv.
    41, 49–51
Whitehead, Beatrice (*née* Case) ii. 272 ('his
  daughters'); v. 15 n.; vii. 124 and n.
Whitehead, Frederick William Newton ii.
  74 n.; v. 15 n.
  paintings of Dorset ii. 74; vii. 124 and n.,
    125, 147 n.
  letters to v. 15; vii. 124, 125–6
Whitehouse, Robert vi. 172 nn.
'Whitewashed Wall, The' (poem):
  pub. in *Reveille* v. 275, 276 n.
Whitfield, Archie Stanton vi. 16 ('educated
  man at Oxford'); vii. 161 n.
  Thomas Hardy: The Artist, the Man, and the
    Disciple of Destiny vi. 17 n.
  letter to vii. 161
Whitman, Walt v. 192, 193 n.
Whitten, Wilfred vii. 57 n.
'Why did I Sketch' (poem) v. 250
Whymper, Edith Mary iv. 80 n., 81 and n.
Whymper, Edward ii. 168 and n.*, 169; iv. 175
  and n.
  at Aldeburgh iv. 80 n., 81 n., 175 n.
  letter to iv. 81
Whymper, Ethel Rose iv. 81 ('the seedling')
  and n.
Whyte, Frederic ii. 271 n.; vii. 37 nn.
  letter to vii. 37
'Widow Betrothed, The' (poem) v. 253
Wiesbaden iv. 306, 307 n.
Wilde, Oscar vi. 70 ('as somebody says'), 71 n.;
  vii. 95 n.
  'The Canterville Ghost' vi. 3 n.
  Salome iii. 209 and n., 210 n.
Wilhelm II, Kaiser v. 57 ('one man') and n.,
  240, 241 n.
  in Tussaud's Chamber of Horrors v. 101
Willcocks & Co. (music publishers):
  letter to iii. 73
Willcocks, Mary Patricia iv. 166 n.
  letter to iv. 166
Williams, (?) Dorothy Rhoda vi. 191 ('his
  daughter'), 192 n.
Williams, Ralph Vaughan:
  setting to music of song from *Dynasts* iii.
    355, 358 and n.; v. 56
  letter to iii. 358
Williams, Colonel Sir Robert vi. 135, 191,
  192 n.
Williams, Sarah i. 31 ('landlady's daughter')
  and n.
Williams, W. H. (Lord Mayor of Liverpool) iv.

64 n.
  letter to iv. 64
Williams & Norgate (publishers) i. 55 n., 102
  letter to i. 55
Williams-Ellis, Amabel vi. 177 n.
Williamson, J. C., Ltd (theatrical manage-
  ment) vi. 357, 358 n.
Willmott, Revd Robert Aris iv. 16 n.
Wilmshurst, George i. 135 n.; vii. 96 n.,
  103 n., 104 n.
  letters to i. 135; vii. 95–6
Wilson, E. B.:
  The Cell in Development and Inheritance v.
    85 n.
Wilson, Henry:
  and Pageant of Construction v. 291, 292 n.
  letter to v. 291
Wilson, (?) Henry Francis vii. 116 n.
  letter to vii. 116
Wilson, (?) Revd James Maurice vii. 116 n.
  letter to vii. 116
Wilson, Rathmell iv. 180 n.
  letters to iv. 180, 181
Wilton House (Wilts) iv. 169, 220
  as setting of 'Marchioness of Stonehenge' iv.
    170 n., 175 and n., 220 n.
Wimbledon:
  Allenswood School v. 344 n.; vi. 34 n.
Wimborne, Ivor Bertie Guest, 1st Baron ii.
  145 n., 252 n.
Wimborne, Cornelia, Lady ii. 144, 145 n.
Wimborne, Simon v. 254 n.
Wimborne Minster (Dorset) i. 95, 110 and n.,
  111 n., 166 n., 242; iii. 283 n.; v. 136,
  137 n.
  move to Lanherne, The Avenue i. 91 and n.,
    92, 95
  as 'Warborne' ii. 133
  move from vii. 98 and n., 110 n.
Winchester, 15th Marquess of ii. 144, 145 n.,
  211, 240, 241 n.
Winchester ii. 216 n., 265; iii. 240; vi. 321,
  322 nn.
  as 'Wintoncester' ii. 133
  Cathedral iv. 220 and n.
  TH invited to re-open Public Library v. 82
    and n.
Windle, Bertram Coghill Alan ii. 133 n.
  (ed.) *Murray's Handbook for Residents and*
    Travellers in Wilts and Dorset ii. 133 n.,
    135 ('the Guide'), 229 n.
  The Wessex of Thomas Hardy ii. 135 n.,
    256 n., 281 ('your book'), 282 n., 302 ('the
    Wessex book') and n.; iii. 16 ('the fourth')
    and n.; iv. 295 and n.
  letters to ii. 131, 135, 242, 281, 302
Windsor Castle iv. 224 and n.

Windsor Castle (*cont.*)
 TH MS in Royal Library iv. 182 and n., 184
Winfrith (Dorset) vi. 283 n.
Wingfield-Digby, Revd Stephen Harold vi. 94 n.
Winkles's Architectural and Picturesque Illustrations of the Cathedral Churches of England and Wales vi. 85 and n.
Winterborne Came (Dorset) i. 120 n., 137 n.; iii. 279 n.
Winterborne Farringdon (Dorset) ii. 30 ('the ruin'), 31 n.
Winterborne Monkton (Dorset) v. 205 and n.
 School vi. 237, 238 n.
Winterborne St Martin (Dorset):
 alternative name of Martinstown iii. 235 n.; v. 4 n.
Winterborne-Tomson ('-Thompson') (Dorset) vi. 226 and n.
'Wintoncester':
 Winchester as ii. 133
Wise, Thomas James v. 26 n., 77 n., 192 n.; vii. 13 n.
 Wordsworth bibliography v. 192 and n.
 Landor reprint v. 202, 203 n.
 The Ashley Library vi. 133 ('the Catalogue') and n., 239 ('Volume IV.') and n., 282 ('fifth volume') and n.; vii. 12 ('seventh volume') and n., 58 ('eighth volume') and n.
 letters to v. 192, 202; vi. 133, 239, 282; vii. 12–13, 58
Wister, Owen iii. 206 and n.
'Withered Arm, The' (story) i. 168 ('short story'), 172 ('the story') and n., 175; iii. 151; iv. 271; vii. 59
 rejected by *Longman's* i. 168 n.
 accepted by *Blackwood's* i. 169 and n., 170 ('proof') and n., 171, 172 n., 173
 'Conjuror Trendle' in iii. 264, 265 n.
Withers, Percy vii. 159 n.
 letter to vii. 159
Withers, Stanley i. 143 n.
 letter to i. 143
Wittersham (Kent):
 Island Cottage iii. 222 n., 226 ('rustication') and n., 305 ('country cottage')
'Wives in the Sere' (poem) ii. 293 ('the lines') and n.
Wix, Revd Cyril Poynder iii. 346 n.
 letters to iii. 346, 350; iv. 15, 16
Wolcomb-Matravers (Dorset) vii. 85 n.
Wolf, Lucien vi. 63 n.
 The Jewish Bogey, and the Forged Protocols of the Learned Elders of Zion vi. 63 and n.
 letter to vi. 63
Wolfeton House (Dorset) ii. 131 ('Wolver-ton'); iii. 328 n.; iv. 241 n.
Wolff, Julia ii. 68 n.
Wolmark, Alfred Aaran vii. 29, 30 n.
Woman at Home ii. 41 n., 115, 190
'Woman I Met, The' (poem):
 pub. in *London Mercury* vi. 50 n.
Wombwell, Lady Julia ii. 19 and n.
women, attitude towards i. 26, 33, 250, 251; ii. 99, 102, 200, 264; iii. 112; vii. 120
Women's Social and Political Union vii. 142 n.
women's suffrage, views on i. 266 (but see vii. 173); ii. 226; iii. 354, 360; iv. 3, 21, 39, 106, 107; v. 186; vii. 142
Women Writers' Club iii. 128 n.
Women's Progressive Society i. 266 and n.; vii. 173
Wood, Charles F. Crosbie vi. 188 n.
 letter to vi. 188
Wood, General Sir Evelyn ii. 258 and n.; v. 85 n.
 letters to v. 85, 122
'Wood Fire, The' (poem) vi. 162, 163 n.
Woodbridge (Suffolk) ii. 288, 289; iv. 150 and n.
Woodbury Hill Fair ii. 230 and n., 294, 295 n.
 as 'Greenhill Fair' ii. 131, 230, 294
Woodlanders, The (novel) i. 167 n., 178 and n., 191; ii. 85 and n.; iv. 154 n.; vi. 61, 62 n., 64; vii. 65 and n., 101 ('the story'), 102 n.
 Gosse poem quoted in i. 153 ('quote you') and n.; iii. 11 n.; v. 222 and n.
 presentation copies i. 165; ii. 32; iii. 213
 dialect in i. 181; ii. 46 n.
 disagreement over rights to ii. 12 and n., 14, 22
 illustrations for 'Wessex Novels' edn ii. 70 and n.
 passage about sparrows over rafters iii. 52, 53 n.
 picture postcards based on iii. 160
 proposed French translation iii. 227, 228 n.
 superstition in iv. 154 ('Fitzpiers'), 155 n.
 non-copyright in N. America vi. 81 and n., 89
 musical setting of scene from vi. 338 n.
 Lytton's impressions of vii. 107, 108 n.
 BACKGROUND AND ORIGINALS OF PLACES:
  i. 163 and n.; ii. 132; vi. 132 and n.; vii. 24
 DRAMATIZATIONS:
  i. 195 and n., 196, 210, 212; iv. 292 ('play') and n.; v. 2; vi. 265, 266 n., 299 n.; vii. 114 n.
  Dorchester performances v. 3 n.; vi. 338 n.; vii. 156 ('proof'), 157 nn.

Woodlanders, The (*cont.*)
London performance iv. 323 and n., 325,
327 ('the play'), 328 n.; v. 3 n.
Weymouth performance v. 2, 3 n.
EDITIONS:
Braille v. 268 and n.
Colonial i. 162
first (three-vol.) i. 159, 161–2, 164 and n.
one-vol. i. 180 and n.
Wessex iv. 212 and n., 216 ('sixth
volume') and n.
'Wessex Novels' ii. 70 and n.
SERIALIZATIONS:
American i. 138 ('a novel') and n., 140
('the story'), 157 n.
Macmillan's Magazine i. 131 ('the
novel'), 138 and n., 139 and n., 140,
141, 143 ('new story'), 148, 149, 153
and n., 161
Woods, Margaret Louisa iii. 279 n.
Poems Old and New iii. 279 and n.
letter to iii. 279
Woodsford (Dorset):
arson of corn ricks at iii. 84 and n.
probable scene of marriage of Tess and
Angel Clare iii. 171 and n.
Woodward, Benjamin iv. 60 and n.
Woodward, Kathleen vii. 28 and n.
Wool (Dorset) iv. 137 n.; vi. 283 n., 371 n.
Wool-Bridge Manor (Dorset):
as scene of wedding night in *Tess* i. 286,
287 n.; ii. 133; iii. 210; iv. 10; vi. 371 n.
and Turberville family iii. 93, 94 n., 209
Woolcombe (Dorset) iii. 234, 260
Woolf, Leonard vi. 90 n.
as literary editor of *Nation and Athenaeum*
vi. 196 and n., 314 n.
Woolf, Virginia v. 77 nn.; vi. 90, 191 n., 307 n.
letters to v. 76; vi. 196, 255
Woolner, Thomas i. 73 n.; v. 145 n.
Poems i. 164 ('kind present') and n.
Pygmalion i. 97 ('charming book') and n.
Worbarrow Bay (Dorset) v. 31
Worcester Cathedral iv. 152 n.
Wordsworth, Dorothy v. 168 n.; vi. 375 n.
Wordsworth, John, Bishop of Salisbury i. 154,
155 n.*, 220 ('the Bishop'), 223
Wordsworth, William i. 218 n.; iii. 245; iv. 24,
26 ('the poet') and n.; v. 167, 168 n.; vi.
375 n.; vii. 22 n., 33 n.
quoted in *Tess* i. 281, 283
Wise bibliography v. 192 and n.
signature on book title-page v. 216 and n.,
218 n.
as 'Wessex worthy' v. 337, 338 n.
at Cambridge vii. 146, 147 n.
The Excursion v. 174 and n.

Preface to *Lyrical Ballads* v. 253, 254 n.
'Two April Mornings' i. 69
World i. 214, 215 n., 250 and n.
comparison of TH with Zola ii. 36 and n.
attack on *Jude* ii. 96 n., 98
attack on *Well-Beloved* ii. 154, 155–7, 159
and nn., 169
World (New York) – see *New York World*
World's Classics iii. 246
'World's Library of Best Books' vii. 47 n.
'Worlingworth, G.' – *see* Henniker, Florence
Worlingworth Hall (Suffolk) iv. 177 n.
Worthing (Sussex) iv. 163 n.; vi. 110
'Wound, The' (poem):
pub. in *Sphere* v. 160 ('two poems'),
161 n.
Wrackleford (Dorset) v. 267 and n.; vi. 43
Wright, Charles Theodore Hagberg iii. 304 n.,
320 n.
letters to iii. 303, 320
Wright, Edward iii. 256 nn.
letter to iii. 255
Wright, Joseph:
English Dialect Dictionary ii. 168 n.; iii.
43 n.
letters to ii. 168; iii. 42
Wyatt, James vi. 30 and n.
Wych, Harold (astrologer) iv. 156 n.
Wyeth, N. C. vi. 271 n.
Wyke Regis (Dorset) iii. 45 n., 84 n.
Wyndham, George:
Ronsard and La Pléiade . . . iii. 242
('Ronsard book'), 243 n.
Wynford, Lady ii. 248, 249 n.

'Xenophanes, the Monist of Colophon'
(poem):
pub. in *Nineteenth Century and After* vi. 231
('the poem'), 232 n., 293

Yale Review vi. 20 and n.
Yale University v. 352 and n.
Yates, Edmund i. 215 n.
letters to i. 214, 250
'Year's Awakening, The' (poem):
pub. in *New Weekly* v. 6 n., 20, 21 and nn.,
23
Yearsley, Louise vi. 197, 198 n.
Yearsley, Percival Macleod (aural surgeon) v.
100 n., 104, 109; vi. 198 nn.
letters to v. 99; vi. 197
Yeats, William Butler iii. 25 n., 124 n.; iv. 37
and n., 152 n., 285 n.
awarded Civil List pension iv. 113 n.
and presentation of R.S.L. medal to TH iv.
216, 217, 218 n.
Kathleen ni Houlihan iv. 92 n., 160 n.

Yeats, William Butler (cont.)
  'The Lake Isle of Innisfree' v. 151 ('Mr Yeats's poem') and n.
  Where There is Nothing iii. 127 n.
Yeovil (Somerset) iii. 135, 224
  St Peter Street (No. 7) i. 43 n.
Yerbury, Francis Rowland (architect) v. 116, 117 n.; vi. 187 n.
  letter to vi. 186
Yokall, Sir James v. 215 n.
Yolland, Florence (ELH's cousin) iv. 250 n.
  letters to iv. 250, 283, 311
York, George, Duke of (later George V, q.v.) ii. 20, 21 n.
York, Princess Mary of Teck, Duchess of (later Queen Mary, q.v.) ii. 20, 21 n.
York, Albert George, Duke of (later George VI) vi. 348 and n.
York, Elizabeth, Duchess of (later Queen Elizabeth the Queen Mother) vi. 348 and n.
York Minster iv. 51
Yorkshire Post ii. 125 n.
Yoshiwara, Shigeo vii. 82 n.
Young, Mrs David Butler ii. 220 n.
Young, Ernest William (mayor of Dorchester) iii. 39 n., 179 n.
  letters to iii. 38, 179
Young, Francis Brett:
  and 'Poets' Tribute' v. 344 and n.
  letter to v. 344
Young, James Carleton iii. 121 n.
  letter to iii. 121
Young, Robert vi. 203 n.

Young, Thomas vi. 203 and n.
'Young Churchwarden, The' (poem) vi. 30 n.
Young Man ii. 44, 45 n., 53 and n.
Younger, Margaret Lucy iv. 232 n.
Youriévitch, Serge vi. 266 n.
  bust of TH vi. 266 and n., 298 and n.
  letter to vi. 266
Youth's Companion i. 116 and n., 123, 127, 129 ('the paper') and n., 158, 159 n.
Ysaÿe, Eugène ii. 285 n.
'Yuletide in a Younger World' (poem) vii. 75 and n.

Zangwill, Israel iv. 44 n.; vii. 30 and n.
  wedding iii. 84 and n., 85, 89 n.
  Merely Mary Ann ii. 13, 14 n.
  letter to iv. 44
Zangwill, Mrs Israel (Edith Ayrton) iii. 84 n., 89 n.
Zermatt ii. 168
'Zermatt: To the Matterhorn' (poem) ii. 168 n.
Zeys, Mathilde ii. 274 n.; vi. 108 n.
Zola, Emile ii. 34, 99, 148 and n.; iii. 34 n.; v. 294 and n.
  Authors' Club dinner to ii. 8 n., 34 n., 36 n.
  compared with TH ii. 36 and n.
  not admired as novelist by TH ii. 157, 230–1; iii. 34
  J'accuse ii. 223 n.
  Nana ii. 36 n.
Zukor, Adolph iv. 303 n.; vi. 195 n.
Zupitza, Julius ii. 39 n.